THIRD EDITION

GAINING AND SUSTAINING COMPETITIVE ADVANTAGE

Jay B. Barney

The Ohio State University

Upper Saddle River, NJ 07458

Library of Congress Cataloging-in-Publication Data

Barney, Jay B.
  Gaining and sustaining competitive advantage / Jay B. Barney.— 3rd ed.
    p.   cm
  Includes bibliographical references and index.
  ISBN 0-13-147094-9
    1. Industrial management.   2.   Strategic planning.   3.   Competition.
  I. Title.

HD31.B27 2007
658.4 — dc22   2006030155

Senior Acquisitions Editor: Michael Ablassmeir
VP/Editorial Director: Jeff Shelstad
Product Development Manager: Ashley Santora
Assistant Editor: Keri Molinari
Marketing Manager: Anne Howard
Marketing Assistant: Susan Osterlitz
Associate Director, Production Editorial: Judy Leale
Managing Editor: Renata Butera
Production Editor: Kelly Warsak
Permissions Coordinator: Charles Morris
Associate Director, Manufacturing: Vinnie Scelta
Manufacturing Buyer: Michelle Klein

Design/Composition Manager: Christy Mahon
Cover Design: Bruce Kenselaar
Cover Photo: Getty Images
Illustration (Interior): Techbooks
Manager, Cover Visual Research & Permissions: Karen Sanatar
Composition: Techbooks
Full-Service Project Management: Penny Walker/Techbooks
Printer/Binder: R.R.D. & Sons Company
Cover printer: Phoenix Color Corp.
Typeface : 10/12 Times Ten Roman

Credits and acknowledgments borrowed from other sources and reproduced, with permission, in this textbook appear on appropriate page within text.

Pearson Prentice Hall™ is a trademark of Pearson Education, Inc.
Pearson® is a registered trademark of Pearson plc
Prentice Hall® is a registered trademark of Pearson Education, Inc.

Pearson Education Ltd.
Pearson Education Singapore Pte. Ltd.
Pearson Education Canada, Ltd.
Pearson Education—Japan

Pearson Education Australia Pty. Limited
Pearson Education North Asia Ltd.
Pearson Educación de Mexico, S.A. de C.V.
Pearson Education Malaysia Pte. Ltd.

10 9 8 7 6 5 4 3 2 1
ISBN: 0-13-147094-9

BRIEF CONTENTS

Contents

PREFACE

So—why do we need another book on business policy and strategic management? What does this book bring to its readers that other books don't? To answer these questions, it is important to understand (1) how business education has evolved in business schools, and (2) strategic management's disciplinary status in colleges of business.

RESEARCH AND TEACHING IN BUSINESS SCHOOLS

In 1959, two evaluations of the status of undergraduate and graduate business education were published. The first, sponsored by the Carnegie Foundation, concluded that "the central problem facing this branch of higher education is that academic standards need to be materially increased."[1] The second, funded by the Ford Foundation, described in more detail what these academic standards should be by arguing that "business educators in increasing numbers are recognizing that it is insufficient to transmit and apply present knowledge. It is the function of higher education to advance the state of knowledge as well. A professional school of business that aspires to full academic status must meet this test."[2]

These evaluations of business education in the 1950s have had a profound effect on the structure and function of business schools. Before the Carnegie and Ford studies, business school professors were often retired managers, and business school classes consisted primarily of discussions about and applications of various informal rules of thumb for managing different business functions. Today, most business school professors have Ph.D.s in either a business discipline or a related nonbusiness discipline, and business school classes focus on discussions about and applications of various models, concepts, and theories that have been developed by academic research. Where previously the discussion of business practices was not well connected to any base academic disciplines, now teaching and research in business draws directly from, and often contribute to, these base disciplines—including economics, psychology, sociology, and mathematics.

Of all the functional areas in the business school, none began making the transition to a theory-grounded, research-based discipline earlier than organizational behavior and finance. As early as the 1930s, organizational behavior researchers were attempting to apply rigorous research methodologies derived from social psychology to study the behavior of individuals and groups in organizations. The now famous studies of the Western Electric plant in Hawthorne, New Jersey, demonstrated not only that social science research methods could be applied in an organizational context, but that they could be used to describe complex social phenomena inside firms.[3] In finance, Modiglliani and Miller's work on capital structure and the cost of capital, and Markowitz's and Tobin's work on portfolio selection, led the way in the application of economic theory to financial decision making in firms.[4] Since this early work, finance has become, in a real sense, a subfield of microeconomics. Moreover, theoretical and empirical work in finance has had a significant effect on the field of microeconomics more generally.

Many of the other disciplines in business schools have gone through similar evolutions. Whereas marketing used to be taught by retired marketing executives, and marketing classes focused on the experiences of these managers, now marketing classes are typically taught by faculty with Ph.D.s in marketing or related disciplines, and marketing classes focus on understanding and applying models and concepts derived from economics, psychology, and statistics. Whereas operations management used to have an uncertain disciplinary grounding, it now has become an arena in which psychological, sociological, mathematical, and statistical models are applied in managing quality, plant location, logistics, and other critical operational activities in firms. Whereas accounting used to focus solely on generally accepted accounting rules, accounting research now draws more broadly on economics, psychology, and computer science to develop those accounting rules and to anticipate their implications for firms.

Some have been concerned that this increased emphasis on rigorous business research has reduced the quality of a business education.[5] These observers have argued that although we now have much more rigorous methods for analyzing a firm's business situation, we have lost the human touch that is required to manage real firms—a human touch that used to be communicated to students by retired executives in the classroom. Of course, there is a great deal of truth in this criticism. It is certainly true that if all a manager did was to apply these research-derived models in a firm, the firm would probably not perform very well. The management of a real organization is not something that can easily be reduced to a computer algorithm. Discipline-based faculty must strive to expose students to this human touch. This is one reason for the continued popularity of case-based teaching in business schools. Not only do cases provide students opportunities to apply the theoretical models they are learning, they also simulate the socially complex context within which the application of these models must actually occur.

It is also true that much of this rigorous business research is irrelevant to real business managers. In any given issue of a research journal, perhaps only one or two articles actually have the potential to be applied in real organizations. The rest of this work is basic research. It is designed to address theoretical problems, problems that often have limited application potential. However, this basic research is often necessary before the applied work can be done. Moreover, when rigorous business research can be applied in real firms, its implications can be staggering. For example, there is little doubt that the way that firms are managed today is fundamentally different from how they were managed 30 years ago and that much of this change is traceable to work done in organizational behavior and related business disciplines.[6] There is also little doubt that theoretical advances in finance have had an enormous effect on the structure and function of the modern economy. Leveraged buy-outs, futures markets, derivatives, and capital budgeting are all examples of economic phenomena that have been fundamentally altered by work in financial economics. Also, there is little doubt that the quality movement that swept the world through the 1980s and early 1990s found its intellectual roots, and many of its management tools, in the work of operations management researchers.

THE ACADEMIC STATUS OF STRATEGIC MANAGEMENT

Where does the discipline of strategic management stand in this evolutionary process? It is probably safe to say that strategic management is one of the least developed and least mature of all the disciplines in the business school. Finance and organizational behavior were well on their way to becoming rigorous discipline-based fields by the 1950s, and marketing, accounting, and operations were well on their way to this same status by the 1960s. However, it was not until the late 1970s and early 1980s that work on a theoretically rigorous underpinning for the field of strategic management was begun. Before this time period, strategic management was often taught by retired managers, and course content focused primarily on describing the activities and decisions of general managers in organizations.

In many ways, the delayed maturity of the field of strategic management is quite understandable. Strategic management is an inherently integrative activity in a firm—forcing managers to bring the skills and expertise of different business functions together to conceive of and implement a strategy. Thus research on strategic management is an inherently multidisciplinary task. To mature fully as an academic discipline, each of the specialties on which strategic management scholars rely must also mature. Therefore it is not surprising that the evolution of the field of strategic management was delayed until other business functions had matured from their preacademic state to become more discipline-based, research-oriented specialties. However, although the maturing of strategic management has been delayed, it is certainly occurring.

Two events signaled the beginning of the evolution of the field of strategic management from its pre-academic stage to a modern, discipline-based research field: the publication (in 1980) of Michael Porter's book, *Competitive Strategy,* and the publication (in 1974) of Richard Rumelt's book, *Strategy, Structure, and Economic Performance.* As is described in Chapters 3 and 4, Porter adapted concepts from a type of industrial organization economics to the analysis of threats and opportunities in a firm's competitive environment. Before Porter, the analysis of a firm's competitive environment was not well structured and involved generating long idiosyncratic lists of threats and opportunities facing a firm. After Porter, the critical threats in a firm's environment, as derived from industrial organization economics, could be described and opportunities facing a firm could be deduced from the structure of a firm's industry. Porter had begun to provide a theoretical structure for analyzing one critical component of the business-level strategy formulation problem.

As indicated in Chapter 12, Rumelt took ideas that had been explored by business historians and business scholars to develop a theory explaining the conditions under which corporate diversification strategies could add economic value to a firm, as well as a model describing the organizational structure firms would need to realize the potential value of a diversification effort.[7] Before Rumelt, discussions of corporate strategy were mired in not very rigorous discussions of synergy and the appropriate level of centralization and decentralization. After Rumelt, the kind of product relatedness needed to achieve economies of scope was described and the specific organizational structure needed to realize these economies was detailed. Rumelt had begun to provide a theoretical structure for analyzing some critical components of the corporate-level strategy formulation and implementation problem.

Just as Porter and Rumelt were completing their work, research in other disciplines began to be published that was destined to have a significant effect on the evolution of the field of strategic management. In organizational behavior, Ouchi's work on Japanese management systems significantly opened up the strategy implementation problem.[8] In economics, transaction costs economics and the evolutionary theory of the firm provided some powerful tools for analyzing a firm's competitive position.[9] In organization theory, population ecology theory was beginning to provide insights to the competitive process facing firms.[10] In finance and accounting, agency theory and positive accounting were providing insights into the economics of organizational structure and organizational processes.[11] Many of these theoretical developments were described in a book I published with Bill Ouchi in 1986 titled *Organizational Economics.*[12]

The result of these theoretical breakthroughs in the field of strategic management and related disciplines has been a rapid growth in the intellectual maturity of strategic management. The number of people studying strategic phenomena in organizations has increased dramatically over the last several years. Currently, the Business Policy and Strategy Division of the Academy of Management is the largest of all Academy divisions. Scholars with a wide variety of disciplinary backgrounds, from finance to organizational behavior, are publishing in the strategic management literature. New ideas are constantly being developed and tested.

Moreover, this growth in interest in strategic management phenomena has not been limited just to business school academics. Much of the best of this work has had important implications for how real firms are managed. Porter's books, including *Competitive Strategy* and *Competitive Advantage,* have been read and applied by many practicing managers. C. K. Prahalad and Gary Hammel's *Harvard Business Review* (*HBR*) article on core competencies—an article solidly grounded in strategic management academic research—is the all-time best-selling reprint at *HBR*. Like earlier work in finance, organizational behavior, and operations, research in strategic management has had, and continues to have, a profound impact on management practice.[13]

THE PURPOSE OF THIS BOOK

Unfortunately, many students of strategic management, whether they are full-time students, part-time students, or practicing managers, have found it difficult to get their minds around this rapidly evolving field. Individual articles or books generally push only a single point of view and do not provide the overall integrative framework necessary to apply strategic management concepts in real organizations. With a couple of exceptions, most textbooks do not include information on the most up-to-date research in strategic management, nor do they provide guidance to students or practitioners about how this research might be applied. *The purpose of this book is to summarize and integrate the latest research in strategic management and related disciplines in a way that is accessible to students and practitioners and in a way that facilitates its application.*

UNIQUE ATTRIBUTES OF THE BOOK

I have taken several actions to ensure the realization of this purpose.

Integrating Strategic Management Research

One of my purposes is to present an integrated view of the field of strategic management. To facilitate this integration, the first five chapters of the book develop a framework (summarized in Chapter 5) that is then used as an organizing framework for the rest of the chapters. Thus, unlike Porter and others, this book is not organized around different types of competitive environments that firms might face. Such a structure unduly emphasizes environmental determinants of firm performance over organizational determinants of performance. Instead, after the organizing framework is developed, chapters focus on specific strategic options that firms may choose to gain competitive advantages. At the business level, these options include cost leadership (Chapter 6), product differentiation (Chapter 7) flexibility (Chapter 8) and tacit collusion (Chapter 9). At the corporate level, these options include vertical integration (Chapter 10), diversification (Chapters 11 and 12), strategic alliances (Chapter 13), mergers and acquisitions (Chapter 14), and international strategies (Chapter 15). How these strategic options help neutralize environmental threats and exploit environmental opportunities is discussed in each of these chapters, in connection with a discussion of how organizational strengths and weaknesses affect the ability of firms pursuing these strategies to gain sustained competitive advantages.

Another way in which the integration of the field of strategic management is facilitated is that strategy formulation and strategy implementation are not discussed in separate parts of the book. Many books and articles seem to adopt the fiction that it is possible to study strategy formulation and strategy implementation independently. This is obviously incorrect. It would clearly be a mistake for firms to formulate their strategies without considering how they were going to implement those strategies. Moreover, it is not possible to evaluate the quality of a firm's strategy implementation efforts independent of the strategy that the firm is trying to implement. Yet many strategy texts address these topics separately, in different parts of the book.

In this book, strategy formulation and strategy implementation are discussed together for each of the strategic options facing firms. Thus, beginning with Chapter 6, the conditions under which pursuing a strategy will be economically valuable, along with the conditions under which pursuing a strategy will be a source of sustained competitive advantage, are discussed. Following this strategy formulation discussion, the actions that a firm must pursue to implement this strategy are also discussed. For all but one of the strategic options facing firms (corporate diversification), the strategy formulation and implementation discussions occur in the same chapter. For corporate diversification strategies, the formulation discussion is in one chapter (Chapter 11), and the implementation discussion is in the subsequent chapter (Chapter 12), because the diversification implementation literature is so large.

Including the Latest Research

Another of my purposes is to summarize the latest research findings in strategic management and related disciplines. Several things have been done to accomplish this purpose. For example, within each chapter, current thinking and research—some of it not yet published—is incorporated in the discussion. In Chapter 2's discussion of firm performance, a variety of measures of firm performance that have only recently begun to appear in the strategy literature are discussed, including the Treynor index, Sharpe's measure, Jensen's alpha, and Tobin's q. Other popular measures of performance that have not been widely discussed in other strategy books are also introduced, including event study methodologies for analyzing firm performance. Also, Chapter 5's discussion of organizational strengths and weaknesses is a state-of-the-art summary of what has come to be known as the resource-based view of the firm.[14] Chapter 9's discussion of tacit collusion draws on recent developments in game theory, and Chapter 13's discussion of trust in strategic alliances draws on some recently published work. Chapter 11's discussion of corporate diversification strategies is well grounded in current work in strategic management and finance. Chapter 15's analysis of international strategies draws on some of the most recent developments in this rapidly growing literature.

To ensure that this text includes the full range of the most recent work in strategic management and related disciplines, each article in each issue of the *Strategic Management Journal*, the *Academy of Management Review,* and the *Academy of Management Journal* for the last 15 years was read and summarized. Then, if it was determined that an article had a strategic focus, the article was classified as being germane to one or more of the chapters of this book. Not all of these articles are cited in the book, but I am quite confident that any current major research stream published in these journals is reflected in the content of my book. For example, I was able to relate every article published in the *Strategic Management Journal* to one of the chapters of this book, with the exception of a few articles on strategic management in small firms.

Ensuring Accessibility and Application

If students and practitioners cannot read, understand, and apply all of this research, it will be of limited value to them. Thus it was not enough to include all the major research streams in strategic management and related disciplines; it was also important to make this work accessible and applicable. I have done several things to accomplish this. First, the book is full of examples. Most of these examples come from *Fortune, Business Week,* or the *Wall Street Journal.* If no examples of a particular strategic phenomenon discussed in the research literature could be found, a discussion of this strategic phenomenon was usually omitted from the book. The logic here is straightforward: If we can't find examples of a phenomenon in the popular business literature, then the phenomenon, though perhaps theoretically interesting, is probably not practically important and thus can be omitted without loss.

In addition, each chapter ends with a chapter summary and review questions. The summary highlights the key issues discussed in the chapter, and the review questions force readers to go beyond what is written in a chapter, to try to understand the implications for managing real firms.

One characteristic that enhances the accessibility and applicability of many strategic management texts is missing in this book—cases. The lack of cases does not mean that cases are irrelevant in the teaching of strategic management. Indeed, I think that case teaching is a very important component of any strategic management class. However, to be most useful, cases should provide students and managers an opportunity to see how a set of ideas, a model, or a technique can actually be used to engage in a strategic analysis and make a strategic decision. In this book I focus on these ideas, models, and techniques, and I assume that teachers will choose their own cases in which these tools can be applied.

There are numerous sources for case material that can be used in conjunction with this book. Moreover, the structure of the text makes choosing cases relatively easy. Because much of the book is organized around specific strategic options facing firms, cases that focus on firms trying to decide whether to pursue a particular strategic option help demonstrate how the ideas and models in a chapter can be applied in a realistic setting. Thus, for example, to help the discussion of cost-leadership competitive business strategies to come alive, cases on Nucor Steel and Wal-Mart are good options, for these firms tend to focus on cost leadership. To help the discussion of vertical integration come alive, cases on Crown Equipment, Pennzoil, and Nucleon are good options, for these firms have all been pursuing interesting vertical integration strategies. The discussion of corporate diversification can be greatly enhanced by cases that focus on diversifying, firms such as Newell-Rubbermaid, Kodak, and Cooper Industries.

Changes in the Third Edition

All the changes I incorporated in the second edition of this book—save one—continue in the third edition. The one change I made in the second edition concerns the location of the vertical integration chapter. I have now included it in Part III of the book, on corporate strategy. Clearly, vertical integration can be important at the business level or at the corporate level. However, it seems that most professors treat it as a corporate strategy, so that is where I decided to put it.

Other important changes in the third edition include: (1) a new introductory section in Chapter 1, (2) integrating a discussion of the strategic management process into Chapter 1, (3) integrating the "willingness to pay" and "cost" characterization of performance into Chapter 2, (4) refocusing the definition of competitive advantage to be consistent with this characterization of performance, (5) a significant revision of Chapter 6's discussion of production differentiation, to increase its readability, (6) some additional discussion of the use of real options logic as an analogy for strategic reasoning in Chapter 8, (7) a simplification of some of the strategic options in Chapter 9's discussion of tacit collusion, (8) a complete rewrite of Chapter 10's discussion of vertical integration to make it easier to understand and apply, and (9) a revision of the review of the empirical research on corporate strategy and firm performance (in Chapter 11) that summarizes the "diversification discount" literature. I have also worked harder to eliminate typographical and other errors in this edition of the book.

ACKNOWLEDGMENTS

In many ways, I began writing the first edition of this book in 1984, while I was an assistant professor at UCLA. Over the years, I continued to work on and refine the text, first as a faculty member at Texas A&M University and most recently as the Chase Chair for Excellence in Corporate Strategy at the Fisher College of Business at The Ohio State University. Colleagues, students, and friends at all these institutions have had a profound effect on my ability to finish this book—a book that, for a long time, I called the "alleged book," as well as its subsequent editions. At UCLA, Bill McKelvey, Bill Ouchi, and Dick Rumelt helped form my approach to academic life and research. Early work with Bill Ouchi and Dick Rumelt had a significant effect on my development as an economically oriented strategy scholar. At UCLA, I was also lucky to have some unusually talented Ph.D. students who influenced me. These students included Kathleen Conner, Bill Hesterly, Julia Liebeskind, Jim Robins, and Todd Zenger.

When I arrived at Texas A&M, I found a thriving strategy group. My colleagues there also had a significant effect on my work. These people included Barry Baysinger,

Bert Cannella, Javier Gimeno, Mike Hitt, Bob Hoskisson, Tom Turk, and Abby McWilliams. My work was also influenced by some talented Ph.D. students at A&M, including Lowell Busenitz, Jim Fiet, Mark Hansen, Doug Moesel, and Beverly Tyler. Much of the hard work of developing the organizing framework and applying it to the analysis of several strategic options occurred while I was at Texas A&M. I am grateful to Don Hellriegel and Mike Hitt, my department heads at A&M, for helping to create a setting within which this kind of work was possible.

Since my arrival at the Fisher College at Ohio State, I have found the support and friendship of my colleagues to be very important. These include Sharon Alvarez, Jay Anand, Kate Conner, Jay Dial, Konstantina Kiousis, Michael Leiblein, Mona Makhija, Mike Peng, Oded Shenkar, Alice Stewart, and Sharon James Wade in the Management Department, and Anil Makhija, Rene Stulz, Ralph Walkling, and Karen Wruck in the Finance Department. My department chair, David Greenberger, Senior Associate Dean Steve Mangum, and Dean Joe Alutto have been instrumental in creating the kind of research atmosphere that makes the completion of a book like this possible. At the Fisher College, I have also been able to work with some very bright Ph.D. students who have influenced this book, including Asli Arikan, Ilgaz Arikan, Doug Bosse, Naga Damaraju, Nilesh Khare, Woonghee Lee, Alison Mackey, Ty Mackey, Doug Miller, Masa Okada, Heli Wang, and Al Warner.

In truth, however, the third edition of this book would never have been completed without the help of Kathy Zwanziger, my very talented and dedicated assistant. Everyone in the field of strategic management who knows me knows Kathy.

Throughout this time period, there has been only one constant in my life—my family. Without them, none of this would have been possible or worthwhile. Thus, it is to my family—my wife, Kim, and my three children, Lindsay (with her husband Ryan and their three children—Isaac, Chloe, and Audrey), Kristian (with his wife Amy and their two children—Dylanie and Lucas), and Erin (with her husband Dave)—that I dedicate this book.

J. B.

ENDNOTES

1. Pierson, F. C. (1959). *The Education of American Businessmen: A Study of University-College Programs in Business Administration*, New York: McGraw-Hill, p. ix.
2. Gordon, R. A., and J. E. Howell (1959). *Higher Education for Business*, New York: Columbia University Press.
3. Roethlisberger, F., and W. Dickson (1939). *Management and the Worker*, Cambridge, MA: Harvard University Press.
4. Modigliani, F., and M. Miller (1958). "The cost of capital, corporation finance, and the theory of investment," *American Economic Review*, 48, pp. 201–297; Modigliani, F., and M. Miller (1963). "Corporate income taxes and the cost of capital," *American Eco-*

nomic Review, 53, pp. 433–443; Markowitz, H. (1959). *Portfolio Selection*, New Haven, CT: Yale University Press; and Tobin, J. (1958). "Liquidity preference as a behavior toward risk," *Review of Economic Studies*, 25, pp. 65–86.
5. See, for example, Hayes, R., and W. Abernathy (1980). "Managing our way to economic decline," *Harvard Business Review*, July–August, pp. 67–77. Many recent criticisms of MBA education strike a similar theme. See, for example, Pfeffer, J., and C. T. Fong (2002). "The end of business schools? Less success than meets the eye," *Academy of Management Learning and Education*, 1(1), pp. 78–95.

6. For example, see Ouchi, W. G. (1981). *Theory Z: How American Business Can Meet the Japanese Challenge*, Reading, MA: Addison-Wesley; and Peters, L. J., and R. H. Waterman, Jr. (1982). *In Search of Excellence*, New York: Harper & Row.

7. The most critical business historian in this context is Alfred Chandler. One of his most influential books is Chandler, A. (1962). *Strategy and Structure: Chapters in the History of the Industrial Enterprise*, Cambridge, MA: MIT Press. Rumelt's path-breaking work was somewhat anticipated by Wrigley, L. (1970). "Divisional autonomy and diversification," unpublished doctoral dissertation, Harvard Business School, Harvard University.

8. Ouchi, W. G. (1981). *Theory Z: How American Business Can Meet the Japanese Challenge*, Reading, MA: Addison-Wesley.

9. See Williamson, O. E. (1975). *Markets and Hierarchies: Analysis and Antitrust Implication*, New York: Free Press; and Nelson, R., and S. Winter (1982). *An Evolutionary Theory of Economic Change*, Cambridge, MA: Belknap Press.

10. See Hannan, M. T., and J. Freeman (1977). "The population ecology of organizations," *American Journal of Sociology*, 72, pp. 267–272.

11. See Jensen, M. C., and W. H. Meckling (1976). "Theory of the firm: Managerial behavior, agency costs, and ownership structure," *Journal of Financial Economics*, 3, pp. 305–360; and Watts, R. L., and J. L. Zimmerman (1978). "Towards a positive theory of determination of accounting standards," *Accounting Review*, 53, pp. 112–133.

12. Barney, J. B., and W. G. Ouchi (1986). *Organizational Economics*, San Francisco: Jossey-Bass.

13. See Porter, M. E. (1980). *Competitive Strategy*, New York; Free Press; Porter, M. E. (1985). *Competitive Advantage*, New York: Free Press; Prahalad, C. K., and G. Hamel (1990). "The core competence of the organization," *Harvard Business Review*, May–June, pp. 79–93. Academic research that predates the Prahalad and Hamel paper includes Prahalad, C. K., and R. A. Bettis (1986). "The dominant logic: A new linkage between diversity and performance," *Strategic Management Journal*, 7(6), pp. 485–501; and Wernerfelt, B. (1984). "A resource-based view of the firm," *Strategic Management Journal*, 5, pp. 171–180.

14. See Wernerfelt, B. (1984). "A resource-based view of the firm," *Strategic Management Journal*, 5, pp. 171–180; Barney, J. B. (1986). "Strategic factor markets: Expectations, luck and business strategy," *Management Science*, 32, pp. 1512–1514; and Barney, J. B. (1991). "Firm resources and sustained competitive advantage," *Journal of Management*, 17, pp. 99–120.

GAINING AND SUSTAINING COMPETITIVE ADVANTAGE

C H A P T E R

1

Introduction:
What Is Strategy?

Most people know the simple card game of blackjack—sometimes known as "21." As played in casinos around the world, the objective of this game is remarkably simple: Players draw cards in an attempt to have their cards sum closer to 21 than their dealer, without going over 21. In blackjack, face cards are equal to 10, aces are equal to 1 or 11, and the remaining cards in the deck are equal to their number (the two of diamonds equals 2, the nine of spades equals 9, and so forth.). The game begins by the dealer passing out two cards to every player. The dealer also gets two cards, but one of the dealer's cards is facing up. All the players play before the dealer plays. Setting aside complications created by different ways players can bet (doubling down, buying insurance, and so forth), playing blackjack requires only one decision: Should you take another card or not?

There are a variety of different theories about when a player should and should not take a card. Some players rely on their intuition and good luck. These players take a card when it "feels like the right thing to do." Sometimes these "intuition players" take a card when their hand sums to 18—and get a 3! Other players have very simple theories of when to take a card: When their cards sum to 16 or more, they stay; 15 or less, they take a card. Simple theories of winning at blackjack are easy to learn and apply. They sometimes even produce wins. Still other players have somewhat more sophisticated theories about how to win this game. For example, some players take a card when their cards sum to 16, but only when the card showing in the dealer's hand is a 10. If the dealer is not showing a 10, these players take a card when their cards sum to 14. These somewhat "contingent theories" of winning blackjack are a bit more complicated than the simple theories and are based on a partial understanding of the probability theory that underlies a game like blackjack.

Of course, it is possible to derive a quite complicated theory of how to win at blackjack by rigorously applying probability theory to the game. The rules of play for such a theory are summarized in Table 1.1. These rules are based on two definitions: a player's stiff (when a player's cards sum to 12, 13, 14, 15, or 16) and a dealer's stiff (when the card showing in the dealer's hand is a 2, 3, 4, 5, or 6). In this approach to playing the game, players assume that the card not showing in the dealer's hand is a 10—because that is the most common value in the deck. If a dealer has a 10 plus a 2, 3, 4, 5, or 6, the odds are very high that the dealer will go over 21 when it is his or her turn to draw cards. Because dealers are likely to go over 21—the casino term is to "bust"—when they are showing a 2, 3, 4, 5, or 6, players should proceed cautiously in asking for more cards. On the other hand, if a dealer is showing an ace, 7, 8, 9, or 10, then players have to be more aggressive, because the most likely outcome is that the dealer will have 16, 17, 18, 19, 20, or 21.

This simple intuition is rigorously implemented in the rules of play presented in Table 1.1.

Of course, there is more to this game than just applying the rules presented in Table 1.1. Setting aside the betting (which can be quite complicated), the way that these rules are implemented can be very important. In particular, although applying the rules in Table 1.1, strictly speaking, is not "cheating," casinos can "ask"—often in pretty forceful ways—those that apply these rules to no longer play in their casino. So, if you are going to play these rules, you need to conceal that you are doing so. This has an impact on numerous aspects of playing the game, everything from the clothes you wear (not too fancy or sloppy—you don't want to stand out), to the beverages you order (water and fruit juices are better than alcoholic beverages), to how you implement the rules (once an hour you should violate the rules in Table 1.1 to throw off casino operators), to how long you should practice before you go into a

---

TABLE 1.1	**Rules for Playing Blackjack Derived from the Application of Probability Theory**

Definitions

Player's stiff—when a player's hand sums to 12, 13, 14, 15, or 16

Dealer's stiff—when the card showing in a dealer's hand is 2, 3, 4, 5, or 6

Rules of Play

Always take a card if you have a stiff (16) and the dealer doesn't (10).

Never take a card if both you (14) and the dealer (5) have stiffs.

Never take a card when your cards sum to 17 and you don't have an ace.

Never take a card if you have three cards that sum to 16 and the dealer shows a 10.

Never take a card if you hold two 7s and the dealer shows a 10.

Taking cards when you hold an ace:
- Ace, 9 and Ace, 8: Never.
- Ace, 7: Only if the dealer shows a 9, 10, or ace.
- Ace, 6: Always.

Derived from: J. Schaffel (2006). *The Pocket Guide to Winning Blackjack*. Summarized at: www.winningblackjack.ca.

CHAPTER 1   Introduction: What Is Strategy? **3** ∎

casino (most experts recommend playing 24 hours straight before you begin playing in a casino).

So, four theories of how to win at blackjack have been described: A theory based on intuition and good luck, a simple theory, a somewhat contingent theory, and a more sophisticated theory based on the application of probability theory to the game along with an understanding of how casinos actually operate. If you were to invest in some-one playing blackjack for you, and if your goal was to maximize your income from this investment, in which of these theories would you invest?[1]

Most potential investors would pick the theory based on probability theory and an understanding of how casinos work. In the long run, this theory of how to win at blackjack is most likely to generate a positive return—in fact, application of this the-ory does enable a player to have a slight advantage over the house. Of course, apply-ing the other theories to the game will also generate positive returns, at least some of the time, but the last of these four theories has the greatest expected value in the long run.

This is a simple version of blackjack. And the theory of how to win this game—the strategy players can adopt—is actually relatively easy to describe and use. Of course, business is a much more complicated game than blackjack. For example, the rules of blackjack remain unchanged, while the "rules" of the game of business can change dramatically, as technology, industry structure, and consumer demands change. However, business is still just a game, and different firms have different theories about how to win their competitive game.

Some firms seem to have a very intuitive approach to business. Some firms choose a course of action because it "feels right." Sometimes these firms get lucky and do well. Other times they don't. Other firms have very simple, easy-to-understand theories: "If a business is not number one or two in a growing industry, we divest it." Simple theories have the huge advantage that everyone in a firm is likely to understand them. And, if these theories happen to be consistent with the underlying economics in an industry, they can generate positive economic returns. If this isn't the case, simple theories can lead to economic failure. Still other firms have somewhat contingent theories, adjusting their strategies based on how their industry is evolving over time. Again, these more complicated theories can sometimes be successful.

Of course, the best theories of how to win a competitive game—like the best the-ories of how to win at blackjack—are based on a complete understanding of the game, both how it is best played and how the rules of play should be implemented in real life. In business, a complete understanding of how a competitive game is best played does not depend on the application of probability theory. Rather, the best we can do is apply economic theory to understand the structure of the competitive game a firm is in, and thereby derive the "rules of play" for this game. The application of these rules requires managers to understand how they can organize, lead, and motivate the people who work in and with a firm to implement these rules efficiently. Also, the implementation of these rules in a business setting does not require an understanding of how casinos work, but a broader understanding of how organizations can implement a firm's theory of how it is going to win. And although this type of theory of how to win the "game of business" cannot guarantee a firm will always have a high level of performance, in the long run investors in firms with these strategies are more likely to maximize their wealth than investors in firms with other kinds of strategies.

1.1 WHAT IS STRATEGY?

If business is like a game—albeit a very complicated one—then a firm's strategy is its theory of how to excel in the game it is playing. More precisely, a firm's **strategy** is its theory of how to achieve high levels of performance in the markets and industries within which it is operating.[2] Evaluating, and choosing a strategy requires an understanding of both the economic logic from which a strategy is derived, and an understanding of the organizational logic through which a strategy is implemented. A failure in either of these areas—in understanding the economics of strategic choice or the organizational elements of strategy implementation—make it less likely that a firm's strategy will generate high levels of performance—although even firms with horrible strategies can sometimes get lucky.[3]

Sometimes a firm's understanding of the critical economic processes in an industry or market and how it can exploit those processes for its own advantage are simply wrong. For example, when Honda Motorcycle Company entered the U.S. motorcycle market in the early 1960s, it believed that the best way to compete against Harley-Davidson, Triumph, and other established motorcycle firms—i.e., Honda's theory of how to perform well in the U.S. motorcycle market—was to sell large and powerful motorcycles. Unfortunately, U.S. consumers did not want to purchase large motorcycles from Honda—after all, they could already purchase large motorcycles from established firms. What U.S. consumers wanted to buy were Honda's smaller motor scooters. Once Honda discovered what customers in the United States really wanted, Honda changed it's strategy and began selling motor scooters. With this niche in smaller motor scooters established, Honda was then able to introduce larger and more powerful motorcycles. This new theory about how Honda could perform well in the U.S. motorcycle market was so successful that Honda, along with several other Japanese motorcycle firms, virtually destroyed all other motorcycle manufacturing firms. Of those firms that competed with Honda in the early 1960s, only Harley-Davidson continues to compete in this industry.[4]

However, Honda's original theory of how to perform well in the U.S. motorcycle market was wrong. However, this company was able to learn that this theory was wrong and change it quickly enough to be successful. Other firms have had what turned out to be incorrect theories of how to perform well in a particular industry or market but have been either unable or unwilling to change that theory. For example, Yugo entered the U.S. automobile market in the mid-1980s. Yugo's theory about how to compete in this market was simple: It would underprice all of its competition. Following this strategy, Yugo felt that it could dominate the low-price automobile segment. What this theory failed to recognize, however, is that performance and safety are concerns for most U.S. car buyers—even those seeking to buy inexpensive automobiles. Yugo's price was certainly lower than that of any other new car in the U.S. market. But its performance and safety were widely perceived to be unacceptable. Moreover, although Yugos cost less than any other new car, they did not cost less than many used cars in the U.S. market—cars with higher levels of performance and safety. Needless to say, Yugo no longer sells cars in the U.S. market and was voted as the worst new car ever sold in the United States.[5]

Honda and Yugo had incorrect theories about how to perform well in the U.S. marketplace. On the other hand, other firms have developed very sophisticated and very successful strategies. Consider, for example, WalMart.[6]

By 1962, Sam Walton and his brother, Bud, owned and operated 16 Ben Franklin "five and dime" stores in rural Arkansas. Early on, Sam Walton recognized the economic potential of locating discount retail outlets in relatively rural cities but was unable to convince the owners of the Ben Franklin chain to pursue this opportunity. In response, he created his own company, and called it Wal-Mart Stores.

Wal-Mart began operations in the fiercely competitive discount retail business. Through the late 1960s, several discount retailers—including King's, Korvette's, Two Guys, and Woolco—were forced out of business. Profit margins in the surviving firms were paper thin—often averaging only 2 or 3 percent of sales. Despite this challenging industry, Wal-Mart began to prosper and grow. By the mid-1980s, while more established retailers, including KMart and Zayre's, had a return on equity averaging about 14 percent, Wal-Mart's return on equity averaged about 33 percent. Despite the fact that Wal-Mart was 4.6 times larger than KMart, Wal-Mart's market value was more than 48 times KMart's market value. By 2005 Wal-Mart's stores had sales of $290 billion and operating income of $17 billion.

Walton's theory of how to perform well in the discount retail market depended on three factors. First, by locating many of its stores in relatively rural cities, Wal-Mart provided a much-needed service to customers who lived in or near these cities. Moreover, these cities were only large enough to support one large discount retail operation. Thus, the Wal-Marts that operated in these rural locations were able to charge prices that were as much as 6 percent higher than the prices at Wal-Marts that were operated in more urban areas—all without attracting additional retail companies into these markets.

Second, Wal-Mart was able to develop one of the most effective and cost-efficient distribution networks in the retail industry. Built around several large warehouse facilities, Wal-Mart's distribution system began with detailed inventory information gathered at each store. This information was used to order just enough product to ensure that inventory would be on hand, but not so much that large amounts of inventory would have to be warehoused. By operating its own fleet of trucks, and by cooperating with its suppliers, Wal-Mart was able to obtain a 6 or 7 percent cost advantage over its competition, including KMart.

Third, Sam Walton himself helped create an organizational culture and a way of doing business that motivated and inspired his employees. To emphasize the importance of low costs, Walton built a headquarters building that looked a great deal like a warehouse. Sam rode around in a beat-up old truck—even though, at the time of his death, he was the richest person in the United States. Employees responded to Sam's way of doing business and generated higher-than-industry-average levels of productivity and lower-than-industry-average levels of shrinkage.

Of course, Wal-Mart faced its own challenges as well. First, by the early 1990s, most of the rural markets that had allowed Wal-Mart to charge relatively higher prices were already exploited. To continue its growth, Wal-Mart had to begin to expand its operations in much more competitive urban settings. Second, in response to developments in the warehouse segment of the retail industry, Wal-Mart introduced Sam's Discount Warehouses. Although discount warehouses have several attractive features, they work on even narrower margins than discount retail stores. Also, Wal-Mart began to experience resistance to its growth efforts. Local merchants and community leaders in several New England states, for example, worked together to keep Wal-Mart from destroying the existing retail distribution network—and the lifestyles associated with it. In addition, several of Wal-Mart's efforts to expand outside of the United States were taking longer to turn profitable than had been anticipated. After almost a decade of struggle, Wal-Mart finally began to turn a profit on its operations in Mexico, and acquisitions in Canada did not generate profits for many years. Acquisitions in Germany were so unprofitable that they were divested in 2006. Finally, some observers had concluded that, with the death of Sam Walton, the special employee spirit that was so important to Wal-Mart's success was beginning to dissipate.

1.2 THE STRATEGIC MANAGEMENT PROCESS

Often a firm develops its strategy—its theory of how to compete successfully—by implementing the strategic management process. The **strategic management process** is a sequential set of analyses and choices that can increase the likelihood that a firm will choose a strategy that enables it to perform well. An example of the strategic management process is presented in Figure 1.1.

A Firm's Mission

The strategic management process begins when a firm defines its mission. A firm's **mission** is its long-term purpose. Missions define both what a firm aspires to be in the long run and what it wants to avoid in the meantime. Missions are often written down in the form of **mission statements.** Table 1.2 shows examples of the mission statements of several well-known firms.

Some Missions May Not Affect Firm Performance

As shown in Table 1.2, most mission statements incorporate many common elements. For example, many define the businesses within which a firm will operate—computer hardware, software, and services for IBM. Some define how a firm will compete in those businesses—doing everything direct at Dell, and just winning at the Oakland Raiders. Many even define the core values that a firm espouses: the "soul of Dell".

Indeed, mission statements often contain so many common elements that some have questioned whether having a mission statement actually creates value for a firm. Moreover, even if a mission statement does say something unique about a company, if that mission statement does not influence behavior throughout an organization, it is

FIGURE 1.1 The Strategic Management Process

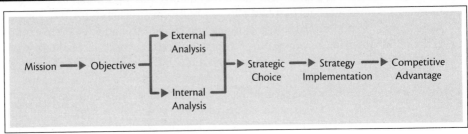

TABLE 1.2	Mission Statements of Some Well-Known Firms

Dell

Dell is building its technology, its business, and its communities through direct relationships with our customers, our employees, and our neighbors. Through this process, we are committed to bringing value to customers and adding value to our company, our neighborhoods, our communities, and our world through diversity, environmental and global citizenship initiatives.

The Core Elements of the "Soul of Dell"

Customers: We believe in creating loyal customers by providing a superior experience at a great value.

The Dell Team: We believe our continued success lies in teamwork and in the opportunity each team member has to learn, develop, and grow.

Direct Relationships: We believe in being direct in all we do.

Global Citizenship: We believe in participating responsibly in the global marketplace.

Winning: We have a passion for winning in everything we do.

IBM

At IBM, we strive to lead in the invention, development, and manufacture of the industry's most advanced information technologies, including computer systems, software, storage systems, and microelectronics. We translate these advanced technologies into value for our customers through our professional solutions, services, and consulting businesses worldwide.

The Oakland Raiders

Just Win—Baby!

Sources: www.dell.com, used with permission of Dell Computer Corporation; www.ibm.com, used with permission of IBM; www.oaklandraiders.com.

unlikely to have much effect on a firm's actions. After all, Enron's 1999 annual report included the following statement of values:

> *Integrity:* We work with customers and prospects openly, honestly and sincerely. When we say we will do something, we will do it; when we say we cannot or will not do something, then we won't do it.[7]

This statement was published at exactly the same time that senior management at Enron was engaging in activities that ultimately defrauded investors, partners, and Enron's own employees—and has landed some Enron executives in jail.[8]

Some Missions Can Improve Firm Performance

Despite these caveats, research by Jim Collins and Jerry Porras in *Built to Last* has identified some firms whose sense of purpose and mission permeates all that they do. Some of these **visionary firms,** or firms whose mission is central to all they do, are listed in Table 1.3.[9] One interesting thing to note about visionary firms is their long-term profitability. From 1926 through 1995, an investment of $1 in one of these firms would

TABLE 1.3 A Sample of Visionary Firms
3M
American Express
Boeing
Citicor
Ford
General Electric
Hewlett-Packard
IBM
Johnson & Johnson
Marriott
Merck
Motorola
Nordstrom
Philip Morris
Procter & Gamble
Sony
Wal-Mart
Walt Disney

Source: Adapted from J. C. Collins and J. I. Porras.
Built to Last: Successful Habits of Visionary Companies.
New York: Harper Collins Publishers Inc. © 1994
James C. Collins and Jerry I. Porras. Reprinted by
permission.

have increased in value to $6,536. That same dollar invested in an average firm over this same time period would have been worth $415 in 1995.

These visionary firms earned substantially higher returns than average firms even though many of their mission statements suggest that profit maximizing, while an important corporate objective, is not their primary reason for existence. Consider what Jim Burke, a former CEO at Johnson & Johnson (one of the visionary firms identified in Table 1.3), says about the relationship between profits and his firm's mission and mission statement:

> All our management is geared to profit on a day-to-day basis. That's part of the business of being in business. But too often, in this and other businesses, people are included to think, "We'd better do this because if we don't, it's going to show up on the figures over the short-term." [Our mission] allows them to say, "Wait a minute. I don't have to do that." The management has told me that they're . . . interested in me operating under this set of principles.[10]

Some Missions Can Hurt Firm Performance

Although some firms have used their missions to develop strategies that create significant competitive advantages, missions can hurt a firm's performance as well. For example, sometimes a firm's mission is very inwardly focused and defined only with reference to the personal values and priorities of its founders or top managers, independent of whether those values and priorities are consistent with the economic realities facing the firm. Strategies derived from such missions or visions are not likely to be a source of competitive advantage.

For example, Ben & Jerry's Ice Cream was founded in 1977 by Ben Cohen and Jerry Greenfield, both as a way to produce super-premium ice cream and as a way to create an organization based on the values of the 1960s counterculture.[11] This strong sense of mission led Ben & Jerry's to adopt some very unusual human resource and other policies. Among these policies, the company adopted a compensation system whereby the highest-paid firm employee could earn no more than five times the income of the lowest-paid firm employee. Later this ratio was adjusted to seven to one. However, even at this level, such a compensation policy made it very difficult to acquire the senior management talent needed to ensure the growth and profitability of the firm without grossly overpaying the lowest-paid employees in the firm. When a new CEO was appointed to the firm in 1995, his $250,000 salary violated this compensation policy.

Indeed, though the frozen dessert market consolidated rapidly through the late 1990s, Ben & Jerry's Ice Cream remained an independent firm, partly because of Cohen's and Greenfield's commitment to maintaining the social values that their firm embodied. Lacking access to the broad distribution network and managerial talent that would have been available if Ben & Jerry's had merged with another firm, the company's growth and profitability lagged. Finally in April 2000, Ben & Jerry's Ice Cream was acquired by Unilever. However, the 66 percent premium finally earned by Ben & Jerry's stockholders in April 2000 had been delayed for several years. In this sense, Cohen's and Greenfield's commitment to a set of personal values and priorities was at least partly inconsistent with the economic realities of the frozen dessert market in the United States.

Obviously, because a firm's mission can help, hurt, or have no effect on its performance, missions by themselves do not necessarily lead a firm to choose and implement strategies that help the firm win its competitive game. Indeed, as suggested in Figure 1.1, although defining a firm's mission is an important step in the strategic management process, it is only the first step in that process.

Objectives

While a firm's mission is a broad statement of its purpose and values, it **objectives** are specific measurable targets a firm can use to evaluate the extent to which it is realizing its mission. Consider, for example, 3M's mission statement in Table 1.4. This statement emphasizes the importance of finding innovative products and producing high returns for shareholders. However, 3M also lists some objectives associated with its mission:

TABLE 1.4   3M's Mission Statement

We are committed to:
- Satisfying our customers with superior quality and value,
- Providing investors with an attractive return through sustained, high-quality growth,
- Respecting our social and physical environment,
- Being a company that employees are proud to be a part of.

Satisfying our customers with superior quality and value—
Providing the highest-quality products and services consistent with our customers requirements and preferences.
Making every aspect of every transaction a satisfying experience for our customers.
Finding innovative ways to make life easier and better for our customers.

Providing investors with an attractive return through sustained, high-quality growth—
Our goals are:
Growth in earnings per share averaging 10 percent a year or better,
A return on capital employed of 27 percent or better,
A return on stockholders' equity of between 20 and 25 percent,
At least 30 percent of our sales each year from products new in the last four years.

Respecting our social and physical environment—
Complying with all laws and meeting or exceeding regulations,
Keeping customers, employees, investors and the public informed about our operations,
Developing products and processes that have a minimal impact on the environment,
Staying attuned to the changing needs and preferences of our customers, employees and society,
Uncompromising honesty and integrity in every aspect of our operations.

Being a company that employees are proud to be a part of—
Respecting the dignity and worth of individuals,
Encouraging individual initiative and innovation in an atmosphere characterized by flexibility, cooperation and trust,
Challenging individual capabilities,
Valuing human diversity and providing equal opportunity for development.

Source: 3M.com (Used with permission of the Director of Corporate Communications at 3M).

growth in earnings per share averaging 10 percent or better per year, a return on employed capital of 27 percent or better; at least 30 percent of sales from products that are no more than four years old; and so forth.

High-quality objectives are tightly connected to elements of a firm's mission and are relatively easy to measure and track over time. Low-quality objectives either do not exist or are not connected to elements of a firm's mission, are not quantitative, and are difficult to measure or difficult to track over time. Obviously, low-quality objectives cannot be used by management to evaluate how well a mission is being realized. Indeed, one indication that a firm is not that serious about realizing part of its mission statement is that there are no objectives, or there are only low-quality objectives, associated with that part of the mission.

External and Internal Analysis

The next two phases of the strategic management process—external analysis and internal analysis—occur more or less simultaneously. By conducting an **external analysis,** a firm identifies the critical threats and opportunities in its competitive environment. It also examines how competition in this environment is likely to evolve and what implications that evolution has for the threats and opportunities a firm is facing. A considerable literature on techniques for and approaches to conducting external analysis has evolved over the last several years. This literature is the primary subject matter of Chapters 3 and 4 of this book.

Whereas external analysis focuses on the environmental threats and opportunities facing a firm, **internal analysis** helps a firm identify its organizational strengths and weaknesses. It also helps a firm understand which of its resources and capabilities are likely to be sources of advantage and which of them are less likely to be sources of such advantages. Finally, internal analysis can be used by firms to identify those areas of its organization that require improvement and change. Just as with external analysis, a considerable literature on techniques for and approaches to conducting internal analysis has evolved over the past several years. This literature is the primary subject matter of Chapter 5 of this book.

The external and internal analyses steps of the strategic management process parallel the steps in SWOT analysis. **SWOT** analysis—an acronym that stands for "strengths, weaknesses, opportunities, and threats"—focuses attention on both the external attributes of a firm's environment (opportunities and threats) and on the internal attributes of a firm (strengths and weaknesses). Traditional SWOT logic suggests that firms should choose strategies that exploit opportunities and neutralize threats through the use of strengths while avoiding or fixing weaknesses.

However, without the analytical tools for analyzing a firm's environment and its internal capabilities presented in Chapters 3, 4, and 5, SWOT analysis does little more than identify the kinds of questions firms should ask in choosing their strategies. By itself, SWOT analysis provides no guidance in how these questions should be answered. Too often, SWOT analysis—without the conceptual tools presented in Chapters 3, 4, and 5—becomes little more than a listing exercise, in which long lists of strengths, weaknesses, opportunities, and threats are generated, and the strategy with the longest list is chosen. With these tools, however, it becomes possible to rigorously identify a firm's strengths and weaknesses, along with its opportunities and threats.

Strategic Choice

Armed with a mission, objectives, and completed external and internal analyses, a firm is ready to make its strategic choices. That is, a firm is ready to choose its "theory of how to win its competitive game."

The strategic choices available to firms fall into two main categories: business-level strategies and corporate-level strategies. **Business-level strategies** are actions firms take to gain advantages in a single market or industry and are the topic of Part II of this book. The four business-level strategies explained in this book are cost leadership (Chapter 6), product differentiation (Chapter 7), flexibility (Chapter 8), and tacit collusion (Chapter 9).

Corporate-level strategies are actions firms take to gain advantages by operating in multiple markets or industries simultaneously and are the topic of Part III of this book. The corporate-level strategies examined in this book include vertical integration strategies (Chapter 10), diversification strategies (Chapters 11 and 12), strategic alliance strategies (Chapter 13), merger and acquisition strategies (Chapter 14), and international strategies (Chapter 15).

Obviously, the details of choosing specific strategies can be quite complex, and a discussion of these details will be delayed until later in the book. However, the underlying logic of strategic choice is not complex. Based on the strategic management process, the objective when making a strategic choice is to choose a strategy that (1) supports the firm's mission, (2) is consistent with the firm's objectives, (3) exploits opportunities in the firm's environment with the firm's strengths, and (4) neutralizes threats in the firm's environment while avoiding the firm's weaknesses. Assuming this strategy is implemented— the last step of the strategic management process—a strategy that meets these four criteria is very likely to be a source of superior performance for a firm.

Strategy Implementation

Of course, simply choosing a strategy means nothing if that strategy is not implemented. **Strategy implementation** occurs when a firm adopts organization policies and practices that are consistent with its strategy. Three specific organizational policies and practices are particularly important in implementing a strategy: a firm's formal organizational structure, its formal and informal management control systems, and its employee compensation policies. A firm that adopts an organizational structure, management controls, and employee compensation that are consistent with and reinforce its strategies is more likely to be able to implement those strategies than a firm that does not do so. Specific organizational structures, management controls, and compensation policies used to implement the business-level strategies are discussed in Part II of this book. Part III focuses on implementing corporate-level strategies.

1.3 EMERGENT STRATEGIES

The simplest way of thinking about a firm's strategy is to assume that firms begin operations with a well-developed theory, that the marketplace provides a test of that theory, and that management makes adjustments to that theory to improve its ability to generate superior performance. There is no doubt that this process describes the strategy process in some firms. For example, FedEx, the world leader in the overnight delivery business, entered this industry with a very well developed theory about how to perform well in that business. Indeed, Fred Smith, the founder of FedEx (known originally as Federal Express), first articulated this theory as a student in a term paper for an undergraduate business class at Yale University. Legend says that he received only a "C" on the paper—but the company that was founded on the theory of competition in the overnight delivery business developed in that paper has done extremely well. Founded in 1971, FedEx had 2005 sales in excess of $29 billion, operating income of $1.4 billion, profits of $31 million, and employed over 100,000 people around the world.[12]

However, other firms do not begin operations with a well-defined, well-formed strategy. Even if they do, often they have to modify this strategy so much once it is actually implemented in the marketplace that it bears little resemblance to the theory with which the firm started. **Emergent strategies** are theories of how to compete successfully in an industry that emerge over time or those that have been radically reshaped once they are initially implemented.[13] The relationship between a firm's intended and emergent strategies is depicted in Figure 1.2.

We have already seen one example of an emergent strategy: Honda's strategy for entering, and later dominating, the U.S. motorcycle market. Also, the current strategies of many firms, including many very successful firms, have been emergent. For example, Johnson & Johnson was originally only a supplier of antiseptic gauze and medical plasters. The firm had no consumer business at all. Then, in response to complaints about irritation caused by some of the firm's medical plasters, J&J began enclosing a small packet of talcum powder with each of the medical plasters it sold. Soon customers were asking to purchase the talcum powder by itself, and the company introduced "Johnson's Toilet and Baby Powder." Later an employee invented a ready-to-use

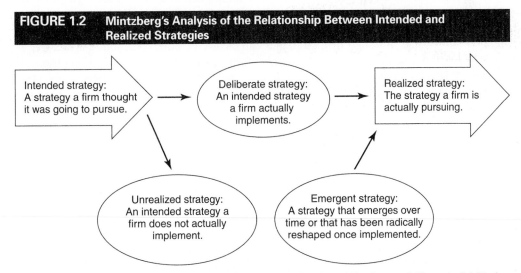

FIGURE 1.2 Mintzberg's Analysis of the Relationship Between Intended and Realized Strategies

Intended strategy: A strategy a firm thought it was going to pursue.

Deliberate strategy: An intended strategy a firm actually implements.

Realized strategy: The strategy a firm is actually pursuing.

Unrealized strategy: An intended strategy a firm does not actually implement.

Emergent strategy: A strategy that emerges over time or that has been radically reshaped once implemented.

Source: Reprinted from "Strategy Formation in an Adhocracy," by Henry Mintzberg and Alexandra McHugh, published in *Administrative Science Quarterly,* Vol. 30, No. 2, June 1985, by permission of *Administrative Science Quarterly.* Copyright © 1985 by Administrative Science Quarterly.

bandage for his wife. It seems she often cut herself while using a knife in the kitchen. When J&J's marketing managers learned of this invention, they decided to introduce it into the market place. J&J's Band-Aid products have become the largest-selling brand category at J&J. Overall, J&J's intended strategy was to compete in the medical products market, but its emergent consumer products strategies now generate over 40 percent of total corporate sales.

Another firm with what turns out to be an emergent strategy is the Marriott Corporation. Marriott was originally in the restaurant business. In the late 1930s, Marriott owned and operated eight restaurants. One of these restaurants was close to an airport in the Washington, D.C., area. Managers at this restaurant noticed that airline passengers came into the restaurant to purchase food to eat on their trip. J. Willard Marriott, the founder of the Marriott Corporation, noticed this trend and negotiated a deal with Eastern Airlines to deliver prepackaged lunches directly to Eastern's planes. This arrangement was later extended to include American Airlines. Over time, providing food service to airlines has become a major business segment for Marriott. Although Marriott's initial intended strategy was to operate in the restaurant business, the company at one time engaged in the emergent food service business at over 100 airports throughout the world. Ultimately, it used this business to expand into the hotel business, for which it is best known today.[14]

Some firms have almost entirely emergent strategies. PEZ Candy, Inc., for example, manufactures and sells small plastic candy dispensers with cartoon and movie character heads, along with candy refills. This privately held firm has made few efforts to speed its growth, yet demand for current and older PEZ products continues to grow. In the 1990s PEZ doubled the size of its manufacturing operation to keep up with demand. Old PEZ dispensers have become something of a collector's item. Several national conferences on PEZ collecting have been held, and some particularly rare PEZ dispensers were once auctioned at Christie's. This demand has enabled PEZ to raise the price of its dispensers to $1.29 and the price of its candy refills to $1.39, all without increases in advertising, sales personnel, and movie tie-ins so typical in the candy industry.[15]

Of course, although firm strategies can clearly be emergent, some have suggested that emergent strategies are relevant only when a firm's strategy formulation process has failed. That is, if managers in a firm were more sophisticated and complete in their strategic analysis, they would have been able to anticipate the economic processes that forced them to abandon their intended strategies in favor of their emergent strategies. In this light, Honda's emergent strategy for entering the U.S. motorcycle market, J&J's emergent consumer products strategy, and Marriott's emergent airline food service strategy, rather than being examples of firms cleverly exploiting opportunities of which they had not been previously aware, are really examples of poor strategic management in the first place.

Certainly, if the economic processes in an industry that determine whether a firm's strategy is valuable could, in principle, have been known and understood before a firm's strategies were chosen, then a firm being forced to abandon its intended strategy in favor of an emergent strategy can be understood as a failure in the strategy creation process. However, even in this situation, the ability to adjust quickly and abandon an intended for an emergent strategy can be seen as an important competitive advantage for a firm. Indeed, some firms adopt an explicit "second mover" approach to strategy, relying on their ability to quickly adopt what other firms demonstrate is a valuable strategy. In general, such "second moving" firms may appear to be pursuing more emergent than deliberate strategies. However, given their resources and capabilities, such second moving may actually be optimal for these firms.[16]

Moreover, in some settings, it is effectively impossible to be able to understand the economic processes that determine the value of a strategy. This is especially the case if a firm is operating in a rapidly changing competitive context. When, in principle, changes that affect the value of a firm's strategies cannot be anticipated, then the ability to adjust rapidly to changing conditions and substitute emergent for intended strategies may be very important. These issues are discussed in more detail in Chapter 4's analysis of opportunities in "hypercompetitive industries" and in Chapter 5's analysis of the role of luck in creating competitive advantages for firms.

1.4 SUMMARY

A firm's strategy is its theory of how to compete successfully. In this sense, a firm's strategy is its best guess about what the critical economic processes in an industry or market are and how it can take advantage of these economic processes to enhance its performance. Some theories of how to compete successfully are better than others, and the study of strategy is the study of alternative theories of how to obtain high levels of performance in different competitive contexts.

A firm's strategy can be based on its mission, or a firm's fundamental purpose and long-term objectives. A firm's mission can imply a set of objectives, or specific measurable performance targets that the firm aspires to in each of the areas covered by its mission, a set of strategies, or the means through which the firm accomplishes its mission and objectives, and tactics or policies, or the actions that the firm takes to implement its strategies.

Sometimes a firm's mission can have a pervasive effect on a firm and its strategies. A vision is a firm mission that is central to all that a firm does. Research suggests that visionary firms can outperform non-visionary firms in the long run. This is true even though the mission in most visionary firms does not emphasize economic performance over other roles and responsibilities of the organization.

Sometimes a firm begins operations with a well-developed, logically complete strategy that is tested by the market and adjusted by managers to improve its ability to generate competitive advantage. Not all strategies, however, are developed and implemented in this way. Emergent strategies are strategies that emerge over time, as a firm operates in a market or industry. When the economic processes in operation in an industry cannot be anticipated, emergent strategies can be very valuable. Moreover, some firms have resources and capabilities that facilitate quick imitation of the successful strategies of other firms. These strategies can also be thought of as emergent.

REVIEW QUESTIONS

1. Some firms publicize their corporate mission statements widely, by including them in annual reports, on company letterheads, and in corporate advertising. What, if anything, does this practice say about the ability of these mission statements to be sources of sustained competitive advantage for a firm? Why?

2. There is little empirical evidence that having a formal, written mission statement improves a firm's performance. Yet many firms spend a great deal of time and money developing mission statements. Why?

3. Is it possible to distinguish between an emergent strategy and an *ad hoc* rationalization of

a firm's past decisions? Can the concept of an emergent strategy be prescriptive? Why or why not?

4. Both internal and external analyses are important in the strategic management process.

Is the order in which these analyses are done important? If yes, which should come first— external analysis or internal analysis? If the order is not important, why not?

ENDNOTES

1. Please note that the author of this textbook has *never* played blackjack in a casino!
2. This approach to defining strategy was discussed by Drucker, P. (1994). "The Theory of Business," *Harvard Business Review*, 75, September/October, pp. 95–105.
3. Luck, as a determinant of a firm's competitive success, has been emphasized by a variety of authors, including Alchian, A. A. (1950). "Uncertainty, evolution, and economic theory," *Journal of Political Economy*, 58, pp. 211–221; Mancke, R. B. (1974). "Causes of Interfirm profitability differences: A new interpretation of the evidence," *Quarterly Journal of Economics*, 108, pp. 181–193; and Barney, J. B. (1986). "Strategic factor markets: Expectations, luck and business strategy," *Management Science*, 32(10), pp. 1231–1241.
4. Honda's early entry into the U.S. motorcycle market is described by Pascale, R. T. (1984). "Perspectives on strategy: The real story behind Honda's success," *California Management Review*, 26(3), pp. 47–72.
5. A description of Yugo's woeful performance in the United States can be found in Hartley, R. F. (1991). *Management Mistakes & Successes*, 3rd ed., New York: John Wiley & Sons.
6. A description of Wal-Mart's history and many of its current challenges can be found in Ghemawat, P. (1986). "Wal-Mart stores' discount operations," Harvard Business School Case no. 90794-039; Ortega, B. (1995). "Life without Sam: What does Wal-Mart do if stock drop cuts into workers' morale?" *Wall Street Journal*, January 4, p. A1; and Troy, M. (1998), "Wal-Mart intensified global push for '99," *Discount Store News*, 37(23), December 14, p. 7.
7. http://www.Enron.com.
8. "On Trial," *Business Week*, January 12, 2004, pp. 80–81.
9. Collins, J. C., and J. I. Porras (1997). *Built to Last: Successful Habits of Visionary Companies*. New York: Harper Collins.
10. Quoted in Collins, J. C., and J. I. Porras (1997). *Built to Last: Successful Habits of Visionary Companies*, New York: Harper Collins.
11. See Theroux, J., and J. Hurstak (1993). "Ben & Jerry's Homemade Ice Cream Inc.: Keeping the mission(s) alive," Harvard Business School Case no. 9-392-025; and Applebaum, A. (2000), "Smartmoney.com: Unilever feels hungry, buys Ben & Jerry's," *Wall Street Journal*, April 13, pp. B1+.
12. FedEx's history is described in Trimble, V. (1993). *Overnight Success: Federal Express and Frederick Smith, Its Renegade Creator*, New York: Crown.
13. Mintzberg, H. (1978). "Patterns in strategy formulation," *Management Science*, 24(9), pp. 934–948; and Mintzberg, H. (1985). "Of strategies, deliberate and emergent," *Strategic Management Journal*, 6(3), pp. 257–272. Mintzberg has been most influential in expanding the study of strategy to include emergent strategies.
14. The J&J and Mariott emergent strategy stories can be found in Collins, J. C., and J. I. Porras (1997). *Built to Last: Successful Habits of Visionary Companies*, New York: Harper Collins.
15. See McCarthy, M. J. (1993). "The PEZ fancy is hard to explain, let alone justify," *Wall Street Journal*, March 10, p. A1, for a discussion of PEZ's surprising emergent strategy.
16. See Lieberman and Montgomery (1988).

CHAPTER

2

Firm Performance and Competitive Advantage

In Chapter 1, strategy was defined as a firm's theory of how to achieve high levels of performance in the markets and industries in which it is operating. In many walks of life, defining performance is easy. In athletics, for example, the team that scores more points outperforms the team that scores fewer points; the athlete who runs faster outperforms the athlete who runs slower. These simple definitions become more complicated, however, when they are applied to a firm. The purpose of this chapter is to introduce one widely accepted definition of firm performance and then to examine several different measures of this definition.

2.1 FIRM PERFORMANCE AND COMPETITIVE ADVANTAGE

Of course, the ultimate objective of the strategic management process (described in Chapter 1) is to enable a firm to choose and implement a strategy that generates a competitive advantage. But what is a competitive advantage? In general, a firm has a **competitive advantage** when it is able to create more economic value than rival firms. **Economic value** is simply the difference between the perceived benefits gained by a customer who purchases a firm's products or services and the full economic cost of these products or services. Thus, the size of a firm's competitive advantage is the difference between the economic value a firm is able to create and the economic value its rivals are able to create.[1]

Consider the two firms presented in Figure 2.1. Suppose these firms compete in the same market for the same customers. Firm I generates $180 of economic value each time it sells a product or service, whereas Firm II generates $150 of economic value each time it sells a product or service. Because Firm I generates more economic value each time it sells a product or service, it has a higher level of performance than Firm II.

The size of this performance difference is equal to the difference in the economic value these two firms create, in this case, $30 ($180 − $150 = $30).

However, as shown in Figure 2.1, Firm I's advantage may come from different sources. For example, Firm I might create greater perceived benefits for its customers than Firm II. In Figure 2.1A, Firm I creates perceived customer benefits worth $230, while Firm II creates perceived customer benefits worth only $200.

Thus, even though the costs of both firms are the same ($50 per unit sold), Firm I creates more economic value ($230 − $50 = $180) than Firm II ($200 − $50 = $150). Indeed, in this situation it is possible for Firm I to have higher costs than Firm II and still create more economic value than Firm II if these higher costs are offset by Firm I's ability to create greater perceived benefits for its customers.

Alternatively, as shown Figure 2.1B, these two firms may create the same level of perceived customer benefit ($210 in this example), but have different costs. If Firm I's costs per unit are only $30, it will generate $180 worth of economic value ($210 − $30 = $180). If Firm II's costs are $60 per unit, it will generate only $150 of economic value ($210 − $60 = $150). Indeed, it might be possible for Firm I to create a lower level of perceived benefits for its customers than Firm II and still create more economic value than Firm II, as long as its disadvantage in perceived customer benefits was more than offset by its cost advantage.

When a firm enjoys a performance advantage over its competition, it is said to enjoy a competitive advantage. Thus, in Figure 2.1, Firm I has a competitive advantage

---

FIGURE 2.1   The Sources of a Firm's Competitive Advantage

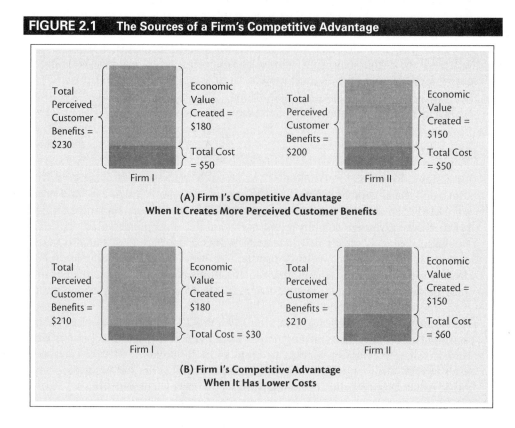

(A) Firm I's Competitive Advantage
When It Creates More Perceived Customer Benefits

(B) Firm I's Competitive Advantage
When It Has Lower Costs

FIGURE 2.2   Types of Competitive Advantage

over Firm II. A firm's competitive advantage can be either temporary or sustained. As summarized in Figure 2.2, a **temporary competitive advantage** is a competitive advantage that lasts for a very short period of time. A **sustained competitive advantage,** on the other hand, can last much longer. Firms that create the same economic value as their rivals experience **competitive parity.** Finally, firms that generate less economic value than their rivals have a **competitive disadvantage.** Not surprisingly, competitive disadvantages can be either temporary or sustained, depending on how long they last.

How long firms are able to sustain competitive advantages has interested scholars for some time. Traditional economic theory predicts that such advantages should be short-lived in highly competitive markets. This theory suggests that any competitive advantages gained by a particular firm will quickly be identified and imitated by other firms, ensuring competitive parity in the long run. In real life, however, competitive advantages often last longer than traditional economic theory predicts.

One of the first scholars to examine this issue was Dennis Mueller. Mueller divided a sample of 472 firms into eight categories, depending on their level of performance in 1949. He then examined the impact of a firm's initial performance on its subsequent performance. The traditional economic hypothesis was that all firms in the sample would converge on an average level of performance. This did not occur. Indeed, firms that were performing well in an earlier time period tended to perform well in later time periods, and firms that performed poorly in an earlier time period tended to perform poorly in later time periods as well.[2]

Geoffrey Waring followed up on Mueller's work by explaining why competitive advantages seem to persist longer in some industries than in others. Waring found that, among other factors, firms that operate in industries that (1) are informationally complex, (2) require customers to know a great deal in order to use an industry's products, (3) require a great deal of research and development, and (4) have significant economies of scale are more like to have sustained competitive advantages compared to firms that operate in industries without these attributes.[3]

Peter Roberts studied the persistence of profitability in one particular industry—the U.S. pharmaceutical industry. Roberts found that not only can firms sustain competitive advantages in this industry, the ability to do so is attributable almost entirely to the firm's capacity to innovate by bringing out new and powerful drugs.[4]

2.2 MEASURING COMPETITIVE ADVANTAGE

A firm has a competitive advantage when it creates more economic value than its rivals, and economic value is the difference between the perceived customer benefits associated with buying a firm's products or services and the cost of producing and selling these products or services. These are deceptively simple definitions, however, and these concepts are not always easy to measure directly. For example, the benefits of a firm's products or services are always a matter of customer perception, and perceptions are hard to measure. Also, the total costs associated with producing a particular product or service may not always be easy to identify or associate with the particular product or service. Despite the very real challenges associated with measuring a firm's competitive advantage, two approaches have emerged. The first estimates a firm's competitive advantage by examining its simple accounting performance; the second does it by examining the firm's adjusted accounting performance. Each of these approaches is discussed below.

Simple Accounting Measures of Competitive Advantage

By far the most popular way of measuring a firm's performance is through the use of simple accounting measures. Simple accounting measures of performance are publicly available for many firms. They communicate a great deal of information about a firm's operations. For these reasons, most early teaching and research in strategy and strategic management focused on the effect of strategy on a firm's accounting performance.

Accounting approaches to characterizing a firm's performance often rely on ratio analysis. Accounting ratios come in various types. Some of the most important accounting ratios, and what they suggest about a firm's performance, are listed in Table 2.1. The major categories of accounting ratios are profitability ratios (ratios with some measure of profit in the numerator and some measure of firm size or assets in the denominator), liquidity ratios (ratios that focus on the ability of a firm to meet its short-term financial obligations), leverage ratios (ratios that focus on the level of a firm's indebtedness), and activity ratios (ratios that focus on the level of activity in a firm's business).

It is also possible to integrate a firm's financial ratios to obtain a more complete picture of the firm's economic performance. Altman applied several statistical techniques to estimate the effect of different financial ratios on the probability that a firm will declare bankruptcy.[5] Altman's estimated equation is

$$\begin{aligned}
Z = \ & .012 \text{ (working capital/total assets)} \\
& + .014 \text{ (retained earnings/total assets)} \\
& + .033 \text{ (earnings before interest and taxes/total assets)} \\
& + .0006 \text{ (market value of equity/book value of total debt)} \\
& + .999 \text{ (sales/total assets)}
\end{aligned} \tag{2.1}$$

Altman concluded that if a firm's Z score is less than 1.8, the firm will fail; if it is between 1.8 and 3.0, it will probably not fail; and if it is more than 3.0, it will not fail. This model successfully predicts corporate failures up to five years prior to their occurrence 69.8 percent of the time. Minor adjustments to this equation can improve the prediction rate.[6]

TABLE 2.1	Ratio Analysis Using Simple Accounting Measures of Historical Firm Performance	
Ratio	*Calculation*	*Interpretation*
Profitability Ratios		
1. Return on total assets (ROA)	$\dfrac{\text{Profits after taxes}}{\text{Total assets}}$	A measure of return on total investment in a firm.
2. Return on equity (ROE)	$\dfrac{\text{Profits after taxes}}{\text{Total stockholders' equity}}$	A measure of return on total equity investment in a firm.
3. Gross profit margin	$\dfrac{\text{Sales} - \text{cost of goods sold}}{\text{Sales}}$	A measure of sales available to operating expenses and still generate a profit.
4. Earnings per share (EPS)	$\dfrac{\text{Profits (after taxes)} - \text{Preferred stock dividends}}{\text{Number of shares of common stock outstanding}}$	A measure of profit available to owners of common stock.
5. Price earnings (p/e)	$\dfrac{\text{Current market price/share}}{\text{After-tax earnings per share}}$	A measure of anticipated firm performance—high p/e ratio tends to indicate that the stock market anticipates strong future performance.
6. Cash flow per share	$\dfrac{\text{After-tax profits} + \text{depreciation}}{\text{Number of common shares outstanding}}$	A measure of funds available to fund activities above current level of costs.
Liquidity Ratios		
1. Current ratio	$\dfrac{\text{Current assets}}{\text{Current liabilities}}$	A measure of the ability of a firm to cover its current liabilities with assets that can be converted into cash in the short term.
2. Quick ratio	$\dfrac{\text{Current assets} - \text{inventory}}{\text{Current liabilities}}$	A measure of the ability of a firm to meet its short term obligations without selling of its current inventory.
Leverage Ratios		
1. Debt to assets	$\dfrac{\text{Total debt}}{\text{Total assets}}$	A measure of the extent to which debt has been used to finance a firm's business activities.
2. Debt to equity	$\dfrac{\text{Total debt}}{\text{Total equity}}$	A measure of the use of debt versus equity to finance a firm's business activities.
3. Times interest earned	$\dfrac{\text{Profits before interest and taxes}}{\text{Total interest charges}}$	A measure of how much a firm's profits can decline and still meet its interest obligations.
Activity Ratios		
1. Inventory turnover	$\dfrac{\text{Cost of goods sold}}{\text{Average inventory}}$	A measure of the speed with which a firm's inventory is turning over.
2. Accounts receivable turnover	$\dfrac{\text{Annual credit sales}}{\text{Accounts receivable}}$	A measure of the average time it takes a firm to collect on credit sales.
3. Average collection period	$\dfrac{\text{Accounts receivable}}{\text{Average daily sales}}$	A measure of the time it takes a firm to receive payment after a sale has been made.

Limitations of Simple Accounting Measures

The simple accounting measures of performance summarized in Table 2.1 are powerful tools for understanding a firm's performance, but they are not without limitations. Three particularly important limitations of accounting measures of performance are discussed below.

Managerial Discretion. Managers often have some discretion in choosing accounting methods, including methods of counting revenues, valuing inventory (for example, last in, first out [LIFO] versus first in, first out [FIFO]), rates of depreciation (straight-line versus accelerated), depletion, amortization, and so forth. Thus, to some degree at least, measures of accounting performance reflect managerial interests and preferences. The relationship between a variety of different managerial interests and accounting methods has been examined in the accounting literature.[7]

When the value of a manager's bonus depends on the firm's accounting performance, managers have a strong incentive to adopt accounting practices that increase the level of reported current-period profit. Empirical work suggests that, under these conditions, managers often do adopt such accounting practices.[8] Indeed, maintaining bonuses, and especially the value of stock options, was a major reason why several firms at the turn of the twenty-first century—including Enron, Tyco, WorldCom, and Health South—adopted fraudulent accounting practices. However, those accounting practices do not have to be fraudulent, and managers can still have a significant effect on a firm's repeated performance.

Also, when a firm's performance violates the expectations of capital markets, managers have an incentive to adopt accounting practices that increase the level of reported current-period profit. In so doing, they may avoid potential employment instability that might be associated with very low stock prices leading to unfriendly takeovers or the violation of debt contract covenants leading to bankruptcy. Managers apparently reason that adopting these accounting methods may give them time to get their organization's performance in order. Again, empirical work is generally consistent with this expectation.[9]

For example, before its turnaround, IBM was able to downplay some of its impending economic problems through such accounting method changes, including booking shipped goods as revenue even though they might be returned by customers, booking the lifetime revenue of long-term computer leases at the time they were signed, and adopting accounting methods that pushed the cost of equipment and retirement into the future. None of these actions was illegal or inconsistent with generally accepted accounting principles. However, they all had the effect of increasing IBM's current-period reported profits. Given IBM's history of very conservative accounting practices, some suggested that these changes were misleading.[10]

Note, again, that none of these changes is necessarily illegal, but they can have a very significant effect on a firm's reported performance.

On the other hand, managers have an incentive to report lower current-period profits when high current-period profits might create potential antitrust liability for themselves and their firm. In this context, high accounting profits could be interpreted as a signal of anticompetitive monopolistic behavior. By adopting accounting methods that reduce the level of reported current profits, managers can avoid this antitrust liability. Empirical results generally support this relationship between the threat of antitrust activity and the adoption of profit-reducing accounting methods.[11]

Finally, managers have an interest in reducing the level of current profitability when doing so gives them power in negotiations with external stakeholders. For example, owners of Major League Baseball teams have at least three reasons for understating the profitability of their teams: (1.) to obtain tax write-offs to offset the profits of other businesses they own; (2.) to present a bleak picture in labor negotiations with players; and (3.) to scare cities into subsidizing the construction of additional baseball infrastructure, including new roads, parking lots, and even stadiums. In 1984, baseball owners reported a collective accounting loss of almost $42 million, although representatives of the players' union concluded, using the same data, that the teams that year collectively had a $9 million accounting profit. Despite these accounting problems, the market value of baseball franchises has doubled every 9 years for the last 90 years. The Baltimore Orioles, for example, were purchased for $70 million in 1989. Their potential sale price in 1993 was $145 million. Recently, this increase in franchise value has accelerated. In 1998 the Los Angeles Dodgers were sold to the News Corporation for $311 million, and in 1999 the Cleveland Indians sold for $320 million. One expert had valued the Indians at $361 million. Richard Jacobs, the former owner of the Indians, turned an eightfold profit on the $40 million that had been paid for that franchise in 1986. In this industry, it may well be that reported accounting performance is not a particularly accurate measure of economic performance.[12]

What this research on managerial interests and accounting methods suggests is that accounting measures of performance cannot be understood independent of the interests and preferences of managers. Thus, if two firms have exactly the same underlying "true" performance, but one firm has large management bonus plans tied to accounting numbers or is not meeting capital market expectations about accounting performance, while the second is under threat of government antitrust action or in the midst of labor negotiations, management choices about accounting methods can lead these firms to have very different "reported" accounting performance.

Short-Term Bias.   Most simple accounting approaches to measuring performance have a built-in short-term bias. This is because longer-term, multiple-year investments in a firm are usually treated, for accounting purposes, simply as costs in those years in which they do not generate revenues that exceed costs. Consider, for example, a firm that has a research and development (R&D) budget of $50,000 per year. For convenience, assume that this firm knows, with absolute certainty, that five years of investing in R&D at this level will create a product that will generate $3 million in revenue in the sixth year. If this firm calculates its return on investment (ROI) in each of the first five years of R&D, the ROI for each of those years looks very bad ($0/$50,000 = 0% ROI). However, if this firm calculates the ROI for the entire six-year period ($3,000,000/$250,000 = 1,200% ROI), the return looks very good. Unfortunately, because most accounting measures of performance are calculated on an annual basis, the longer-term positive effect of R&D for this firm can easily be understated.

Valuing Intangible Resources and Capabilities.   A third limitation of accounting measures of firm performance is that they generally do not fully value a firm's intangible resources and capabilities. A firm's **intangible resources and capabilities** are productive assets that are difficult to observe, describe, and value but that nevertheless can have a significant effect on a firm's performance. Intangible resources and capabilities such as "close relationships with customers," "close cooperation among managers," "a sense of loyalty to the firm," and "brand awareness" are difficult to measure yet are often important determinants of a firm's success.[13]

The challenge facing users of simple accounting measures of performance is that intangible resources and capabilities, just like their more tangible counterparts, are the result of investments that firms make over long periods of time. However, instead of investing in such physical assets as plant and equipment, firms invest in nonphysical assets such as teamwork, reputations, loyalty, and relationships. If these investments in intangible resources and capabilities are not included in a measure of firm performance, computed accounting rates of return may substantially overstate a firm's actual performance.

Effects of Accounting Limitations

Simple accounting measures of performance are limited, but if these limitations are inconsequential, accounting numbers may still be an extremely accurate—and convenient—measure of firm performance. Several researchers have examined the magnitude of these measurement problems.[14] Unfortunately, this research suggests that these measurement problems may, in fact, be very large. Indeed, two of the most influential of these researchers have concluded that "[t]he[se] effects can be large enough to account for the entire inter-firm variation in the accounting rates of return among the largest firms in the United States. A ranking of firms by accounting rates of return can easily [be] invert[ed]."[15]

This assertion has created controversy among those interested in understanding the determinants of a firm's performance.[16] Recall that most of the early teaching and research focused on the link between a firm's strategies and its performance had adopted accounting measures of performance. However, most subsequent empirical work has consistently supported the conclusion that simple accounting measures of firm performance can be very inaccurate.[17]

All this does not suggest that simple accounting measures of performance are somehow bad, nor does it suggest that these accounting numbers should be ignored. It does suggest, however, that care and judgment must be used when applying accounting measures to characterize firm performance.

Adjusted Accounting Measures of Competitive Advantage

Although simple accounting measures of firm performance have important limitations, they have the enormous advantage of being widely available for publicly traded firms. For some time now, finance and accounting scholars have been exploring ways to adjust publicly available accounting numbers so that they can be used to measure more accurately the economic value that a firm is generating. Such adjusted accounting measures take advantage of the broad availability of accounting numbers, but do so in a way that avoids many of the limitations of simple accounting measures of firm performance. Some of these adjusted accounting performance measures are discussed in this section.[18]

At the simplest level, these adjusted accounting measures of firm performance just compare a firm's revenues and costs. For some of these measures, estimating a firm's costs relies heavily on the concept of a firm's cost of capital. In efficient capital markets, a firm's **cost of capital** is the return that capital suppliers (both debt and equity) expect to receive from investing in a firm. A firm that generates a return that is less than its cost of capital will be unable to continue to attract capital; a firm that generates a return that is greater than its cost of capital will be able to attract additional capital. Thus, a firm's cost of capital is an important component of a firm's costs. Estimating a firm's revenues, on the other hand, requires a thorough understanding of current accounting practices and the implications of those practices on a firm's reported profits.

Four Adjusted Accounting Measures of a Firm's Economic Performance

Four adjusted accounting measures of a firm's economic performance are described in this section: return on invested capital (ROIC), economic profit (EP), market value added (MVA),[19] and Tobin's *q*. Taken together, these four adjusted accounting measures of performance can provide a clear picture of a firm's true economic performance. Calculation of the first two of these measures, ROIC and EP, in turn, depends on three numbers that must be calculated from a firm's profit-and-loss statement and balance sheet, and from information about a firm's capital market performance. These three numbers are net operating profit less adjusted taxes (NOPLAT), invested capital, and the weighted average cost of capital (WACC). Calculation of these three building-block numbers is described first, followed by a description of how these numbers are combined to calculate a firm's ROIC and EP. The calculation of MVA and Tobin's *q* are then described. Calculation of ROIC, EP, and Tobin's *q* is completed for a hypothetical firm, with the profit-and-loss statement and balance sheet presented in Table 2.2 and 2.3. MVA, on the other hand, is reported for a sample of 100 firms in the United States.[20]

TABLE 2.2	Profit-and-Loss Statement for a Hypothetical Firm ($million)					
	2001	*2002*	*2003*	*2004*	*2005*	*2006*
Net sales	182.3	193.4	205.3	231.1	229.2	255.3
Cost of goods sold	(125.1)	(132.3)	(145.1)	(168.2)	(162.1)	(182.2)
Selling, general, & admin. expenses	(18.3)	(21.7)	(24.5)	(28.7)	(32.3)	(29.2)
Other expenses	0	0	0	0	0	0
Depreciation expense	(8.5)	(10.1)	(13.1)	(8.2)	(15.4)	(14.2)
Amortization of goodwill	(3.0)	(4.2)	(3.5)	(2.1)	(1.1)	(1.2)
Interest income	.4	.3	.7	1.2	.2	.4
Interest expense	(.6)	(.8)	(.9)	(2.1)	(.4)	(.8)
Provision for income taxes	(10.2)	(9.1)	(8.6)	(12.1)	(10.1)	(11.2)
Other income	0	0	0	0	0	0
Net income	17.0	15.5	10.3	10.9	8.0	16.9

TABLE 2.3	Balance Sheet for a Hypothetical Firm ($million)					
	2001	*2002*	*2003*	*2004*	*2005*	*2006*
Assets						
Operating cash	2.8	3.1	4.2	5.3	5.4	6.8
Accounts receivable	17.0	19.2	27.3	28.7	32.1	36.5
Inventories	2.0	3.1	8.5	7.6	28.7	27.9
Other current assets	3.2	10.3	4.8	8.1	12.1	12.2
Total current assets	25.0	35.7	44.8	49.7	78.2	83.4
Gross property, plant, and equipment	81.3	89.3	96.1	107.3	138.2	149.3
Accumulated depreciation	(24.2)	(31.2)	(35.1)	(38.4)	(44.4)	(41.2)
Book value of fixed assets	57.1	58.1	61.0	68.9	93.8	108.1
Goodwill	17.4	27.1	28.1	20.0	15.9	15.0
Other operating assets	3.4	12.7	11.1	14.2	33.3	44.4
	102.9	133.6	145.0	152.8	221.3	250.9

	2001	*2002*	*2003*	*2004*	*2005*	*2006*
Liabilities & equity						
Short-term debt	.3	.5	.9	2.3	9.8	12.0
Accounts payable	6.4	12.2	10.8	8.9	24.7	22.2
Accrued liabilities	4.3	7.7	8.3	9.2	21.7	24.5
Total current liabilities	11.0	20.4	20.0	20.4	56.2	58.7
Long-term debt	5.0	12.8	14.3	19.2	37.5	49.2
Deferred income taxes	9.2	11.3	14.4	11.2	21.3	22.3
Preferred stock	0	0	0	0	0	0
Retained earnings	55.1	57.2	58.1	56.2	55.1	56.0
Common stock & paid-in capital	22.3	32.0	38.2	45.8	51.2	63.7
Other long-term liabilities	0	0	0	0	0	0
Total liabilities & equity	102.6	133.7	145.0	152.8	221.3	249.9
Shares outstanding	1.3	1.5	1.8	1.7	1.4	1.7
Average price/share (high-low/trading days)	18	19.5	21.2	16.3	10.1	12.2
Bond rating	AA	A	AB	BB	BB	BB
β	1.1	1.1	1.2	1.4	1.4	1.3
Risk-free rate	3.5	3.8	3.9	3.8	3.9	3.9
Market rate of return	11.1	12.2	14.3	15.3	14.2	15.1

Calculating Net Operating Profits Less Adjusted Taxes

In order to calculate NOPLAT, it is first necessary to calculate three numbers from a firm's profit-and-loss statement and balance sheet: (1) earning before interest and taxes (EBIT), (2) taxes on EBIT, and (3) changes in deferred income taxes. EBIT is calculated as

$$\text{EBIT} = \text{net sales} - (\text{cost of goods sold} + \text{selling, general, and} \\ \text{administrative expenses} + \text{depreciation expense}) \qquad \textbf{(2.2)}$$

EBIT is calculated for our hypothetical firm in Panel A of Table 2.4.

Taxes on EBIT is calculated as

$$\text{Taxes on EBIT} = \text{provision for income taxes} + \text{tax shield on interest} \\ \text{expense} - (\text{tax on interest income} + \text{tax on nonoperating profit}) \qquad \textbf{(2.3)}$$

Provision for income taxes is usually reported in a firm's financial statements. To calculate tax shield on interest expense, tax on interest income, and tax on nonoperating profit, it is usually necessary to multiply a firm's interest expense, interest income, and nonoperating profit by its marginal tax rate. The marginal tax rate is set by statute and should include all national and regional taxes. Taxes on EBIT are calculated for our hypothetical firm in Panel B of Table 2.4.

Changes in deferred income taxes are calculated by comparing a firm's deferred income taxes in a year with its deferred income taxes in the previous year. The calculation of changes in deferred income taxes for our hypothetical firm is presented in Panel C of Table 2.4.

NOPLAT is calculated by combining EBIT, taxes on EBIT, and changes in deferred income taxes in the following way:

$$\text{NOPLAT} = \text{EBIT} - \text{taxes on EBIT} + \text{changes in deferred income taxes} \quad \textbf{(2.4)}$$

NOPLAT is calculated for our hypothetical firm in Panel D of Table 2.4.

Calculating Invested Capital
Invested capital is the amount of money a firm has invested in the operations of its businesses. Invested capital is calculated as

$$\text{Invested capital} = (\text{operating current assets} \\ + \text{book value of fixed current assets}) \\ - (\text{net other operating assets} \\ + \text{non-interest-bearing current liabilities}) \qquad \textbf{(2.5)}$$

As shown in Panel A of Table 2.5, operating current assets equals the sum of a firm's operating cash, accounts receivable, inventories, and other current assets. Panel B of Table 2.5 shows that the book value of current fixed assets equals the sum of a firm's gross property, plant, and equipment less accumulated depreciation. Panel C of Table 2.5 calculates net other operating assets as equal to a firm's other assets minus its other liabilities. Non-interest-bearing current liabilities equal a firm's accounts payable plus other accrued liabilities and is calculated in Panel D of Table 2.5. Finally, invested capital is calculated for our hypothetical firm in Panel E of Table 2.5.

Calculating the Weighted Average Cost of Capital
A firm's weighted average cost of capital (WACC) is the weighted average of the marginal costs of all of a firm's sources of capital, including its debt and equity. The precise

TABLE 2.4 Calculating NOPLAT from the Profit-and-Loss Statement (Table 2.2) and Balance Sheet (Table 2.3) for a Hypothetical Firm Assuming This Firm's Deferred Income Tax in 2000 Equaled $8.8 Million and Its Marginal Tax Rate Is 40% ($million)

Panel A:
Calculating EBIT

	2001	2002	2003	2004	2005	2006
Net sales ($)	182.3	193.4	205.3	231.1	229.2	255.3
Cost of goods sold ($)	125.1	132.8	145.1	168.2	162.1	182.2
SGA ($)	18.3	21.7	24.5	28.7	32.3	29.2
Depreciation expense ($)	8.5	10.1	13.1	8.2	15.4	14.2
EBIT ($)	30.4	28.8	22.6	26.0	19.4	29.7

EBIT = net sales − (cost of goods sold + selling, general, and administrative expense [SGA] + depreciation expense)

Panel B:
Calculating Taxes on EBIT

	2001	2002	2003	2004	2005	2006
Provision for income taxes ($)	10.2	9.1	8.6	12.1	10.1	11.2
Tax shield on interest expense[1] ($)	.24	.32	.36	.84	.16	.32
Tax on interest income[2] ($)	.16	.12	.28	.48	.08	.16
Tax on nonoperating profit[3] ($)	0	0	0	0	0	0
Taxes on EBIT ($)	10.28	9.3	8.68	12.46	10.18	11.36

Taxes on EBIT = Provision for income taxes + tax shield on interest expense − (tax on interest income + tax on nonoperating profit)

Panel C:
Calculating Changes in Deferred Income Taxes

	2001	2002	2003	2004	2005	2006
Changes in deferred income tax ($)	0.4	2.1	3.1	3.2	10.1	1.0

Changes in deferred income taxes = (deferred tax $_{t-1}$ − deferred tax$_t$)

Panel D:
Calculating NOPLAT

	2001	2002	2003	2004	2005	2006
EBIT	30.4	28.81	22.6	16.0	19.4	29.7
Taxes on EBIT	10.28	9.3	8.68	12.46	10.18	11.36
Changes in deferred income tax	.4	2.1	3.1	3.2	10.1	1.0
NOPLAT	19.72	17.4	10.82	10.34	(.88)	17.34

NOPLAT = EBIT − taxes on EBIT + changes in deferred income taxes

[1]Marginal tax rate × interest expense

[2]Marginal tax rate × interest income

[3]Marginal tax rate × nonoperating profit

TABLE 2.5   **Calculating Invested Capital from the Profit-and-Loss Statement (Table 2.2) and Balance Sheet (Table 2.3) for a Hypothetical Firm Assuming This Firm's Deferred Income Tax in 2000 Equaled $8.8 Million and Its Marginal Tax Rate Is 40% ($million)**

Panel A:
Calculating Operating Current Assets

	2001	2002	2003	2004	2005	2006
Operating cash ($)	2.8	3.1	4.2	5.3	5.1	6.8
Accounts receivable ($)	17.0	19.2	27.3	28.7	32.1	36.5
Inventory ($)	2.0	3.1	8.5	7.6	28.7	17.9
Other current assets ($)	3.2	10.3	4.8	8.1	12.1	21.2
Operating current assets ($)	25.0	35.7	44.8	49.7	78.0	82.4

Operating current assets = operating cash + accounts
receivable + inventory + other current assets

Panel B:
Calculating Book Value of Fixed Current Assets

	2001	2002	2003	2004	2005	2006
Gross property, plant, and equipment ($)	81.3	89.3	96.1	107.3	138.2	149.3
Accumulated depreciation ($)	24.2	31.2	35.1	38.4	44.4	41.2
Book value of fixed current assets ($)	57.1	58.1	61.0	68.9	93.8	108.1

Book value of fixed current assets = gross property,
plant, and equipment − accumulated depreciation

Panel C:
Calculating Net Operating Other Assets

	2001	2002	2003	2004	2005	2006
Other operating assets ($)	3.4	12.7	11.1	14.2	33.3	44.4
Other long-term liabilities ($)	0	0	0	0	0	0
Net other operating assets ($)	3.4	12.7	11.1	14.2	33.3	44.4

Net operating other assets = other operating
assets − other long-term liabilities

Panel D:
Calculating Non-Interest-Bearing Current Liabilities

	2001	2002	2003	2004	2005	2006
Accounts payable ($)	6.6	12.2	10.8	8.9	24.7	22.2
Accrued liabilities ($)	4.3	7.7	8.3	9.2	21.7	24.5
Non-interest-bearing current liabilities ($)	10.9	19.9	19.1	18.1	46.4	46.7

Non-interest-bearing current liabilities = accounts payable + accrued liabilities

TABLE 2.5	continued					

Panel E:
Calculating Invested Capital

	2001	2002	2003	2004	2005	2006
Operating current assets ($)	25.0	35.7	44.8	49.7	78.0	82.4
Book value of fixed current assets ($)	57.1	58.1	61.0	68.9	93.8	108.1
Net other operating assets ($)	3.4	12.7	11.1	14.2	33.3	44.4
Non-interest-bearing current liabilities ($)	10.9	19.9	19.1	18.1	46.4	46.7
Invested capital ($)	68.0	61.2	75.6	86.3	92.1	99.4

Invested capital = (operating current assets + book value of fixed current assets) − (net other operating assets + non-interest-bearing current liabilities)

calculation of a firm's WACC can be quite complicated. However, a simplified approach involves estimating a firm's cost of debt, estimating a firm's cost of equity, weighting the cost of each of these sources of capital, and then summing these figures.

The Cost of Debt.   Different kinds of debt have different costs. In general, the cost of a firm's debt can be estimated based on the quality of that debt as evaluated by Moody's, Standard and Poor's, or some other bond-rating service. If a firm's debt is rated say, AA, and the cost of AA-rated debt is currently 12 percent, then 12 percent is not an unreasonable estimate of the current pretax cost of this debt. If a firm's debt is rated CCC (a high-yield or "junk-bond" rating), and the cost of CCC-rated debt is currently 22 percent, then the pretax cost of this high-yield debt is currently 22 percent. If a firm's debt is not rated by one of the major bond-rating services, then it is necessary to identify a firm similar to the firm whose cost of capital is being estimated whose debt is rated. This rating can be used as a basis for calculating the pretax cost of debt.

If a firm's interest payments are tax-deductible, then the pretax cost of debt must be adjusted to reflect the tax benefits of debt. This is done by multiplying the cost of a firm's debt times one minus that firm's marginal tax rate:

$$\text{After-tax cost of debt} = (1 - \text{marginal tax rate}) \text{ cost of debt} \qquad \textbf{(2.6)}$$

The calculation of a firm's cost of debt is complicated by the existence, for many firms, of quasi-debt forms of financing such as operating leases, capital leases, and preferred stock. If these quasi-debt forms of financing are a significant part of a firm's capital structure, additional work must be done to calculate the cost of a firm's debt. On the other hand, if these quasi-debt forms of financing are not a significant portion of a firm's capital structure, then the approach to calculating a firm's after-tax cost of debt, as in equation 2.6, is sufficient. This is done for our hypothetical firm in Panel A of Table 2.6.

The Cost of Equity.   There are two approaches to estimating a firm's cost of equity. One applies the capital asset pricing model (CAPM), the other applies arbitrage pricing theory (APT). Only the CAPM approach to estimating the cost of equity will be described here. The CAPM can be written as

$$\text{Cost of equity} = RFR_t + \beta_j \left[E(R_{m,t}) - RFR_t \right] \qquad \textbf{(2.7)}$$

TABLE 2.6	Calculating the Weighted Average Cost of Capital from the Profit-and-Loss Statement (Table 2.2) and Balance Sheet (Table 2.3) for a Hypothetical Firm Assuming This Firm's Deferred Income Tax in 2000 Equaled $8.8 Million and Its Marginal Tax Rate Is 40%

Panel A:
Calculating the After-Tax Cost of Debt

	2001	2002	2003	2004	2005	2006
Cost of debt[1] (%)	.08	.083	.094	.102	.104	.106
After-tax cost of debt (%)	.048	.049	.056	.061	.062	.064

After-tax cost of debt $= (1 - \text{marginal tax rate})$ cost of debt

Panel B:
Calculating the Cost of Equity

	2001	2002	2003	2004	2005	2006
Risk-free rate (%)	.035	.038	.039	.038	.039	.039
β	1.1	1.1	1.2	1.4	1.4	1.3
Market rate (%)	.111	.122	.143	.153	.142	.151
Cost of equity (%)	.119	.130	.164	.199	.183	.185

Cost of equity $=$ risk-free rate $+ \beta$ (market rate $-$ risk-free rate)

Panel C:
Calculating the Weighted Average Cost of Capital

	2001	2002	2003	2004	2005	2006
After-tax cost of debt (%)	.048	.049	.056	.061	.062	.064
Cost of equity (%)	.119	.130	.164	.199	.183	.185
Liabilities/firm market value (%)	.25	.33	.34	.33	.52	.52
Equity/firm market value (%)	.75	.67	.66	.67	.48	.48
Weighted average cost of capital (%)	.101	.139	.127	.1534	.120	.121

$$\text{Weighted average after-tax cost of debt} = \frac{\text{market value of debt}}{\text{firm's market value}}(\text{after-tax cost of debt})$$

$$\text{Weighted average cost of equity} = \frac{\text{market value of equity}}{\text{firm's market value}}(\text{cost of equity})$$

Weighted average cost of capital $=$ weighted average after-tax cost of debt $+$ weighted average cost of equity

[1]Based on bond rating in Table 2.5

where

$RFR_t =$ the risk-free rate of return in time t
$\beta_j =$ firm j's systematic risk
$E(R_{m,t}) =$ the expected rate of return on a fully diversified portfolio of securities at time t

and where, theoretically,

$$\beta_j = \frac{\text{COV}(R_j, R_m)}{\text{VAR}(R_m)} \qquad (2.8)$$

where

$$\text{COV}(R_j, R_m) = \text{the covariance between returns from firm } j\text{'s securities and the overall securities market}$$
$$\text{VAR}(R_m) = \text{the variance of overall security market returns}$$

Empirically, each of the variables in the capital asset pricing model, except one, can be measured directly. For example, a reasonable measure of the risk-free rate of return in a time period (RFR_t) is the interest rate on government securities during that time period. A reasonable measure of the expected market rate of return during a time period [$E(R_{m,t})$] is the actual rate of return of various stock market indices, including the New York Stock Exchange common stock index or the Standard and Poor's composite index. The remaining variable in equation 2.7, β_j, can be estimated by rewriting equation 2.7 in the form of a statistical multiple-regression equation as

$$R_{j,t} = a_j + b_j R_{m,t} + e_{j,t} \tag{2.9}$$

where

$R_{j,t}$ = the actual return of firm j's securities at time t
a_j = a constant equal to $(1 - b_j)\text{RFR}_t$
b_j = an estimate of β_j
$R_{m,t}$ = the rate of return on a fully diversified portfolio of securities at time t
$e_{j,t}$ = the error in estimating $R_{j,t}$

The value of b_j in equation 2.9 can be estimated through regression analysis, and is an empirical estimate of β_j.

The cost of equity for our hypothetical firm is calculated in Panel B of Table 2.6.

Weighting the Components of a Firm's Cost of Capital. The cost of each source of capital needs to be weighted by the percentage of a firm's total capital that takes that form. This is done for debt and equity by

$$\text{Weighted after-tax cost of debt} = \frac{\text{market value of debt}}{\text{firm's market value}} (\text{after-tax cost of debt})$$
$$\tag{2.10}$$

$$\text{Weighted cost of equity} = \frac{\text{market value of equity}}{\text{firm's market value}} (\text{cost of equity}) \tag{2.11}$$

A reasonable estimate of the market value of a firm's debt is simply the book value of that debt. This information is usually found in a firm's balance sheet. The market value of equity is calculated by multiplying the number of a firm's shares outstanding by the price per share. In order to avoid significant changes in the market value of equity due to short-term stock price fluctuations, it is usually appropriate to calculate a firm's price per share as an average over some period of time. These calculations are done for our hypothetical firm in Panel C of Table 2.6.

Finally, a firm's WACC is calculated as

$$\text{WACC} = (\text{weighted after-tax cost of debt}) + (\text{weighted cost of equity}) \tag{2.12}$$

The WACC for our hypothetical firm is also calculated in Panel C of Table 2.6.

Calculating a Firm's Return on Invested Capital

With a firm's NOPLAT, invested capital, and WACC now calculated, it is possible to calculate ROIC and EP. This is done in Table 2.7. In this table, ROIC is calculated as

$$ROIC = \frac{NOPLAT}{invested\ capital} \qquad (2.13)$$

TABLE 2.7 **Calculating ROIC and EP from the Profit-and-Loss Statement (Table 2.2) and Balance Sheet (Table 2.3) for a Hypothetical Firm Assuming This Firm's Deferred Income Tax in 2000 Equaled $8.8 Million and Its Marginal Tax Rate Is 40%**

Panel A:
Calculating ROIC

	2001	2002	2003	2004	2005	2006
NOPLAT ($)	19.72	17.4	10.82	10.34	(.88)	17.34
Invested capital ($)	68.0	61.2	75.6	86.3	92.3	99.4
ROIC (%)	.29	.284	.143	.119	(.009)	.174
Weighted average cost of capital (%)	.101	.139	.127	.153	.120	.121

$$ROIC = \frac{NOPLAT}{invested\ capital}$$

Panel B:
Calculating ROIC Adjusted for Goodwill

	2001	2002	2003	2004	2005	2006
NOPLAT ($)	19.72	17.4	10.82	10.34	(.88)	17.34
Invested capital ($)	68.0	61.2	75.6	86.3	92.3	99.4
Goodwill ($)	17.4	27.1	28.1	20.0	15.9	15.0
Amortization of goodwill ($)	3.0	4.2	3.5	2.1	1.1	1.2
Adjusted ROIC (%)	.275	.257	.143	.119	.002	.164
Weighted average cost of capital (%)	.101	.139	.127	.153	.120	.121

$$ROIC\ adjusted\ for\ goodwill = \frac{NOPLAT + amortization\ of\ goodwill}{invested\ capital + (goodwill - amortization\ of\ goodwill)}$$

Panel C:
Calculating EP

	2001	2002	2003	2004	2005	2006
Invested capital	68.0	61.2	75.6	86.3	92.3	99.4
ROIC (%)	.29	.284	.143	.119	(.009)	.174
Weighted average cost of capital (%)	.101	.139	.127	.153	.120	.121
EP ($)	12.9	8.9	1.2	(2.9)	(11.1)	5.3

$$EP = invested\ capital \times (ROIC - WACC)$$

ROIC equals a firm's operating profits divided by the amount of capital invested in a company and characterizes a firm's return on its capital (in percentage terms) for a given time period. If a firm's ROIC is greater than its WACC, that firm is generating profits in excess of the capital required to generate these profits. This is consistent with a firm achieving superior performance. In a similar way, a firm with an ROIC less than its WACC is achieving inferior economic performance.

Goodwill in Calculating ROIC. The treatment of one important component of the balance sheet of many firms in calculating ROIC has yet to be discussed. This component is goodwill. **Goodwill** is defined as the difference between the market value of an asset and the price a firm paid to acquire that asset. Firms pursuing an acquisition strategy will often have to pay a premium over the market price of a target to complete the acquisition of that target. The reasons why this premium must usually be paid are discussed in Chapter 14.

From an accounting point of view, goodwill is included as an asset on a firm's balance sheet. Some firms can accumulate substantial amounts of goodwill, especially if they have engaged in numerous acquisitions. For example, in 1999, Cooper Industries had total assets valued at $3.8222 billion. Over $1.516 billion of these assets, or almost 40 percent, were accounted for as goodwill and represented the premiums that Cooper had paid to make numerous acquisitions over the previous years.[21]

Technically, it is not difficult to incorporate goodwill into the calculation of a firm's ROIC. In calculating a firm's invested capital, the total amount of goodwill on a firm's balance sheet, before cumulative amortization of goodwill, should simply be added to equation 2.5. Also, in calculating NOPLAT, the amortization of goodwill should not be subtracted from equation 2.4. Incorporating goodwill into the calculation of a firm's ROIC in this way implicitly recognizes that goodwill, unlike the physical assets a firm purchases, does not wear out and is not replaced. The incorporation of goodwill is done for our hypothetical firm in Panel B of Table 2.7.

It has been suggested that a firm's ROIC should be calculated both including its goodwill and not including its goodwill.[22] ROIC without including goodwill measures the operating performance of a firm; it can be used to compare the performance of different firms and of a single firm over time. On the other hand, calculating ROIC including goodwill measures how well a firm has invested its capital—in particular, whether it has generated a return on its capital in excess of the cost of its capital, taking into consideration the premiums it has paid to gain access to some assets. If a firm has overpaid for several assets (that is, if it has paid in expectation of an operating profit that has not been forthcoming), then that firm could have an ROIC, excluding goodwill, greater than the cost of capital, but an ROIC, including goodwill, less than the cost of capital.

Calculating a Firm's Economic Profit

Not surprisingly, a firm's EP and its ROIC are closely related. Whereas ROIC characterizes a firm's performance in terms of a percentage return on invested capital, EP calculates the actual economic value created by a firm in a given time period in dollar terms. EP is calculated as

$$EP = \text{invested capital} \times (\text{ROIC} - \text{WACC}) \qquad \textbf{(2.14)}$$

If a firm is earning superior performance, the difference between ROIC and WACC will be positive. Suppose this difference is 8 percent. Then the economic value that this firm would have created during a given time period would be 8 percent times its invested capital. Note that WACC is subtracted from a firm's ROIC, and the result is multiplied by the capital invested in a firm to see how much wealth (measured in dollars) a firm created over and above the cost of the capital required to generate these profits in a given time period.

Of course, if a firm's WACC is greater than its ROIC, then the firm's calculated EP will be negative and becomes a measure of how much value the firm destroyed in a given time period. The calculation of EP for our hypothetical firm is presented in Panel C of Table 2.4.

Calculating a Firm's Market Value Added

ROIC and EP provide information about a firm's performance over some defined period of time. If, on the other hand, one is interested in characterizing a firm's long-term performance, a helpful measure of performance is MVA. One approach to calculating a firm's MVA sums the market value of a firm's equity and debt, and then subtracts its economic book value, or the amount that investors have contributed to produce whatever value a firm has created:

MVA = (market value of equity + market value of debt) − economic book value **(2.15)**

In an important sense, a firm's MVA can be thought of as the sum of its annual economic performance. A firm that consistently generates positive annual EP numbers will have very large MVA numbers. On the other hand, firms that fail to generate consistently positive EP numbers will usually have lower MVAs. Of course, MVA can also be negative, when the market value of equity plus the book value of debt is less than the amount invested in a firm since its inception.

The primary challenge in calculating a firm's MVA is determining the amount invested in a firm since its inception. This is particularly problematic if a firm has been in existence for a long time. Fortunately, Stern Stewart, a consulting firm, calculates annually the MVA for the 3,000 largest publicly owned U.S. companies. A sample of the MVAs of 100 well-known U.S. firms is presented in Table 2.8. The MVAs of these firms in 1999 and 2004 are both presented.[23]

Several interesting findings emerge from Table 2.8. First, wherease General Electric had the highest MVA in 2004, its MVA had dropped by over $170 billion since 1999. Thus, according to this measure of performance, GE was still creating an enormous amount of value, but not as much value as it used to.

However, GE did not have the biggest drop between 1999 MVA and 2004 MVA—that honor goes to Cisco, with a 1999 MVA over $513 billion and a 2004 MVA of $71 billion—a difference of $442 billion. This drop probably reflects, first, the high value of Cicso at the height of the technology bubble, and second, the much more competitive markets in which Cisco is currently operating. Following close behind Cisco, in terms of MVA reductions, are fellow technology firms Microsoft ($340 billion reduction) and Intel ($304 billion reduction). Indeed, most technology firms—including Dell, IBM, Yahoo, Hewlett Packard, and Amazon.com—saw their MVAs drop from 1999. One notable exception to this trend is Apple Computer, which saw its MVA

TABLE 2.8	MVA for a Sample of Large U.S. Firms in 2004 and 1999				
	2004 MVA	1999 MVA		2004 MVA	1999 MVA
GE	299,810	473,898	US Bancorp	30,334	14,877
Exxon	197,782	125,579	Carnival Corp	30,247	11,071
Microsoft	178,032	518,856	Schlumberger	30,211	33,961
Wal-Mart	161,693	222,588	Target	29,806	24,879
J&J	138,199	70,595	Bristol-Meyers Squibb	27,654	96,752
United Health	112,755	17,119	Apple Computer	26,965	16,808
P&G	105,858	54,970	McDonald's	23,288	38,917
Citigroup	99,485	148,172	Disney	22,717	61,100
Intel	97,468	401,417	Boeing	21,717	5,732
Dell	88,086	132,523	Hewlett Packard	19,347	111,930
IBM	85,707	155,969	Starbucks	18,020	7,143
HSBC	83,665	6,038	Emerson Electric	17,916	14,287
CISCO	71,381	513,337	Avon Products	16,921	4,975
Bank of America	68,514	35,528	Merrill Lynch	16,511	20,178
UBS	64,723	—	MBNA Corp	16,207	15,646
UPS	62,097	60,016	Sprint Corp	13,591	42,625
Pepsico	57,999	39,266	Harley Davidson	13,369	10,589
Home Depot	57,575	135,322	Amazon.com	13,152	22,333
Wells Fargo	56,553	40,180	Hershey	12,969	4,724
Abbott Labs	52,883	43,645	Gap	12,839	39,294
3M	52,443	25,879	Best Buy	12,059	16,381
Genetech	48,368	31,650	Accenture	11,529	—
Qualcomm	48,029	102,315	Electronic Arts	11,480	3,154
American Express	47,953	58,653	DirecTV	10,625	40,577
Berkshire Hathaway	47,915	29,216	Marriott	10,262	4,049
ING	44,798	23,218	Bed Bath & Beyond	8,589	4,899
Google	44,498	—	Genzyme	7,748	2,776
EBay	42,575	21,689	Southwest Airlines	5,601	7,297
ComCast	42,555	32,967	XM Satellite	5,546	1,030
Amgen	42,033	56,706	Nordstrom	5,350	2,383
Merck	39,934	122,530	Nucor	5,297	1,999
Lilly	39,555	56,699	UAL	5,266	(2,109)
Gillette	35,771	25,821	Whole Foods	5,168	467
Walgreen	35,384	21,323	Ford Motor	5,119	4,967
United Technologies	35,355	18,665	Cardinal Health	5,117	470
DuPont	32,840	31,739	Tyco	4,911	52,567
Morgan Stanley	31,804	75,965	Tribune Co.	4,820	5,489
Chevron	31,799	33,391	Harrah's Entertainment	4,515	554
Yahoo	30,985	81,863	Pixar	4,430	1,330
Anheuser-Busch	30,833	22,053	Abercrombie & Fitch	4,347	1,263
Lowe's	30,707	16,664	New York Times	3,737	5,792
Barclays	30,647	24,672	Ball, Corp.	3,156	93
Wyeth	30,402	55,509	Tiffany & Co.	3,071	5,068

TABLE 2.8 continued	2004 MVA	1999 MVA		2004 MVA	1999 MVA
Cooper Industries	3,058	(184)	Xerox	291	4,285
AEP	3,021	755	Circuit City	278	9,691
Petsmart	2,938	(295)	FootLocker	193	(2,219)
Sun Microsystems	2,791	157,111	Maytag Corp	(160)	1,231
Safec Corp.	2,435	(1,101)	MCI	(214)	—
Car Max	2,385	(314)	Whirlpool	(227)	286
Molson Coors Brewery	2,273	294	Federated Dept. Stores	(758)	(1,286)
NCR Corp	2,213	(176)	Six Flags	(815)	(170)
Cheesecake Factory	2,212	654	Service Corp. International	(1,000)	(3,226)
Verizon Communications	1,924	70,380	Goodyear Tires & Rubber	(1,095)	(3,344)
Caesar's Entertainment	1,822	(551)	Safeway, Inc.	(1,379)	17,042
Revlon Inc.	1,811	1,217	Winn-Dixie Stores	(1,736)	1,101
Wendy's	1,790	642	Newell Rubbermaid	(2,689)	(1,396)
Monster Worldwide	1,634	5,713	Blockbuster	(2,704)	(5,339)
Corning	1,531	47,194	Kroger	(3,343)	3,542
Electronic Data Systems	1,465	23,676	Eastman Kodak	(4,340)	3,604
Amerisource Bergen	1,276	240	Pfizer	(5,130)	125,073
Jet Blue Airways	1,216	—	Quest Comm.	(11,044)	29,585
Scotts Miracle Gro	975	581	General Motors	(12,393)	22,876
Talbotts	956	1,277	Time Warner	(22,362)	—
Motorolla	861	67,431	DaimerChrysler	(26,941)	10,662
Barnes & Noble	741	618	Lucent Tech.	(37,476)	146,141
ToysRUs	592	(1,037)	SBC (now AT&T)	(44,226)	33,354
Office Max	366	279	AT&T	(72,800)	46,230

Data provided by Stern Stewart Consulting. Information about how to access the entire list can be found at http://www.sternstewart.com.

increase almost $10 billion over this time period, probably reflecting Apple's success in its laptop, PC, and iPod businesses.

Wal-Mart, the largest U.S. company in terms of sales, continued to create substantial MVA in 2004, at $161 billion. However, its MVA also slipped from 1999, when it was $222 billion. Other well-known firms whose MVA dropped over this five-year period include Citigroup, Home Depot, Qualcomm, American Express, Amgen, Merck, Eli Lilly, Morgan Stanley, and Chevron.

Some firms experienced significant growth in their five-year MVA. The MVA growth leader was UnitedHealth, with an increase of MVA of $95 billion. Johnson & Johnson, another diversified health care company, also saw its MVA increase, by $68 billion—although several pure pharmaceutical companies (including Merck and Lilly) saw their MVAs drop. In financial services, HSBC saw its MVA increase by $77 billion. All the other banks included in Table 2.8 also saw their MVAs increase. Proctor and Gamble's MVA increased by $51 billion, perhaps reflecting the aggressive restructuring in which the firm engaged during this time period, as did Exxon, with an increase of $72 billion in its MVA. Interestingly, other energy companies—including Chevron and Shlumberger—did not fare as well as Exxon.

Finally, the two biggest value destroyers in 2004 were SBC and AT&T, destroying $44 billion and $72 billion in value, respectively. In what can only be characterized as an incredible irony, these two firms merged in 2005.

Calculating Tobin's Q

ROIC and EP provide a great deal of information about the performance of a firm over a defined period of time. Unfortunately, both these performance measures require information about a firm's cost of capital. And, as was suggested earlier, calculating a firm's WACC can be very difficult, especially if a firm is using a wide variety of domestic and international sources of capital. In this setting, it can be convenient to adopt an approach to characterizing a firm's performance that avoids many of the problems of simple accounting measures of performance but does not rely on the explicit calculation of a firm's WACC. This is what Tobin's q does.

Conceptually, **Tobin's q** is defined as the ratio of a firm's market value to the replacement cost of its assets.[24] If a firm has assets that would cost, say, $10,000 to replace, and the market perceives the value of this firm to be, say, $50,000, this firm has taken assets worth $10,000 and generated $50,000 with them—a condition consistent with creating economic value. Thus, a q greater than 1.0 is an indicator that a firm is generating superior performance. Similarly, a q less than 1.0 suggests that a firm is generating low levels of performance.

As with the other adjusted accounting measures of performance discussed here, the numerator and denominator of q must be estimated from numbers on a firm's profit-and-loss statement and balance sheet.[25] The market value of a firm can be calculated as

$$\text{Firm market value} = \text{market value of common stock}$$
$$+ \text{ market value of preferred stock}$$
$$+ \text{ book value of a firm's short-term debt}$$
$$+ \text{ book value of a firm's long-term debt} \qquad \textbf{(2.16)}$$

The market value of common stock is calculated as the number of firm shares outstanding times the price per share at the end of a given time period. Alternatively, one can calculate the average number of shares outstanding over some time period, as well as the average price per share over this same time period, and obtain the market value of common stock.

If a firm's preferred stock is traded frequently, then the market value of preferred stock can be calculated in a way that parallels the calculation of the market value of common stock—that is, number of shares of preferred stock outstanding times the ending price per share of preferred stock. If the stock is not traded frequently, then the market value of preferred stock will equal a firm's total preferred dividends capitalized by the Standard and Poor's preferred stock yield index. Fortunately, the market value of preferred stock is reported by one of the most widely available sources of accounting information about a firm—Compustat.

The book value of a firm's short-term debt is the difference between the value of a firm's short-term liabilities and its short-term assets. The book value of a firm's long-term debt is taken directly from a firm's balance sheet.

Several different approaches have been proposed for calculating the replacement value of a firm's assets. The simplest of these approaches is to take a firm's period-ending book value of total assets as an estimate of the replacement value of those assets and calculate q as

$$q = \frac{\text{firm market value}}{\text{book value of total assets}} \qquad \textbf{(2.17)}$$

Obviously, it is important to calculate the numerator and denominator of q over the same time periods.

This simple approach to estimating q has been criticized on several grounds.[26] For example, it has been suggested that the market value of a firm's total short- and long-term debt is more appropriated to include in q's numerator than the book value of debt. Also, a variety of techniques has been used to develop more accurate estimates of the actual replacement cost of a firm's assets.[27] Clearly, if a firm has had assets in place for some time, the actual replacement cost of those assets, and the book value of those assets, can be significantly different, thereby inflating q.

Although these are real limitations to the calculation of an accurate q, they are at least partially compensated for by the simplicity of calculating q in this manner. Moreover, some recent research suggests that this simple form of calculating q is highly correlated with more sophisticated, and presumably more accurate, approaches to this calculation.[28] Tobin's q is calculated for our hypothetical firm in Table 2.9.

Weaknesses of Adjusted Accounting Measures of Firm Performance

Although ROIC, EP, MVA, and Tobin's q all provide important information about the historical performance of a firm, and although all these measures avoid some of the weaknesses of simple accounting measures of firm performance, these measures, nevertheless, have some important weaknesses.

Measurement Problems in Estimating β. Theoretically, it should be possible to estimate β_j with b_j, as in equation 2.9. However, this estimation can be problematic. The

TABLE 2.9 Calculating Tobin's q for a Hypothetical Firm	2001	2002	2003	2004	2005	2006
Shares outstanding	1.3	1.5	1.8	1.7	1.4	1.7
Average market price	18.0	19.5	21.2	16.3	10.1	12.2
Market value of common stock	23.4	29.25	38.16	27.71	14.14	20.74
Current assets	25.0	35.8	44.8	49.7	78.2	82.4
Current liabilities	11.0	20.4	20.0	20.4	56.2	58.7
Book value of short-term debt	14.0	15.4	24.8	29.3	22.0	23.7
Book value of long-term debt	5.0	12.8	14.3	19.2	37.5	49.2
Firm market value	42.4	57.45	77.26	76.2	73.64	93.64
Book value of fixed assets	57.1	58.1	61.0	68.9	93.8	108.1
Tobin's q	.74	.99	1.27	1.11	.79	.87

traditional approach for estimating β_j described previously seems straightforward enough—that is, simply estimate the statistical regression in equation 2.9. However, slight modifications in how the variables in equation 2.9 are measured can lead to different β_j estimates. For example, Merrill Lynch's approach to estimating b_j is based on monthly capital gains for an individual security $(R_{j,\,t})$ and for the market as a whole $(R_{m,\,t})$, where market returns are estimated using the Standard and Poor's 500 Index. The resulting regression equation is then adjusted according to the criteria developed by Blume.[29] Value Line, on the other hand, estimates b_j using weekly capital gains return data and uses the New York Stock Exchange Composite Index as a measure of market returns. The resulting regression equation is again adjusted according to Blume's method. Unfortunately, the betas calculated in these different ways can vary. Indeed, research has shown that these two estimates of β are statistically different from one another even though they use the same empirical equation—equation 2.9—and only slightly different measures of variables.[30]

Further, the estimate of β_j typically requires a relatively long data series, both for the returns of an individual firm's securities and for expected market rates of returns. This requirement is not a problem for firms that have existed for long periods of time or for calculating expected market rates of return. However, if a firm has a relatively brief history, it may be statistically impossible to estimate its β_j.

Theoretical Mis-specification of the CAPM. Another limitation of adjusted accounting measures of performance concerns the theoretical validity of the capital asset pricing model. As suggested previously, the capital asset pricing model can be used to calculate a firm's cost of equity. Unfortunately, there is a growing consensus that the capital asset pricing model is an incomplete explanation of how returns on a firm's securities are generated.

If the CAPM is complete, and if capital markets are efficient, then empirical estimations of equation 2.9 should reveal that a_j is not significantly different from zero and that b_j should be the only statistically significant factor to explain a firm's security performance. Unfortunately, empirical research is simply not consistent with these expectations: a_j is often significantly different from zero, and other factors, besides b_j, have a significant effect in explaining a firm's security returns, even when controlling for b_j.[31] These results suggest that the CAPM is an incomplete model, that capital markets are not efficient, or both. Roll has concluded that it is logically *impossible* to conduct separate tests of the completeness of the CAPM and capital market efficiency, and thus not possible to evaluate the completeness of the CAPM fully.[32] The development of the arbitrage pricing theory is an effort to overcome the limitations of the CAPM.[33]

Intangible Resources and Capabilities and Adjusted Accounting Measures of Performance. One of the important limitations of simple accounting measures of firm performance discussed earlier was the inability of these measures to incorporate information about the cost of acquiring or developing intangible resources and capabilities in a firm. Many of these limitations carry over to adjusted accounting measures of firm performance.

Consider, for example, Tobin's q. This measure uses the replacement cost of a firm's assets as its denominator. The simple approach to calculating q presented in this chapter uses the book value of a firm's assets as an estimate of replacement costs. More sophisticated approaches to calculating q use more complicated approaches to estimating the replacement value of a firm's assets. However, none of these approaches incorporates the full cost of replacing a firm's intangible resources and capabilities, because the full cost of these intangible assets is not incorporated into a firm's balance sheet. This can lead to significant inaccuracies in calculating a firm's q, especially when a firm has significant investments in intangible resources and capabilities such as brand name, relationships with suppliers, relationships with buyers, teamwork among employees, and so forth.

Other Measures of Firm Performance

Although the simple accounting and adjusted accounting approaches to measuring firm performance have received a great deal of attention in literature, a variety of other techniques are also useful. Some of the most important of these are discussed in this section.

Event Study Measures of Performance

It is possible to use the stock market's reaction to the implementation of a particular strategy to gauge the value created (or destroyed) by that strategy. This approach is rooted firmly in the theory of finance and assumes that capital markets are efficient in the **semistrong form**—that is, the price of a firm's debt and equity fully reflects all publicly available information about the economic value of the firm.[34] This approach has been come to be known as the **event study method**.[35]

The logic behind these event studies is quite simple. Imagine that a firm chooses and implements a valuable new strategy. A valuable new strategy will generate higher levels of economic performance for a firm after it is implemented, compared to the economic performance of that firm before the strategy is implemented. In efficient capital markets, this greater economic performance will be reflected in higher stock market performance for this firm, compared with its stock market performance before the strategy was implemented. In this approach to measurement, the implementation of a new strategy marks the beginning of an **event.** An event ends when the capital markets adjust fully to the additional value created by the firm's new strategy. The period of time between the beginning of an event and the end of an event is called the **event window.**

A measure of the total value created by a strategic event is that event's **cumulative abnormal return,** or CAR. An event's CAR is computed in several stages. First, an individual firm's capital asset pricing model parameters (a_j and b_j) are estimated. This is done by regressing the stock market rate of return in time $t(R_{m,t})$ on a firm's actual rate of return in the stock market in time t ($R_{j,t}$), as in equation 2.18:

$$R_{j,t} = a_j + b_j R_{m,t} + e_{j,t} \qquad (2.18)$$

All these variables are defined as in equation 2.19.

It is important that these parameters be estimated using a firm's market return data *outside* the event window of interest. Thus if a firm implements a new strategy in January 2006, the estimates of a_j and b_j for that firm should be based on its returns before January 2006. These parameter estimates can then be used to calculate excess returns for that firm $(XR_{j,t})$ in the event window, as in equation 2.19:

$$XR_{j,t} = R_{j,t} - (a_j + b_j R_{m,t}) \tag{2.19}$$

In this equation, $R_{j,t}$ is the actual stock market return a firm experiences in the event window—that is, after the firm has implemented its new strategy—and $(a_j + b_j R_{m,t})$ is the return this firm would have obtained if its historical performance had continued. If $XR_{j,t}$ is greater than zero for each time period, t, then the firm earned a greater than historically expected return in that period. $XR_{j,t}$ thus becomes a measure of superior performance. Of course, if $XR_{j,t}$ is less than zero, then a firm will have earned less than its historically expected return on its new strategy in each time period t. If $XR_{j,t}$ is equal to zero, the firm would have earned just its historically expected return in each time period t.

The cumulative effect of a new strategy on a firm's stock market performance is then measured by its cumulative abnormal return:

$$CAR_j = \sum_{t=T_1}^{T_2} XR_{j,t} \tag{2.20}$$

where T_1 is the beginning of the strategic event and T_2 is the end of the strategic event. Whether a firm's cumulative abnormal return is large enough to conclude that it did not occur by chance (that is, large enough to be statistically significant) can be calculated by dividing a firm's CAR by the standard deviation of excess returns during the event window:

$$t_j = \frac{CAR_j}{s_j} \tag{2.21}$$

where s_j is the standard deviation of $XR_{j,t}$ from time T_1 to time T_2. This statistic is normally distributed when the number of time periods in an event window is large. A t_j greater than 2.0 means the probability that a firm's CAR was generated by chance is less than .05.

Event studies are powerful measures of a firm's performance, but they, too, have limitations. First, it is sometimes difficult to specify a strategic event's beginning date. As described in Chapter 5, firms sometimes have a strong incentive to keep the implementation of new and valuable strategies proprietary. Thus, specifying with any precision when a strategy is implemented can be difficult. Moreover, emergent strategies, in an important sense, have no starting date. They are described as strategies only after they have been implemented.

Second, even when a strategic event does have an explicit beginning date, information about a pending strategy may leak out to the capital markets before the strategy is officially implemented. As this information becomes public, it will be reflected in a firm's stock prices. Thus, by the time of the official announcement, much of the rise in the price of a firm's stock will already have occurred, because investors will have anticipated the valuable strategy that was announced. In this situation, a firm's CAR in the event window may not be statistically significant even though the strategy itself added significant value to the firm.[36]

Given these limitations, event study measures of economic performance are most applicable for analyzing the performance implications of intended and discrete strategies, such as mergers and acquisitions, organizational restructurings, and changes in management compensation.

Finally, these event study methods depend on the capital asset pricing model. Measurement problems associated with the CAPM, along with possible theoretical mis-specification, continue to be limitations for event study measures of firm performance.

Sharpe's Measure

In Sharpe's measure of firm performance, a firm's stock market performance is compared to a firm's total risk.[37] Stock market performance is computed by taking the difference between a firm's stock market performance in some time interval ($R_{j,t}$) and the average risk-free rate of return during that same interval (RFR_t). A firm's total risk is measured as the standard deviation of its stock market returns in the time interval (sd_t). Thus, S_j is computed as

$$S_j = \frac{R_{j,t} - \text{RFR}_t}{\text{sd}_t} \qquad (2.22)$$

The numerator in equation 2.22 can be thought of as a measure of the risk premium earned by a firm, and the denominator is the firm's total risk. Thus, S_j is a measure of a firm's return dollars per unit of risk. The higher the value of S_j, the greater the dollar return per unit of risk, and the greater the economic performance of a firm.

The Treynor Index

Treynor's index is similar to Sharpe's measure.[38] Whereas Sharpe's measure compares a firm's returns to total risk, Treynor's index compares returns to the firm's systematic risk, measured by β_j:

$$T_j = \frac{R_{j,t} - \text{RFR}_t}{\beta_j} \qquad (2.23)$$

Jensen's Alpha

Another alternative market-based measure of performance was proposed by Jensen.[39] This measure is computed by comparing a firm's stock market performance to its risk-adjusted expected performance:

$$R_{j,t} - \text{RFR}_t = a_j + b_j(R_{m,t} - \text{RFR}_t) + e_j \qquad (2.24)$$

where

$R_{j,t}$ = Firm j's stock market returns at time t
RFR_t = the risk-free rate of return at time t
a_j = an empirically determined CAPM parameter
b_j = an estimate of Firm j's systematic risk, β_j
$R_{m,t}$ = the stock market return for a fully diversified portfolio of stocks at time t
e_j = error

Notice that in equation 2.24, a_j is the only difference between the risk premium actually earned by Firm j ($R_{j,t}$ − RFR$_t$) and that firm's expected market performance, given its economic history $[b_j(R_{m,t} - RFR_t) + e_j]$. A Jensen's alpha greater than zero suggests that a firm is outperforming the market (superior returns); an alpha less than zero suggests that a firm is underperforming the market; and an alpha equal to zero suggests that a firm is performing at market levels.

Limitations of Alternative Market Measures

Each of these alternative performance measures was originally designed to evaluate the performance of an investment portfolio. Only recently have they begun to be applied to measuring firm performance. However, they continue to rely on assumptions that are usually more appropriate for valuing investment portfolios than for valuing firms. For example, both Sharpe's and Treynor's measures implicitly assume that the cost of capital for firms is equal to the risk-free interest rate. This is why both of these measures, in the numerator, calculate the difference between a firm's actual returns ($R_{j,t}$) with the risk-free return (RFR$_t$). Fully diversified investment portfolios are more likely to be able to obtain capital at this low risk-free rate. However, a firm's cost of capital is usually higher than this risk-free rate. Also, the Treynor index compares a firm's actual returns only to systematic risk (β_j), implicitly assuming that the firm has fully diversified away any unsystematic risk. Again, this may be a reasonable assumption for investment portfolios, but relatively few firms diversify away all unsystematic risk. Indeed, in Chapter 11, we argue that such unrelated diversification often reduces the wealth of a firm's shareholders. Finally, both Treynor's index and Jensen's alpha depend on the capital asset pricing model to compute a firm's systematic risk. All the limitations of the CAPM also apply to these measures.

Despite these limitations, these three alternative market measures, in combination with other measures of firm performance, can provide insight into a firm's economic position. Empirically, Sharpe's measure, Treynor's index, and Jensen's alpha are highly correlated. In a study of 160 diversified and nondiversified firms, it was found that the correlation among these performance measures ranged from .84 to .90 and were all statistically significant. However, the correlation between these three measures and two accounting measures of performance (firm ROA and ROE minus industry average ROA and ROE), although consistent, were much lower, ranging from .15 to .30. These correlations were still statistically significant. These results suggest that these alternative market measures of firm performance provide information about performance over and above simple accounting measures of performance.[40]

2.3 STAKEHOLDERS' ALTERNATIVES

All of the definitions and measures of firm performance discussed so far in this chapter share a common, often unstated assumption—that the primary objective of a firm is (and should be) maximizing the wealth of its shareholders. As **residual claimants,** shareholders receive any cash in excess of what is required to pay off a firm's other claimants. Those other claimants, according to this approach, largely determine a firm's costs. Generating revenues in excess of these costs creates cash that can be paid to shareholders, as residual claimants.

From another point of view, shareholders are just one of several different stakeholders in a firm. A firm's **stakeholders** are those institutions and groups that provide a firm resources and thus have an interest in how a firm performs. Stakeholders include a firm's employees, customers, management, suppliers, debt holders, and even society at large. Because stakeholders provide resources, they have an interest in how those resources are used and applied. Also because each stakeholder provides different resources to a firm, each stakeholder can have a different interest in how it would like to see the firm managed. In this multiple-stakeholders approach, one set of stakeholders may believe that a firm is a very high performer; another set may conclude that a firm is only a mediocre performer, and still another might conclude that a firm is performing poorly.[41]

Because different firm stakeholders use different criteria to judge a firm's performance, rarely will it be possible for an organization to implement strategies that completely satisfy all of its stakeholders. For example, a firm that, fully satisfies its employees and managers by providing expensive non-business-related perquisites (such as chauffeur-driven limousines, numerous corporate jets, extrathick carpeting in offices) may be reducing the economic wealth of its stockholders. Both of these stakeholding groups will not be fully satisfied simultaneously. A firm that fully satisfies its customers by selling high-quality products at very low prices may be reducing its profits, an action that reduces the potential gain of stockholders. Also, a firm that fully meets the needs of its stockholders by borrowing money for low-risk projects, by investing in high-risk projects, can end up increasing the risks borne by its debt holders.[42]

Understanding the performance implications of strategies becomes extremely complex in these situations. The implications of a particular strategy for each of a firm's numerous stakeholders would need to be isolated. As long as there is significant variance in these stakeholders' interests, this task can be challenging.

Several authors have argued that the unique status of equity holders as residual claimants reduces the need to think about a firm's stakeholders in evaluating performance. This argument suggests that because equity holders are residual claimants, they gain access to a firm's cash only after all other legitimate claims are paid. In this logic, a firm that maximizes the wealth of its equity holders automatically satisfies the legitimate demands of its other stakeholders.[43]

Recently, however, some scholars have begun observing that whenever a stakeholder makes an investment in a firm that is more valuable in that firm than any other firm, that stakeholder also becomes, to some extent at least, a residual claimant. For example, when an employee works for a single firm for many years, he or she develops a great deal of knowledge about how to get work done in that firm that is of little value in other firms. However, this kind of knowledge can be very valuable in the firm in which it was developed. As will be shown in Chapter 5, it can even be a source of competitive advantage and superior performance. In general, however, employees (and other stakeholders) will only be willing to make these kinds of investments in a firm if they are able to share some of the economic profits they generate. In this sense, these employees (and other stakeholders) become residual claimants in the firm.

When multiple stakeholders have claims on a firm's residual cash flows, questions about how this cash should be divided among them, and what actions firms should engage in to satisfy these different stakeholders, both emerge. That is, questions about stakeholder interests—though they are complex—must nevertheless be addressed. The field of strategic management is only beginning to come to terms with these ideas (see, for example, the discussion of employee interests in corporate diversification in Chapter 11).[44]

2.4 SUMMARY

This chapter has examined the role of performance in strategic management. Conceptually, firm performance was defined by comparing the willingness of a firm's customers to pay and a firm's cost of developing and selling its products or services. The difference between these is known as economic value. Firms that create greater economic value than their competitors gain competitive advantages, which can be temporary or sustained; firms that create the same economic value as their competitors gain competitive parity; those that create less end up with competitive disadvantages, which also can be temporary or sustained.

Two classes of measures of this conceptualization of firm performance have been described: simple accounting measures and adjusted accounting measures (including ROIC, economic profit, MVA, event studies, Sharpe's measure, Treynor's index, and Jensen's alpha). All of these measures have both strengths and weaknesses. Finally, the challenges associated with applying a stakeholder approach to evaluating firm performance have also been described.

REVIEW QUESTIONS

1. A firm is currently earning an economic profit. What effect will this current performance have on the expected performance of this firm in the future? What implications, if any, does your answer have for the strategizing efforts of managers?
2. Should a firm's managers attempt to gain superior profits from their strategizing efforts? Justify your answer from the point of view of stockholders, employees, customers, and society at large.
3. Economic definitions of firm performance have been criticized for focusing on only one of a firm's stakeholders—stockholders. Do you agree with this criticism? Why or why not?
4. You are on an airplane, sitting next to the president of a company, and she begins boasting about her firm's high ROA. What questions should you ask her to fully evaluate the performance of her firm? Suppose she is boasting about her firm's high EPS. What questions should you ask her to fully evaluate her firm's performance? Suppose she is boasting about her firm's ability to attract managerial and professional talent. What questions should you ask her to fully evaluate her firm's performance?
5. In the following tables, the profit-and-loss statement and balance sheet for Apple Computer in 2004 and 2005 are reproduced. Using these numbers, calculate Apple's ROA, ROE, gross profit margin, quick ratio, debt-to-equity ratio, inventory turnover, ROIC, and EP. Assume that Apple's marginal tax rate is .4 and that its deferred tax in 1997 was $35 million.

Financial Results for Apple Computer in 2004 and 2005 ($millions)		
	2005	**2004**
Net sales	13,931	8,279
Cost of goods sold	(9,888)	(6,020)
Selling, general, & administrative expense	(1,859)	(1,421)
Other expenses[1]	(534)	(512)
Amortization of goodwill	0	0
Interest income (net)[2]	72	68
Provision for income taxes[3]	(480)	(107)
Other income	0	0
Net income	1,335	276
	*	*
Assets	**2005**	**2004**
Operating cash	8,261	5,464
Accounts receivable	895	774
Inventories	165	101
Other current assets	975	716
Total current assets	10,300	7,055
Book value of fixed assets[4]	817	707
Goodwill	69	80
Net other operating assets	338	191
	11,551	8,050
	*	*
Liabilities and equity	**2005**	**2004**
Net current liabilities[5]	3,484	2,651
Long-term debt	601	323
Deferred income taxes	0	0
Preferred stock	0	0
Retained earnings	3,945	2,562
Shareholders' equity	3,521	2,514
Total liabilities & equity	11,551	8,050
	*	*
Other financial information	**2005**	**2004**
Shares outstanding	166 million	152 million
Price/share (average)	37.12	13.75
Bond rating	AA	AA
Beta	.57	.57
Risk-free rate	.01	.01
Market rate	.111	.12

[1]Includes R&D and restructuring costs

[2]Interest income − interest expense = interest income (net)

[3]Provision for income taxes in 2003: 24

[4]Property, plant, and equipment net of depreciation

[5]Includes account payable, accrued expenses

Answers to Question 5

	2005	2004
ROA:	$\dfrac{1{,}335}{11{,}551} = 11.56\%$	$\dfrac{276}{8{,}050} = 3.43\%$
ROE:	$\dfrac{1{,}335}{3{,}521} = 37.91\%$	$\dfrac{276}{2{,}514} = 10.99\%$
Gross profit margin	$13{,}931 - 9{,}888 = \$4{,}043$	$8{,}279 - 6{,}020 = \$2{,}259$
Quick ratio	$\dfrac{10{,}300}{3{,}484} = 2.96$	$\dfrac{7{,}055}{2{,}651} = 2.66$

Calculating ROIC and EP

$\text{EBIT}_{2005} = 113{,}931 - (9{,}888 + 1{,}859 + 534) = 1{,}650$

$\text{EBIT}_{2004} = 8{,}279 - (6{,}020 + 1{,}421 + 512) = 1{,}407$

$\text{Taxes on EBIT}_{2005} = 480 + .4(165) + .4(0) = 546$

$\text{Taxes on EBIT}_{2004} = 107 + .4(57) + .4(0) = 129.8$

$\text{Change in Deferred Income Tax}_{2005-2004} = 0 - 0$

$\text{Change in Deferred Income Tax}_{2004-2003} = 0 - 24$

$\text{NOPLAT}_{2005} = 1{,}650 - (546) + 0 = 1{,}104$

$\text{NOPLAT}_{2004} = 1{,}407 - (129.8) + (-24) = 1{,}301.2$

	2005	2004
Total current assets	10,300	7,055
Book value of fixed assets	817	707
Other operating assets (net)	(338)	(191)
Invested capital	10,779	7,571
ROIC_{2005}	$= \dfrac{1{,}104}{10{,}779} = 10.24\%$	
ROIC_{2004}	$= \dfrac{1{,}391.2}{7{,}571} - 17.19\%$	
EP_{2005}	$= 10{,}779 \times (10.24\% - 6.13\%) = \$443$	
EP_{2004}	$= 7{,}571 \times (17.19\% - 6.52\%) = \$807.8$	

Calculating WACC

	2005	2004
After-tax cost of debt	.048	.049
Cost of equity	$.01 + .57(.11 - .01) = .067$	$.01 + .57(.12 - .01) = .0727$
Weight of equity	$\dfrac{2{,}514}{8{,}058} = .30$	$\dfrac{2{,}514}{8{,}050} = .31$
Weight of debt	.70	.69
WACC	$.3(.048) + .7(.067) = .0613$	$.31(.049) + .69(.073) = .0652$

ENDNOTES

1. This definition of competitive advantage has a long history in the field of strategic management. For example, it is closely related to the definitions provided by Barney (1986, 1991) and Porter (1985). It is also consistent with the value-based approach described by Peteraf (2001), Brandenburger and Stuart (1999), and Besanko, Dranove, and Shanley (2000). For more discussion on this definition, see Peteraf and Barney (2004).
2. Mueller, D. C. (1977). "The persistence of profits above the norm." *Economica*, 44, pp. 369–380.
3. Waring, G. F. (1996). "Industry differences in the persistence of firm-specific returns." *The American Economic Review*, 86, pp. 1253–1265.
4. Roberts, P. W. (1999). "Product innovation, product-market competition, and persistent profitability in the U.S. pharmaceutical industry." *Strategic Management Journal*, 20, pp. 644–670.
5. See Altman, E. I. (1968). "Financial ratios, discriminate analysis and the prediction of corporate bankruptcy," *Journal of Finance*, 23, pp. 589–609.
6. See Dambolona, I. G., and S. J. Khoury (1980). "Ratio stability and corporate failure," *Journal of Finance*, 35(4), pp. 1017–1026; and Altman, E. I., R. G. Haldemen, and P. Narayanan (1977). "Zeta analysis: A new model to identify bankruptcy risk of corporations," *Journal of Banking and Finance*, 1, pp. 29–54. These adjustments include the standard deviation of some financial ratios in equation 2.1.
7. This literature is called *positive accounting*. Two important papers in this tradition are Watts, R. L., and J. L. Zimmerman (1978). "Towards a positive theory of determination of accounting standards," *Accounting Review*, 53, pp. 112–133; and Watts, R. L., and J. L. Zimmerman (1990). "Positive accounting theory: A ten-year perspective," *Accounting Review*, 65, pp. 131–156.
8. See Watts, R. L., and J. L. Zimmerman (1986). *Positive Accounting Theory*, Upper Saddle River, NJ: Prentice Hall; and Healy, P. M. (1985). "The effect of bonus schemes on accounting decisions," *Journal of Accounting & Economics*, 7, pp. 85–107.
9. See Kalay, A. (1982). "Stockholder-bondholder conflict and dividend constraints," *Journal of Financial Economics*, 10, pp. 211–233; Press, E. G., and J. B. Weintrop (1990). "Accounting-based constraints in public and private debt agreements: Their association with leverage and impact on accounting choice," *Journal of Accounting & Economics*, 12, pp. 65–95; Duke, J., and H. Hunt (1990). "An empirical examination of debt covenant restrictions and accounting-related debt proxies," *Journal of Accounting & Economics*, 12, pp. 45–63; and Bowen, R. M., E. W. Noreen, and J. M. Lacey (1981). "Determinants of the corporate decision to capitalize interest," *Journal of Accounting & Economics*, 3(2), pp. 151–179.
10. This incident at IBM is described in Miller, M. W., and Berton, L. (1993). "Softer numbers: As IBM's woes grew, its accounting tactics got less conservative," *Wall Street Journal*, April 7, p. A1.
11. See Zmijewski, M. E., and R. L. Hagerman (1981). "An income strategy approach to the positive theory of accounting standard setting/choice," *Journal of Accounting & Economics*, 3(2), pp. 129–149; and Zimmerman, J. L. (1983). "Taxes and firm size," *Journal of Accounting & Economics*, 5(2), pp. 119–149.
12. See Smith, T. K., and E. Norten (1993). "Throwing curves: One baseball statistic remains a mystery," *Wall Street Journal*, April 2, p. A1; and Hymon, M. (1999). "Pity the Poor Owners? That's Rich," *Business Week*, November 22, pp. 91+.
13. The role of intangible assets in creating competitive advantage is discussed in detail in Chapter 5. Some of the best discussions of the role can be found in Barney, J. B. (1991). "Firm resources and sustained competitive advantage," *Journal of Management*, 17, pp. 99–120; Dierickx, I., and K. Cool (1989). "Asset stock accumulation and sustainability of competitive advantage," *Management Science*, 35, pp. 1504–1511; and

Itami, H. (1987). *Mobilizing Invisible Assets*, Cambridge, MA: Harvard University Press.

14. Some of the best of this work can be found in Fisher, F. M., and J. J. McGowan (1983). "On the misuse of accounting rates of return to infer monopoly profits," *American Economic Review*, 73, pp. 82–97; Fisher, F. M. (1979). "Diagnosing monopoly," *Quarterly Review of Economics & Business*, 19, pp. 7–33; Livingstone, J. L., and G. L. Salamon (1971). "Relationship between the accounting and the internal rate of return measures: A synthesis and analysis," in J. L. Livingstone and T. J. Burns (eds.), *Income Theory and Rate of Return*, Columbus: Ohio State University Press; Solomon, E. (1970). "Alternative rate of return concepts and their implications for utility regulation," *Bell Journal of Economics*, 1, pp. 65–81; and Stauffer, T. R. (1971). "The measurement of corporate rates of return: A generalized formulation," *Bell Journal of Economics*, 2, pp. 434–469.

15. Fisher, F. M., and J. J. McGowan (1983). "On the misuse of accounting rates of return to infer monopoly profits," *American Economic Review*, 73, p. 83. In this particular study, Fisher and McGowan only examined the implications of changing the accounting treatment of depreciation. And, using just this one potential adjustment to a firm's accounting procedures, they found these very substantial effects.

16. Long, W. F., and D. J. Ravenscraft (1984). "The misuse of accounting rates of return: Comment," *American Economic Review*, 74, pp. 494–500.

17. For example, see Injiri, Y. (1980). "Recovery rate and cash flow accounting," *Financial Executive*, 48(3), pp. 54–60; and Salamon, G. L. (1985). "Accounting rates of return," *American Economic Review*, 75, pp. 495–504.

18. Much of the discussion in this section is taken from Copeland, T., T. Koller, and J. Murrin (1995). *Valuation: Measuring and Managing the Value of Companies*, 2nd ed., New York: John Wiley & Sons.

19. EVA, a technique closely related to MVA, will be discussed in Chapter 12.

20. The methods described for calculating these four measures of economic performance are widely applicable. However, they may need to be adjusted according to specific accounting practices in an industry or country. Industries such as oil and gas exploration, movie production, and financial services have all developed specific accounting conventions that require additional adjustments to reported accounting numbers in order to calculate accurate estimates of the true conventions used in the United States, although some research suggests that these accounting differences are not very important [see Choi, F. D. S., and R. M. Levich (1990). *The Capital Market Effects of International Accounting Diversity*, Homewood, IL: Dow-Jones Irwin]. When accounting conventions used by a firm are significantly different than generally accepted accounting principles in the United States, the approach to calculating the adjusted accounting measures described here will have to be modified. See Copeland, T., T. Koller, and J. Murrin (1995). *Valuation: Measuring and Managing the Value of Companies*, 2nd ed., New York: John Wiley & Sons, for more information.

21. This information was taken from Cooper's 10K filings.

22. Copeland, T., T. Koller, and J. Murrin (1995). *Valuation: Measuring and Managing the Value of Companies*, 2nd ed., New York: John Wiley & Sons, pp. 165–166.

23. I would like to thank Stern Stewart for making this information available.

24. See Tobin, J. (1978). "Monetary policies and the economy: The transmission mechanism," *Southern Economic Journal*, 37, pp. 421–431; Tobin, J. (1969). "A general equilibrium approach to monetary theory," *Journal of Money, Credit and Banking*, 1, pp. 15–29; Tobin, J., and W. Brainard (1968). "Pitfalls in financial model building," *American Economic Review*, 58, pp. 99–122; Lindenberg, E. B., and S. A. Ross (1981). "Tobin's q ratio and industrial organization," *Journal of Business*, 54(1), pp. 1–32; Chappell, H. W., and D. C. Cheng (1984). "Firms' acquisition decisions and

Tobin's *q* ratio," *Journal of Economics & Business*, 36(1), pp. 29–42; and Smirlock, M., T. Gillingan, and W. Marshall (1984). "Tobin's *q* and the structure-performance relationship," *American Economic Review*, 74(5), pp. 1051–1060.

25. This approach to estimating *q* is suggested by Chung, K. H., and S. W. Pruitt (1994). "A simple approximation of Tobin's *q*," *Financial Management*, 23(3), pp. 70–74.

26. See Perfect, S. B., and K. K. Wiles (1994). "Alternative constructions of Tobin's *q*: An empirical comparison," *Journal of Empirical Finance*, 1, pp. 313–341.

27. See Perfect, S. B., and K. K. Wiles (1994). "Alternative constructions of Tobin's *q*: An empirical comparison," *Journal of Empirical Finance*, 1, pp. 313–341; Hall, B. H. (1990). "The manufacturing sector master file: 1959–1987," National Bureau of Economic Research, Working Paper Series no. 3366; and Lindenberg, E. B., and S. A. Ross (1981). "Tobin's *q* ratio and industrial organization," *Journal of Business*, 54(1), pp. 1–32.

28. In a regression between the approach to calculating *q* in equation 2.17 (and more sophisticated approaches to calculating *q*), Chung and Pruitt (1994) found that R^2 never fell below .966. Perfect and Wiles found simple correlation between a simple approach to calculating *q* and more complex approaches to be equal to .93.

29. Blume, M. E. (1975). "Betas and their regression tendencies," *Journal of Finance*, 30, pp. 785–795.

30. Statman, M. (1981). "Betas compared: Merrill Lynch vs. Value Line," *Journal of Portfolio Management*, 7(2), pp. 41–44.

31. See Copeland, T. E., and J. F. Weston (1983). *Financial Theory and Corporate Policy*, Reading, MA: Addison-Wesley, p. 207; Basu, S. (1977). "Investment performance of common stocks in relation to their price-earnings ratios: A test of the efficient markets hypothesis," *Journal of Finance*, June, pp. 663–682; Banz, R. W. (1981). "The relationship between return and market value of common stocks," *Journal of Financial Economics*, March, pp. 3–18; Reinganum, M. R. (1981). "Misspecification

of capital asset pricing: Empirical anomalies based on earnings yields and market values," *Journal of Financial Economics*, March, pp. 19–46.

32. Roll, R. (1977). "A critique of the asset pricing theory's tests; Part I: On past and potential testability of the theory," *Journal of Financial Economics*, March, pp. 129–176.

33. Ross, S. A. (1976). "The arbitrage theory of capital asset pricing," *Journal of Economic Theory*, December, pp. 343–362.

34. This definition was first suggested by Fama, E. F. (1970). "Efficient capital markets: A review of theory and empirical work," *Journal of Finance*, May, pp. 383–417.

35. More technical discussion of the event study method can be found in Fama, E. F., L. Fisher, M. C. Jensen, and R. Roll (1969). "The adjustment of stock prices to new information," *International Economic Review*, 10(1), pp. 1–21; Ball, R. and P. Brown (1968). "An empirical examination of accounting income numbers," *Journal of Accounting Research*, Autumn, pp. 159–178; Brown, S. J., and J. B. Warner (1980). "Measuring security price performance," *Journal of Financial Economics*, 8, pp. 205–258; Brown, S. J., and J. B. Warner (1985). "Using daily stock returns: The case of event studies," *Journal of Financial Economics*, 14(1), pp. 3–31. Cautions in applying this method are discussed in McWilliams, A., and D. Siegel (1997). "Event Studies in Management Research: Theoretical and Empirical Issues," *Academy of Management Journal*, 40(3), pp. 626–657.

36. See Bettis, R. A. (1983). "Modern financial theory, corporate strategy and public policy: Three conundrums," *Academy of Management Review*, 8(3), pp. 406–415; and Bromiley, P., M. Govekar, and A. Marcus (1988). "On Using Event-Study Methodology in Strategic Management Research," *Technovation*, 8, pp. 25–42.

37. See Sharpe, W. F. (1966). "Mutual fund performance," *Journal of Business*, January, pp. 119–138.

38. Treynor, J. L. (1965). "How to rate mutual fund performance," *Harvard Business Review*, January/February, pp. 63–75.

39. See Jensen, M. C. (1968). "The performance of mutual funds in the period 1945-64," *Journal of Finance*, May, pp. 389–416.

40. See Hoskisson, R. E., M. A. Hitt, R. A. Johnson, and D. D. Moesel (1993). "Construct validity of an objective (entropy) categorical measure of diversification strategy," *Strategic Management Journal*, 14, pp. 215–235.

41. See Cameron, K. (1986). "Effectiveness as paradox: Consensus and conflict in conceptions of organizational effectiveness," *Management Science*, 32, pp. 539–553.

42. Several authors have studied the implications of conflicts of interest among a firm's stakeholders. Conflicts between managers and equity holders is the object of much of agency theory, as first developed by Jensen, M. C., and W. H. Meckling (1976). "Theory of the firm: Managerial behavior, agency costs, and ownership structure," *Journal of Financial Economics*, 3, pp. 305–360. Agency theory is discussed in more detail in Chapter 13. Conflicts between equity holders and debt holders are discussed in Copeland, T. E., and J. F. Western (1983). *Financial Theory and Corporate Policy*, Reading, MA: Addison-Wesley. Conflicts between customers and stockholders are discussed in Titman, S. (1984). "The effect of capital structure on a firm's liquidation decisions," *Journal of Financial Economics*, 13(1), pp. 137–151.

43. Copeland, Koller, and Murrin (1995) provide a particularly articulate example of this argument.

44. See Wang and Barney (2006).

CHAPTER

$$\boxed{3}$$

Evaluating Environmental Threats

Chapter 1 defined a firm's strategy as its theory of how to achieve high levels of performance in the markets and industries in which it is operating. Defining and measuring performance was then explored in Chapter 2. Armed with these sets of ideas, it is now possible to explore the specific attributes that a firm's strategy must possess if it is to generate competitive advantages.

Some of these specific attributes have already been mentioned in Chapter 1. In the strategic management process described in that chapter, both internal analysis—to understand a firm's strengths and weaknesses—and external analysis—to understand a firm's opportunities and threats—are required if firms expect to choose high-performance-generating strategies.

However, as was also suggested in Chapter 1, observing that it is important to understand threats and opportunities in a firm's environment and a firm's strengths and weaknesses is not the same as providing a rigorous theory-based set of tools to actually accomplish these analyses. These tools are the subjects of this and the following two chapters. This chapter focuses on environmental threats—how they can be identified and how they can be neutralized. Chapter 4 focuses on environmental opportunities, and Chapter 5 focuses on organizational strengths and weaknesses. Applying these tools can enable a firm to choose a strategy that will generate competitive advantages.

The primary objective in analyzing the threats and opportunities in a firm's environment is to evaluate the overall economic attractiveness of an industry. **Industry attractiveness** depends on the level of opportunity and threat in an industry. Highly attractive industries are characterized by significant opportunities and only limited threats; highly unattractive industries are characterized by significant threats and only limited opportunities. The average performance of firms in economically very attractive industries will be greater than the average performance of firms in economically unattractive industries. Thus, firms in the pharmaceutical industry, an industry that most observers agree is economically attractive, typically outperform firms in the worldwide consumer electronics industry, an industry that most agree is not as attractive economically. Of course, industry analysis must go beyond an arbitrary and incomplete listing of threats and opportunities in an industry. Rather, what is required is an approach to analyzing industry attractiveness that is grounded in a theory of competition in an industry.

This chapter discusses a general theoretical framework that can be used to inform the analysis of environmental threats and opportunities: the structure-conduct-performance (S-C-P) model in industrial organization economics. The chapter examines how the S-C-P model has been used to develop frameworks for analyzing environmental threats and applies those frameworks to the analysis of threats in the pharmaceutical and consumer electronics industries.

3.1 THE STRUCTURE-CONDUCT-PERFORMANCE MODEL

In the 1930s, a group of economists began developing an approach for understanding the relationships among a firm's environment, its behavior, and performance. The original objective of this work was to describe conditions under which perfect-competition dynamics would *not* develop in an industry. Understanding when perfect-competition dynamics were not developing assisted government regulators in isolating those industries in which competition-enhancing regulations should be implemented.[1]

The theoretical framework that developed out of this effort became known as the structure-conduct-performance model (SCP). The term **structure** in this model refers to industry structure, measured by such factors as the number of competitors in an industry, the heterogeneity of products, and the cost of entry and exit. **Conduct** refers to specific firm actions in an industry, including price taking, product differentiation, tacit collusion, and exploitation of market power. **Performance** in the S-C-P model has two meanings: the performance of individual firms and the performance of the economy as a whole. The structure-conduct-performance model is summarized in Figure 3.1.

The logic that links industry structure to conduct and performance is well known. Attributes of the industry structure within which a firm operates define the range of options and constraints facing a firm. In some industries, firms have very few options and face many constraints. Firms in these industries generate, at best, returns that just cover their cost of capital in the long run, and social welfare (as traditionally defined in economics) is maximized. In this setting, industry structure completely determines both firm conduct and long-run firm performance (normal).

In other less competitive industries, firms face fewer constraints and a greater range of conduct options. Some of these options may enable firms to obtain competitive advantages. Even when firms have more conduct options, industry structure still constrains the range of those options. Also, other attributes of industry structure—including barriers to entry—determine how long firms in an industry will be able to sustain their advantages. Without barriers to entry, any competitive advantages by firms

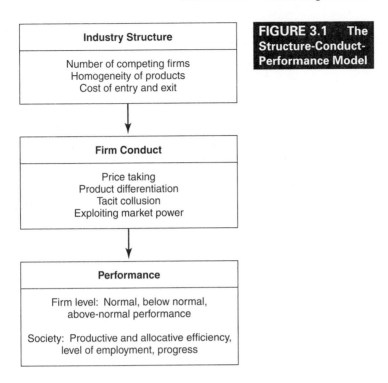

FIGURE 3.1   The Structure-Conduct-Performance Model

in an industry will be quickly competed away by new entrants. Thus, even in this case, industry structure still has an important effect on firm conduct and firm performance even though firms in these industries can sometimes have competitive advantages.

One way of describing the competitive structure of different industries is presented in Table 3.1. As shown in this table, industries can be described as perfectly competitive, monopolistically competitive, oligopolistic, or monopolistic.

Industries are **perfectly competitive** when there are large numbers of competing firms, products being sold are homogeneous with respect to cost and product attributes, and entry and exit are very low-cost. Examples of such perfectly competitive industries include the spot market for crude oil. As is well known, firms operating in perfectly competitive industries can act only as price takers. A firm is a **price taker** when it responds to changes in industry supply or demand by adjusting prices rather than attempting to influence the level of supply or demand. Price-taking firms can expect to gain only competitive parity.

Other industries can be described as monopolistically competitive. In these industries, firms carve out market niches within which they act as quasi-monopolists. However, these monopoly positions are always threatened by the competitive actions of other firms in the industry. In **monopolistically competitive industries,** there are large numbers of competing firms and low-cost entry and exit into and out of the industry. However, unlike the case of perfect competition, products in these industries are not homogeneous with respect to costs or product attributes. Rather, firms in this type of industry are successfully implementing product differentiation strategies—strategies that

TABLE 3.1   Types of Industry Structure, Firm Conduct Options, Firm Performance, and Social Welfare Implications

Type of Industry	Industry Attributes	Examples	Firm Conduct Options	Expected Firm Performance	Social Welfare Implications
Perfect competition	Large number of competing firms Homogenous products Low-cost entry and exit	Stock market Crude oil	Price taking	Normal	Social welfare maximized
Monopolistic competition	Large number of competing firms Heterogeneous products Low-cost entry and exit	Toothpaste Shampoo Golf balls Automobiles	Product differentiation (see Chapter 8)	Above normal	Less than perfect competition
Oligopoly	Small number of competing firms Homogenous or heterogeneous products Costly entry and exit	U.S. steel and autos in the 1950s U.S. breakfast cereal	Collusion (see Chapter 10)	Above normal	Less than monopolistic competition
Monopoly	One firm Costly entry	Polaroid in instant photography Microsoft in PC operating systems	Use market power to set prices	Above normal	Less than oligopoly

will be discussed in more detail in Chapter 7. Examples of monopolistically competitive industries include toothpaste, shampoo, golf balls, and automobiles. Firms in such industries have a variety of conduct options and can gain competitive advantages.

Still other industries can be described as oligopolies. **Oligopolies** are characterized by a small number of competing firms, by either homogeneous or heterogeneous products, and by costly entry and exit. Examples of oligopolistic industries include the U.S. automobile and steel industries in the 1950s and the U.S. breakfast cereal market today. Currently, the top four producers of breakfast cereal account for about 90 percent of the breakfast cereal sold in the United States, and the top eight account for almost 100 percent of the breakfast cereal sold in the United States. Firms in such industries also face a variety of conduct options, including tacit collusion, a strategy described in more detail in Chapter 10. Firms in oligopolistic industries can earn significant economic profits.

Finally, a few industries can be described as monopolistic. **Monopoly industries** consist of only a single firm. Entry into this type of industry is very costly. There are few examples of purely monopolistic industries. However, one industry that comes close to being a monopoly is the personal computer operating systems industry—an industry almost completely dominated by Microsoft. One of the critical conduct options facing firms in this kind of industry is the use of market power to set prices that generate significant economic value.

The regulatory implications of the S-C-P paradigm depend on the level of social welfare associated with each of the types of competition presented in Table 3.1. Social welfare is maximized in perfectly competitive industries, it is somewhat lower in monopolistically competitive industries, it is somewhat lower still in oligopolies, and it is very low in monopolies. Thus, the information in Table 3.1 can be used to identify when and how competition in an industry varies from the perfectly competitive ideal. Once identified remedies that increase the level of competitiveness in an industry can be instituted.[2]

Strategy researchers have turned the traditional objectives of the S-C-P model upside down. Instead of seeking ways to increase the competitiveness of industries, strategy researchers have used the S-C-P model as a way to describe the attributes of an industry that make it *less* than perfectly competitive, and thus help firms find ways to obtain competitive advantages.

3.2 THE FIVE FORCES MODEL OF ENVIRONMENTAL THREATS

To a firm seeking a competitive advantage, an **environmental threat** is any individual, group, or organization outside the firm that seeks to reduce the level of that firm's performance.[3] Threats increase a firm's costs, decrease the willingness of a firm's customers to pay, or in other ways reduce a firm's performance. In S-C-P terms, **threats** are forces that tend to increase the competitiveness of an industry and force firm performance to competitive parity.[4]

The objective of developing a model of environmental threats is to assist managers in analyzing these threats so that they can be more effective in developing strategies to neutralize them. The most widely known model of environmental threats in the field of strategic management was developed by Professor Michael Porter of Harvard Business School. In this model, known as the *five forces framework,* Porter suggests that five specific attributes of industry structure can threaten the ability of a firm to either maintain or create competitive advantages. These five forces are: (1) the threat of entry, (2) the threat of rivalry, (3) the threat of substitutes, (4) the threat of suppliers, and (5) the threat of buyers. The five forces framework is summarized in Figure 3.2.[5]

The Threat of Entry

The first environmental threat identified in the five forces framework is the threat of new entry. **New entrants** are firms that have either recently begun operations in an industry or that threaten to begin operations in an industry soon. For Amazon.com, in the online book-ordering business, Barnes & Noble.com and Borders.com are new entrants.[6] Even though Amazon invented this way of selling books, both Barnes & Noble and Borders recently entered this market. For ESPN in the television sports industry, both the Fox Sports Regional Network and the College Sports Television (CSTV) network are new entrants. The Fox Regional Sports Network consists of several regional sports channels that broadcast both national and regional sporting events, sports news shows, and sports entertainment shows—including *The Best Damn Sports Show, Period.* CSTV is a new (founded in spring of 2003) sports cable and satellite channel that specializes in college sports.

According to the S-C-P model, new entrants are motivated to enter into an industry by the superior performance that some incumbent firms in that industry may be achieving. Firms seeking these high profits enter the industry, thereby increasing the level of industry competition and reducing the performance of incumbent firms. With the absence of any barriers, entry will continue as long as any firms in the industry are earning superior performance. Entry will cease when the competitive advantages of all incumbent firms are competed away.

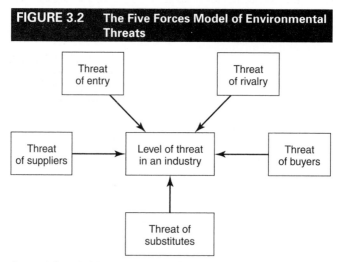

FIGURE 3.2 The Five Forces Model of Environmental Threats

TABLE 3.2   Barriers to Entry into an Industry
1. Economies of scale
2. Product differentiation
3. Cost advantages independent of scale
4. Contrived deterrence
5. Government regulation of entry

The extent to which new entry acts as a threat to an incumbent firm's performance depends on the cost of entry. If the cost of entry into an industry is greater than the potential profits a new entrant could obtain by entering, then entry will not be forthcoming, and new entrants are not a threat to incumbent firms. But if the cost of entry is lower than the return from entry, entry will occur until the profits derived from entry are less than the costs of entry.

The threat of entry depends on the cost of entry, and the cost of entry, in turn, depends on the existence and "height" of barriers to entry. **Barriers to entry** are attributes of an industry's structure that increase the cost of entry. The greater the height of these barriers, the greater is the cost of entry. With significant barriers to entry in place, potential entrants will not enter into an industry even though incumbent firms are earning substantial profits. Five barriers to entry are broadly cited in the S-C-P and strategy literatures. These five barriers, listed in Table 3.2, are (1) economies of scale, (2) product differentiation, (3) cost advantages independent of scale, (4) contrived deterrence, and (5) government regulation of entry. Three other barriers to entry often cited in the literature are actually special cases of these basic five.[7]

Economies of Scale as a Barrier to Entry

For economies of scale to act as a barrier to entry, the relationship between the volume of production and firm costs must have the shape of line A in Figure 3.3. This curve

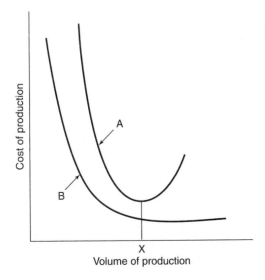

FIGURE 3.3   Economies of Scale and the Cost of Production

The figure shows two economies of scale: steeply curved (line A) and not steeply curved (line B).

Cost of production

A

B

X
Volume of production

suggests that any deviation, positive or negative, from an optimal level of production (point X in Figure 3.3) will lead a firm to experience much higher costs of production. Empirical research seems to suggest that the economies-of-scale curves in many industries are not as steeply sloped as line A in Figure 3.3.[8] Rather, in many industries there is a broad range of volume of production that can lead to low costs of production, as depicted by line B in Figure 3.3. Nevertheless, some industries including metal-can manufacturing, steel manufacturing, and aluminum smelting seem to have very narrow ranges of optimal sizes of production.

To see how economies of scale can act as a barrier to entry, consider the following: Imagine an industry with the following attributes: There are five incumbent firms (each firm has only one plant); the optimal level of production in each of these plants is 4,000 units (X in Figure 3.3 = 4,000 units); total demand for the output of this industry is fixed at 22,000 units; the economies-of-scale curve is as depicted by line A in Figure 3.3; and there are few, if any, opportunities to differentiate products in this industry. Total demand in this industry (22,000 units) is greater than total supply (5 × 4,000 units = 20,000). From traditional price theory, it follows that the five incumbent firms in this industry will be earning high levels of economic profit. The S-C-P model suggests that, absent barriers, these profits should motivate entry.

However, look at the entry decision from the point of view of potential entrants. Certainly, incumbent firms are earning profits, but potential entrants face an unsavory choice. On the one hand, new entrants could enter the industry with an optimally efficient plant and produce 4,000 units. However, this form of entry will lead industry supply to rise to 24,000 units (20,000 + 4,000). Suddenly, supply will be greater than demand (24,000 > 22,000), and all the firms in the industry, including the new entrant, will lose money. On the other hand, the new entrant might enter the industry with a plant of smaller-than-optimal size (for example, 1,000 units). This kind of entry leaves total industry demand larger than industry supply (22,000 > 21,000). However, the new entrant faces a serious cost disadvantage in this case, because it does not produce at the low-cost position on the economies-of-scale curve. Faced with these bleak alternatives— if it enters at scale, it loses money; if it does not enter at scale, it loses money—the potential entrant simply does not enter, even though incumbent firms are earning significant profits.

In order for economies of scale to act as a barrier to entry in this manner, the optimal size of entry has to be a relatively large percentage of supply in an industry. In this way, entry at the optimal size will easily drive industry supply greater than demand, and potential losses will deter entry. If, on the other hand, efficient new entrants have very little effect on total supply in an industry, then new entry will occur, and incumbent profits will be competed away.

Of course, there are other options for potential entrants besides entering at the efficient scale and losing money or entering at an inefficient scale and losing money. For example, potential entrants can attempt to expand primary demand (that is, increase total demand from 22,000 to 24,000 units or more) and enter at the optimal size. This alternative relaxes the condition that industry demand is fixed. Potential entrants can also attempt to develop new production technology, shift the economies-of-scale curve to the left (thereby reducing the optimal plant size), and enter. Such new technology makes production in this industry less "lumpy" and may enable firms to enter and gain some profits. This alternative relaxes the condition that the economies-of-scale curve has the shape of line A of Figure 3.3. Finally, potential entrants may try to differentiate their products. In order to charge higher prices to offset higher production costs associated with a smaller-than-optimal plant. This relaxes the zero product differentiation condition.[9]

Any of these firm actions, or combinations of them, may enable entry into an industry. However, these actions are often costly. If the cost of engaging in these "barrier busting" activities is greater than the return from entry, entry will not occur, even if incumbent firms are earning substantial profits. Not only can potential entrants engage in these activities, so can incumbent firms. If incumbent firms act to increase primary demand, introduce new production technology, or differentiate their product, these incumbent firms may be able to obtain any of the competitive advantages that could have been appropriated by new entrants and new entry will not occur.

Historically, economies of scale acting as a barrier to entry discouraged entry into the worldwide steel market. To exploit economies of scale fully, traditional steel plants had to be very large. If new entrants into the steel market had built these efficient and large steel manufacturing plants, they would have had the effect of increasing the steel supply over the demand for steel, and the outcome would have been reduced margins for established and incumbent firms. The likelihood of this outcome tended to discourage new entry. However, in the 1970s, the development of alternative mini-mill technology shifted the economies-of-scale curve to the left by making smaller plants very efficient in addressing some segments of the steel market. This shift had the effect of decreasing barriers to entry into the steel industry. Recent entrants, including Nucor Steel and Chappenell Steel, have significant cost advantages over firms still using outdated, less efficient production technology.[10]

Product Differentiation as a Barrier to Entry

Product differentiation means that incumbent firms possess brand identification and customer loyalty that potential entrants do not possess. Brand identification and customer loyalty serve as entry barriers because new entrants not only have to absorb the standard costs associated with starting production in a new industry but also have to absorb the costs associated with overcoming incumbent firms' differentiation advantages. If the cost of overcoming these advantages is greater than the potential return from entering an industry, entry will not occur, even if incumbent firms are earning substantial profits.

Care must be taken when comparing the costs that incumbent firms face in creating product differentiation barriers to entry and the costs that potential entrants face in overcoming those barriers. In general, if the cost of entry deterrence borne by incumbent firms is equal to the value of entry deterrence, then incumbent firms will not enjoy superior performance, even though they have successfully deterred entry. For example, suppose a firm could earn $1,000 of profits if there was no entry into its industry. However, because there are potential entrants, this firm may feel compelled to invest in product differentiation (through advertising, customer service, and so forth) to deter entry. These activities are costly. If the total cost of the product differentiation needed to deter new entry is $1,000, then this incumbent firm would not earn any profits ($1,000 in potential economic profit − $1,000 in costs for deterring entry = $0 economic profit), even if it successfully deterred entry. Only if the cost of entry deterrence is less than the value of deterred entry can incumbent firms obtain superior performance.

There are numerous examples of industries in which product differentiation tends to act as a barrier to entry. In the brewing industry, for example, substantial investments by Budweiser, Miller, and Coors (among other incumbent firms) in advertising (will we ever forget the Budweiser frogs?) and brand recognition have made large-scale entry into the U.S. brewing industry very costly. Whether these efforts to forestall entry have reduced the returns to these incumbent firms is a difficult question, although some research seems to suggest that this may have occurred to some extent for the largest firms in U.S. brewing.[11]

E. & J. Gallo Winery, a U.S. wine maker, faces product differentiation barriers to entry in its efforts to sell Gallo wine in the French market. The market for wine in France is huge—the French consume 16.1 gallons of wine per person per year, for a total consumption of over 400 million cases of wine, while U.S. consumers drink only 1.8 gallons of wine per person per year, for a total consumption of less than 200 million cases. Despite this difference, intense loyalties to local French vineyards have made it very difficult for Gallo to break into this huge French market—a market where American wines are still given as "gag gifts" and only American-theme restaurants carry U.S. wines on their menus. Gallo is attempting to overcome this product differentiation advantage of French wineries by emphasizing its California roots—roots that many French consider to be exotic—and downplaying the fact that it is a U.S. company, consumers.[12]

Cost Advantages Independent of Scale as a Barrier to Entry

In addition to the barriers cited previously, incumbent firms may have a whole range of cost advantages, independent of economies of scale, compared to new entrants. These cost advantages can act to deter entry, because new entrants find themselves at a cost disadvantage vis-à-vis incumbent firms with these cost advantages. New entrants can engage in activities to overcome the cost advantages of incumbent firms, but as the cost of overcoming them increases, the economic profit potential from entry is reduced. In some settings, incumbent firms enjoying cost advantages independent of scale, can earn superior profits and still not be threatened by new entry —because the cost of overcoming those advantages can be prohibitive. Five of these cost advantages, independent of scale, will be discussed: (1) proprietary technology, (2) know-how, (3) favorable access to raw materials, (4) favorable geographic locations, and (5) learning-curve cost advantages. These are summarized in Table 3.3.

Proprietary Technology. In some industries, proprietary (secret or patented) technology gives incumbent firms important cost advantages over potential entrants. To enter these industries, potential entrants must develop their own substitute technologies or copy the proprietary technologies. Both of these activities can be costly. Developing substitute technology can involve expensive and risky research and development efforts. Copying proprietary technology can be costly in terms of potential lawsuits over patent violations. If the cost to new entrants of duplicating incumbent firms' cost positions is greater than the economic potential from entering an industry, new entry will not be forthcoming even though incumbent firms may be earning substantial profits. Notice that this proprietary technology need not be linked with economies of scale to act as a barrier to entry.

TABLE 3.3	Sources of Cost Advantage, Independent of Scale, That Can Act as Barriers to Entry

Proprietary Technology: When incumbent firms have secret or patented technology that reduces their costs below the costs of potential entrants, potential entrants must develop the source of substitute technologies to compete. The cost of developing this technology can act as a barrier to entry.

Know-how: When incumbent firms have knowledge, skills, and information that take years to develop and are not possessed by potential entrants. The cost of developing this know-how can act as a barrier to entry.

Favorable Access to Raw Materials: When incumbent firms have low-cost access to critical raw materials that is not enjoyed by potential entrants. The cost of gaining similar access can act as a barrier to entry.

Favorable Geographic Locations: When incumbent firms have all the best locations already locked up. The cost of duplicating these locations can act as a barrier to entry.

Learning-Curve Cost Advantages: When incumbent firms have high levels of cumulative volume of production, which give them cost advantages over potential entrants.

Know-how.   Even more important than technology per se as a barrier to entry is the know-how built up by incumbent firms over their history.[13] Know-how is the often-taken-for-granted knowledge and information that is needed to compete in an industry on a day-to-day basis.[14] Know-how includes information about countless details that has taken years, sometimes decades, to accumulate in a firm, which enables the firm to interact with customers and suppliers, to be innovative and creative, to manufacture quality products, and so forth. Typically, new entrants will not have access to this know-how and thus may find themselves at a cost disadvantage compared to incumbents. It may be difficult (costly) for new entrants to build this know-how in a relatively short period of time. Together, these attributes of know-how can discourage new entry.

One industry in which this kind of know-how is very important is the pharmaceutical industry. Success in this industry depends critically on having high-quality research and development skills. The development of world-class research and development skills takes decades, as firms accumulate the knowledge, abilities, ideas—the know-how—needed to succeed. New entrants face enormous cost disadvantages for decades as they attempt to develop these abilities, and thus entry into the pharmaceutical industry has been quite limited.

Favorable Access to Raw Materials.   Incumbent firms may also have cost advantages, compared to new entrants, based on favorable access to raw materials. If, for example, there are only a few sources of high-quality iron ore in a specific geographic region, steel firms that have access to these sources may have a cost advantage over steel firms that must ship their ore in from distant sources.

Of course, in order for favorable access to raw materials to be a source of cost advantage for incumbent firms, firms with this access must not have paid its full value when they acquired it. If a firm is able to save a million dollars a year because it does not have to ship its raw materials long distances, but it has to pay an extra million dollars a year for access to its raw materials, this firm obviously does not earn above-normal economic profits. However, if a million-dollar savings was obtained for a $25,000 investment, then this firm has a cost advantage over potential entrants and can be expected to have a competitive advantage that will not motivate entry.

There are a variety of reasons why an incumbent firm may pay less for access to raw materials than what that access is ultimately worth. First, at the time access to raw materials is obtained, the full value of this access may not be known. Thus, for example, a farmer may purchase land to grow cotton, only to discover that the land rests on a very valuable reservoir of oil. Second, changes in technology or demand may increase the value of a source of raw materials in ways that were not anticipated when the source was acquired.[15] Porter cites certain deposits of sulfur that were thought to have relatively little value when they were sold by some oil companies to several sulfur-mining companies. However, changes in sulfur-mining technology made these sources of raw materials much more valuable than had been anticipated.[16]

In general, new entrants are less likely to be able to acquire favorable access to raw materials for a price less than the full value of that access, compared to incumbent firms. When incumbent firms earn economic profits on their favorable access to raw materials, these economic profits reveal the full value of that access. In the future, firms that attempt to duplicate that access will have to pay its full economic value. Thus the profits earned by incumbent firms that motivate new entry ensure that new entrants will not be able to earn profits from acquiring special access to raw materials.

Favorable Geographic Locations. Incumbent firms may have all the favorable locations locked up, thereby gaining a cost advantage compared to potential entrants. Like favorable access to raw materials, favorable locations are a source of cost advantage only if incumbent firms acquire these locations at a price that is less than their true value.

One firm that has built its success at least partly on the early acquisition of favorable geographic locations is Wal-Mart. By moving early to put its large retail outlets in small and medium-size markets, Wal-Mart was able to acquire many retail locations before the full value of these locations was apparent. New entrants into these markets would have to compete not only with Wal-Mart's impressive economies of scale but also with Wal-Mart's cost advantage stemming from the timing of the acquisition of its locations. Given these two factors, it is not surprising that few other retail firms have moved into these same small and medium-size markets.[17]

Learning-Curve Cost Advantages. It has been shown that in certain industries (such as airplane manufacturing), the cost of production falls with the cumulative volume of production. Over time, as incumbent firms gain experience in manufacturing, their costs fall below those of potential entrants. Potential entrants, in this context, must endure substantially higher costs while they gain experience, and thus they may not enter, despite possible above-normal returns being earned by incumbent firms. These learning-curve economies are discussed in more detail in Chapter 6.

Contrived Deterrence as a Barrier to Entry

Economies of scale, product differentiation, and cost advantages independent of scale can all be thought of as **natural barriers to entry.** In each of these cases, incumbent firms are engaging in activities designed to improve their efficiency (economies of scale and cost advantages independent of scale) or give themselves an advantage over current competition (product differentiation). A secondary consequence of these activities is that they also deter entry. A firm would engage in these activities even if they did not deter entry because they improve its efficiency and enhance its competitive position in an industry.

An alternative approach to studying entry focuses on **contrived deterrence.** Here, incumbent firms engage in activities whose sole objective is to deter new entry, even if these activities may *reduce* the efficiency of incumbent firms.[18]

Most of the barriers previously cited could be used as contrived deterrents. For example, to prevent possible entry, a firm might invest in more product differentiation than current competition requires. Also, a firm might invest in more than economy-of-scale-maximizing levels of manufacturing capacity only to deter entry. In all cases, the objective of this additional investment is to send a signal to potential entrants that if they enter, they are likely to face intense competitive pressures from incumbent firms.

Of course, these contrived deterrence investments are costly and can actually reduce the efficiency of incumbent firms. As with all strategic decisions, the benefits of these investments (in the form of deterred entry) must be weighed against the costs (reduced efficiency).

Consider, for example, the situation presented in Figure 3.4.[19] Here, there is one incumbent firm and one potential entrant. In Figure 3.4A, the incumbent firm has made no contrived deterrence investments and the potential entrant has to decide whether to enter. If this firm decides not to enter this industry (perhaps because of substantial "natural" barriers to entry), the incumbent firm will earn a monopolist profit (P_m) and the new entrant will earn (at least in this industry) zero profits (0).

If, on the other hand, the potential entrant decides to enter, the incumbent firm has to decide whether to accommodate the new entry (for example, by reducing its level of output) or fight the new entry (for example, by maintaining or even increasing its output in order to drive the new entrant out of business). If the incumbent firm decides to accommodate the new entrant, then both the new firm and the incumbent firm earn profits equal to P_d (the **duopolist profit,** or the profit each firm in this industry earns by tacitly colluding with the other firm). If the incumbent firm decides not to accommodate, both the incumbent and the new entrant earn profits equal to P_w (the **warring profit,** or the profit each firm in this industry earns by attempting to drive its competitor out of business). By applying the information in Table 3.1, it is not difficult to see that $P_m > P_d > P_w$. Accommodating new entrants through tacit collusion is discussed in more detail in Chapter 9.

These profitability results present a dilemma for the incumbent firm. Clearly, the incumbent firm is much better off if the potential entrant decides not to enter. In this case, the incumbent firm earns profits equal to P_m. To help ensure this level of profitability, the incumbent is likely to "threaten" the potential entrant with dire consequences if it actually enters—especially if there are no "natural" barriers to entry protecting the incumbent firm. However, these threats, in general, are not credible. Once entry actually occurs, the incumbent firm has a strong incentive to accommodate the new entrant because P_d is greater than P_w. Of course, accommodating a new entrant sends to other potential entrants the signal that the original incumbent firm will accommodate, which increases the probability of subsequent entry.

An incumbent firm can partially resolve its dilemma by engaging in a contrived deterrence strategy. This is shown in Figure 3.4B. In Figure 3.4B, the incumbent makes the first decision about whether to invest in contrived deterrence. If the incumbent does not invest in contrived deterrence, then the outcomes are as shown in Figure 3.4A. However, if the incumbent decides to invest in contrived deterrence, the potential entrant must then decide whether to enter, and the incumbent must then decide whether

FIGURE 3.4   Contrived Deterrence Strategies

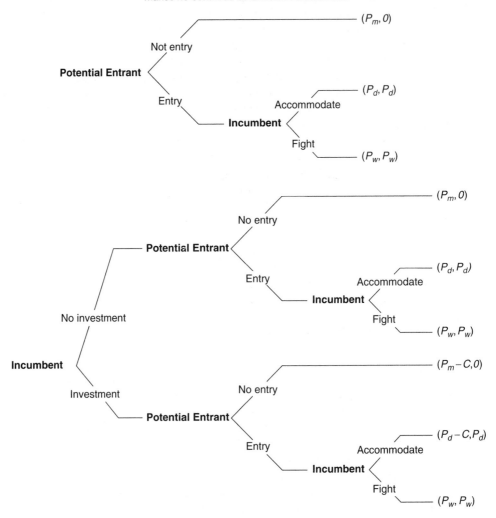

(A)
There is one incumbent and one new entrant, and the incumbent makes no contrived deterrence investments.

(B)
There is one incumbent and one new entrant, and the incumbent makes a contrived deterrence investment that costs C.

Profit implications:
$P_m > (P_m - C) > P_d > (P_d - C) > P_w > 0$

to accommodate or fight if a new entry is forthcoming. If the investment is made and no new entry is forthcoming, the incumbent firm earns $P_m - C$ (where C is the cost of the entry-deterring investment, and the potential entrant earns nothing (at least in this industry). If the investment is made, new entry occurs, and the incumbent accommodates, then the incumbent earns $P_d - C$, and the new entrant earns P_d. If the investment is made, entry occurs, and the incumbent fights, then both the incumbent and the new entrant earn P_w. The cost of deterring entry is not counted against the incumbent firm in this case because it is being used in a productive activity.

If the cost of deterring entry (C) is less than the profits of a duopolist (P_d), then the following relationships hold in Figure 3.4B: $P_m > (P_m - C) > P_d > (P_d - C) > P_w$. The implications of these inequalities for an incumbent are clear. The best situation to be in is to be a monopolist not threatened by entry (or a monopolist protect by "natural" barriers to entry) and to earn the highest level of performance (P_m). Thus incumbent firms should invest in contrived deterrence only if they are not protected from entry by "natural" barriers—economies of scale, product differentiation, or cost advantages independent of scale. If this is not the case, the next best situation is to *effectively* deter entry (because $P_m - C$ is assumed to be greater than P_d). Indeed, there may be significant leeway in making these entry-deterring investments. As long as the cost of deterrence (C) does not reduce an incumbent firm's performance to the level of a duopolist profit (P_d), this investment should be made. Also, this analysis suggests that if an investment to deter entry is going to be made, it should not fail, for ($P_d - C$) is less than P_d.

Researchers have suggested that contrived deterrence investments are most likely to succeed if they have three attributes.[20] First, an incumbent firm should invest in ways that, to the extent possible, forces it to fight if entry occurs. The object of these investments should be to reduce managerial discretion to accommodate to zero. It is perhaps ironic, but firms in this contrived deterrence world gain advantage by limiting their strategic options.[21]

Second, contrived deterrence investments must be highly specific. **Specific investments** have value in a limited range of economic activities. Nonspecific investments can be used to engage in a wide range of activities, including those that could accommodate new entrants. Specific investments should not be useful in accommodating new entrants. Indeed, their only use may be to fight new entrants. Thus an investment in excess general-purpose manufacturing space or in general-purpose warehouse space does not pose a credible threat to a potential entrant, but an investment in highly specialized excess manufacturing capacity or in highly specialized warehouse space does. Also, the cost of transforming these specialized investments into alternative uses must be high, so that they remain specific.

Finally, contrived deterrence investments must be made in a very public setting. If an incumbent firm makes these investments but fails to inform a potential entrant, their deterrence effect is limited. It is much more effective for an incumbent to announce its deterring investment publicly and as widely as possible.

This model applies to a monopolist attempting to deter entry into its industry. It can easily be generalized to industries with closely cooperating oligopolists.[22] Indeed, as we describe in detail in Chapter 9, virtually all contrived deterrence research focuses either on monopolists or on closely cooperating oligopolists. When numerous firms of equal size are competing in an industry, no one firm is likely to be able to create a sufficiently creditable threat to be able to deter entry.

One industry in which this kind of contrived deterrence seems to have been operating was the U.S. electric turbine industry. All indications were that this industry was significantly over capacity, yet the two incumbent firms (General Electric and Westinghouse) continued to add highly specialized manufacturing capacity in highly public ways (such as announcements in *Wall Street Journal* advertisements and press releases). Much of this effort seemed designed to try to deter entry into the U.S. market by several European competitors.[23]

Contrived deterrence may have also played an important role in the titanium dioxide market. Titanium dioxide is a whitener used in paints, paper, and plastics. Regulatory changes meant that DuPont's approach to manufacturing titanium dioxide had a substantial cost advantage over other approaches to manufacturing this product. Moreover, these regulatory changes meant that there would be substantial amounts of excess demand for titanium dioxide. In order to forestall the creation of new manufacturing capacity to meet this excess demand, DuPont announced that it was going to rapidly increase its own manufacturing capacity for titanium dioxide. When another firm (Kerr-McGee) began construction of a new titanium dioxide plant, DuPont falsely announced that it had begun construction of a very large facility—a facility that would largely satisfy excess demand for titanium dioxide. Records suggest that this announcement was designed to deter Kerr-McGee from completing this plant. Unfortunately for DuPont, overall demand for titanium dioxide fell, and entry into this industry subsided—not because of DuPont's efforts to deter entry but because the industry no longer promised profits for new entrants.[24]

Government Policy as a Barrier to Entry

Governments, for their own reasons, may decide to prevent entry into an industry. This can be the case even though incumbent firms are earning substantial profits.

In the United States and most other developed economies, government regulation of entry is most often coupled with government regulation of the profitability of incumbent firms. Thus although incumbent firms may be protected from entry by government policy, this protection comes at the cost of firms seeking above-normal performance that might have been earned. This was the case, for example, when the Civil Aeronautics Board regulated routes and prices in the U.S. airline industry. Deregulation left U.S. airlines vulnerable to new entry (which has certainly occurred), but also gave them the right to earn economic profits (something that has apparently yet to occur for most U.S. airlines).[25]

However, in some economies, government policy may enable incumbent firms to earn very high levels of economic profit while still prohibiting entry. For example, entry into Japanese markets has historically been very difficult, largely because of tariff and nontariff trade barriers.[26] In the early 1990s, International Game Technology (IGT), a leading U.S. manufacturer of slot machines, sought entry into the large Japanese gambling market (Japan has over two-thirds of the world's slot machines, approximately 800,000 in total). IGT's entry was deterred, however, because its slot machines did not meet government slot machine standards. Unfortunately, knowledge about what these standards were was available only to members of the Japanese industry's trade association, and to become a member of this trade association, a firm needed to have been manufacturing slot machines in Japan for at least 3 years. It took several years for IGT to be able to overcome these challenges and start selling slot machines in the Japanese market.[27]

Similar barriers exist to entry into the Japanese beer industry. This industry is dominated by four firms (Kirin, Asahi, Sapporo, and Suntory) that, collectively, have 78 percent of the Japanese beer market. In order for foreign firms to enter into this market and begin producing beer in Japan, they must obtain a license from the ministry of finance (MOF). However, to obtain such a license, a firm must already be producing 2 million liters of beer in Japan. This government-sponsored "Catch 22" has effectively limited non-Japanese beers to the expensive import market in Japan.[28]

Other quasi-government bodies can also act to deter entry. For example, the ruling body of the IndyCar racing series once passed a rule requiring all new engine-manufacturing entrants into the series to make their engines available to all competitors for purchase. At the time, the only firm considering entry into this engine-manufacturing competition was the Honda Motor Company. Honda believed that the cost of making its new engines available to all competitors upon entry into IndyCar racing would be prohibitive. The effect of this rule was to deter Honda's entry into the IndyCar series. Not surprisingly, this rule was supported both by General Motors and Ford, incumbent IndyCar engine suppliers who receive substantial advertising advantages from their involvement in this racing series. Ultimately, this rule was relaxed, and Honda began selling engines to just a few IndyCar racing teams.[29]

Other Barriers to Entry

Several other barriers to entry have been cited in the literature. Usually, however, these other entry barriers turn out to be special cases of the five just discussed.

For example, capital requirements of entry have been cited as a barrier. Upon reflection, however, it is difficult to see how capital requirements, per se, can act as barriers. If capital markets are efficient—in at least the semistrong form—then firms should be able to obtain capital to invest in any positive net-present-value strategies.[30] Entry into an industry will have a positive present value when the cost of entry is less than the (discounted) positive net cash flows coming as a result of entry. The sheer size of the capital investment needed is not relevant in this decision—only whether the discounted returns from entry are greater than the cost of entry. Certainly, there has been substantial evidence that the sheer size of capital requirements per se has been not enough to deter the entry of many firms into new industries through the use of multi-billion dollar acquisitions.

However, it *may* be the case that incumbent firms have a lower cost of capital than new entrants. This lower cost of capital for incumbents can reflect any "natural" barriers to entry cited previously (for example, economy-of-scale advantages, product differentiation advantages, cost advantages independent of scale). These factors could combine to make investing in new entry into an industry more risky than investing in an incumbent firm's ongoing business operations. In efficient capital markets, this risk differential will be reflected in a cost-of-capital differential between incumbent and new entry firms.

A very high cost of capital for potential new entrants into an industry can turn what otherwise would be a positive net-present-value investment into a negative net-present-value investment. In this case, even if firms wanted to enter, they would not be able to obtain the capital to do so. However, entry is not deterred by the sheer size of capital required but by the advantages incumbent firms possess that raise the discount rates of potential entrants. Thus if capital is a barrier to entry, it is a barrier because one (or several) "natural" barriers are in place.

Customer-switching costs have also been cited as a possible barrier to entry. Customer-switching costs are one-time costs borne by customers when switching from one firm's products to another's. For certain products and services, customers must make substantial investments to learn how to use the product, support it, and to exploit it fully. For example, when a company purchased a mainframe computer system from IBM, it made substantial investments in buildings and rooms that were designed specifically for those computers, for hardware peripherals (including printers, disk drives, and terminals) that supported their operations, and for software and trained computer operators that made the system work. The value of these investments could easily be larger than the cost of the mainframe computer itself.

When customers have made these investments to use incumbent firms' products, new entrants must convince these customers not only that their products are preferable to the incumbent firms' but also that their products or services will add value greater than the costs of switching. If switching costs are substantial, potential entrants may not be able to begin operations, even though incumbent firms are earning profits.[31]

However, upon reflection, it becomes clear that customer-switching costs are a special case of either cost or product differentiation barriers to entry. In the absence of monopoly, customers in an industry will be willing to accept high switching costs as a condition for using a firm's products only if they perceive the value of that firm's products to be much greater than the value of alternatives. Higher perceived value, in turn, is a function of the level of product differentiation or lower costs of incumbent firms in an industry. Thus, customer-switching costs operate as a barrier only under conditions of product differentiation or cost advantage.

Finally, access to distribution channels has also been cited as a barrier to entry. If incumbent firms have all the logical distribution channels in an industry already locked up, then new entrants will have to absorb substantial costs to create new distribution channels to compete. However, if it is recognized that prior access to distribution channels is logically equivalent to having special access to some important raw material, geographic location, or know-how, then distribution channels become a special case of cost advantages independent of scale acting as a barrier to entry. Because of this, all the conditions that must hold for these cost advantages to generate entry deterrence must also hold for access to distribution channels. Most notably, the full value of access to distribution channels should not have been reflected in the cost to incumbent firms when that access was originally obtained.

Even when incumbent firms have prior access to distribution channels, new entrants may still be able to create new channels. This has occurred in the U.S. television broadcasting industry with the entry of several newer television networks, including the Fox, Warner Brothers, and UPN networks.[32] In the end, if the profit potential of new entry is greater than the cost of new entry, entry is likely to occur even if the cost of creating new distribution networks is significant.

Low Levels of Entry and the Existence of Barriers to Entry

One common confusion in analyzing the threat of new entry into an industry is to conclude that the low level of actual entry into an industry means that there must be high barriers to entry in that industry. Of course, there are always two reasons why the level of entry into an industry may be low. First, there may be substantial barriers to entry.

Second, there may be low levels of profit in an industry. If no incumbent firms are making substantial economic profits, it is unlikely that any firm will choose to enter, independent of whether barriers to entry exist.

Because low profits can lead to low levels of entry, it is not possible to conclude that low levels of entry necessarily means that there are high barriers to entry in an industry. In conducting this type of analysis, the appropriate question to ask is: "If some incumbent firms were earning high levels of profit, would entry be possible?" This focuses attention on the structural attributes of an industry that actually define the level to which an industry is characterized by barriers to entry rather than on the actual level of entry into an industry. The actual level of entry into an industry may be a function of both the barriers to entry that might exist in an industry and the level of profitability enjoyed by incumbent firms in an industry.

The Threat of Rivalry

New entrants are an important threat to the ability of firms to maintain or improve their level of performance, but they are not the only threat in a firm's environment. A second environmental threat in the five forces framework is **rivalry**—the intensity of competition among a firm's direct competitors. Both BarnesandNoble.com and Borders.com have become rivals of Amazon.com. CBS, NBC, Fox, USA Networks, and TNN—to name a few—are all ESPN rivals.

High levels of rivalry are indicated by such actions as frequent price cutting by firms in an industry (for example, price discounts in the airline industry), frequent introduction of new products by firms in an industry (for example, continuous product introductions in consumer electronics), intense advertising campaigns (Pepsi versus Coke in the soft-drink industry), and rapid competitive actions and reactions in an industry (competing airlines quickly matching the discounts of other airlines).

Some of the attributes of an industry that are likely to generate high levels of rivalry are listed in Table 3.4. First, rivalry tends to be high when there are numerous firms in an industry and when these firms tend to be roughly the same size. Such is the case in the laptop personal computer industry. Worldwide, over 120 firms have entered the laptop computer market, and no one firm dominates in market share. Since the early 1990s, prices in the laptop market have been declining 25 to 30 percent a year. Profit margins for laptop personal computer firms that used to be in the 10–13 percent range have fallen rapidly to 3–4 percent.[33] With large numbers of equal-sized firms, it is very difficult for firms in an industry to establish any rivalry-reducing tacit collusion strategies. This difficulty is discussed in more detail in Chapter 9.

TABLE 3.4   Attributes of an Industry that Increase the Threat of Rivalry
1. Large number of competing firms.
2. Competing firms that are the same size and have the same influence.
3. Slow industry growth.
4. Lack of product differentiation.
5. Productive capacity added in large increments.

Second, rivalry tends to be high when industry growth is slow. When industry growth is slow, firms seeking to increase their sales must acquire market share from established competitors. This tends to increase rivalry. Intense price rivalry emerged in the U.S. fast-food industry—with 99-cent Whoppers at Burger King and "dollar menus" at Wendy's and McDonald's—when the growth in this industry declined.[34]

Third, rivalry tends to be high when firms are unable to differentiate their products in an industry. When product differentiation is not a viable strategic option, firms are often forced to compete only on the basis of price. Intense price competition is typical of high-rivalry industries. In the airline industry, for example, intense competition on longer routes—such as between Los Angeles and New York and between Los Angeles and Chicago—has kept prices on these routes down. There are relatively few product differentiation options on these routes. However, by creating hub-and-spoke systems, certain airlines (American, United, Delta) have attempted to develop regions of the United States in which they are the dominant carrier. These hub-and-spoke systems enable airlines to partially differentiate their products geographically and thus reduce the level of rivalry in segments of this industry.[35]

Finally, rivalry tends to be high when production capacity is added in large increments. If, in order to obtain economies of scale, production capacity must be added in large increments, an industry is likely to experience periods of oversupply after new capacity comes on line. This overcapacity often leads to price cutting. Much of the growing rivalry in the commercial jet industry between Boeing and AirBus can be traced to the large manufacturing capacity additions made by AirBus when it entered this industry.[36] This dynamic is discussed in more detail in Chapters 4 and 9.

The Threat of Substitutes

A third environmental threat in the five forces framework is substitutes. The products or services provided by a firm's **rivals** meet approximately the same customer needs in the same ways as the products or services provided by the firm itself. **Substitutes** meet approximately the same customer needs but do so in different ways. Close substitutes for Amazon.com include Barnes & Noble, Borders, and Waldenbooks book stores. Television is a somewhat more distant substitute for Amazon, because the popularity of television comedies, dramas, and documentaries dampens demand for books. Substitutes for ESPN include sports magazines, sports sections in newspapers, and actually attending sporting events.

Substitutes place a ceiling on the prices firms in an industry can charge and on the profits firms in an industry can earn. For example, during the oil price "shocks" of the 1970s and 1980s, members of OPEC were able to collude, reduce output, and drive the price of crude oil over $40 per barrel. At this price, a broad range of substitutes that had previously not been economically viable suddenly became more attractive. Substitutes included oil shale, oil sands, solar energy, and even conservation. If the price of oil had remained at (inflation-adjusted) over $40 per barrel, several of these substitutes might have reached a critical mass and become long-term viable alternatives to crude oil, and they could have acted as constraints on the profits of oil companies and oil-producing countries. The collapse of crude oil prices in the 1980s made these substitute products less attractive, but at the cost of reducing the profits of oil-producing countries. Recent increases in the price of crude oil may, once again, make these substitutes economically more viable, especially if these higher prices last for several years.

In the extreme, substitutes can ultimately replace an industry's products and services. This happens when a substitute is clearly superior to previous products. Examples include electronic calculators as substitutes for slide rules and mechanical calculators, electronic watch movements as substitutes for pin-lever mechanical watch movements, and compact discs as substitutes for long-playing (LP) records (although some audiophiles continue to argue for the sonic superiority of LPs).

Substitutes are playing an increasingly important role in reducing the profit potential in a wide variety of industries. For example, in the legal profession, private mediation and arbitration services are becoming viable substitutes for lawyers. Computerized texts are becoming viable substitutes for printed books in the publishing industry. Television news programs, especially services such as CNN and Fox News, are very threatening substitutes for weekly news magazines, including *Time* and *Newsweek*. In Europe, so-called superstores are threatening smaller food shops. Minor league baseball teams are partial substitutes for major league teams. Cable television is a substitute for broadcast television. Groups of "big box" retailers are substitutes for traditional shopping centers. Private mail delivery systems (such as those in the Netherlands and Australia) are substitutes for government postal services. Home financial planning software is a partial substitute for professional financial planners.[37]

The Threat of Suppliers

A fourth environmental threat in the five forces framework is suppliers. Suppliers provide a wide variety of raw materials, labor, and other critical assets to firms. Suppliers can threaten the performance of firms in an industry by increasing the prices of their supplies or by reducing the quality of those supplies. Any profits that were being earned in an industry can be transferred to suppliers in this way. For Amazon.com, book publishers and, more recently, book authors are critical suppliers, along with the employees who provide programming and logistics capabilities to the firm. Critical suppliers for ESPN include sports leagues—such as the NFL and the NHL—as well as TV personalities who staff ESPN television shows.

Some supplier attributes that can lead to high levels of threat are listed in Table 3.5. First, a firm's suppliers are a greater threat if the *suppliers'* industry is dominated by a small number of firms. In this setting, a firm has few options but to purchase supplies from these firms. These few firms thus have enormous flexibility to charge high prices, to reduce quality, or to squeeze the profits of the firms to which they sell in other ways. Much of Microsoft's power in the software industry reflects its dominance in the operating system market, where Windows remains the de facto standard for most personal

TABLE 3.5   Indicators of the Threat of Suppliers in an Industry
1. The suppliers' industry is dominated by a small number of firms.
2. Suppliers sell unique or highly differentiated products.
3. Suppliers are *not* threatened by substitutes.
4. Suppliers threaten forward vertical integration.
5. Firms are *not* important customers for suppliers.

computers. For now, at least, if a company wants to sell personal computers, it is going to need to interact with Microsoft.

Conversely, when a firm has the option of purchasing from a large number of suppliers, suppliers have less power to threaten the firm's profits. For example, as the number of attorneys in the United States has increased over the years (up 40 percent since 1981, currently close to 1 million), lawyers and law firms have been forced to begin competing for work. Some corporate clients have forced law firms to reduce their hourly fees and to handle repetitive simple legal tasks for low flat fees.[38] Also, as the percentage of a firm's workers in a labor union shrinks, the ability of that union to threaten the firm falls.[39]

Second, suppliers are a greater threat when what they supply is unique or highly differentiated. There was only one Michael Jordan, as a basketball player, as a spokesperson, and as a celebrity (but *not* as a baseball player). Jordan's unique status gave him enormous bargaining power as a supplier and enabled him to extract much of the economic profit that would otherwise have been earned by the Chicago Bulls. In the same way, Intel's unique ability to develop, manufacture, and sell microprocessors gives it significant bargaining power as a supplier in the personal computer industry.

Supplier uniqueness can operate in almost any industry. For example, in the highly competitive world of television talk shows, some guests, as suppliers, can gain surprising fame for their unique characteristics. For example, one woman was a guest on eight talk shows. Her claim to fame: She was the tenth wife of a gay, con-man bigamist. Talk show hosts can also exercise significant power as suppliers. King World, the distributor of the *Oprah* talk show, has depended on *Oprah* for as much as 40 percent of its revenues. This, of course, has given the show's host, Oprah Winfrey, significant leverage in negotiating with King World.[40]

Third, suppliers are a greater threat to firms in an industry when suppliers are *not* threatened by substitutes. When there are no effective substitutes, suppliers can take advantage of their position to extract economic profits from firms they supply. Both Intel (in microprocessors) and Microsoft (in PC operating systems) have been accused of exploiting their unique product positions to appropriate rents from customers. When there are substitutes for supplies, supplier power is checked. In the metal-can industry, for example, steel cans are threatened by aluminum cans as a substitute. In order to continue to sell to can manufacturers, steel companies have had to keep their prices below the price of aluminum. In this way, the potential power of the steel companies is checked by the existence of a substitute product, aluminum.[41]

Fourth, suppliers are a greater threat to firms when they can credibly threaten to enter into and begin competing in a firm's industry. This is called **forward vertical integration,** and suppliers cease to be suppliers alone but become suppliers *and* rivals. The threat of forward vertical integration is partially a function of barriers to entry into an industry. When an industry has high barriers to entry, suppliers face significant costs of forward vertical integration, and thus forward integration is not as serious a threat to the profits of incumbent firms (vertical integration is discussed in detail in Chapter 10).

Finally, suppliers are a threat to firms when firms are *not* an important part of suppliers' business. Steel companies, for example, are not too concerned about losing the business of a sculptor or of a small construction company. However, they are very concerned about losing the business of the major can manufacturers, major white-goods manufacturers (that is, manufacturers of refrigerators, washing machines, dryers, and so forth), and automobile companies. Steel companies, as suppliers, are likely to be very accommodating and willing to reduce prices and increase quality for can manufacturers, white-goods manufacturers, and auto companies. Smaller, "less important" customers, however, are likely to be subject to greater price increases, lower-quality service, and lower-quality products.

The Threat of Buyers

The final environmental threat in the five forces framework is buyers. **Buyers** purchase a firm's products or services. Whereas sellers actions may increase a firm's costs, buyers actions may decrease a firm's revenues. Amazon.com's buyers include all those who purchase books online as well as those who purchase advertising space on Amazon's Web site. ESPN's buyers include all those who watch sports on television as well as those who purchase advertising space on the network. Some of the important indicators of the threat of buyers are listed in Table 3.6.

First, if a firm has only one buyer, or a small number of buyers, these buyers can be very threatening. Firms that sell a significant amount of their output to the U.S. Department of Defense recognize the influence of this buyer on their operations. Reductions in defense spending have forced defense companies to try even harder to reduce costs and increase quality to satisfy government demands. All these actions reduce the economic profits of these defense-oriented companies.[42]

Firms that sell to large retail chains have also found it difficult to maintain high levels of profitability. Powerful retail firms can make significant and complex logistical and other demands on firms that sell to them and, if these firms fail to meet these demands, buyers can "fire" them. These demands can have the effect of reducing the profits of firms that sell to powerful buyers.

Wal-Mart is notorious for exercising this kind of power over its suppliers. For example, when Rubbermaid was unable to meet Wal-Mart's deliveries, product quality, and product mix demands, Wal-Mart threatened to cut Rubbermaid off as a supplier. Rather than losing the Wal-Mart account, Rubbermaid sought out a partner that had the resources required to supply Wal-Mart effectively. Ultimately, Newell, Inc., acquired Rubbermaid. Newell is generally seen as one of Wal-Mart's most successful suppliers. Thus, Wal-Mart's influence over Rubbermaid at least partially determined Rubbermaid's ownership structure.[43]

Second, if the products or services that are being sold to buyers are standard and not differentiated, then the threat of buyers can be greater. For example, farmers sell a very standard product. It is very difficult to differentiate products such as wheat, corn, or tomatoes (although this can be done to some extent through the development of new strains of crops, the timing of harvests, the use of no pesticides, and so forth). In

---

TABLE 3.6   Indicators of the Threat of Buyers in an Industry

1. The number of buyers is small.
2. Products sold to buyers are undifferentiated and standard.
3. Products sold to buyers are a significant percentage of a buyer's final costs.
4. Buyers are *not* earning significant economic profits.
5. Buyers threaten backward vertical integration.

general, wholesale grocers and food brokers can always find alternative suppliers of basic food products. These numerous alternative suppliers increase the threat of buyers and force farmers to keep their prices, and profits, low. If any one farmer attempts to raise prices, wholesale grocers and food brokers simply purchase their supplies from some other farmer.

Third, buyers are likely to be more of a threat when the supplies they purchase are a significant portion of the costs of their final products. In this context, buyers are likely to be very concerned about the costs of their supplies and constantly on the lookout for cheaper alternatives, including the possibility of backward vertical integration. For example, the metal can is approximately 40 percent of the final cost of a can of Campbell's soup. In order to reduce this cost and gain control over a significant portion of its total costs, Campbell's Soup Company was once one of the largest can-manufacturing companies in the world.[44]

Fourth, buyers are likely to be more of a threat when they are *not* earning significant economic profits. In these circumstances, buyers are likely to be very sensitive to the costs of the products or service they buy and insist on the lowest possible cost and the highest possible quality from suppliers. This effect can be exacerbated when the profits suppliers earn are greater than the profits buyers earn. In this setting, buyers have a strong incentive to enter into their supplier's business to capture some of the economic profits being earned by suppliers. This strategy of **backward vertical integration** is discussed in more detail in Chapter 10.

Finally, buyers are more of a threat to firms in an industry when they have the ability to vertically integrate backward. In this case, buyers become both buyers and rivals and lock in a certain percentage of an industry's sales. The extent to which buyers represent a threat to vertically integrate, in turn, depends on the barriers to entry that are in place in an industry. If there are significant barriers to entry, buyers may not be able to engage in backward vertical integration, and their threat to firms is reduced.

It is interesting to note, for example, that Home Box Office (HBO) began producing its own movies (that is, it vertically integrated backwards) when the level of competition in cable services increased. One explanation of this move is that HBO could no longer gain high levels of performance in the cable business, so instead began operations in a higher-profit film production industry.[45]

3.3 APPLYING THE FIVE FORCES MODEL

The five forces model has three important implications for managers seeking to choose and implement strategies. First, this model describes the most common sources of threat in industries. Second, it can be used to characterize the overall threat in those industries. Finally, it can be used to anticipate the average level of performance in an industry.

In an important sense, the five forces model describes processes that tend to move an industry toward the economic condition of perfect competition. In general, industries are perfectly competitive when there are high levels of threat from new entry, rivalry, substitutes, suppliers, and buyers. Firms in this kind of industry generally enjoy only competitive parity. Any profits that might exist in this type of industry are quickly competed away by potential entrants, rivals reducing their prices, substitutes becoming more attractive, suppliers raising their prices or lowering their quality, and buyers demanding lower prices or higher quality.

When a firm operates in an industry that is not perfectly competitive, it may be possible to earn some profits. Industries in which the threat of new entrants entering, rivals, substitutes, suppliers, and buyers is less pronounced will, on average, have higher levels of performance. To see how the five forces model can be used to analyze the threats in an industry, consider the performance potential of the two industries described in Table 3.7: the pharmaceutical industry and the consumer electronics industry.

Analyzing the Pharmaceutical Industry

The pharmaceutical industry consists of organizations that develop, patent, and distribute drugs. Some of the major players in this industry include Merck, Eli Lilly, Johnson & Johnson, and Bristol-Myers Squibb.

The Threat of Entry

The threat of new entry into the pharmaceutical industry is quite low. Although there are not significant production economies of scale in this industry, there are very important economies in the research and development process. Firms with large R&D labs are able to engage in basic research that can simultaneously benefit several lines of inquiry. For example, basic research on retroviruses in the 1970s enabled Burroughs Wellcome to develop AZT, an AIDS-fighting drug, in the 1980s (HIV, which causes AIDS, is a type of retrovirus).[46]

TABLE 3.7   Application of Five Forces Model to Analysis of Threats in the U.S. Pharmaceutical Industry and the Consumer Electronics Industry

Pharmaceutical Industry

The pharmaceutical industry consists of firms that develop, patent, and distribute drugs. Although there are not significant production economies in this industry, there are important economies in research and development. Product differentiation exists as well, because firms often sell branded products. Firms compete in research and development. However, once a product is developed and patented, competition is significantly reduced. Recently, the increased availability of generic, nonbranded drugs has threatened the profitability of some drug lines. Once an effective drug is developed, there are usually few, if any, alternatives to that drug. Drugs are manufactured from commodity chemicals, usually available from numerous suppliers. Major customers include doctors and patients. Recently, increased costs have led the federal government and insurance companies to pressure drug companies to reduce their prices.

The Consumer Electronics Industry

The consumer electronics industry consists of firms that develop, manufacture, and distribute electronics for the home and consumer. Common products include portable CD players, televisions, video game consoles, and so forth. There are several very large firms in this industry. Many of these firms have strong brand names. Despite this, some smaller firms—such as Bose in speakers and home entertainment systems and Play Station in video game consoles—are able to enter this industry in niche markets. Much of the production in this industry is located in low-cost countries internationally, including Southeast Asia and Mexico. Although companies are constantly introducing new consumer technologies, many of these technologies are quickly duplicated by rivals. Raw materials in this industry are widely available, although the engineering talent required to develop new technologies is not. Retail outlets for consumer electronics are plentiful, but competition in this industry has recently forced several retail chains out of business.

Source: Performance information taken from *Fortune* (2000). "The Fortune 500, 1999," April 26, pp. F1–F77.

There are also important product differentiation advantages for incumbent firms in the pharmaceutical industry. Brand names such as Tylenol, Bayer, and Sudafed help differentiate what would otherwise be commodity products.

Incumbent firms also enjoy cost advantages independent of scale over potential entrants. These cost advantages reflect the proprietary technology and R&D know-how that has developed in pharmaceutical firms over decades. Government policy also plays a role in deterring entry, because approval of new drugs for sale in the United States can take up to 12 years. New entrants face not only the challenge of developing the R&D skills to compete in this industry, they also must wait several years before selling their products.

The Threat of Rivalry

Historically, the level of rivalry in the pharmaceutical industry has been low. Firms competed in research and development to be the first to develop a drug to treat a particular disease. However, once these drugs were developed, patents protected the firm from significant competition.

Over the last several years, however, competition among pharmaceutical firms has begun to heat up. Most of that competition still takes place in the form of research and development races to develop new drugs. Now, however, the cost of research and development has accelerated. Moreover, different firms will often develop similar drugs to address similar conditions, although in different way. For example, both Viagra and Cialis treat male impotence, but do so in somewhat different ways. They are manufactured by two different companies.

Over this same time period, on the other hand, the total number of large pharmaceutical firms has fallen, as several previously large independent firms have merged. And while price increases have slowed over the last five years or so, overall demand for pharmaceutical drugs continues to grow as the population ages and as drugs are used as a low-cost substitute for hospitalization.

Thus, given these multiple trends, it seems reasonable to conclude that the level of rivalry in this industry is moderate.

The Threat of Substitutes

The threat of substitutes in the pharmaceutical industry is moderate to low. Substitutes do exist for some key products. Acetaminophen (the key ingredient in Tylenol), for example, is a substitute for aspirin (the key ingredient in Bayer aspirin). However, fewer substitutes exist for prescription drugs, especially during the time when a firm holds a patent on a drug. After the patent expires, so-called generic drugs can be substitutes for brand-name drugs.

The Threat of Suppliers

The threat of suppliers is low in the pharmaceutical industry. There are large numbers of suppliers of the basic raw materials. These supplies, more often than not, are commodity chemicals. Because of the barriers to entry cited previously, the threat of forward vertical integration by suppliers into this industry is small.

The Threat of Buyers

Historically, the threat of buyers has been very small in the pharmaceutical industry. Recently, however, pressures by insurance companies, health maintenance organizations, and the federal government to reduce the price of drugs have become more intense.[47] Legislation that limits the time that pharmaceutical companies can retain patents on drugs has been introduced. Also, many states have passed legislation that requires pharmacists to offer consumers nonbranded generics in place of branded drugs. However, much of this threat has been reduced by the strong product differentiation that exists in the pharmaceutical industry. Thus, overall, the threat of buyers is moderate.

Expected Performance

Given this five forces analysis of the pharmaceutical industry, the expected level of performance in this industry is quite high. Indeed, the pharmaceutical industry is consistently one of the most profitable industries in the world.

Analyzing the Consumer Electronics Industry

The consumer electronics industry consists of firms that develop, manufacture, and distribute electronics for the home and consumer. Major players in this industry include Sony, Matsushita (known as Panasonic in the United States), and Phillips.

The Threat of Entry

The threat of entry is moderate in the consumer electronics industry. This is because some barriers to entry exist. Although economies of scale in manufacturing do not act as a barrier to entry in this industry (because these are realized at the level of a particular plant, and individual plants are small relative to the total size of these markets), product differentiation (in the form of the well-known brand names of a few incumbent firms), cost advantages independent of scale (in the form of the innovative know-how of some incumbent firms), and government barriers to entry (in the form of some tariff barriers) do act to increase the cost of entry. However, despite these barriers, new firms can still enter this industry by developing new technologies and building brand names associated with these technologies. Firms such as Bose and Play Station have been able to enter into new segments of this industry and garner relatively high levels of profit.

The Threat of Rivalry

The threat of rivalry is high in this industry. There are numerous firms in this industry and overall industry growth has been slow. Although the brand names of some incumbent firms help moderate rivalry, the fact that innovative technologies are often rapidly duplicated suggests an ongoing high level of rivalry.

The Threat of Substitutes

At the broadest level, firms in the consumer electronics industry are in the "entertainment" industry. Thus, all forms of entertainment—everything from hiking in the mountains to movies to sporting events—are at least partial substitutes for consumer electronics. For this reason, the threat of substitutes in this industry is quite high.

The Threat of Suppliers

The threat of suppliers is low in this industry. Most raw materials are widely available in very competitive markets. The only critical factor of production that may be in short supply is engineering talent. Sometimes, consumer electronics firms find themselves competing for the services of the best engineering talent.

The Threat of Buyers

Historically, the retail consumer electronics industry was relatively fragmented. However, with bankruptcies and consolidation, a few large firms are beginning to play a larger role. These firms—including Wal-Mart and Best Buy—are beginning to exercise some influence on the prices and products of consumer electronics companies. Thus, the overall threat of buyers in this industry is moderate.

Expected Performance

Given this five forces analysis of the consumer electronics industry, the expected level of performance in this industry is moderate—certainly lower than the level of performance of the pharmaceutical industry. Indeed, the performance of firms in the consumer electronics industry has historically been significantly lower than the performance of firms in the pharmaceutical industry.

3.4 ANOTHER INDUSTRY FORCE: COMPLEMENTORS

Recently, Professors Adam Brandenburger and Barry Nalebuff have suggested that another force needs to be added to Porter's five forces framework.[48] These authors distinguish between competitors and what they call a firm's complementors. Another firm is a **competitor** if your customers value your product less when they have this other firm's product than when they have your product alone. Rivals, new entrants, and substitutes can all be seen as specific examples of competitors. On the other hand, another firm is a **complementor** if your customers value your product more when they have this other firm's product than when they have your product alone.

Consider, for example, the relationship between producers of television programming and cable television companies. The value of these firms' products depends partially on the existence of each other. Television producers need outlets for their programming. The growth in the number of channels on cable television provides more of these outlets and thus increases the value of these production firms. On the other hand, cable television companies can continue to add channels, but those channels need content. So the value of cable television companies depends partly on the existence of television production firms. Because the value of television production companies is greater when cable television firms exist, and because the value of cable television companies is greater when television production companies exist, these types of firms are complementors.

Brandenburger and Nalebuff go on to argue that an important difference between complementors and competitors is that a firm's complementors help increase the size of a firm's market, while a firm's competitors divide this market among a set of firms. Based on this logic, these authors suggest that although a firm will usually want to discourage the entry of competitors into its market, it will usually want to encourage the entry of complementors. Returning to the television producers/cable television example, television producers actually want cable television companies to grow and prosper and constantly add new channels, while cable television firms want television producers to grow and constantly create new and innovative programming. If the growth of either of these businesses slows, it hurts the growth of the other.

Of course, the same firm can be a complementor for one firm and a competitor for another. For example, the invention of satellite television and the popularization of DirecTV and the Dish Network represent a competitive challenge to cable television companies. That is, DirecTV and, say, Time Warner Cable, are competitors. However, DirecTV and television production companies are complementors to each other. In deciding whether to encourage the entry of new complementors, a firm has to weigh the extra value these new complementors will create against the competitive effect of this entry on a firm's current complementors.

A single firm can also be both a competitor and a complementor to another firm. This is very common in industries in which it is important to have technological standards. Without standards about, for example, the size of a CD, how information will be stored on a CD, how this information will be read, and so forth, many consumers would have been unwilling to purchase a CD player. With standards in place, however, sales of a particular technology may soar. To develop technology standards, firms must be willing to cooperate. This cooperation means that, with respect to the technology standard, these firms are complementors. And indeed, when these firms act as complementors, their actions have the effect of increasing the total size of the market. However, once these firms cooperate to establish standards, they begin to compete to try to obtain as much of the market they jointly created as possible. In this sense, these firms are also competitors.

Understanding when firms in an industry should behave as complementors and when they should behave as competitors is sometimes very difficult. It is even more difficult for a firm that has interacted with other firms in its industry as a competitor to change its organizational structure, formal and informal control systems, and compensation policy and start interacting with these firms as a complementor, at least for some purposes. Learning to manage what Brandenburger and Nalebuff call the "Jekyll and Hyde" dilemma associated with competitors and complementors can distinguish excellent from only average firms.

3.5 THREATS IN AN INTERNATIONAL CONTEXT

One of the most important benefits of the five forces framework is that it forces strategic managers to broaden their definition of competition. Traditionally, a firm's competitors have been defined as those firms whose products or services meet approximately the same customer needs as a particular firm's products or services. In five forces' language, these competitors are a firm's rivals. However, in an important sense, any individual, group, or organization that seeks to reduce a firm's economic performance can be thought of as a competitor. The five forces framework gives us a tool for describing the forms these other sources of competition can take. Thus new and potential entrants, substitutes, suppliers, buyers, and rivals can all be a firm's competitors and can all reduce an industry's attractiveness.

Although the five forces framework extends the definition of the kinds of competition that may exist in an industry, care must be taken to apply this framework broadly, to develop a complete understanding of the structure of threats facing firms. One way to broaden the application of this framework is to apply it to sources of threat that may exist outside a firm's domestic market. Firms from different countries are just as important in determining the level of threat in an industry as firms operating in a domestic market. Failure to recognize nondomestic firms within the five forces framework can lead to the conclusion that an industry is more attractive than it really is or less attractive than it really is.

Overstating an industry's attractiveness by failing to recognize nondomestic threats has occurred in numerous instances. For example, in the U.S. automobile industry, failure to recognize the threat posed by Japanese and European manufacturers— first as new entrants, then as rivals—led U.S. domestic firms, including General Motors, Ford, and Chrysler, to underestimate the level of threat in their industry. This, in turn, led these U.S. firms to not respond to their European and Japanese competitors until those competitors were well established in the U.S. market.[49] Similarly, failure to recognize Japanese motorcycle manufacturers as new entrants and rivals led U.S. and European motorcycle manufacturers to underestimate the level of threat in this industry. Ultimately, this threat almost destroyed U.S. and European motorcycle manufacturing.[50]

In the 1970s, firms in the Swiss mechanical watch manufacturing industry underestimated the level of threat they faced from nondomestic substitutes. Although international rivals and new entrants did not pose significant threats in this industry, electronic time-keeping movements, as substitutes for mechanical watch movements, did emerge as an important threat to the traditional industry. U.S. and Japanese electronics firms developed these electronic time-keeping devices. It took several years for the Swiss watch industry to recover from this unanticipated threat. Indeed, the Swiss industry may have permanently lost significant market share to some of its non-Swiss rivals.[51]

In general, failure to recognize nondomestic suppliers and buyers can lead to an understatement of an industry's attractiveness because including nondomestic suppliers and buyers in a five forces analysis generally has the effect of increasing the total number of potential suppliers and buyers associated with an industry. As the number of these potential suppliers and buyers goes up, the relative power of domestic suppliers and buyers goes down, and the overall attractiveness of an industry increases.

Thus, for example, although the U.S. market for metal containers is very mature and slow-growing, the worldwide market for metal containers still has a great deal of growth potential. Recognizing these nondomestic buyers can lead to the conclusion that the metal container industry is much more attractive than would be the case if only domestic buyers were included in a five forces analysis.[52]

Indeed, nondomestic competition is such an important consideration in five forces analyses of the attractiveness of industries that the U.S. Department of Justice and the Federal Trade Commission (FTC) now include nondomestic competition in evaluating the concentration of an industry. Although the U.S. automobile industry appears to be highly concentrated (and therefore possibly subject to antitrust enforcement), the global automobile industry is not concentrated and thus the domestic industry is highly competitive, even though there are only three major U.S. firms. Put in five forces terminology, the U.S. automobile industry appears to be very attractive— because, with only three firms, there is presumably low rivalry in this industry. However, by considering non-U.S. rivals and new entrants, the U.S. automobile industry is actually much less attractive—and thus not a likely candidate for Department of Justice or FTC scrutiny for possible antitrust activities.

3.6 SUMMARY

The structure-conduct-performance framework was originally designed to evaluate the competitiveness of industries to assist government regulators. This framework suggests that a firm's conduct and performance are determined largely by industry structure. Thus sources of above-normal economic performance must be sought in the structural characteristics of industries.

Strategy scholars have turned the original objectives of the S-C-P framework upside down by attempting to describe industry conditions under which firms may be able to obtain competitive advantages and superior economic returns. In doing so, strategy scholars have developed powerful models of environmental threats and opportunities, two key components of SWOT analysis.

Michael Porter developed the most influential model of environment threats. His five forces (threats) in an industry are (1) the threat of entry, (2) the threat of rivals, (3) the threat of substitutes, (4) the threat of suppliers, and (5) the threat of buyers. The level of threat of new entrants is a function of barriers to entry, including economies of scale, product differentiation, cost advantages independent of scale, contrived deterrence, and government regulation of entry. There are also numerous indicators of the other threats in an industry.

Recently, it has been suggested that a sixth force—complementors—also has a significant effect on industry attractiveness. A firm is a complementor if its existence increases the value of another firm's products or services.

Although S-C-P-based models of environmental threat are important tools in strategic analyses, they must be linked with models of environmental opportunities and models of organizational strengths and weaknesses to choose strategies that maximize the performance of firms. These models are examined in the next two chapters.

REVIEW QUESTIONS

1. Your former college roommate calls you and asks to borrow $10,000 so that he can open a pizza restaurant in his hometown. In justifying this request, he argues that there must be significant demand for pizza and other fast food in his hometown because there are lots of such restaurants already there and three or four new ones are opening each month. He also argues that demand for convenience food will continue to increase and he points to the large number of firms that now sell frozen dinners in grocery stores. Will you lend him the money? Why or why not?

2. According to the five forces model, one potential threat in an industry is buyers. Yet unless buyers are satisfied, they are likely to look for satisfaction elsewhere. Can the fact that buyers can be threats be reconciled with the need to satisfy buyers?

3. If several competing firms are aware of the five forces model of environmental threats and make their strategic choices solely on the basis of this model, what is the expected level of performance for these firms? Why?

4. Government policies can have a significant effect on the average profitability of firms in an industry. Government, however, is not included as a potential threat in the five forces model. Should the model be expanded to include government? If yes, why? If no, why not?

5. Strategic management scholars turned the original social welfare-maximizing objectives of the S-C-P framework upside down. What, if any, are the social welfare implications of this approach, and should managers be concerned about these implications (if they exist)?

ENDNOTES

1. Early contributors to the structure-conduct-performance model include Mason, E. S. (1939). "Price and production policies of large scale enterprises," *American Economic Review,* 29, pp. 61–74; and Bain, J. S. (1956). *Barriers to New Competition,* Cambridge, MA: Harvard University Press. The major developments in this framework are summarized in Bain, J. S. (1968). *Industrial Organization,* New York: John Wiley & Sons; and Scherer, F. M. (1980). *Industrial Market Structure and Economic Performance,* Boston: Houghton Mifflin. The links between this framework and work in strategic management are discussed by Porter, M. E. (1981a). "The contribution of industrial organization to strategic management," *Academy of Management Review,* 6, pp. 609–620, and Barney, J. B. (1986c). "Types of competition and the theory of strategy: Toward an integrative framework," *Academy of Management Review,* 1, pp. 791–800.

2. The S-C-P framework was originally developed as a social policy tool; however, its antitrust implications are not without controversy. For example, a naive application of this logic suggests that whenever a firm enjoys a sustained competitive advantage, it must be engaging in anticompetitive behavior. Demsetz, H. (1973). "Industry structure, market rivalry, and public policy," *Journal of Law and Economics,* 16, pp. 1–9, and others have noted that, sometimes, the reason a firm has a sustained competitive advantage is that it meets customer needs more efficiently than other firms. This logic is an important precursor to the model of organizational strengths and weaknesses discussed in Chapter 5.

3. See Christensen, C. R., K. R. Andrews, J. L. Bower, G. Hamermesh, and M. E. Porter (1980). *Business Policy: Text and Cases,* Homewood, IL: Irwin.

4. Porter, M. E. (1980). *Competitive Strategy.* New York: Free Press.

5. The five forces framework is described in detail in Porter, M. E. (1979). "How competitive forces shape strategy," *Harvard Business Review,* March/April, pp. 137–156; and Porter, M. E. (1980). *Competitive Strategy,* New York: Free Press.

6. Note that Barnes & Noble and Borders were both already operating in the book store market. However, they are new entrants in the on-line book selling market.

7. These barriers were originally proposed by Bain, J. S. (1968). *Industrial Organization.* New York: John Wiley & Sons; and Porter, M. E. (1980). *Competitive Strategy,* New York: Free Press. It is actually possible to estimate the "height" of barriers to entry in an industry by comparing the cost of entry into an industry with barriers and the cost of entry into that industry if barriers did not exist. The difference between these costs is the "height" of the barriers to entry into an industry.

8. Scherer, F. M. (1980). *Industrial Market Structure and Economic Performance,* Boston: Houghton Mifflin.

9. Another alternative would be for a firm to own and operate more than one plant. If there are economies of scope in this industry, a firm might be able to enter this industry and earn superior profits. An economy of scope exists when the value of operating in two businesses simultaneously is greater than the value of operating in these two businesses separately. The concept of economy of scope is explored in more detail in Part III of this book.

10. See Ghemawat, P., and H. J. Stander III (1992). "Nucor at a crossroads," Harvard Business School Case no. 9-793039.

11. See Montgomery, C. A., and B. Wernerfelt (1991). "Sources of superior performance: Market share versus industry effects in the U.S. brewing industry," *Management Science,* 37, pp. 954–959.

12. Stecklow, S. (1999). "Gallo woos French, but don't expect Bordeaux by the jug," *Wall Street Journal,* March 26, pp. A1+.

13. See Kogut, B., and U. Zander (1992). "Knowledge of the firm, combinative capabilities, and the replication of technology," *Organization Science,* 3, pp. 383–397; and Dierickx, I., and K. Cool (1989). "Asset stock accumulation and

sustainability of competitive advantage," *Management Science,* 35, pp. 1504–1511. Both emphasize the importance of know-how as a barrier to entry into an industry. More generally, intangible resources are seen as particularly important sources of sustained competitive advantage. This will be discussed in more detail in Chapter 5.

14. See Polanyi, M. (1962). *Personal Knowledge: Towards a Post Critical Philosophy,* London: Routledge & Kegan Paul; and Itami, H. (1987). *Mobilizing Invisible Assets,* Cambridge, MA: Harvard University Press.

15. See Barney, J. B. (1986). "Strategic factor markets: Expectations, luck and business strategy," *Management Science,* 32, pp. 1512–1514, for the logic that underlies this discussion. This logic, discussed in detail in Chapter 5, is traceable to the work of Ricardo, D. (1817). *Principles of Political Economy and Taxation,* London: J. Murray.

16. Porter, M. E. (1980). *Competitive Strategy,* New York: Free Press.

17. See Ghemawat, P. (1986). "Wal-Mart store's discount operations," Harvard Business School Case no. 9-387-018.

18. This class of contrived deterrence strategies is summarized by Tirole, J. (1988). *The Theory of Industrial Organization,* Cambridge, MA: MIT Press. See also the discussion of contrived deterrence in Chapter 10.

19. Dixit, A. K. (1982). "Recent developments in oligopoly theory," *Papers and Proceedings of the American Economic Association,* 94th annual meeting, 72(2), pp. 12–17.

20. Tirole, J. (1988). *The Theory of Industrial Organization,* Cambridge, MA: MIT Press.

21. For an interesting theory of negotiation based on these ideas, see Schelling, T. C. (1960). *Strategies of Conflict,* Cambridge, MA: Harvard University Press.

22. For examples, see Tirole, J. (1988). *The Theory of Industrial Organization,* Cambridge, MA: MIT Press.

23. Porter, M. E. (1980). *Competitive Strategy,* New York: Free Press.

24. For a detailed description of this contrived deterrence strategy, see Ghemawat, P. (1984). "Capacity expansion in the titanium dioxide industry," *Journal of Industrial Economics,* 33(2), pp. 145–163.

25. See O'Brien, B. (1993). "Losing altitude: After long soaring, Delta Air Lines runs into financial clouds," *Wall Street Journal,* June 25, p. A1; Carey, S. (1993). "USAir declares war over fares in California," *Wall Street Journal,* June 9, p. B1; Woods, W. (1991). "Misery in the air," *Fortune,* December 16, pp. 88–89; and McGahan, A., and J. Kou (1995). "The U.S. airline industry in 1995," Harvard Business School Case no. 9-795-113.

26. See Tuller, L. W. (1991). *Going Global: New Opportunities for Growing Companies to Compete in World Markets,* Homewood, IL: Irwin. Given Japan's economic troubles throughout the 1990s, some of these difficulties in entering the Japanese markets seem to be going away.

27. Schlesinger, J. M. (1993). "Tough gamble: A slot-machine maker trying to sell in Japan hits countless barriers," *Wall Street Journal,* May 11, p. A1.

28. "Only here for the biru," *The Economist,* May 14, 1994, pp. 69–70.

29. Suris, O. (1993). "IndyCar 'Honda rule' blocks fast track," *Wall Street Journal,* May 28, p. B1.

30. Semistrong capital market efficiency means that the price of a firm's assets will reflect all publicly available information about their value. See Fama, E. F. (1970). "Efficient capital markets: A review of theory and empirical work," *Journal of Finance,* May, pp. 383–417. See also Copeland, T. E., and J. F. Weston (1983). *Financial Theory and Corporate Policy,* Reading, MA: Addison-Wesley.

31. See Klein, B., R. Crawford, and A. Alchian (1978). "Vertical integration, appropriable rents, and the competitive contracting process," *Journal of Law and Economics,* 21, pp. 297–326.

32. See Jensen, E., and M. Robichaux (1993). "Fifth network sparks interest of TV industry," *Wall Street Journal,* June 28, p. B1.

33. See Saporito, B. (1992). "Why the price wars never end," *Fortune,* March 23, pp. 68–78; and Allen, M., and M. Siconolfi (1993). "Dell Computer drops planned share offering," *Wall Street Journal,* February 25, p. A3.

34. See Wahlgreen, E. (2005). "Salads days for burger joints," *Business Week Online,* June 3, 2005; and Gogoi, P., and M. Romen (2003). "Arch support," *Business Week,* April 21, p. 52.

35. This will be discussed in more detail in Chapter 4.

36. Labich, K. (1992). "Airbus takes off," *Fortune,* June 1, pp. 102–108.

37. See Pollock, E. J. (1993). "Mediation firms alter the legal landscape," *Wall Street Journal,* March 22, p. B1; Cox, M. (1993). "Electronic campus: Technology threatens to shatter the world of college textbooks," *Wall Street Journal,* June 1, p. A1; Reilly, P. M. (1993). "At a cross-roads: The instant-new age leaves Time magazine searching for a mission," *Wall Street Journal,* May 12, p. A1; Rohwedder, C. (1993). "Europe's smaller food shops face finis," *Wall Street Journal,* May 12, p. B1; Fatsis, S. (1995). "Major leagues keep minors at a distance," *Wall Street Journal,* November 8, p. B1+; Norton, E., and G. Stem (1995). "Steel and aluminum vie over every ounce in a car's construction," *Wall Street Journal,* May 9, p. A1+; Paré, T. P. (1995). "Why the banks lined up against gates," *Fortune,* May 29, p. 18; "Hitting the mail on the head," *The Economist,* April 30, 1994, pp. 69–70; Pacelle, M. (1996). "'Big boxes' by discounters are booming," *Wall Street Journal,* January 17, p. A2; and Pope, K., and L. Cauley (1998). "In battle for TV ads, cable is now the enemy," *Wall Street Journal,* May 6, p. B1+.

38. Tully, S. (1992). "How to cut those #$%* legal costs," *Fortune,* September 21, pp. 119–124.

39. Nulty P. (1993). "Look what the unions want now," *Fortune,* February 8, pp. 128–135.

40. Jensen, E. (1993). "Tales are oft told as TV talk shows fill up airtime," *Wall Street Journal,* May 25, p. A1; "King World ponders life without Oprah," *Wall Street Journal,* September 26, 1995, p. B1.

41. See DeWitt, W. (1997). "Crown Cork & Seal/Carnaud Metalbox," Harvard Business School Case no. 9-296-019.

42. Perry, N. J. (1993). "What's next for the defense industry," *Fortune,* February 22, pp. 94–100.

43. See Osterland, A. (1999). "Fixing Rubbermaid is no snap," *Business Week,* September 20, p. 108.

44. See DeWitt, W. (1997). "Crown Cork & Seal/Carnaud Metalbox," Harvard Business School Case no. 9-296-019; and Hamermesh, R. G., and R. S. Rosenbloom (1989). "Crown Cork & Seal, Inc. in 1989," Harvard Business School Case no. 9-388-096.

45. "Time Warner, Inc.: HBO unit expands push into original programming," *Wall Street Journal,* January 16, 1992, p. 136.

46. O'Reilly, B. (1990). "The inside story of AIDS drug," *Fortune,* November 5, pp. 112–129.

47. Starr, C. (1993). "Orphan drug act: Celebration a decade and 87 drugs later," *Drug Topics,* April 5, pp. 26–31; Birnbaum, J. H., and M. Waldholz (1993). "Harsh medicine: Attack on drug prices opens Clinton's fight for healthcare plan," *Wall Street Journal,* February 16, p. A1.

48. Brandenburger, A., and B. Nalebuff (1996). *Co-opetition,* New York: Doubleday.

49. For a discussion of global competition in the automobile industry, the failure of U.S. firms to recognize international threats, and how U.S. firms have responded to this increased level of threat in this industry, see Womack, J. P., D. Jones, and D. Roos (1990). *The Machine That Changed the World,* New York: Rawson.

50. See Pascale, R. T. (1984). "Perspectives on strategy: The real story behind Honda's success," *California Management Review,* 26(3), pp. 47–72.

51. See Enright, M. J., and U. Bumbacher (1995). "Swiss watch industry," Harvard Business School Case no. 9792-046.

52. See Hamermesh, R. G., and R. S. Rosenbloom (1989). "Crown Cork & Seal, Inc. in 1989," Harvard Business School Case no. 9-388-096.

CHAPTER

$$\boxed{4}$$

Evaluating Environmental Opportunities

In Chapter 3, the structure-conduct-performance (S-C-P) model was used to describe a framework for analyzing a firm's environmental threats. Chapter 4 also applies the S-C-P model. However, instead of focusing on environmental threats, this chapter describes frameworks for analyzing environmental opportunities. Models for analyzing organizational strengths and weaknesses are discussed in Chapter 5.

Chapter 4 begins by examining some generic industry structures that have been identified in the literature, along with the kinds of opportunities that are likely to exist in each of these industry structures. Another tool that can be useful in identifying environmental opportunities—strategic groups analysis—is then described. The chapter ends with a discussion of some of the limitations of the S-C-P framework as it is applied to the study of environmental threats and opportunities.

4.1 OPPORTUNITIES AND INDUSTRY STRUCTURE

S-C-P logic suggests that one approach to understanding opportunities in a firm's environment is to examine the industry's structure and the opportunities associated with that structure.[1] Several generic industry structures are described in the literature, along with opportunities that are likely to exist for firms that operate in these types of industries. Porter examined opportunities in five types of industries: (1) fragmented industries, (2) emerging industries, (3) mature industries, (4) declining industries, and (5) international industries. Three other types of industries identified in the literature are network industries, hypercompetitive industries, and empty-core industries. The kinds of opportunities typically associated with these industry structures are shown in Table 4.1.

TABLE 4.1 Industry Structure and Environmental Opportunities	
Industry Structure	*Opportunities*
Fragmented industry	Consolidation:
	• Discover new economies of scale
	• Alter ownership structure
Emerging industry	First-mover advantages:
	• Technological leadership
	• Preemption of strategically valuable assets
	• Creation of customer-switching costs
Mature industry	Product refinement
	Investment in service quality
	Process innovation
Declining industry	Leadership strategy
	Niche strategy
	Harvest strategy
	Divestment strategy
International industry	Multinational opportunities
	Global opportunities
	Transnational opportunities
Network industry	First-mover advantages and
	"winner takes all" strategies
Hypercompetitive industry	Flexibility
	Proactive disruption
Empty-core industry	Collusion
	Government regulation
	Significant product differentiation
	Demand management

Opportunities in Fragmented Industries: Consolidation

Fragmented industries are industries in which a large number of small or medium-sized firms operate, and no small set of firms has dominant market share or creates dominant technologies. Most service industries, retailing, fabrics, and commercial printing, to name just a few are fragmented industries.

Industries can be fragmented for a wide variety of reasons. For example, there may be few barriers to entry into a fragmented industry, thereby encouraging numerous small firms to enter. There may be few, if any, economies of scale, and even some important diseconomies of scale, thus encouraging firms to remain small. Also, there may be a need for close local control over enterprises in an industry—for example, local movie houses and local restaurants—to ensure quality and to minimize losses from theft.

The major opportunity facing firms in fragmented industries is the implementation of strategies that begin to consolidate the industry into a smaller number of firms. Firms that are successful in implementing this **consolidation strategy** can become industry leaders and obtain benefits from this kind of effort.

Consolidation can occur in several ways. For example, an incumbent firm may discover new economies of scale in an industry. In the highly fragmented funeral home industry, Service Corporation International (SCI) found that the development of a chain of funeral homes gave it advantages in acquiring key supplies (coffins) and in the allocation of scarce resources (morticians and hearses). By acquiring numerous previously independent funeral homes, SCI was able to reduce its costs substantially and to gain higher levels of economic performance.[2]

In the highly fragmented paper and office supplies industry, Century Paper found that owning several geographically contiguous supply outlets enabled the organization to reduce warehousing costs, reduce corporate overhead, and apply professional management techniques to otherwise inefficiently managed operations. Building on its base in Houston, Texas, Century Paper was able to acquire supply operations in San Antonio, Dallas, New Orleans, and other locations in a way that helped make the company one of the largest suppliers in the United States.[3]

Incumbent firms may also adopt different ownership structures to help consolidate an industry. Kampgrounds of America (KOA) uses franchise agreements with local operators to provide camping facilities to travelers in the fragmented private camping grounds industry. KOA provides local operators with professional training, technical skills, and access to its brand-name reputation. Local operators, in return, provide KOA with local managers who are intensely interested in the financial and operational success of their campgrounds. Similar franchise agreements have been instrumental in the consolidation of other fragmented industries, including fast foods (McDonalds), muffler repair (Midas), and motels (La Quinta, Holiday Inn, Howard Johnson's).[4]

The benefits of implementing a consolidation strategy in a fragmented industry turn on the advantages that larger firms in such industries gain from their larger market share. As will be discussed in Chapter 6, firms with large market share can have important cost advantages over firms in the same industry with small market share. However, as is the case with all opportunities facing a firm, the benefits must be weighed against the cost of exploiting this opportunity. If the value of becoming an industry leader (by implementing consolidation) is less than the cost of becoming an industry leader, then exploiting this opportunity will lead to below-normal economic performance. However, as will be discussed in the case of mergers and acquisitions (Chapter 14), there is reason to believe that consolidation strategies in fragmented industries will sometimes (but not always) enable firms to earn superior economic profits.

Opportunities in Emerging Industries: First-Mover Advantages

Emerging industries are newly created or newly re-created industries formed by technological innovations, changes in demand, the emergence of new customer needs, and so forth. Over the last 30 years, the world economy has been flooded with emerging industries, including the microprocessor industry, the personal computer industry, the medical imaging industry, and the biotechnology industry, to name a few. Firms in emerging industries face a unique set of opportunities, the exploitation of which can be a source of superior performance for some time for some firms.

The opportunities that face firms in emerging industries fall into the general category of first-mover advantages. **First-mover advantages** are advantages that come to firms that make important strategic and technological decisions early in the development of an industry.[5] In emerging industries, many of the rules of the game and standard operating procedures for competing and succeeding are yet to be established. First-moving firms can sometimes help establish the rules of the game and create an industry's structure that is uniquely beneficial to them. In general, first-mover advantages can arise from three primary sources: (1) technological leadership, (2) preemption of strategically valuable assets, and (3) the creation of customer-switching costs.

Technological Leadership

Firms that make early investments in particular technologies in an industry are implementing a **technological leadership strategy.** Such strategies can generate two advantages in emerging industries. First, firms that have implemented these strategies may obtain a low-cost position based on their greater cumulative volume of production with a particular technology. These cost advantages have had important competitive implications in such diverse industries as the manufacture of titanium dioxide by DuPont and Procter & Gamble's competitive advantage in disposable diapers.

As was mentioned in Chapter 3, because DuPont had already invested in an environmentally friendly process for manufacturing titanium dioxide, it was able to gain important first-mover advantages when government regulations made other approaches to manufacturing this product too costly. Procter & Gamble gained a similar first-mover advantage by investing heavily in the technology needed to manufacture disposable diapers before any other firms. With this technology in place, Procter & Gamble was able to sell a low-cost, high-quality product that dominated the disposable diaper market with the Pampers brand name for several years.[6]

However, even though technological leadership can enable a firm to gain important first-mover advantages, these advantages will be sustained only if the technologies on which they are based do not diffuse rapidly among competitors in an industry. Research has shown that most technologies in most industries, in fact, diffuse rather rapidly, and thus the first-mover advantages that technological leadership can create for a firm are usually short-lived.[7] In fact, in both the titanium dioxide and disposable diaper industries, the first-mover advantages described earlier lasted only a relatively short period of time. After a year or so, many of DuPont's competitors began using the same environmentally friendly production process as DuPont. Indeed, this is why DuPont was motivated to implement the contrived deterrence strategy discussed in Chapter 3. In the same way, many of Procter & Gamble's disposable diaper competitors invested in similar, and then better, production technologies. Ultimately, Procter & Gamble was unable to sustain the head start that technological leadership gave them in the disposable diaper industry.

Second, firms that make early investments in a technology may obtain patent protections that enhance their performance.[8] Xerox's patents on the xerography process and General Electric's patent on Edison's original light bulb design were important for these firms' success when these two industries were emerging.[9] However, although there are some exceptions (for example, the pharmaceutical industry and specialty chemicals), patents, per se, seem to provide relatively small profit opportunities for first-moving firms in most emerging industries. One group of researchers found that imitators can duplicate first movers' patent-based advantages for about 65 percent of the first mover's costs.[10] Thus, as was suggested in Chapter 1, there may be cost advantages in being an efficient "second mover," especially in industries in which returns on investing early are very uncertain. These researchers also found that 60 percent of all patents are imitated within 4 years of being granted—without legally violating patent rights obtained by first movers. As we will discuss in detail in Chapter 5, patents are rarely a source of sustained competitive advantage for firms, even in emerging industries.

Preemption of Strategically Valuable Assets

First movers that invest only in technology usually do not obtain sustained competitive advantages. However, first movers that move to tie up strategically valuable resources in an industry before their full value is widely understood can gain sustained competitive advantages. Firms that are able to acquire these resources have, in effect, erected formidable barriers to imitation in an industry. Some strategically valuable assets that can be acquired in this way include access to raw materials, particularly favorable geographic locations, and particularly valuable product market positions.

When an oil company such as Royal Dutch Shell (because of its superior exploration skills) acquires leases with greater development potential than was expected by its competition, the company is gaining access to raw materials in a way that is likely to generate sustained competitive advantages. When Wal-Mart opens stores in medium-size cities before the arrival of its competition, Wal-Mart is making it difficult for the competition to enter this market. And when breakfast cereal companies expand their product lines to include all possible combinations of wheat, oats, bran, corn, and sugar, they are using a first-mover advantage to deter entry.[11]

Of course, in order for actions that tie up strategically valuable resources to create economic profits, they must be implemented before the full value of these resources is widely known. Suppose, for example, that the true value of a particular oil lease is widely known. In this setting, competition to gain access to this resource will continue until the point that the price a firm pays to gain the right to drill for oil equals the value of that right. If a particular lease is widely expected to generate (in net-present-value terms) $10 million worth of crude oil over its productive life, then the price that a firm will have to pay to gain access to this lease will be approximately $10 million. This will be so because as long as the price of this lease is less than $10 million, another firm will always be willing to increase the amount of money it is willing to pay to gain access to this lease. However, once the price of acquiring this lease equals its value, no firm will be willing to pay more. Thus, if the true value of this lease is widely known, then the price paid to gain access to this lease will approximately equal the value of this lease, and thus no economic profit is created. This will be the case even though, in the end, only one firm actually gains the right to exploit this lease and thus it appears that only this firm has tied up this strategically valuable resource in this industry.

Consider, also, Wal-Mart's experience in medium-size towns. When Wal-Mart first implemented this strategy, the advantages of operating in these towns were not widely understood. Thus, in the beginning, Wal-Mart was able to enter into these towns at a very low cost and gain the economic profits associated with this strategy. However, once the value of these locations became well known, several of Wal-Mart's competitors began competing for the right to provide discount retail services to medium-size towns that did not have them. Moreover, the towns themselves began making demands on Wal-Mart and other competitors—to invest in roads and other infrastructure improvements, to change the mix of products, to change the design of the stores—that effectively increased the cost of doing business in these towns. Once the value of this strategically valuable resource became widely known, it became more difficult to acquire it in ways that would generate economic profits.

Creating Customer-Switching Costs

Early decisions by firms in an emerging industry can also have the effect of increasing **customer-switching costs.** Customer-switching costs exist when, for example, a firm's customers make investments in order to use this firm's particular products or services, and when these investments are not useful in using other firm's products or services. These investments tie customers to a particular firm, and make it more difficult for customers to begin purchasing from different firms.[12]

As will be suggested in Chapter 7, switching costs can be thought of as a form of product differentiation. Customer investments to use an early mover's product help differentiate that product from other firms' products. Such switching costs are important factors in industries as diverse as applications software for personal computers, prescription pharmaceuticals, and groceries.[13]

In applications software for personal computers, users make very significant investments to learn how to use a particular software package. Once computer users have learned how to operate a particular software, they are very unlikely to switch to new software, even if that new software system is superior to what they currently use. Such a switch would require learning the new software, how it is similar to the old software, and how it is different from that software. For these reasons, some computer users will continue to use outdated software, even though new software performs much better.[14] This is also why firms that bring out new software applications spend so much time and effort to make the transition from old to new software as painless as possible.

Similar switching costs can exist in some segments of the prescription pharmaceutical industry. Once medical doctors become familiar with a particular drug, its applications, and side effects, they are sometimes reluctant to change to a new drug, even if that new drug promises to be more effective than the older, more familiar drug. Trying the new drug requires learning about its properties and side effects. Even if the new drug has received government approvals, its use requires doctors to be willing to "experiment" with the health of their patients. Given these issues, many physicians are less willing to adopt new drug therapies. This is one reason that pharmaceutical firms spend so much time and money having their sales force educate their physician customers. This kind of education is necessary for a doctor to be willing to switch from an old drug to a new drug. Moreover, once doctors switch and become familiar with a new drug, they are not likely to switch again any time soon. Thus, in the prescription pharmaceutical industry, customer-switching costs make it difficult to gain new customers, but once customers are obtained, these costs make it easier to retain them.

Customer-switching costs can even play a role in a very mature and competitive industry such as grocery stores. Each grocery store has a particular layout of products. Once customers learn where different products are located in a particular store, they are not likely to change stores, because in so doing they will have to learn the location of products in the new store. Many customers want to avoid the time and frustration associated with wandering around a new store looking for some obscure product. Indeed, the cost of switching stores may be great enough to enable some grocery stores to charge higher prices than what would be the case without customer-switching costs. As long as the high prices that are charged by a particular store are less than the cost of switching stores, customers will not switch. If a particular store already has numerous customers, new grocery store competitors may not be able to attract at least some of these customers—despite lower prices on similar kinds of products—because of customer-switching costs.

First-Mover Disadvantages

Of course, the opportunities for investing in new technologies, acquiring strategically valuable resources, and creating buyer-switching costs must be balanced against the risks associated with first moving in emerging industries. These kinds of industries are characterized by a great deal of uncertainty. When first-moving firms are making critical strategic decisions, it may not be at all clear what the right decisions are. In general, first moving is desirable when first movers can influence the way that uncertainty is resolved in an industry. However, when the evolution of technology, consumer demand, and production technology cannot be influenced by first-moving firms, whether first-moving efforts will be successful is indeterminate.[15] In these highly uncertain settings, a reasonable strategic alternative to first moving may be retaining flexibility. Whereas first-moving firms attempt to resolve the uncertainty they face by making decisions early in the evolution of an emerging industry, firms use flexibility to resolve this uncertainty by delaying decisions until the economically correct path is clear and then moving quickly to take advantage of that path. As will be discussed in Chapter 9, delaying decisions and then moving quickly to exploit opportunities when they present themselves has broad strategic implications for firms. For example, firms that choose this flexibility approach will, in general, be less vertically integrated than firms that choose to try to reduce the uncertainty they face through first moving.

Indeed, as was suggested in Chapter 1, there are organizations that specialize in being fast and flexible "second movers." In computer technology, IBM has usually been described as a second mover, waiting for other firms to develop new technology and then moving quickly to duplicate that technology. Crown Cork & Seal historically adopted an explicit "second-mover" strategy in food-container research and development. Even Procter & Gamble has generally been seen as a very effective second mover in its industry. Given that a second mover's product development costs can be just 65 percent of a first mover's product development costs, the advantages that accrue to a first mover must be very substantial to justify first moving as a strategy.[16]

Opportunities in Mature Industries: Product Refinement, Service, and Process Innovation

Emerging industries are often formed by the creation of new products or technologies that radically alter the rules of the game in an industry. Over time, however, as these new ways of doing business become widely understood, as technologies diffuse through competitors, and as the rate of innovation in new products and technologies drops, an industry begins to enter the mature phase of its development. Common characteristics of **mature industries** include: (1) slowing growth in total industry demand, (2) the development of experienced repeat customers, (3) a slowdown in increases in production capacity, (4) a slowdown in the introduction of new products or services, (5) an increase in the level of international competition, and (6) an overall reduction in the profitability of firms in the industry.[17]

The fast-food industry in the United States has become mature over the last 10 to 15 years. In the 1960s, there were only three large national fast-food chains in the United States: McDonald's, Burger King, and Dairy Queen. Through the 1980s, all three of these chains grew rapidly, although the rate of growth of McDonald's outstripped the rate of growth of the other two firms. During this period, however, other fast-food chains also entered the market. These included some national chains, such as Kentucky Fried Chicken, Wendy's, and Taco Bell, and some strong regional chains such as Jack in the Box and In-and-Out Burger. By the early 1990s, growth in this industry had slowed considerably. McDonald's announced that it was having difficulty finding locations for new McDonald's stores that did not impinge on the sales of existing. In order to create the perception of introducing new products, firms such as McDonald's had to resort to introducing products for defined periods of time, taking these products off the market, and then reintroducing them as new products some time later. Except for non-U.S. operations, where competition in the fast-food industry is not as mature, the profitability of most U.S. fast-food companies has not grown as much as it did in the 1960s through the 1980s. Recently, these firms have been refining their product mix to regain their profitability.[18]

Opportunities for firms in mature industries typically shift from the development of new technologies and products in an emerging industry to greater emphasis on refining a firm's current products, an emphasis on increasing the quality of service, and a focus on reducing manufacturing costs and increasing quality through process innovations.

Refining Current Products

In mature industries such as home detergents, motor oil, and kitchen appliances, there are likely to be few, if any, major technological breakthroughs. However, this does not mean that there is not innovation in these industries. Innovation in these industries focuses on extending and improving current products and technologies. In home detergents, innovation recently has focused on changes in packaging and on selling more highly concentrated detergents. In motor oil, packaging changes (from fiber foil cans to plastic containers), additives that keep oil cleaner longer, and oil formulated to operate in four-cylinder engines are examples of this kind of innovation. In kitchen appliances, the availability of refrigerators with crushed ice and water through the door, commercial-grade stoves for home use, and dishwashers that automatically adjust the cleaning cycle depending on how dirty dishes are are examples of such improvements.[19]

Emphasis on Service

When firms in an industry have only limited ability to invest in radical new technologies and products, efforts to differentiate products often turn toward the quality of customer service. A firm that is able to develop a reputation for high-quality customer service may be able to obtain superior performance even though the products it sells are not highly differentiated.

Process Innovation

A firm's **processes** are the activities in which it engages to design, produce, and sell its products or services. **Process innovation,** then, is an effort to refine and improve a firm's current processes. Several authors have studied the relationships among process innovation, product innovation, and the maturity of an industry.[20] This work, summarized in Figure 4.1, suggests that in the early stages of industry development, product innovation is very important as firms struggle to create technological advantages, preempt valuable strategic resources, and create buyer-switching costs. Over time, however, product innovation becomes less important, and process innovations designed to reduce manufacturing costs, increase product quality, and streamline management become more important. In mature industries, firms can often gain an advantage by manufacturing the same product as competitors, but at a lower cost. Alternatively, firms can manufacture a product that is perceived to be of higher quality, and do so at a competitive cost. Process innovations facilitate both reduction of costs and increases in quality.

Research on manufacturing in the automobile industry points to the importance of process innovations. In a study of over 70 auto assembly plants, Krafcik and MacDuffie measured both the quality of the assembled cars and the cost of these cars. The cars assembled in these plants were mid-size family sedans—a relatively mature segment of a relatively mature industry, the automobile business. These researchers found six plants in their sample that simultaneously had very high quality and very low costs. These six plants were designated "world-class manufacturers." The management of these plants had several things in common; among them was a constant, unending focus on improving the manufacturing process as well as the process for managing the entire plant.

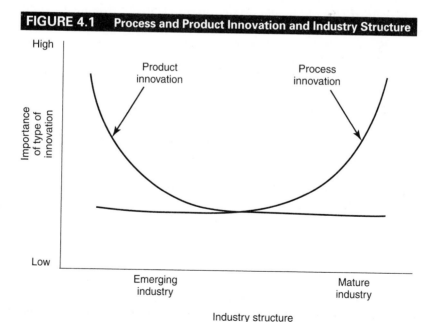

FIGURE 4.1   Process and Product Innovation and Industry Structure

Source: Hayes, R. H., and S. G. Wheelwright (1979). "The dynamics of process-product life cycles," *Harvard Business Review*, March–April, pp. 127–136.

This emphasis on process innovation enabled these plants to gain competitive advantages in an otherwise very mature segment of the industry.[21]

Opportunities in Declining Industries: Leadership, Niche, Harvest, and Divestment

A **declining industry** is an industry that has experienced an absolute decline in unit sales over a sustained period of time.[22] Obviously, firms in a declining industry face more threats than opportunities. Rivalry in a declining industry is likely to be very high, as is the threat of buyers, suppliers, and substitutes. However, even though threats are significant, there are opportunities that firms can exploit. The major strategic opportunities that firms in this kind of industry face are leadership, niche, harvest, and divestment.

Market Leadership

An industry in decline is often characterized by overcapacity in manufacturing, distribution, and so forth. Reduced demand often means that firms in this kind of industry will have to endure a significant shakeout period, until this overcapacity is reduced and capacity is brought more in line with demand. But after this shakeout has occurred, a smaller number of lean and focused firms may enjoy a relatively benign environment with few threats and several opportunities. If the industry structure that is likely to exist after a shakeout is quite attractive, firms in an industry before the shakeout may have an incentive to weather the storm of decline—to survive until the situation improves to the point that they can begin to earn higher profits.

If a firm has decided to wait out the storm of decline in hopes of better environmental conditions in the future, it should consider various steps to increase its chances of survival. Most important of these is that a firm must establish itself as a **market leader** in the preshakeout industry, most typically by becoming the firm with the largest market share in that industry. The purpose of becoming a market leader is *not* to facilitate tacit collusion (see Chapter 9) or to obtain lower costs from economies of scale (see Chapter 6). Rather, in a declining industry, the leader's objective should be to try to facilitate the exit of firms that are not likely to survive a shakeout, thereby obtaining a more favorable competitive environment as quickly as possible.

Market leaders in declining industries can facilitate exit in a variety of ways, including: purchasing and then deemphasizing competitors' product lines, purchasing and retiring competitors' manufacturing capacity, manufacturing spare parts for competitors' product lines, and sending unambiguous signals of their intention to stay in an industry and remain a dominant firm. For example, overcapacity problems in the European petrochemical industry were partially resolved when ICI traded its polyethylene plants to British Petroleum for BP's polyvinylchloride (PVC) manufacturing plants. In this case, both firms were able to close some excess capacity in the market where they wanted to remain.[23]

Market Niche

A firm in a declining industry following a leadership strategy attempts to facilitate exit by other firms; a firm following a **niche strategy** in a declining industry reduces its scope of operations and focuses on narrow segments of the declining industry. If only a few firms choose this niche, then these firms may have a favorable competitive setting, even though the industry as a whole is facing shrinking demand.

Two firms that used this niche approach in a declining market are GTE Sylvania and General Electric in the vacuum-tube industry. The invention of the transistor and then of the semiconductor just about destroyed demand for vacuum tubes in new products. GTE Sylvania and GE rapidly recognized that new product sales in vacuum tubes were drying up. In response, these firms began specializing in supplying *replacement* vacuum tubes to the consumer and military markets. To earn high profits, these firms had to refocus their sales efforts and scale down their sales and manufacturing staffs. Over time, as fewer and fewer firms manufactured vacuum tubes, GTE Sylvania and GE were able to charge very high prices for their replacement parts.[24]

Harvest

Leadership and niche strategies, though differing along several dimensions, have one attribute in common: Firms that implement these strategies intend to remain in the industry despite its decline. Firms that pursue a **harvest** strategy in a declining industry do not expect to remain in the industry over the long term. Instead, they engage in a long, systematic, phased withdrawal, extracting as much value as possible during the withdrawal period.

The extraction of value during the implementation of a harvest strategy presumes that there is some value to harvest. Thus, firms that implement this strategy must ordinarily have enjoyed at least some profits at some time in their history, before the industry began declining. Firms can implement a harvest strategy by reducing the range of products they sell, reducing their distribution network, eliminating less profitable customers, reducing product quality, reducing service quality, deferring maintenance and equipment repair, and so forth. In the end, after a period of harvesting in a declining industry, firms can either sell their operations in an industry (to a market leader) or simply cease operations.

In principle the harvest opportunity sounds simple, but in practice it presents some significant management challenges. The movement toward a harvest strategy often means that some of the characteristics of a business that have long been a source of pride to managers may have to be abandoned. Thus, whereas prior to harvest a firm may have specialized in high-quality service, quality products, and excellent customer value, during harvest the quality of service may fall, product quality may deteriorate, and prices may rise. These changes may be difficult for managers to accept, and higher turnover in a harvesting firm may be the result. It is also difficult to hire quality managers into a harvesting business, because such individuals are likely to seek more satisfying opportunities elsewhere.

For these reasons, few firms explicitly announce a harvest strategy. However, examples can be found. General Electric seems to be following a harvest strategy in the electric turbine business. Also, United States Steel and the International Steel Group seem to be following this strategy in certain segments of the steel market.[25]

Divestment

The final opportunity facing firms in a declining industry is divestment. Like a harvest strategy, the objective of **divestment** is to extract a firm from a declining industry. However, unlike harvest, divestment occurs quickly, often soon after a pattern of decline is established. Firms without established competitive advantages may find divestment a superior option to harvest, because they have few competitive advantages they can exploit through harvesting.

In the 1980s, General Electric used this rapid divestment approach to virtually abandon the consumer electronics business. Total demand in this business was more or less stable during the 1980s, but competition (mainly from Asian manufacturers) increased substantially. Rather than remain in this business, GE sold most of its consumer electronics operations and used the capital to enter the medical imaging industry, where this firm has found an environment more conducive to superior performance.[26]

In the defense business, divestment is the stated strategy of General Dynamics, at least in some of its business segments. General Dynamics managers recognized early that the changing defense industry could not support all the incumbent firms. When General Dynamics concluded that it could not remain a leader in some of its businesses, it decided to divest those to concentrate on a few remaining businesses. Since 1991, General Dynamics has sold businesses worth over $2.83 billion, including its missile systems business, its Cessna aircraft division, and its tactical aircraft division (maker of the very successful F-16 aircraft and partner in the development of the next generation of fighter aircraft, the F-22). These divestitures have left General Dynamics in just three defense businesses: armored tanks, nuclear submarines, and space launch vehicles. During this time, the market price of General Dynamics stock has returned almost $4.5 billion to its investors, has risen from $25 per share to a high of $110 per share, and has provided a total return to stockholders of 555 percent.[27]

Of course, not all divestments are caused by industry decline. Sometimes firms divest certain operations to focus their efforts on remaining operations, sometimes they divest to raise capital, and sometimes they divest to simplify operations. These types of divestments reflect a firm's diversification strategy and are explored in detail in Chapter 11.

Opportunities in International Industries: Multinational, Global, and Transnational Opportunities

It is an assumption of business in the twenty-first century that competition is becoming more international in scope. Even industries that appear likely to be national or regional in focus (Broadway plays, for example, are by definition produced only in New York City) have, over the last several years, become more international in character (many major Broadway hits are transfers from the West End in London, and regional traveling companies perform these plays throughout the world). International competition has some very obvious effects on the level and kinds of threats in an industry. International competition tends to increase rivalry, the threat of new entry, and the threat of substitutes. However, the internationalization of a business also creates opportunities for firms.[28]

These opportunities exist for both large firms and small ones. For example, based on 2002 results, total revenue for the 500 largest international firms in the world was over $9.1 trillion. By contrast, the total sales of the 500 largest firms in the United States in 2002 was $6.7 trillion.[29] Many of these large international firms—including Nestlé (Switzerland), Nokia (Finland), and Sony (Japan)—sell more outside their home markets then they do in their home markets. For all these large firms, there are significant opportunities associated with international operations.

International opportunities are increasingly important for smaller firms as well. Arby's (a U.S. fast-food restaurant), Domino's Pizza, DryClean USA, and Page Boy Maternity have all begun operations in Mexico and are attempting to expand their international operations, despite currency fluctuations and political risks. Logitech, a manufacturer of personal computer mice and other electronic pointing devices, had headquarters in California and Switzerland when it was first founded, and R&D and manufacturing operations in Taiwan and Ireland just a couple of years later. In an important sense, Logitech began operations pursuing opportunities in an international industry. Momenta Corporation (a firm in the pen-based computer industry), Oxford Instruments (which supplies high-field magnets to physics laboratories), SPEA (a firm in the graphics software business), and Technomed (a medical products firm) were all very small, and very new, companies when they began pursuing business opportunities in international industries.[30]

Given the importance of international opportunities for business, an entire chapter (Chapter 15) is dedicated to international strategies. At this point, it is sufficient to observe that these opportunities in international industries generally fall into three large categories: multinational opportunities, global opportunities, and transnational opportunities.

Multinational Opportunities

Firms that pursue **multinational opportunities** in international industries operate simultaneously in several national or regional markets, but these operations are independent of each other and free to choose how to respond to the specific needs of each national or regional marketplace. Some well-known firms that have pursued multinational international opportunities include Nestlé and General Motors (GM). Only a small percentage of Nestlé's products are sold throughout the world. Rather, managers in each country where Nestlé operates have the responsibility to discern local tastes, design products to be consistent with those tastes, and market these specially designed products locally. In a similar way, GM encourages very little interaction between its U.S. and European operations. Cars designed for the European market and sold under GM's Opal brand name have been sold only very infrequently in the United States, and relatively few Chevrolets and Oldsmobiles designed for the U.S. market are sold in Europe.

Pursuing multinational opportunities in international industries has at least two advantages. First, this strategy enables firms to respond rapidly to changing conditions in a country or region. If threats or opportunities appear in one part of the world but not in others, a multinational firm can move quickly to neutralize threats or exploit opportunities in those geographic regions where it is needed. For example, by operating at least partially as a multinational, McDonald's enables many of its European franchises to sell beer and wine alongside Big Macs and fries. Such sales do not represent an opportunity in McDonald's home market of the United States.

Second, although there are relatively few operational interactions between divisions and headquarters in a multinational company, impressive organizational resources can be marshaled quickly should they be required to exploit an opportunity or neutralize a threat in a particular country or region. McDonald's, for example, has been able to use all of its technological and management skills to open franchises in Moscow and other Eastern European cities.[31]

Global Opportunities

Whereas firms that pursue multinational opportunities operate in countries or regions in an independent manner, those that pursue **global opportunities** seek to optimize production, distribution, and other business functions throughout the world in addressing all the markets in which they operate. If manufacturing costs are very low and quality is very high in plants located in Singapore, global organizations will locate manufacturing facilities there. If particular research and development skills and technology are widely available in Great Britain, global organizations will locate their R&D operations there. If capital is less costly in New York, global organizations will locate their financial functions there. In this manner, the cost and quality of each organizational function can be optimized.

Of course, there are some costs and risks associated with global strategies. First, because the delivery of products or services in a global organization requires inputs from numerous operations all over the world, a global strategy puts a great deal of emphasis on coordination. Coordination can be difficult across divisions within a single country; it can be even more difficult across divisions between different countries or regions. Differences in language, culture, legal systems, and traditional business practices may complicate these coordination efforts.

Second, locating interdependent units in geographically disparate areas can create significant transportation costs. The very low cost of manufacturing automobile transmissions in Mexico may be effectively negated by the need to transport those transmissions to Japan to be installed in automobiles. This is less of a problem for a firm that ships products that are relatively light, small, and have very high profit margins.

Finally, exploiting global strategies may limit a firm's ability to respond to local needs, opportunities, and threats. Firms that pursue global opportunities in international industries are well designed to respond to global markets and less well designed to respond to a series of local markets. If the structure of the markets in which a firm operates does not vary significantly by country or region, a global approach may be a particularly attractive opportunity.

Transnational Opportunities

Recently, another opportunity has been described in international industries: operating as a transnational firm. Some have argued that the traditional trade-off between global integration and local responsiveness can be replaced by this transnational approach that exploits the advantages of both global integration and local responsiveness. Firms that exploit a **transnational opportunity** in an international industry treat their global operations as an integrated network of distributed and interdependent resources and capabilities.[32] In this context, a firm's operations in each country are not simply independent activities attempting to respond to local market needs; they are also repositories of ideas, technologies, and management approaches that the firm might be able to use and apply in its other global operations. Put differently, operations in different countries can be thought of as "experiments" in the creation of capabilities. Some of these experiments will work and generate important new capabilities for an entire firm; others will fail to create such benefits for a firm.

When an operation in a particular country develops a capability in manufacturing a particular product, providing a particular service, or engaging in a particular activity that can be used by other countries, the country operating with this capability can achieve global economies of scale by becoming the firm's primary supplier of this product, service, or activity. In this way, local responsiveness is retained as country managers search for new capabilities that will enable them to maximize profits in their particular markets, and global integration and economies of scale are realized as country operations that have developed unique capabilities become suppliers for all other country operations.

Managing a firm that is attempting to be both locally responsive and globally integrated is not an easy task. Some of these organizational challenges are discussed in Chapter 15.

Opportunities in Network Industries: First-Mover Advantages and "Winner Take All" Strategies

The opportunities associated with the first five industry structures identified in Table 4.1 are derived from S-C-P theory as it has developed since the late 1960s. Certainly, these industry structures, and the kinds of opportunities associated with them, continue to exist today. Emerging industries, with important first-mover opportunities, continue to be created. Fragmented, mature, declining, and international industries also exist, and the opportunities associated with each of these types of industries continue to be important for firms that operate in them.

However, several other industry structures have recently been identified. Consistent with S-C-P logic, these recently described industry structures have a significant effect on the kinds of opportunities facing firms that operate in them. Three of these other industry structures are described here: network industries, hypercompetitive industries, and empty-core industries.

An industry is said to be a **network industry** if the value of a product or service being sold depends, at least in part, on the number of those products or services being sold. For example, a telephone is not a very valuable product if only a small number of people own telephones, because it can be used to contact only this small number of people. However, if many people own a telephone, its value as a communications tool increases dramatically. Thus, the value created by owning a telephone increases as the number of people who own a phone increases. Because of the relationship between product value and the number of products that have been sold, network industries are sometimes also called **increasing-returns industries**.[33]

Each of the industry structures identified in Table 4.1 can manifest the attributes of a network industry, at least to some extent. Thus, when fax machines were first introduced, the fax machine industry was an emerging industry. However, fax machines are subject to increasing returns, so this industry was not only emerging, it was also a network industry. The telephone industry is currently mature. However, it also has many of the attributes of a network industry.

Not only can different kinds of industries manifest the attributes of a network industry, the extent to which these network attributes define the opportunities in an industry can also vary. The extent to which network attributes determine the opportunities in an industry depends on the degree to which increasing returns determine the value of a product or service. In telephone and fax machines, the number of people using these products has a very significant effect on their value. Thus, the opportunities in these industries are determined almost entirely by their network characteristics.

In applications software for personal computers, the number of people that use a specific software also has an effect on the value of that software. In particular, if a large number of people use a particular software application, they will find it easier to communicate with each other, share files, and so forth. However, the value of a particular software application also depends on the features, ease of use, and speed of that software—attributes that do not depend on the number of people who use that software, per se. The breadth to which network attributes of a product or service determines the value of that product or service is an indicator of the extent to which network opportunities are important in an industry.

The primary opportunity in a network industry is **first-mover advantages.** At first glance, this appears to be the same opportunity that exists in emerging industries. However, there are important differences between how first moving acts as an opportunity in emerging industries and how it acts as an opportunity in network industries.

As suggested earlier in this chapter, first moving in an emerging industry can be important in at least three ways. First, to the extent that first moving in an emerging industry generates technological advantages—either through generating larger cumulative volumes of production in an industry that can lead to important cost advantages or through obtaining patents on critical technologies in an industry—it can generate value for a firm. Second, to the extent that first moving enables firms to preempt strategically valuable assets in an emerging industry—including access to raw materials, geographic locations, or product market positions—it can generate value for a firm. Third, to the degree that first moving in an emerging industry creates customer-switching costs, it can generate value for a firm.

In network industries, first moving can create value to the extent that a firm's products or services become the de facto standard. In a network industry, when a firm's products or services become the de facto standard, that product or service is likely to end up with virtually all the market share in the industry. In pure network industries, virtually the entire value of a product or service depends on the number of those using a product or service. If a particular product or service happens to be among the first to be introduced to the market, and the first adopted by a significant minority of potential customers, it often grows to completely dominate the market. In network industries, first moving often becomes a **winner-take-all strategy.**

This winner-take-all aspect of first moving in a network industry is very different from creating customer-switching costs in an emerging industry. In the latter case, customer-switching costs are the result of investments that customers make to use a particular product or service. The decision facing these customers involves comparing the value gained by using a particular product or service plus the costs of making new investments to use the new product or service. In this setting, a firm may decide not to switch to a new product or service, even though it is superior to its current product or service, because of the cost of making the investments needed to use this new product or service.

In a network industry, reluctance to change products or services does not depend on the cost of the investments needed to use a new product or service. Indeed, in a network industry, no investments may be required to use a new product or service, and firms may still not switch to this new product or service. Rather, in a network industry, reluctance to switch to a new product or service depends on the number of users of this new product or service, not on the cost of the investments necessary to use it. If the number of users of this new product or service is low, then, in a network industry, its value to customers is low, and thus customers will be unwilling to switch.

Of course, in some industries, both switching costs and network effects can be substantial. In these settings, customer will be unwilling to switch to new products or services because of both the cost of the investments necessary to use these new products or services and the lower value these new products or services promise, because they are used by a small number of firms.

Given the winner-take-all characteristic of first moving in a network industry, firms in this setting have a very strong incentive to be first to the market and first to be adopted by a significant number of customers. This can lead firms to make decisions that, at first, appear to be counterintuitive.

For example, network dynamics turned out to be very important in the home videotape player market. The value of a home videotape player depends on the availability of movies on videotape to play on that player; that is, video-taped movies are a complement to videotape players. The availability of movies on tape to play on a videotape player depends, in turn, on the number of video players that have been purchased. Thus, the larger the number of videotape players of a particular type purchased, the more valuable is that type of videotape player. This is a classic network industry.

In the early days of this industry, two different video standards were competing: Sony's Beta technology and Matsushita's VHS technology. Most experts agreed that Beta technology was superior to VHS. However, Sony was only willing to license the manufacture of its Beta technology at a high fee. Sony reasoned that because it had a superior technology, customers would naturally be drawn to the Beta format, other firms would want to adopt this technology to satisfy customer demand, and thus Sony could charge very high licensing fees to these other manufacturers. Matsushita, on the other hand, charged a very low fee for licensing VHS technology. Numerous manufacturers started selling VHS machines. As the number of VHS machines being purchased increased, the value of VHS machines increased, and it became the de facto standard in the industry—despite the fact that Beta was a clearly superior product.[34]

In the extreme, firms that operate in a network industry may have an incentive to sell their products at very low prices, or even give them away, in order to increase the number of their products in use. As this number increases, the value of this product increases, and it can become the de facto standard in the industry. Once it becomes the de facto standard, a firm can then raise its prices and obtain an economic profit. Thus, in some settings, giving a product away can become a source of sustained competitive advantage.[35]

This may have been Microsoft's strategy in the Internet browser market. By bundling its Internet Explorer software with its Windows operating system, Microsoft was essentially giving this software to its customers for free. One explanation of this behavior is that Microsoft believed that the Internet browser market was a network industry. In order to become the de facto standard in this segment of the software market, Microsoft may have reasoned that it was important to increase the number of customers using Internet Explorer quickly. The simplest way to do this was simply not to charge for this software.

However, the U.S. Department of Justice was apparently not convinced that the Internet browser market was a network industry. If the Internet browser market is not a network industry, then Microsoft's decision to give Internet Explorer away for free was not an effort to become the de facto standard in this segment of the industry but rather was an effort to extend its monopoly position in the personal computer operating system market to a specific application. It is left to the reader to decide whether the Internet browser segment of the software applications industry is characterized by increasing returns or not. Recall that the critical question to be asked in determining this is: Does the value of a particular software application increase as the number of people using this application increases?[36]

Opportunities in Hypercompetitive Industries: Flexibility and Proactive Disruption

In each of the six industry structures discussed so far, the way that competition in an industry unfolds is assumed to be either stable or evolving in predictable ways. The relative stability and predictability of how new firms in an industry can compete and gain competitive advantages make it possible to describe specific identifiable strategic opportunities. Even in emerging industries—industries in which the bases on which firms compete is only being established—it is assumed that the primary task facing firms is to exploit first-mover advantages that can be used to sustain competitive advantages. Thus, the search for such advantages is the constant that underlies the technological innovation and creativity that typically exists in emerging industries. Stable and predictable bases of competition make it easier to understand the range of opportunities that may exist in an industry.

However, suppose that the way competition in an industry evolves is both unstable and unpredictable. Such industries are called **hypercompetitive**.[37] In hypercompetitive industries, firms cannot assume that the bases of competition will remain stable or predictable. Rather, the bases of competition in such industries are constantly evolving and are doing so in unpredictable ways. Suppose, for example, that at one point an industry appears to be emerging, in which case the primary opportunity in this industry is first-mover advantages. However, what if this industry structure were suddenly to shift to a mature industry, in which product refinement, service, and process improvement are critical opportunities. What if, just as suddenly, this industry shifted from mature to declining and then from declining back to emerging? Given the unstable and unpredictable way that this industry's structure is evolving, what, if anything, can be said about the opportunities facing a firm?

There are several examples of industries that may currently be hypercompetitive, including the music download industry and the biotechnology industry. Right now in these industries, the bases of competition are difficult to understand because they are constantly changing. In the music download business, for example, some observers have suggested that the critical determinant of success is having a low per-song fee for downloads. Others have suggested that the critical determinant of success is an easy interface between the web site and digital music players, and so forth. If music download is an emerging industry, the critical determinants of firm success will become clear over time and there will no longer be ambiguity about why some music download firms are more successful than others. On the other hand, if music download is a hypercompetitive industry, the determinants of business success will be continually changing, in unpredictable ways. If e-commerce is hypercompetitive, different, even contradictory, assertions about what determines a firm's success in this industry may all be correct at different times and for different firms.

At first glance, it may appear that because the bases of competition in a hyper-competitive industry cannot be known, there can be no obvious opportunities in these kinds of industries. In fact, there are two important strategic opportunities in hyper-competitive industries: flexibility and proactive disruption.

A firm exploits a **flexibility** opportunity when it retains the ability to change from one strategy to another at low cost. In less uncertain environments, the advantages of flexibility generally do not outweigh the advantages of being able to focus a firm's efforts to exploit particular environmental opportunities. In hypercompetitive industries, however, where specific opportunities cannot be anticipated, the ability to change strategic direction quickly once an opportunity develops may be a viable strategy.

A broad range of firm-level policies are consistent with exploiting flexibility opportunities in hypercompetitive industries. For example, as will be discussed in Chapters 8 and 10, flexible firms will be less vertically integrated than less flexible firms. Flexible firms will not invest in firm-specific or strategy-specific training, but rather will invest in broad, general-purpose training. As described in Chapter 8, firms that exploit flexibility opportunities will adopt a real options approach to valuing strategic initiatives, will engage in more broadly diversified research and development efforts, and will adopt nonrestrictive employee contracts, including the use of temporary employees and self-organizing work teams. All this flexibility can reduce a firm's effectiveness in implementing any one strategy, but can increase a firm's ability to move from one strategy to another under conditions of high uncertainty.

The second major opportunity in hypercompetitive industries is **proactive disruption.**[38] Rather than waiting for an industry's structure to evolve in unpredictable ways, proactive disruption suggests that a firm should take charge of the competitive process by pursuing strategies that shift the bases of competition in an industry. In this way, a firm can gain at least temporary competitive advantages. Proactive disruption is similar to a first-mover advantage in that a firm that pursues this opportunity will act before its competitors. However, unlike first-moving opportunities, firms that pursue proactive disruption opportunities do not expect their actions to result in long-term advantages. Rather, they seek only short-term advantages, advantages that will be destroyed by the proactive disruption activities of competing firms or proactive disruption activities of the firm itself. Thus, firms that pursue proactive disruption strategies commit themselves to doing things to consistently disrupt the structure of competition in an industry over time.

Seven attributes of successful proactive disruption strategies have been identified.[39] These attributes are listed in Table 4.2. As suggested in this table, firms that pursue proactive disruption should not simply abandon their current customers in order to create new bases of competition in an industry. Rather, the task is to satisfy current customers and create new customers simultaneously. New customers are created by understanding and meeting customer needs that customers themselves cannot fully articulate. Indeed, most major technological breakthroughs involve the development of new products and services that neither the firm making the technological breakthrough nor that firm's original customers could have anticipated. Just as Edison did not anticipate the ultimate value of the phonograph in playing music (he was convinced that this technology's highest-valued use was going to be as a dictation machine to be used in offices), the initial inventors of the integrated circuit could not have anticipated the numerous ways this technology has affected modern society. Firms that exploit

TABLE 4.2   Attributes of Successful Proactive Disruption Opportunities in Hypercompetitive Industries

Vision for disruption
1. Stakeholder satisfaction: Satisfy current stakeholders, especially customers.
2. Strategic soothsaying: Anticipate unarticulated customer needs and identify whole new classes of customers.

Capability for disruption
3. Use speed: Make disrupting decisions quickly, before competitors make these decisions.
4. Use surprise: Make decisions that could not have been anticipated by competitors.

Tactics for disruption
5. Shift the rules of the game: Make decisions that change the bases of competition in an industry.
6. Signal: Use signals of competitive intent to discourage the proactive disruption efforts of other firms.
7. Make simultaneous and sequential strategic thrusts: Invest in a series of proactive disruption efforts all at once and in sequence.

proactive disruption opportunities do not wait until demand for a new product or technology is well established. Rather, they create that demand.

With this vision for disruption in place, these firms then move quickly and with surprise to restructure the competitive rules in an industry. Moreover, given the high uncertainty in this industrial context, it is not uncommon for firms that pursue proactive disruption opportunities to engage in many of these actions simultaneously. Firms in this industry context do not have the luxury of gradually unveiling a series of products or strategies over time. Always bordering on managerial chaos, these firms pursue multiple—and even contradictory—avenues of innovation all at once.

Opportunities in Empty-Core Industries: Collusion, Government Regulation, Significant Product Differentiation, and Demand Management

Whereas hypercompetitive industries are industries in which the bases of competition are constantly changing in unpredictable ways, the bases of competition in empty-core industries are all too stable. Unfortunately, these rules of the game make it virtually impossible for firms to profitably pursue traditional competitive strategies. Instead, the primary opportunities in empty-core industries are collusion, government regulation, significant product differentiation, and demand management.

Empty-Core Industries

Markets exist when buyers and sellers enter voluntarily into economic exchanges they each find to be more beneficial than any other exchange into which they could enter. A person seeking to buy a car, for example, ends up buying a particular car when the price, quality, performance, and safety of that car is better than the price, quality, performance, and safety of other cars he or she could have purchased. A person seeking to sell a car ends up selling that car to a particular person when the total price of selling that car (that is, the direct sales price minus the cost of continuing to try to sell the car) is greater than the price that could be obtained by selling it to someone else. When both the buyer and seller believe that they are getting the best deal they can, the exchange is completed and the buyer gets a new car while the seller gets money.[40]

In some settings, however, buyers and sellers may never conclude that a particular exchange is more beneficial than any other exchanges into which they could enter. In these settings, buyers are always shopping and sellers are always selling, but exchanges do not occur. These kinds of markets are called **empty-core markets.**

Consider a very simple example of an empty-core market.[41] Suppose there are two taxicab companies, Firm A and Firm B. Suppose also that four customers want to take a cab from the taxi stand to the airport and each is willing to pay up to $3 to do so— although all of them would be happy to pay less than $3 for the trip. Finally, suppose Firm A and Firm B each owns one cab: Firm A's cab can carry two passengers and costs $5 to go to the airport no matter how many passengers it takes, while Firm B's cab can carry three passengers and costs $7 to go to the airport no matter how many passengers it takes.

Clearly, Firms A and B both want to fill up their cabs for trips to the airport. Suppose that Firm B approaches three customers and offers to drive them to the airport for $2.34 each. At this price, Firm B will break even on its trip to the airport (3 passengers at $2.34 each is $7, the cost of Firm B driving to the airport). However, there is one customer left, and she still needs to get to the airport. Suppose this last customer goes to Firm A and offers $3 to be taken to the airport. This is as much as this customer is willing to pay, but it does not cover Firm A's cost of driving to the airport (for Firm A, this trip costs $5). To cover its costs of driving to the airport, Firm A might contact one of Firm B's customers and offer a seat to the airport for only $2. Selling this seat for $2 would cover Firm A's cost of driving to the airport ($3 + $2 = $5), and this customer is likely to want to shift to Firm A's taxi because he is currently paying $2.34 to Firm B to travel to the airport. However, as soon as one of Firm B's customers shifts to Firm A, Firm B's costs of driving to the airport are not covered, because it now has only two passengers, paying $2.34 each (2 × $2.34 < $7). So Firm B is likely to contact the customer at Firm A who is currently paying $3 to go to the airport and offer to drive her to the airport for only $2.34. Once this customer shifts from Firm A to Firm B, Firm A no longer can cover its costs. Its one remaining passenger might be willing to increase the amount she will pay to go to the airport from $2 to $3, at which point Firm A can lure one of Firm B's passengers currently paying $2.34 by offering a fare of $2, and so on. This is an empty-core market, where buyers are always shopping and sellers are always selling but exchanges do not occur.

One could easily imagine a scene in a Three Stooges movie in which customers are constantly getting into and then out of these two cabs as prices are constantly being adjusted to lure customers away from the competition in a way that the taxicab companies can at least break even. The one thing that never occurs in this scene is that the taxicabs actually travel to the airport in a way that allows them to at least break even.

Strategically speaking, the problem facing firms in empty-core markets is that there are often real costs to not completing an exchange. In the taxicab example, all the time that customers and the companies are negotiating and renegotiating who will go to the airport in which cab and at what price, the two firms are paying for the cabs they purchased. These costs mean that even if these cabs never go to the airport (and thus the variable costs of going to the airport are avoided altogether), these cab companies will still lose money.

When markets have empty cores (that is, when no exchanges are completed) and when firms in these markets have large irreversible sunk costs, firms have strong incentives to set prices below their average costs. Setting prices in this way assures that these firms will lose money. However, these firms will often not lose as much money in this setting as they would if exchanges in this market are never completed. Competition in an industry in which prices are set below average costs is called **cutthroat competition.**

Return again to the taxicab example. Suppose it costs Firm A $2 to own its taxi, whether or not it is used to travel to the airport. Also, suppose it costs Firm B $3 to own its taxi, whether or not it is used to travel to the airport. If these companies and the four customers wanting to get to the airport can never complete an exchange, Firm A will lose $2 and Firm B will loose $3. Because Firm B knows that it will loose $3 if it does not take a trip to the airport, it might be willing to offer its seats at $2 each. Recall that the cost of Firm B going to the airport is $7, and thus when this firm sells its seats at $2 each, it does not cover its costs of going to the airport (3 × $2 = $6 and $6 < $7). However, Firm B may be willing to do this anyway, because it is better for it to lose $1 than it is to lose $3 by not going to the airport at all. Of course, if Firm B sells its seats for $2 each, then Firm A will have to respond. If Firm A sells its seats for $1.90 each, it will get the customers it needs to go to the airport. At the end of this trip, Firm A will have lost $1.20 ($5 cost − 2 × $1.90 revenue). However, this $1.20 loss is better than the $2 it would have lost if it did not take the trip at all.

In traditional economic settings, it is not unusual for less efficient firms to suffer economic losses while more efficient firms gain either competitive parity or advantage. However, in empty-core industries, even the most efficient firms lose money. Recall that it costs Firm A in our example $5 to take two people to the airport (a cost of $2.50 per person) and it costs Firm B $7 to take three people to the airport (a cost of $2.33 per person). In non-empty-core markets, prices would fall to somewhere between $2.33 per person and $2.50 a person, at which point Firm A (the less efficient firm) would lose money and Firm B (the more efficient firm) would earn normal or above-normal profits. However, with cutthroat competition, prices fall below the average cost of even the most efficient firms in a market, and all competing firms lose money.

When will a market have an empty core and when will cutthroat competition emerge in an industry? Research has shown that empty cores and cutthroat competition are likely to emerge in markets in which capacity is added in relatively large increments, there are large unavoidable fixed costs, there is little product differentiation, and demand is unpredictable.[42]

In some markets, capacity can only be added in large discrete units. For example, capacity on a particular air route is not added a seat at a time; it is added an airplane at a time. Similarly, capacity in the ocean shipping market is added only a ship at a time, electric generation capacity is added only a power plant at a time, and capacity in gas pipelines is added only a pipeline at a time.[43] When these discrete units of additional capacity are large relative to the total supply in an industry, an industry's supply curve is not smooth and continuous; rather, it is "lumpy" and discontinuous.

To see the effects of the lumpy and discontinuous industry supply curves, compare the situation in Figure 4.2A (in which industry supply and demand curves are continuous and smooth) to the situation in Figure 4.2B (in which industry supply is discontinuous and lumpy). In Figure 4.2A, there will always be a market-determined price

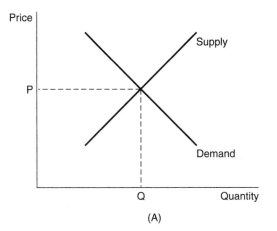

FIGURE 4.2   Industry Supply and Demand (A) When Supply Is Continuous and (B) When Supply Is Discontinuous

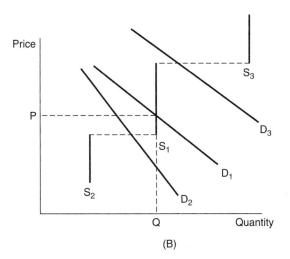

because industry supply and demand will always intersect. At this price, customers are willing to purchase Q units of output and producers are willing to produce Q units of output.

The situation is very different in Figure 4.2B. First, notice that industry supply is discontinuous. This is because capacity in this industry is added in large increments. Second, notice that each of the segments of this supply curve is vertical. This means that, within each of these segments, supply is inelastic. For example, a particular oil tanker has a fixed capacity. If that capacity comes on the market, no more or less than the full capacity of this oil tanker can be offered on the market. If the capacity of a second oil tanker is offered on the market, no more or no less than the full capacity of two oil tankers can be offered on the market. For a given level of capacity offered in this type of market, changes in demand do not affect the level of supply. In this sense, supply for a given level of capacity is fixed.

When industry demand happens to intersect a segment of this discontinuous supply curve (see demand curve D_1 in Figure 4.2B), a market-determined price exists, customers will be willing to pay this price for Q units of capacity, and producers will be willing to offer Q units of capacity. However, when industry demand does not intersect a segment of the discontinuous supply curve (as is the case for curves D_2 and D_3), no market-determined price exists that will satisfy customers and producers simultaneously. In these settings, the market will be chronically under capacity (for example, when the total amount of oil that needs to be shipped is greater than what can be shipped with one tanker, but only one tanker's capacity is on the market) or chronically over capacity (for example, when the total amount of oil that needs to be shipped is greater than what can be shipped with one tanker but less than what can be shipped with two tankers and the capacity of two tankers is on the market). In this scenario, buyers and sellers will always have other exchange opportunities that are more attractive than their current exchange opportunities. Thus, this kind of a market has an empty core.

Cutthroat competition emerges in empty-core markets when, in addition to capacity being added in large increments, firms have large unavoidable fixed costs, product differentiation is not possible, and demand is unpredictable. When a firm has large unavoidable fixed costs, a firm that fails to bring its capacity to market (because no price exists that fully satisfies both itself and its customers) loses money because it has to pay those costs no matter what. Rather than losing this much money, a firm may be willing to set prices that do not cover its *full costs,* but that do cover its *unavoidable fixed costs*. Thus, if it costs a firm $200 million to own an oil tanker, whether or not it is being used to transport oil, that firm is likely to use its tanker to ship oil. It will do so even if it loses money by shipping oil, as long as the amount of money it loses is less than the $200 million it would lose if it did not use the tanker to ship oil. Like the taxicab example, if the choice is between losing a great deal of money and losing less money, the profit-maximizing decision is to lose less money. When prices fall below a firm's average total costs, the firm loses money every time it brings its capacity to market. However, this outcome may be better than a firm keeping its prices above average total costs, being unable to bring its capacity to market, and having to pay large unavoidable fixed costs. Unfortunately, in the long run, firms cannot survive if they continuously set prices below their average total costs.[44]

If firms can significantly differentiate their products in markets in which capacity is added in large increments and there are large unavoidable fixed costs, cutthroat competition problems can still be avoided. If product differentiation leads to the creation of several noncompeting groups of customers in a market, then different firms can satisfy the demand of different customer groups and cutthroat competition will not emerge. Thus, cutthroat competition will emerge in a market only when capacity is added in large increments, there are large unavoidable fixed costs, and there is not significant product differentiation.

Unpredictable demand also contributes to the emergence of cutthroat competition in a market. With predictable demand, it is possible to build a technology that adds just the right amount of capacity to a market to meet industry demand, which partially avoids the competitive problems created by being able to add only large increments of capacity in a market. However, when demand is unpredictable, it is difficult to build just the right amount of capacity to ensure that industry supply-and-demand curves will intersect and thus difficult to ensure that a market price that satisfies both buyers and sellers will be determined.

Cutthroat Competition in the Postderegulation U.S. Airline Industry: An Example

One industry that had many of the attributes of an empty core was the postderegulation U.S. airline industry.[45] Before 1978, the U.S. airline industry was highly regulated. An agency of the U.S. federal government—the Civil Aeronautics Board—determined which airlines would fly which routes, the frequency of flights, and the prices that could be charged. During this highly regulated period, the U.S. airline industry was very stable. There was very little entry or exit, and U.S. airline firms were profitable.

Beginning in 1978, regulatory processes for determining routes, flight frequency, and prices in the U.S. airline industry were replaced by market processes. This deregulation increased the level of competitive intensity in the industry considerably. There was competitive entry, competitive exit, consolidation, and a restructuring of employment contracts with airline unions. Not surprisingly, prices for airline tickets dropped significantly post-deregulation.

Most observers expected this period of intense competition to last a relatively short period of time—a time during which vigorous competition would lead to a shakeout by which the least efficient airlines would cease operations and only the most efficient would remain. Post-shakeout, most observers believed that the most efficient airlines would remain in operation and that they would be able to be profitable.

However, this shakeout period lasted much longer than anyone had suspected. In fact, for a period of over 15 years, virtually all U.S. airlines lost money, several went into bankruptcy, and the survival of the industry was in jeopardy. With the exception of Southwest Airlines (discussed in detail in Chapter 5), the total losses experienced by U.S. airlines in the 15 years after deregulation were greater than the total profits that firms had earned since their creation and operation in a highly regulated situation. Both inefficient and relatively efficient airlines lost money, and did so for many years. And this was before the additional disruption to demand caused by the 9/11 attacks.

One of the reasons for these massive losses is that the nonregulated airline industry has many of the attributes of an empty-core market with cutthroat competition. Capacity in this industry is added only in large increments—one airplane at a time, not one airplane seat at a time. There are very large irreversible sunk costs associated with owning an airplane. A new Boeing 747 can cost over $300 million—a cost that has to be paid by an airline whether an airplane is being used to carry passengers or not. Given these large irreversible sunk costs, airline companies were unwilling not to fly a plane, even if they lost money flying it, because they would lose less money flying the plane than not flying the plane. Right after deregulation, most airlines had similar route structures, so there was very little product differentiation in this industry. Finally, because there was very little history of demand in an unregulated industry, predicting market-determined demand was very difficult. Given this competitive context, it is not surprising that most U.S. airlines lost a great deal of money.

Opportunities in Empty-Core Markets

Of course, U.S. airline companies engaged in a wide variety of activities to try to become profitable in this deregulated industry. For example, many renegotiated their contracts with unions and reduced the quality of their services in order to reduce their costs of operations. However, cost leadership (as discussed in Chapter 6) is not a viable opportunity in empty-core industries. Opportunities in mature markets, including product refinement, service, and process innovation—do not solve the competitive problems in empty-core markets. In the same way, leadership, niche, harvest, and divestment—opportunities in declining markets—in general do not solve the competitive problems in empty-core markets. In short, cutthroat competition is not the same as the vigorous competition that often exists in mature or declining industries. Instead, the major opportunities in empty-core markets with cutthroat competition are collusion, government regulation, significant product differentiation, and demand management.[46]

Collusion. Competition in empty-core markets can lead to prices that are lower than the average total costs of firms in these markets. One way to avoid the losses associated with such prices is for firms in these markets to engage in **collusion,** the voluntary restraining of competition by, for example, taking turns in bringing their capacity to the market. Returning to the taxi example, if Firms A and B agree that on Monday, Wednesday, and Friday only Firm A will transport customers to the airport, and that on Tuesday, Thursday, and Saturday only Firm B will transport customers to the airport, both Firm A and Firm B can charge prices for their services that exceed their average costs. In this way, Firms A and B can both earn above-normal profits and avoid the problems of cutthroat competition.

Collusion, as an example of interfirm cooperation, is discussed in more detail in Chapter 9. In general, while collusion can generate superior profits for firms, it usually does so by hurting consumers. Most commonly, colluding firms hurt customers by raising prices above the competitive level. However, in the case of empty-core industries, customers are actually better off if formerly competing firms collude. After all, if firms continue to compete in these empty-core markets, they will gain competitive disadvantages and go out of business. When this occurs, customers will not be able to gain access to those firms' products or services. With collusion, at least some customer needs will be satisfied, and satisfying some customers is better than satisfying no customers. Thus, collusion in empty-core markets may be the best outcome that customers can expect. Although it is not perfect, it is better than customers not having access to the products or services that firms in these markets have to offer.[47]

Government Regulation. It is often difficult for firms to create and maintain voluntary collusive arrangements (see Chapter 9). Once firms agree to cooperate by reducing their output—thereby increasing prices in a market—there are strong incentives for firms to "cheat" on these collusive agreements. Although cheating on collusive agreements can take many forms in empty-core markets, it generally takes the form of firms making more capacity available to the market than what was agreed to.[48] When more capacity is brought to the market in empty-core industries, cutthroat competition is likely to emerge.

When firms cannot discipline themselves sufficiently to avoid cutthroat competition in an empty-core market, they may seek government regulation as a way to maintain order and discipline in the industry. Rather than relying on tacit collusion as a nonmarket mechanism for setting prices above a firm's total average costs, government regulation uses the bureaucratic and administrative processes in a government to set prices that will lead to firm survival. Although these prices will always be higher than what would be the prices determined through cutthroat competition, these prices will ensure that firms in an industry will survive, and thus that consumers will have access to the products and services of that industry. As was the case with tacit collusion, the cost of using government regulation to ensure that customers will have access to an industry's products or services will generally be higher prices.

Significant Product Differentiation.   Product differentiation also provides an opportunity for firms in empty-core markets to solve competition problems. However, the level of product differentiation required to solve empty-core competitive problems is very significant. As suggested earlier, product differentiation must have the effect of creating groups of noncompeting customers. As will be described in Chapter 7, when this occurs, a firm enjoys some of the advantages of monopoly within the group of customers to whom it sells. With this partial monopoly in place, firms do not have to cooperate with each other for customers, and thus cutthroat competition does not emerge.

Predicting Demand.   A final opportunity in empty-core markets is predicting demand. Here the task is to learn how to predict demand in a market and then to have a range of capacity options to bring to market supply that just meets demand. By developing very sophisticated tools for predicting demand in particular markets, firms can add only that amount of additional capacity that is needed to meet the chronic undersupply or oversupply problems that would otherwise characterize empty-core markets. When supply can be adjusted to meet demand, cutthroat competition will not exist.

Solving Empty-Core Problems in the Deregulated U.S. Airline Industry

The deregulated airline industry is an excellent example of an empty-core industry with cutthroat competition. It is also an example of how firms in this kind of industry can exploit opportunities for collusion, government regulation, significant product differentiation, and predicting demand to solve their cutthroat competition problems.[49] Although it took the U.S. airline industry several years to fully exploit these competitive opportunities in this industry, since the mid-1990s this industry has become more stable, and most U.S. airline companies have become profitable. Unfortunately, the effectiveness of most of these strategies was condemned by the event of September 11, 2001.

By the mid-1980s, it became clear that none of the opportunities that existed in mature or declining industries were viable options in the empty-core U.S. airline industry. Although firms continued to increase their efficiency, it was becoming obvious that they could not cut costs enough to be financially viable. During this time period, airlines began to collude. In fact, the U.S. Department of Justice has identified at least two efforts to create collusion in this post-deregulation industry: an (unsuccessful) attempt by American Airlines to raise prices in cooperation with several other U.S. airlines in the mid-1980s, and a successful cooperative attempt to raise prices in the late 1980s. Collusion was proved in the second case, and most major U.S. airlines signed a consent decree admitting their guilt and reimbursing passengers.

Because collusion proved difficult to achieve, by the early 1990s several industry observers began calling for the re-regulation of the U.S. airline industry. Although price and route regulations were never re-established, the U.S. government has created a regulatory regime that enables U.S. airlines to engage in activities that would probably be considered illegal in other industries but are deemed necessary for U.S. airlines to be able to avoid cutthroat competition.

In particular, the U.S. government has allowed U.S. airlines to create effective geographic monopolies through hub-and-spoke systems. Different airlines dominate different geographic hubs: Delta in Atlanta and Cincinnati, American in Dallas and Chicago, United in Chicago and Denver, USAirways in Pittsburgh and Philadelphia, Continental in Houston and Cleveland, Northwest in Detroit and Minneapolis. These airlines dominate these hubs by providing the most flights to and from these cities. They also operate the most attractive gates in these hubs. Someone flying into or out of any of these hubs is more likely to have to fly on the airline that dominates the hub than on any other airline. More important, anyone who lives near these major hub cities has few options other than to fly with the airline that dominates the hub.

This dominance gives airlines geographically limited market power—power they can use to increase their ticket prices above what would be the prices in a more competitive market. This effect on ticket prices can be quite substantial. For example, people who live near Detroit (a Northwest hub) have few options except Northwest if they want to fly to Orlando, Florida. People who live near Columbus, Ohio (an airport without a hub), can fly Northwest (through Detroit) to Orlando, Delta (through Cincinnati) to Orlando, Continental (through Cleveland) to Orlando, American or United (through Chicago) to Orlando, or USAirways (through Pittsburgh) to Orlando. Because the air travel market in Columbus is more competitive than the air travel market in Detroit, prices from Detroit to Orlando on Northwest are often higher than prices from Columbus to Orlando, via Detroit, on Northwest. This is the case even though the latter trip is longer than the former.

Put differently, the dominance of certain city hubs creates very significant product differentiation in the airline industry. Northwest's air travel products are much more highly differentiated in Detroit than they are in Columbus. This differentiation enables Northwest to set prices above the level that would otherwise prevail. It has already been suggested that this price might fall below Northwest's average total costs and thus not be sustainable over the long run. Thus, in addition to any other benefits they may create, hub-and-spoke systems enable airlines to differentiate their product significantly, thereby avoiding cutthroat competition.

However, hub-and-spoke systems can also increase the predictability of demand for an airline. Day-to-day demand for air travel between smaller communities and larger destinations is often very unpredictable. For example, the number of people who want to fly from South Bend, Indiana, to Orlando may vary substantially from day to day. In a similar way, the number of people who want to fly from State College, Pennsylvania, to Orlando may also vary unpredictably day by day. However, by flying passengers from smaller cities to large airport hubs, the unpredictabilities of demand between smaller cities and a destination tend to cancel each other out, making the resulting level of aggregate demand more predictable. Thus, while on any given day, demand for air travel between South Bend and Orlando may be down, it may be up for air travel between State College and Orlando. In the aggregate, demand between a hub (where passengers from these smaller cities gather) and Orlando is more predictable than demand between these smaller cities and Orlando.

When airlines can predict demand on a particular route more precisely, they can make just the right amount of capacity available on that route. This helps avoid the overcapacity and undercapacity problems that are characteristic of empty-core industries with uncertain demand and thus helps avoid the cutthroat competition that can develop on these routes. The availability of airplanes with very different seating capacities, from Boeing 737s that seat 135 passengers to Boeing 747s that can seat up to 500 passengers, means that airlines can add just the right level of capacity to a particular route to meet demand but not exceed demand.

More recently, airlines have adopted "yield management" systems to increase the predictability of demand on particular routes even more. This is done by adjusting the prices on a route based on historical patterns of demand on that route. For example, if anticipated ticket sales fall below the expected level five days before a flight, airlines will lower prices. If anticipated ticket sales are greater than what was expected five days before the flight, prices can be increased. By adjusting prices on a flight, demand can be managed such that it meets the supply available on that route, without the risks of having either not enough or too much capacity on that route. Yield management is one reason why a ticket on a flight may cost $150 one day, and $350 the next.

Of course, it has taken U.S. airlines some time to exploit all these different opportunities. First, they had to realize that they were operating in an empty-core industry and that traditional approaches to improving performance, by themselves, would not work in this industry structure. Once they recognized the market context within which they were operating, it took some time to build the hub-and-spoke systems and to develop the databases needed to implement yield management strategies. And, after all this work, the events of 9/11 reduced total industry demand by about 20%. Since 2001, U.S. airlines have been faced, once again, with cutthroat competition.

All this said, there is one U.S. airline—Southwest—that never experienced the huge losses associated with cutthroat competition, has never adopted a hub-and-spoke system, flies only one type of aircraft, and does not engage in yield management. As suggested above, how Southwest has been able to succeed will be discussed in Chapter 5.

4.2 STRATEGIC GROUPS ANALYSIS OF ENVIRONMENTAL THREATS AND OPPORTUNITIES

The analysis of environmental threats and opportunities outlined in Chapter 3 and thus far in Chapter 4 assumes that the appropriate unit of analysis for this type of strategic work is the industry. On the threat side, entry into an industry, rivalry among firms within an industry, substitutes for products in an industry, the power of suppliers to firms in an industry, and the power of an industry's buyers are the most relevant points of analysis. On the opportunity side, different opportunities are assumed to depend on the structure of the industry in which a firm operates. This industry focus is not too surprising, because the theoretical underpinnings of the models presented in these two chapters—the structure-conduct-performance paradigm—also takes the industry as its unit of analysis.

Unfortunately, adopting the industry as the unit of analysis in evaluating a firm's threats and opportunities is not without limitations. First, the definition of what constitutes an industry is often ambiguous. The traditional definition of an industry focuses on cross-elasticities of demand among a set of firms. When increases in the price of one firm's products or services lead to an increase in demand for another firm's products or services, then these two firms have a **high cross-elasticity of demand** and can be thought of as being in the same industry.

In practice, however, studies of such cross-elasticities of demand between firms are rarely done. Even when they are done, how high cross-elasticities need to be to constitute an industry is somewhat of a judgment call. More often than not, firms are classified into the same industry when they seem, to some outside observers, to produce similar goods or services. Rigorous definitions of how similar products or services need to be, the dimensions along which products or services are similar, and other important issues are rarely examined. Indeed, most decisions about what industry a firm is in depend more on a firm's standard industrial classification (SIC) code and less on the economic situation facing the firm.

Second, the adoption of the industry as the unit of analysis implicitly assumes that firms in an industry are essentially identical in terms of the threats and opportunities they face. However, even when there is high cross-elasticity in demand between firms, it does not follow that different firms, or different groups of firms, will face exactly the same threats and opportunities. For example, there is probably high cross-elasticity of demand between Mercedes and Lexus. Both are at the luxury end of the automobile market, and changes in the price of one of these types of cars are likely to affect demand for the other, yet the threats these two firms face are different. For example, Lexus, a division of Toyota Motor Corporation, needs to deal with the threat of import quotas being applied to Japanese automobile firms—a threat that has yet to emerge for Mercedes and other German automotive companies.

Given these limitations of using the industry as a unit of analysis, several scholars have suggested that a level of analysis between the individual firm and the industry may be appropriate. This level of analysis is the strategic group.

The Concept of Strategic Groups

A **strategic group** is a set of firms that face similar threats and opportunities that are different from the threats and opportunities facing other firms in an industry.[50] Notice that this definition requires that a set of firms face threats and opportunities that are similar to each other yet simultaneously different from the threats and opportunities faced by other firms in an industry. If only the first criterion holds (similar threats and opportunities), and not the second, the strategic group is logically equivalent to an industry, and traditional S-C-P–based analyses of threats and opportunities are appropriate.

This concept of strategic groups allows both for ambiguity about the boundaries of an industry and for variance in the structure of threats and opportunities that face firms in an industry. Boundary ambiguity is made less relevant by focusing on the set of firms that face very similar threats and opportunities. In this context, defining industry boundaries becomes less important than defining group boundaries. If more than one group exists in an industry, then variance in the structure of threats and opportunities can be included in an industry analysis.

Many of the concepts that are applicable in the analysis of industry structure have analogies in the analysis of strategic groups. Most important of these is **a mobility barrier,** a concept that is directly analogous to entry barriers at the industry level. Whereas entry barriers restrict entry into an industry, mobility barriers restrict movement of firms between strategic groups in an industry. Industry characteristics that limit entry into an industry can also limit mobility between strategic groups. Thus, for example, economies of scale, product differentiation, cost advantages independent of scale, government policy, and even contrived deterrence can all be mobility barriers within an industry. Firms that seek to reduce mobility by erecting mobility barriers face the same cost/benefit kinds of constraints as firms that seek to erect barriers to entry.[51]

Applying the Strategic Groups Concept

The concept of strategic groups has been applied in order to understand the structure of threat and opportunity in a wide variety of industries. One recent application focused on the evolution of competition within and between strategic groups in the pharmaceutical industry.[52] The first task in this type of analysis is to isolate several key mobility barriers that might be operating in an industry. Recall that these mobility barriers are intra-industry versions of many of the barriers to entry cited in Chapter 3. Three major mobility barriers have been identified in the pharmaceutical industry: research and development skills, marketing skills, and product positioning skills (that is, differentiated versus generic drugs). These mobility barriers are all examples of combinations of economies of scale, product differentiation, and cost advantages independent of scale barriers to entry operating *within* the pharmaceutical industry.

With these mobility barriers isolated, it is then possible to measure the conduct of firms in an industry with respect to these barriers. Some firms emphasize their own R&D skills; others rely on the R&D skills of other firms by licensing products that these other firms develop. Some firms have invested in huge sales and marketing forces to sell their drugs; others have invested in less elaborate sales and marketing organizations.

With the conduct of each firm measured relative to the mobility barriers in an industry, a similarity matrix can then be formed. Different measures of similarity can be used, but simple correlational analysis can be used to form an $(n \times n)$ correlation matrix (where n is the number of firms in an industry). Each element of this correlation matrix (i, j) is the correlation between the vector of measures of conduct for firm i with the vector of measures of conduct for firm j.

To form groups of firms that face similar threats and opportunities but that are also different from the threats and opportunities facing other firms in an industry, this similarity matrix can be subjected to cluster analysis. The resulting clusters are strategic groups—that is, sets of firms that are pursuing similar sets of strategies and actions, and thus are likely to face similar sets of threats and opportunities. This type of analysis has been conducted on firms in the pharmaceutical industry. The results of these analyses are presented in Figure 4.3.

This analysis makes it possible to describe the evolution of competition within and between strategic groups in the pharmaceutical industry in some detail. For

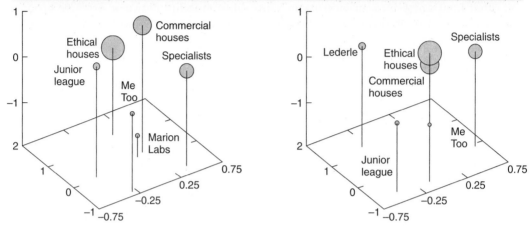

FIGURE 4.3   Strategic Groups in the U.S. Pharmaceutical Industry, 1963 to 1969 and 1980 to 1982. Groups are represented in three dimensions. Each axis represents a critical attribute or firm conduct in this industry: research and development skills, marketing skills, and product positioning skills. The size of the spheres reflects the total sales of the firms in each strategic groups.

Source: Cool, K. O., and D. Schendel. "Strategic group formation and performance: The case of the U.S. pharmaceutical industry, 1963–1982," *Management Science*, 33 1985, pp. 1102–1124. © 1987 The Institute of Management Sciences (currently INFORMS), 290 Westminster Street, Providence, RI 02901.

example, the strategic group labeled "ethical houses" lost some of its members over time, as three firms (Abbott, Lederle, and Squibb) were unable to keep pace with the innovative output of the R&D leaders in the industry (Lilly, Merck, and UpJohn). Also, as revealed in the dimensional analysis in Figure 4.3, the "ethical houses" strategic group had some difficulty remaining distinct from the "commercial houses" strategic group in the pharmaceutical industry. Also, Lederle, a traditional member of the "ethical houses" strategic group, left this group in the late 1980s and seemed to follow a unique strategy. During the 1980s, Lederle used its relatively large marketing group to push commodity generic drugs, a strategy that was not pursued by any firm in the earlier period.

Limitations of Strategic Groups Analysis

If strategic groups analysis is applied carefully, it can be an important supplemental tool for analyzing environmental threats and opportunities in an industry. In particular, it can be used to study the evolution of competition between sets of firms in an industry over time. Unfortunately, the use of this concept can also be misleading.[53] Because there is little probability theory associated with cluster analysis, it is usually not possible to tell if a strategy group defined through cluster analysis is real—in a statistically meaningful way—or simply an artifact of cluster analysis. Thus, great care must be taken in interpreting the results of a strategic groups analysis. This said, when groups that are identified in an industry are real and meaningful, the use of strategic groups as a unit of analysis can significantly improve the quality of the analysis of threats and opportunities facing a firm.

4.3 LIMITATIONS OF S-C-P–BASED MODELS OF ENVIRONMENTAL THREATS AND OPPORTUNITIES

There is little doubt that S-C-P models of environmental threats and opportunities are important strategic tools and vital tools for firms looking to choose strategies. Like all models, however, they have some important limitations, and managers and scholars alike must be aware of these limitations as they attempt to apply S-C-P models. Four particularly important limitations are (1) assumptions about firm profits and entry, (2) the role of inefficient firm strategies, (3) the limited concept of firm heterogeneity, and (4) the percentage of variance in firm profits that is explained by the industry within which a firm operates.

Assumptions About Firm Profits and Entry

Traditional S-C-P logic suggests that entry into an industry is motivated by incumbent firms earning above-normal economic profits—that above-normal profits are a signal to potential entrants that opportunities exist in an industry. Empirically, S-C-P logic suggests that the rate of entry into an industry is positively correlated with the level of firm performance in that industry.

There is, however, an alternative point of view. According to this point of view, a high level of performance by incumbent firms sends exactly the opposite signal to potential entrants: Instead of encouraging entry, high performance by incumbents discourages entry because it suggests that incumbent firms are very effective and efficient.[54] Incumbent firms with important competitive advantages are able to meet customer needs very effectively and at very low cost and thus generate above-normal performance. Potential entrants may decide against entering because of the likelihood that they will not be able to duplicate the effectiveness and efficiency of incumbent firms. Empirically, this alternative view suggests that the rate of entry into an industry will be negatively correlated with the level of firm performance in that industry.

Not surprisingly, there is mixed empirical evidence concerning these alternative views of profits and entry. It seems that when incumbent firms gain competitive advantages based on monopolistic/oligopolistic price and output strategies, high levels of performance in an industry generally encourage entry. The reason for this outcome is that incumbent firms in this context are usually not very efficient or effective in meeting customer needs and are easy prey for efficient and effective new entrants. However, if incumbent firms are earning superior levels of performance because of their exceptional ability to meet customer needs in a low-cost and efficient manner, high levels of firm performance in an industry actually discourages entry.

These conflicting points of view concerning profits and entry have a wide variety of implications. At a societal level, antitrust regulation has traditionally been based on the S-C-P assumption that high levels of firm performance in an industry are evidence of collusion, contrived deterrence, monopoly, or some other anticompetitive actions. The alternative view of profits and entry is now beginning to have an influence on government policy. In fact, sometimes it is difficult to tell whether high profits encourage or deter entry. This, in many ways, was the core question in the Microsoft antitrust case. There is no doubt that Microsoft dominates both the PC operating systems and application software markets. However, did Microsoft's dominance result from its anticompetitive monopolistic behavior, or did it result from Microsoft's ability to develop operating systems and applications software in a timely and efficient manner? Suppose Microsoft has engaged in anticompetitive behavior *and* has efficiently anticipated and solved consumer problems with new products and services. What proportion of its market value can be attributed to its anticompetitive actions and what part to efficient and timely production of new products and services? Even more problematic, if Microsoft engaged in both these kinds of activities, would government remedies designed to address Microsoft's anticompetitive actions have the effect of reducing its ability to serve its customers efficiently?

At the firm level, assumptions about whether high incumbent profits encourage or deter entry go a long way in determining whether a firm should choose to enter an industry. If incumbent firms are earning high profits because of their oligopoly/monopoly actions, then entry may be an attractive alternative. However, if the profits of incumbent firms are high because of competitive advantages they possess, entry is likely to be more costly and thus a less desirable option.

The Role of Inefficient Firm Strategies

Most of the strategic options that emerge from an S-C-P analysis of environmental threats and opportunities have the effect of improving a firm's ability to meet customer needs or reduce a firm's costs. These strategies focus on improving a firm's efficiency and effectiveness in order to gain competitive advantages and superior profits. These strategies suggest that the best way to gain and maintain advantages is to be more effective and efficient than current or potential competitors.

However, certain S-C-P strategies (such as contrived deterrence strategies) seem to suggest that decreasing a firm's efficiency and effectiveness can maximize firm performance. This occurs when an S-C-P model suggests that a firm invest in more productive capacity than is required for current and anticipated operations, invest in more product differentiation than is required to meet customer needs, or gain access to more low-cost factors of production than are required for efficient operations.

In general, implementing strategies that *decrease* firm efficiency in order to improve a firm's performance seems likely to be very risky and applicable only in very unusual circumstances. For example, in the model of contrived deterrence, presented in Chapter 3, there was only one incumbent firm and one potential entrant. More typically, firms that reduce their efficiency encourage new entry rather than discourage it. As suggested earlier, inefficient and ineffective incumbent firms are easy prey for efficient and effective rivals and new entrants. In general, the most reasonable strategic advice must be for incumbent firms to learn how to meet customer needs more efficiently and effectively. This choice will not only give firms the opportunity for competitive advantages within an industry, it will usually have the effect of deterring new entry as well.[55]

The Limited Concept of Firm Heterogeneity

S-C-P models of environmental threats and opportunities provide only a weakly developed sense of the heterogeneity of firms in an industry. Firms in an industry may differ in an S-C-P framework, but the differences are restricted to variance in the threats and opportunities a firm faces. This variance, in turn, reflects differences in economies of scale, product differentiation, production costs, and so forth. This level of firm hetero-geneity in the S-C-P approach is significantly less than the level of firm heterogeneity assumed to exist in traditional approaches to strategic management.[56]

This lack of firm heterogeneity in S-C-P models of environmental threats and oppor-tunities is not surprising and stems directly from the unit of analysis in these models: the industry. The S-C-P framework is designed to study industry structure and leads to a powerful model of environmental threats and opportunities. It was never intended to be a general model of strategic choice. A general model of strategic choice must in-clude both environmental analyses (of threats and opportunities) and organizational analyses (of strengths and weaknesses). Alternative theoretical frameworks that focus on unique firm characteristics must be used to complete internal analyses. These frame-works are described in the next chapter.

Industry and Firm Effect on Performance

For some time now, scholars have been interested in the relative effects of the attributes of the industry in which a firm operates and the attributes of the firm itself on its performance. The first work in this area was published by Richard Schmalansee.[57] Using a single year's worth of data, Schmalansee estimated the vari-ance in the performance of firms that was attributable to the industries in which firms operated versus other sources of performance variance. Schmalansee's con-clusion was that approximately 20 percent of the variance in firm performance can be explained by the industry in which a firm operates—a conclusion consistent with the S-C-P model and its emphasis on industry as a primary determinant of a firm's performance.

Richard Rumelt identified some weaknesses in Schmalansee's research.[58] Most important of these was that Schmalansee had only one year's worth of data with which to examine the effects of industry and firm attributes on firm performance. Rumelt was able to use four years' worth of data, which allowed him to distinguish between stable and transient industry and firm effects on firm performance. Rumelt's results were con-sistent with Schmalansee's in one sense: Rumelt also found that about 16 percent of the variance in firm performance was due to industry effects, versus Schmalansee's 20 per-cent. However, only about half of this industry effect was stable. The rest represented year-to-year fluctuations in the business conditions in an industry. This result is broadly inconsistent with the S-C-P model.

Rumelt also examined the effect of firm attributes on firm performance and found that over 80 percent of the variance in firm performance was due to these firm attrib-utes, but over half of this 80 percent (46.38 percent) was due to stable firm effects. The importance of stable firm differences in explaining differences in firm performance is also inconsistent with the S-C-P framework. These results are consistent with another model of firm performance called the resource-based view, which will be described in Chapter 5.

More recent work by McGahan and Porter is consistent with Rumelt's work, al-though McGahan and Porter show that the size of the industry effect can vary substantially, depending on an industry's structure.[59] However, in virtually all cases reported by these authors, the size of the firm effect on firm performance was substantially larger than the industry effect.

These results have clear implications for the role of external analysis in the strategic management process. Although such analysis is still important for firms making strategic choices, the resources and capabilities a firm brings to its competitive environment, on average, have a much larger effect on a firm's performance.

4.4 SUMMARY

One way to think about identifying opportunities in an industry is to isolate a set of generic industry structures and then to identify opportunities that exist in these different types of industries. Porter and others have described several generic industries: fragmented industries, emerging industries, mature industries, declining industries, international industries, network industries, hypercompetitive industries, and empty-core industries. The most common types of opportunity in each of these industries have also been identified.

In identifying the threats and opportunities facing firms, it can sometimes be helpful to recognize groups of firms within an industry that face similar threats and opportunities, but threats and opportunities that are different from those faced by other firms in the industry. Such firms constitute strategic groups in an industry. Techniques for discovering strategic groups in an industry have been described.

Although S-C-P–based models of environmental threats and opportunities are very powerful, they are subject to some limitations. Some of the most important of these are the effect of incumbent firms' profits on entry by new firms, the effect of strategies that reduce incumbent firms' efficiency and effectiveness on new entries, and an underdeveloped sense of firm heterogeneity. These limitations suggest that the S-C-P framework is not a general model of strategy formulation, but must be coupled with additional theoretical frameworks that enable managers to analyze the strengths and weaknesses of individual firms.

REVIEW QUESTIONS

1. How should firms choose from among the four opportunities they face in declining industries?
2. Given the ideas developed in Chapter 4, is it appropriate to say that there are really no unattractive industries? If yes, what implications does this statement have for the ideas presented in Chapter 3? If no, describe an industry that has no opportunities.
3. Is the evolution of industry structure from an emerging industry to a mature industry to a declining industry inevitable? Why or why not?
4. Imagine two firms competing in a hypercompetitive industry. Firm A has focused on re-

taining its flexibility; Firm B has focused on becoming a "proactively disruptive" firm. In the long run, which of these firms will perform better, and why?
5. The electric utility industry in the United States has historically been very highly regulated. However, it is currently experiencing deregulation. In your view, are U.S. electric utilities likely to face cutthroat competition? Why or why not?
6. Under what conditions, if any, would it make sense for firms to implement strategies that reduce their competitive efficiency?

ENDNOTES

1. See Bain, J. S. (1956). *Barriers to New Competition,* Cambridge, MA: Harvard University Press.
2. Jacob, R. (1992). "Service Corp. International: Acquisitions done the right way," *Fortune,* November 16, p. 96.
3. Personal communication, 1997.
4. Porter, M. E. (1980). *Competitive Strategy,* New York: Free Press.
5. For the definitive discussion of first-mover advantages, see Lieberman, M., and C. Montgomery (1988). "First-mover advantages," *Strategic Management Journal,* 9, pp. 41–58.
6. Ghemawat, P. (1984). "Du Pont in titanium dioxide (A)," Harvard Business School Case no. 9-385-140; and Porter, M. E. (1981). "Disposable diaper industry in 1974," Harvard Business School Case no. 9-380-175.
7. See Spence, A. M. (1981). "The learning curve and competition," *Bell Journal of Economics,* 12, pp. 49–70; Mansfield, E. (1985). "How rapidly does new industrial technology leak out?" *Journal of Industrial Economics,* 34(2), pp. 217–223; Lieberman, M. B. (1982). "The learning curve, pricing and market structure in the chemical processing industries," unpublished doctoral dissertation, Harvard University; and Lieberman, M. B. (1987). "The learning curve, diffusion, and competitive strategy," *Strategic Management Journal,* 8, pp. 441–452, for discussions of the importance of proprietary learning and why it is difficult to keep learning proprietary. These issues are also discussed in more detail in Chapter 6.
8. See Gilbert, R. J., and D. M. Newbery (1982). "Preemptive patenting and the persistence of monopoly," *American Economic Review,* 72(3), pp. 514–526.
9. See Bresnahan, T. F. (1985). "Post-entry competition in the plain paper copier market," *American Economic Review,* 85, pp. 15–19, for a discussion of Xerox's patents; and Bright, A. A. (1949). *The Electric Lamp Industry,* New York: Macmillan, for a discussion of General Electric's patents.
10. See Mansfield, E., M. Schwartz, and S. Wagner (1981). "Imitation costs and patents: An empirical study," *Economic Journal,* 91, pp. 907–918.
11. See Main, O. W. (1955). *The Canadian Nickel Industry,* Toronto: University of Toronto Press, for a discussion of asset preemption in the oil and gas industry; Ghemawat, P. (1986). "Wal-Mart store's discount operations," Harvard Business School Case no. 9-387-018, for Wal-Mart's preemption strategy; Schmalansee, R. (1978). "Entry deterrence in the ready-to-eat breakfast cereal industry," *Bell Journal of Economics,* 9(2), pp. 305–327; and Robinson, W. T., and C. Fornell (1985). "Sources of market pioneer advantages in consumer goods industries," *Journal of Marketing Research,* 22(3), pp. 305–307, for a discussion of preemption in the breakfast cereal industry. In this latter case, the preempted valuable asset is shelf space in grocery stores.
12. Klemperer, P. (1986). "Markets with consumer switching costs," doctoral thesis, Graduate School of Business, Stanford University; and Wernerfelt, B. (1986). "A special case of dynamic pricing policy," *Management Science,* 32, pp. 1562–1566.
13. See Gross, N. (1995). "The technology paradox," *Business Week,* March 6, pp. 691–719; Bond, R. S., and D. F. Lean (1977). *Sales, Promotion, and Product Differentiation in Two Prescription Drug Markets,* Washington, DC: U. S. Federal Trade Commission; Montgomery, D. B. (1975). "New product distribution: An analysis of supermarket buyer decision," *Journal of Marketing Research,* 12, pp. 255–264; Ries, A., and J. Trout (1986). *Marketing Warfare,* New York: McGraw-Hill; and Davidson, J. H. (1976). "Why most new consumer brands fail," *Harvard Business Review,* 54, March/April, pp. 117–122, for a discussion of switching costs in these industries.
14. I, myself, was probably the last user of Wordstar on the planet. I stopped using it only because printer drive software was no longer available.

15. A point made very well by Wernerfelt, B., and A. Karnani (1987). "Competitive strategy under uncertainty," *Strategic Management Journal,* 8, pp. 187–194.

16. IBM's second-mover strategy is described by Carroll, P. (1993). *Big Blues: The Unmaking of IBM,* New York: Crown; Crown Cork & Seal's second-mover strategy is described by Hamermesh, R. G., and R. S. Rosenbloom (1989). "Crown Cork and Seal Co., Inc.," Harvard Business School Case no. 9-388-096; and Proctor & Gamble's second-mover strategy is described by Porter, M. E. (1981b). "Disposable diaper industry in 1974," Harvard Business School Case no. 9-380-175.

17. Porter, M. W. (1980). *Competitive Strategy,* New York: Free Press.

18. Gibson, R. (1991). "McDonald's insiders increase their sales of company's stock," *Wall Street Journal,* June 14, p. A1; and E. Wahlgreen (2005). "Salads days for burger joints," *Business Week Online,* June 3, 2005.

19. Descriptions of these product refinements can be found in Demetrakakes, P. (1994). "Household-chemical makers concentrate on downsizing," *Packaging,* 39(1), p. 41; Reda, S. (1995). "Motor oil: Hands-on approach," *Stores,* 77(5), pp. 48–49; and Quinn, J. (1995). "KitchenAid," *Incentive,* 169(5), pp. 46–47.

20. See Hayes, R. H., and S. G. Wheelwright (1979). "The dynamics of process-product life cycles," *Harvard Business Review,* March/April, p. 127.

21. See Krafcik, J. K., and J. P. MacDuffie (1989). *Explaining High Performance Manufacturing: The International Automotive Assembly Plant Study,* International Motor Vehicle Program, Cambridge, MA: Massachusetts Institute of Technology.

22. See Porter, M. E. (1980). *Competitive Strategy,* New York: Free Press; and Harrigan, K. R. (1980). *Strategies for Declining Businesses,* Lexington, MA: Lexington Books.

23. See Aguilar, F. J., J. L. Bower, and B. Gomes-Casseres (1985). "Restructuring European Petrochemicals: Imperial Chemical Industries, P.L.C.," Harvard Business School Case no. 9-385-203.

24. See Harrigan, K. R. (1980). *Strategies for Declining Businesses,* Lexington, MA: Lexington Books.

25. See Klebnikov, P. (1991). "The powerhouse," *Forbes,* September 2, pp. 46–52; and Rosenbloom, R. S., and C. Christensen (1990). "Continuous casting investments at USX Corporation," Harvard Business School Case no. 9-391-121.

26. Finn, E. A. (1987). "General Eclectic," *Forbes,* March 23, pp. 74–80.

27. See Smith, L. (1993). "Can defense pain be turned to gain?," *Fortune,* February 8, pp. 84–96; Perry, N. J. (1993). "What's next for the defense industry," *Fortune,* February 22, pp. 94–100; and Dial, J., and K. J. Murphy (1995). "Incentive, downsizing, and value creation at General Dynamics," *Journal of Financial Economics,* 37, pp. 261–314.

28. See Bartlett, C. A., and S. Ghoshal (1989). *Managing Across Borders: The Transnational Solution,* Boston: Harvard Business School Press; and Bartlett, C., and S. Ghoshal (1993). Beyond the M-form: Toward a managerial theory of the firm," *Strategic Management Journal,* 14, pp. 23–46.

29. www.forbes.com.

30. See Moffett, M. (1993). "U.S. firms yell olé to future in Mexico," *Wall Street Journal,* August 9, p. B1; and Oviatt, B. M., and P. P. McDougall (1995). "Global start-ups: Entrepreneurs on a worldwide stage," *Academy of Management Executive,* 9, pp. 30–44. Logitech, Oxford Instruments, SPEA, and Technomed are all still successful independent firms pursing global strategies. Momenta Corporation, on the other hand, failed three years after it was founded.

31. Blackman, A. (1990). "Moscow's Big Mac attack," *Time,* February 5, p. 51; and Bartlett, C. A., and S. Ghoshal (1989). *Managing Across Borders: The Transnational Solution,* Boston: Harvard Business School Press.

32. Bartlett, C. A., and S. Ghoshal (1989). *Managing Across Borders: The Transnational Solution,* Boston: Harvard Business School Press.

33. See Conner, K. (1995). "Obtaining strategic advantage from being imitated: When can encouraging 'clones' pay?" *Management Science,* 41, pp. 209–225.

34. Sony's strategies are described in more detail in Chapter 5 and in Davidson, J. H.

(1976). "Why most new consumer brands fail," *Harvard Business Review,* 54, March/April, pp. 117–122.

35. Conner, K. R., and R. P. Rumelt (1991). "Software piracy: An analysis of protection strategies," *Management Science,* 37(2), pp. 125–139.

36. See, for example, Mandel, M. (2000). "Antitrust in the digital age," *Business Week,* May 15, pp. 46–48.

37. See D'Aveni, R. (1994). *Hypercompetition: Managing the Dynamics of Strategic Maneuvering,* New York: Free Press.

38. This is my term, not D'Aveni's, although I believe this term captures many of the specific opportunities D'Aveni identifies in hypercompetitive industries.

39. See D'Aveni, R. (1995). "Coping with hypercompetition: Utilizing the new 7S's framework," *Academy of Management Executives,* 9(3), pp. 45–60.

40. The notion of an empty core was first developed by Telser, L. (1978). *Economic Theory and the Core,* Chicago: University of Chicago Press.

41. This example was first suggested to me by Abigail McWilliams.

42. How these industry attributes generate empty-core markets and cutthroat competition is demonstrated analytically by Telser, L. (1978). *Economic Theory and the Core,* Chicago: University of Chicago Press.

43. Empty-core analyses of various markets have been published. See, for example, Bittlingmayer, G. (1982). "Decreasing average cost and competition: A new look at the Addyston Pipe case," *Journal of Law and Economics,* 25, pp. 201–229, for a discussion of empty cores in pipe manufacturing; McWilliams, A. (1990). "Rethinking horizontal market restrictions: In defense of cooperation in empty core markets," *Quarterly Review of Economics and Business,* 30, pp. 3–14, for a discussion of the turn-of-the-century trusts in empty-core terms; Pirrong, S. C. (1992). "An application of core theory to the analysis of ocean shipping markets," *Journal of Law and Economics,* 35, pp. 89–132; and Sjostrom, W. (1989). "Collusion in ocean shipping: A test of monopoly and empty core models," *Journal*

of Political Economy, 97, pp. 1160–1179, for a discussion of empty cores in ocean shipping markets.

44. However, as Keynes put it so well, in the long run, we are all dead.

45. Ghemewat, P., and A. McGahan (1995). "The U.S. airline industry in 1995," Harvard Business School Case no. 9-795-113.

46. McWilliams, A., and J. Barney (1994). "Managing cutthroat competition in empty core markets: An additional motive for inter-firm cooperation," unpublished manuscript, Arizona State University West, describes in more detail how these and other traditional opportunities fail to solve empty-core and cutthroat competition problems.

47. The social welfare benefits of collusion in empty-core markets are discussed in more detail in Telser, L. (1987). *A Theory of Efficient Cooperation and Competition,* Cambridge, MA: MIT Press.

48. Firms will want to cheat this way in order to exploit the higher prices that collusion has created in this market. This, however, is an example of what will be called Cournot cheating in Chapter 10. However, unlike the situation described in Chapter 10, Cournot cheating in empty-core industries will lead to cutthroat competition and low levels of economic performance.

49. Ghemewat, P., and A. McGahan (1995). "The U.S. airline industry in 1995," Harvard Business School Case no. 9-795-113.

50. See Hunt, M. S. (1972). "Competition in the Major Home Appliance Industry 1960–1970," unpublished doctoral dissertation, Harvard University; and Caves, R. E., and M. E. Porter (1977). "From entry barriers to mobility barriers: Conjectural decisions and contrived deterrence to new competition," *Quarterly Journal of Economics,* 91, pp. 241–262. This literature is reviewed in McGee, J., and H. Thomas (1986). "Strategic groups: Theory, research and taxonomy," *Strategic Management Journal,* 7, pp. 141–160; and Barney, J. B., and R. E. Hoskisson (1990). "Strategic groups: Untested assertions and research proposals," *Managerial and Decision Economics,* 11, pp. 187–198.

51. Mobility barriers are described in Caves, R. E., and M. E. Porter (1977). "From entry barriers to mobility barriers: Conjectural decisions and contrived deterrence to new competition," *Quarterly Journal of Economics,* 91, pp. 241–262.

52. Cool, K. O., and I. Dierickx (1993). "Rivalry, strategic groups and firm profitability," *Strategic Management Journal,* 14, pp. 47–59. This research builds on the work of Cool, K. O., and D. Schendel (1987). "Strategic group formation and performance: The case of the U. S. pharmaceutical industry, 1963–1982," *Management Science,* 33, pp. 1102–1124.

53. See Barney, J., and R. Hoskisson (1990). "Strategic groups: Untested assertions and research proposals," *Managerial and Decision Economics,* 11, pp. 187–198.

54. A point that was originally made by Demsetz, H. (1973). "Industry structure, market rivalry, and public policy," *Journal of Law and Economics,* 16, pp. 1–9.

55. Williamson argues that "efficiency is the best strategy." Williamson, O. E. (1991). "Strategizing, economizing, and economic organization," *Strategic Management Journal,* 12 (Winter), pp. 75–94.

56. See Barney, J. B. (1991). "Firm resources and sustained competitive advantage," *Journal of Management,* 17, pp. 99–120; and Conner, K. R. (1991). "A historical comparison of resource based theory and five schools of thought within industrial organization economics: Do we have a new theory of the firm?" *Journal of Management,* 17(1), pp. 121–154.

57. R. Schmalansee (1985). "Do markets differ much?" *American Economic Review,* 75, pp. 341–351.

58. R. P. Rumelt (1991). "How much does industry matter?" *Strategic Management Journal,* 12, pp. 167–185.

59. See, for example, McGahan, A., and M. Porter (2003). "The emergence and sustainability of abnormal profits," *Strategic Organization,* 1, pp. 79–108; McGahan, A., and M. Porter (2002). "What do we know about variance in accounting profitability?" *Management Science,* 48, pp. 834–851; and McGahan, A. (1999). "The performance of U.S. corporations: 1981–1994," *Journal of Industrial Economics,* 47, pp. 373–398.

5

Evaluating Firm Strengths and Weaknesses: The Resource-Based View

Consider the performance of Dell Computer. Dell is in the highly competitive personal computer (PC) business, with 2005 sales of $54.2 billion. A five forces analysis of the personal computer industry reveals numerous threats and relatively few opportunities. The level of rivalry in this industry is very high; hundreds of electronics firms around the world build and sell personal computers for the home and business. Fierce price competition periodically erupts in the industry. Large corporate buyers are able to use their volume to leverage ever-lower prices from PC makers, and critical suppliers to the industry, including Intel and Microsoft, have enormous power and influence. The growth of hand held personal digital assistants (PDAs) and related electronic technology are rapidly becoming important substitutes for PCs.

Given this industry environment, it is not surprising that many personal computer manufacturers have found this industry to be unattractive. In 2004, for example, Compaq Computer and Hewlett Packard merged to try to restore profitability to their PC business, and IBM sold its PC business to China's Lenovo Group for $1.25 billion in cash and equity. After helping create the personal computer business in the first place, IBM finally concluded that it simply could not make enough money in this business to justify its continuing investment.

In the face of what can only be described as a very competitive environment, Dell Computer was able to earn relatively high levels of profit through most of the 1990's and the first few years of the 21st century. Dell created and sustained a high level of performance over a long period of time in this difficult industry by eliminating virtually all finished-products inventory and through a consistent emphasis on efficient assembly and delivery to customers.[1]

Dell Computer is not the only firm that has been able to obtain high levels of economic performance despite conducting business in a very competitive industry. Wal-Mart operates in the highly competitive discount retail sales industry, an industry that has consistently experienced price competition and margin erosion since it was founded in the mid-1960s. Indeed, several discount retail store chains—including Kmart—have declared bankruptcy over the years. Despite these challenges, Wal-Mart has consistently earned a return on sales over twice the industry average. The airline business is another industry racked by profit-destroying competition. But while total losses among U.S. airlines have totaled over $20 billion since the early 1990s, Southwest Airlines' profits have continued to grow. Indeed, Southwest Airlines has been one of the few consistently profitable airlines in the world. In the highly competitive steel industry, the market value of almost all vertically integrated steel producers in the United States has been falling for at least two decades. Despite these results, the market value of Nucor Steel has continued to soar, giving its shareholders one of the consistently highest rates of return for any investment in its industry.[2]

The performance of Dell, Wal-Mart, Southwest Airlines, and Nucor Steel in industries with so many threats and few opportunities reminds us that a firm's competitive environment is not the only determinant of a firm's profit potential. Some firms are able to develop and implement strategies that generate high levels of profit in competitively difficult industries. Other firms conduct business in industries with relatively few threats and enormous opportunities, only to choose and implement strategies that generate poor performance. To understand the performance of both kinds of firms, it is necessary to look beyond the analysis of threats and opportunities that exist in a firm's environment and examine the unique strengths and weaknesses that a firm might possess.

In this chapter, we examine models for analyzing a firm's strengths and weaknesses. We discuss economic and other theories underlying models of strengths and weaknesses, describe how these models have been used to develop a framework for analyzing strengths and weaknesses, and examine some of the limitations of this framework.

5.1 TRADITIONAL RESEARCH ON FIRM STRENGTHS AND WEAKNESSES

Whereas models of environmental threats and opportunities are grounded in a single approach to economic analysis—the structure-conduct-performance paradigm—the study of firm strengths and weaknesses draws on a wider variety of research traditions, some in economics and others in noneconomic disciplines. Among the most important of these are traditional research on distinctive firm competencies, Ricardian economics, and the theory of firm growth.

Theories of Distinctive Competence

The first of the research traditions that underpins the modern study of firm strengths and weaknesses is work on distinctive competencies. This work falls into two broad categories. The first examines general managers as distinctive competencies; the second examines other organizational attributes as distinctive competencies.

General Managers as Distinctive Competencies

Research on the competitive implications of a firm's internal strengths and weaknesses has a long tradition. Much of this work was begun at the Harvard Business School as early as 1911 by Shaw, Copeland, Smith, and Learned with the analysis of the role of general managers in organizations. In this early work, it was assumed that decisions made by **general managers** (that is, managers with significant profit-and-loss responsibility in an organization, who typically have more than one function reporting to them) had a very large effect on a firm's performance. General managers, it was argued, were the individuals in an organization who had the responsibility for analyzing the firm's environment, understanding the firm's internal strengths and weaknesses, and choosing strategies to maximize value. Although general managers might call on a variety of line and staff managers to assist in this strategy-making effort, the quality of general managers in a firm was thought to determine the performance of the firm. High-quality general managers were thought of as organizational strengths, and low-quality general managers were thought of as weaknesses.[3]

   This general management approach to understanding firm strengths and weaknesses has a great deal of validity, but two problems limit its applicability. First, even if one accepts the notion that general management decisions are the most important determinants of firm performance, the qualities and characteristics that make up a "high-quality" general manager are ambiguous and difficult to specify. General managers with widely different skills and styles have been quite effective. For example, Jack Welch, the recently retired chief executive officer (CEO) at General Electric, is usually described as a relatively "hands-off" manager. Instead of becoming deeply involved in day-to-day activities, Welch was said to set the general strategic and operational direction in the firm and then hold subordinates accountable in meeting their profit and performance targets. On the other hand, Bill Gates, co-founder and former CEO at Microsoft, was intensely involved in the detailed operations of his firm. And yet, both Jack Welch and Bill Gates were generally recognized as successful general managers. Although some authors argue that there are some attributes common to all successful general managers, it must nevertheless be admitted that there is significant variance in style and approach even among the most successful general managers.[4]

   Second, general managers are an important possible strength (or weakness) for an organization, but they are not the only organizational strengths or weaknesses. An exclusive emphasis on general managers as a source of competitive advantage ignores a wide variety of other firm attributes that may be important for understanding firm performance. General managers in organizations are probably similar to baseball managers: They receive too much credit when things go well and too much blame when things go poorly.

Institutional Leadership as a Distinctive Competence

While faculty members at the Harvard Business School were studying the effect of general managers on firm performance, some sociologists led by Phillip Selznick were studying the internal characteristics of organizations from a completely different perspective. In a series of articles and books, culminating in his book, *Leadership and Administration,* Selznick examined the relationship between what he called institutional leadership and distinctive competence.[5]

According to Selznick, **institutional leaders** in organizations do more than carry out the classic managerial activities of planning, organizing, leading, and controlling. In addition, they create and define an organization's purpose or mission. In more contemporary terms, institutional leaders help create a vision for an organization around which its members can rally. Institutional leaders also organize and structure a firm so that it reflects this fundamental purpose and vision. With this organization in place, Selznick suggests that institutional leaders then focus their attention on safeguarding a firm's distinctive values and identity—the distinctive vision of a firm—from internal and external threats. This organizational vision, in combination with organizational structure, helps define a firm's **distinctive competencies**—those activities that a particular firm does better than any competing firms.

Selznick did not go on to analyze the competitive or performance implications of institutional leadership or distinctive competence in any detail. However, it is not difficult to see that firms with distinctive competencies have strengths that may enable them to obtain competitive advantages, and that leaders as visionaries and institution builders, rather than just as managers and administrators, may be an important source of this competitive advantage. This form of reasoning is similar to the models of organizational strengths and weaknesses that will be discussed later in this chapter.

Selznick's analysis of distinctive competence has much to recommend it, but it has limitations as well. Most important of these is that Selznick's analysis focuses only on senior managers (his institutional leaders) as the ultimate source of competitive advantage for a firm and on a single tool (the development of organizational vision) that senior managers can use to create distinctive competencies. Although these are important possible strengths and weaknesses in a firm, they are not the only possible strengths and weaknesses.

Ricardian Economics

Research on general managers and institutional leaders as possible strengths and weaknesses focuses exclusively on top managers, but the next major influence on the study of organizational strengths and weaknesses—Ricardian economics—traditionally included little or no role for managers as possible strengths or weaknesses. Instead, David Ricardo was interested in the economic consequences of the "original, unaugmentable, and indestructible gifts of Nature." Much of this early work focused on the economic consequences of owning land.[6]

Unlike many factors of production, the total supply of land is relatively fixed and cannot be increased significantly in response to higher demand and prices. Such factors of production are perfectly inelastic, because their quantity of supply is fixed and does not respond to price increases. In these settings, it is possible for those who own higher-quality factors of production with inelastic supply to earn an economic rent. An **economic rent** is a payment to an owner of a factor of production in excess of the minimum required to induce that factor into employment.

Ricardo's argument concerning land as a factor of production is summarized in Figure 5.1. Imagine that there are many parcels of land suitable for growing wheat. Also suppose that the fertility of these different parcels varies from high fertility (low costs of production) to low fertility (high costs of production). The long-run supply curve for wheat in this market can be derived as follows. At low prices, only the most fertile land will be cultivated; as prices rise, production continues on the very fertile land and additional crops are planted on less fertile land; at still higher prices, even less fertile land will be cultivated. This analysis leads to the simple market supply curve presented in Figure 5.1A. Given market demand, P^* is the market-determined price of wheat in this market.

Now consider the situation facing two different kinds of firms. Both these firms follow traditional profit-maximizing logic by producing a quantity (q) such that marginal cost equals marginal revenue. However, this profit-maximizing decision for the firm with less fertile land (in Figure 5.1B) generates competitive parity and zero economic profit. On the other hand, the firm with more fertile land (Figure 5.1C) has average total costs less than the market-determined price and thus is able to earn superior profits.

In traditional economic analysis, the economic profit earned by the firm with more fertile land should lead other firms to enter into this market, to obtain some land and begin production of wheat. However, all the land that can be used to produce wheat in a way that generates at least competitive parity given the market price P^* is already in production. In particular, there is no more very fertile land left, and fertile land (by assumption) cannot be created. This is what is meant by land being inelastic in supply. Thus the firm with more fertile land and lower production costs has a sustained competitive advantage over firms with less fertile land and higher production costs and is able to earn an economic rent.

Of course, at least two events can threaten this sustained competitive advantage. First, market demand may shift down and to the left. This would force firms with less fertile land to cease production, and would also reduce the economic rent of the firm with more fertile land. If demand shifted far enough, this economic rent might disappear altogether.

FIGURE 5.1   Ricardian Rents and the Economics of Land with Different Levels of Fertility

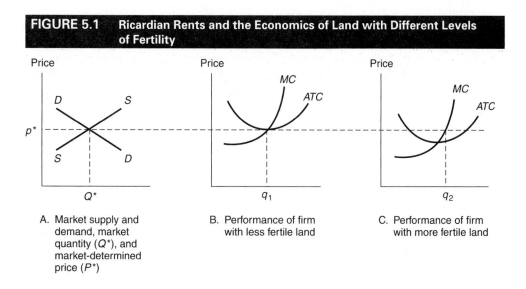

A. Market supply and demand, market quantity (Q^*), and market-determined price (P^*)

B. Performance of firm with less fertile land

C. Performance of firm with more fertile land

Second, firms with less fertile land may discover low-cost ways to increase their land's fertility, thereby reducing the competitive advantage of the firm with more fertile land. For example, firms with less fertile land may be able to use inexpensive fertilizers to increase their land's fertility, or they may be able to reduce their production costs to be closer to the costs of the firm that had the more fertile land initially. The existence of such low-cost fertilizers suggests that whereas *land* may be in fixed supply, *fertility* may not be. If enough firms can increase the fertility of their land, then the rents originally earned by the firm with the more fertile land will disappear.

Traditionally, most economists have implicitly assumed that relatively few factors of production are inelastic in supply. Most economic models presume that if prices for a factor of production rise, more of that factor will be produced, increasing supply and ensuring that suppliers will earn only normal economic returns. More recently, however, there has been a growing recognition that numerous resources used by firms are inelastic in supply and are possible sources of economic rents. Thus, although labor per se is probably not inelastic in supply, highly skilled and creative laborers may be. Although individual managers are probably not inelastic in supply, managers who can work effectively in teams may be. And although top managers may not be inelastic in supply, top managers who are also institutional leaders (as suggested by Selznick and others) may be. Firms that own (or control) these kinds of resources may be able to earn economic rents by exploiting them. This observation is critical in the model of organizational strengths and weaknesses described in Section 5.2.

Penrose's Theory of Firm Growth

In 1959, Edith Penrose published a book titled *The Theory of the Growth of the Firm* that has much to say about resources and competitive advantage. Penrose's objective was to understand the process through which firms grow and the limits of growth. Traditional economic models had analyzed firm growth using the assumptions and tools of neoclassical microeconomics.[7] The most problematic of these, for Penrose, was the assumption that firms could be appropriately modeled as if they were relatively simple production functions. In other words, traditional economic models assumed that firms simply observed supply-and-demand conditions and translated these conditions into levels of production that maximized firm profits.[8]

This abstract notion of what a firm is had and continues to have utility in some circumstances. However, in attempting to understand constraints on the growth of firms, Penrose concluded that this abstraction was not helpful. Instead, she argued that firms should be understood, first, as an administrative framework that links and coordinates activities of numerous individuals and groups, and second, as a bundle of productive resources. The task facing managers was to exploit the bundle of productive resources controlled by a firm through the use of the administrative framework that had been created in a firm. According to Penrose, the growth of a firm is limited by the productive opportunities that exist as a function of the bundle of productive resources controlled by a firm and by the administrative framework used to coordinate the use of these resources.

Besides looking inside a firm to analyze the ability of firms to grow (in a way that parallels internal analyses in the SWOT-organizing framework), Penrose made several other contributions to the study of a firm's strengths and weaknesses. First, she observed that the bundles of productive resources controlled by firms can vary significantly by firm—that firms, in this sense, can be fundamentally heterogeneous even if they are in the same industry. Second, Penrose adopted a very broad definition of what might be considered a productive resource. Whereas traditional economists (including Ricardo) focused on just a few resources that might be inelastic in supply (such as land), Penrose began to study the competitive implications of such inelastic productive resources as managerial teams, top management groups, and entrepreneurial skills. Finally, Penrose recognized that, even within this extended typology of productive resources, there might still be additional sources of firm heterogeneity. Thus, in her analysis of entrepreneurial skills as a possible productive resource, Penrose observed that some entrepreneurs are more versatile than others, some are more ingenious in fund raising, some are more ambitious, and some exercise better judgment.

5.2 ANALYZING ORGANIZATIONAL STRENGTHS AND WEAKNESSES

Research on the skills of general managers, institutional leaders, economic rents, and firm growth have recently been brought together to develop a rigorous model that can be used to analyze a firm's strengths and weaknesses. This general framework, usually called the **resource-based view of the firm,** focuses on the idiosyncratic, costly-to-copy resources controlled by a firm—resources whose exploitation may give a firm a competitive advantage. A growing number of authors are focusing their efforts on understanding the resource-based view, its implications for firm performance, and its relationship with the frameworks for studying environmental threats and opportunities discussed in Chapters 3 and 4.[9]

Basic Assumptions of the Resource-Based View of the Firm

This approach to studying a firm's internal strengths and weaknesses rests on two fundamental assumptions. First, building on Penrose's work, this work assumes that firms can be thought of as bundles of productive resources and that different firms possess different bundles of these resources. This is the assumption of firm **resource heterogeneity.** Second, drawing from the work of Selznick and Ricardo, this approach assumes that some of these resources are either very costly to copy or inelastic in supply. This is the assumption of **resource immobility.** If the resources a firm possesses enable the firm to exploit opportunities or neutralize threats, these resources are possessed by only a small number of competing firms, and if they are costly to copy or inelastic in supply, then they may be firm strengths and thus potential sources of competitive advantage.

Resource Categories

Any of a wide range of firm attributes could be considered resources in this context. In general, **firm resources** are all assets, capabilities, competencies, organizational processes, firm attributes, information, knowledge, and so forth, that are controlled by a firm and that enable the firm to conceive of and implement strategies designed to improve its efficiency and effectiveness.

Several authors have generated lists of firm attributes that may be thought of as resources.[10] Generally, these resources can be conveniently divided into four categories: financial capital, physical capital, human capital, and organizational capital. **Financial capital** includes all the different money resources that firms can use to conceive of and implement strategies—capital from entrepreneurs, equity holders, from bondholders, and from banks. Retained earnings are also an important type of financial capital.

Physical capital includes the physical technology used in a firm, a firm's plant and equipment, its geographic location, and its access to raw materials. Specific examples of physical capital are a firm's computer hardware and software technology, robots used in manufacturing, and automated warehouses to control inventory costs. Geographic location, as a type of physical capital, is an important resource for firms as diverse as Wal-Mart (with its operations in rural markets generating, on average, higher returns than its operations in more competitive urban markets) and L.L. Bean (a catalog retail firm that believes that its rural Maine location helps its employees identify with the outdoor lifestyle of many of its customers).[11]

Human capital includes the training, experience, judgment, intelligence, relationships, and insight of *individual* managers and workers in a firm.[12] The importance of the human capital of well-known entrepreneurs such as Bill Gates (Microsoft) and Steve Jobs (Apple) is broadly understood. However, valuable human capital resources are not limited to just entrepreneurs or just senior managers and can include managers and others at all levels in a firm.[13]

Whereas human capital is an attribute of single individuals, **organizational capital** is an attribute of collections of individuals. Organizational capital includes a firm's formal reporting structure (what Penrose called the administrative framework); its formal and informal planning, controlling, and coordinating systems; and its culture and reputation; as well as informal relations among groups within a firm and between a firm and those in its environment. Firms as diverse as Merck and Harley-Davidson use their management reputations as a type of organizational capital, to gain access to managerial labor markets, distribution networks, and customer groups.[14]

Resources, Capabilities, and Competencies

As the resource-based view of the firm has developed, different authors have used different terms to describe strategically relevant financial, physical, individual, and organizational attributes. One of the earliest strategic management references to these organizational attributes was by Wernerfelt, who simply called them "resources." Barney and others have adopted Wernerfelt's terminology. Prahalad and Bettis, in their analysis of the implications of these kinds of organizational attributes for diversification strategies, called them a firm's dominant logic. In more recent work on managing diversification, Prahalad and Hamel called these internal attributes of firms core competencies. Stalk, Evans, and Shullman, in some closely related work, called them core capabilities.[15]

In practice, the differences among these various terms are subtle at best. Some have suggested that a firm's "resources" include its fundamental financial, physical, individual, and organizational capital attributes. "Capabilities," in contrast, include only those internal firm attributes that enable a firm to coordinate and exploit its other resources. General practice seems to suggest that core competencies are restricted to firm attributes that enable managers to conceive of and implement certain corporate diversification strategies.

Although these distinctions among resources, capabilities, and competencies can be drawn in theory, it is likely that they will become badly blurred in practice. In particular, it seems unlikely that a debate about whether a particular firm attribute is a "resource" and "capability" or a "competence" will be of much value to managers or firms. Given this state of affairs, the following conventions are adopted throughout the remainder of this book. First, the terms **resources** and **capabilities** will be used interchangeably and often in parallel. Second, the term **core competence** is applied only in discussions of the conception or implementation of diversification strategies. Thus, core competence is largely restricted in use until Part III.

Using Value-Chain Analysis to Identify Resources and Capabilities

One way to identify resources and capabilities that have the potential for creating competitive advantage for a firm is to engage in **value-chain analysis.** Most goods or services are produced through a series of vertical business activities—acquiring raw materials, manufacturing intermediate products, manufacturing final products, sales and distribution, after-sales service, and so forth. For example, as shown in Figure 5.2, the sale of oil-based products such as gasoline and motor oil involves several vertically related business activities including exploring for crude oil, drilling for crude oil, pumping crude oil, shipping crude oil, buying crude oil, refining crude oil, selling refined products to distributors, shipping refined products, and selling refined products to final customers. This set of vertically related business activities is a product's **value chain.**

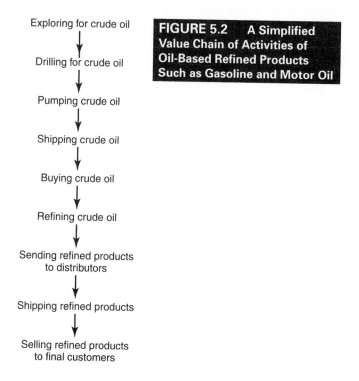

Exploring for crude oil

Drilling for crude oil

Pumping crude oil

Shipping crude oil

Buying crude oil

Refining crude oil

Sending refined products to distributors

Shipping refined products

Selling refined products to final customers

FIGURE 5.2   A Simplified Value Chain of Activities of Oil-Based Refined Products Such as Gasoline and Motor Oil

Each stage in a product's value chain typically has financial, physical, individual, and organizational resources associated with it. Exploring for crude oil, for example, is very expensive and thus requires substantial financial resources. It requires access to land (a physical resource), the application of substantial scientific and technical knowledge (individual resources), and an organizational commitment to risk taking and exploration (organizational resources). Selling refined oil products to final customers requires very different resources. Retail outlets (such as stores and gas stations) are costly to build and require both financial and physical resources. These outlets must be staffed by knowledgeable salespeople who can be thought of as individual resources—and marketing these products to customers through advertisements and other means can require a commitment to creativity that is an organizational resource.

Of course, different firms can choose to focus on different aspects of a particular product's value chain. Thus, some firms in the oil industry focus only on exploration and production, others focus only on refining, and still others on selling refined products. A firm's choices about which activities in a value chain it will focus on can have significant effects on the kinds of resources and capabilities it will control. Thus, for example, a firm that specializes in oil exploration is likely to have very different financial, physical, individual, and organizational resources than a firm that specializes in refining or a firm that specializes in selling refined products. Consequently, understanding in which stages in a product's value chain a firm operates can be helpful in identifying the types of financial, physical, individual, and organizational resources a firm is likely to control. The ability of these resources and capabilities to generate competitive advantages can then be analyzed.

However, even firms that operate in the same set of value-chain activities may approach these activities very differently and therefore may develop very different resources and capabilities associated with these activities. For example, two firms may both sell refined oil products to final customers. However, one of these firms may sell only through retail outlets that it owns, whereas the second may sell only through retail outlets that it doesn't own. The first firm's financial and physical resources are likely to be very different from the second firm's financial and physical resources, although these two firms may have similar individual and organizational resources.

What value-chain analysis does is to force analysts to think about firm resources and capabilities at a very micro level. Although it is possible to characterize a firm's resources and capabilities more broadly, it is usually more helpful to think about how each of the activities in which a firm engages affects the financial, physical, individual, and organizational resources in the firm. With this understanding, it is possible to begin to understand potential sources of competitive advantage for a firm in a much more detailed way. Moreover, as will become clear shortly, this approach to identifying a firm's resources and capabilities suggests that firms simultaneously gain competitive advantages in some value-chain activities, competitive parity in other activities, and even competitive disadvantages in other activities. That is, not only should a firm's resources and capabilities be understood at a micro level, the concept of competitive advantage can also be applied at this level. This can lead to a much richer and complex understanding of a firm's overall competitive position in an industry.

Because value-chain analysis can be so helpful in identifying the financial, physical, individual, and organizational resources and capabilities controlled by a firm, several generic value chains for identifying firm resources and capabilities have been developed.

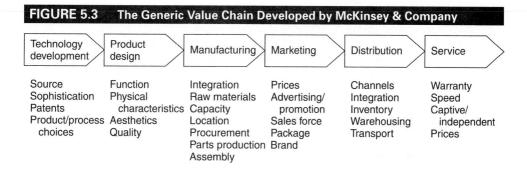

FIGURE 5.3   The Generic Value Chain Developed by McKinsey & Company

Technology development	Product design	Manufacturing	Marketing	Distribution	Service
Source	Function	Integration	Prices	Channels	Warranty
Sophistication	Physical	Raw materials	Advertising/	Integration	Speed
Patents	characteristics	Capacity	promotion	Inventory	Captive/
Product/process	Aesthetics	Location	Sales force	Warehousing	independent
choices	Quality	Procurement	Package	Transport	Prices
		Parts production	Brand		
		Assembly			

The first, proposed by the management consulting firm McKinsey & Company, is presented in Figure 5.3.[16] This relatively simple model suggests that the creation of value almost always involves six distinct activities: technology development, product design, manufacturing, marketing, distribution, and service. Firms can develop distinctive capabilities in any one, or any combination, of these activities. For example, many have suggested that Japanese firms have developed distinctive competencies in manufacturing and are now attempting to develop similar competencies in product design. One of the key questions facing Japanese firms concerns their ability to develop distinctive competencies in technology development, because until recently, most of the technology used by Japanese firms was developed elsewhere. Other firms may have no distinctive competencies in manufacturing, but may have valuable capabilities in product design, marketing, and distribution (such as The Limited in retail clothing).

Porter has proposed a second generic value chain.[17] This value chain, presented in Figure 5.4, divides value-creating activities into two large categories: primary activities and support activities. Primary activities include inbound logistics (purchasing, inventory, and so forth), production, outbound logistics (warehousing and distribution), sales and marketing, and service (dealer support and customer service). Support activities include infrastructure (planning, finance, information services, legal), technology development (research and development, product design), and human resource management

FIGURE 5.4   The Generic Value Chain Developed by Porter

Support Activities	Infrastructure activities: Planning, finance, MIS, legal services				
	Technology: Research, development, design				
	Human resource management and development				
Primary Activities	Purchasing Inventory holding Materials handling	Production	Warehousing and distribution	Sales and marketing	Dealer support and customer service

Margin

Source: Reprinted with permission of The Free Press, an imprint of Simon and Schuster, from *Competitive Advantage* by Michael E. Porter. Copyright © 1985 by The Free Press.

and development. Primary activities are associated directly with the manufacture and distribution of a product. Support activities assist a firm in accomplishing its primary activities. As is the case with the McKinsey value chain, a firm can develop strengths or weaknesses in any one, or in any combination, of the activities listed in Porter's value chain. These activities, and how they are linked to one another, can be thought of as a firm's resources and capabilities.

A Framework for Analysis: VRIO

The definition of a firm's resources and capabilities, and the two assumptions of resource heterogeneity and resource immobility, are quite abstract and are not directly amenable to the analysis of a firm's strengths and weaknesses. However, it is possible to develop a framework, based on this definition and on these two assumptions, that is more generally applicable. This framework is called the **VRIO framework.** It is structured in a series of four questions to be asked about the business activities in which a firm engages: (1) the question of **value,** (2) the question of **rarity,** (3) the question of **imitability,** and (4) the question of **organization.**[18] The answers to these questions determine whether a particular firm resource or capability is a strength or a weakness. Table 5.1 summarizes the questions; each question is discussed in detail later.

The Question of Value

The **question of value** is: Do a firm's resources and capabilities enable the firm to respond to environmental threats or opportunities? In order for a firm's resources and capabilities to be strengths, they must enable a firm to exploit environmental opportunities or neutralize environmental threats. Firm resources and capabilities that make it difficult for a firm to exploit opportunities or neutralize threats can be thought of as weaknesses. The question of value thus links internal analyses of strengths and weaknesses with external analyses of threats and opportunities. Throughout this book, the question of value will be addressed for different strategic options facing firms by applying the models of environmental threats and opportunities, developed in Chapters 3 and 4 and elsewhere. Thus, despite observations by some strategic management scholars, S-C-P–based models of environmental threats and opportunities are complements to resource-based models of organizational strengths and weaknesses.

The answer to the question of value, for many firms, has been "yes." For example, Sony has a great deal of experience in designing, manufacturing, and selling miniaturized electronic technology. Sony has used these resources and capabilities to exploit

---

TABLE 5.1   Questions for Conducting a Resource-Based Analysis of a Firm's Internal Strengths and Weaknesses

1. The Question of Value: Do a firm's resources and capabilities enable the firm to respond to environmental threats or opportunities?
2. The Question of Rarity: Is a resource currently controlled by only a small number of competing firms?
3. The Question of Imitability: Do firms without a resource face a cost disadvantage in obtaining or developing it?
4. The Question of Organization: Are a firm's other policies and procedures organized to support the exploitation of its valuable, rare, and costly-to-imitate resources?

numerous market opportunities, including portable tape players, portable disc players, portable televisions, and easy-to-hold video cameras. 3M has used its resources and capabilities in substrates, coatings, and adhesives, along with an organizational culture that rewards risk taking and creativity, to exploit numerous market opportunities in office products, including invisible tape and Post-it notes. Sony's and 3M's resources and capabilities—including their specific technological skills and their creative organizational cultures—made it possible for these firms to respond to, and even create, new environmental opportunities.[19]

Unfortunately, for other firms, the answer to the question of value has been "no." For example, long experience in traditional vertically integrated steel making made it almost impossible for United States Steel (USS) to recognize or respond to fundamental changes in the structure of the steel industry. Unable to respond to fundamental changes, USS decided to delay its investment in continuous casting steel-manufacturing technology. Nucor Steel, in contrast, was not shackled by its past, made these investments, and has become a major player in the international steel industry. In a similar way, Sears was unable to recognize and respond to changes in the retail market that had been created by Wal-Mart and specialty retail boutiques. In a sense, Sears's historical success, along with a commitment to stick with a traditional way of doing things, led it to miss some significant market opportunities. For both USS and Sears, resources and capabilities—in particular, their experience operating in an older competitive environment—were not valuable and prevented them from responding to competitive opportunities or threats. Only recently have USS and Sears begun to modify their resources and capabilities to become more valuable.[20]

Changes in Resource Value.   Obviously, that a firm's resources and capabilities have been valuable in the past does not necessarily imply that they will always be valuable. Changes in customer tastes, industry structure, or technology can render a firm's resources and capabilities less valuable. For example, General Electric's resources and capabilities in transistor manufacturing became much less valuable when semiconductors were invented. American Airlines's skills in managing their relationship with the Civil Aeronautics Board became much less valuable after airline deregulation. IBM's numerous resources and capabilities in the mainframe computing business became less valuable with the rise in power and reduction in price of personal computers.

A firm that no longer possesses valuable resources and capabilities has two fundamental choices. One choice is to develop new and valuable resources and capabilities. Crown Equipment, for example, was a leading manufacturer of motors used to rotate television antennas. With the rise of cable and satellite systems, this industry virtually disappeared. However, rather than liquidating, Crown developed new capabilities and is currently one of the leading manufacturers of electric forklifts in the world.

The other choice is to apply traditional strengths in new ways, instead of developing new resources and capabilities. For example, the invention and diffusion of air conditioning in manufacturing plants significantly reduced the value of the electric fan manufacturing skills of the Hunter Fan Company, a traditional fan manufacturer. However, rather than abandoning its skills altogether, Hunter Fan exploited a new market in which its traditional strengths would be valued: electric ceiling fans for homes and apartments. To address this new opportunity, Hunter Fan had to develop some additional resources and capabilities, including brass-plating skills and new distribution networks, but the resources and capabilities that had made Hunter successful in the industrial market were still valuable in the home market.[21]

Valuable Resources and Economic Performance. The effect of valuable resources and capabilities on a firm's economic performance can be derived directly from the definition of performance presented in Chapter 2. In particular, a firm's resources and capabilities are valuable if, and only if, they reduce a firm's net costs or increase how much a firm's customers are willing to pay compared to what would have been the case if this firm did not possess those resources.[22] When using firm resources and capabilities to develop strategies that do not exploit opportunities or neutralize threats, using these resources and capabilities will not increase how much a firm's customers are willing to pay. In fact, often the use of these resources and capabilities will actually reduce the economic value compared to what would have been the case if these nonvaluable resources had not been exploited. Such resources and capabilities are **weaknesses.**

Of course, as was suggested earlier, the resources and capabilities of different firms can be valuable in different ways. This can be true even if firms are competing in the same industry. For example, both Rolex and Timex manufacture watches, but they exploit very different valuable resources and capabilities. Rolex emphasizes its quality manufacturing, commitment to excellence, and high-status reputation in marketing its watches, focusing on increasing how much customers are willing to pay. Timex emphasizes its high-volume and low-cost manufacturing skills and abilities and thus focuses on reducing its costs. Rolex exploits its resources and capabilities in response to demand for very expensive watches. Timex exploits its resources and capabilities in response to demand for practical, reliable, low-cost timekeeping.

The Question of Rarity

Understanding the value of a firm's resources and capabilities is an important first consideration in understanding the firm's internal strengths and weaknesses. However, if a particular resource or capability is controlled by numerous competing firms, then that resource is unlikely to be a source of competitive advantage for any one of them. Instead, valuable but common (that is, not rare) resources and capabilities are sources of competitive parity. These observations lead to the question of rarity: How many competing firms already possess particular valuable resources and capabilities?

To observe that common resources or capabilities cannot generate a competitive advantage is not to dismiss them as unimportant for strategic managers. Instead, valuable but common resources and capabilities can help ensure a firm's survival when they are exploited to create competitive parity in an industry. Under conditions of competitive parity, though no one firm gains a competitive advantage, firms do increase their probability of survival.

Consider, for example, a telephone system as a resource or capability. Because telephone systems are widely available and because virtually all organizations have access to telephone systems, these systems are not rare and thus not a source of competitive advantage. However, firms that do not possess a telephone system are likely to give their competitors an important competitive advantage and place themselves at a competitive disadvantage. Unless firms with a competitive disadvantage change their activities, they are likely to earn poor economic returns. In the long run, the survival of these kinds of firms can be jeopardized.

How rare a valuable firm resource or capability must be in order to have the potential for generating a competitive advantage varies from situation to situation. It is not difficult to see that if a firm's valuable resources and capabilities are absolutely unique among a set of current and potential competitors, they can generate a competitive advantage. However, it may be possible for a small number of firms in an industry to possess a particular valuable resource or capability and still obtain a competitive advantage. In general, as long as the number of firms that possess a particular valuable resource or capability is less than the number of firms needed to generate perfect competition dynamics in an industry, that resource or capability can be considered rare and a potential source of competitive advantage.

Valuable but common resources and capabilities can only be sources of competitive parity, but valuable and rare resources and capabilities can be sources of at least temporary competitive advantage. For example, skills in developing and using point-of-purchase data collection to control inventory and product ordering gave Wal-Mart a competitive advantage over Kmart—a firm that, for many years, did not have access to this same timely information, and even when it did have access, did not exploit the information the way Wal-Mart did. For many years, Wal-Mart's valuable point-of-purchase inventory-control system was rare, at least relative to Kmart, its major U.S. competitor.

Managers at Kmart, however, were aware of these advantages possessed by Wal-Mart and began to develop similar technological skills and abilities.[23] Over time, Kmart became successful in developing these capabilities. Thus, they are no longer rare for Wal-Mart and are not a source of competitive advantage. In other words, Wal-Mart's competitive advantage based on these particular skills was only temporary. However, it may be that other Wal-Mart's resources—including the geographic location of some of its stores—will be more difficult for Kmart to imitate. These resources may be sources of sustained competitive advantage for Wal-Mart.

The Question of Imitability

Valuable and rare organizational resources may be a source of competitive advantage. Indeed, firms with such resources are often strategic innovators that are able to conceive of and engage in strategies other firms could either not conceive of, could not implement, or both, because these other firms lacked the relevant resources and capabilities. These firms may gain the first-mover advantages discussed in Chapter 4.

Valuable and rare organizational resources, however, can be sources of sustained competitive advantage only if firms that do not possess them face a cost disadvantage in obtaining them compared to firms that already possess them. In language developed by Lippman and Rumelt and also by Barney, these kinds of resources are **imperfectly imitable**.[24] These observations lead to the question of imitability: Do firms without a resource or capability face a cost disadvantage in obtaining it compared to firms that already possess it?

Imagine an industry with five essentially identical firms. Each of these firms manufactures the same products using the same raw materials, and sells the products to the same customers through the same distribution channels. It is not hard to see that firms in this kind of industry will gain only average economic performance. Now, suppose that one of these firms, for whatever reason, discovers or develops a heretofore unrecognized valuable resource and uses that resource either to exploit an environmental opportunity or neutralize an environmental threat. Obviously, this one firm will gain a competitive advantage over its competitors.

This firm's competitors can respond to this competitive advantage in at least two ways. First, they can ignore the success of this one firm and continue as before. This action, of course, keeps them at a competitive disadvantage. Second, these firms can attempt to understand why this one firm is able to be successful and then duplicate the resources of this one firm and implement a similar strategy. If competitors have no cost disadvantages in acquiring or developing the needed resources, then this imitative approach will generate competitive parity in the industry.

However, sometimes, for reasons that are discussed later, competing firms may face an important cost disadvantage in duplicating a successful firm's valuable resources. If this is the case, this one innovative firm may gain a **sustained competitive advantage**—an advantage that is not competed away through strategic imitation. Firms that possess and exploit costly-to-imitate, rare, and valuable resources in choosing and implementing their strategies may enjoy a period of sustained competitive advantage.

Forms of Imitation: Direct Duplication and Substitution. In general, imitation occurs in one of two ways: direct duplication or substitution. Imitating firms can attempt to duplicate directly the resources possessed by the firm with a competitive advantage. Thus, if a firm has a competitive advantage because of its research and development skills, imitating firms can attempt to develop their own R&D skills. If a firm has a competitive advantage because of its marketing expertise, imitating firms can attempt to develop their own marketing expertise. If the cost of direct duplication of a firm's resources or capabilities is greater than the cost of developing these resources and capabilities for the firm with the competitive advantage, then this advantage may be sustained. If direct duplication is no more costly than the original development of these resources or capabilities, then any competitive advantage will be only temporary.

The relative costs of direct duplication directly parallel the situation facing a firm with less fertile land competing with a firm with more fertile land studied by Ricardo and described in Figure 5.1. Costly duplication suggests that the resources or capabilities in question are inelastic in supply and thus those firms that already possess these resources may earn an economic rent.

Imitating firms can also attempt to substitute other resources for a costly-to-imitate resource possessed by a firm with a competitive advantage. For example, if one firm has a competitive advantage because of the interpersonal communication skills of its top management team, a competing firm may try to substitute a sophisticated management information system for interpersonal communication skills. If the effects of interpersonal communication skills and sophisticated management information systems are the same, then these resources can be thought of as substitutes. If substitute resources exist, and if imitating firms do not face a cost disadvantage in obtaining them, then the competitive advantage of other firms will be only temporary. However, if these resources have no substitutes, or if the cost of acquiring these substitutes is greater than the cost of obtaining the original resources, then competitive advantages can be sustained.

Again, the relative cost of substitutes in imitating the sources of a firm's competitive advantage directly parallels the role of substitutes in the analysis of Ricardian rents in Figure 5.1. In that example, if less fertile land with low-cost fertilizer is strategically equivalent to more fertile land, then very fertile land is not likely to be a source of economic rents. However, if less fertile land with low-cost fertilizer is not a strategic substitute for very fertile land, or if fertilizer is very costly, then owning more valuable land can be a source of economic rents.

Sources of Cost Disadvantages in Imitating Resources. Why might a competing firm facing a cost disadvantage in imitating a firm's resources? A variety of authors have studied a range of reasons why imitation might be costly.[25] Four of these reasons are discussed here.

Unique Historical Conditions. It may be that the low-cost acquisition or development of a resource for a particular firm depended on certain unique historical conditions. The ability of firms to acquire, develop, and exploit resources often depends on their place in time and space. Once time and history pass, firms that do not have space-and-time-dependent resources face a significant cost disadvantage in obtaining and developing them, because doing so would require these other firms to re-create history. Dierickx and Cool suggest that these resources have important **time-compression diseconomies.**[26]

Consider, for example, Caterpillar, the heavy-duty construction equipment firm. During the years just before the entry of the United States into World War II, the federal government decided that it would need a primary supplier of construction equipment to build and maintain military bases and landing fields throughout the world. This single supplier not only would need to build high-quality construction equipment but also would need to develop an effective and efficient global service and supply network to support construction efforts throughout the world. At the time, no construction equipment firm in the world had this global service and supply network.

After a brief competition among several medium-sized construction equipment firms, the federal government chose Caterpillar as its primary supplier. The government agreed to pay Caterpillar high enough prices for its equipment to enable Caterpillar to develop the required worldwide service and supply network. Caterpillar gladly accepted this opportunity and went about building high-quality construction equipment, along with a new worldwide service and supply network.

After the war, Caterpillar was the only firm in the world with a worldwide service and supply network. Indeed, Caterpillar still advertises its ability to deliver any part, for any piece of Caterpillar equipment, to any place in the world, in under 2 days. By using this valuable resource, Caterpillar was able to become the dominant firm in the heavy-construction-equipment industry. Even today, despite recessions and labor strife, Caterpillar remains the market-share leader in virtually every category of heavy-construction equipment.[27]

Now consider the position of a firm trying to compete with Caterpillar by duplicating its worldwide service and supply network. In order to develop this network at the same cost as Caterpillar, this competing firm would have to receive the same kind of government support that Caterpillar received during World War II. This kind of support is not likely to be forthcoming. A firm might decide that, in order to build this network at low cost, it must simply re-create World War II. This would be, to say the least, difficult to do and very costly to imitate.

Interestingly, although no firm has ever been able to duplicate Caterpillar's global service and supply network directly, other firms have been successful in this industry by competing in ways that did not require this costly-to-imitate resource. These competitors have developed resources that are substitutes for Caterpillar's global service and supply network. In particular, Komatsu, the Japanese construction equipment firm, circumvented the need to have a highly developed global service and supply network by simply building construction equipment that broke down less frequently.[28]

There are at least two ways that unique historical circumstances can give a firm a sustained competitive advantage. First, it may be that a particular firm is the first in an industry to recognize and exploit an opportunity, and being first gives a firm one or more of the first-mover advantages discussed in Chapter 4. Thus, although in principle other firms in an industry could have exploited an opportunity, that only one firm did so makes it more costly for other firms to imitate this original firm.

A second way that history can have an effect on a firm builds on the concept of **path dependence.**[29] A process is said to be path-dependent when events early in the evolution of a process have significant effects on subsequent events. In the evolution of competitive advantage, path dependence suggests that a firm may gain a competitive advantage in the current period based on the acquisition and development of resources in earlier periods. In these earlier periods, it was often not clear what the full future value of particular resources would be. Because of this uncertainty, firms are able to acquire or develop these resources for less than what will turn out to be their full value. However, once the full value of these resources is revealed, other firms seeking to acquire or develop these resources will need to pay their full known value, which (in general) will be greater than the costs incurred by the firm that acquired or developed these resources in some earlier period. The cost of acquiring both duplicate and substitute resources rise once their full value becomes known.

Consider, for example, a firm that purchased land for ranching some time ago and discovered a rich supply of oil on this land in the current period. Just as Ricardo would suggest, the difference between the value of this land as a supplier of oil (high) and the value of this land for ranching (low) is an economic rent for this firm. Moreover, other firms attempting to acquire this or adjacent land will now have to pay for the full value of the land in its use as a supply of oil (high) and thus will be at a cost disadvantage compared to the firm that acquired it some time ago for ranching.

Causal Ambiguity. A second reason why a firm's resources and capabilities may be costly to imitate is that imitating firms may not understand the relationship between the resources and capabilities controlled by a firm and that firm's competitive advantage. In other words, the relationship between firm resources and capabilities and competitive advantage may be causally ambiguous.

At first, it seems unlikely that causal ambiguity about the sources of competitive advantage for a firm would ever exist. Managers in a firm seem likely to understand the sources of their own competitive advantage. If managers in one firm understand the relationship between resources and competitive advantage, then it seems likely that managers in other firms will also be able to discover these relationships and thus will have a clear understanding of which resources and capabilities they should duplicate or seek substitutes for. If there are no other sources of cost disadvantage for imitating firms, imitation should lead to competitive parity.[30]

However, managers in a particular firm may not always fully understand the relationship between the resources and capabilities they control and competitive advantage. This lack of understanding might occur for at least three reasons. First, it may be that the resources and capabilities generate competitive advantage are so taken for granted, so much a part of the day-to-day experience of managers in a firm, that these managers are unaware of them. Itami calls these kinds of taken-for-granted organizational characteristics **invisible assets.**[31] Organizational resources and capabilities such as teamwork among top managers, organizational culture, relationships among other employees, and relationships with customers and suppliers may be "invisible" in this sense.[32] If managers in firms that have such capabilities do not understand their relationship to competitive advantage, managers in other firms face significant challenges in understanding which resources they should imitate.

Second, managers may have multiple hypotheses about which resources and capabilities enable their firm to gain a competitive advantage, but they may be unable to evaluate which of these resources and capabilities, alone or in combination, actually create the competitive advantage. For example, if one asks successful entrepreneurs what enabled them to become successful, they are likely to reply with hypotheses such as "hard work, willingness to take risks, and a high-quality top management team." However, if one asks what happened to unsuccessful entrepreneurs, they too are likely to suggest that their firms were characterized by "hard work, willingness to take risks, and a high-quality top management team." It may be that "hard work, willingness to take risks, and a high-quality top management team" are important resources and capabilities for entrepreneurial firm success. However, other factors may also play a role. Without rigorous experiments, it is difficult to establish which of these resources have a causal relationship with competitive advantage and which do not.

Finally, it may be that not just a few resources and capabilities enable a firm to gain a competitive advantage, but that literally thousands of these organizational attributes, bundled together, generate these advantages. Dierickx and Cool emphasize the importance of the **interconnectedness of asset stocks** and **asset mass efficiencies** as barriers to imitation. When the resources and capabilities that generate competitive advantage are complex networks of relationships among individuals, groups, and technology, imitation can be costly.

Historically, the field of strategic management has been enamored with the ability that some firms have to make correct "big decisions." This emphasis on "big" strategic decisions as the source of sustained competitive advantage reflects the original emphasis on general managers discussed in Section 5.1. The success of some organizations may be traceable to their ability to make correct big decisions (for example, IBM's decision about the 360 series in the 1960s, Boeing's decision about the 747 in the 1970s). In other cases, however, competitive advantage depends not on the ability to make a few big decisions well but on the ability to make numerous small decisions well. The ability to make these numerous small decisions well is almost invisible to those outside the firm, for each of these decisions, by itself, is inconsequential. Collectively, however, they may provide a firm a competitive advantage that is costly to imitate.

Consider, for example, The Mailbox, Inc., a very successful firm in the bulk mailing business in Dallas, Texas. If there ever was a business in which it seems unlikely that a firm would have sustained competitive advantages, it is bulk mailing. Firms in this industry gather mail from customers, sort it by Zip Code, and then take it to the post office to be mailed. Where is the competitive advantage? Yet The Mailbox has enjoyed an enormous market share advantage in the Dallas–Fort Worth area for several years. Why?

When asked, senior managers at The Mailbox have some difficulty explaining their success. Indeed, they can point to no "big decisions" they have made to generate this advantage. However, as one examines their finance function, their operations, their human resource function, their marketing and sales function, as well as the way they treat their employees, it becomes clear that The Mailbox's success depends not on the ability to do one thing well but rather on the ability to do the hundreds of thousands of things needed to run a bulk mailing business well. Individually, each one of these resources and capabilities is not costly to imitate. Collectively, however, they are very costly to imitate. These hundreds of thousands of resources and capabilities are difficult to describe. Their relationship with this firm's overall competitive advantage is not clear. Firms seeking to imitate The Mailbox's success face significant challenges in even understanding what they might want to imitate, let alone how they should go about imitating this firm.[33]

Whenever the sources of competitive advantage for a firm are widely diffused across people, locations, and processes in a firm, those sources of competitive advantage will be costly to imitate. Perhaps the best example of such a resource is knowledge itself. To the extent that valuable knowledge about a firm's products, processes, customers, and so on, is widely diffused throughout an organization, competitors will have difficulty imitating that knowledge and it can be a source of sustained competitive advantage. The recognition that knowledge can be an important resource has led some to suggest that the resource-based view of the firm should actually be called the knowledge-based view of the firm. However, although knowledge is clearly an important resource for firms, it is not the only resource that a firm can control that can generate competitive advantages.[34]

Social Complexity. A third reason that a firm's resources and capabilities may be costly to imitate is that they may be socially complex phenomena, beyond the ability of firms to systematically manage and influence. When competitive advantages are based on such complex social phenomena, the ability of other firms to imitate these resources and capabilities either through direct duplication or substitution is significantly constrained. Efforts to influence these kinds of phenomena are likely to be much more costly than they would be if these phenomena developed in a natural way over time in a firm.[35]

A wide variety of firm resources and capabilities may be socially complex. Examples include the interpersonal relations among managers in a firm, a firm's culture, and a firm's reputation among suppliers and customers.[36] Notice that in most of these cases it is possible to specify how these socially complex resources add value to a firm. Thus there is little or no causal ambiguity surrounding the link between these firm resources and capabilities and competitive advantage. However, understanding that an organizational culture with certain attributes or quality relations among managers can improve a firm's efficiency and effectiveness does not necessarily imply that firms that lack these attributes can engage in systematic effort to create them, or that low-cost substitutes for them exist. For the time being, such social engineering may be beyond the abilities of most firms. At the very least, such social engineering is likely to be much more costly than it would be if socially complex resources evolved naturally within a firm.[37]

This discussion does not mean to suggest that complex resources and capabilities do not change and evolve in an organization. They clearly do. Nor does this discussion mean to suggest that managers can never radically alter an organization's socially complex resources and capabilities. Such transformational leaders do seem to exist and do have an enormous effect on the socially complex resources and capabilities in a firm. As suggested earlier, CEOs such as Jack Welch and Bill Gates seem to have the attributes of transformational leaders, as did the late Robert Goizueta at Coca-Cola and Arthur Martinez at Sears Roebuck. However, transformational leaders themselves are socially complex phenomena. The fact that a leader in one firm can transform the firm's socially complex resources and capabilities does not necessarily mean that other firms will be able to duplicate this feat at low cost. It may even be the case that although a particular leader may be able to transform the socially complex resources and capabilities in one firm, this same leader will be unable to transform the socially complex resources and capabilities in another firm.[38]

Although the ability of socially complex resources and capabilities to generate sustained competitive advantages has been emphasized so far, *nonvaluable* socially complex resources and capabilities can create sustained competitive *disadvantages* for a firm. For example, large integrated steel firms, such as United States Steel, are saddled with organizational cultures, values, and management traditions that prevent them from adopting new technologies in a timely and efficient manner. These firms face significant competitive disadvantages compared to mini-mill producers such as Nucor, Florida Steel, North Star Steel, and Chaparral.[39]

It is interesting to note that firms seeking to imitate complex physical technology often do not face the cost disadvantages of imitating complex social phenomena. A great deal of physical technology (machine tools, robots, and so forth) can be purchased in supply markets. Even when a firm develops its own unique physical technology, reverse engineering tends to diffuse this technology among competing firms in a low-cost manner. Indeed, the costs of imitating a successful physical technology are often lower than the costs of developing a new technology.[40]

Although physical technology is usually not costly to imitate, the application of this technology in a firm is likely to call for a wide variety of socially complex organizational resources and capabilities. These organizational resources may be costly to imitate, and, if they are valuable and rare, the combination of physical and socially complex resources may be a source of sustained competitive advantage.

For example, most medium-size and large firms own management information systems that provide information about accounting performance, personnel, and operations. The computers, other hardware, and software that are used in these systems can usually be purchased. Even customized software developed by a firm can be imitated (by direct duplication or by a firm developing equivalent substitute software) without a significant cost disadvantage. In some firms, however, management information systems are tightly integrated with management decision making, information systems managers have close working relationships with line managers, and the management information system is a vital day-to-day tool in running the firm. These kinds of firms are likely to have a competitive advantage compared to firms that own a management information system but do not fully utilize it. Firms at a competitive disadvantage can purchase the most up-to-date hardware and software, but these purchases by themselves will not generate competitive parity, because it is the socially complex link between the management information system and other parts of the organization that is the source of the advantage.[41]

Patents.   At first glance, it might appear that a firm's patents would make it very costly for competitors to imitate a firm's products.[42] Patents do have this effect in some industries. For example, patents in the pharmaceutical industry effectively foreclose other firms from marketing the same drug until a firm's patents expire. Patents raised the cost of imitation in the instant photography market as well.

From another point of view, however, a firm's patents may decrease, rather than increase, the costs of imitation. This is especially true for product patents and less true for patents that attempt to protect a process from imitation. When a firm files for patent protection, it is forced to reveal a significant amount of information about its product. Governments require this information to ensure that the technology in question is patentable. In obtaining a patent, a firm may provide important information to competitors about how to imitate its technology.

Moreover, as suggested in Chapter 4, most technological developments in an industry are diffused throughout firms in that industry in a relatively brief period of time, even if the technology in question is patented and patented technology is not immune to low-cost imitation. Patents may restrict direct duplication for a time, but they may actually increase the chances of substitution by functionally equivalent technologies.[43]

Although patents may not be immune to low-cost imitation, the skills and abilities that enable a firm to develop numerous new products or services over time can be a source of sustained competitive advantage even though any one of these products or services may be imitated. Consider, for example, the performance of Sony. Most observers agree that Sony possesses some special management and coordination skills that enable it to conceive, design, and manufacture high-quality miniaturized consumer electronics. However, virtually every time Sony brings out a new miniaturized product, several of its competitors quickly duplicate that product through reverse engineering, thereby reducing Sony's technological advantage. In what way can Sony's socially complex miniaturization resources and capabilities be a source of sustained competitive advantage when most of Sony's products are quickly imitated through direct duplication?

After Sony introduces each new product, it experiences a rapid increase in profits attributable to the new product's unique features. This increase, however, leads other firms to reverse-engineer the Sony product and introduce their own version. Increased competition results in a reduction in the profits associated with a new product. Thus at the level of individual products, Sony apparently enjoys only temporary competitive advantages. However, looking at the total returns earned by Sony across all of its new products over time makes clear the source of Sony's sustained competitive advantage: By exploiting its resources and capabilities in miniaturization, Sony is able to constantly introduce new and exciting personal electronics products. No one of these products generates a sustained competitive advantage. Over time, however, and across several such product introductions, Sony's resource and capability advantages lead to sustained competitive advantages.[44]

The Question of Organization

A firm's potential for competitive advantage depends on the value, rarity, and imitability of its resources and capabilities. However, to realize this potential fully, a firm must be organized to exploit its resources and capabilities. These observations lead to the question of organization: Is a firm organized to exploit the full competitive potential of its resources and capabilities?

Numerous components of a firm's organization are relevant to the question of organization, including its formal reporting structure, its explicit management control systems, and its compensation policies. These components are often called **complementary resources and capabilities** because they have limited ability to generate competitive advantage in isolation. However, in combination with other resources and capabilities, they can enable a firm to realize its full potential for competitive advantage potential.[45]

For example, it has already been suggested that much of Caterpillar's sustained competitive advantage in the heavy construction industry can be traced to its becoming the primary supplier of this equipment to Allied forces during World War II. However, if Caterpillar's management had not taken advantage of this opportunity by implementing a global formal reporting structure, global inventory and other control systems, and compensation policies that created incentives for employees to work around the world, then Caterpillar's potential for competitive advantage would not have been fully realized. By themselves, these attributes of Caterpillar's organization could not be a source of competitive advantage—that is, adopting a global organizational form was relevant for Caterpillar only because it was pursuing a global opportunity. However, this organization was essential for Caterpillar to realize its full competitive advantage potential.

In a similar way, much of Wal-Mart's continuing competitive advantage in the discount retailing industry can be attributed to its early entry into rural markets in the southern United States. However, to exploit this geographic advantage fully, Wal-Mart needed to implement appropriate reporting structures, control systems, and compensation policies. One component of Wal-Mart's organization—its point-of-purchase inventory control system—is being imitated by Kmart and thus by itself is not likely to be a source of sustained competitive advantage. However, this inventory control system has enabled Wal-Mart to take full advantage of its rural locations by decreasing the probability of stock-outs in those locations.

Having an appropriate organization in place has enabled Caterpillar and Wal-Mart to realize the full competitive advantage potential of their other resources and capabilities. Having an inappropriate organization in place prevented Xerox from taking full advantage of some of its most critical valuable, rare, and costly-to-imitate resources and capabilities.

Through the 1960s and early 1970s, Xerox invested in a series of very innovative technology development research efforts. Xerox managed this research effort by creating a stand-alone research center in Palo Alto, California (Palo Alto Research Center—PARC), and by assembling a large group of highly creative and innovative scientists and engineers to work there. Left to their own devices, these scientists and engineers at Xerox PARC developed an amazing array of technological innovations—the personal computer, the "mouse," Windows-type software, the laser printer, the "paperless office," Ethernet, and so forth. In retrospect, it is clear that the market potential of these technologies was enormous. Moreover, because they were developed at Xerox PARC, they were rare. Xerox might have been able to gain some important first-mover advantages if the organization had been able to translate these technologies into products, thereby increasing the cost to other firms of imitating these technologies.

However, although Xerox possessed very valuable, rare, and costly-to-imitate resources and capabilities in the technologies developed at Xerox PARC, it did not have an organization in place to take advantage of these resources. No structure existed whereby Xerox PARC innovations could become known to managers at Xerox.

Indeed, most Xerox managers—even many senior managers—were unaware of these technological developments through the mid-1970s. Once they finally became aware of them, very few of the technologies survived Xerox's highly bureaucratic product development process, a process whereby product development projects were divided into hundreds of minute tasks and progress in each task was reviewed by dozens of large committees. Even innovations that survived the product development process were not exploited by Xerox managers, because management compensation at Xerox depended almost exclusively on maximizing current revenue. Short-term profitability was relatively less important in compensation calculations, and the development of markets for future sales and profitability was essentially irrelevant. Xerox's formal reporting structure, its explicit management control systems, and its compensation policies were all inconsistent with exploiting the valuable, rare, and costly-to-imitate resources developed at Xerox PARC. Not surprisingly, Xerox failed to exploit any of these potential sources of sustained competitive advantage.[46]

5.3 APPLYING THE VRIO FRAMEWORK

The questions of value, rarity, imitability, and organization can be brought together into a single framework to understand the return potential associated with exploiting any of a firm's resources or capabilities. This is done in Table 5.2. The relationship of the VRIO framework to strengths and weaknesses is presented in Table 5.3.

If a resource or capability controlled by a firm is not valuable, that resource will not enable a firm to choose or implement strategies that exploit environmental opportunities or neutralize environmental threats. Organizing to exploit this resource will increase a firm's costs or decrease the amount customers are willing to pay. These types of resources are weaknesses. Firms will either have to fix these weaknesses or avoid using them when choosing and implementing strategies. If firms do exploit these kinds of resources and capabilities, they can expect to put themselves at a competitive disadvantage compared to firms that either do not possess these nonvaluable resources or do not use them in conceiving and implementing strategies.

If a resource or capability is valuable but not rare, exploiting this resource in conceiving and implementing strategies will generate competitive parity. However, failure to exploit these kinds of resources can put a firm at a competitive disadvantage. In this sense, valuable-but-not-rare resources can be thought of as organizational strengths.

TABLE 5.2   The VRIO Framework

Is a resource or capability. . .

Valuable?	Rare?	Costly to Imitate?	Exploited by Organization?	Competitive Implications
No	—	—	No	Competitive disadvantage
Yes	No	—	—	Competitive parity
Yes	Yes	No	—	Temporary competitive advantage
Yes	Yes	Yes	Yes	Sustained competitive advantage

TABLE 5.3   The Relationship Between the VRIO Framework and Organizational Strengths and Weaknesses

Is a resource or capability...

Valuable?	*Rare?*	*Costly to Imitate?*	*Exploited by Organization?*	*Strength or Weakness*
No	—	—	No	Weakness
Yes	No	—	—	Strength
Yes	Yes	No	—	Strength and distinctive competence
Yes	Yes	Yes	Yes	Strength and sustainable distinctive competence

If a resource or capability is valuable and rare but not costly to imitate, exploiting this resource will generate a temporary competitive advantage for a firm. A firm that exploits this kind of resource is, in an important sense, gaining a first-mover advantage, because it is the first firm that is able to exploit a particular resource. However, once competing firms observe this competitive advantage, they will be able to acquire or develop the resources needed to implement this strategy through direct duplication or substitution at no cost disadvantage compared to the first-moving firm. Over time, any competitive advantage that the first mover obtained will be competed away as other firms imitate the resources needed to compete. However, between the time a firm gains a competitive advantage by exploiting a valuable and rare but imitable resource or capability, and the time that competitive advantage is competed away through imitation, the first-moving firm shows superior performance. Consequently, this type of resource or capability can be thought of as an organizational strength and distinctive competence.

If a resource or capability is valuable, rare, and costly to imitate, exploiting this resource will generate a sustained competitive advantage. In this case, competing firms face a significant cost disadvantage in imitating a successful firm's resources and capabilities, and thus cannot imitate this firm's strategies. As suggested earlier in this chapter, this cost advantage may reflect the unique history of the successful firm, causal ambiguity about which resources to imitate, or the socially complex nature of these resources and capabilities. In any case, attempts to compete away the advantages of firms that exploit these resources will not generate superior performance for imitating firms. Even if these firms are able to acquire or develop the resources or capabilities in question, the very high costs of doing so will put them at a competitive disadvantage compared to the firm that already possesses the valuable, rare, and costly-to-imitate resources. These kinds of resources and capabilities are organizational strengths and sustainable distinctive competencies.

The question of organization operates as an adjustment factor in the VRIO framework. For example, if a firm has a valuable, rare, and costly-to-imitate resource and capability but fails to organize itself to take full advantage of this resource, some of its potential competitive advantage may be lost (this is the Xerox example).

To examine how the VRIO framework can be applied in analyzing real strategic issues, consider the examples of Dell Computer and competition in the soft drink industry.

Dell Computer

Earlier in this chapter, it was suggested that Dell Computer was able to gain a sustained competitive advantage in a very competitive industry, the personal computer industry through the 1990's. It is possible to use value-chain analysis, in combination with the resource-based view of the firm and the VRIO framework, to begin to identify the sources of that advantage. Figure 5.5 applies a version of the generic value chain developed by McKinsey & Company (see Figure 5.3) to Dell Computer.[47]

Notice that Dell is not highly vertically integrated. Indeed, one of the critical aspects of Dell's ability to generate economic value has been that it has adopted a strategy that enables it to focus only on those aspects of its operations in which it has either a temporary or a sustained competitive advantage. This approach to vertical integration is discussed in more detail in Chapter 10.

Dell has at least a temporary competitive advantage in purchasing. This advantage stems from several factors, including Dell's volume of sales, which makes it an important customer to its suppliers. Dell has been able to use its volume to obtain price reductions on many of the supplies it purchases. However, although its size is a valuable asset in this function, it is neither rare nor costly to imitate. After all, other PC firms have sales almost as large as Dell and thus enjoy similar volume advantages.

More important than Dell's size is the way that Dell manages its purchasing function. Dell purchases just the supplies it needs to complete production and expects its suppliers—both large and small—to make numerous deliveries to its production facilities, sometimes several times a day. In this way, Dell has been able to shift the costs of having an inventory of supplies from itself to its suppliers. This approach to purchasing has been relatively unusual (that is, rare) in the personal computer industry. However, it is becoming the standard for efficient manufacturing in large numbers of industries,

FIGURE 5.5   An Extended Generic Value Chain for Dell Computers with an Application of the VRIO Framework

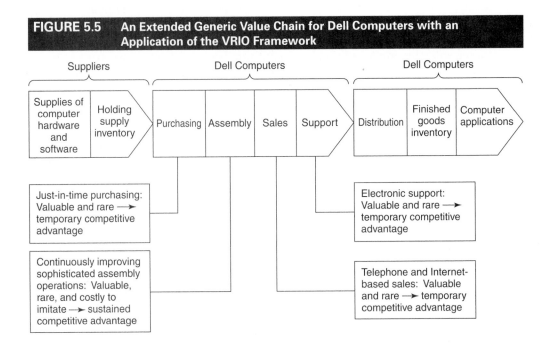

including the automobile industry. For this reason, although purchasing may be a source of temporary competitive advantage, it seems imitable, and thus not likely to be a source of sustained competitive advantage.

Dell assembly operations may have also been a source of at least a temporary competitive advantage. Attention to detail, increased speed and efficiency, and high quality are all built into Dell assembly operations. This is so even though Dell assembles customized personal computers with numerous different option combinations available. For example, in building one type of computer, Dell engineers were able to reduce the number of times a computer had to be touched during the assembly process from 130 to 60. In another stage of the operation, Dell was able to modify the assembly process so that instead of requiring six screws to secure a subassembly, only a single screw was required—without the loss of quality. This attention to detail has led Dell to obtain over 200 patents on assembly operations. And unlike product patents, patents on assembly operations are often costly to imitate because they are usually part of an integrated production system. Using language developed earlier in this chapter, Dell's advantage in assembly is based on numerous small decisions, decisions that are virtually invisible to competitors. Moreover, Dell's relentless emphasis on process improvement is deeply engrained in its socially complex culture. These attributes of assembly process suggest that it is valuable and rare. They may also be costly to imitate, at least in the short to medium term

Sales and support at Dell are both managed through telephone and Internet operations. Although Dell has held a head start in these areas of its business, it is unlikely that other personal computer firms ignored similar opportunities.[48] However, Dell currently does have a reputation for its direct-to-customer capabilities. This reputation among customers will probably mean that Dell will continue to enjoy these advantages beyond the time that competitors actually catch up to Dell's sales and service strategy (see Chapter 7 for a discussion of reputation as a basis of product differentiation).

Dell outsources distribution, transportation, inventory holding, and computer applications. Again, this enables Dell to concentrate on only those aspects of the value chain that are sources of either temporary or sustained competitive advantage. Given its strategy, it is not surprising that Dell's performance has been outstanding—even though it operates in a very competitive industry. However, it seems likely that many of the resources that have enabled Dell to implement its strategy may diffuse among its competitors in the long run. After all, HP, Lenovo, and many other PC firms have watched Dell carefully and have learned how to operate more efficiently. If this analysis is correct, then Dell's period of sustained superior performance may be ending. Dell's recent performance suggests that this might be the case.

Competition in the U.S. Soft Drink Industry

The decades-long "cola wars" between Pepsi and Coke in the United States and throughout the world are well known. Huge advertising campaigns, celebrity endorsements, sponsorship of major sporting events, and millions of dollars spent on Super Bowl television commercials are all part of this history. Over the years, PepsiCo and the Coca-Cola Corporation have become two of the most efficient and effective marketing organizations in the world.[49]

One episode in the cola wars exemplifies this competition between Coke and Pepsi. Beginning in the 1970s, Pepsi ran numerous blind taste tests among consumers. Results of these tests suggest that, on average, consumers preferred the taste of Pepsi to the taste of Coke. Pepsi, of course, wanted to use these taste preferences in its marketing efforts to try to catch up to or even surpass Coke's sales in certain markets. To this end, over the years Pepsi developed a comprehensive marketing campaign called the "Pepsi Challenge." After choosing a market, Pepsi would increase advertising, increase access to coupons, discount prices, fly in celebrities, and increase sponsorship of local events in that market, all under the Pepsi Challenge banner.

One of the markets that Pepsi chose for the Pepsi Challenge was the Dallas–Fort Worth, Texas, market. In the Dallas–Fort Worth market there are three important soft drinks: Coke, Pepsi, and Dr Pepper. At that time, Dr Pepper was still an independent company headquartered in Dallas. Although it had national and international distribution aspirations, Dr Pepper had its strongest sales in the southern part of the United States, especially in Texas.

In implementing the Pepsi Challenge, Pepsi tried to increase its market share in the Dallas–Fort Worth market. There is little doubt that, in the soft drink industry, market share is very valuable. Aside from the bottling operations owned by PepsiCo, Coca-Cola, and independent bottlers, there is relatively little manufacturing in the soft drink industry. The primary way that soft drink firms can increase their sales and profitability in soft drinks, per se, is to increase their market share through marketing efforts like the Pepsi Challenge.

As Pepsi implemented the challenge to acquire market share in Dallas–Fort Worth, the organization brought to bear an enormous wealth of resources and capabilities, including high-quality marketing and sales staffs, an excellent distribution system, and sufficient financial backing to do the job. All these resources were valuable, but were they also rare? Put another way, was there any resource or capability that Pepsi could use to implement the Pepsi Challenge that Coca-Cola could not use to defend its market share? The answer is "probably not." Both firms possessed enormous marketing, sales, and distribution skills, and both had enormous financial strength. It seems likely that Coke could quickly imitate any action that Pepsi took. Assuming that both these firms are efficiently organized (a reasonable assumption in this case), the resources and capabilities that Pepsi brought to bear in the Pepsi Challenge were valuable but not rare (compared to Coke's resources and capabilities), and thus would generate only competitive parity.

The situation was very different in the competition for market share between Pepsi and Dr Pepper. Resources and capabilities that would enable Pepsi to acquire share were still valuable. However, Pepsi had a broad range of resources that Dr Pepper did not have. Moreover, it would be very costly for Dr Pepper to acquire resources comparable to Pepsi's reputation in the market, huge advertising budget, and high-powered distribution network. Thus, in the competition between Pepsi and Dr Pepper for market share, Pepsi possessed not only valuable but also rare and costly-to-imitate resources and capabilities. In this competitive battle, Pepsi seemed likely to gain sustained competitive advantage.

The results of the Pepsi Challenge in Dallas–Fort Worth are quite interesting. After six months of intensive competition, including retail discounts, coupons, and increased advertising, Coke's market share increased from 33 percent to 37 percent, Pepsi's share doubled from 7 percent to 14 percent, and Dr Pepper's share went down "significantly." However, after six months of the Pepsi Challenge, the retail price of soft drinks in this market was half the pre-Challenge level. Pepsi doubled its market share but cut its revenue in half to do so. This outcome is very consistent with competitive parity. Apparently, both Pepsi and Coke took market share away from Dr Pepper. However, the cost of acquiring that share increased so that the cost of acquiring share approximately equaled its value and thus was a source of competitive parity for Pepsi (and Coke) in Dallas–Fort Worth.

Each of the firms in this competition learned some valuable lessons. Dr Pepper learned that if it wanted to be a major player in the soft drink industry, it would need to develop resources and capabilities that rivaled those of Pepsi and Coke. It was very unlikely that Dr Pepper could develop these resources on its own; thus Dr Pepper has gone through a series of acquisitions, joint ventures, and other cooperative activities to try to develop a resource base large enough to survive in this industry. First, Dr Pepper merged with 7UP. In 1995, Britain's Cadbury Schweppes acquired this merged firm.

PepsiCo and Coca-Cola learned that head-to-head competition for market share is not likely to be a source of competitive advantage for firms with equally matched resources and capabilities. Instead of continuing this head-to-head competition, PepsiCo and Coca-Cola have searched for alternative strategic directions. PepsiCo has diversified away from sole reliance on soft drinks and has moved into other, noncola drinks, the fast-food business, and the snack-food business. Although the fast-food business has been divested, Pepsi's snack-food operations have been very profitable. In its cola operations, Pepsi continues to seek out younger cola drinkers. Coca-Cola, after abandoning some unsuccessful diversification moves, remains focused on cola and other soft drinks but now emphasizes international sales. Indeed, over 60 percent of Coca-Cola's profits come from overseas sales, where Pepsi is not as strong a competitor. In the domestic market, Coca-Cola has steered its marketing efforts more toward older cola drinkers. All this is not to suggest that Pepsi and Coca-Cola no longer compete in the soft drink industry. They clearly do. However, both of these firms seem to have backed away from the intense rivalry of the cola wars.

5.4 IMPLICATIONS OF THE RESOURCE-BASED VIEW

The resource-based view and the VRIO framework can be applied to individual firms to understand whether these firms will gain competitive advantages, how sustainable these competitive advantages are likely to be, and what the sources of these competitive advantages are. In this way, the resource-based view and the VRIO framework can be understood as important complements to the five forces analysis described in Chapter 3 and the opportunities analysis described in Chapter 4 for analyzing the competitive situation of individual firms.

However, beyond what these frameworks can say about the competitive performance of a particular firm, the resource-based view has some broader implications for managers seeking to gain competitive advantages. Some of these broader implications are listed in Table 5.4.

TABLE 5.4 Broader Implications of the Resource-based View

1. The responsibility for competitive advantage in a firm:
   - Competitive advantage is every employee's responsibility.
2. Competitive parity and competitive advantage:
   - If all a firm does is what its competition does, it can gain only competitive parity.
   - In gaining competitive advantage, it is better for a firm to exploit its own valuable, rare, and costly-to-imitate resources than to imitate the valuable and rare resources of a competitor.
3. Difficult-to-implement strategies:
   - As long as the cost of strategy implementation is less than the value of strategy implementation, the relative cost of implementing a strategy is more important for competitive advantage than the absolute cost of implementing a strategy.
   - Firms can systematically overestimate and underestimate their uniqueness.
4. Socially complex resources:
   - Not only can employee empowerment, organizational culture, and teamwork be valuable, they can also be sources of sustained competitive advantage.
5. The role of the organization:
   - Organization should support the use of valuable, rare, and costly-to-imitate resources. If conflicts between these attributes of a firm arise, change the organization.

Where Does the Responsibility for Competitive Advantage in a Firm Reside?

First, the resource-based view suggests that competitive advantages can be found in several of the various resources and capabilities a firm controls. These resources and capabilities are not limited to those that are controlled directly by a firm's senior managers. Thus, the responsibility for creating, nurturing, and exploiting valuable, rare, and costly-to-imitate resources and capabilities for competitive advantage is not restricted to senior managers. Rather, every employee in a firm should accept the responsibility of creating, nurturing, and exploiting resources and capabilities that can generate competitive advantages for a firm. To do this, employees should go beyond defining their jobs in functional terms to defining their jobs in competitive and economic terms.

Consider a simple example.[50] In a recent visit to a very successful automobile manufacturing plant, the plant manager was asked to describe his job responsibilities. He said, "My job is to manage this plant in order to help the firm make and sell the best cars in the world." In response to a similar question, the person in charge of the manufacturing line also said, "My job is to manage this manufacturing line in order to help the firm make and sell the best cars in the world." A janitor was asked to describe his job responsibilities. Although he had not been present in the two earlier interviews, the janitor responded, "My job is to keep this facility clean in order to help the firm make and sell the best cars in the world."

Which of these three employees is most likely to be a source of sustained competitive advantage for this firm? Certainly, the plant manager and the manufacturing line manager *should* define their jobs in terms of helping the firm make and sell the best cars in the world. However, it is unlikely that their responses to this question would be any different than the responses of other senior managers at other manufacturing plants around the world. Put differently, while the definition of these two manager's jobs in terms of enabling the firm to make and sell the best cars in the world is valuable, it is unlikely to be rare and thus is likely to be a source of competitive parity, not competitive advantage. On the other hand, a janitor who defines his or her job as helping the firm make and sell the best cars in the world instead of simply cleaning the facility is, most would agree, quite unusual. Because it is rare, it might be a source of at least a temporary competitive advantage.

Of course, the value created by one janitor defining his or her job in these competitive terms rather than functional terms is not huge—but suppose that all the employees in this plant defined their jobs in these terms. Then the value that might be created could be substantial. Moreover, the organizational culture and tradition in a firm that would lead employees to define their jobs in this way is likely to be costly for other firms to imitate. Thus, if this approach to defining job responsibilities is broadly diffused in a particular plant, it seems likely to be valuable, rare, and costly to imitate and thus a source of sustained competitive advantage, assuming the firm is organized to take advantage of this unusual resource.

In the end, it is clear that competitive advantage is too important to remain the property of senior management alone. To the extent that employees throughout an organization are empowered to develop and exploit valuable, rare, and costly-to-imitate resources and capabilities in the accomplishment of their job responsibilities, a firm may actually be able to gain sustained competitive advantages.

Competitive Parity and Competitive Advantage

Second, the resource-based view suggests that if all a firm does is create value in the same way as its competitors, the best performance it can ever expect is competitive parity. To do better than competitive parity, firms must engage in valuable and rare activities. They must do things to create economic value that other firms have not even thought of, let alone implemented.

This is especially critical for firms that find themselves at a competitive disadvantage. Such firms should examine their more successful competition, understand what has made this competition so successful, and, when imitation is very low-cost, should imitate the successful actions of its competitors. In this sense, benchmarking a firm's performance against the performance of its competitors can be extremely important.

However, if this is all that a firm does, it can only expect to achieve competitive parity. Gaining competitive advantage depends on a firm discovering its own unique resources and capabilities and how they can be used in choosing and implementing strategies. For a firm seeking competitive advantage, it is better to be excellent in how it develops and exploits its own unique resources and capabilities than it is to be excellent in how it imitates the resources and capabilities of other firms.

This does not imply that firms must always be first movers to gain competitive advantages. As was suggested in Chapters 1 and 4, some firms develop valuable, rare, and costly-to-imitate resources and capabilities as efficient second movers—that is, rapidly imitating and improving on the product and technological innovations of other firms. Rather than suggesting that firms must always be first movers, the resource-based view suggests that, in order to gain competitive advantages, firms must implement strategies that rely on valuable, rare, and costly-to-imitate resources and capabilities, whatever those strategies or resources might be.

Difficult-to-Implement Strategies

Third, as firms contemplate different strategic options, they often ask how difficult and costly it will be to implement those strategies. As long as the cost of implementing a strategy is less than the value that a strategy creates, the resource-based view suggests that the critical question facing firms is not "Is a strategy easy to implement or not?" but rather is "Is this strategy easier for us to implement than it is for our competitors to implement?" Firms that already possess the valuable, rare, and costly-to-imitate resources needed to implement a strategy will, in general, find it easier (that is, less costly) to implement a strategy than firms that first have to develop the required resources and then implement the proposed strategy. For firms that already possess a resource, strategy implementation can be natural and swift.

In understanding the relative costs of implementing a strategy, firms can make two errors. First, they can overestimate the uniqueness of the resources they control. Although every firm's history is unique and no two management teams are exactly the same, this does not always mean that a firm's resources and capabilities will be rare. Firms with similar histories operating in similar industries will often develop similar capabilities. If a firm overestimates the rarity of its resources and capabilities, it can overestimate its ability to generate competitive advantages.

For example, when asked what their most critical sources of competitive advantage are, many managers will cite the quality of their top management team, the quality of their technology, and their commitment to excellence in all that they do. When pushed about their competitors, these same managers will admit that they too have high-quality top management teams, high-quality technology, and a commitment to excellence in all that they do. Although these three attributes of firms can be sources of competitive parity, they cannot be sources of competitive advantage.

Second, firms can sometimes underestimate their uniqueness and thus underestimate the extent to which the strategies they pursue can be sources of sustained competitive advantage. When firms possess valuable, rare, and costly-to-imitate resources, they may find it relatively easy to implement their strategies. Sometimes, firms that have found strategy implementation easy assume that other firms will also be able to easily implement these strategies. Of course, this is not the case if these resources controlled by a firm are, in fact, rare and costly to imitate.

Problems associated with underestimating the uniqueness of a firm are most common when a firm's resources and capabilities are invisible and taken for granted. In these settings, managers may not fully appreciate what it is that makes their firm special and thus not fully appreciate the competitive potential these resources create.

In general, firms must take great care not to overestimate or underestimate their uniqueness. An accurate assessment of the value, rarity, and imitability of a firm's resources is necessary to develop an accurate understanding of the relative costs of implementing a firm's strategies and thus the ability of those strategies to generate competitive advantages. Often, firms must employ outside assistance in helping them describe the rarity and imitability of their resources, even though managers in firms will generally be much more familiar with the resources controlled by a firm than outsiders. However, outsiders can provide a measure of objectivity in evaluating the uniqueness of a firm.

Socially Complex Resources

Over the last several decades, much has been written about the importance of employee empowerment, organizational culture, and teamwork for firm performance. Most of this work suggests that firms that empower employees, have an enabling culture, and encourage teamwork will, on average, make better strategic choices and implement them more efficiently than firms that do not have these organizational attributes. Using the language of the resource-based view, most of this work has suggested that employee empowerment, organizational culture, and teamwork, at least in some settings, are economically valuable.

Resource-based logic acknowledges the importance of the value of these organizational attributes. However, it also suggests that these socially complex resources and capabilities can be rare and costly to imitate—and it is their rarity and costly imitation that makes it possible for socially complex resources and capabilities to be sources of sustained competitive advantage.

Put differently, the resource-based view actually extends and broadens traditional analyses of the socially complex attributes of firms. Not only can these attributes be valuable, they can also be rare and costly to imitate and become sources of sustained competitive advantage. Several organizational behavior and human resource management scholars have become interested in understanding the implications of socially complex individual and organizational resources for sustained competitive advantage. Early empirical research in the area is consistent with resource-based expectations.

The Role of Organization

Finally, resource-based logic suggests that an organization's structure, control systems, and compensation policies should support and enable a firm's efforts to exploit fully the valuable, rare, and costly-to-imitate resources and capabilities it controls. These attributes of organization, by themselves, are usually not sources of sustained competitive advantage.

These observations suggest that if there is a conflict between these resources a firm controls and that firm's organization, the organization should be changed. Often, however, once a firm's structure, control systems, and compensation policies are put in place, they remain, regardless of whether they are consistent with the firm's underlying resources and capabilities. In such a setting, the firm will not be able to realize the full competitive potential of its underlying resource base.

To the extent that a firm's resources and capabilities are continuously evolving, its organizational structure, control systems, and compensation policies must also evolve. For these attributes of organization to evolve, managers must be aware of their link to the firm's resources and capabilities and of organizational alternatives. In each of the chapters in Parts II and III of this book, the organizational alternatives associated with different strategies will be discussed.

5.5 LIMITATIONS OF THE VRIO FRAMEWORK

The resource-based view of the firm and the VRIO framework presented in Table 5.2 provide a powerful tool for analyzing a firm's internal organizational strengths and weaknesses. However, this approach, like S-C-P–based models of the analysis of environmental threats and opportunities, has limitations. A discussion of three of the most important limitations follows.

Sustained Competitive Advantage and Environmental Upheaval

Earlier it was suggested that a sustained competitive advantage does not last forever, even though it is founded on valuable, rare, and costly-to-imitate resources and capabilities. If the threats and opportunities that face a firm in its competitive environment remain relatively stable, then a firm with these resources (if it is organized correctly) will be able to continue to exploit them to gain a competitive advantage. Also, if the types of threats and opportunities in a firm's environment evolve in predictable ways, a firm with these kinds of resources and capabilities will often be able to exploit and modify them to maintain a sustained competitive advantage. However, if a firm's threats and opportunities change in a rapid and *unpredictable* manner, it will often be unable to maintain a sustained competitive advantage.

These sudden and unpredictable changes in the threats and opportunities that a firm faces are called **Schumpeterian revolutions,** after Joseph Schumpeter, the economist who first described them and analyzed their economic consequences.[51] Schumpeterian revolutions have the effect of drastically changing the value of a firm's resources by changing the threats and opportunities that face the firm. This may happen because of unanticipated changes in demand, radical new technological developments, violent political upheavals, and other events. These are the hypercompetitive industries identified in Chapter 4.

Numerous industries are characterized by Schumpeterian revolutions. For example, the development of personal computers significantly altered the value of the manufacturing skills of typewriter companies. The development of electronic calculators significantly altered the value of the design and manufacturing skills of mechanical calculator firms. And the skills of manufacturing high-quality vinyl long-playing records changed in value because of the introduction of compact disc technology.

The resource-based view of the firm can help managers choose strategies to gain sustained competitive advantage only as long as the rules of the game in an industry remain relatively fixed. After a Schumpeterian revolution, however, what were weaknesses may become strengths and what were strengths may become weaknesses. Notice that the competitive advantages of firms in this context are not competed away through imitation. Rather, they are replaced through a Schumpeterian revolution. Thus sustained competitive advantages will not last forever even if they are not competed away through imitation; they can be displaced through revolutionary environmental changes.

Managerial Influence

A second limitation of the VRIO approach to studying organizational strengths and weaknesses is that it suggests that managers have a limited ability to create sustained competitive advantages. These limitations are summed up best, perhaps, by what might be called the **imitability paradox:** The less costly it is for managers in a firm to develop or acquire resources that could generate competitive advantage, the less likely it is that these resources will be a source of sustained competitive advantage. In general, if any firm can develop or acquire a set of valuable resources at no cost disadvantage, then those resources will be imitable and a source only of competitive parity in the long run.

What the imitability paradox suggests is that not all firms can gain sustained competitive advantages. Managers in firms that have developed valuable, rare, and costly-to-imitate resources or capabilities over long periods of time (because of path dependence, causal ambiguity, or social complexity) may be able to help their firms gain sustained competitive advantages. However, firms that do not have any of these special skills and capabilities, but attempt to acquire them without any cost disadvantage, will not gain sustained competitive advantages, because if one firm can acquire these resources, others will be able to as well.

Although the observation that not all firms can obtain a sustained competitive advantage does suggest some limitations on managers' ability to affect firm performance, it is consistent with most research on the performance of firms in various industries. In most industries, several firms (perhaps even the majority) apparently discover their own unique resources and capabilities and exploit them in ways that generate superior performance. However, there are often firms in an industry that are perpetually generating only competitive parity, or even competitive disadvantages. These perpetually failing firms simply have not developed valuable resources that would enable them to gain a sustained competitive advantage. Of course, at some point in the future, a Schumpeterian revolution may occur in these industries, making these perpetually losing firms suddenly able to gain competitive advantages and excel.[52]

The Unit of Analysis

In S-C-P–based models of environmental opportunities and threats, the unit of analysis is the industry. This unit of analysis has several advantages for strategic analysts, not the least of which is access to data. Most government reports about firms are organized into industry categories, making information about the number of rivals, the power of suppliers and buyers, and so forth, relatively accessible.

In resource-based models of organizational strengths and weaknesses, however, the unit of analysis shifts downward, to inside the firm. In these models the firm is thought of as a bundle of resources and capabilities, and the analysis of the return potential of these resources must be conducted one resource, or bundle of resources, at a time. Gaining access to this kind of intraorganizational information can be very difficult. These data problems are exacerbated when it is recognized that resources and capabilities can be utilized to generate sustained competitive advantages precisely because they are difficult to describe and are invisible.

In the face of these challenges, it is tempting to raise the level of analysis of a firm's strengths and weaknesses to the level of a firm and analyze the value, rarity, imitability, and organization of a firm's products or services. This kind of analysis can be helpful, but it also can be misleading. Research on the diffusion of product technology cited in Chapter 4 suggests that new products and services, with a few important exceptions, rapidly become diffused among a set of competing firms. However, as was suggested earlier for the Sony Corporation, although a firm's particular products may be imitated, that firm may still have a sustained competitive advantage based on its underlying abilities to be innovative and creative.

Thus, despite the significant challenges associated with firm resources as the unit of analysis in models of organizational strengths and weaknesses, a proper analysis seems to require an investigation of these intraorganizational phenomena. In the end, it is not surprising that understanding the implications of these intraorganizational resources is critical to completing an analysis of a firm.

5.6 SUMMARY

This chapter has developed a framework for analyzing a firm's organizational strengths and weaknesses. This framework is based on several literatures, including research on the effect of general managers on an organization, research on other types of distinctive competencies in a firm, work on Ricardian economics, and economic models of firm growth. The framework builds most directly on the resource-based view of the firm and on two critical assumptions: that firms have different resources and capabilities (the assumption of resource heterogeneity) and that these differences can persist over time (the assumption of resource immobility).

On the basis of these two assumptions, it has been suggested that the answers to four questions can be used to determine the competitive potential of a firm's resources and capabilities. The four questions that make up the VRIO framework are the question of value, the question of rarity, the question of imitability, and the question of organization. This VRIO framework has been applied to several real strategic situations. Three limitations of this approach—the effect of unanticipated changes in a firm's environment, limited managerial effect on performance, and data challenges associated with the unit of analysis—have also been discussed.

REVIEW QUESTIONS

1. Which approach to strategy formulation is more likely to generate economic profits: (a) evaluating environmental opportunities and threats and then developing resources and capabilities to exploit these opportunities and neutralize these threats; or (b) evaluating internal resources and capabilities and then searching for industries in which they can be exploited? Why?

2. Which firm will have a higher level of economic performance: (a) a firm with valuable, rare, and costly-to-imitate resources and capabilities operating in a very attractive indus-

try; or (b) a firm with valuable, rare, and costly-to-imitate resources and capabilities operating in a very unattractive industry? Assume both these firms are appropriately organized. Explain your answer.

3. Which is more critical to sustaining human life—water or diamonds? Why do firms that provide water to customers generally earn lower economic profits than firms that provide diamonds?

4. Will a firm that is currently experiencing competitive parity be able to gain sustained competitive advantages by studying another

firm that is currently experiencing sustained competitive advantage? Why or why not?

5. Your former college roommate calls you and asks to borrow $10,000 so that he can open a pizza restaurant in his hometown. He acknowledges that there is a high degree of rivalry in this market, that the cost of entry is low, and that there are numerous substitutes for pizza, but he believes that his pizza restaurant will have some sustained competitive advantages. For example, he is going to have sawdust on his floor, a variety of imported beers, and a late-night delivery service. Will you lend him the money? Why or why not?

ENDNOTES

1. Information on Dell Computers and the computer industry is taken from Brown, E. (1999). "America's most admired companies," *Fortune,* March 1, pp. 68+; Kirkpatrick, D. (1997). "Now everyone in PCs wants to be like Mike," *Fortune,* August 9, pp. 91+; Kirkpatrick, D. (1998). "The second coming of Apple," *Fortune,* November 8, pp. 86+; and "Ranked within states" (2006). "The Fortune 500," *Fortune,* April 17, pp. F1+.

2. See Ghemawat, P. (1986). "Wal-Mart stores' discount operations," Harvard Business School Case no. 9-387-018; Heskett, J. L., and R. H. Hallowell (1993). "Southwest Airlines: 1993 (A)," Harvard Business School Case no. 9-695-023; and Ghemawat, P., and H. J. Stander III (1992). "Nucor at a crossroads," Harvard Business School Case no. 9-793-039.

3. See Learned, E. P., C. R. Christensen, K. R. Andrews, and W. Guth (1969). *Business Policy.* Homewood, IL: Irwin.

4. See Curran, J. (1997). "GE Capital: Jack Welch's secret weapon," *Fortune,* November 10, pp. 116+, for a discussion of Welch's management style; and Schlender, B. (1997). "On the road with Chairman Bill," *Fortune,* May 20, pp. 72+. Charan, R., and G. Colvin (1999). "Why CEOs fail," *Fortune,* June 21, pp. 69+, suggest that successful CEOs share eight common attributes: (1) integrity, maturity, and energy; (2) business acumen; (3) people acumen; (4) organizational acumen; (5) curiosity, intellectual capacity, and a global mindset; (6) superior judgment; (7) an insatiable appetite for accomplishment and profits; and (8) a powerful motivation to grow and convert learning into practice. Although there is little doubt that these personal attributes

of CEOs contribute to their success, there still remains a great deal of variability in the management style, approach, and method of general managers—too much variability to conclude that we know exactly what it takes to be a successful general manager. For a discussion of the relationship between this problem and the theory of leadership, see Yukl, G. (1989). "Managerial leadership: A review of theory and research," *Journal of Management,* 15(2), pp. 251–289.

5. See Selznick, P. (1957). *Leadership in Administration,* New York: Harper & Row.

6. See Ricardo, D. (1817). *Principles of Political Economy and Taxation,* London: J. Murray.

7. See Penrose, E. T. (1959). *The Theory of the Growth of the Firm,* New York: John Wiley & Sons.

8. This criticism of traditional price theory models has also been voiced by Williamson, O. E. (1975). *Markets and Hierarchies: Analysis and Antitrust Implications,* New York: Free Press; Williamson, O. E. (1985). *The Economic Institutions of Capitalism,* New York: Free Press; Nelson, R., and S. Winter (1982). *An Evolutionary Theory of Economic Change,* Cambridge, MA: Belknap Press; and others. See Barney, J. B., and W. G. Ouchi (1986). *Organizational Economics,* San Francisco: Jossey-Bass, for a discussion of these and related criticisms of traditional economics. All this does not suggest that there is never any value in adopting the "simple production function" approach of traditional economics. However, it has limited utility in developing models of organizational strengths and weaknesses.

9. The term "the resource-based view" was coined by Wernerfelt, B. (1984). "A resource-based view of the firm," *Strategic Management Journal, 5,* pp. 171–180. Some important early contributors to this theory include Rumelt, R. P. (1984). "Toward a strategic theory of the firm," in R. Lamb (ed.), *Competitive Strategic Management,* pp. 556–570,Upper Saddle River, NJ: Prentice Hall; and Barney, J. B. (1986). "Strategic factor markets: Expectations, luck and business strategy," *Management Science, 32,* pp. 1512–1514. A second wave of important early resource-based theoretical work includes Barney, J. B. (1991). "Firm resources and sustained competitive advantage," *Journal of Management, 7,* pp. 49–64; Dierickx, I., and K. Cool (1989). "Asset stock accumulation and sustainability of competitive advantage," *Management Science, 35,* pp. 1504–1511; Conner, K. R. (1991). "A historical comparison of resource-based theory and five schools of thought within industrial organization economics: Do we have a new theory of the firm?" *Journal of Management, 17*(1), pp. 121–154; and Peteraf, M. A. (1993). "The cornerstones of competitive advantage: A resource-based view," *Strategic Management Journal, 14,* pp. 179–191. A review of much of this early theoretical literature can be found in Mahoney, J. T., and J. R. Pandian (1992). "The resource-based view within the conversation of strategic management," *Strategic Management Journal, 13,* pp. 363–380. The theoretical perspective has also spawned a growing body of empirical work, including Brush, T. H., and K. W. Artz, (1999). "Toward a Contingent Resource-Based Theory," *Strategic Management Journal, 20,* pp. 223–250; Marcus, A., and D. Geffen (1998). "The dialectics of competency acquisition," *Strategic Management Journal, 19,* pp. 1145–1168; Brush, T. H., P. Bromiley, and M. Hendrickx (1999). "The relative influence of industry and corporation on business segment performance," *Strategic Management Journal, 20,* pp. 519–547; Yeoh, P.-L., and K. Roth (1999). "An empirical analysis of sustained advantage in the U.S. pharmaceutical industry," *Strategic Management Journal, 20,* pp. 637–653; Roberts, P. (1999). "Product innovation, product-market competition and persistent profitability in the U.S. pharmaceutical industry," *Strategic Management Journal, 20,* pp. 655–670; Gulati, R. (1999). "Network location and learning," *Strategic Management Journal, 20,* pp. 397–420; Lorenzoni, G., and A. Lipparini (1999). "The leveraging of interfirm relationships as a distinctive organizational capability," *Strategic Management Journal, 20,* pp. 317–338; Majumdar, S. (1998). "On the utilization of resources," *Strategic Management Journal,* pp. 809–831; Makadok, R. (1997). "Do inter-firm differences in capabilities affect strategic pricing dynamics?" *Academy of Management Proceedings '97,* pp. 30–34; Silverman, B. S., J. A. Nickerson, and J. Freeman (1997). "Profitability, transactional alignment, and organizational mortality in the U.S. trucking industry," *Strategic Management Journal, 18* (Summer special issue), pp. 31–52; Powell, T. C., and A. Dent-Micallef (1997). "Information technology as competitive advantage," *Strategic Management Journal, 18*(5), pp. 375–405; Miller, D., and J. Shamsie (1996). "The resource-based view of the firm in two environments," *Academy of Management Journal, 39*(3), pp. 519–543; Maijoor, S., and A. Van Witteloostuijn (1996). "An empirical test of the resource-based theory," *Strategic Management Journal, 17,* pp. 549–569; Barnett, W. P., H. R. Greve, and D. Y. Park (1994). "An evolutionary model of organizational performance," *Strategic Management Journal, 15* (Winter special issue), pp. 11–28; Levinthal, D., and J. Myatt (1994). "Co-evolution of capabilities and industry: The evolution of mutual fund processing," *Strategic Management Journal, 17,* pp. 45–62; Henderson, R., and I. Cockburn (1994). "Measuring competence? Exploring firm effects in pharmaceutical research," *Strategic Management Journal, 15,* pp. 63–84; Pisano, G. P. (1994). "Knowledge, integration, and the locus of learning: An empirical analysis of process development," *Strategic Management Journal, 15,* pp. 85–100; and Zajac, E. J., and J. D. Westphal (1994). "The costs and

benefits of managerial incentives and monitoring in large U.S. corporations: When is more not better?" *Strategic Management Journal,* 15, pp. 121–142.

10. See Hitt, M. A., and R. D. Ireland (1986). "Relationships among corporate-level distinct competencies, diversification strategy, corporate strategy and performance," *Journal of Management Studies,* 23, pp. 401–416; Thompson, A. A., Jr., and A. J. Strickland, III (1987). *Strategic Management: Concepts and Cases,* 4th ed., Plano, TX: Business Publications.

11. See Ghemawat, P. (1986). "Wal-Mart stores' discount operations," Harvard Business School Case no. 9-387-018, on Wal-Mart; Kupfer, A. (1991) and Holder, D. (1989). "L.L. Bean, Inc.—1974," Harvard Business School Case no. 9-676-014, on L.L. Bean. Some of Wal-Mart's more recent moves, especially its international acquisitions, are described in Laing, J. R. (1999). "Blimey! Wal-Mart," *Barron's,* 79, p. 14. L.L. Bean's lethargic performance in the 1990s, together with its turnaround plan, is described in Symonds, W. (1998). "Paddling harder at L.L. Bean," *Business Week,* 3607, p. 72.

12. For an early discussion of the importance of human capital in firms, see Becker, G. S. (1964). *Human Capital,* New York: Columbia University Press.

13. See Rigdon, J. E. (1993). "Workplace: Using new kinds of corporate alchemy, some firms turn lesser lights into stars," *Wall Street Journal,* May 3, p. B1; and Alpert, M. (1992). "The care and feeding of engineers," *Fortune,* September 21, pp. 86–95. A discussion of the importance of human resources as a source of competitive advantage can be found in Barney, J., and P. Wright (1998). "On becoming a strategic partner," *Human Resource Management,* 37, pp. 31–46.

14. For a discussion of organizational capital in general, see Tomer, J. F. (1987). *Organizational Capital: The Path to Higher Productivity and Well-Being,* New York: Praeger; Caminiti, S. (1992). "The payoff from a good reputation," *Fortune,* February 10, pp. 74–77; Leana, C. R., and H. J. Van Buren, III (1999). "Organizational social capital and employment practices,"

Academy of Management Review, 24(3), pp. 538–555, for a discussion of how firms use their organizational capital in labor and other markets; and Yoder, S. K. (1991). "A 1990 reorganization at Hewlett Packard is already paying off," *Wall Street Journal,* July 22, p. 1+, for how Hewlett Packard uses its organizational capital to manage change. The organizational capital implications of HP's recent decision to spin off its measurement technology business is discussed in Nee, E. (1999). "Lew Platt: Why I dismembered HP," *Fortune,* 139, pp. 167–170.

15. Wernerfelt, B. (1984). "A resource-based view of the firm," *Strategic Management Journal,* 5, pp. 171–180; Barney, J. B. (1991). "Firm resources and sustained competitive advantage," *Journal of Management,* 17, pp. 99–120; Prahalad, C. K., and R. A. Bettis (1986). "The dominant logic: A new linkage between diversity and performance," *Strategic Management Journal,* 7(6), pp. 485–501; Prahalad, C. K., and G. Hamel (1990). "The core competence of the organization," *Harvard Business Review,* May/June, pp. 79–93; Stalk, G., P. Evans, and L. Shulman (1992). "Competing on capabilities: The new rules of corporate strategy," *Harvard Business Review,* March/April, pp. 57–69.

16. See Grant, R. M. (1991). *Contemporary Strategy Analysis,* Cambridge, MA: Basil Blackwell.

17. Porter, M. E. (1987). *Competitive Advantage,* New York: Free Press.

18. First developed in Barney, J. B. (1991). "Firm resources and sustained competitive advantage," *Journal of Management,* 17, pp. 99–120. The resource-based view and the VRIO framework describe ways that firms can expect to be successful. However, a firm may also be successful simply because it is lucky. See, for example, Mancke, R. B. (1974). "Causes of interfirm profitability differences: A new interpretation of the evidence," *Quarterly Journal of Economics,* 88, pp. 181–193; Mancke, R. B. (1977). "Interfirm profitabilty differences: Reply," *Quarterly Journal of Economics,* pp. 677–680; and Lippman, S., and R. Rumelt (1982). "Uncertain imitability: An analysis

of interfirm differences in efficiency under competition," *Bell Journal of Economics,* 13, pp. 418–438.

19. See Schlender, B. R. (1992). "How Sony keeps the magic going," *Fortune,* February 24, pp. 75–84; and Anonymous (1999). "The weakling kicks back," *The Economist,* 352(8126), p. 46, for a discussion of Sony. See Krogh, L., J. Praeger, D. Sorenson, and J. Tomlinson (1988). "How 3M evaluates its R&D programs," *Research Technology Management,* 31, pp. 10–14.

20. See Rosenbloom, R. S., and C. Christensen (1990). "Continuous casting investments at USX Corporation," Harvard Business School Case no. 9-391-121; and Baker, S. (1995). "A real steelman for USX," *Business Week,* 3424, p. 47, for a discussion of USX. See Montgomery, C. A. (1989). "Sears, Roebuck and Co. in 1989," Harvard Business School Case no. 9-391-147; and Weimer, D. (1998). "The softest side of Sears," *Business Week,* 3610, December 8, p. 6, for a discussion of Sears.

21. Personal communication for both Crown and Hunter Fan.

22. Of course, a firm cannot compare its performance with resources and capabilities to itself without these resources and capabilities. In this context, a firm comparing itself with other successful firms can be an important benchmark. See Martin, J. (1996). "Are you as good as you think you are?" *Fortune,* September 30, pp. 142+. Cautions about identifying the strength of your resources and capabilities can be found in Coyne, K., S. Hall, and P. Clifford (1997). "Is your core competence a mirage?" *McKinsey Quarterly,* pp. 41–54.

23. Steven, L. (1992). "Front line systems," *Computerworld,* March 2, pp. 61–63. Of course, other problems at Kmart has prevented it from becoming fully competitive with Wal-Mart. Davids, M. (1997). "More attention to Kmart shoppers," *Journal of Business Strategy,* 18, p. 36.

24. Lippman, S., and R. Rumelt (1982). "Uncertain imitability: An analysis of interfirm differences in efficiency under competition," *Bell Journal of Economics,* 13, pp. 418–438; Barney, J. B. (1986). "Strategic factor markets: Expectations, luck and business strategy," *Management Science,* 32, pp. 1512–1514; and Barney, J. B. (1986). "Organizational culture: Can it be a source of sustained competitive advantage?" *Academy of Management Review,* 11, pp. 656–665.

25. These explanations of costly imitation were first developed by Dierickx, I., and K. Cool (1989). "Asset stock accumulation and sustainability of competitive advantage," *Management Science,* 35, pp. 1504–1511; Barney, J. B. (1991). "Firm resources and sustained competitive advantage," *Journal of Management,* 7, pp. 49–64; Mahoney, J. T., and J. R. Pandian (1992). "The resource-based view within the conversation of strategic management," *Strategic Management Journal,* 13, pp. 363–380; and Peteraf, M. A. (1993). "The cornerstones of competitive advantage: A resource-based view," *Strategic Management Journal,* 14, pp. 179–191.

26. Dierickx, I., and K. Cool (1989). "Asset stock accumulation and sustainability of competitive advantage," *Management Science,* 35, pp. 1504–1511. In economics, the role of history in determining competitive outcomes was first examined by Arthur, W. B. (1989). "Competing technologies, increasing returns, and lock-in by historical events," *Economic Journal,* 99, pp. 116–131.

27. See Rukstad, M. G., and J. Horn (1989). "Caterpillar and the construction equipment industry in 1988," Harvard Business School Case no. 9-389-097. In the late 1990s, Caterpillar's performance was rocked by downturns in Asian markets. However, Caterpillar's long-term competitive advantage continues, despite its short-term difficulties.

28. See Bartlett, C. A., and U. S. Rangan (1985). "Komatsu Ltd.," Harvard Business School Case no. 9-385-277.

29. This term was first suggested by Arthur, W. B. (1989). "Competing technologies, increasing returns, and lock-in by historical events," *Economic Journal,* 99, pp. 116–131. A good example of path dependence is the development of Silicon Valley and the important role that Stanford University and a

few early firms played in creating the network of organizations that has since become the center of much of the electronics business. See Alley, J. (1997). "The heart of Silicon Valley," *Fortune,* July 7, pp. 86+.

30. Reed, R., and R. J. DeFillippi (1990). "Causal ambiguity, barriers to imitation, and sustainable competitive advantage," *Academy of Management Review,* 15(1), pp. 88–102, suggest that causal ambiguity about the sources of a firm's competitive advantage need only exist among a firm's competitors for it to be a source of sustained competitive advantage. Managers in a firm, they argue, may fully understand the sources of their advantage. However, in a world in which employees move freely and frequently from firm to firm, such special insights into the sources of a firm's competitive advantage will not remain proprietary very long. For this reason, for causal ambiguity to be a source of sustained competitive advantage, both the firm trying to gain such an advantage and those trying to imitate it must face similar levels of causal ambiguity. Indeed, Wal-Mart recently sued Amazon.com for trying to steal some of its secrets by hiring employees away from Wal-Mart. See Nelson, E. (1998). "Wal-Mart accuses Amazon.com of Stealing its secrets in lawsuit," *Wall Street Journal,* October 19, pp. B10. For a discussion of how difficult it is to maintain secrets, especially in the world of the World Wide Web, see Farnham, A. (1997). "How safe are your secrets?" *Fortune,* September 8, pp. 114+. The international dimensions of the challenges associated with maintaining secrets are discussed in Robinson, E. (1998). "China spies target corporate America," *Fortune,* March 30, pp. 118+.

31. Itami, H. (1987). *Mobilizing Invisible Assets,* Cambridge, MA: Harvard University Press.

32. See Barney, J. B., and B. Tyler (1990). "The attributes of top management teams and sustained competitive advantage," in M. Lawless and L. Gomez-Mejia (eds.), *Managing the High Technology Firm,* pp. 33–48, Greenwich, CT: JAI Press, on teamwork in top management teams; Barney, J. B. (1986). "Organizational culture:

Can it be a source of sustained competitive advantage?" *Academy of Management Review,* 11, pp. 656–665, on organizational culture; Henderson, R. M., and I. Cockburn (1994). "Measuring competence? Exploring firm effects in pharmaceutical research," *Strategic Management Journal,* 15, pp. 63–84, on relationships among employees; and Dyer, J. H., and H. Singh (1998). "The relational view: Cooperative strategy and sources of interorganizational competitive advantage," *Academy of Management Review,* 23(4), pp. 660–679, on relationships with suppliers and customers.

33. Personal communication.

34. For a discussion of knowledge as a source of competitive advantage in the popular business press, see Stewart, T. (1995). "Getting real about brain power," *Fortune,* November 27, pp. 201+; Stewart, T. (1995). "Mapping corporate knowledge," *Fortune,* October 30, pp. 209+. For the academic version of this same issue, see Simonin, B. L. (1999). "Ambiguity and the process of knowledge transfer in strategic alliances," *Strategic Management Journal,* 20(7), pp. 595–623; Spender, J. C. (1996). "Making knowledge the basis of a dynamic theory of the firm," *Strategic Management Journal,* 17 (Winter special issue), pp. 109–122; Hatfield, D. D., J. P. Liebeskind, and T. C. Opler (1996). "The effects of corporate restructuring on aggregate industry specialization," *Strategic Management Journal,* 17, pp. 55–72; and Grant, R. M. (1996). "Toward a knowledge-based theory of the firm," *Strategic Management Journal,* 17 (Winter special issue), pp. 109–122.

35. Porras, J., and P. O. Berg (1978). "The impact of organizational development," *Academy of Management Review,* 3, pp. 249–266, have done one of the few empirical studies on whether systematic efforts to change socially complex resources are effective. They found that such efforts are usually not effective. Although this study is getting older, it is unlikely that current change methods will be any more effective than the methods examined by these authors.

36. See Hambrick, D. (1987). "Top management teams: Key to strategic success," *California*

Management Review, 30, pp. 88–108, on top management teams; Barney, J. B. (1986). "Organizational culture: Can it be a source of sustained competitive advantage?" *Academy of Management Review,* 11, pp. 656–665, on culture; Porter, M. E. (1980). *Competitive Strategy,* New York: Free Press; and Klein, B., and K. Leffler (1981). "The role of market forces in assuring contractual performance," *Journal of Political Economy,* 89, pp. 615–641, on relations with customers.

37. See Harris, L. C., and E. Ogbonna (1999). "Developing a market oriented culture: A critical evaluation," *Journal of Management Studies,* 36(2), pp. 177–196.

38. See Tichy, N. M., and M. A. Devanna (1986). *The Transformational Leader,* New York: John Wiley & Sons, on transformational leaders; Huey, J. (1997). "In search of Robert's secret formula," *Fortune,* December 29, p. 230, for a discussion of Robert Goizueta as a CEO; and Sellers, P. (1995). "Sears: In with the new, out with the old," *Fortune,* October 16, pp. 98+, for a discussion of Martinez as he took over at Sears. Information about Welch and Gates can be found in Curran, J. (1997). "GE Capital: Jack Welch's secret weapon," *Fortune,* November 10, pp. 116+, for a discussion of Welch's management style; and Schlender, B. (1997). "On the road with Chairman Bill," *Fortune,* May 20, pp. 72+. Welbourne, T., and A. Andrews (1998). "Predicting the performances of initial public offerings." *Academy of Management Journal,* 39, pp. 891–919, provide empirical evidence that socially complex human resources can have an effect on the validation of firms undergoing initial public offering.

39. Ghemawat, P., and H. J. Stander, III (1993). "Nucor at a crossroads," Harvard Business School Case no. 9-793-039.

40. Lieberman, M. B. (1987). "The learning curve, diffusion, and competitive strategy," *Strategic Management Journal,* 8, pp. 441–452, has a very good analysis of the cost of imitation in the chemical industry. See also Lieberman, M. B., and D. B. Montgomery (1988). "First-mover advantages," *Strategic Management Journal,* 9, pp. 41–58.

41. This argument was articulated in detail by Fuerst, B., F. Mata, and J. Barney (1996).

"Information technology and sustained competitive advantage: A resource based analysis," *MIS Quarterly,* 19, pp. 487–505; and tested in Ray, G., J. Barney, and W. Muhanna (2004). "Capabilities, business processes, and competitive advantage," *Strategic Management Journal,* 25, pp. 23–57; and Ray, G., W. Muhanna, and J. Barney (2005). "Information technology and the performance of the customer service process," *MIS Quarterly,* 29, pp. 625–651.

42. Rumelt, R. P. (1984). "Toward a strategic theory of the firm," in R. Lamb (ed.), *Competitive Strategic Management,* pp. 556–570, Upper Saddle River, NJ: Prentice Hall, among others, cites patents as a source of costly imitation.

43. There is currently significant debate about the patentability of different kinds of products. For example, although typefaces are not patentable (and cannot be copyrighted), the process for displaying typefaces may be. See Thurm, S. (1998). "Copy this typeface? Court ruling counsels caution," *Wall Street Journal,* July 15, p. B1+.

44. Schlender, B. R. (1992). "How Sony keeps the magic going," *Fortune,* February 24, pp. 75–84.

45. For an insightful discussion of these complementary resources, see Amit, R., and P. J. H. Schoemaker (1993). "Strategic assets and organizational rent," *Strategic Management Journal,* 14(1), pp. 33–45.

46. See Kearns, D. T., and D. A. Nadler (1992). *Prophets in the Dark,* New York: Harper-Collins; and Smith, D. K., and R. C. Alexander (1988). *Fumbling the Future,* New York: William Morrow.

47. Information about Dell Computers was taken from Brown, E. (1999). "America's most admired companies," *Fortune,* March 1, pp. 68+; Kirkpatrick, D. (1998). "The second coming at Apple," *Fortune,* November 9, pp. 96+; and Hamel, G., and J. Sampler (1998). "The E-corporation," *Fortune,* December 7, pp. 80+.

48. Indeed, many other firms, including Compaq and Hewlett Packard, have begun using the Internet to sell their products. See McWilliams, G. (1998). "Mimicking Dell, Compaq to sell its PC directly," *Wall Street*

Journal, November 11, pp. B1+; and McHugh, J. (1999). "Emerging channels—sort of," *Fortune,* 163, p. 55.

49. Information about Pepsico, Coca-Cola, and Dr Pepper was taken from Pearson, A. E., and C. L. Irwin (1988). "Coca-Cola vs. Pepsi-Cola (A)," Harvard Business School Case no. 9-387-108; Light, L. (1999). "Now that's a Pepsi Challenge," *Business Week,* 3627, May 3, pp. 15+; Anonymous (1999). "Sweet success," *Harvard Business Review,* 77, May/ June, p. 192; Sellers, P. (1999). "Crunch time for Coke," *Fortune,* 140, July 19, pp. 72–78; and Doherty, J. (1997). "A sparkling strategy?" *Barron's,* 77, September 15, p. 12.

50. Personal communication.

51. See Schumpeter, J. A. (1934). *The Theory of Economic Development,* Cambridge, MA: Harvard University Press.

52. See Jacobsen, R. (1988). "The persistence of abnormal returns," *Strategic Management Journal,* 9(5), pp. 415–430.

C H A P T E R

Cost Leadership

A firm pursues a business-level strategy when it seeks competitive advantage in a single market or industry. A variety of business strategies have been identified. Four of these—cost leadership, product differentiation, flexibility, and tacit collusion—are examined in this part of the book. The first two of these business strategies—cost leadership and product differentiation—are so important in the literature that they have sometimes been called *generic business strategies*.[1]

6.1 DEFINING COST LEADERSHIP

A firm that chooses a **cost leadership business strategy** focuses on gaining advantages by reducing its economic costs below all of its competitors. This does not mean that the firm abandons other business or corporate strategies. Indeed, a single-minded focus on *just* reducing costs can lead a firm to make low-cost products that no one wants to buy. However, a firm pursuing a cost leadership strategy focuses much of its effort on reducing its economic costs below those of competitors.

Numerous firms have pursued cost leadership strategies. For example, Proctor & Gamble has established Ivory Soap as a cost leader in the home soap market. Ivory is packaged in plain paper wrappings and does not use costly deodorants and fragrances. Many of Ivory's competitors (including Dial, Dove, and Irish Spring) are packaged in expensive foil wrappers and include deodorants and fragrances. Ivory is still advertised, but advertisements tend to emphasize Ivory's low price, high value, and purity. Most of its competitors advertise their soaps' deodorizing effectiveness, ability to soften skin, sex appeal, and so forth. Ivory continues to be a successful product by keeping production costs low and providing solid value for customers.[2]

In automobiles, Hyundai has implemented a cost leadership strategy with its emphasis on low-priced cars for basic transportation. Like Ivory Soap, Hyundai spends a significant amount of money advertising its products, but advertisements tend to emphasize Hyundai's sporty styling and high gas mileage. Hyundai is positioned as a fun and inexpensive car, not a high-performance sports car or a luxurious status symbol. Hyundai's ability to sell these fun and inexpensive automobiles depends on its design choices (keep it simple) and its low manufacturing costs.[3]

Among watchmakers, Timex has very successfully implemented a cost leadership strategy. Timex originally developed a low-cost replacement for expensive watch movements by substituting high-density steel pins (pin levers) for jewels. However, with the development of more accurate and even less expensive electronic movements, Timex quickly moved to incorporate electronic movements into its watch line. Timex continues to advertise its low prices, reliability, and overall value. A person wearing a Timex is unlikely to make any fashion or status statements but is likely to know what time it is.[4]

Sources of Cost Advantages

There are many reasons why an individual firm may have a cost advantage over its competitors. A cost advantage is possible even when competing firms produce similar products. A discussion of some important sources of cost differences among firms follows.

Size Differences and Economies of Scale

One of the most widely cited sources of cost advantages for a firm in a single business is its size. When there are significant **economies of scale** in manufacturing, marketing, distribution, service, or other functions of a business, larger firms (up to some point) have a cost advantage over smaller firms. The relationship between firm size (measured in terms of volume of production) and costs (measured in terms of average costs per unit of production) when there are significant economies of scale is illustrated in Figure 6.1. As the volume of production increases, the average cost per unit decreases until some optimal volume of production (point X) is reached, after which the average

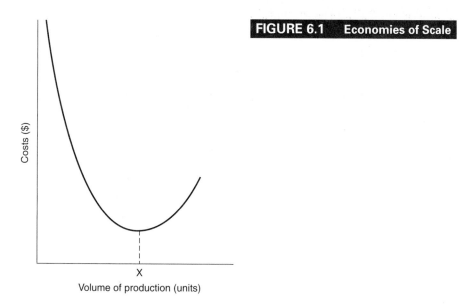

FIGURE 6.1   **Economies of Scale**

Costs ($)

X

Volume of production (units)

costs per unit of production begin to rise because of **diseconomies of scale** (a concept discussed in more detail later in this chapter). If the relationship between volume of production and average costs per unit of production shown in Figure 6.1 holds, and if a firm in an industry has the largest volume of production (but not greater than the optimal level, X), then that firm will have a cost advantage in that industry.

The **economies of scale curve** depicted in Figure 6.1 can also be represented mathematically. If the quantity of a good or service being produced equals Q and the total cost of producing this quantity of a good or service equals $TC(Q)$, then the average cost, $AC(Q)$, of producing this good or service, if economies of scale exist, is

$$AC(Q) = \frac{TC(Q)}{Q} \qquad (6.1)$$

Economies of scale exist in producing this product or service as long as $AC(Q)$ decreases when Q increases.

For example, if the relationship between total costs, $TC(Q)$, and the quantity of production, Q, is given by

$$TC(Q) = 200 + 5Q^2 \qquad (6.2)$$

Then

$$AC(Q) = \frac{200 + 5Q^2}{Q}$$

$$= \frac{200}{Q} + 5Q \qquad (6.3)$$

As shown in Table 6.1, the average cost of production for this product or service falls as the quantity produced increases from one unit [$AC(1) = 205$] to six units [$AC(6) = 63.3$]. However, diseconomies of scale begin at seven units of production [$AC(7)$] = 63.57.

This approach to estimating economies of scale was once applied in the U.S. savings and loan industry.[5] The average cost function for S&Ls was estimated to be

$$AC = 2.38 - .615A + .54A^2 \qquad (6.4)$$

TABLE 6.1	Calculating Economies and Diseconomies of Scale When $TC(Q) = 200 + 5Q^2$
Q	$AC(Q)$
1	205
2	110
3	81.6
4	70
5	65
6	63.3
7	63.57
8	65
9	67.22
10	70

where *AC* equals an S&L's long-run average cost and *A* is an S&L's dollar value of assets. This equation is at a minimum when total assets equal $574 million. Institutions with assets less than $574 million, according to this analysis, will have a cost disadvantage, as will institutions with assets worth more than $574 million.

There are various reasons why large volumes of production are often associated with lower average per-unit costs. Important sources of economies of scale are listed in Table 6.2 and discussed later.

Volume of Production and Specialized Machines.   When a firm has high levels of production, it is typically able to purchase and use specialized manufacturing tools that cannot be kept in operation in small firms. Manufacturing managers at BIC Corporation, for example, have emphasized this important advantage of high volumes of production. A former director of manufacturing at BIC once observed:

> We are in the automation business. Because of our large volume, one tenth of 1 cent in savings turns out to be enormous. . . . One advantage of the high-volume business is that you can get the best equipment and amortize it entirely over a short period of time (4 to 5 months). I'm always looking for new equipment. If I see a cost-saving machine, I can buy it. I'm not constrained by money.[6]

Only firms with BIC's level of production in the pen industry have the ability to reduce their costs in this manner.

Volume of Production and the Cost of Plant and Equipment.   High volumes of production may also allow a firm to build larger manufacturing operations. In some industries, the cost of building these manufacturing operations, per unit of production, is lower than the cost, per unit of production, of building smaller manufacturing operations. Thus large-volume firms, other factors being equal, will be able to build lower per-unit-cost manufacturing operations and will have lower average costs of production.

The link between volume of production and the cost of building manufacturing operations is particularly important in industries characterized by **process manufacturing**—chemical, oil refining, paper and pulp manufacturing, and so forth. Because of the physical geometry of process manufacturing facilities, the costs of constructing a processing plant with increased capacity can be expected to rise as the two-thirds power of a plant's capacity. This is because the area of the surface of some three-dimensional containers (such as spheres and cylinders) increases at a slower rate than the volume of these containers. Thus larger containers hold greater volumes and require less material per unit volume for the outside skins of these containers. Up to some point, increases in capacity come at a less-than-proportionate rise in the cost to build this capacity.[7]

TABLE 6.2   Major Sources of Economies of Scale

1. Volume of production and specialized machines
2. Volume of production and cost of plant and equipment
3. Volume of production and employee specialization
4. Volume of production and overhead costs

For example, it might cost a firm $100 to build a plant with a capacity of 1,000 units, for a per-unit average cost of $.1. But, assuming the "two-thirds rule" applies, it might cost a firm $465 to build a plant with a capacity of 10,000 units ($465 = 10,000^{2/3}$), for a per-unit average cost of $.0465. The difference between $.1 per unit and $.0465 per unit represents a cost advantage for a large firm. Because it costs less per unit to build a large-capacity plant, firms with large volumes of production that build large-capacity plants may have lower average per-unit costs than firms with lower volumes of production and small-capacity plants.

Volume of Production and Employee Specialization. High volumes of production are also associated with high levels of employee specialization. As workers specialize in accomplishing a narrow task, they can become more and more efficient at this task, thereby reducing their firm's costs. This reasoning applies both in specialized manufacturing tasks (such as the highly specialized manufacturing functions in an assembly line) and in specialized management functions (such as the highly specialized managerial functions of accounting, finance, and sales). As Adam Smith first observed in 1776, cost advantages may be associated with the division of labor.

Smaller firms often do not possess the volume of production needed to justify this level of employee specialization. With smaller volumes of production, highly specialized employees may not have enough work to keep them busy an entire workday. This low volume of production is one reason why smaller firms often have employees who perform multiple business functions and often use outside contract employees and part-time workers to accomplish highly specialized functions such as accounting, taxes, and human resource management.

Volume of Production and Overhead Costs. A firm with high volumes of production has the luxury of spreading its overhead costs over more units and thereby reducing the overhead costs per unit. Suppose that, in a particular industry, the operation cost of a variety of accounting, control, and research and development functions, regardless of how large a firm is, is $100,000. Clearly, a firm that manufactures 1,000 units is imposing a cost of $100 per unit to cover overhead expenses. However, a firm that manufactures 10,000 units is imposing a cost of $10 per unit to cover overhead. Again, the larger-volume firm's average per-unit costs are lower than the small-volume firm's average per-unit costs.

Obviously, for a firm to generate a cost advantage in this manner, a firm's overhead costs cannot be highly and positively correlated with a firm's volume of production. If the overhead costs of a firm are highly and positively correlated with the firm's volume of production, then any increase in the volume of production will lead to a correspondingly large increase in the cost of overhead. A firm with overhead costs of $100,000 and a volume of production of 1,000 units will have an overhead cost of $1 million if it increases its volume of production to 10,000 units and if overhead costs are highly and positively correlated with a firm's volume of production. Obviously, the average overhead cost per unit ($100) is the same in each of these situations. However, as long as the volume of production and overhead costs are not correlated in this way, large-volume-of-production firms will have an advantage over low-volume-of-production firms in spreading overhead costs across units.

Size Differences and Diseconomies of Scale

Just as economies of scale can generate cost advantages for larger firms, important diseconomies of scale can actually increase costs if firms grow too large. As Figure 6.1 and Table 6.1 show, volumes of production beyond some optimal point (point x in Figure 6.1, seven units of production in Table 6.1) can actually lead to an increase in costs. If other firms in an industry have grown beyond the optimal firm size, a smaller firm (with a level of production closer to the optimal) may obtain a cost advantage even when all firms in the industry are producing very similar products. Sources of diseconomies of scale for a firm are listed in Table 6.3 and discussed below.

Physical Limits to Efficient Size.   Applying the two-thirds rule to the construction of manufacturing facilities seems to imply, for some industries at least, that larger is always better. However, there are some important physical limitations to the size of some manufacturing processes. Engineers have found, for example, that cement kilns develop unstable internal aerodynamics above 7 million barrels per year capacity. Others have suggested that scaling up nuclear reactors from small installations to huge facilities generates forces and physical processes that, though non-detectable in smaller facilities, can become significant in larger operations. These physical limitations on manufacturing processes reflect the underlying physics and engineering in a manufacturing process and suggest when the cost curve in Figure 6.1 will begin to rise.[8]

Managerial Diseconomies.   Although the underlying physics and engineering in a manufacturing process have important effects on a firm's costs, managerial diseconomies are perhaps even more important causes of these cost increases. As a firm increases in size, it often increases in complexity, and the ability of managers to control and operate it efficiently becomes limited.

One well-known example of a manufacturing plant that grew too large and thus became inefficient is Crown Cork & Seal's can manufacturing plant in Philadelphia. Through the early part of this century, this Philadelphia facility handled as many as 75 different can manufacturing lines. The most efficient plants in the industry, however, were running from 10 to 15 lines simultaneously. The huge Philadelphia facility was simply too large to operate efficiently and was characterized by large numbers of breakdowns, a high percentage of idle lines, and poor-quality products.[9]

Worker Motivation.   A third source of diseconomies of scale depends on the relationships among firm size, employee specialization, and employee motivation. It has already been suggested that one of the advantages of increased volumes of production is that it allows workers to specialize in smaller and more narrowly defined production

---

TABLE 6.3   Major Sources of Diseconomies of Scale

1. Physical limits to efficient size
2. Managerial diseconomies
3. Worker motivation
4. Distance to markets and suppliers

---

tasks. With specialization, workers become more and more efficient at the particular task facing them.

However, a significant stream of research suggests that these types of very specialized jobs can be very demotivating for employees. Based on motivational theories taken from social psychology, this job design literature suggests that as workers are removed further from the complete product that is the end result of a manufacturing process, the role that a worker's job plays in the overall manufacturing process becomes more and more obscure. As workers become mere "cogs in a manufacturing machine," worker motivation wanes, and productivity and quality both suffer.[10]

Several manufacturing facilities in the U.S. automobile industry have experienced this lack of worker motivation and reduced quality due to worker overspecialization. Among others, Ford Motor Company has made significant efforts to help workers understand how their particular job contributes to the final product and to the success of the company. Ford has accomplished this by the use of a variety of employee participation schemes, including quality circles in which each worker's point of view is sought.

Distance to Markets and Suppliers. A final source of diseconomies of scale can be the distance between a large manufacturing facility and the place where the goods in question are to be sold, or the places where essential raw materials are purchased. Any reductions in cost attributable to the exploitation of economies of scale in manufacturing may be more than offset by large transportation costs associated with moving supplies and products to and from the manufacturing facility. Firms that build highly efficient plants without recognizing these significant transportation costs may put themselves at a competitive disadvantage compared to firms with slightly less efficient plants but plants that are located nearer suppliers and key markets.

Experience Differences and Learning-Curve Economies

A third possible source of cost advantages for firms in a particular business depends on their different cumulative levels of production. In some circumstances, firms with the greatest experience in manufacturing a product or service will have the lowest costs in an industry and thus will have a cost-based advantage. The link between cumulative volumes of production and cost has been formalized in the concept of the **learning curve.** The relationship between cumulative volumes of production and per-unit costs is represented graphically in Figure 6.2.

The Learning Curve and Economies of Scale. As illustrated in Figure 6.2, the learning curve is very closely linked to economies of scale. Indeed, there are only two differ-

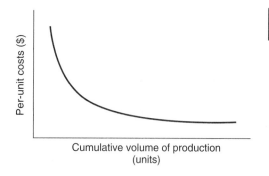

FIGURE 6.2   The Leaning Curve and the Cost of Production

ences between these concepts. First, whereas economies of scale focuses on the relationship between the volume of production at a given point in time and average unit
costs, the learning curve focuses on the relationship between the *cumulative* volume of
production and average unit costs. Second, whereas diseconomies of scale are pre-
sumed to exist if a firm gets too large, there is no corresponding increase in costs in the
learning-curve model as the cumulative volume of production grows. Rather, costs continue to fall until they approach the technologically possible lowest cost.

In general, the learning-curve model can be thought of as a dynamic generalization of the concept of economies of scale. Instead of simply examining the volume of
production and costs at a given point in time, the learning-curve model attempts to relate the volume of production and costs over time.

The Learning Curve and Cost Advantages.   The learning-curve model is based on the
empirical observation that the costs of producing a unit of output fall as the cumulative
volume of output increases. This relationship was first observed in the construction of
aircraft before World War II. Research then showed that the labor costs per aircraft fell
by 20 percent each time the cumulative volume of production doubled.[11] A similar pattern has been observed in numerous industries, although the rate of cost reduction may
vary. Some of these industries include the manufacture of ships, computers, spacecraft,
and semiconductors. In all these cases, increases in cumulative production have been
associated with the improvement of work methods, a fine-tuning of the production operation, and detailed learning about how to make the production of products as efficient as possible.

However, learning curve-cost advantages are not restricted to manufacturing.
Learning can be associated with any business function, from purchasing raw materials
through distribution and service. Also, there can be important learning effects in service industries as well. The learning curve is most often applied in the analysis of manufacturing costs, but it is important to recognize that the learning curve applies whenever
the cost of accomplishing a business function falls as a function of the cumulative number of times a firm has engaged in that function.[12]

The curve in Figure 6.2 can be represented in equation form as

$$y = ax^{-\beta} \tag{6.5}$$

where a is the amount of time spent producing (that is, acquiring raw materials, manufacturing, distributing, and so forth) the first unit, x is the total number of units produced, β is a coefficient that describes the rate of learning in producing output, and y is
the average time to produce all x units. In general, firms that produce the same products and services as their competitors, but do so in less time, will have an important cost
advantage.

It is possible to use the learning-curve equation to anticipate the average time
costs of producing a product. Suppose that it takes a team of workers 45 minutes to produce their first snipe trap. Given learning, it should take these same workers less time
to produce their second snipe trap, say 27 minutes. With these two observations, it is
possible to estimate the rate of learning for snipe trap manufacturing. The time to produce the first snipe trap, a, is 45 minutes. The total number of snipe traps produced, x, is
two, and the average time to produce these snipe traps, y, is 36 minutes: (45 + 27)/2.
Plugging this information into the learning-curve equation, it is possible to calculate β,

the rate of learning. In this example, β, the rate of learning in the production of snipe traps, is .3219. With this estimate of β, the learning curve for snipe trap production is

$$y = (45)(x)^{-.3219} \tag{6.6}$$

This equation can be used to anticipate the costs of producing products (snipe traps) in the future. It can also be used to compare the relative costs of producing for two different firms. Suppose there are two firms in the snipe trap business, Firm A and Firm B. Suppose that Firm A has just entered this business and has just produced its first snipe trap. It has already been shown that this first snipe trap will take approximately 45 minutes to produce. Firm B has been in the snipe trap business much longer than Firm A. Indeed, Firm B is building its sixth snipe trap. Using the learning-curve equation, the time costs of building this sixth trap can be estimated.

To estimate the cost of producing this sixth trap, one must first estimate the average time it takes to build each of six traps, multiply this average by 6 (to obtain the total time it takes to build six traps), estimate the average time it takes to build five traps, multiply this average by 5 (to obtain the total time it takes to build five traps), and then subtract the total time it takes to make five traps from the total time it takes to make six traps. This difference is the amount of time it takes to make just the sixth trap. These calculations are shown in Table 6.4 for snipe traps.

It turns out that the sixth trap will take approximately 16.8 minutes to produce. This compares with the 45 minutes that Firm A must take to produce its first snipe trap.

TABLE 6.4   Application of the Learning Curve to Estimate Costs of Producing Snipe Traps for Two Firms: Firm A (Just Starting Production) and Firm B (Producing Its Sixth Snipe Trap)

Step 1:   Estimate the learning-curve equation for production of snipe traps (done in text).
$y = (45)(x)^{-.3219}$

Step 2:   How long will it take Firm A to produce its first snipe trap?
45 minutes (same as for Firm B)

Step 3:   What is the average time it will take Firm B to produce six snipe traps?
$y = (45)(6)^{-.3219}$
$= 25.3$ minutes

Step 4:   What is the total time it will take for Firm B to produce these six snipe traps?
151.8 minutes = (6)(25.3) minutes

Step 5:   What is the average time it took Firm B to produce five snipe traps?
$y = (45)(5)^{-.3219}$
$= 26.8$ minutes

Step 6:   What is the total time it took Firm B to produce five snipe traps?
134 minutes = (5)(26.8) minutes

Step 7:   How much time will it take Firm B to produce only its sixth snipe trap?
Total time to produce six = 151.8 minutes
Total time to produce five = 134.0 minutes
Time to produce sixth trap = 16.8 minutes

Therefore, it will cost Firm A 45 minutes to make its snipe trap, and Firm B only 16.8 minutes to make its snipe trap.

The difference between 45 minutes and 16.8 minutes represents a significant cost advantage for Firm B over Firm A.

Learning-Curve Names. Different learning curves have different names. Unfortunately, the name of a learning curve does not appear in the learning-curve equation but instead must be derived from that equation. The name of a learning curve is derived from the effect that learning has on average production costs when production is doubled. If it takes 10 hours to produce the first unit, and an average of 9 hours to produce the second unit (notice that total production has doubled from one unit to two), this manufacturing process is said to have a 90 percent learning curve (9/10 = .90). If it averages 20 minutes to produce six products, and averages of 16 minutes to produce 12 products (production has doubled), this manufacturing process is said to have an 80 percent learning curve (16/20 = .80).

There is a mathematical relationship between the name of a learning curve and β in the learning-curve equation. For most purposes, however, the value of β and the learning curves listed in Table 6.5 are sufficient to calculate most learning-curve–based cost advantages.

The Learning Curve and Competitive Advantage. The learning-curve model summarized in Figure 6.2 has been used to develop a model of cost-based competitive advantage that links learning with market share and average production costs. The

TABLE 6.5 Learning-Curve Names and β Values for Common Learning Curves	
Learning-Curve Name (in percent)	*Value of β*
99	.1044
98	.0291
97	.0439
96	.0589
95	.0740
94	.0893
93	.1047
92	.1203
91	.1361
90	.1520
89	.1681
88	.1844
87	.2009
86	.2176
85	.2345
84	.2515
83	.2688
82	.2863
81	.3040
80	.3219

major proponent of the application of this learning-curve logic to create competitive advantage has been the Boston Consulting Group.[13]

The logic behind this application of the learning-curve model is straightforward. It seems clear that the first firm that moves successfully down the learning curve will obtain a cost advantage over rivals, just as Firm B in the snipe trap example has a cost advantage over Firm A. To move a production process down the learning curve, and thereby obtain costs lower than rivals' costs, a firm needs to have higher levels of cumulative volume of production. Of course, firms that are successful at producing high volumes of output need to sell that output to customers. Manufacturing to increase inventory may reduce a firm's manufacturing costs, but it will lead to disaster in the long run. In selling this output, firms are, in effect, increasing their market share. Thus, to drive down the learning curve and obtain a cost advantage, firms must be aggressive in acquiring market share.

This application of learning-curve logic has been criticized by a wide variety of authors.[14] Two criticisms are particularly salient. First, although the acquisition of market share is likely to allow a firm to reduce its production costs, the acquisition of share itself is expensive. To acquire share, firms must often increase advertising and other marketing expenditures and reduce prices. Indeed, a significant amount of research suggests that the costs that firms will need to absorb in order to acquire market share will often equal the value of that market share in lowering a firm's production costs. Thus, efforts to move down the learning curve quickly by acquiring market share are likely to generate only competitive parity.[15]

The second major criticism of this application of the learning-curve model is that there is, in this logic, no room for any other business- or corporate-level strategies. In other words, this application of the learning curve implicitly assumes that firms can compete only on the basis of low costs and that any other strategies are not possible. Most industries, however, are characterized by opportunities for at least some other strategies, and thus this strict application of the learning-curve model can be misleading.[16]

These criticisms aside, it is still true that in many industries, firms with larger cumulative levels of production, other things being equal, will have lower average production costs. Thus experience in all the facets of production can be a source of cost advantage even if the single-minded pursuit of market share to obtain these cost reductions may not give a firm economic profits.

Differential Low-Cost Access to Factors of Production

Besides economies of scale, diseconomies of scale, and learning-curve cost advantages, differential low-cost access to factors of production may create cost differences among firms producing similar products in an industry. **Factors of production** are any inputs used by a firm in conducting its business activities; they include labor, capital, land, and raw materials. A firm that has differential low-cost access to one or more of these factors is likely to have lower economic costs compared to rivals.

Consider, for example, an oil company with fields in Saudi Arabia compared to an oil company with fields in the North Sea. The costs of obtaining crude oil for the first firm are considerably less than the cost of obtaining crude oil for the second. North Sea drilling involves the construction of giant offshore drilling platforms, housing workers on floating cities, and transporting oil across an often-stormy sea. Drilling in Saudi Arabia requires only the simplest drilling technologies because the oil is found relatively close to the surface. It is not hard to believe that the costs of the Saudi Arabia–based firm will be lower than the costs of the North Sea–based firm.

Low-cost access to factors of production is an important determinant of firm performance in the global copper industry. From 1984 to 1986, world copper prices were only 61 cents a pound. By the late 1980s, however, demand for copper outstripped supply, and prices rose to as high as $1.46 per pound in the mid-1990s. Of course, this excess demand led to competitive entry. Entry took the form of global mining firms, including Broken Hill Property Corporation (from Australia), Mitsubishi Corporation (from Japan), Minorco (from South Africa), and Phelps Dodge (from the United States), opening new copper mines in Chile and other locations in South America. Compared to copper mines in Africa, Australia, Canada, and Russia, these South American mines are much richer sources of copper ore. By applying mining technologies developed in less productive mines, South American miners are able to extract more ore at lower costs than competitors. As world copper supplies increased and prices fell, it became difficult for traditional but less rich sources of copper ore to remain profitable.[17]

Of course, in order to create a cost advantage, the cost of acquiring low-cost factors of production must be less than the cost savings generated by these factors. For example, even though it may be much less costly to drill for oil in Saudi Arabia than in the North Sea, if it is very expensive to purchase the rights to drill in Saudi Arabia compared to the costs of the rights to drill in the North Sea, the potential cost advantages of drilling in Saudi Arabia can be lost. As with all sources of cost advantages, firms must be careful to weigh the cost of acquiring that advantage against the value of that advantage for the firm.

Differential access to raw materials such as oil, coal, and copper ore can be important determinants of a cost advantage. However, differential access to other factors of production can be just as important. For example, it may be easier (that is, less costly) to recruit highly trained electronics engineers for firms located near where these engineers receive their schooling than for firms located some distance away. This lower cost of recruiting is a partial explanation of the development of geographic technology centers such as Silicon Valley in California, Route 128 in Massachusetts, and the Research Triangle in North Carolina. In all three cases, firms are located physically close to several universities that train the engineers that are the lifeblood of high-technology companies.

Volume of firm production may also affect differential access to factors of production. A firm with very high volumes of production may be able to use its market share as a lever to obtain discounts for raw materials and other supplies. These volume discounts may not be available to smaller firms. The search for volume discounts is one explanation for the recent development of hospital chains in the hospital industry and chains of retail stores in various retail markets. Chains of hospitals can purchase many of their supplies at a lower cost than can individual hospitals. Even individual hospitals are beginning to join together in purchasing consortia to reduce their costs of supplies. Individual retail outlets find it difficult to use volume leverage to purchase from suppliers. However, by joining together in purchasing groups, these firms can gain such advantages. These purchasing advantages explain, for example, the growth of the Ace Hardware and True Value Hardware groups of companies in the United States.[18]

Technological Advantages Independent of Scale

Another possible source of cost advantage in an industry may be the different technologies that firms employ to manage their business. It has already been suggested that larger firms may have technology-based cost advantages that reflect their ability to exploit economies of scale (for example, the two-thirds rule). Here, technology-based cost advantages that do not depend on economies of scale are discussed.

Traditionally, discussion of technology-based cost advantages has focused on the machines, computers, and other physical tools that firms use to manage their business. Clearly, in some industries, these physical technology differences between firms can create important cost differences—even when the firms in question are approximately the same size in terms of volume of production. In the steel industry, for example, technological advances can substantially reduce the cost of producing steel. Firms with the latest steel-manufacturing technology will typically enjoy some cost advantage compared to similar-sized firms without the latest technology. The same applies in the manufacturing of semiconductors, automobiles, consumer electronics, and a wide variety of other products.[19]

These physical technology cost advantages apply in service firms as well as in manufacturing firms. At various points in their history, firms such as broker Charles Schwab and Kaiser Permanente, the largest health maintenance organization (HMO) in the United States, have used technology to gain important cost advantages.[20]

However, the concept of technology can be easily broadened to include not just the physical tools that firms use to manage their business, but any processes within a firm that are used in this way. This concept of firm technology includes not only the **technological hardware** of companies—the machines and robots—but also the **technological software** of firms—things such as the quality of relations among labor and management, an organization's culture, and the quality of managerial controls. All these characteristics of a firm can have an effect on a firm's economic costs.[21]

Research in the automobile industry, for example, suggests that although "hard technology," including automation and robots, is an important component of low-cost manufacturing, "soft technology" such as the use of quality circles on the manufacturing floor, a sense of loyalty from the worker to the firm, and an organizational culture that emphasizes cost control is just as important, if not more important, in explaining the cost position of some firms.[22]

Policy Choices

Thus far, this discussion has focused on reasons why a firm can gain a cost advantage despite producing products that are similar to competing firms' products. When firms produce essentially the same outputs, differences in economies of scale, learning-curve advantages, differential access to factors of production, and differences in technology can all create cost advantages (and disadvantages) for firms. However, firms can also make choices about the kinds of products and services they will sell—choices that have an effect on their relative cost position. In general, firms that are attempting to implement a cost leadership strategy will choose to produce relatively simple standardized products that sell for relatively low prices compared to the products and prices of firms pursuing other business or corporate strategies. These kinds of products often tend to have high volumes of sales, which (if significant economies of scale exist) tend to reduce costs even further.

These kinds of choices in product and pricing tend to have a very large effect on a cost leader's operations. In these firms, the task of reducing costs is not delegated to a single function or a special task force within the firm but is the responsibility of every manager and employee. Cost reduction sometimes becomes the central objective of the firm. Indeed, in this setting, management must be constantly alert to cost-cutting efforts that reduce the ability of the firm to meet customers' needs.

In this all-out effort to reduce costs, firms must avoid manufacturing or selling low-cost products that no one wants to buy. In the end, a firm's performance depends on the relationship between revenues and costs. However, if cutting costs threatens revenues, a low-cost firm may not remain profitable.

6.2 THE ECONOMIC VALUE OF COST LEADERSHIP

There is little doubt that cost differences can exist among firms, even when those firms are manufacturing very similar products. Policy choices about the kinds of products firms in an industry choose to produce can also create important cost differences. The effects of these cost differences on economic performance can be seen in Figure 6.3.

The firms depicted in this figure are price takers—that is, the price of the products or services they sell is determined by market conditions and not by individual decisions of firms (see Chapter 3). This implies that there is effectively no product differentiation in this market and that no one firm's sales constitute a large percentage of this market. (Markets with product differentiation are discussed in Chapter 7; markets with dominant firms are discussed in Chapter 9).

The price of goods or services in this type of market (P^*) is determined by aggregate industry supply and demand. This industry price determines the demand facing an individual firm in this market. Because these firms are price takers, the demand facing an individual firm is horizontal—that is, firm decisions about levels of output have a negligible effect on overall industry supply and thus a negligible effect on the market-determined price. As is well known, a firm in this setting maximizes its economic

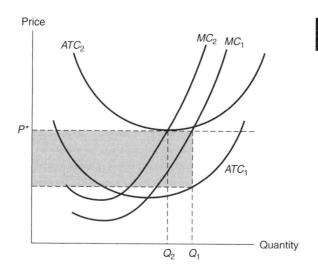

FIGURE 6.3   Cost Leadership and Economic Performance

performance by producing a quantity of output (Q) so that marginal revenue equals marginal cost (MC). The ability of firms to earn economic profits in this setting depends on the relationship between the market-determined price (P^*) and the average total cost (ATC) of a firm at the quantity it chooses to produce.

Firms in the market depicted in Figure 6.3 fall into two categories. All but one firm have the average total cost curve ATC_2 and the marginal cost curve MC_2. However, one firm in this industry has the average total cost curve ATC_1 and a marginal cost curve MC_1. Notice that ATC_1 is less than ATC_2 at the performance-maximizing quantities produced by these two kinds of firms (Q_1 and Q_2, respectively). In this particular example, firms with common average total cost curves are earning zero economic profits, while the low-cost firm is earning an economic profit (equal to the shaded area in Figure 6.3). A variety of other examples could also be constructed: The cost leader firm could be earning zero economic profits while other firms in the market are incurring economic losses; the cost leader firm could be earning substantial economic profits while other firms are earning smaller economic profits; the cost leader firm could be incurring small economic losses while the other firms are incurring substantial economic losses; and so forth. However, in all these examples, the cost leader's economic performance is greater than the economic performance of other firms in the industry. Thus cost leadership can have an important effect on a firm's economic performance.

Cost Leadership and Environmental Threats

The value of cost leadership can also be analyzed relative to the models of environmental threats and opportunities presented in Chapters 3 and 4. How cost leadership reduces the threat of new entrants, rivalry, substitutes, buyers, and suppliers is discussed here. Describing the ways that cost leadership can enable a firm to exploit environmental opportunities is left as an exercise for the reader.

Cost Leadership and the Threat of Entry

A cost leadership competitive strategy helps reduce the threat of new entrants by creating cost-based barriers to entry. Recall that many of the barriers to entry cited in Chapter 3, including economies of scale and cost advantages independent of scale, presume that incumbent firms have lower costs than potential entrants. If an incumbent firm is a cost leader, for any of the reasons just listed, then new entrants may have to invest heavily to reduce their costs prior to entry. Often, new entrants will enter using another business strategy (for example, product differentiation) rather than attempting to compete on costs.

The relationship between Caterpillar and Komatsu in the construction equipment industry (described briefly in Chapter 5) can be understood in these terms. Caterpillar obtained an important competitive advantage by gaining low-cost access to an important factor of production (a worldwide service and supply network). Komatsu was unable to match Caterpillar's cost advantage in this area and thus entered the worldwide construction equipment industry with high-quality machines that break down less frequently. Because it could not match Caterpillar's cost advantage in service and supply, Komatsu choose to differentiate its product on the basis of high reliability.[23]

Cost Leadership and the Threat of Rivalry

Firms with a low-cost position also reduce the threat of rivalry. The threat of rivalry is reduced through pricing strategies that low-cost firms can engage in and through their relative effect on the performance of a low-cost firm and its higher-cost rivals.

Cost leader firms have two choices in pricing their products or services. First, these firms can set their prices equal to the prices of higher-cost competitors. Assuming that there are few opportunities for other firms to implement product differentiation strategies, customers will be indifferent about purchasing goods or services from the low-cost firm or from its high-cost rivals. However, at these competitive prices, high-cost firms are not likely to earn an economic profit, whereas the cost leader firm is.

Second, low-cost firms can price their goods or services slightly below the prices of their high-cost rivals. Again, assuming little product differentiation, customers will no longer be indifferent about which firm they prefer to buy from. Obviously, the lower prices of the low-cost firm will attract numerous customers, rapidly increasing the market share of the low-cost firm.

Each of these alternatives has strengths and weaknesses. Keeping prices equal to the competition's prices enables a low-cost firm to earn large margins on its sales. As important, this pricing approach at least partially conceals the fact that the low-cost firm has a cost advantage. Concealing this information reduces the chances that competitors will imitate the low-cost firm, thereby reducing its cost advantage. However, keeping prices equal to a competitor's prices does sacrifice market share and sales volume. Setting the low-cost firm's prices below the prices of competing firms has the opposite effects. Such a pricing strategy can significantly increase a firm's market share and total volume of sales, but at the cost of some of the profit margin of the low-cost firm. Also, setting prices to this lower level sends a signal to competitors that lower costs are possible. Such a signal may motivate competitors to try to reduce their costs, either through implementing their own cost leadership competitive strategies or through implementing strategies that reduce costs.

In the end, the choice between these two pricing strategies depends on the ability of competing firms to respond to the cost advantages of cost leaders. If the potential responses of competing firms are likely to be very detrimental to the cost leader, then this firm should set its prices equal to competitors' prices, sacrificing some market share for increased profit margins and the release of less information. However, if competitive reactions are not likely to threaten the cost leader, then dropping prices below competitors' prices should increase overall economic performance through increased volumes of profitable sales.

More generally, these strategic pricing options, and the potential superior economic performance they hold, are available only to cost leaders. These strategies enable a low-cost firm to earn economic profits even if the industry within which this firm operates is characterized by intense rivalry.

Cost Leadership and the Threat of Substitutes

As suggested in Chapter 3, substitutes become a threat to a firm when their cost and performance, relative to the firm's current products or services, become more attractive to customers. Thus, when the price of crude oil goes up, substitutes for crude oil become more attractive. When the cost and performance of electronic calculators improve, demand for mechanical adding machines disappears.

In this situation, cost leaders have the ability to keep their products and services attractive relative to substitutes. While high-cost firms may have to charge high prices to cover their costs, thus making substitutes more attractive, cost leaders can keep their prices low and still earn economic profits.

Cost Leadership and the Threat of Suppliers

Suppliers can become a threat to a firm by charging higher prices for the goods or services they supply or by reducing the quality of those goods or services. However, when a supplier sells to a cost leader, that firm has greater flexibility in absorbing higher-cost supplies than does a high-cost firm. Higher supply costs may destroy any economic profits for high-cost firms but still allow a cost leader firm to gain such profits.

Cost leadership based on large volumes of production and economies of scale can also reduce the threat of suppliers. Large volumes of production imply large purchases of raw materials and other supplies. Suppliers are not likely to jeopardize these sales by threatening their customers. Indeed, as was suggested earlier, buyers are often able to use their purchasing volume to extract volume discounts from suppliers.

Cost Leadership and the Threat of Buyers

Cost leadership can also reduce the threat of buyers. Powerful buyers are a threat to firms when they insist on low prices or higher quality and service from their suppliers. Lower prices threaten firm revenues; higher quality can increase a firm's costs. Cost leaders can have their revenues reduced by buyer threats and still gain economic profits. These firms can also absorb the greater costs of increased quality or service and may still have a cost advantage over their competition.

Buyers can also be a threat through backward vertical integration. Being a cost leader deters buyer backward vertical integration, because a buyer that vertically integrates backward will often not have costs as low as an incumbent cost leader. Rather than vertically integrating backwards and increasing their cost of supplies, powerful buyers usually prefer to continue purchasing from their low-cost suppliers.

Finally, if cost leadership is based on large volumes of production, then the threat of buyers may be reduced, because buyers may depend on just a few firms for the goods or services they purchase. This dependence reduces the willingness of buyers to threaten a selling firm.[24]

6.3 COST LEADERSHIP AND SUSTAINED COMPETITIVE ADVANTAGE

Given that cost leadership can be valuable, an important question becomes, "Under what conditions will firms implementing this business strategy be able to maintain that leadership to obtain a sustained competitive advantage?" If cost leadership strategies can be implemented by numerous firms in an industry, or if no firms face a cost disadvantage in imitating a cost leadership strategy, then being a cost leader does not generate a sustained competitive advantage for a firm. As was suggested in Chapter 5, the ability of a valuable cost leadership strategy to generate a sustained competitive advantage depends on that strategy being rare and costly to imitate, either through direct duplication or substitution. As suggested in Tables 6.6 and 6.7, the rarity and imitability of a cost leadership strategy depends, at least in part, on the sources of that cost advantage.

TABLE 6.6   The Rarity of Sources of Cost Advantage

Likely to Be Rare Sources of Cost Advantage	*Less Likely to Be Rare Sources of Cost Advantage*
Learning-curve economies of scale (especially in emerging businesses)	Economies of scale (except when efficient plant size approximately equals total industry demand)
Differential low-cost access to factors of production	Diseconomies of scale
Technological "software"	Technological hardware (unless a firm has proprietary hardware development skills)
	Policy choices

The Rarity of Sources of Cost Advantage

Some of the sources of cost advantage listed in Table 6.6 are likely to be rare among a set of competing firms; others are less likely to be rare. Sources of cost advantage that are likely to be rare include learning-curve economies (at least in emerging industries), differential low-cost access to factors of production, and technological "software." The remaining sources of cost advantage are less likely to be rare.

Rare Sources of Cost Advantage

Early in the evolution of an industry, substantial differences in the cumulative volume of production of different firms are not unusual. Indeed, this was one of the major benefits associated with first-mover advantages, discussed in Chapter 4. These differences in cumulative volume of production, in combination with substantial learning-curve economies, suggest that in some settings learning-curve advantages may be rare and thus a source of at least temporary competitive advantage.

TABLE 6.7   Direct Duplication of Cost Leadership

		Basis for Costly Duplication		
	Source of Cost Advantage	*History*	*Uncertainty*	*Social Complexity*
Low-cost duplication possible	1. Economies of scale	—	—	—
	2. Diseconomies of scale	—	—	—
May be costly to duplicate	3. Learning-curve economies	*	—	—
	4. Technological "hardware"	—	*	*
	5. Policy choices	*	—	—
Usually costly to duplicate	6. Differential low-cost access to factors of production	***	—	**
	7. Technological "software"	***	**	***

— = not a source of costly imitation

* = somewhat likely to be a source of costly imitation

** = likely to be a source of costly imitation

*** = very likely to be a source of costly imitation

The definition of differential access to factors of production implies that this access is often rare. Certainly, if large numbers of competing firms have this same access, then it cannot be a source of competitive advantage.

Technological software is also likely to be rare among a set of competing firms. These software attributes represent each firm's path through history. If these histories are unique, then the technological software they create may also be rare. Of course, if several competing firms experience similar paths through history, the technological software in these firms is less likely to be rare.

Less Rare Sources of Cost Advantage

When the efficient size of a firm or plant is significantly smaller than the total size of an industry, there will usually be numerous efficient firms/plants in that industry, and a cost leadership strategy based on economies of scale will not be rare. For example, if the efficient firm/plant size in an industry is 500 units, and the total size of the industry (measured in units produced) is 500,000 units, then there are likely to be numerous efficient firms/plants in this industry, and economies of scale are not likely to give any one firm a cost-based competitive advantage.

Cost advantages based on diseconomies of scale are also not likely to be rare. It is unusual for numerous firms to adopt levels of production in excess of optimal levels. If only a few firms are too large in this sense, then several competing firms in an industry that are *not* too large will have cost advantages over the firms that are too large. However, because several firms will enjoy these cost advantages, they are not rare.

One important exception to this generalization may be when changes in technology significantly reduce the most efficient scale of an operation. Given such changes in technology, several firms may be inefficiently large. If a small number of firms happens to be sized appropriately, then the cost advantages these firms obtain in this way may be rare. Such changes in technology have made large integrated steel producers "too big" relative to smaller mini-mills. Thus mini-mills have a cost advantage over larger integrated steel firms.

Technological hardware is also not likely to be rare, especially if it is developed by suppliers and sold on the open market. However, if a firm has proprietary technology development skills, it may possess rare technological hardware that creates cost advantages.

Finally, policy choices by themselves are not likely to be a rare source of cost advantage, particularly if the product or service attributes in question are easy to observe and describe.

The Imitability of Sources of Cost Advantage

Even when a particular source of cost advantage is rare, it must be costly to imitate in order to be a source of sustained competitive advantage. Both direct duplication and substitution, as forms of imitation, are important. Again, the imitability of a cost advantage depends, at least in part, on the source of that advantage.

Easy-to-Duplicate Sources of Cost Advantage

In general, economies of scale and diseconomies of scale are relatively easy-to-duplicate bases of cost leadership. As can be seen in Table 6.7, these sources of cost advantage do not build on history, uncertainty, or socially complex resources and capabilities and thus are not protected from duplication for these reasons.

For example, if a small number of firms do obtain a cost advantage based on economies of scale, and if the relationship between production scale and costs is widely understood among competing firms, then firms at a cost disadvantage will rapidly adjust their production to exploit these economies of scale. This can be done by either increasing a firm's current operations to the point that the firm exploits economies or by combining previously separate operations to obtain these economies. Both actions enable a firm at a cost disadvantage to begin using specialized machines, reduce the cost of plant and equipment, increase employee specialization, and spread overhead costs more effectively.

Indeed, perhaps the only time economies of scale are not subject to low-cost duplication is when the efficient size of operations is a significant percentage of total demand in an industry. Of course, this is the situation described in Chapter 3's discussion of economies of scale as a barrier to entry. For example, as suggested earlier, BIC Corporation, with its dominant market share in the disposable pen market, has apparently been able to gain and retain an important cost advantage in that market based on economies of scale. BIC's ability to retain this advantage reflects the fact that the optimal plant size in the disposable pen market is a significant percentage of the pen market, and thus economies of scale act as a barrier to entry in that market.

Like economies of scale, in many settings diseconomies of scale will not be a source of sustained competitive advantage for firms that have *not* grown too large. In the short run, firms experiencing significant diseconomies can reduce the size of their operations to become more efficient. In the long run, firms that fail to adjust their size will destroy economic value and cease operations.

Although in many ways reducing the size of operations to improve efficiency seems like a simple problem for managers in firms/plants, in practice it is often a difficult change to implement. Because of uncertainty, managers in a firm/plant that is too large may not understand that diseconomies of scale have increased their costs. Sometimes, managers conclude that the problem is that employees are not working hard enough, that problems in production can be fixed, and so forth. These firms/plants may continue their inefficient operations for some time, despite costs that are higher than the industry average.[25]

Other psychological processes can also delay the abandonment of operations that are too large. One of these phenomena is known as **escalation of commitment:** Managers committed to an incorrect (cost-increasing or revenue-reducing) course of action *increase* their commitment to this action as its limitations become manifest. For example, a manager who believes that the optimal firm size in an industry is larger than the actual optimal size may remain committed to large operations despite costs that are higher than the industry average.[26]

For all these reasons, firms suffering from diseconomies of scale must often turn to outside managers to assist in reducing costs. Outsiders bring a fresh view to the organization's problems and are not committed to the practices that generated the problems in the first place.[27]

Bases of Cost Leadership That May Be Costly to Duplicate
Although cost advantages based on learning-curve economies are rare (especially in emerging industries), they are usually not costly to duplicate. As suggested in Chapter 4, for learning-curve cost advantages to be a source of sustained competitive advantage,

the learning obtained by a firm must be proprietary. Most recent empirical work suggests that in most industries learning is not proprietary and thus can be rapidly duplicated as competing firms move down the learning curve by increasing their cumulative volume of production.[28]

However, the fact that in *most* industries learning is not costly to duplicate does not mean that learning is not costly to duplicate in all industries. In some industries, the ability of firms to learn from their production experience may vary significantly. For example, some firms treat production errors as failures and systematically punish employees who make those errors. These firms effectively reduce risk taking among their production employees and thus reduce the chances of learning how to improve their production process. Alternatively, other firms treat production errors as opportunities to learn how to improve their production process. These firms are likely to move rapidly down the learning curve and retain cost advantages, despite the cumulative volume of production of competing firms. These different responses to production errors reflect the organizational cultures of these different firms. Because organizational cultures are socially complex, they can be very costly to duplicate.[29]

Because technological hardware can usually be purchased across supply markets, it is also not likely to be difficult to duplicate. Sometimes, however, technological hardware can be proprietary, or closely bundled with other unique, costly-to-duplicate resources controlled by a firm. In this case, technological hardware can be costly to duplicate.

It is unusual, but not impossible, for policy choices, per se, to be a source of sustained competitive cost advantages for a firm. As suggested earlier, if the policies in question focus on easy-to-observe and easy-to-describe product characteristics, then duplication is likely, and cost advantages based on policy choices will be temporary. However, if policy choices reflect complex decision processes within a firm, teamwork among different parts of the design and manufacturing process, or any of the software commitments discussed previously, then policy choices can be a source of sustained competitive advantage, as long as only a few firms have the ability to make these choices.

Indeed, most of the successful firms that operate in unattractive industries, described in Chapter 5, make policy choices that are costly to imitate because they reflect historical, causally ambiguous, and socially complex firm processes. Thus, for example, Dell's low product inventory strategy—a policy with clear low-cost implications—actually reflects the complex links among various parts of the value chain within Dell, an unwavering commitment to manufacturing flexibility and efficiency, and an organizational culture that focuses on Web-based sales. Wal-Mart's supply chain management strategy—again, a policy with clear low-cost implications—actually reflects Wal-Mart's unique history, its socially complex relations with suppliers, and its unique organizational culture. And Southwest Airlines' low-price pricing strategy—a strategy that reflects Southwest's low-cost position—is possible because of the kind of airplane fleet Southwest has built over time, the commitment of its employees to Southwest's success, a charismatic founder (Herb Kelleher), and its unique organizational culture. Because these firms' policies reflect costly-to-imitate attributes of these firms, they can be sources of sustained competitive advantage.

However, for these and other firms, it is not these policy choices, per se, that create sustainable cost leadership advantages. Rather, it is how these policies flow out of the historical, causally ambiguous, and socially complex processes within a firm that make them costly to duplicate.

Costly-to-Duplicate Sources of Cost Advantage

Differential low-cost access to factors of production and technological software, because they build on historical, uncertain, and socially complex resources and capabilities, are usually costly-to-duplicate bases of cost leadership. As suggested earlier, differential access to factors of production often depends on the location of a firm. Moreover, to be a source of economic profits, this valuable location must be obtained before its full value is widely understood.

Both these attributes of differential access to factors of production suggest that if, in fact, it is rare, it will often be costly to duplicate. First, some locations are effectively unique and cannot be duplicated. For example, most private golf clubs would like to own courses with the spectacular beauty of Pebble Beach in Monterey, California, but there is only one Pebble Beach—a course that runs parallel to some of the most beautiful oceanfront scenery in the world. Although "scenery" is an important factor of production in running and managing a golf course, the re-creation of Pebble Beach's scenery at some other location is simply beyond our technology.

Second, even if a location is not totally unique, once its value is revealed, acquisition of that location is not likely to generate economic profits. Thus, for example, although being located in Silicon Valley provides low-cost access to some important factors of production for electronics firms, firms that moved to this location after its value was revealed have substantially higher costs than firms that moved there before its full value was revealed. These higher costs effectively reduce the economic profit that otherwise could have been generated. Referring to the discussion in Chapter 5, these arguments suggest that gaining differential access to factors of production in a way that generates economic profits may reflect a firm's unique path through history.

When differential access to factors of production depends on the volume of production, then much of the analysis of economies of scale as a source of sustained competitive advantage applies. Only if the special (and probably unusual) conditions outlined previously hold is it likely that economies of scale leading to differential access to factors of production will be a source of sustained competitive advantage.

Technological software is also likely to be difficult to duplicate and often can be a source of sustained competitive advantage. As suggested in Chapter 5, the values, beliefs, culture, and teamwork that constitute this software are socially complex and may be immune from competitive duplication. Firms with cost advantages rooted in these socially complex resources incorporate cost savings in every aspect of their firm. These firms constantly focus on improving the quality and cost of their operations, and they have employees firmly committed to, and understand, what it takes to be a cost leader. Other firms may talk about low costs; these firms live cost leadership. Dell, Wal-Mart, and Southwest are all examples of such firms. If there are few firms in an industry with these kinds of beliefs and commitments, then these firms can gain a sustained competitive advantage from their cost advantage.

Substitutes for Sources of Cost Advantage

In an important sense, all of the sources of cost advantage listed in this chapter are at least partial substitutes for each other. Thus, for example, one firm may reduce its cost through exploiting economies of scale in large-scale production, and a competing firm may reduce its costs through exploiting learning-curve economies and large cumulative volume of production. If these different activities have similar effects on a firm's cost position, and if they are equally costly to implement, then they are strategic substitutes for each other.

Because of the substitute effects of different sources of cost advantage, it is not unusual for firms pursuing cost leadership to pursue *all* the cost reduction activities discussed in this chapter simultaneously. Implementing this *bundle* of cost-reducing activities may have few substitutes. If duplicating this bundle of activities is also rare and difficult, then a firm may be able to gain a sustained competitive advantage from doing so.

Several of the other strategies discussed in later chapters can also have the effect of reducing a firm's costs and thus may be substitutes for the sources of cost reduction discussed in this chapter. For example, one common motivation for firms to implement strategic alliance strategies is to exploit economies of scale in combination with other firms. Thus a strategic alliance that reduces a firm's costs may be a substitute for a firm exploiting economies of scale on its own to reduce its costs. As is discussed in more detail in Chapter 13, many of the strategic alliances among aluminum mining and smelting companies are motivated by realizing economies of scale and cost reduction. Also, corporate diversification strategies often enable firms to exploit economies of scale across different businesses within which they operate. In this setting, each of these businesses—treated separately—may have scale disadvantages; but collectively, their scale creates the same low-cost position as that of an individual firm that fully exploits economies of scale to reduce costs in a single business (see Chapter 11).

6.4 ORGANIZING TO IMPLEMENT COST LEADERSHIP

As with all strategies, firms that seek to implement cost leadership strategies must adopt an organizational structure, management controls, and compensation policies that reinforce this strategy. Some key issues associated with using these organizing tools to implement cost leadership are summarized in Table 6.8.

TABLE 6.8   Organizing to Realize the Full Potential of Cost Leadership Strategies

Organization Structure

1. Few layers in the reporting structure
2. Simple reporting relationships
3. Small corporate staff
4. Focus on narrow range of business functions

Management Control Systems

1. Tight cost control systems
2. Quantitative cost goals
3. Close supervision of labor, raw material, inventory, and other costs
4. A cost-leadership philosophy

Compensation Policies

1. Reward for cost reduction
2. Incentives for all employees to be involved in cost reduction

Organizational Structure in Implementing Cost Leadership

As suggested in Table 6.8, a firm implementing cost leadership strategies will generally adopt what is known as a **functional organizational structure.**[30] An example of a functional organization structure is presented in Figure 6.4. Indeed, this functional organizational structure is the structure used to implement all business-level strategies a firm might pursue, although this structure is modified when used to implement these different strategies.

In a functional structure, each of the major business functions is managed by a **functional manager.** For example, if manufacturing, marketing, finance, accounting, and sales are all included within a functional organization, then a manufacturing manager leads that function, a marketing manager leads that function, a finance manager leads that function, and so forth. In a functional organizational structure, all these functional managers report to one person. This person may have any of many different titles—including president, CEO, chair, or founder. However, for purposes of this discussion, this person will be called the **chief executive officer (CEO).**

The CEO in a functional organization has a unique status. Everyone else in this company is a functional specialist. The manufacturing people manufacture, the marketing people market, the finance people finance, and so forth. Indeed, there is only one person in the functional organization who has to have a multifunctional perspective—the CEO. This role is so important that sometimes the functional organization is called a **U-form structure,** where the "U" stands for "unitary"—because there is only one person in this organization who has a broad, multifunctional corporate perspective.

When this U-form structure is used to implement a cost leadership strategy, it is kept as simple as possible. As suggested in Table 6.8, firms that implement cost leadership strategies have relatively few layers in their reporting structure. Complicated reporting structures, including **matrix structures** in which one employee reports to two or more people, are usually avoided.[31] Corporate staff in these organizations is kept small. Such firms do not operate in a wide range of business functions, but instead operate only in those few business functions in which they have valuable, rare, and costly-to-imitate resources and capabilities.

One excellent example of a firm that pursues a cost leadership strategy is Nucor Steel. A leader in the mini-mill industry, Nucor has only five layers in its reporting structure, compared to 12 to 15 in its major higher-cost competitors. Most operating decisions at Nucor are delegated to plant managers, who have full profit-and-loss responsibility for their operations. Corporate staff at Nucor is small and focuses its efforts on accounting for revenues and costs and on exploring new manufacturing processes to further reduce Nucor's operating expenses and expand its business opportunities. Nucor's former president, Ken Iverson, believed that Nucor does only two things well: build plants efficiently and run them effectively. Thus Nucor focuses its efforts in these areas

FIGURE 6.4   An Example of the U-Form Organizational Structure

Chief Executive Officer (CEO)

Manufacturing   Sales   Research and Development   Human Resources   Legal and subcontracts many of its other business functions, including the purchase of its raw materials, to outside vendors.[32]

Responsibilities of the CEO in a Functional Organization

The CEO in a U-form organization has two basic responsibilities: (1) to formulate the strategy of the firm and (2) to coordinate the activities of the functional specialists in the firm to facilitate the implementation of this strategy. In the special case of a cost leadership strategy, the CEO must decide on which bases such a strategy should be founded and then must coordinate functions within the firm to make sure that the economic potential of this strategy is fully realized.

Strategy Formulation

The CEO in a U-form organization engages in strategy formulation by applying the strategic management process described in Chapter 1. A CEO establishes the firm's mission and associated objectives. He or she evaluates environmental threats and opportunities, understands the firm's strengths and weaknesses, and then chooses one or more of the business and corporate strategies discussed in this book. In the case of a cost leadership strategy, the application of the strategic management process must lead a CEO to conclude that the best chance for achieving a firm's mission is for that firm to adopt a cost leadership business-level strategy.

Although the responsibility for strategy formulation in a U-form organization rests ultimately with the CEO, this individual needs to draw on the insights, analysis, and involvement of functional managers throughout the firm. CEOs who fail to involve functional managers in strategy formulation run several risks. First, strategic choices made in isolation from functional managers may be made without complete information. Second, limiting the involvement of functional managers in strategy formulation can limit their understanding of, and commitment to, the chosen strategy. This can severely limit their ability, and willingness, to implement any strategy—including cost leadership—that is chosen.[33]

Coordinating Functions for Strategy Implementation

Even the best-formulated strategy is competitively irrelevant if it is not implemented. And strategies can be implemented effectively only if all the functions within a firm are aligned in a way that is consistent with this strategy.

For example, compare two firms pursuing a cost leadership strategy. All but one of the first firm's functions—marketing—are aligned with this cost leadership strategy. All of the second firm's functions—including marketing—are aligned with this cost leadership strategy. Because marketing is not aligned with the first firm's cost leadership strategy, this firm is likely to advertise products that it does not sell. That is, this firm might advertise its products on the basis of their style and performance, but sell product that are reliable (but not stylish) and inexpensive (but not high performers).

A firm that markets products it does not actually sell is likely to disappoint its customers. On the other hand, the second firm that has all of its functions—including marketing—aligned with its chosen strategy is more likely to advertise products it actually sells and thus is less likely to disappoint its customers. In the long run, it seems reasonable to expect this second firm to outperform the first firm, at least with respect to implementing a cost leadership strategy.

Of course, alignment is required of all of a firm's functional areas, not just marketing. Also, misalignment can emerge in any of a firm's functional areas. Some common misalignments between a firm's cost leadership strategy and its functional activities are listed in Table 6.9.

Management Controls in Implementing Cost Leadership

As suggested in Table 6.8, cost leadership firms are typically characterized by very tight cost control systems; frequent and detailed cost control reports; an emphasis on quantitative cost goals and targets; and close supervision of labor, raw materials, inventory, and other costs. Again, Nucor is an example of a cost leadership firm that has implemented these kinds of control systems. At Nucor, groups of employees are given weekly cost and productivity improvement goals. Groups that meet or exceed these goals receive extra compensation. Plant managers are held responsible for cost and profit performance. A plant manager who does not meet corporate performance expectations cannot expect a long career at Nucor. Similar group-oriented cost-reduction systems are in place at some of Nucor's major competitors, including Chaparral Steel.[34]

Less formal management control systems also drive a cost-reduction philosophy at cost leadership firms. For example, although Wal-Mart is one of the most successful retail operations in the world, its Arkansas headquarters is plain and simple. Indeed, some have suggested that Wal-Mart's headquarters looks like a warehouse. Its style of interior decoration was once described as "early bus station." Regional vice-presidents at Wal-Mart travel every week, from Monday to Thursday, meet all day Friday, attend a company-wide meeting on Saturday morning, and then have late Saturday and Sunday off, just in time to start traveling again on Monday. This schedule enables Wal-Mart to reduce its costs by 2 percent of sales by *not* opening independent regional offices. Wal-Mart even involves its customers in reducing costs by asking them to "help keep your costs low" by returning shopping carts to the designated areas in Wal-Mart's parking lots.[35]

TABLE 6.9	Common Misalignments Between Business Functions and a Cost Leadership Strategy	
	When Function Is **Aligned** *with Cost Leadership Strategies*	*When Function Is* **Misaligned** *with Cost Leadership Strategies*
Manufacturing	Lean, low cost, good quality	Inefficient, high cost, poor quality
Marketing	Emphasize value, reliability, and price	Emphasize style and performance
R&D	Focus on product extensions and process improvements	Focus on radical new technologies and products
Finance	Focus on low cost and stable financial structure	Focus on nontraditional financial instruments
Accounting	Collect cost data and adopt conservative accounting principles	Collect no cost data and adopt very aggressive accounting principles
Sales	Focus on value, reliability, and low price	Focus on style and performance and high price

Compensation Policies and Implementing Cost Leadership Strategies

As suggested in Table 6.8, compensation in cost leadership firms is usually tied directly to cost-reduction efforts. Such firms often provide incentives for employees to work together to reduce costs and increase or maintain quality, and they expect *every* employee to take responsibility for both costs and quality. For example, an important expense for retail stores such as Wal-Mart is "shrinkage"—a nice way of saying people steal stuff. About half the shrinkage in most stores comes from employees stealing their own companies' products.

Wal-Mart used to have a serious problem with shrinkage. Among other solutions (including hiring "greeters" whose real job is to discourage shoplifters), Wal-Mart developed a compensation scheme that took half the cost savings created by reduced shrinkage and shared it with employees in the form of a bonus. With this incentive in place, Wal-Mart's shrinkage problems dropped significantly.

Even apparently small cost savings can be important for firms implementing a cost leadership strategy. Ford Motor used compensation policies to help discover cost reductions in manufacturing the Ford Taurus. Cost reductions included redesigning door hinge pins (to save $2 per car), the use of splash shields under wheel wells made out of recycled plastic (to save 45 cents per car), and the use of a part from the Lincoln Continental to reinforce sheet metal under seats (to save $1.50 per car). Collectively, these small improvements have trimmed $180 from the cost of producing each Taurus. This could lead to additional profits of almost $73 million for the Taurus line of products.[36]

6.5 SUMMARY

Firms that produce essentially the same products can have very different costs. Some of the most important reasons are (1) size differences and economies of scale, (2) size differences and diseconomies of scale, (3) learning-curve economies, (4) differential access to factors of production, and (5) technological advantages independent of scale. In addition, firms competing in the same industry can make policy choices about the kinds of products and services to sell that can have significant effects on their relative cost position. Cost leadership in an industry can generate economic profits and can assist a firm in reducing the threat of each of the five forces in an industry outlined in Chapter 3.

All of the sources of cost advantage discussed in this chapter can be sources of sustained competitive advantage if they are rare and costly to imitate. Overall, differential access to factors of production and technological software advantages independent of scale have the greatest potential to create cost-based sustained competitive advantages.

Of course, to realize the full potential of these competitive advantages, a firm must be organized appropriately. Organizing to implement a strategy always involves a firm's organizational structure, its management control systems, and its compensation policies. As with all business strategies, the most appropriate organizational structure to implement leadership is a U-form structure. In the case of cost leadership, the U-form structure should have a few layers, simple reporting relationships, a small corporate staff, and focus on a narrow range of business functions. Budgets in firms that implement cost leadership should focus on costs. Quantitative cost objectives should be built into budgets; management committees should supervise labor, raw material, inventory, and other costs closely; and management committees should create and diffuse a cost leadership philosophy throughout the firm. In firms implementing cost leadership strategies, compensation systems should reward all employees for reducing costs.

REVIEW QUESTIONS

1. Porter originally argued that there are *three* generic competitive strategies: cost leadership, product differentiation, and focus. Others have suggested that focus is just a special case of cost leadership or product differentiation and thus there are only *two* competitive strategies. It could also be argued that firms can choose from among numerous strategic alternatives, but whatever alternative they choose, the critical task is to implement that strategy efficiently. This suggests that there is *one* competitive strategy—efficiency. So, how many competitive strategies are there: three, two, or one? Does your answer affect the strategic decisions firms should make?

2. Proctor & Gamble (Ivory Soap), Hyundai, and Timex are all cited as examples of firms that pursue cost leadership strategies, but these firms make substantial investments in advertising, which seems more likely to be associated with a product differentiation strategy. Are these firms really pursuing a cost leadership strategy, or are they pursuing a product differentiation strategy by emphasizing their lower costs?

3. When economies of scale exist, firms with large volumes of production will have lower costs than firms with smaller volumes of production. The realization of these economies of scale, however, is far from automatic. What

actions can firms take to ensure that they realize whatever economies of scale are created by their volume of production?

4. Firms engage in forward pricing when they establish, during the early stages of the learning curve, a price for their products that is lower than their actual costs, in anticipation of lower costs later on, after significant learning has occurred. Under what conditions, if any, does forward pricing make sense? What risks, if any, do firms that engage in forward pricing face?

5. One way of thinking about organizing to implement cost leadership strategies is that firms that pursue this strategy should be highly centralized, have high levels of direct supervision, and keep employee wages to an absolute minimum. Another approach is to decentralize decision-making authority—to ensure that individuals who know the most about reducing costs make decisions about how to reduce costs. This, in turn, implies less direct supervision and somewhat higher levels of employee wages (why?). Which of these two approaches seems more reasonable? Under what conditions would these different approaches make more or less sense?

6. How can being a cost leader enable a firm to exploit the environmental opportunities discussed in Chapter 4?

ENDNOTES

1. Porter, M. E. (1980). *Competitive Strategy,* New York: Free Press.
2. Lawrence, J., and P. Sloan (1992). "P&G plans big new Ivory push," *Advertising Age,* November 23, p. 12.
3. Weiner, S. (1987). "The road most traveled," *Forbes,* October 19, pp. 60–64.
4. Roush, C. (1993). "At Timex, they're positively glowing," *Business Week,* July 12, p. 141.

5. Wilson, J. H. (1981). "A note on scale economies in the savings and loan industry," *Business Economics,* January, pp. 45–49.

6. Christensen, C. R., N. A. Berg, and M. S. Salter (1980). *Policy Formulation and Administration: A Casebook of Senior Management Problems in Business,* 8th ed., p. 163, Homewood, IL: Irwin.

7. Scherer, F. M. (1980). *Industrial Market Structure and Economic Performance,* Boston: Houghton Mifflin; Moore, F. T. (1959). "Economies of scale: Some statistical evidence," *Quarterly Journal of Economics,* 73, pp. 232–245; and Lau, L. J., and S. Tamura (1972). "Economies of scale, technical progress, and the nonhomothetic Leontief production function," *Journal of Political Economy,* 80, pp. 1167–1187.

8. Scherer, F. M. (1980). *Industrial Market Structure and Economic Performance,* Boston: Houghton Mifflin; and Perrow, C. (1984). *Normal Accidents: Living with High-Risk Technologies,* New York: Basic Books.

9. Hamermesh, R. G., and R. S. Rosenbloom (1989). "Crown Cork and Seal Co., Inc.," Harvard Business School Case no. 9-388-096.

10. See Hackman, J. R., and G. R. Oldham (1980). *Work Redesign,* Reading, MA: Addison-Wesley.

11. This relationship was first noticed in 1925 by the commander of Wright-Patterson Air Force Base in Dayton, Ohio.

12. Learning curves have been estimated for numerous industries. Boston Consulting Group (1970). *Perspectives on Experience,* Boston: BCG, presents learning curves for over 20 industries; Lieberman, M. (1984). "The learning curve and pricing in the chemical processing industries," *Rand Journal of Economics,* 15, pp. 213–228, estimates learning curves for 37 chemical products.

13. Henderson, B. (1974). *The Experience Curve Reviewed III—How Does It Work?* Boston: Boston Consulting Group; and Boston Consulting Group (1970). *Perspectives on Experience,* Boston: BCG.

14. Hall, G., and S. Howell (1985). "The experience curve from the economist's perspective," *Strategic Management Journal,* 6, pp. 197–212.

15. See, for example, Montgomery, C. A., and B. Wernerfelt (1991). "Sources of superior performance: Market share versus industry effects in the U. S. brewing industry," *Management Science,* 37, pp. 954–959. More generally, while there is usually a positive cross-sectional correction between market share and firm performance [Buzzell, R. D., B. T. Gale, and R. Sultan (1975). "Market share: A key to profitability," *Harvard Business Review,* 53(1), January/February, pp. 97–106], it does not follow that firms that engage in activities to increase their share will earn economic profits. If there is a competitive market for market share, then acquiring share will generate only average economic returns. Only when the value of share is not widely known among competing firms can acquiring share be a source of competitive advantage. This is most likely to be the case in emerging industries, in which the source of value in a strategy may not yet be widely understood.

16. Hill, C. W. L. (1988). "Differentiation versus low cost or differentiation and low cost: A contingency framework," *Academy of Management Review,* 13(3), pp. 401–412.

17. Friedland, J., and B. Ortega (1995). "U.S. copper producers are deeply worried as Chile surges ahead," *Wall Street Journal,* July 25, pp. A1+.

18. See Aguilar, F. J., and A. Bhambri (1983). "Johnson & Johnson (A)," Harvard Business School Case no. 9-384-053, for a discussion of hospital chains; and Taylor, D., and J. S. Archer (1994). *Up Against the Wal-Marts,* New York: Amacon, for a discussion of chains in the hardware and related retail industries.

19. See Ghemawat, P., and H. J. Stander III (1992), "Nucor at a crossroads," Harvard Business School Case no. 9-793-039 on technology in steel manufacturing and cost advantages; Shaffer, R. A. (1995). "Intel as conquistador," *Forbes,* February 27, p. 130, on technology in semiconductor manufacturing and cost advantages; Monteverde, K., and D. Teece (1982). "Supplier switching costs and vertical integration in the automobile industry," *Rand Journal of Economics,* 13(1), pp. 206–213; and McCormick, J., and

N. Stone (1990). "From national champion to global competitor: An interview with Thomson's Alain Gomez," *Harvard Business Review,* May/June, pp. 126–135, on technology in consumer electronic manufacturing and cost advantages.

20. Schultz, E. (1989). "Climbing high with discount brokers," *Fortune,* Fall (special issue), pp. 219–223; Schonfeld, E. (1998). "Can computers cure health care?" *Fortune,* March 30, pp. 111+.

21. See Barney, J. (1991). "Firm resources and sustained competitive advantage," *Journal of Management, 17,* pp. 99–120.

22. For work on Japan, see Ouchi, W. G. (1981). *Theory Z: How American Business Can Meet the Japanese Challenge,* Reading, MA: Addison-Wesley; and Pascale, R. T., and A. G. Athos (1981). *The Art of Japanese Management,* New York: Simon & Schuster. For work on U.S. firms, see Peters, T. J., and R. H. Waterman (1982). *In Search of Excellence,* New York: Harper & Row. The role of the interaction between technological hardware and software in obtaining low-cost, high-quality manufacturing is cited in Womack, J. P., D. I. Jones, and D. Roos (1990). *The Machine That Changed the World,* New York: Rawson, on "lean manufacturing."

23. Bartlett, C. A., and U. S. Rangan (1985). "Komatsu Ltd.," Harvard Business School Case no. 9-385-277.

24. Pfeffer, J., and G. R. Salancik (1978). *The External Control of Organizations: A Resource Dependence Perspective,* New York: Harper & Row.

25. See Meyer, M. W., and L. B. Zucker (1989). *Permanently Failing Organizations,* Newbury Park, CA: Sage.

26. Staw, B. M. (1981). "The escalation of commitment to a course of action," *Academy of Management Review,* 6, pp. 577–587.

27. Hesterly, W. S. (1989). "Top management succession as a determinant of firm performance and de-escalation: An agency problem," unpublished doctoral dissertation, University of California, Los Angeles.

28. See Spence, A. M. (1981). "The learning curve and competition," *Bell Journal of Economics,* 12, pp. 49–70, on why learning needs to be proprietary; Mansfield, E. (1985). "How rapidly does new industrial technology leak out?" *Journal of Industrial Economics,* 34(2), pp. 217–223; Lieberman, M. B. (1982). "The learning curve, pricing and market structure in the chemical processing industries," unpublished doctoral dissertation, Harvard University; Lieberman, M. B. (1987). "The learning curve, diffusion, and competitive strategy," *Strategic Management Journal,* 8, pp. 441–452, on why it usually is not proprietary.

29. Barney, J. B. (1986). "Organizational culture: Can it be a source of sustained competitive advantage?" *Academy of Management Review,* 11, pp. 656–665.

30. See Krafcik, J. K., and J. P. MacDuffie (1989). *Explaining High Performance Manufacturing: The International Automotive Assembly Plant Study,* International Motor Vehicle Program, Cambridge, MA: Massachusetts Institute of Technology.

31. Tetzeli, R. (1993). "Johnson controls: Mining money in mature markets," *Fortune,* 127(6), pp. 77–80.

32. See Porter, M. E. (1980). *Competitive Strategy,* New York: Free Press; and Harrigan, K. R. (1980). *Strategies for Declining Businesses,* Lexington, MA: Lexington Books.

33. The beginning of the decline in the defense industry is well documented by Perry, N. J. (1993). "What's next for the defense industry," *Fortune,* February 22, pp. 94–100; and Smith, L. (1993). "Can defense pain be turned to gain?" *Fortune,* February 8, pp. 84–96.

34. See Porter, M. E. (1980). *Competitive Strategy,* New York: Free Press; and Harrigan, K. R. (1980). *Strategies for Declining Businesses,* Lexington, MA: Lexington Books.

35. Collins, J. (2003). "Bigger, better, faster," *Fast Company,* June, pp. 74+; Breen, B. (2003). "What's selling in America?" *Fast Company,* January, pp. 80+; Ghemawat, P. (1993). "Wal-Mart discount store operations," Harvard Business School Case no. 9-387-018.

36. See Harrigan, K. R. (1980). *Strategies for Declining Businesses,* Lexington, MA: Lexington Books.

C H A P T E R

7

Product Differentiation

7.1 DEFINING PRODUCT DIFFERENTIATION

Product differentiation is a business strategy whereby firms attempt to gain a competitive advantage by increasing the willingness of customers to pay for the products or services they sell. Attempts to increase this willingness to pay are often made by altering the objective properties of those products or services. Rolex attempts to differentiate its watches from Timex watches by manufacturing Rolex watches with solid gold cases. Mercedes attempts to differentiate its cars from Hyundai's cars through sophisticated engineering and high performance. McDonald's attempts to differentiate its fast food from the fast food sold by locally owned, single-outlet fast-food stores by selling the same food, at the same quality and prices, and in the same way at all of its thousands of outlets.

Firms often alter the objective properties of their products or services to implement a product differentiation strategy, but the existence of product differentiation, in the end, is *always* a matter of customer perception. Products sold by two different firms may be very similar, but if customers believe the first is more valuable than the second, then the first product has a differentiation advantage.

For example, in the world of "craft" or "microbrewery" beers, image among consumers about where a beer is brewed may be very different than how a beer is actually brewed. Boston Beer Company, for example, sells Samuel Adams beer. Customers can tour the Boston Beer Company, where they will see a small row of fermenting tanks and two 10-barrel kettles being tended by a brew master wearing rubber boots. However, Samuel Adams Beer is not actually brewed in this small factory. Instead, it is brewed—in 200-barrel steel tanks—in Cincinnati, Ohio, by the Hudepohl-Schoenling Brewing Company, a contract brewing firm that also manufactures Hudy Bold beer and Little Kings Cream Ale. Maui Beer Company's Aloha Lager brand is brewed in

Portland, Oregon, and Pete's Wicked Ale (a craft beer that claims it is brewed "one batch at a time. Carefully.") is brewed in batches of 400 barrels each by Stroh Brewery Company, makers of Old Milwaukee Beer. However, to the extent that consumers perceive there to be important differences between these "craft" beers and more traditional brews—despite many of their common manufacturing methods—important bases of product differentiation exist.[1] If products or services are *perceived* as being different, then product differentiation exits.

Just as perceptions can create product differentiation between products that are essentially identical, the lack of perceived differences between products with very different characteristics can prevent product differentiation. For example, many potential customers are likely to believe that Rolex watches (because they are so expensive) use state-of-the-art timekeeping technology and that watches manufactured by Casio (because they are less expensive) use less advanced technology. In fact, Rolex still uses an old timekeeping technology (a self-winding mainspring), and Casio uses the most sophisticated electronic timekeeping technology in the world (battery-driven quartz crystals). However, because Casio is perceived to be less sophisticated than Rolex, Casio's potential technology-based product differentiation advantage over Rolex does not exist.

Sometimes, customer perceptions create bases of product differentiation that are neither designed nor desired by firms. For example, in the 1970s, children throughout the United States believed that Bubblicious (a brand of soft, easy-to-chew bubble gum) was made out of spiders. Since the 1980s, persistent rumors have suggested that Proctor & Gamble (P&G) is linked to a satanic cult. At one time, P&G had a Web site dedicated to disabusing this rumor (www.pg.com/rumor). In the 1990s, teenagers throughout the United States believed that drinking Mountain Dew (a citric-flavored soft drink manufactured and distributed by PepsiCo) reduced the sperm count in males. Obviously, customer perceptions that a firm's product is made out of spiders, that a firm is tied to a satanic cult, or that a firm's product can adversely affect male sexuality are not valuable bases of product differentiation (except for very small and unusual segments of consumers). Each of these firms has had to engage in efforts to alter these consumer perceptions.[2]

Product differentiation is always a matter of customer perceptions, but firms can take a variety of actions to influence these perceptions. These actions can be thought of as bases of product differentiation.

Bases of Product Differentiation

A wide variety of authors, drawing on both theory and empirical research, have developed lists of ways firms can differentiate their products or services.[3] Some of these are listed in Table 7.1. Although the purpose of all these bases of product differentiation is to create the perception that a firm's products or services are unusually valuable, different bases of product differentiation attempt to accomplish this objective in different ways. For example, the first four bases of product differentiation listed in Table 7.1 attempt to create this perception by focusing directly on the attributes of the products or services a firm sells. The second three attempt to create this perception by developing a relationship between a firm and its customers. The last five attempt to create this perception through linkages within and between

TABLE 7.1 Ways That Firms Can Differentiate Their Products

To differentiate their products, firms can focus directly on the attributes of its products or services, or
  1. Product features
  2. Product complexity
  3. Timing of product introduction
  4. Location

On relationships between itself and its customers, or
  5. Product customization
  6. Consumer marketing
  7. Product reputation

On linkages within or between firms
  8. Linkages among functions within a firm
  9. Linkages with other firms
 10. Product mix
 11. Distribution channels
 12. Service and support

Sources: Adapted from Porter, M. C. (1980). *Competitive Strategy,* New York: Free Press; and Caves, R. E., and P. Williamson (1985). "What is product differentiation, really?" *Journal of Industrial Economics,* 34, pp. 113–132.

firms. Of course, these bases of product differentiation are not mutually exclusive. Indeed, firms often attempt to differentiate their products or services along multiple dimensions simultaneously.

Focusing on the Attributes of a Firm's Products or Services

Product Features. The most obvious way in which firms can try to differentiate their products is by altering the features of the products they sell. One industry in which firms are constantly modifying product features in an attempt to differentiate their products is the automobile industry. Chrysler, for example, introduced the "cab forward" design to try to give its cars a distinctive look, whereas Audi went with a more radical flowing and curved design to differentiate its cars. For emergency situations, General Motors introduced the On Star system which instantly connects drivers to GM operators 24 hours a day, whereas Mercedes-Benz continued to develop its Crumple Zone system to ensure passenger safety in a crash. In body construction, General Motors continues to develop its Uni-body construction system, in which different parts of a car are welded to each other rather than built on a single frame, whereas Jaguar introduced a 100 percent aluminum body to help differentiate its top-of-the-line model from other luxury cars. Mazda continues to tinker with the motor and suspension of its sporty Miata, whereas Nissan introduced the 350Z—a continuation of the famous 240Z line—and Porsche changed from air-cooled to water-cooled engines in its 911 series of sports cars. All these—and many more—changes in the attributes of automobiles are examples of firms trying to differentiate their products by altering product features.

Product Complexity.   Product complexity can be thought of as a special case of altering a product's features to create product differentiation. In a given industry, products can vary significantly in their complexity. The BIC "crystal pen," for example, has only a handful of parts, whereas a Cross pen or a Mont Blanc pen has many more parts. To the extent that these differences in product complexity convince consumers that the products of some firms are more valuable than the products of other firms, product complexity can be a basis of product differentiation.

Timing of Product Introduction.   Introducing a product at the right time can also help create product differentiation. As suggested in Chapter 2, in some industry settings (that is, in emerging industries), *the* critical issue is to be a first mover—to introduce a new product before all other firms. Being first in emerging industries can enable a firm to set important technological standards, preempt strategically valuable assets, and develop customer-switching costs. These first-mover advantages can create a perception among customers that the products or services of the first-moving firm are somehow more valuable than the products or services of other firms.[4]

First moving has been an important determinant of perceived differences in the quality of education at universities in the United States and worldwide. In the United States, the first few universities founded (for example, Harvard and Yale) are seen as being more prestigious than more recently founded state schools. In the United Kingdom, the oldest universities (including Oxford and Cambridge) are also widely perceived to be superior to more recently founded universities. Regardless of whether the date of founding of a university has an effect on the quality of education, if there is a *perceived* link between founding date and quality, founding date acts as a timing-based source of product differentiation.[5]

Timing-based product differentiation, however, does not depend only on being a first mover. Sometimes, a firm can be a later mover in an industry but introduce products or services at just the right time and thereby gain a competitive advantage. This can happen when the ultimate success of a product or service depends on the availability of complementary products or technologies. For example, the domination of Microsoft's MS-DOS operating system, and thus ultimately the domination of Windows, was possible only because IBM introduced its version of the personal computer. Without the IBM PC, it would have been difficult for any operating system—including MS-DOS— to have such a large market presence.[6]

Location.   The physical location of a firm can also be a source of product differentiation.[7] Consider, for example, Disney's operations in Orlando, Florida. Beginning with The Magic Kingdom and Epcot Center, Disney built a world-class destination resort in Orlando. Over the years, Disney has added numerous attractions to its core entertainment activities, including MGM Studios, over 11,000 Disney-owned hotel rooms, a $100 million sports center, an automobile racing track, an after-hours entertainment district, and most recently, a $1 billion theme park called "The Animal Kingdom"—all in and around Orlando. Now, families travel to Orlando from around the world, knowing that in a single location they can enjoy a full range of Disney adventures.[8]

Focusing on the Relationship Between a Firm and Its Customers

Product Customization.   Products can also be differentiated by the extent to which they are customized for particular customer applications. Product customization is an important basis for product differentiation in a wide variety of industries, from enterprise software to bicycles.

Enterprise Software.   is software that is designed to support all of a firm's critical business functions, including human resources, payroll, customer service, sales, quality control, and so forth. Major competitors in this industry include PeopleSoft and Oracle. However, although these firms sell basic software packages, most firms find it necessary to customize these basic packages to meet their specific business needs. The ability to build complex software packages that can also be customized to meet the specific needs of a particular customer is an important basis of product differentiation in this marketplace.

In the bicycle industry, consumers can spend as little as $50 on a bicycle, and as much as—well, almost as much as they want on a bicycle, easily in excess of $10,000. High-end bicycles use, of course, the very best components—such as brakes and gears. But what really distinguishes these bicycles is their customized fit. Firms that sell these customized bicycles build a strong and lightweight frame that is custom-fit to you and to your individual riding style. Much of the competition in this high end of the industry focuses on different ways of customizing this fit and different space-age materials that can be used to build the frames. Once a serious rider becomes accustomed to a particular customization approach, it is very difficult for that rider to switch to suppliers that might have an alternative approach to customization.

Consumer Marketing.   Differential emphasis on consumer marketing has been a basis for product differentiation in a wide variety of industries. Through advertising and other consumer marketing efforts, firms attempt to alter the perceptions of current and potential customers, whether or not specific attributes of a firm's products or services are altered.

For example, in the soft drink industry, Mountain Dew—a product of PepsiCo—was originally marketed as a fruity, lightly carbonated drink, that tasted "as light as a morning dew in the mountains." However, beginning in the late 1990s, Mountain Dew's marketing efforts changed dramatically. "As light as a morning dew in the mountains" became "Do the Dew," and Mountain Dew focused its marketing efforts on young, mostly male, extreme-sports-oriented consumers. Young men riding snowboards, roller blades, mountain bikes, and skateboards—mostly upside down—became central to most Mountain Dew commercials. Mountain Dew became a sponsor of a wide variety of extreme sports contests and an important sponsor of the X-games on ESPN. And will we ever forget the confrontation between the young Dew enthusiast and a mountain ram over a can of Mountain Dew in a meadow? Note that this radical repositioning of Mountain Dew depended entirely on changes in consumer marketing. The features of the underlying product were not changed at all.

Reputation.   Perhaps the most important relationship between a firm and its customers depends on a firm's reputation in its marketplace. Indeed, a firm's **reputation** is really no more than a socially complex relationship between a firm and its customers.

Once developed, a firm's reputation can last a long time, even if the basis for that reputation no longer exists.[9]

A firm that has tried to exploit its reputation for cutting-edge entertainment is MTV, a division of Viacom, Inc. While several well-known video artists—including Madonna—have had their videos banned from MTV, it has still been able to develop a reputation for risk-taking on television. MTV believes that its viewers have come to expect the unexpected in MTV programming. One of the first efforts to exploit, and reinforce, this reputation for risk taking was *Bevis and Butthead,* an animated series on MTV starring two teenage boys with serious social and emotional development problems. More recently, MTV exploited its reputation by inventing an entirely new genre of television—reality TV—through its *Real World* and *House Rules* programs. Not only are these shows cheap to produce, they build on the reputation that MTV has for providing entertainment that is a little risky, a little sexy, and a little controversial. Indeed, MTV has been so successful in providing this kind of entertainment that it had to form an entirely new cable station—MTV 2—to actually show music videos.[10]

Focusing on Links Within and Between Firms

Linkages Between Functions.   A less obvious but still important way in which a firm can attempt to differentiate its products is by linking different functions within the firm. For example, research in the pharmaceutical industry suggests that firms vary in the extent to which they are able to integrate different scientific specialties—such as genetics, biology, chemistry, and pharmacology—to develop new drugs. Firms that are able to form effective multidisciplinary teams to explore new drug categories have what some have called an **architectural competence,** that is, the ability to use organizational structure to facilitate coordination among scientific disciplines to conduct research. Firms that have this competence are able to pursue product differentiation strategies more effectively—by introducing new and powerful drugs—compared to firms that do not have this competence. And in the pharmaceutical industry, in which firms that introduce such drugs can experience very large positive returns, the ability to coordinate across functions is an important source of competitive advantage.[11]

Linkages with Other Firms.   Another basis of product differentiation is linkages with other firms. Here, instead of differentiating products or services on the basis of linkages between functions within a single firm or linkages between different products, differentiation is based on explicit linkages between one firm's products and the products or services of other firms.

This form of product differentiation has increased in popularity over the last several years. For example, with the growth in popularity of stock car racing in the United States, more and more corporations are looking to link their products or services with famous names and cars in NASCAR. Firms such as Kodak, Circuit City, Gatorade, McDonald's, Home Depot, The Cartoon Network, True Value, and Pfizer (manufacturer of Viagra) have all been major sponsors of NASCAR teams. In one year, the Coca-Cola Corporation filled orders for over 200,000 NASCAR-themed vending machines. VISA struggled to keep up with demand for its NASCAR affinity cards, and over 1 million NASCAR Barbie dolls were once sold by Mattel—generating revenues of about $50 million. Notice that none of these firms sells products for automobiles. Rather, these firms seek to associate themselves with NASCAR because of the popularity of this sport.[12]

Another product with which firms often seek to link their own products and services is movies, especially summer "blockbuster" movies. This can be done in at least two ways. First, firms may **co-brand** their product with a movie.[13] That is, they may tie the brand of their product to the brand of another firm's product. For example, McDonald's often uses characters from movies as toys in their Happy Meals. This first occurred in 1979, when a McDonald's Happy Meal featured action figures from *Star Trek: The Motion Picture*. Second, firms can attempt to place their products in a movie. Such product placements can be as simple as having an actor drink from a can of Coca-Cola after defeating the bad guys, or as complicated as introducing a new product to the market by having an actor use this product in a movie. Both BMW and Aston-Martin used this kind of product placement in James Bond movies to introduce new cars to the automobile market—although the cars that were actually sold did not include machine guns and rockets.

In general, linkages between firms to differentiate their products are examples of cooperative strategic alliance strategies. The conditions under which cooperative strategic alliances create value and are sources of sustained competitive advantage are discussed in detail in Chapter 13.

Product Mix.   One of the outcomes of linkages among functions within a firm and linkages between firms can be changes in the mix of products a firm brings to the market. This mix of products or services can be a source of product differentiation, especially when (1) those products or services are technologically linked or (2) when a single set of customers purchase several of a firm's products or services.

For example, technological interconnectivity is an extremely important selling point in the information technology business and thus an important basis of potential product differentiation. However, seamless interconnectivity—in which Company A's computers talk to Company B's computers across Company C's data line, merging a database created by Company D's software with a database created by Company E's software, to be used in a calling center that operates with Company F's technology—has been extremely difficult to realize. For this reason, some information technology firms try to realize the goal of interconnectivity by adjusting their product mix, that is, by selling a bundle of products whose interconnectivity they can control and thus whose interconnectivity they can guarantee to customers. This goal of selling a bundle of interconnected technologies can influence a firm's research and development, strategic alliance, and merger and acquisition strategies, because all these activities can influence the set of products a firm brings to market.

Shopping malls are an example of the second kind of linkage among a mix of products—a linkage in which products have a common set of customers. Many customers prefer to go to one location to shop at several stores at once, rather than traveling to a series of separate locations to shop. This one-stop shopping reduces travel time and helps turn shopping into a social experience. Mall development companies have recognized that the value of several stores brought together in a particular location is greater than the value of those stores if they were isolated, and they have invested to help create this mix of retail shopping opportunities.[14]

Distribution Channels.   Linkages within and between firms can also have an effect on how a firm chooses to distribute its products. And distribution channels can be a basis of product differentiation. For example, in the soft drink industry, Coca-Cola,

PepsiCo, and Seven-Up all distribute their drinks through a network of independent and company-owned bottlers. These firms manufacture key ingredients for their soft drinks and ship these ingredients to local bottlers, who add carbonated water, package the drinks in bottles or cans, and distribute the final product to soft drink outlets in a given geographic area. Each local bottler has exclusive rights to distribute a particular brand in a geographic location.

Canada Dry has adopted a completely different distribution network. Instead of relying on local bottlers, Canada Dry packages its final product in several locations and then ships its soft drinks directly to wholesale grocers, who distribute them to local grocery stores, convenience stores, and other retail outlets.

One of the consequences of these alternative distribution strategies is that Canada Dry has a relatively strong presence in grocery stores but a relatively small presence in soft drink vending machines. The vending machine market is dominated by Coca-Cola and PepsiCo. These two firms have local distributors that maintain and stock vending machines. Canada Dry has no local distributors and is able to get its products into vending machines only when they are purchased by local Coca-Cola or Pepsi distributors. These local distributors are likely to purchase and stock Canada Dry products such as Canada Dry ginger ale, but they are contractually forbidden from purchasing Canada Dry's various cola products.[15]

Service and Support.   Finally, products have been differentiated by the level of service and support associated with them. Some firms in the home appliance market, including General Electric, have not developed their own service and support network and instead rely on a network of independent service and support operations throughout the United States. Other firms in the same industry, including Sears, have developed their own service and support network.[16]

Differences in service and support have recently become a major point of differentiation in the automobile industry. Firms such as Lexus (a division of Toyota) and Saturn (a division of General Motors) compete not only on the basis of product quality but also on the basis of the level of service and support they provide. To emphasize Saturn's willingness to provide service and support, Saturn once advertised a need that one of its customers had to replace a defective seat in a Saturn car. The customer lived in the Alaska wilderness, and Saturn sent a customer service representative there for just a single day to replace the defective seat.

Product Differentiation and Creativity

The bases of product differentiation listed in Table 7.1 indicate a broad range of ways in which firms can differentiate their products and services. In the end, however, any effort to list all possible ways to differentiate products and services is doomed to failure. Product differentiation is ultimately an expression of the creativity of individuals and groups within firms and is limited only by the opportunities that exist, or that can be created, in a particular industry and by the willingness and ability of firms to explore creatively various ways to take advantage of those opportunities. It is not unreasonable to expect that the day some academic researcher claims to have developed the definitive list of bases of product differentiation, some creative engineer, marketing specialist, or manager will think of yet another way to differentiate his or her product.

7.2 IDENTIFYING BASES OF PRODUCT DIFFERENTIATION

Because bases of product differentiation are limited only by the creativity of managers, an important management skill is to learn how to describe the ways that products in a market have already been differentiated in order to find market segments in which unfulfilled demand might still exist.

Two statistical techniques can be used to accomplish these tasks: multidimensional scaling and regression analysis of determinants of a product's price.

Multidimensional Scaling

Multidimensional scaling is a mathematical technique for analyzing the perceived similarity of a set of products or services. This approach begins by asking a sample of customers to describe how similar several products sold in a single product market are to each other. For example, for the automobiles listed in Figure 7.1, customers could be asked how similar a Ford Taurus is overall to a Chevrolet Lumina, a Honda Accord to a Mercedes 300E, and so forth. After numerous customers have been asked to characterize the similarity among these cars, an estimate of the perceived similarity of these cars, taken two at a time, can be developed. These measures of product similarity can be arranged in matrix form, as is done in Figure 7.1.

This similarity matrix is used as input into a multidimensional scaling computer program. The object of the program is to discover a relatively small number (usually two or three) of underlying product dimensions that can be used to mathematically re-create the entire similarity matrix. If two or three underlying product dimensions allow the (reasonably) accurate re-creation of the entire similarity matrix, then those dimensions usually reflect the key bases of product differentiation used in a market. In Figure 7.1, the hypothetical analysis of the automobile similarity matrix yields two interpretable dimensions: perceived performance and perceived reliability.

These dimensions can be used to analyze which products in a market compete directly against each other, which products are differentiated, and which segments of the market are not being exploited by currently available products. In Figure 7.1, each of the automobiles is plotted on a two-dimensional surface in which the x-axis represents a product's dimension score on the perceived performance dimension and the y-axis represents a product's dimension score on the perceived reliability dimension. As can be seen in this hypothetical analysis, the Ford Taurus and Honda Accord compete against each other in the medium-performance/high-reliability segment of the market, the Chevrolet Lumina and Chrysler LeBaron compete in the medium-performance/medium-reliability segment, and Mercedes 300E is relatively isolated in the high-performance/medium-reliability segment.

Beyond revealing the bases of product differentiation that have been used in an industry, this type of analysis can also suggest new product differentiation opportunities. For example, an actual multidimensional scaling study of competing pain relievers revealed the pattern presented in Figure 7.2. Notice that in this market, there seems to be room for products that are perceived to be very gentle and very effective (the upper-right quadrant of Figure 7.2). Over the years, several firms have moved to fill this void with the development of extra-strength non-aspirin pain relievers.[17]

FIGURE 7.1	**Hypothetical Multidimensional Scaling Analysis of 10 Midsize Automobiles: Measures of Perceived Similarity (1.0 = cars are the same; 0.0 = cars not similar at all)**

	Taurus	Lumina	Accord	LeBaron	. . .	Mercedes
Taurus	1.0	.65	.76	.42	. . .	.54
Lumina	.65	1.0	.53	.47	. . .	.23
Accord	.76	.53	1.0	.65	. . .	.78
LeBaron	.42	.47	.65	1.0	. . .	.81
•	•	•	•	•		
•	•	•	•	•		
•	•	•	•	•		
Mercedes	.54	.23	.78	.81	. . .	1.0

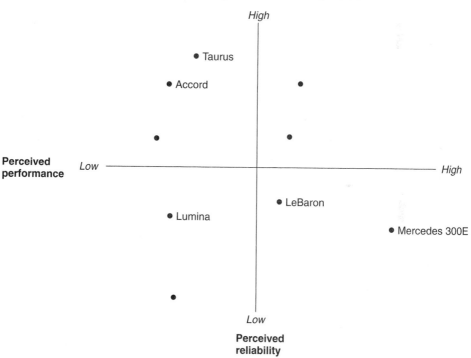

Two-dimensional analysis of this similarity matrix

Source: A. J. Rowe, R. O. Mason, and K. E. Dickel (1982). *Strategic Management: A Methodological Approach.* Reading, MA: Addison-Wesley.

Regression Analysis

Multidimensional scaling is a purely inductive method for describing the bases of product differentiation in an industry. Analysts are not required to hypothesize which particular product attributes might be used as the basis of product differentiation, but rather allow dimensions to emerge inductively from an analysis of perceived product similarities. Regression analysis of the determinants of product price is a more deductive approach to the empirical analysis of bases of product differentiation.

FIGURE 7.2 Multidimensional Scaling of Perceived Differences Among Pain Relievers

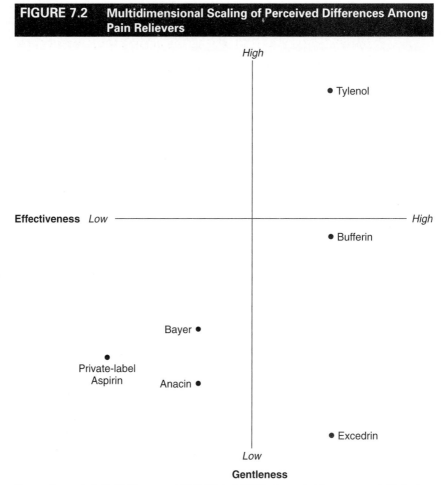

Source: Rowe, A. J., R. O. Mason, and K. E. Dickel (1982). *Strategic Management: A Methodological Approach,* Reading, MA: Addison-Wesley.

Consider the simple example presented in Table 7.2. Here, once again, the industry under consideration is automobiles. In this approach, however, the analyst proposes a wide range of characteristics that may have an effect on a car's price. In automobiles, product attributes such as engine displacement, passenger room, trunk size, perceived quality, acceleration, and braking capabilities may all have an effect on the price of a car. Each car being studied is measured relative to these possible bases of product differentiation. The product's price (in this case, the wholesale price of each automobile) is then taken as a dependent variable in a multiple regression analysis. The form of the equation is

$$\text{Price}_i = b_0 + b_1 \text{ attribute}_1 + b_2 \text{ attribute}_2 + b_3 \text{ attribute}_3 + \cdots + b_j \text{ attribute}_j \quad \textbf{(7.1)}$$

TABLE 7.2	Hypothetical Regression Analysis of Bases of Product Differentiation in Automobiles (Dependent Variable: Price)	
Independent Variable	*Regression Coefficient*	*Statistical Significance*
Constant	1.78	*
Engine displacement	.23	
Passenger room	2.89	
Trunk size	4.87	*
Perceived quality	.21	
Acceleration	21.34	**
Braking capabilities	.256	*

* = Significant at the .05 level
** = Significant at the .01 level

where

$$\text{Price}_i = \text{the price of product } i$$
$$\text{Attribute}_j = \text{a measure of attribute } j \text{ for product } i$$
$$b_j = \text{the regression coefficient measuring the impact of attribute } j \text{ on the price of product } i, \text{ controlling for other product attributes}$$

This regression model estimates the effect of each product attribute on the price of a product. A statistically significant regression coefficient in this equation suggests that a particular product attribute has a significant effect on a product's price and, by implication, can be thought of as a basis of product differentiation. In Table 7.2, it turns out that acceleration, braking capabilities, and trunk size all have significant effects on the price of cars and thus are likely to be bases of product differentiation in this market.

7.3 THE ECONOMIC VALUE OF PRODUCT DIFFERENTIATION

To have the potential for generating competitive advantages, the bases of product differentiation on which a firm competes must be valuable. Economically valuable bases of product differentiation can enable a firm to increase its revenues, neutralize threats, and exploit opportunities.

Product Differentiation and Economic Performance

Given the wide variety of ways in which firms can differentiate their products and services, it is not surprising that the effect of this particular strategy on firm performance and industry structure has received a great deal of attention in the economic literature. The two classic treatments of these relationships, developed independently and published at approximately the same time, are by Edward Chamberlin and Joan Robinson.[18]

Both Chamberlin and Robinson examine product differentiation and firm performance relative to perfect competition. As explained in Chapter 3, under perfect competition, there are assumed to be numerous firms in an industry, each controlling a small proportion of the market, and the products or services sold by these firms are assumed to be identical. Under these conditions, firms face a horizontal demand curve (because they have no control over the price of the products they sell), and they maximize their economic performance by producing and selling output such that marginal revenue equals marginal costs. The maximum economic performance a firm in a perfectly competitive market can obtain, assuming no cost differences across firms, is a normal economic profit.

When firms sell differentiated products, they gain some ability to adjust their prices. A firm can sell its output at very high prices and produce relatively smaller amounts of output, or it can sell its output at very low prices and produce relatively greater amounts of output. These trade-offs between price and quantity produced suggest that firms selling differentiated products face a downward-sloping demand curve, rather than the horizontal demand curve for firms in a perfectly competitive market. Firms selling differentiated products and facing a downward-sloping demand curve are in an industry structure described as **monopolistic competition** by Chamberlin. It is as if, within the market niche defined by a firm's differentiated product, a firm possesses a monopoly.

Monopolistically competitive firms still maximize their economic profit by producing and selling a quantity of products such that marginal revenue equals marginal cost. The price that firms can charge at this optimal point depends on the demand they face for their differentiated product. If demand is large, then the price that can be charged is higher; if demand is low, then the price that can be charged is lower. However, if a firm's average total cost is below the price it can charge (that is, if average total cost is less than the demand-determined price), then a firm selling a differentiated product can earn an economic profit.

Consider the example presented in Figure 7.3. Several curves are relevant in this figure. First, notice that the demand (D) facing a firm in this industry is downward-sloping.

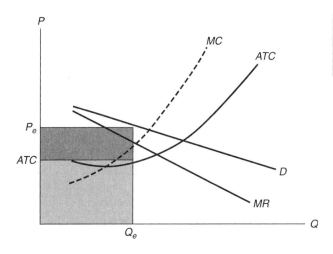

FIGURE 7.3   Product Differentiation and Firm Performance: The Analysis of Monopolistic Competition

This means that the industry is not perfectly competitive and that a firm has some control over the prices it can charge for its products. Also, the marginal revenue curve (*MR*) is downward-sloping and everywhere lower than the demand curve. Marginal revenue is downward-sloping because in order to sell additional levels of output of a single product, a firm must be willing to lower its price. The marginal revenue curve is lower than the demand curve because this lower price applies to all the products sold by a firm, not just to any additional products the firm sells. The marginal cost curve (*MC*) in Figure 7.3 is upward-sloping, indicating that in order to produce additional outputs, a firm must accept additional costs. The average total cost curve (*ATC*) can have a variety of shapes, depending on the economies of scale, the cost of factors of production, and other cost phenomena described in Chapter 6.

These four curves (demand, marginal revenue, marginal cost, and average total cost) can be used to determine the level of economic profit for a firm under monopolistic competition. In order to maximize profit, the firm produces an amount (Q_e) such that marginal costs equal marginal revenues. To determine the price of a firm's output at this level of production, a vertical line is drawn from the point where marginal costs equal marginal revenues. This line will intersect with the demand curve. Where this vertical line intersects demand, a horizontal line is drawn to the vertical (price) axis to determine the price a firm can charge. In Figure 7.3, this price is P_e. At the point Q_e, average total cost is less than the price. The total revenue obtained by the firm in this situation (price × quantity) is indicated by the shaded area in Figure 7.3. The economic profit portion of this total revenue is indicated by the darker-shaded section of the shaded portion of the figure. Because this darker-shaded section is above average total costs in Figure 7.3, it represents superior economic profit. If this section were below average total costs, it would represent below-average economic profits.

Chamberlin and Robinson also discuss the effect of entry into the market niche defined by a firm's differentiated product. As discussed in Section 3.1, a basic assumption of structure-conduct-performance (S-C-P) models is the existence of superior profits motivating entry into an industry or into a market niche within an industry. In monopolistically competitive industries, such entry means that the demand curve facing incumbent firms shifts downward and to the left. This implies that an incumbent firm's customers will buy less of its output if it maintains its prices, or (equivalently) that a firm will have to lower its prices to maintain its current volume of sales. In the long run, entry into this market niche can lead to a situation in which the price of goods or services sold when a firm produces output such that marginal cost equals marginal revenue is exactly equal to that firm's average total cost. At this point, a firm earns a normal economic return even if it still sells a differentiated product.

Much of Chamberlin and Robinson's analysis of competition and performance in monopolistically competitive industries has implications for a strategic analysis of product differentiation. The ability of a firm to market a differentiated product, and obtain superior economic profits, depends on that product either neutralizing threats or exploiting opportunities. The ability of a firm to maintain its competitive advantage depends, in turn, on the rarity and imitability of its organizational strengths and weaknesses.

Product Differentiation and Environmental Threats

Successful product differentiation helps a firm respond to each of the environmental threats identified in the five forces framework. For example, product differentiation helps reduce the threat of new entry by forcing potential entrants to an industry to absorb not only the standard costs of beginning business but also the additional costs associated with overcoming incumbent firms' product differentiation advantages. The relationship between product differentiation and new entry has already been discussed in Chapter 3.

Product differentiation reduces the threat of rivalry, because each firm in an industry attempts to carve out its own unique product niche. Rivalry is not reduced to zero, for these products still compete with one another for a common set of customers, but it is somewhat attenuated, because the customers each firm seeks are different. For example, both a Rolls Royce and a Hyundai satisfy the same basic consumer need—transportation—but it is unlikely that potential customers of Rolls Royces will also be interested in purchasing a Hyundai or vice versa.

Product differentiation also helps firms reduce the threat of substitutes by making a firm's current products appear more attractive than substitute products. For example, fresh food can be thought of as a substitute for frozen processed foods. In order to make its frozen processed foods more attractive than fresh foods, products such as Stouffer's and Swanson meals are marketed heavily through television advertisements, newspaper ads, point-of-purchase displays, and coupons.

Product differentiation can also reduce the threat of suppliers. Powerful suppliers can raise the prices of the products or services they provide. Often, these increased supply costs must be passed on to a firm's customers in the form of higher prices if a firm's profit margin is not to deteriorate. A firm without a highly differentiated product may find it difficult to pass its increased costs on to customers, because these customers will have numerous other ways to purchase similar products or services from a firm's competitors. However, a firm with a highly differentiated product may have loyal customers or customers who are unable to purchase similar products or services from other firms. These types of customers are more likely to accept increased prices due to a firm passing on increased costs caused by a powerful supplier. Thus a powerful supplier may be able to raise its prices, but these increases often do not reduce the profitability of a firm selling a highly differentiated product.

Of course, the ability of a firm that sells a highly differentiated product to be somewhat immune from powerful suppliers may actually encourage suppliers to exercise their power. Because firms can pass increased costs on to customers, suppliers may decide to increase costs. At some point, even the most loyal customers of the most differentiated products or services may find a firm's prices too high. These price barriers suggest a limit to a firm's ability to raise prices. Any increase in supply costs once these barriers are reached results in reduced economic profits for a firm.

However, at these price and supply-cost levels, a firm may find it possible to obtain substitute supplies, or other firms may have entered into the supply market. The existence of substitute supplies or more suppliers both attenuates the power of suppliers and enables a firm selling a differentiated product to maintain positive economic profits.

The relationship between sugar suppliers and soft drink manufacturers over the last 30 years has had many of these characteristics. In the 1970s, sugar was a major ingredient in soft drinks. However, in the early 1980s, sugar prices rose suddenly. At first, soft drink companies were able to pass these increased costs on to customers in the form of increased prices. Customer loyalty to soft drink brands, and dislike for soft drink substitutes, kept customers purchasing soft drinks despite increased prices. However, as sugar prices continued to rise, several alternatives to sugar were developed. First, expensive sugar from sugar cane was supplemented by less expensive high-fructose corn syrup. Second, aspartame, a low-calorie sugar substitute (marketed under the brand name NutraSweet) was developed. Thus, although soft drink firms could raise their prices in response to increased sugar costs, ultimately these higher prices led to the development of sugar substitutes that reduced the power of sugar companies as suppliers to the soft drink industry.[19]

Finally, product differentiation can reduce the threat of buyers. As both Chamberlin and Robinson observed, when a firm sells a highly differentiated product, it enjoys a quasi-monopoly in that segment of the market. Buyers interested in purchasing this particular product must buy it from a particular firm. Any potential buyer power is reduced by the ability of a firm to withhold highly valued products or services from a buyer.

Product Differentiation and Environmental Opportunities

Product differentiation can also help a firm take advantage of environmental opportunities. For example, in fragmented industries firms can use product differentiation strategies to help consolidate a market. In the office paper industry, Xerox used its brand name to become a leading seller of paper for office copy machines and printers. Arguing that its paper was manufactured specially to avoid jamming in its own copy machines, Xerox was able to brand what had been a commodity product and used this advantage to partially consolidate this industry.[20]

The role of product differentiation in emerging industries has been discussed in Chapter 4. By being a first mover in these industries, a firm can gain product differentiation advantages based on perceived technological leadership, preemption of strategically valuable assets, and buyer loyalty due to high switching costs.

In mature industries, product differentiation efforts often switch from attempts to introduce radically new technologies to product refinement as a basis of product differentiation. For example, in the mature retail gasoline market, firms attempt to differentiate their products by selling slightly modified gasolines (cleaner-burning gasoline, gasoline that cleans fuel injectors, and so forth) and by altering the product mix (linking gasoline sales with convenience stores).

Product differentiation can also be an important strategic option in a declining industry. Product-differentiating firms may be able to become leaders in this kind of industry (based on their reputation, on unique product attributes, or on some other product differentiation basis). Alternatively, highly differentiated firms may be able to discover a viable market niche that will enable them to survive despite the overall decline in the market.

Finally, the decision to implement a product differentiation strategy can have a significant effect on how a firm acts in a global industry. This is discussed in more detail in Chapter 15.

7.4 PRODUCT DIFFERENTIATION AND SUSTAINED COMPETITIVE ADVANTAGE

Product differentiation strategies add value by enabling firms to charge for their products or services prices that are greater than a firm's average total cost. Firms that implement this strategy successfully can reduce a variety of environmental threats and exploit a variety of environmental opportunities. However, as discussed in Chapter 5, the ability of a strategy to add value to a firm must be linked with rare and costly-to-imitate organizational strengths and weaknesses in order to generate a sustained competitive advantage. Each of the bases of product differentiation listed earlier in this chapter varies with respect to how likely it is to be rare and how likely it is to be costly to imitate.

Rare Bases for Product Differentiation

The concept of product differentiation generally assumes that the number of firms that have been able to differentiate their products in a particular way is, at some point in time, less than the number of firms needed to generate perfect competition dynamics. When Chamberlin and Robinson suggest that highly differentiated firms can charge a price for their product that is greater than average total cost, they are asserting that these firms are implementing a rare competitive strategy.

Ultimately, the rarity of a product differentiation strategy depends on the ability of individual firms to be creative. As suggested earlier, highly creative firms will be able to discover or create new ways to differentiate their products or services. These kinds of firms will always be one step ahead of the competition, for rival firms will often be trying to imitate these firms' last product differentiation move while creative firms are working on their next product differentiation move.

The Imitability of Product Differentiation

Valuable and rare bases of product differentiation must be costly to imitate if they are to be sources of sustained competitive advantage. Both direct duplication and substitution, as approaches to imitation, are important.

Direct Duplication of Product Differentiation

Once a firm has discovered a new way to differentiate its product, it usually is forced to reveal that new source of product differentiation to its competitors when it begins selling its new products or services. For example, when Chrysler Corporation began selling its line of minivans—a new and creative way to differentiate Chrysler's station wagons from other firms' station wagons—Chrysler revealed minivans as a basis of product differentiation in this segment of the automobile market. When Seven-Up revealed its effort to differentiate its soft drink product on the basis of its lack of caffeine, Seven-Up revealed "caffeine-free" as a potential basis of product differentiation in that market. Also, when Proctor & Gamble began selling concentrated laundry detergent in smaller boxes, it revealed concentration and container size as potential bases of product differentiation in the laundry detergent market. Thus, although the rarity of product differentiation depends on the creativity of individual firms, the marketing of differentiated products or services often provides a road map to other firms seeking to duplicate a successful firm's differentiation efforts.

Bases of Product Differentiation That Are Easy to Duplicate. Selling a differentiated product often reveals the basis of product differentiation, but such bases vary in the extent to which they are easy to duplicate and thus are subject to imitation. As can be seen in Table 7.3, easy-to-duplicate bases of product differentiation tend *not* to build on historical, uncertain, or socially complex firm resources or capabilities.

For example, although many firms spend a great deal of time and energy trying to differentiate their products on the basis of product features, product features by themselves are usually relatively easy to duplicate. Rival firms can usually purchase the differentiated product and take it apart to discover the features that act as a basis of differentiation. Such reverse engineering has occurred for many products in numerous markets.

Reverse engineering can even be applied to products that cannot be purchased and taken apart. For example, in the early 1990s, a new offensive football system, the run-and-shoot offense, began to become popular in the National Football League. This wide-open offensive system emphasizes quick play calling, multiple pass options, and a limited running attack. It was diffused throughout much of the league in at least two ways.

TABLE 7.3   Bases of Product Differentiation and the Cost of Duplication

		Source of Costly Duplication		
	Basis of Product Differentiation	*History*	*Uncertainty*	*Social Complexity*
Low-cost duplication possible	1. Product features	—	—	—
May be costly to duplicate	2. Product mix	*	*	*
	3. Linkages with other firms	*	—	**
	4. Product customization	*	—	**
	5. Product complexity	*	—	*
	6. Consumer marketing	—	**	—
Usually costly to duplicate	7. Linkages among functions within a firm	*	*	**
	8. Timing of product introduction	***	*	—
	9. Location	***	—	—
	10. Product reputation	***	**	***
	11. Distribution channels	**	*	**
	12. Service and support	*	*	**

— = not likely to be a source of costly duplication
 * = somewhat likely to be a source of costly duplication
** = likely to be a source of costly duplication
*** = very likely to be a source of costly duplication

Source: R. E. Caves and P. Williamson (1985). "What is product differentiation, *really*" *Journal of Inustrial Economics,* 34, pp. 113–132.

Coaches who had experience working with the run-and-shoot offense began working for new teams, and teams that did not have an experienced run-and-shoot coach on their staff spent hours watching videotape of run-and-shoot offenses to discover how the system worked. This "reconstruction" can be thought of as an example of reverse engineering Over time, as this new offensive system became widely understood, its effectiveness waned. Currently, no NFL teams claim to be implementing the run-and-shoot offense.[21]

Bases of Product Differentiation That May Be Costly to Duplicate.   Some bases of product differentiation may be costly to duplicate, at least in some circumstances. A firm's product mix can be easy to duplicate if numerous competing firms possess the resources and capabilities that the firm uses to develop its product mix. The ability to offer both personal computers and printers to customers is not unique to Hewlett-Packard; IBM, Apple, Dell, and numerous other firms provide this similar product mix.

Links with other firms may be easy to duplicate in some situations and costly to duplicate in others. For example, the first car rental firm that established a linkage with a credit card company, so that the credit card company would pay for a customer's extra insurance, may have obtained a brief product differentiation-based competitive advantage. However, as soon as the relationship was revealed (through advertising), numerous other credit card and car rental firms rapidly duplicated these linkages. Indeed, currently every major credit card firm has this type of relationship with at least one car rental firm. This suggests that these particular interfirm relations were not a source of sustained competitive advantage.

Some linkages between firms, however, can be very costly to imitate. This is especially likely when specific kinds of linkages can exist between only a few firms (that is, when only a few firms have the needed complementary resources and capabilities to link together), and when these linkages themselves are based on socially complex relationships. These kinds of cooperative interfirm relations are discussed in detail in Chapter 13.

In the same way, product customization and product complexity are often easy-to-duplicate bases of product differentiation. However, sometimes the ability of a firm to customize its products for one of its customers depends on close relationships it has developed with those customers. Product customization of this sort depends on the willingness of a firm to share often-proprietary details about its operations, products, research and development, or other characteristics with a supplying firm. Willingness to share this kind of information, in turn, depends on the ability of each firm to trust and rely on the other. The firm opening its operations to a supplier must trust that that supplier will not make this information broadly available to competing firms. The firm supplying the customized products must trust that its customer will not take unfair advantage by requiring the development of a customized product that has no other potential customers and then insisting on a lower-than-agreed-to price, higher-than-expected quality, and so forth. If two firms have developed these kinds of socially complex relationships, and few other firms have, then these linkages with other firms will be costly to duplicate and a source of sustained competitive advantage.

Finally, consumer marketing, though a very common form of product differentiation, is often easy to duplicate. Many consumer marketing efforts seem to follow very tried-and-true paths, including advertising, point-of-purchase displays, and coupons. Rarely are these efforts difficult to duplicate. For example, in advertising beer, attractive bathing suit–clad men and women engaging in some sporting contest (baseball, basketball, volleyball) or having a party are very common. Rarely will these characteristics of advertisements be difficult to duplicate, and thus rarely will they be a source of sustained competitive advantage.

Periodically, however, an advertising campaign or slogan, a point-of-purchase display, or some other attribute of a consumer marketing campaign will unexpectedly catch on and create greater-than-expected product awareness. In marketing beer, campaigns such as "Tastes great, less filling," "Why ask why," the "Budweiser Frogs," and "What's Up?" have had these unusual effects. If a firm, in relation with its various consumer marketing agencies, is systematically able to develop superior consumer marketing campaigns, then this firm may be able to obtain a sustained competitive advantage. However, if such campaigns are unpredictable and largely a matter of a firm's good luck, they cannot be expected to be a source of sustained competitive advantage.

Bases of Product Differentiation That Are Usually Costly to Duplicate.   The remaining bases of product differentiation listed in Table 7.3 are usually costly to duplicate. Firms that differentiate their products on these bases may be able to obtain sustained competitive advantages.

Linkages across functions within a single firm are usually a costly-to-duplicate basis of product differentiation. Whereas linkages with other firms can be either easy or costly to duplicate, depending on the nature of the relationship that exists between firms, linkages across functions within a single firm usually require socially complex, trusting relations. As discussed in detail in Chapter 6, there are numerous built-in conflicts between functions and divisions within a single firm. Organizations that have a history and culture that support cooperative relations among conflicting divisions may be able to set aside functional and divisional conflicts, to cooperate in delivering a differentiated product to the market. However, firms with a history of conflict across functional and divisional boundaries face a significant, and costly, challenge in altering these socially complex, historical patterns.

One firm that has been attempting to eliminate conflicts across its functions is the Division of Damler Chrysler. Since its founding, different functions involved in design, engineering, and manufacturing at Chrysler have had adversarial relationships. Design engineers would develop body styles that conflicted with the requirements of engineer designers; engine designers would develop power plants that were very costly to build, and so forth. The results of these adversarial relations were long delays in product development, product compromises, and lower quality. Recently, however, Chrysler has attempted to set aside traditional conflicts in developing automobile platforms. Reports suggest that this new cooperative approach has been successful, although it is still limited to a small group of engineers working on specific projects. Whether Chrysler will be able to develop these kinds of cooperative relations between other critical functions, and the costs of these attempts, and how Chrysler's merger with Daimler-Benz will affect these efforts, are still not known.[22]

Timing is also a difficult-to-duplicate basis of product differentiation. As suggested in Chapter 5, it is difficult (if not impossible) to re-create a firm's unique historical position.

Rivals of a firm with a timing-based product differentiation advantage may need to seek alternative ways to differentiate their products.

Location is often a difficult-to-duplicate basis of product differentiation. This is especially the case when a firm's location is unique. For example, research on the hotel preferences of business travelers suggests that location is a major determinant of the decision to stay in a hotel. Hotels that are convenient to both major transportation and commercial centers in a city are preferred, other things being equal, to hotels in other types of locations. Indeed, location has been shown to be a more important decision criterion for business travelers than price. If only a few hotels in a city have these prime locations, and if no further hotel development is possible, then hotels with these locations can gain sustained competitive advantages.

Of all the bases of product differentiation listed in this chapter, perhaps none is more difficult to duplicate than a firm's reputation. A firm's reputation is actually a socially complex relationship between a firm and its customers, based on years of experience, commitment, and trust. Reputations are not built quickly, nor can they be bought and sold. Rather, they can only be developed over time by consistent investment in the relationship between a firm and its customers. A firm with a positive reputation can enjoy a significant competitive advantage, whereas a firm with a negative reputation, or no reputation, may have to invest significant amounts over long periods of time to match the differentiated firm.

Distribution channels can also be a costly-to-duplicate basis of product differentiation. This can be the case for at least two reasons. First, relations between a firm and its distribution channels are often socially complex and thus costly to duplicate. Second, the supply of distribution channels may not be completely elastic. Firms that already have access to these channels may be able to use them, but firms that do not have such access may be forced to create their own or develop new channels. Creating new channels, or developing entirely new means of distribution, can be difficult and costly undertakings.[23] These costs are one of the primary motivations underlying many international joint ventures (see Chapter 13).

Finally, level of service and support can be a costly-to-duplicate basis of product differentiation. In most industries, it is usually not too costly to provide a minimum level of service and support. In home electronics, this minimum level of service can be provided by a network of independent electronic repair shops. In automobiles, this level of service can be provided by service facilities associated with dealerships. In fast foods, this level of service can be provided by a minimum level of employee training.

However, moving beyond this minimum level of service and support can be difficult to duplicate for at least two reasons. First, increasing the quality of service and support may involve substantial amounts of costly training. McDonald's has created a sophisticated training facility (Hamburger University) to maintain its unusually high level of service in fast foods. General Electric has invested heavily in training for service and support over the last several years. Many Japanese automakers have spent millions on training employees to help support auto dealerships, before they opened U.S. manufacturing facilities.[24]

More important than the direct costs of the training needed to provide high-quality service and support, these bases of product differentiation often reflect an attitude of a firm and its employees toward customers. In many firms throughout the world, the customer has become "the bad guy." This is, in many ways, understandable.

Employees tend to interact with their customers less frequently than they interact with other employees. When they do interact with customers, they are often the recipients of complaints directed at the firm. In these settings, hostility toward the customer can develop. Such hostility is, of course, inconsistent with a product differentiation strategy based on customer service and support.

In the end, high levels of customer service and support are based on socially complex relations between firms and customers. Firms that have conflicts with their customers may face some difficulty duplicating the high levels of service and support provided by competing firms.

Substitutes for Product Differentiation

The bases of product differentiation outlined in this chapter vary in how rare they are likely to be and in how difficult they are to duplicate. However, the ability of the bases of product differentiation to generate a sustained competitive advantage also depends on whether low-cost substitutes exist.

Substitutes for bases of product differentiation can take two forms. First, many of the bases of product differentiation listed in Table 7.3 can be partial substitutes for each other. For example, product features, product customization, and product complexity are all very similar bases of product differentiation and thus can act as substitutes for each other. A particular firm may try to develop a competitive advantage by differentiating its products on the basis of product customization, only to find that its customization advantages are reduced as another firm alters the features of its products.

Thus, for example, there used to be personal computer word-processing software designed specifically for use in publishing. The level of customization of this publishing software was quite substantial. However, over the years, the addition of more features to standard word-processing packages narrowed the product differentiation gap between publishing-oriented word-processing software and general-use word-processing software.

In a similar way, linkages between functions, linkages between firms, and product mix, as bases of product differentiation, can also be substitutes for each other. IBM links its sales, service, and consulting functions to differentiate itself in the mainframe computer market. Other computer firms, however, may develop close relationships with computer service companies and consulting firms to close this product differentiation advantage.

Second, other strategies discussed throughout this book can be substitutes for many of the bases of product differentiation listed in Table 7.3. For example, one firm may try to gain a competitive advantage through adjusting its product mix, and another firm may substitute strategic alliances to create the same type of product differentiation.

For example, the Grateful Dead, REM, and the Dave Matthews Band have all differentiated themselves in the world of rock-and-roll bands on the basis of concert performances that have built steady and very loyal groups of fans. Phil Collins, Michael Bolton, and Cher have built their fan bases through numerous corporate tie-ins, including live concerts broadcast by cable networks. In this sense, the grass-roots differentiation approach of REM and Dave Matthews can be seen as a partial substitute for the strategic alliances of Phil Collins and Cher. In personal computers,

Dell's use of Internet ordering systems can be seen as a partial substitute for Gateway's recent entry into retail computer stores. Both serve to differentiate these computer makers in the crowded PC market, but do so in different ways. Also, Southwest Airlines' continued emphasis on friendly, on-time, low-cost service and United Airlines' emphasis on its links to Lufthansa and other worldwide airlines through the Star Alliance can both be seen as product differentiation efforts that are at least partial substitutes.[25]

In contrast, some of the other bases of product differentiation discussed in this chapter have few obvious close substitutes. These include timing, location, distribution channels, and service and support. To the extent that these bases of product differentiation are also valuable, rare, and difficult to duplicate, they may be sources of sustained competitive advantage.

7.5 ORGANIZING TO IMPLEMENT PRODUCT DIFFERENTIATION

Firms that seek to implement product differentiation strategies can use all the organizing tools mentioned in previous chapters, including organizational structure, management controls, and compensation policies. In using these tools, firms implementing product differentiation strategies must learn how to balance a set of conflicting organizing demands. On the one hand, these firms need to use these organizing tools to encourage creativity, innovativeness, and risk taking among their employees so that new, highly differentiated products can be developed and brought to market. On the other hand, these firms need to implement a structure, management controls, and compensation policies that bring coherence and order to a firm's product differentiation strategies. Balancing the tensions between encouraging creativity on the one hand and order on the other is the critical organizing problem facing firms that implement product differentiation strategies.

The Process of Developing Highly Differentiated Products

The need for a firm that implements a product differentiation strategy to manage the tension between creativity on the one hand and order on the other, reflects the special attributes of the innovation process in firms. One description of this process is presented in Table 7.4. As suggested in this table, at one level the innovation process is simple and logical. It moves from the **initiation stage,** at which an innovation is conceived, to the **development stage,** at which it is developed into real products and services, and ends in the **implementation/termination stage,** at which an innovation is implemented (if it turns out to have market value) or terminated (if it turns out not to have market value). This logical progression from initiation to development to implementation/ termination suggests that the innovations that enable a firm to pursue a product differentiation strategy proceed in an orderly process.

However, this sense of orderliness is contradicted by many of the processes that occur within and between each of the stages of the innovation process presented in Table 7.4.[26] For example, in the initiation stage, innovation gestation usually takes place over several years as random and coincidental innovations occur in a firm. Firms are often only motivated to coordinate these separate events into a coherent innovation effort

TABLE 7.4   The Process of Developing Innovative Products and Services

Initiation

1. *Gestation:* Innovations are not initiated on the spur of the moment, by a single dramatic incident, or by a single entrepreneur. In most cases, there was an extended gestation period lasting several years in which seemingly coincidental events occurred that preceded and set the stage for the initiation of innovations.

2. *Shock:* Concentrated efforts to initiate innovations are triggered by "shocks" from sources internal or external to the organization.

3. *Plans:* Plans are developed and submitted to resource controllers to obtain the resources needed to launch innovation development. In most cases, the plans served more as "sales vehicles" than as realistic scenarios of innovation development.

Development

4. *Proliferation:* When developmental activities begin, the initial innovative idea soon proliferates into numerous ideas and activities that proceed along divergent, parallel, and convergent paths of development.

5. *Setbacks:* Setbacks and mistakes are frequently encountered because plans go awry or unanticipated environmental events significantly alter the ground assumptions of the innovation. As setbacks occur, resource and development time lines diverge. Initially, resource and schedule adjustments are made and provide a "grace" period for adapting the innovation. With time, however, unattended problems often "snowball" into vicious cycles.

6. *Criteria shift:* To compound the problems, criteria of success and failure often change, differ between resource controllers and innovation managers, and diverge over time, often triggering power struggles between insiders and outsiders.

7. *Fluid participation of organizational personnel:* Innovation personnel participate in highly fluid ways. They tend to be involved on a part-time basis, have high turnover rates, and experience euphoria in the beginning, frustration and pain in the middle period, and closure at the end of the innovation journey. These changing human emotions represent some of the most "gut-wrenching" experiences for innovation participants and managers.

8. *Investors/top management:* Investors and top managers are frequently involved throughout the development process and perform contrasting roles that serve as checks and balances on one another. In no cases were significant innovation development problems solved without intervention by top managers or investors.

9. *Relationships with others:* Innovation development entails developing relationships with other organizations. These relationships lock innovation units into specific courses of action that often result in unintended consequences.

10. *Infrastructure development:* Innovation participants are often involved with competitors, trade associations, and government agencies to create an industry or community infrastructure to support the development and implementation of their innovations.

Implementation/Termination

11. *Adoption:* Innovation adoption and implementation occurs throughout the developmental period by linking and integrating the "new" with the "old" or by reinventing the innovation to fit the local situation.

12. *Termination:* Innovations stop when implemented or when resources run out. Investors or top managers make attributions about innovation success or failure. These attributions are often misdirected but significantly influence the fate of innovations and the careers of innovation participants.

Source: Adapted from Van de Ven, A., D. Polley, R. Garud, and S. Vankataraman (1999). *The Innovation Journey,* New York: Oxford University Press, pp. 23–24.

when they face an important competitive shock. Even then, the innovation "plans" that are developed often do not actually describe the innovation process. Rather, they are often used only as political tools within a firm to "sell" continuing investment in an innovation. The actual process of innovation within a firm may be very different than the process as described in its "innovation plans."

In the development stage, the innovation process is characterized by proliferation, setbacks, shifting criteria for evaluating an innovation, a constantly changing group of employees involved in an innovation, and changes in top managers who are sponsoring an innovation. To be successful, those associated with innovations must often develop relationships with other firms to support this and related innovations. As will be described in Chapter 13, these interfirm relationships often evolve in unpredictable ways. Indeed, it is not unusual for an innovation that has moved from the initiation stage to the development stage to move back to the initiation stage, and for this recycling of the innovative process to occur several times.

One response to this confusion and potential chaos is for a firm to attempt to impose order on the innovation process. Certainly, some of the most wasteful aspects of this innovative process can be made more efficient. For example, many firms have found it necessary to establish explicit criteria for stopping a particular innovative effort. If this effort is not stopped, it may continue indefinitely, recycling from the initiation to the development stage, never moving to either implementation or termination. One way to ensure that a terminated innovative process is actually terminated is to reassign all the people associated with that innovation to other innovative projects. This increases the chance that this rejected innovative effort will actually go away.

Although it is appropriate for a firm to bring some order to the innovative process, an attempt to routinize and structure this process to too great a degree can actually destroy its creativity. This is because the chaos and disorder of this process may actually encourage the development of truly innovative products and technologies that a firm may be able to use to implement a product differentiation strategy. Put differently, if the only innovation a firm allows is innovation it can anticipate, it will never be able to exploit innovations it could not have anticipated.

One way firms sometimes try to impose structure and order on the innovation process is to shorten the time that an innovation takes to go through the initiation, development, and implementation/termination stages. However, because the ultimate economic value of many important technological innovations is very difficult to anticipate early in the development of these technologies, moving too quickly from initiation to implementation/termination can limit a firm's ability to introduce differentiated products. There was, for example, widespread skepticism about the need for the electric light bulb when it was first introduced, because oil lamps had demonstrated their value for centuries. Early investors could see little value, beyond amusement, in the Wright brothers' airplane. In the early 1950s, the president of IBM asserted that the total demand for computers in the world would never exceed seven. In the 1960s, a consultant evaluating the market potential of Xerox machines concluded, "Nothing will ever replace carbon paper." And in the 1980s, the Internet was considered little more than an efficient way for academics around the world to share their research papers. If the firms that ultimately developed these technologies into products had moved too quickly from initiation to implementation/termination, the products would not have been introduced.

The organizing dilemmas that firms using innovation to implement a product differentiation strategy face have recently been examined in detail. Some of the most important of these are summarized in Figure 7.4 and include organizing dilemmas associated with interfunctional collaboration, institutional control, connections with the past, and commitment to a market vision.[27] To the extent that firms fail to strike a balance between the contradictory organizing imperatives summarized by these dilemmas, they risk being able to develop the innovative products and services required to implement a product differentiation strategy successfully.

Interfunctional Collaboration

Interfunctional collaboration in the innovation process is necessary if firms are to develop products and technologies that can actually be marketed to customers. Without this collaboration, new products and services are usually optimized from the point of view of one function within the firm. Thus, for example, when manufacturing dominates the innovative process, a new product may be very easy to manufacture but difficult to sell. On the other hand, if the sales department dominates the innovative process, a new product may be very easy to sell but costly to manufacture. It was already suggested in Chapter 6 that one of the primary responsibilities of a CEO in implementing a business-level strategy is to resolve and manage conflicts between functions in a U-form structure.

On the other hand, too much interfunctional collaboration can slow the innovation process dramatically, because each functional manager in a firm has to "sign off" on each major component of a new technology or product. Moreover, products that are developed in this interfunctional way may end up being technological and

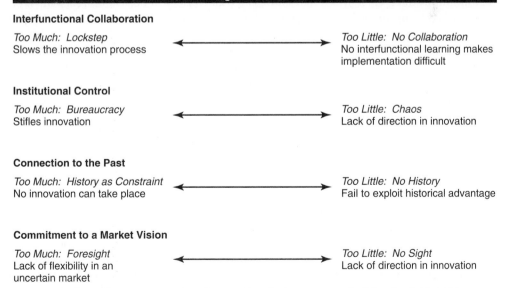

FIGURE 7.4   Organizing Dilemmas for Firms Implementing Innovative Product Differentiation Strategies

Interfunctional Collaboration

Too Much: Lockstep
Slows the innovation process

Too Little: No Collaboration
No interfunctional learning makes implementation difficult

Institutional Control

Too Much: Bureaucracy
Stifles innovation

Too Little: Chaos
Lack of direction in innovation

Connection to the Past

Too Much: History as Constraint
No innovation can take place

Too Little: No History
Fail to exploit historical advantage

Commitment to a Market Vision

Too Much: Foresight
Lack of flexibility in an uncertain market

Too Little: No Sight
Lack of direction in innovation

Source: Adapted from Brown, S., and K. Eisenhardt (1998). *Competing on the Edge,* Cambridge, MA: Harvard Business School Press.

functional compromises—not easy enough to manufacture to give a firm a cost leadership advantage, not easy enough to sell to give a firm a product differentiation advantage.

There are numerous examples of firms that have emphasized either not enough interfunctional collaboration in the innovative process or too much interfunctional collaboration in the innovative process. Time Warner is an example of a firm that probably does not have enough interfunctional collaboration.[28] It is not unusual for the publishing division of Time Warner to own the copyright to an important novel but be unwilling to work with the movie production division of Time Warner to develop this novel into a movie. That lack of interfunctional cooperation limits the ability of Time Warner's movie production division to differentiate its products in the marketplace. It also has led many observers to be skeptical about the ability of Time Warner to exploit relationships with America Online, despite the recent merger of these firms.

A firm that may have emphasized too much interfunctional collaboration is Quaker, especially in how it managed its acquisition of Snapple. Before its acquisition by Quaker, Snapple prospered through its close relationships with its distributors, a strong product concept, and strong advertising that featured a Snapple employee from New York in apparently "homemade" television commercials. However, integrating Snapple with similar Quaker products (including Gatorade) led Quaker to abandon Snapple's traditional strengths. Purchased for $1.7 billion, the Snapple division lost over $100 million over 3 years and was finally sold off for $300 million.[29]

Institutional Control

Without some institutional control, a firm's innovative processes will often lack strategic direction and focus. Instead of producing and selling a well-designed portfolio of products or services that address a wide variety of customer needs in an efficient and comprehensive way, firms without an innovative focus may end up trying to sell a hodge-podge of products or services to very different customers in very different ways. Some of those products may be differentiated on the basis of their reliability, others on the basis of their effectiveness, others on the basis of their ease of use, and still others on the basis of how they look. Rather than developing a single integrated product differentiation strategy to sell to a well-defined market segment, this unfocused firm may find itself selling in multiple markets each of which makes very different demands on suppliers. In an effort to try to satisfy the multiple conflicting needs of very different customers, this unfocused firm is likely to end up satisfying none of them.

On the other hand, too much institutional control can stifle creativity. By instituting multiple bureaucratic hurdles to control the innovation process, a firm can slow that process to a crawl. Instead of deciding how to address customer needs, too much institutional control can lead innovators to spend most of their time trying to decide how to satisfy internal control systems so that they can continue innovating. In the extreme, potential innovators may conclude that the costs of engaging in innovation are so high, and the probability of success so low, that innovative efforts do not even begin. Without innovation, the ability of a firm to implement a product differentiation strategy can be significantly limited.

An example of a firm that fell victim to chaos—in which no rules, loose structure, and random communication make it difficult to create new highly differentiated products—is Ben and Jerry's Ice Cream. During the 1980s, Ben and Jerry's was a relatively small producer of highly differentiated expensive ice cream. Known for having few operating rules, a strong team orientation, value-based capitalism, and an emphasis on "anything but vanilla" flavors, Ben and Jerry's prospered through the 1980s. However, in the 1990s, as Ben and Jerry's grew larger and as competition increased (from firms such as Häagen-Daz), the chaotic management that had served Ben and Jerry's for so long became part of the firm's financial problems. By being slow to introduce low-fat products, Ben and Jerry's lost some of its competitive advantage, and saw its stock price drop from a high of $30 to only $12 per share. The acquisition of Ben and Jerry's by Unilever can be understood as an effort to institute more institutional controls in this firm.[30]

Of course, the number of firms that fall victim to bureaucratic impediments to implementing product differentiation strategies is larger than the number that fall victim to chaos. Examples of these highly bureaucratic firms include Daimler-Benz and Campbell Soup. Both of these firms were once dominant in their market niche, but both have failed to keep up with the introduction of new products and services. By the mid-1990s, BMW sold more cars worldwide than Mercedes, and by the mid-1990s, Campbell Soup's dominant market position was being threatened by innovative new products offered by competitors.[31]

Connection to the Past

It has already been suggested (in Chapter 5) that a firm's unique history can be a source of sustained competitive advantage. This is because firms typically find it costly to imitate valuable and rare resources that a competing firm was able to develop or acquire because it happened to be in the right place at the right time to develop or acquire them. Caterpillar is an example of a firm with a unique history that gave it an important competitive head start in pursuing global opportunities in the heavy construction equipment industry. This head start reflected the heavily subsidized worldwide service and support network that Caterpillar was able to build because of its role as the primary supplier of heavy construction equipment to the Allies during World War II. And because of its history, Caterpillar's head start has become a sustained competitive advantage. Firms that are not connected with their own past can fail to gain the competitive advantages that their own history may promise for them.

However, not only can history be a source of sustained competitive advantage, it can also be a source of sustained competitive disadvantage. This can happen in at least two ways. First, a firm that was *unable* to develop or acquire valuable resources because of its history may find itself at a sustained competitive disadvantage compared to firms that have been able to develop those resources. Rather than focusing on strategies that require the resources and capabilities this firm does not possess, such a firm must find alternative bases of competitive advantage to exploit. Thus, for example, when Komatsu (a Japanese heavy construction equipment firm) found itself at a historically derived sustained competitive disadvantage to Caterpillar, instead of trying to compete head to head with Caterpillar's worldwide service and support network, Komatsu designed and built heavy construction equipment that did not break down as frequently.

Although it did not completely neutralize Caterpillar's competitive advantage, this strategy did allow Komatsu to become a viable second supplier in many of Caterpillar's markets.[32] A firm that fails to find these alternative bases of competitive advantage, that is, a firm that is too connected to its nonvaluable past, will be unable to gain even competitive parity.

Second, in some circumstances, the value of history-derived competitive advantages can change with changes in technology, demand, and customer tastes. In this setting, what was once a source of competitive advantage can be a source of competitive disadvantage. If a firm remains wedded to its historically derived resources and capabilities, even if those resources and capabilities are no longer valuable, its performance can fall significantly. In this sense, being too connected to what has become a nonvaluable past can hurt a firm's performance.

Another firm that has, at some times in its history, been too disconnected from its past is Apple Computer. Consider, for example, Apple's Newton personal digital assistant. The Newton was a new product category, built on hardware and software technologies that were very different than Apple's traditional strengths, and which competed in the consumer electronics market, in which Apple had not historically competed. Because the Newton was such a break with Apple's past, management made a series of technical mistakes (emphasizing handwriting recognition rather than communication capabilities) and marketing mistakes (too high of a price), mistakes that they probably would not have made if this new product had been more similar to Apple's historical products.[33]

One of the best-known examples of a firm being too connected to its now nonvaluable past is Disney in the days before Michael Eisner took over as CEO. During that period, decision making, innovation, and creativity were stifled by managers at Disney always asking, "What would Walt do?," referring of course to Walt Disney, the founder of the firm. This question, however, created two problems for the company. First, Walt was dead, so it was difficult to know what he would have done. Second, consumer tastes were changing. What Walt would have done in the 1960s was not terribly relevant to what needed to be done in the mid-1980s. As described in Chapter 1, being so closely linked with the past significantly hurt Disney's performance. When Eisner became CEO, he did not abandon Disney's past, but he adapted it to modern tastes.[34]

Finally, firms can sometimes be overcommitted to a single vision of the future of a marketplace and refuse to acknowledge competitively possible alternatives. This can interfere with the firm's efforts to introduce differentiated products desired by customers. For example, in the mid-1980s Monsanto invested over $1 billion on genetically engineered agricultural products, anticipating the rapid growth in demand for these products. And over several years, Monsanto, in fact, had developed a broad range of these highly differentiated products. However, one part of the genetically engineered agricultural product market that Monsanto failed to anticipate was consumer reluctance to purchase and consume genetically engineered products. This has slowed the development of this marketplace, and made it much more difficult for Monsanto to earn a positive return on its investment.[35]

On the other hand, having no vision about the future of a market can also make it very difficult to implement a product differentiation strategy. In the deregulated telecommunications market in the United States, AT&T often seemed to lack a clear strategic focus or vision about how this market would evolve. Mostly, AT&T seemed to react to the strategic actions of others, including local phone service providers and long-distance carriers such as MCI and Sprint. For example, AT&T only began exploring international opportunities after MCI merged with WorldCom to form a truly international telecommunications company. More frequently, AT&T's primary strategy seemed to have been to engage in very large employee layoffs every 3 years or so; not surprisingly, in 2005, AT&T was purchased by SBC.[36]

Managing the Innovative Process for Product Differentiation

Firms can use their organizational structure, management control processes, and compensation policies to help resolve the organizing problems described in Figure 7.4. How this can be done is described in Figure 7.5. Firms that manage these tensions well will be able to conceive of and implement innovative product differentiation strategies.

Organizational Structure and Implemention of Product Differentiation

As with all business-level strategies, the most efficient organizational structure for implementing product differentiation strategies is the U-form structure introduced in Chapter 6. However, unlike the U-form used to implement cost leadership strategies—in which a simple and lean structure is important—the U-form structure used to implement product differentiation strategies is often augmented with numerous temporary product development teams. Product development teams are multifunctional groups of managers who work together to develop and implement new, highly differentiated products.

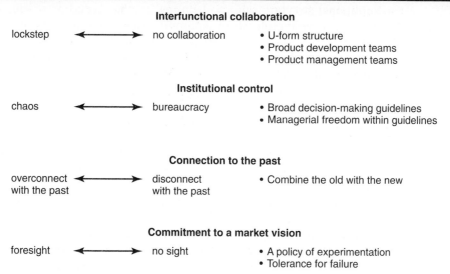

| FIGURE 7.5 | Using Organizational Structure, Management Controls, and Compensation Policy to Resolve Organizing Dilemmas Associated with Implementing Product Differentiation Strategies |

Interfunctional collaboration

lockstep ←——————→ no collaboration
- U-form structure
- Product development teams
- Product management teams

Institutional control

chaos ←——————→ bureaucracy
- Broad decision-making guidelines
- Managerial freedom within guidelines

Connection to the past

overconnect ←——————→ disconnect
with the past   with the past
- Combine the old with the new

Commitment to a market vision

foresight ←——————→ no sight
- A policy of experimentation
- Tolerance for failure

The product development team is a structural tool that a firm can use to resolve the first of the four organizing dilemmas identified in Figure 7.5: the appropriate level of interfunctional collaboration. Because product development teams are usually temporary and are created to help manage the introduction of new, highly differentiated products, they avoid the lockstep problem of trying to link all of a firm's business functions all the time in implementing this strategy. Because they are multifunctional in character, they can facilitate learning across business functions.

A firm that has excelled at using cross-functional product development teams to help introduce new, highly differentiated products and services is Disney. For example, when Disney anticipates introducing new characters in an animated feature, professionals in the retail business, in Disney's theme park businesses, and in their book publishing business get together in product development teams to plan on how to take advantage of these new characters in multiple businesses. By anticipating these linkages, Disney is actually able to enhance its product differentiation strategies, because its retail, theme park, and book publishing activities tend to reinforce the unique attributes of its animated characters, while its animated characters tend to help differentiate its retail, theme park, and book publishing activities.[37]

In some organizations, product development teams are such an important part of implementing a product differentiation strategy that they cease to be temporary. When this occurs, a **product management team** has developed. A product management team is a permanent cross-functional team that is assigned the responsibility of managing the ongoing product differentiation of a product or service. Firms such as Proctor & Gamble, American Express, and The Limited all use product management teams to implement their product differentiation strategies.

When a firm uses product management teams to implement its product differentiation strategies, and when those product management teams have the responsibility for managing a product's profitability, that firm has begun shifting its organizational structure from the U-form structure described in Chapter 6 to the M-form, or multidivisional structure, described in Chapter 12. A detailed discussion of this M-form structure will be delayed until Chapter 12.

Organizational structure can also help resolve the second organizing dilemma identified by Brown and Eisenhardt: the appropriate level of institutional control in the innovation process. This can be done through the use of different leadership roles in a firm's structure, leadership roles that can create some institutional control in the innovation process without creating so much control that it stifles creativity.

Five leadership roles that can have the effect of facilitating the innovation process have been identified in the literature. These five roles are presented in Table 7.5 and include the role of **the institutional leader, the critic, the sponsor, the mentor,** and **the entrepreneur.**[38] Firms that do not have all these leadership roles in their organizational structure are unlikely to experience successful innovation. And without innovation, it is usually difficult for a firm to implement a product differentiation strategy. For example, without someone in the organization adopting the role of an institutional leader, the organizational infrastructure needed for innovation will not likely be in place. Without a critic, those engaged in an innovative process will not face pressures that force them to make decisions and choices that will lead ultimately to a new, highly differentiated product. Without sponsors and mentors, those working

TABLE 7.5	Leadership Roles in the Innovation Process
Institutional leader	Creates the organizational infrastructure needed for innovation
	Resolves disputes among other leaders
Critic	Challenges investments, goals, and progress
Entrepreneur	Manages the innovative unit
Sponsor	Procures, advocates, and champions
Mentor	Coaches, counsels, and advises

Source: Adapted from Van de Ven, A., D. Polley, R. Garud, and S. Vankataraman (1999). *The Innovation Journey,* New York: Oxford University Press, p. 91.

on an innovation can be chronically short of vital resources, and the entire innovation process can get badly off track. Finally, without an entrepreneur, there is no one individual in a firm who is assigned the task of managing the innovation process, and thus no one individual who has an incentive to make sure that the innovation process is successful.

Management Controls and Implementing Product Differentiation

Management control systems are also a very important part of implementing a product differentiation strategy. Management controls can be used to resolve three of the organizing dilemmas presented in Figure 7.5. For example, in resolving the dilemma between chaos and bureaucracy, firms can develop management controls that allow creative decision making within a broader structure of rules and expectations about behavior.

A firm that has worked hard to reach this balance between chaos and bureaucracy is 3M. In an effort to provide a set of guiding principles that define the range of acceptable decisions at 3M, senior managers at 3M have developed a set of innovating principles. These principles, presented in Table 7.6, define the boundaries of innovative chaos in 3M. Within the boundaries defined by these principles, managers and engineers are expected to be creative and innovative in developing highly differentiated products and services.[39]

Another firm that has managed this tension well is British Airways (BA). BA has extensive training programs to teach its flight attendants how to provide world-class service, especially for its business-class customers. This training constitutes the standard operating procedures that define the rules that give purpose and structure to BA's efforts to provide a differentiated service in the highly competitive airline industry. Interestingly, however, BA also provides its flight attendants training in when to violate these standard policies and procedures. By recognizing that no set of management controls can ever anticipate all the special situations that can occur in providing service to customers, BA empowers its employees to meet specific customer needs. This enables BA to have both a clearly defined product differentiation strategy and the flexibility to adjust this strategy as the situation dictates.[40]

TABLE 7.6   Guiding Innovation Principles at 3M as Expressed by W. Coyne[a] (1996)

1. *Vision.* Declare the importance of innovation; make it part of the company's self-image.

   "Our efforts to encourage and support innovation are proof that we really do intend to achieve our vision of ourselves . . . that we intend to become what we want to be . . . as a business and as creative individuals."

2. *Foresight.* Find out where technologies and markets are going. Identify articulated and unarticulated needs of customers.

   "If you are working on a next-generation medical imaging device, you'll probably talk to radiologists, but you might also sit down with people who enhance images from interplanetary space probes."

3. *Stretch goals.* Set goals that will make you and the organization stretch to make quantum improvements. Although many projects are pursued, place your biggest bets on those that change the basis of competition and redefine the industry.

   "We have a number of stretch goals at 3M. The first states that we will derive 30 percent of all sales from products introduced in the past 4 years. . . . To establish a sense of urgency, we've recently added another goal, which is that we want 10 percent of our sales to come from products that have been in the market for just 1 year. . . . Innovation is time sensitive . . . you need to move quickly."

4. *Empowerment.* Hire good people and trust them, delegate responsibilities, provide slack resources, and get out of the way. Be tolerant of initiative and the mistakes that occur because of that initiative.

   "William McKnight [a former chairman of 3M] came up with one way to institutionalize a tolerance of individual effort. He said that all technical employees could devote 15 percent of their time to a project of their own invention. In other words, they could manage themselves for 15 percent of the time. . . . The number is not so important as the message, which is this: The system has some slack in it. If you have a good idea, and the commitment to squirrel away time to work on it and the raw nerve to skirt your lab manager's expressed desires, then go for it.

   Put another way, we want to institutionalize a bit of rebellion in our labs. We can't have all our people off totally on their own. . . we do believe in discipline . . . but at the same time 3M management encourages a healthy disrespect for 3M management. This is not the sort of thing we publicize in our annual report, but the stories we tell—with relish—are frequently about 3Mers who have circumvented their supervisors and succeeded.

   We also recognize that when you let people follow their own lead . . . everyone doesn't wind up at the same place. You can't ask people to have unique visions and march in lockstep. Some people are very precise, detail-oriented people . . . and other are fuzzy thinkers and visionaries . . . and this is exactly what we want."

5. *Communications.* Open, extensive exchanges according to ground rules in forms that are present for sharing ideas and where networking is each individual's responsibility. Multiple methods for sharing information are necessary.

   "When innovators communicate with each other, you can leverage their discoveries. This is critically important because it allows companies to get the maximum return on their substantial investments in new technologies. It also acts as a stimulus to further innovation. Indeed, we believe that the ability to combine and transfer technologies is as important as the original discovery of a technology."

6. *Rewards and recognition.* Emphasize individual recognition more than monetary rewards through peer recognition and by choice of managerial or technical promotion routes.
   "Innovation is an intensely human activity."

   "I've laid out six elements of 3M's corporate culture that contribute to a tradition of innovation: vision, foresight, stretch goals, empowerment, communication, and recognition. . . . The list is . . . too orderly. Innovation at 3M is anything but orderly. It is sensible, in that our efforts are directed at reaching our goals, but the organization . . . and the process . . . and sometimes the people can be chaotic. We are managing in chaos, and this is the right way to manage if you want innovation. It's been said that the competition never knows what we are going to come up with next. The fact is, neither do we."

[a]Senior Vice President, Research and Development, 3M
Source: "Building a Tradition of Innovation," The Fifth U.K. Innovation Lecture, Department of Trade and Industry, London. Cited in Van de Ven et al. (1999), pp. 198–200.

In resolving the tension between overconnecting with the past and not connecting with the past at all, managerial controls can again be very helpful. In particular, controls can require that innovative products combine both the old and the new. These combinations can help firms avoid the liabilities associated both with relying only on the old or only on the new.

Finally, firms can use management controls to resolve the dilemmas associated with having too narrow a vision about the future of a marketplace, on the one hand, and no vision about the future of a marketplace, on the other. Two sets of management controls that are important in resolving this dilemma are a policy of experimentation and policies that tolerate, and even celebrate, failure.

A policy of experimentation means that firms are committed to engage in several related small product differentiation efforts simultaneously. That these product differentiation efforts are related suggests that a firm has some vision about how a particular market is likely to unfold over time. That vision is the way that these innovative efforts are related to each other. However, that there are several of these product differentiation efforts occurring simultaneously suggests that a firm is not overly committed to a particular narrow vision about how a market is going to evolve. Rather, several different experiments facilitate the exploration of different futures in a marketplace. Indeed, successful experiments can actually help define the future evolution of a marketplace.

Consider, for example, Charles Schwab, the innovative discount broker. In the face of increased competition from full-service and Internet-based brokerage firms, Schwab engaged in a series of experiments to discover the next generation of products it could offer to its customers and the different ways it could differentiate those products. For example, Schwab investigated software for simplifying online mutual fund selection, online futures trading, and online company research. Schwab also formed an exploratory alliance with Goldman Sachs to evaluate the possibility of enabling Schwab customers to trade in initial public offerings. Not all of Schwab's experiments led to the introduction of highly differentiated products. For example, based on some experimental investments, Schwab decided to not get into the credit card market. However, by experimenting with a range of possible product differentiation moves, Schwab was able to develop a range of new products for the fast-changing financial services industry.[41]

Of course, a policy of experimentation will only be viable if a firm also has a policy that tolerates, and even celebrates, failure. Without this tolerance, no experimentation will occur in a firm, for no managers will be willing to take the risks that will necessarily be associated with experimentation.

Compensation Policies and Implementing Product Differentiation: The Balanced Scorecard

Organizational structure can be used to manage the first two of the four organizing dilemmas associated with implementing a product differentiation strategy described in Figure 7.4. Different managerial controls can be used to manage the last three of these organizing dilemmas associated with implementing a product differentiation strategy described in Figure 7.4. In general, however, the use of these tools to implement a product differentiation strategy is substantially assisted when they are supported by an appropriate compensation policy.

In implementing a cost leadership strategy, compensation should focus on providing appropriate incentives for managers and employees to reduce costs. Various forms of cash payments, stock, and stock options can all be tied to the attainment of specific cost goals, and thus can be used to create incentives for realizing cost advantages. Similar techniques can be used to create incentives for helping a firm implement its product differentiation advantage.

However, since the implementation of a product differentiation strategy generally involves the integration of multiple business functions, often through the use of product development teams, compensation schemes designed to help implement this strategy must generally recognize its multifunctional character. Many firms, facing this multifunctional compensation task, have chosen to implement what is now known as the **balanced scorecard** approach to compensation.[42]

Compensation policies that reward individuals in a firm for realizing only a single objective—whether that objective is lower costs, higher accounting profit, or higher economic profits—may or may not create incentives for cross-functional cooperation, depending on the extent to which such cooperation is seen as essential in reaching this single objective. The balanced scorecard approach to compensation can build incentives for cross-functional cooperation into organizational policies by recognizing what the key components of success in an organization are.

Suppose, for example, that in order for a firm to implement its product differentiation strategy, it must create a perception of high-quality service on the part of customers, it must deliver products to distribution channels in a timely manner, it must provide a string of creative new products to the marketplace, and it must generate a positive economic profit. Notice that the first three critical elements in the successful implementation of this product differentiation strategy are activities that are usually associated with different business functions: service with the sales function, product delivery with the manufacturing function, and the creation of new products with the R&D function. The balanced scorecard approach to compensation recognizes this multidimensional nature of performance. Under this approach, specific measurements for each of these critical dimensions of performance are identified. For example, one measure of high-quality service might be an annual survey of important customers; a measure of timely delivery of products to distribution channels might be the average dollar value of final product inventory in a firm; one measure of the number new products introduced to the market might be the number of patents obtained; and one measure of positive economic profit might be return on invested capital.

As shown in Figure 7.6, once the critical elements of firm performance are identified and concrete measures of these elements specified, then each of these elements must be weighted and combined to form an overall measure of the performance of an individual, a function, or a business. In this manner, incentives are created for managers throughout the firm to cooperate across multiple functions in order to implement successfully a strategy such as product differentiation.

Of course, the balanced scorecard can be used to help implement other business-level strategies besides product differentiation. In particular, this approach can be used to help implement cost leadership strategies. Indeed, to the extent that the implementation of cost leadership requires intense multifunctional cooperation in a firm, this approach to compensation can be very helpful as part of the process of implementing that

FIGURE 7.6 **Using the Balanced Scorecard to Help Implement a Product Differentiation Strategy**

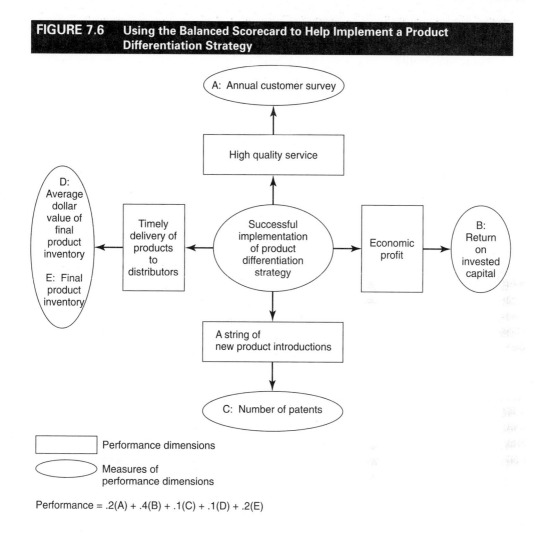

Performance = .2(A) + .4(B) + .1(C) + .1(D) + .2(E)

strategy. However, because product differentiation strategies require a high level of multifunctional integration, the balanced scorecard approach to compensation is described here.

7.6 IMPLEMENTING PRODUCT DIFFERENTIATION AND COST LEADERSHIP STRATEGIES

The arguments developed in Chapter 6 and in this chapter suggest that cost leadership and product differentiation competitive business strategies can, under certain conditions, create sustained competitive advantages. Given the beneficial effects of both strategies on a firm's competitive position, an important question becomes:

"Can a single firm implement both strategies simultaneously?" After all, if each separately can improve a firm's performance, wouldn't it be better for a firm to implement both?

Simultaneous Low-Cost and Product Differentiation Strategies Hurt Firm Performance

A quick comparison of some of the organizational requirements for the successful implementation of cost leadership strategies and product differentiation strategies is presented in Table 7.7 and summarizes one perspective on the question of whether these strategies can be implemented simultaneously. In this view, the organizational requirements of these strategies are essentially contradictory. Cost leadership requires simple reporting relationships, but product differentiation requires cross-divisional/cross-functional linkages. Cost leadership requires intense labor supervision, but product differentiation requires less intense supervision of creative employees. Cost leadership requires rewards for cost reduction, but product differentiation requires rewards for creative flair. It is reasonable to ask: "Can a single firm combine these multiple contradictory skills and abilities?"

Porter has argued that firms that attempt to implement both strategies end up doing neither well. This logic leads to the curve pictured in Figure 7.7. This figure suggests that there are two ways to earn superior economic performance within a single industry: (1) by selling high-priced products and gaining small market share (product differentiation) or (2) by selling low-priced products and gaining large market share (cost leadership). Firms that do not make this choice of strategies (medium price, medium market share) or that attempt to implement both strategies will fail. Porter calls these firms "stuck in the middle."[43]

TABLE 7.7	Organizational Requirements for Implementing Cost Leadership and Product Differentiation Strategies
Cost Leadership	**Product Differentiation**
Organizational Structure	*Organizational Structure*
1. Few layers in the reporting structure	1. Cross-divisional/cross-functional product development teams
2. Simple reporting relationships	2. Willingness to explore new structures to exploit new opportunities
3. Small corporate staff	3. Isolated pockets of intense creative efforts
4. Focus on narrow range of business functions	
	Management Control Systems
Management Control Systems	1. Broad decision-making guidelines
1. Tight cost control systems	2. Managerial freedom within guidelines
2. Quantitative cost goals	3. Policy of experimentation
3. Close supervision of labor, raw material, inventory, and other costs	
4. A cost-leadership philosophy	*Compensation Policies*
	1. Rewards for risk taking, not punishment for failures
Compensation Policies	2. Rewards for creative flair
1. Reward for cost reduction	3. Multidimensional performance measurement
2. Incentives for all employees to be involved in cost reduction	

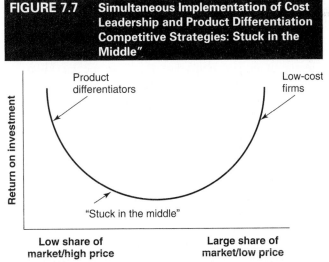

FIGURE 7.7   Simultaneous Implementation of Cost Leadership and Product Differentiation Competitive Strategies: Stuck in the Middle"

Source: Adapted with the permission of The Free Press, a Division of Simon & Schuster Adult Publishing Group, from COMPETITIVE STRATEGY: Techniques for Analyzing Industries and Competitors by Michael E Porter. Copyright © 1980, 1998 by The Free Press. All Rights Reserved.

Simultaneous Low-Cost and Product Differentiation Strategies Help Firm Performance

More recent work contradicts Porter's assertion about firms being "stuck in the middle." This work suggests that firms that are successful in both cost leadership and product differentiation can often expect to gain a sustained competitive advantage. This advantage reflects at least two processes.

Differentiation, Market Share, and Low-Cost Leadership

Firms that are able to differentiate their products and services successfully are likely to see an increase in their volume of sales. This is especially so if the basis of product differentiation is attractive to a large number of potential customers. Thus product differentiation can lead to increased volume of sales. It has already been established (in Chapter 6) that an increased volume of sales can lead to economies of scale, learning, and other forms of cost reduction. So, successful product differentiation can, in turn, lead to cost reductions and a cost leadership position.[44]

This is the situation that best describes McDonald's. McDonald's has traditionally followed a product differentiation strategy, emphasizing cleanliness, consistency, and fun in its fast-food outlets. Over time, McDonald's has used its differentiated product to become the market-share leader in the fast-food industry. This market position has enabled McDonald's to reduce its costs, so that McDonald's is now the cost leader in fast foods as well. Thus McDonald's level of profitability depends on both its product differentiation strategy and its low-cost strategy. Either one of these two strategies by itself would be difficult to overcome; together they give McDonald's a very costly-to-imitate competitive advantage.[45]

Managing Organizational Contradictions

Product differentiation can lead to high market share and low costs. Some firms may also develop special skills in managing the contradictions that are part of implementing low-cost and product differentiation strategies simultaneously. Some recent research on automobile manufacturing helps describe these special skills.

Traditional thinking in automotive manufacturing was that plants could either reduce manufacturing costs by speeding up the assembly line or increase the quality of the cars they made by slowing the line, emphasizing team-based production, and so forth. In general, it was thought that plants could not build low-cost/high-quality (that is low cost *and* highly differentiated) automobiles simultaneously.

Several researchers at the Massachusetts Institute of Technology examined this traditional wisdom. They began by developing rigorous measures of the cost and quality performance of automobile plants and then applied these measures to over 70 auto plants throughout the world that assembled mid-sized sedans. What they discovered was six plants in the entire world that had, at the time this research was done, very low costs *and* very high quality.[46]

In examining what made these six plants different from other auto plants, these researchers focused on a broad range of manufacturing policies, management practices, and cultural variables. Three important findings emerged. First, these six plants had the best manufacturing technology hardware available—robots, laser-guided paint machines, and so forth. However, manufacturing hardware by itself was not enough to make these plants special. In addition, policies and procedures at these plants implemented a range of highly participative, group-oriented management techniques, including participative management, quality circles, team production, and total quality management. As important, employees in these plants had a sense of loyalty and commitment toward the plant they worked for—a belief that they would be treated fairly by their plant managers.

What this research shows is that firms *can* implement cost leadership and product differentiation strategies simultaneously if they learn how to manage the contradictions inherent in these two strategies. The management of these contradictions, in turn, depends on socially complex relations among employees, between employees and the technology they use, and between employees and the firm for which they work. These relations are not only valuable (because they enable a firm to implement cost leadership and differentiation strategies) but also socially complex and thus likely to be costly to imitate and a source of sustained competitive advantage.

Recently, even Porter has backed off his original "stuck in the middle" argument and now suggests that low-cost firms must have competitive levels of product differentiation to survive and that product differentiation firms must have competitive levels of cost to survive.[47]

7.7 SUMMARY

Product differentiation exists when customers perceive a particular firm's products to be more valuable than other firms' products. Although differentiation can have several bases, it is, in the end, always a matter of customer perception.

A variety of bases of product differentiation have been described in the literature. These bases of product differentiation can be discovered by the use of multidimensional scaling or by regression analysis of the determinant of product prices. In the end, however, product differentiation is limited only by environmental opportunities and creativity in exploiting those opportunities.

The value of product differentiation has been studied by both Chamberlin and Robinson. Their work suggests that a firm with a differentiated product can set its prices higher than average total costs and thus obtain an above-normal profit. Each of the bases of product differentiation can be used to neutralize environmental threats and exploit environmental opportunities.

The rarity and imitability of bases of product differentiation vary. Highly imitable bases include product features. Somewhat imitable bases include product mix, links with other firms, product customization, and consumer marketing. Cost-to-imitate bases of product differentiation include linking business functions, timing, location, reputation, and service and support.

The implementation of a product differentiation strategy involves managing several organizing tensions, including (1) lockstep collaboration across all of a firm's functions versus no collaboration, (2) chaos versus bureaucracy, (3) overconnecting with a firm's past versus disconnecting with a firm's past, and (4) overcommitment to one view of how a market is likely to evolve versus no vision about how a market is likely to evolve. Firms can use organizational structure, managerial controls, and compensation policies to help manage these dilemmas. Organizational structure can be used to manage the first dilemma through a U-form structure with cross-functional product development/management teams when appropriate. Leadership roles can also help to resolve the second of these organizing dilemmas. Managerial controls can be used to manage the last three remaining organizing dilemmas through the use of broad decision-making guidelines that provide managerial flexibility within those guidelines, a policy of combining the old and the new in an organization, and a policy of small experiments. Compensation policy can be helpful in resolving these dilemmas by creating appropriate managerial incentives for implementing a product differentiation strategy. Because of the multifunctional nature of this implementation, firms often have to use a balanced score card approach to compensation.

A variety of organizational attributes are required to implement a product differentiation strategy successfully. Porter has argued that contradictions between these organizational characteristics and those required to implement a cost leadership strategy mean that firms that attempt to do both will perform poorly. More recent research notes the relationships among product differentiation, market share, and low costs and observes that some firms have learned to manage the contradictions between cost leadership and product differentiation.

REVIEW QUESTIONS

1. Although cost leadership is perhaps less relevant for firms that pursue product differentiation, costs are not totally irrelevant. What advice about costs would you give a firm pursuing a product differentiation strategy?

2. Product features are often the focus of product differentiation efforts, yet product features

are among the easiest-to-imitate bases of product differentiation and thus among the least likely bases of product differentiation to be a source of sustained competitive advantage. Does this seem paradoxical to you? If not, why not? If yes, how can you resolve this paradox?

3. What are the strengths and weaknesses of the different empirical approaches to describing the bases of product differentiation discussed in the chapter? What can these empirical approaches do for a manager that more conceptual approaches cannot do? What can the conceptual approaches do for a manager that the more empirical approaches cannot do?

4. "Monopolistic competition" is the term that Chamberlin developed to describe firms pursuing a product differentiation strategy in a competitive industry. In Chapter 4 it was sug-

gested that one of the limitations of firms applying the S-C-P framework to make strategic choices is that often they can begin to behave as a monopolist, and monopolists generally are not able to maintain high levels of productive efficiency. Does this same problem exist for firms operating in a "monopolistic competition" context? Why or why not?

5. A firm with a highly differentiated product can increase the volume of its sales. Increased sales volumes can enable a firm to reduce its costs. High volumes with low costs can lead a firm to very high profits, some of which the firm can use to invest in further differentiating its products. What advice would you give a firm whose competition is enjoying this product differentiation and cost leadership advantage?

ENDNOTES

1. See Ono, Y. (1996). "Who really makes that cute little beer? You'd be surprised," *Wall Street Journal,* April 15, pp. A1+. Since this 1996 article, some of these craft beers have changed the way they are manufactured to be more consistent with the image they are trying to project.

2. Proctor & Gamble has sued many Amway distributors for spreading this rumor. Information about Mountain Dew can be found in Pollock, E. (1999). "Why Mountain Dew is now the talk of the teen circuit," *Wall Street Journal,* October 14, pp. A1+.

3. See, for example, Porter, M. C. (1980). *Competitive Strategy,* New York: Free Press; and Caves, R. E., and O. Williamson (1985). "What is product differentiation, really?" *Journal of Industrial Economics,* 34, pp. 113–132.

4. Lieberman, M. B., and D. B. Montgomery (1988). "First-mover advantages," *Strategic Management Journal,* 9, pp. 41–58.

5. London, H. (1995). "Bait and switch in academe," *Forbes,* 155(12), p. 120.

6. Carroll, P. (1993). *Big Blues: The Unmaking of IBM.* New York.: Crown Publishers.

7. These ideas were first developed in Hotelling, H. (1929). "Stability in competition," *Economic Journal,* 39, pp. 41–57; and Ricardo, D. (1817). *Principles of political economy and taxation.* London: J. Murray.

8. See Gunther, M. (1998). "Disney's Call of the Wild." *Fortune,* April 13, pp. 120–124.

9. The idea of reputation is explained in Klein, B., and K. Leffler (1981). "The role of market forces in assuring contractual performance," *Journal of Political Economy,* 89, pp. 615–641.

10. See Robichaux, M. (1995). "It's a book! A T-shirt! A toy! No, just MTV trying to be Disney." *Wall Street Journal,* February 8, pp. A1+.

11. See Henderson, R., and I. Cockburn (1994). "Measuring competence? Exploring firm effects in pharmaceutical research," *Strategic Management Journal,* 15, pp. 63–84.

12. See Johnson, R. (1999). "Speed sells," *Fortune,* April 12, pp. 56–70. In fact, NASCAR fans either love or hate Jeff Gordon.

13. See Carvell, T. (1998). "How Sony created a monster," *Fortune,* June 8, pp. 162+; and Gibson, R. (1999). "Star Wars' tie-in is more a menace than a hit at Tricon," *Wall Street Journal,* July 21, p. A5.

14. Kotler, P. (1986). *Principles of Marketing,* Upper Saddle River, NJ: Prentice Hall.

15. Porter, M. E., and R. Wayland (1991). "Coca-Cola vs. Pepsi-Cola and the soft drink industry," Harvard Business School Case no. 9-391-179.

16. Ghemawat, P. (1993). "Sears, Roebuck and Company: The Merchandise Group," Harvard Business School Case no. 9-794-039.

17. From Rowe, A. J., R. O. Mason, and K. E. Dickel (1982). *Strategic Management: A Methodological Approach,* Reading, MA: Addison-Wesley.

18. Chamberlin, E. H. (1933). *The Theory of Monopolistic Competition,* Cambridge, MA: Harvard University Press; and Robinson, J. (1934). "What is perfect competition?" *Quarterly Journal of Economics,* 49, pp. 104–120.

19. Casey, J. (1976). "High fructose corn syrup," *Research Management,* 19, pp. 27–32.

20. Welsh, J. (1998). "Office-paper firm pursues elusive goal: brand loyalty," *Wall Street Journal,* September 21, pp. B6.

21. Oates, B. (1992). "What happened to the run-and-shoot revolution?" *Football Digest,* 22(2), p. 28.

22. Moritz, M., and B. Seaman (1984). *Going for Broke: Lee Iacocca's Battle to Save Chrysler,* Garden City, NY: Anchor Press/Doubleday; Taylor, A., III (1994). "Iacocca's minivan," *Fortune,* 129(11), pp. 56–66; and Loeb, M. (1995). "Empowerment that pays off," *Fortune,* 131(5), pp. 145–146.

23. See Hennart, J. F. (1988). "A transaction cost theory of equity joint ventures," *Strategic Management Journal,* 9, pp. 361–374.

24. Deutsch, C. H. (1991). "How is it done? For a small fee . . . ," *New York Times,* October 27, p. 25; Armstrong, L. (1991). "Services: The customer as 'honored guest,'" *Business Week,* October 25, p. 104.

25. See Rankin, A. (1998). "Dave Mathews Band succeeds by marching to its own drummer," *Columbus Dispatch,* August 2, pp. F1+; and Yoffie, D. (1994). "Swissair's alliances (A)," Harvard Business School Case no. 9-794-152.

26. Van de Ven, A., D. Polley, R. Garud, and S. Venkatraman (1999). *The Innovation Journey,* New York: Oxford University Press.

27. Brown, S., and K. Eisenhardt (1998). *Competing on the Edge,* Cambridge, MA: Harvard Business School Press.

28. Garvin, D., and J. West (1995). "Time Life Inc. (A)," Harvard Business School Case no. 9-395-012.

29. Burns, G. (1997). "What price the Snapple debacle?" *Business Week,* April 14, p. 42.

30. Judge, P. (1996). "Is it rainforest crunch time?" *Business Week,* July 15, p. 70.

31. Berman, P., and A. Alger (1994). "Reclaiming the patrimony," *Forbes,* March 14, p. 50.

32. See Rukstad, M.G., and J. Horn (1989). "Caterpillar and the construction equipment industry in 1988," Harvard Business School Case no. 9-389-097.

33. Burgess, J. (1993). "Apple bets on Newton, new direction," *Washington Post,* July 30.

34. Collis, D. (1995). "The Walt Disney Company (A)," Harvard Business School Case no. 1-388-147.

35. Grant, L. (1997). "Monsanto's bet: There's gold in going green," *Fortune,* April 14, p. 116.

36. Arnst, C. (1998). "AT&T: Will the bad news ever end?" *Business Week,* October 7, p. 122.

37. Collis, D. (1995). "The Walt Disney Company (A)," Harvard Business School Case no. 1-388-147.

38. Van de Ven, A., D. Polley, R. Garud, and S. Venkatraman (1999). *The Innovation Journey,* New York: Oxford University Press, pp. 198–200.

39. Ibid.

40. Prokesch, S. (1995). "Competing on customer service: An interview with British Airways' Sir Colin Marshall," *Harvard Business Review,* November/December, p. 101.

41. Position, L. L. (1999). "David S. Pottruck," *Business Week,* September 27, p. EB 51.

42. Kaplan, R. S., and D. P. Norton (1996). *The Balanced Scorecard: Translating Strategy into Action,* Boston: Harvard Business School Press.

43. Porter, M. E. (1980). *Competitive Strategy,* New York: Free Press.

44. Hill, C. W. L. (1988). "Differentiation versus low cost or differentiation and low cost: A contingency framework," *Academy of Management Review,* 13(3), pp. 401–412.

45. Gibson, R. (1995). "Food: At McDonald's, new recipes for buns, eggs," *Wall Street Journal,* June 13, p. B1.

46. Womack, J. P., D. I. Jones, and D. Roos (1990). *The Machine That Changed the World,* New York: Rawson.

47. Porter, M. E. (1985). *Competitive Advantage,* New York: Free Press.

C H A P T E R

8

Flexibility: Real Options Analysis Under Risk and Uncertainty

8.1 Introducing Risk and Uncertainty into Strategic Choices: Traditional Approaches
8.2 Defining Flexibility and Options
8.3 The Economic Value of Flexibility
8.4 Flexibility and Sustained Competitive Advantage
8.5 Organizing to Implement Flexibility
8.6 Summary

The strategic analysis tools and options discussed so far in this book have, for the most part, ignored the effect that uncertainty can have on a firm's strategic choices. For example, in pursuing a cost leadership strategy, it is implicitly assumed that firms can anticipate the relationship between their actions (for example, increasing their volume of sales) and their cost position and thus choose strategies that will give them cost advantages. A similar ability to anticipate the relationship between a firm's actions and its product positioning in a marketplace is assumed in the discussion of product differentiation strategies.

Indeed, uncertainty about the relationship between a firm's actions and competitive outcomes has been discussed only once, in the discussion of hypercompetitive industries in Chapter 4. In that discussion it was suggested that in these kinds of industries, firms cannot anticipate the dimensions along which competition will unfold because these dimensions evolve in unpredictable ways. Thus, strategic decision making in this context is uncertain. It was also suggested that an important attribute of any strategy pursued under conditions of high uncertainty is **flexibility**—that is, the ability to change direction quickly and at low cost, given unanticipated changes in the competitive situation within which a firm is operating.

This chapter builds on the discussion of strategy in hypercompetitive industries by extending the discussion of the role of flexibility as a strategic option for firms.

This discussion begins by examining traditional ways of introducing risk and uncertainty into strategic analysis. Limitations of these traditional approaches lead to a discussion of real options theory as a way to understand the importance of flexibility in strategic choices under uncertainty.

8.1 INTRODUCING RISK AND UNCERTAINTY INTO STRATEGIC CHOICES: TRADITIONAL APPROACHES

A decision-making setting is said to be **risky** when its future state cannot be characterized by a single point but rather must be characterized by a probability distribution of possible outcomes. For example, if the level of rivalry in a particular industry is risky, then at some point in the future there might be a 15 percent chance that rivalry in that industry would be very high, a 25 percent chance that it would be high, a 40 percent chance that it would be moderate, a 25 percent chance that it would be low, and a 5 percent chance that it would be very low. Similar outcome distributions may exist for other environmental threats; for environmental opportunities; for the value, rarity, and imitability of a firm's resources and capabilities; and for the value of the strategic actions a firm may take to implement, cost leadership, product differentiation, or other strategies.

The level of risk associated with the future value of an attribute of a firm or industry can vary across firms and industries. In general, the greater the dispersion of possible future values of an attribute of a firm or an industry, the greater is the riskiness associated with that attribute. For example, suppose that, in a second industry, there is 10 percent chance that the level of rivalry in the future will be very high, a 20 percent chance it will be high, a 40 percent chance it will be moderate, a 20 percent chance it will be low, and a 10 percent chance it will be very low. Compared to the industry described earlier, the dispersion of possible future levels of rivalry in this second industry is greater. Thus, the level of risk about the future level of rivalry in this second industry is greater than the level of risk about the future level of rivalry in the first industry.

It is often convenient to measure the level of risk about the future value of an attribute of a firm or an industry by the standard deviation of the probability distribution of those future values. This is done in Table 8.1 for the two industries just described. As suggested earlier, decisions made about the future level of rivalry in the second industry—with a standard deviation of 1.095—are riskier than decisions made about the future level of rivalry in the first industry—with a standard deviation of .948.

Sometimes, the level of ignorance about the attributes of a firm or an industry is so high that it is not possible to specify all future states of that attribute, and thus it is not possible to specify the probability of these different states occurring. Indeed, some authors distinguish between **risk,** or situations in which the future value of an attribute of an industry or firm is not known but the probability distribution of those future values is known, and **uncertainty,** or situations in which the future value of an attribute of an industry or firm is not known and the probability distribution of those future values is also not known.[1]

A variety of industries are characterized by high levels of uncertainty. For example, whereas demand for some toys (for example, blocks) may be quite predictable year

TABLE 8.1   Comparing the Riskiness of Making Decisions About the Future Level of Rivalry in Two Industries Using Standard Deviation Measures of Dispersion

Standard deviation $= \sqrt{\sum_{i=1}^{N} P_i(V_i - \overline{V})^2}$

where

P_i = probability of outcome i
V_i = value of outcome i
V = mean value of all outcomes
N = number of outcomes

Industry One		Industry Two	
P_i *Probability of an Outcome*	V_i *Value of an Outcome*	P_i *Probability of an Outcome*	V_i *Value of an Outcome*
.05	5 = future rivalry very high	.10	5 = future rivalry very high
.25	4 = future rivalry high	.20	4 = future rivalry high
.40	3 = future rivalry moderate	.40	3 = future rivalry moderate
.25	2 = future rivalry low	.20	2 = future rivalry low
.05	1 = future rivalry very low	.10	1 = future rivalry very low
Standard deviation = .948		Standard deviation = 1.095	

to year, the blockbuster success of Pet Rocks, Cabbage Patch Kids, Tickle Me Elmo, and Bratz is very difficult to anticipate. Biotechnology firms also have a very difficult time predicting which of their technologies, if any, will ultimately generate significant cash flows. And, despite enormous efforts to pre-test and re-edit their movies, the success of individual movies is very difficult to predict.

Uncertainty and risk are important variables in strategic decision making for at least two reasons. First, all things being equal, most of a firm's stakeholders, in general, prefer less uncertainty and risk to more uncertainty and risk. A failure to consider uncertainty and risk in strategic decision making may make it difficult for a firm to satisfy many of its critical stakeholders. Second, some strategic choices are more valuable under conditions of high uncertainty and risk than others. For example, as suggested earlier, strategic choices that enhance a firm's flexibility and keep its strategic options open are generally of greater value under conditions of high uncertainty and risk than under conditions of low uncertainty and risk. A failure to incorporate uncertainty and risk in the strategic decision-making process may lead a firm to be too flexible if uncertainty and risk are low, or not flexible enough if uncertainty and risk are high.

Using Present Value to Introduce Risk in Strategic Decision Making

Traditionally, risk has been introduced into strategic decision making through adjustments to the discount rate that is applied to evaluating the cash flows associated with a strategy a firm is going to pursue. As is well known, a firm maximizes its market value when it implements strategies that generate cash flows with positive net present value. The models presented in Part I of this book, and in Chapters 6 and 7, can all be thought of as tools to help a firm predict what the cash flows associated with implementing a strategy will be. Armed with these cash flow estimates, the net present value of a firm's strategies are calculated by

$$NPV_j = \sum_{t=0}^{N} \frac{NCF_{j,t}}{(1+k)^t} \qquad (8.1)$$

where

NPV_j = net present value of Firm j's cash flows
N = the economic life of the investment
$NCF_{j,t}$ = the net cash flow of Firm j at time t
k = the discount rate

$NCF_{j,t}$ is calculated as

$$NCF_{j,t} = (1 - T_j)(Rev_{j,t} - C_{j,t}) + T_j(dep_{j,t}) - I_{j,t} \qquad (8.2)$$

where

$Rev_{j,t}$ = Firm j's operating revenues in time t
$C_{j,t}$ = Firm j's operating costs at time t
T_j = Firm j's marginal tax rate
$dep_{j,t}$ = Firm j's depreciation in time t
$I_{j,t}$ = Firm j's new investment in time t

In applying this net present value formula, an important question becomes: "What is the appropriate discount rate?" If there is no risk in generating the cash flows associated with a strategy, then the appropriate discount rate is the risk-free opportunity cost of capital. Generally, this is taken to be equal to the rate of return on government securities, a relatively low discount rate. Relatively few of the strategies that a firm might pursue generate these completely risk-free cash flows.[2]

Alternatively, if a firm is continuing to implement strategies that it has been successfully implementing for some time, then the level of risk associated with the cash flows these strategies are generating is generally already known. If capital markets are efficient, a firm's cost of capital will reflect publicly available information about the risk associated with the cash flows that the firm's strategies have been generating.[3] In this setting, the appropriate discount rate to apply in equation 8.1 is the firm's opportunity cost of capital—that is, the cost of the capital that the firm acquires to help implement its ongoing strategies.

For example, suppose General Motors (GM) is currently building a particular automobile by running two shifts in a single factory. Suppose also that GM anticipates demand for this automobile to increase. In this situation, GM has to decide whether to add a third shift to the production process in the factory at which this automobile is built. The value that might be created for GM by adding a third shift is somewhat risky, because it depends on forecasted increases in demand actually occurring. However, because this decision simply extends and augments General Motors' already implemented strategy of building this particular type of automobile, the risk associated with it is moderate. In this setting, the appropriate discount rate in estimating the present value of this decision is General Motors' opportunity cost of capital.

But what is the appropriate discount rate when a firm is implementing new and innovative strategies? For example, suppose instead of GM deciding whether to add a third shift to manufacture a current product, GM is deciding whether to build a whole new kind of automobile (for example, a minivan), an automobile using an entirely new technology (such as a car powered by a hydrogen fuel cell), or to introduce a nonautomotive product (perhaps a software product). Obviously, there is substantial risk associated with the cash flows that may be generated by these new and innovative strategies. Thus, the risk-free opportunity cost of capital is an inappropriate discount rate. Moreover, because the capital market does not have all the information it needs to estimate the risk associated with the cash flows these new and innovative strategies generate, a firm's opportunity cost of capital may also not be the appropriate discount rate.

The traditional solution to this problem has been to assign a discount rate to the cash flows that may be generated by implementing new and innovative strategies on the basis of the **risk class** of those strategies. Thus, all strategies that are perceived as being very risky are given the same high discount rate, while those strategies that are perceived as being less risky are given the same low discount rate. If two strategies generate the same cash flows, the riskier of the two will receive the higher discount rate and the less risky will generate a higher net present value.

Limitation of Using Present Value in Uncertain Settings

This traditional approach to determining the discount rate of risky new strategies has at least three important limitations. First, this approach requires information about the cash flows a strategy may generate that is often not known in uncertain settings. To assign a strategy to a risk class, one must know how risky the cash flows associated with that strategy are. Characterizing the level of risk associated with implementing a new and innovative strategy is itself an uncertain undertaking. Misclassifying a strategy's risk class can lead to the choice of an inappropriate discount rate, which, in turn, can lead firms either to choose to implement a strategy they should not have chosen, or fail to choose to implement a strategy they should have chosen.

For example, of the three innovative new strategies that GM might consider, which is the least risky: building a new type of car, building cars with entirely new technology, or building non-automotive products? At first glance, it might appear that building non-automotive products would be the most risky of these three options because it forces GM to stray the farthest from its core strategy of building automobiles. However, if GM has developed this non-automotive product as part of its automobile production process, then the introduction of this product may actually be less risky than either building a new type of car or building a car with new technology. In the end, knowing how risky a particular investment is and what the appropriate discount rate for that investment should be can be very difficult problems for a firm making strategic decisions under conditions of high uncertainty.

Second, this approach to including risk into strategic decision making implicitly assumes that the risk associated with implementing a new strategy remains constant over the life of that strategy. This is often not the case. Strategies may be very risky during some periods of time (for example, in the beginning, when they are first being introduced) and much less risky during other periods of time (for example, after a strategy has been implemented for some time). Moreover, decisions made as a strategy is being implemented can have the effect of either increasing or decreasing the riskiness of a strategy. That is, changes in the level of risk associated with implementing a new strategy do not always increase or decrease in simply predictable ways over time. Indeed, a firm may commit to a particular course of action with an associated level of risk, only to revise its strategy and adopt a different course of action with a different level of risk.

Finally, this approach fails to incorporate information about the full range of strategic opportunities that a new and innovative strategy may create for a firm in the future. A new and innovative strategy may not have positive direct consequences for a firm, but it may create strategic opportunities for a firm in the future. Those future strategic opportunities may be very valuable. Choosing a discount rate based on a strategy's risk class typically focuses only on that strategy's direct effects and does not incorporate information about the value that a strategy may generate by creating strategic opportunities for a firm in the future.

In principle, it may be possible to respond to these first two problems by adjusting the level of risk associated with implementing a new strategy for each period during which a strategy is being implemented.[4] However, in practice, this approach to strategic decision making places unrealistic demands on the abilities of managers to anticipate cash flows, the level of risk associated with those cash flows, changes in strategy, and changes in the level of uncertainty and risk associated with implementing a new strategy over time. Moreover, it does nothing to address questions of valuing the future opportunities inherent in a strategic investment—that is, the strategic flexibility certain investments may create for a firm. Rather than modifying traditional net present value methods to incorporate the high levels of risk associated with implementing new and innovative strategies, many scholars have turned to an alternative. This alternative builds on options theory, as it has been developed in finance.[5] However, because strategic decision making typically involves making investments in real strategic assets, this approach to strategic decision making is called **real options theory.**

8.2 DEFINING FLEXIBILITY AND OPTIONS

An **option** is the right, but not obligation, to buy or sell a specified asset at a prespecified price on a prespecified date. Most managers are familiar with options written on financial assets. For example, if an investor has a **stock option,** he or she has the right, but not the obligation, to purchase a stock at a prespecified price on or before a prespecified day.[6] Suppose this prespecified price (called the **exercise** or **strike price**) is $45. Also suppose that the market price on this stock on the agreed date (called the

expiration or **maturity date**) is $65. Clearly, this investor will want to exercise this option by buying the stock at the prespecified price, because in doing so, he or she will be able to buy financial assets that are worth $65 for $45. On the other hand, if the market price on the expiration date is $30, the investor will not want to exercise the option. Rather, the option will simply expire on the expiration date.

The ability to delay the decision about whether to buy a stock at any point up until the maturity date of a stock option is what introduces flexibility into this financial instrument. Without a stock option, the decision about whether to buy a stock must be made immediately, regardless of uncertainty about the future value of that stock. With a stock option, that decision can be delayed while uncertainty about the future value of the stock resolves over time. With this uncertainty at least partly resolved, the owner of the stock option can then decide whether to exercise the option to purchase the stock, thus retaining flexibility. The cost of retaining this flexibility is simply the cost of the stock option.

Although it is widely understood that options can be written on financial assets, they can also be written on real assets, that is, the physical, human, and organizational capital a firm uses to implement its strategies. These options are called **real options.** Just as with financial options, the owners of a real option have the right, but not the obligation, to expand or contract their investment in a real asset at some future date. This provides a firm the same kind of flexibility that a stock option provides someone investing in stock.

For example, suppose that a pharmaceutical firm invests in research and development. That R&D may have the direct effect of creating a new product (Product A) that can be sold to the marketplace. However, it may also have the effect of creating new ways of thinking about developing drugs that could, at some future date, lead to the development of two additional drugs for the marketplace, Products B and C. Put differently, the opportunity to exploit the R&D used to develop Product A in creating Products B and C in the future is a real option associated with this research and development effort.

Now suppose that, given that this firm has already developed Product A, it would cost an additional $100,000 to develop Products B and C.[7] This is this real option's **exercise price.** If, at some point in the future, the market value of Products B and C rises to be much greater than $100,000, then this firm will exercise its real option, invest in additional product development, and introduce Products B and C to the marketplace. At this point, this firm will be able to buy cash flows worth much more than $100,000 for $100,000. On the other hand, if the market value of Products B and C never rises above $100,000, then the firm will never exercise this option. At some point, when the R&D in which this firm has invested becomes obsolete, this real option will expire. Notice that, as with financial options, this firm does not have to decide whether it will invest in additional R&D to introduce Products B and C until after uncertainty about the value of those products is reduced, one way or another. The original R&D that led to the development of Product A created flexibility around the development of Products B and C.

This example of a real option helps clarify why traditional net present value (NPV) approaches to valuing uncertain strategies over time may be significantly limited. Strategies that a firm implements now can affect the range of strategic choices it can make in the future. Traditional present value methods only incorporate information about the value a strategy creates now. They do not incorporate information about the value that a current strategy may create in the future. If the present value of a current strategy is negative, traditional methods lead that strategy to be rejected, even if the present value of its possible effects on future strategies a firm might pursue is very positive.

For example, suppose that Product A has a negative net present value, but the only way that Products B and C can be developed is first to learn how to produce Product A. An evaluation of Product A by itself using traditional NPV techniques would lead a firm not to invest in this R&D. However, this decision would ignore the potential benefits that this R&D might have for Products B and C at some time in the future. If Products B and C turn out to be very valuable, then the positive cash flow they generate may more than compensate for the negative cash flow generated by Product A by itself.

In general, both the direct and delayed effects of a firm's strategies must be considered in strategic decision making. This is especially important under conditions of high uncertainty, when the ability to exploit future options is likely to be very important for a firm. Real options logic is perfectly adapted to strategic decision making in this setting.

Types of Flexibility

Of course, the flexibility associated with a firm's real options can take many forms. Some of the most important types of flexibility that a firm can possess, and examples of actions that can create these different types of flexibility, are listed in Table 8.2.

For example, a firm can make strategic choices that enhance its ability to defer additional investment in a strategy until some later time period. This is the **option to defer.** An oil and gas company creates this option when it leases land for potential exploration and oil extraction instead of buying it. By leasing the land, this firm defers the decision about whether to fully invest in exploration and extraction on that land

TABLE 8.2 Types of Flexibility and Examples of Actions That Can Create Each Type	
Type of Flexibility	*Example*
The option to defer	An oil company leases land for potential exploration instead of buying it.
The option to grow	A firm builds a plant with the ability to add capacity at low cost.
The option to contract	A firm hires contract and temporary employees instead of full-time employees.
The option to shut down and restart	A firm outsources distribution to a firm that distributes the products of many firms instead of outsourcing distribution to a firm that distributes only its production.
The option to abandon	A firm builds a manufacturing plant that employs only general-purpose machinery.
The option to expand	A firm invests to create one product because that investment could lead to the development of other products in the future.

until after uncertainty about future oil prices is resolved and until after the production potential of that land is more completely understood. An oil company that buys this land instead of leasing it forgoes the option of not investing in this land in the future and thus is less flexible than the firm that leases the land.

Firms can also make choices that enhance their ability to "grow" an investment in the future, should that option turn out to be valuable. This is the **option to grow.** Thus, for example, a manufacturing firm creates this option by building a plant with a capacity that can be increased at relatively low cost. This can be done by, say, running several smaller manufacturing lines in a single plant simultaneously and bringing them on line as demand increases. A firm that builds a plant that is very difficult to increase in capacity is less flexible than this firm.

Firms can also make choices that enhance their ability to get smaller and reduce investment in a strategy, should that option turn out to be valuable in the future. This is the **option to contract.** One way to create this option is to use contract and temporary employees instead of full-time employees. In most countries, contract and temporary employees are much less costly to lay off than full-time employees. Indeed, in some countries—including Germany and France—full-time employment growth is significantly limited by the costliness of laying off full-time employees.[8] For this reason, firms that employ a high percentage of contract and temporary employees are more flexible than firms that employ only full-time employees.[9]

A firm can also make choices that enhance its ability to shut down and restart a business should this option be valuable in the future. This is the **option to shut down and restart.** Compare, for example, two firms: one outsources its distribution to a company that distributes only its products and a second that outsources its distribution to a company that distributes the products of numerous firms. Suppose that market conditions compel both of these firms to shut down their operations for some time period. Which of these two firms is likely to have a lower cost of restarting operations? Because the first firm's distributor was probably unable to distribute anything during this downtime, it may have suffered significantly. Indeed, it may not have even survived this downtime. The second firm's distributor, on the other hand, because it distributes the products of numerous firms, was probably able to survive during this downtime. Upon restart, the second firm can simply reestablish its relationship with its distributor and go on as before. The first firm may have to find an entirely new distributor. Thus, the cost of restarting the business for the second firm is likely to be much lower than the cost of restarting business for the first firm. In this sense, working with a firm that distributes the products of numerous firms has the effect of increasing the flexibility of a firm to shut down and restart a business should it decide this is necessary to do.

Firms can also make choices that enhance their ability to abandon a particular strategy. This is the **option to abandon.** For example, a firm creates this option if it builds a manufacturing plant that employs only general-purpose machinery. Compared to highly customized manufacturing equipment, general-purpose machinery has significant salvage and resale value. The ability to extract more residual value from an investment in a strategy reduces the cost of abandoning that strategy and thus has the effect of increasing the flexibility of a firm to abandon a strategy should it decide to do so.

Finally, a firm can also make choices that enhance its ability to expand its strategy beyond its current boundaries. This is the **option to expand.** We have already seen an example of this option in the discussion of the pharmaceutical firm that does R&D to create Product A. This firm creates the option to expand because the R&D it invested in to create Product A can, with some additional investment, be used to create Products B and C in the future, should these products turn out to be valuable. A firm that does not invest in the original R&D does not have the flexibility to decide whether to invest to create Products B and C in the future.

This example also shows that the actions a firm takes can create more than one type of flexibility simultaneously. Thus, not only does investing in Product A have the effect of creating the option to expand, it also has the effect of creating the option to defer investment (in Products B and C) until some future date.

8.3 THE ECONOMIC VALUE OF FLEXIBILITY

As with all the strategic alternatives discussed in this book, the decision about whether to adopt a real options approach to making strategic choices begins with an analysis of the economic value of this approach.

Trade-Offs Between Flexibility and Other Business Strategies

Of course, the actions that firms can take to create flexibility are not costless. Indeed, creating flexibility can have the effect of reducing the ability of a firm to engage in some of the other strategic alternatives discussed thus far. For example, it has already been suggested that a firm can create an option to grow by building a plant with a capacity that can be increased at low cost. One way to do this is to build a plant with several small manufacturing lines that can be brought on line as demand increases. However, building such a plant may not be the lowest-cost way to manufacture a product. Low-cost manufacturing may require a firm to build a plant with a specific capacity. In this way, the entire manufacturing process can be optimized relative to this capacity. However, this kind of plant is very costly to grow. Put differently, the decision to commit to being a low-cost producer may reduce a firm's flexibility to grow a plant in the future. Alternatively, one of the costs associated with retaining the option to grow a plant at low cost may be the ability to become a low-cost producer. In making this choice, a firm must again weigh the value gained by remaining flexible against any lost opportunities from being a low-cost producer.

Of course, all this does not mean there will always be a trade-off between retaining the flexibility to grow and being a low-cost producer. For example, recent developments in lean manufacturing, automated machine tools, and robotics all suggest that, in some circumstances, it is possible for a firm to be both flexible and a low-cost producer. In this setting, all the opportunities described in Chapter 6 and in this chapter for a firm to gain a competitive advantage exist.[10]

Conflicts can also arise between a firm attempting to retain its flexibility and attempting to implement a product differentiation strategy. As discussed in Chapter 7, successful product differentiation requires a firm to position its products or services consistently in a market over time. Rapid changes in how a product or service is positioned can lead to confusion in customers' minds, making it difficult to differentiate that product or service in the marketplace. However, retaining the option to expand is all about retaining the flexibility to reposition a firm or its products in new ways, depending on how demand in an industry evolves. It is difficult for most firms to implement strategies that both differentiate a product or service and enable a firm to change rapidly how that product or service is differentiated.[11] In this sense, one of the costs associated with retaining flexibility may be the limited ability to differentiate one's products or services. The relative value of these two strategies must be weighed before a firm can make a fully informed strategic choice.

Flexibility and Uncertainty

Because there are significant costs associated with implementing a strategy of flexibility, an important question becomes: "When is strategic flexibility likely to be valuable for a firm?" The answer to this question has already been suggested: Flexibility is valuable under conditions of high uncertainty.

Consider first the strategic decision facing a firm when there is no uncertainty. In this setting, a firm can apply the tools and frameworks presented thus far in this book to anticipate the competitive implications of its decisions. In this simple world, a firm compares the competitive implications of one strategic choice with other strategic choices and chooses the strategy that is most beneficial to it. Or, using the language of finance, the firm calculates the present value of these strategic alternatives and chooses that alternative with the highest present value. Because there is no uncertainty in this setting, retaining flexibility is unnecessary. Indeed, in this extreme case, if there are any costs associated with retaining flexibility, not retaining flexibility will be preferred over retaining flexibility.

On the other hand, if there is a great deal of uncertainty facing a firm, it may be very difficult to know which of several strategic options will be most beneficial to a firm. Rather than committing to one of these options in a way that will be costly to reverse, real options logic suggests that a firm should keep its options open, retain flexibility, and engage in activities that do not foreclose strategic options whose value may be substantial in some future period. Thus, only under conditions of high uncertainty are the advantages of creating flexibility likely to outweigh its costs. The more uncertain a strategic decision-making setting, the more important retaining flexibility becomes. The less uncertain this setting, the less important retaining flexibility becomes.

Valuing Flexibility

Fortunately, it is possible to estimate the value of strategic flexibility for a firm. This can be done by recognizing the relationship between real options and financial options, then using techniques developed to value financial options to value real options.

Valuing Financial Options

It has been shown that the value of an option depends on five variables: (1) the value of the underlying asset, S (for example, the value of the stock on which a stock option is written); (2) the option's exercise price, X; (3) the time to an option's maturity, T; (4) the variance in the price of the asset on which an option is written, σ^2 (for example, the variance in the price of the stock on which a stock option is written); and (5) the risk-free rate of interest, r_f.[12] These variables combine to determine an option's value through the following formula:

$$c = S\, N(d_1) - [Xe^{-r_f T} N(d_2)] \tag{8.3}$$

where

c = the value of this option
S = the value of the underlying asset
X = exercise price of the option
T = time to maturity
r_f = risk-free rate

$$d_1 = \frac{\ln(S/X) + r_f T}{\sigma\sqrt{T}} + \frac{1}{2}\sigma\sqrt{T}$$

$d_2 = d_1 - \sigma\sqrt{T}$ σ^2 = variance in the price of the underlying asset

$N(d_1)$ and $N(d_2)$ are the cumulative area of d_1 and d_2, respectively, in a normal distribution. This formula is known as the **Black-Scholes formula.**

Although this equation can look formidable, its application can be simplified into three steps. First, identify the inputs needed to calculate d_1 and d_2. Second, using a chart of the areas under the normal curve, calculate $N(d_1)$ and $N(d_2)$. Third, calculate the option value.

This is done for an option with the following attributes: (1) the value of the underlying asset, S (for example, the current stock price if this is a stock option), is $50; (2) the exercise price of this option, X, is $45; (3) the time to this option's maturity, T, is 3 months (expressed as a percentage of 1 year, $T = .25$); (4) the variance in the price of the underlying asset, σ^2, is 20 percent; and (5) the risk-free interest rate, r_f, is 6 percent.[13] Putting these values into the equation for estimating d_1 and d_2 yields

$$d_1 = \frac{\ln(50/45) + .06(.25)}{\sqrt{.2}\sqrt{.25}} + \frac{1}{2}(\sqrt{.2}\sqrt{.25})$$

$$= \frac{.12036}{.2236} \tag{8.4}$$

$$d_2 = d_1 - \sigma\sqrt{2}$$

$$= .65 - (\sqrt{.2}\sqrt{.25}) = .426 \tag{8.5}$$

Substituting these numbers back into equation 8.3 yields

$$c = S\, N(.65) - Xe^{r_f T} N(.426) \tag{8.6}$$

$N(d_1)$ and $N(d_2)$ are calculated using the chart of the areas under the normal curve presented in Table 8.3 and available as a built-in option on many calculators. Table 8.3 presents the area under the normal curve between the mean of this distribution and points to the right of this distribution. Thus, the area between the mean of this distribution (0) and .65 standard deviation to the right of this mean (remember, $d_1 = .65$) is approximately .242. The total area under this curve to the left of this mean is .5. Thus, the cumulative (that is, total) area under this curve for

TABLE 8.3	Areas Under the Standard Normal Distribution Function								
Z	.00	.01	.02	.03	.04	.05	.06	.07	.08	.09
0.0	.0000	.0040	.0080	.0120	.0160	.0199	.0239	.0279	.0319	.0359
0.1	.0398	.0438	.0478	.0517	.0557	.0596	.0636	.0675	.0714	.0753
0.2	.0793	.0832	.0871	.0910	.0948	.0987	.1026	.1064	.1103	.1141
0.3	.1179	.1217	.1255	.1293	.1331	.1368	.1406	.1443	.1480	.1517
0.4	.1554	.1591	.1628	.1664	.1700	.1736	.1772	.1808	.1844	.1879
0.5	.1915	.1950	.1985	.2019	.2054	.2088	.2123	.2157	.2190	.2224
0.6	.2257	.2291	.2324	.2357	.2389	.2422	.2454	.2486	.2517	.2549
0.7	.2580	.2611	.2642	.2673	.2704	.2734	.2764	.2794	.2823	.2852
0.8	.2881	.2910	.2939	.2967	.2995	.3023	.3051	.3078	.3106	.3133
0.9	.3159	.3186	.3212	.3238	.3264	.3289	.3315	.3340	.3365	.3389
1.0	.3413	.3438	.3461	.3485	.3508	.3531	.3554	.3577	.3599	.3621
1.1	.3643	.3665	.3686	.3708	.3729	.3749	.3770	.3790	.3810	.3830
1.2	.4032	.4049	.4066	.4082	.4099	.4115	.4131	.4147	.4162	.4177
1.4	.4192	.4207	.4222	.4236	.4251	.4265	.4279	.4292	.4306	.4319
1.5	.4332	.4345	.4357	.4370	.4382	.4394	.4406	.4418	.4429	.4441
1.6	.4452	.4463	.4474	.4484	.4495	.4505	.4515	.4525	.4535	.4545
1.7	.4554	.4564	.4573	.4582	.4591	.4599	.4608	.4616	.4625	.4633
1.8	.4641	.4649	.4656	.4664	.4671	.4678	.4686	.4693	.4699	.4706
1.9	.4713	.4719	.4726	.4732	.4738	.4744	.4750	.4756	.4761	.4767
2.0	.4772	.4778	.4783	.4788	.4793	.4798	.4803	.4808	.4812	.4817
2.1	.4821	.4826	.4830	.4834	.4838	.4842	.4846	.4850	.4854	.4857
2.2	.4861	.4864	.4868	.4871	.4875	.4878	.4881	.4884	.4887	.4890
2.3	.4893	.4896	.4898	.4901	.4904	.4906	.4909	.4911	.4913	.4916
2.4	.4918	.4920	.4922	.4925	.4927	.4929	.4931	.4932	.4934	.4936
2.5	.4938	.4940	.4941	.4943	.4945	.4946	.4948	.4949	.4951	.4952
2.6	.4953	.4955	.4956	.4957	.4959	.4960	.4961	.4962	.4963	.4964
2.7	.4965	.4966	.4967	.4968	.4969	.4970	.4971	.4972	.4973	.4974
2.8	.4974	.4975	.4976	.4977	.4977	.4978	.4979	.4979	.4980	.4981
2.9	.4981	.4982	.4982	.4982	.4984	.4984	.4985	.4985	.4986	.4986
3.0	.4987	.4987	.4987	.4988	.4988	.4989	.4989	.4989	.4990	.4990

$d = .65$ is $.5 + .242 = .742$. Thus, $N(d_1) = .742$. Repeating this procedure yields the result that $N(d_2) = .665$.

Armed with these estimates of $N(d_1)$ and $N(d_2)$, the value of this option can be calculated as

$$c = 50 (.742) - [45e^{-.06\,(.25)}(.665)]$$
$$= 37.10 - 45(.9851)\,(.665)$$
$$= 37.10 - 28.48$$
$$= 7.62 \qquad\qquad (8.7)$$

Thus, the value of this option is $7.62. That is, an investor should be willing to pay up to $7.62 for the right, but not the obligation, to buy a stock that is currently selling for $50 for $45 in 3 months, given the historical variance in this stock's value and the risk-free interest rate.

Valuing Real Options

Financial options have several attributes that make it possible to estimate their value by applying the Black-Scholes formula. For example, financial options generally have a well-defined value of the underlying asset (S), a prespecified exercise price (X), a prespecified time to maturity (T), and an easy-to-calculate variance in the price of the underlying asset (σ^2).

Unfortunately, real options usually do not have many of these characteristics and thus the direct application of the Black-Scholes formula to value real options is more problematic. In real options, the underlying asset might be a manufacturing plant, a distribution center, or a firm's reputation. All of these assets are real, but none is traded in liquid markets. Thus it is difficult to know with certainty what the value of these assets is at any given time. This also makes it difficult to calculate the variance in the price of the underlying asset. And unlike financial options, real options usually do not have prespecified exercise prices and maturity dates. Rather, the exercise price and maturity date are factors that are at least partly under the control of the firm that is creating the real option.

Despite these difficulties, it is possible to use analogies to the Black-Scholes formula to value real options, at least approximately.[14] For example, imagine the following two-stage investment. In year 1, a firm invests $135 million to build Phase One of a plant. This Phase One investment generates the cash flow and terminal value presented in Panel A of Table 8.4. The net present value of this Phase One investment, using conventional means and a discount rate of 12 percent, is $14.24 million. Then, in year 3, this firm can invest an additional $487 million in Phase Two of this plant. This Phase Two investment generates the cash flow and terminal value presented in Panel B of Table 8.4. The net present value of the Phase Two investment (also using a 12 percent discount rate) is −$41.68 million. The traditional net present value of this entire investment is, as shown in Panel C of Table 8.4: −$30.62. Based on this analysis, this firm should not invest in this plant. For future considerations, the risk-free rate of interest during this entire time period is 5.5 percent.

However, this traditional valuation implicitly assumes that the firm has to make the decision about whether to invest in Phase One and Phase Two at the same time. It fails to recognize a real option that is embedded in this phased investment: the option to delay the decision to invest in Phase Two of this plant for 3 years. Thus the valuation question facing this firm is "Is the value created by this real option sufficient to justify investing in Phase One of the plant, even though traditional valuation techniques suggest that investing in Phase One and Two will not create value for the firm?" As is shown in Table 8.5, this kind of investment can be valued in six steps.

Step One: Recognize Real Options Step One is to recognize any real options associated with an investment. The two-stage investment in this example clearly creates the kind of flexibility-enhancing strategy described in this chapter. By investing in this plant in two stages over time, a firm creates for itself the option to defer, the option to grow, and the option to expand—all depending on how the market happens to evolve—compared to what would have been the case if it built the entire plant all at once. Thus this investment has real options associated with it.

Step Two: Describe a Real Option Using Financial Option Parameters Step Two in valuing this kind of investment is to describe it in terms of the five parameters that

TABLE 8.4 An Example Two-Phase Investment
Discount rate = 12 percent; risk-free rate = 5.5 percent

(A)
Phase One of the Investment

Year	0	1	2	3	4	5	6
Cash flow	0	10.0	12.0	13.4	14.5	15.1	12.8
Terminal value							185.0
Investment	(135)						
Discount factor	1.0	.893	.797	.712	.636	.567	.507
Present value	(135)	8.93	9.56	12.69	9.22	8.56	100.28
Net present value = 13.24							

(B)
Phase Two of the Investment

Year	0	1	2	3	4	5	6
Cash flow	0	0	0	0	26.2	28.3	27.0
Terminal value							510.1
Investment				(487)			
Discount factor	1.0	.893	.797	.712	.636	.567	.507
Present value	0	0	0	(346.7)	16.7	16.1	272.3
Net present value = (41.68)							

(C)
Combined Phase One and Two

Year	0	1	2	3	4	5	6
Cash flow	0	10.0	12.0	13.4	40.7	43.4	38.8
Terminal value							695.1
Investment	(135)			(487)			
Discount factor	1.0	.893	.797	.712	.636	.567	.507
Present value	(135)	8.93	8.56	(337.2)	25.9	24.6	372.6
Net present value = (30.6)							

determine the value of a financial option: S, X, T, σ^2, and r_f. This is done by recognizing the correspondence between the five value-determining attributes of a financial option and similar attributes of a real option. The correspondence of the five parameters of the Black-Scholes option pricing model, attributes of real option investments, and attributes of the example are presented in Table 8.6.

Consider first the exercise price of a real option. A financial option's exercise price, X, is analogous to the amount of money that a firm would have to invest if and when it actually exercised a real option. In the example, X is $487 million, the amount of money that this firm would have to invest in net working capital and fixed assets if it decides to proceed with the Phase Two investment in year 3.

The price of the underlying asset in a financial option, S, corresponds to the present value of the cash flows generated by the assets built or acquired if and when a firm exercises its real option. In the example, S is the present value now (at time zero) of the cash flows that the Phase Two addition to the plant is expected to generate in the fourth

TABLE 8.5   Steps in Valuing a Real Option

Step One:

Recognize the real option ————————➤ The two-stage investment allows the decision about whether to invest in Phase Two to be deferred for three years. This creates an option to defer, grow, or expand.

Step Two:

Describe the real option using ————➤ See Table 8.6.
financial option parameters

Step Three:

Establish a benchmark ——————————➤ The *NPV* of the investment valued as if the decision about Phase Two has to be made at the same time as the decision about Phase One is −$30.62 million.

Step Four:

Calculate option value metrics ————➤ $NPV_q = S/PV(X)$
$$= S/[X/(1 + r_f)^T]$$
$$= .775$$
$$\sigma\sqrt{T} = .4\sqrt{3}$$
$$= .693$$

Step Five:

Estimate the value of the ——————➤ $(NPV_q, \sigma\sqrt{T}) = (.775, .693)$
option from the Black-Scholes $= 19.7$
option pricing table $.197 \times S = $ present value
                        $.197 (\$305.02) = \$60.09$

Step Six:

Compare full present value ————————➤ Benchmark value −$30.62
with option value   Full present value $= NPV$ of Phase One
                                            + option value of Phase Two
                                            $= \$14.24 + \$60.09$
                                            $= \$74.33$

Because $74.33 > ($30.62), this firm should invest in Phase One, keeping open its option for investing in Phase Two.

Source: Adapted from Luehrmen, T. (1998). "Investment opportunities as real options: Getting started on the numbers," *Harvard Business Review,* 76(4), pp. 51–67; and Luehrmen, T. (1998). "Strategy as a portfolio of real options," *Harvard Business Review,* 76(5), pp. 89–98.

year onward. As shown in Panel B of Table 8.4, in this case, *S* equals $305.02 million (16.67 + 16.05 + 272.3 = 305.02).

A financial option's time to maturity, *T*, is analogous to the length of time a company can defer the decision about whether to exercise a real option. In the example, *T* is 3 years. The time value of money for both financial and real options is the risk-free rate of interest (r_f). In the example, this is given as 5.5 percent.

Finally, the variance in the price of the asset underlying financial options, σ^2, corresponds to the uncertainty about the actual cash flows an exercised real option will generate. Of course, the level of uncertainty associated with a real option's cash flow is usually not known when a real option is first created. Indeed, the whole idea behind

TABLE 8.6	**Correspondence of Value-Determining Parameters of Financial Options to the Attributes of Real Options, Applied to the Example in Table 8.4**	
Financial Parameter	*Real Option Analogy*	*Value of Real Option Analogy in the Example*
Exercise price: X	Amount of money a firm would have to invest if and when it actually exercised a real option	X = $487 million (i.e., the Phase Two investment in year 3 in Table 8.4)
Price of underlying asset: S	Present value of cash flow generated by assets built or acquired if and when a firm exercised its real option	S = $305.02 (i.e., the present value of the cash flows generated by the Phase Two investment in years 4, 5, and 6 plus the present value of the terminal value of this investment)
Time to maturity: T	Length of time a decision to invest can be deferred	T = 3 years
Risk-free interest rate: r_f	Risk-free interest rate	r_f = 5.5%
Variance in the price of the underlying asset: σ^2	Uncertainty in the cash flow associated with the deferred investment	σ^2 = .16

investing in ways that create real options is to avoid overcommitting to a particular course of action before this uncertainty is reduced. Thus, estimating σ^2 to value a real option can be difficult.

However, there are at least two practical approaches to estimating σ^2 for real options. First, using their prior experience, managers can estimate how uncertain the cash flows associated with exercising a real option in the future are likely to be and choose an appropriate value of σ^2. Uncertain cash flows should have a σ^2 equal to around .09; more uncertain cash flows should have a σ^2 equal to around .20; and still more uncertain cash flows should have a σ^2 equal to around .36.

Second, if managers do not have prior experience to guide them, they can estimate all the Black-Scholes parameters associated with a real option except σ^2. Then, various values of σ^2 can be used to calculate the value of the real option. By examining the relationship between cash flow uncertainty and real option value, managers can decide whether to invest in a real option. For example, if the only way a real option has a significant positive value is if the cash flow uncertainty associated with that option is very high (for example, σ^2 = .5), risk-averse managers might decide that investing to create this real option is not worthwhile. Alternatively, if a real option is valuable even when the cash flow uncertainty associated with it is quite low (for example, σ^2 = .02), even risk-averse managers would probably be willing to invest to create this real option.[15] In the example, it is assumed that σ^2 equals .16.

Step Three: Establishing a Benchmark   To see if valuing an investment as a real option creates any extra value for a firm, it is necessary to establish a benchmark. This benchmark is simply the present value of an investment valued without recognizing any real options embedded in that investment. As shown in Panel C of Table 8.3, that benchmark figure is −$30.62.

Step Four: Calculate Option Value Metrics Several authors have shown that it is possible to combine the parameters of the Black-Scholes option pricing model into two variables, called **option value metrics.** These metrics incorporate all the information about the five option valuation parameters, but do so in two numbers.[16] This can significantly simplify the valuation of a financial option.

Similar metrics can be calculated for real options. The first, often called NPV_q, is simply the ratio between the present value now of the cash flows that would be generated by the assets built or acquired if and when a real option is exercised and the present value of the amount of money needed to invest in an option if and when it is exercised. From Table 8.5, we know that this ratio is simply

$$NPV_q = \frac{S}{PV(X)}$$

$$= \frac{S}{X(1+r_f)^T} \qquad (8.8)$$

For the example, S = $305.02 million and X = $487 million. With a discount rate of 12 percent, NPV_q can be calculated as

$$NPV_q = \frac{305.01}{487(1 + .055)^3}$$

$$= .775 \qquad (8.9)$$

The second metric has been called **cumulative volatility** and is found as

$$\text{Cumulative volatility} = \sigma\sqrt{T} \qquad (8.10)$$

Notice that, up to this point, the uncertainty associated with the cash flow generated by a real option has been described by the variance in those cash flows (σ^2). However, in calculating cumulative volatility, the standard deviation of those cash flows (σ) is used. Of course, the standard deviation of these cash flows is simply the square root of their variance. Because in the example, $\sigma^2 = .16, \sigma^1 = .4$. Because $T = 3$,

$$\text{Cumulative volatility} = .4\sqrt{3}$$

$$= .693 \qquad (8.11)$$

Step Five: Estimate the Value of the Option from a Black-Scholes Option Pricing Table One of the advantages of using the two option value metrics to parameterize a real option is that it is then possible to use a precalculated table to determine the value of a specific call option as a percentage of the underlying project's value. That is, these two metrics define a particular call option, and this call option's value is known to be equal to a percentage of an underlying project's (or assets) value.[17] A Black-Scholes option pricing table lists this known percentage as a function of these two parameters. Such a table is presented in Table 8.7.

With NPV_q = .775 and $\sigma\sqrt{T}$ = .693, the value of the real option in the investment described in Table 8.3 is approximately 18.7 percent of the value of the underlying asset, S. Because S = 305.02 in this case, the value of this option is $60.08.

Step Six: Compare Full Present Value with the Benchmark Value Recall that the benchmark value of this investment, using traditional present value techniques, was

TABLE 8.7   **Black-Scholes Option Pricing Table**

$$\sigma\sqrt{T}$$

	0.05	0.10	0.15	0.20	0.25	0.30	0.35	0.40	0.45	0.50
0.50	*	*	*	*	0.0003	0.0015	0.0044	0.0094	0.0167	0.0261
0.60	*	*	*	0.004	0.0024	0.0070	0.0144	0.0243	0.0366	0.0506
0.70	*	*	0.0005	0.0035	0.0103	0.0204	0.0333	0.0482	0.0645	0.0820
0.75	*	0.0001	0.0018	0.0077	0.0178	0.0310	0.0463	0.0632	0.0810	0.0997
0.80	*	0.0005	0.0050	0.0148	0.0283	0.0442	0.0615	0.0799	0.0989	0.1183
0.82	*	0.0010	0.0072	0.0186	0.0334	0.0502	0.0682	0.0870	0.1063	0.1259
0.84	*	0.0018	0.0099	0.0230	0.0390	0.0566	0.0752	0.0943	0.1139	0.1337
0.86	*	0.0031	0.0133	0.0280	0.0450	0.0633	0.0824	0.1019	0.1216	0.1415
0.88	0.0001	0.0051	0.0175	0.0336	0.0516	0.0705	0.0899	0.1096	0.1295	0.1494
0.90	0.0003	0.0079	0.0225	0.0399	0.0586	0.0779	0.0976	0.1175	0.1374	0.1573
0.92	0.0010	0.0118	0.0283	0.0467	0.0660	0.0857	0.1055	0.1255	0.1454	0.1653
0.94	0.0027	0.0169	0.0349	0.0542	0.0738	0.0937	0.1136	0.1336	0.1535	0.1733
0.96	0.0060	0.0232	0.0424	0.0622	0.0821	0.1020	0.1219	0.1418	0.1616	0.1813
0.98	0.0116	0.0309	0.0507	0.0707	0.0906	0.1105	0.1304	0.1501	0.1698	0.1894
1.00	0.0199	0.0399	0.0598	0.0797	0.0995	0.1192	0.1389	0.1585	0.1780	0.1974
1.02	0.0311	0.0501	0.0695	0.0891	0.1086	0.1281	0.1476	0.1670	0.1862	0.2054
1.04	0.0445	0.0613	0.0799	0.0988	0.1180	0.1372	0.1563	0.1754	0.1945	0.2134
1.06	0.0595	0.0734	0.0907	0.1090	0.1276	0.1463	0.1651	0.1839	0.2027	0.2214
1.08	0.0754	0.0863	0.1020	0.1193	0.1373	0.1556	0.1740	0.1925	0.2109	0.2293
1.10	0.0914	0.0996	0.1136	0.1299	0.1472	0.1649	0.1829	0.2010	0.2191	0.2372
1.12	0.1073	0.1132	0.1255	0.1407	0.1572	0.1743	0.1918	0.2095	0.2273	0.2451
1.14	0.1229	0.1270	0.1376	0.1516	0.1672	0.1837	0.2007	0.2018	0.2354	0.2529
1.16	0.1380	0.1407	0.1497	0.1626	0.1773	0.1932	0.2096	0.2264	0.2435	0.2606
1.18	0.1525	0.1544	0.1619	0.1736	0.1874	0.2026	0.2185	0.2349	0.2515	0.2683
1.20	0.1667	0.1679	0.1741	0.1846	0.1975	0.2120	0.2273	0.2432	0.2595	0.2759
1.25	0.2000	0.2004	0.2040	0.2119	0.2227	0.2353	0.2492	0.26398	0.2791	0.2946
1.30	0.2308	0.2309	0.2329	0.2385	0.2473	0.2583	0.2707	0.2841	0.2983	0.3129
1.35	0.2593	0.2593	0.2604	0.2643	0.2713	0.2806	0.2916	0.3039	0.3169	0.3306
1.40	0.2857	0.2857	0.2863	0.2889	0.2994	0.3023	0.3120	0.3230	0.3351	0.3478
1.45	0.3103	0.3103	0.3106	0.3124	0.3166	0.3232	0.3316	0.3416	0.3526	0.3645
1.50	0.3333	0.3333	0.3335	0.3346	0.3378	0.3432	0.3506	0.3595	0.3696	0.3806
1.75	0.4286	0.4286	0.4286	0.4287	0.4294	0.4313	0.4347	0.4395	0.4457	0.4530
2.00	0.5000	0.5000	0.5000	0.5000	0.5001	0.5007	0.5022	0.5047	0.5083	0.5131
2.50	0.6000	0.6000	0.6000	0.6000	0.6000	0.6001	0.6003	0.6009	0.6021	0.6041

−$30.62. The full investment, recognizing the option value inherent in it, is the present value of Phase One of this investment plus the option value of Phase Two of this project, or

$$\text{Present value} = \$14.24 + \$60.09$$
$$= \$74.33 \tag{8.12}$$

TABLE 8.7 continued

$$\sigma\sqrt{T}$$

0.55	0.60	0.65	0.70	0.75	0.80	0.85	0.90	0.95	1.00
0.0375	0.0506	0.0651	0.0808	0.0976	0.1151	0.1333	0.1520	0.1712	0.1906
0.0661	0.0827	0.1003	0.1185	0.1373	0.1565	0.1761	0.1958	0.2157	0.2356
0.1003	0.1191	0.1384	0.1580	0.1778	0.1977	0.2176	0.2376	0.2575	0.2773
0.1188	0.1383	0.1580	0.1779	0.1978	0.2178	0.2377	0.2575	0.2772	0.2968
0.1380	0.1578	0.1777	0.1977	0.2176	0.2374	0.2572	0.2768	0.2963	0.3156
0.1457	0.1657	0.1856	0.2055	0.2254	0.2452	0.2648	0.2843	0.3037	0.3228
0.1536	0.1735	0.1935	0.2133	0.2331	0.2528	0.2724	0.2918	0.3110	0.3300
0.1614	0.1814	0.2013	0.2211	0.2408	0.2604	0.2798	0.2991	0.3181	0.3370
0.1693	0.1892	0.2091	0.2288	0.2484	0.2679	0.2872	0.3063	0.3252	0.3439
0.1772	0.1971	0.2168	0.2364	0.2559	0.2752	0.2944	0.3134	0.3321	0.3507
0.1852	0.2049	0.2245	0.2440	0.2634	0.2825	0.3016	0.3204	0.3390	0.3507
0.1931	0.2127	0.2322	0.2515	0.2707	0.2898	0.086	0.3272	0.3457	0.3639
0.2010	0.2204	0.2398	0.2590	0.2780	0.2969	0.3156	0.3340	0.3523	0.3704
0.2088	0.2282	0.2473	0.2664	0.2852	0.3039	0.3224	0.3407	0.3588	0.3767
0.2167	0.2358	0.2548	0.2737	0.2923	0.3108	0.3292	0.3473	0.3652	0.3829
0.2245	0.2434	0.2622	0.2809	0.2994	0.3177	0.3358	0.3538	0.3715	0.3890
0.2323	0.2510	0.2696	0.2880	0.3063	0.3244	0.3424	0.3601	0.3777	0.3890
0.2400	0.2585	0.2769	0.2951	0.3132	0.3311	0.3489	0.3664	0.3838	0.4010
0.2477	0.2659	0.2841	0.3021	0.3200	0.3377	0.3552	0.3726	0.3898	0.4068
0.2553	0.2733	0.2912	0.3091	0.3267	0.3442	0.3615	0.3787	0.3957	0.4125
0.2629	0.2806	0.2983	0.3158	0.3333	0.3506	0.3677	0.3747	0.4015	0.4181
0.2704	0.2878	0.3052	0.3226	0.3398	0.3569	0.3738	0.3906	0.4072	0.4236
0.2778	0.2950	0.3121	0.3292	0.3462	0.3631	0.3798	0.3964	0.4128	0.4291
0.2852	0.3021	0.3190	0.3358	0.3525	0.3692	0.3857	0.4021	0.4184	0.4344
0.2925	0.3091	0.3257	0.3423	0.3588	0.3722	0.3916	0.4077	0.4238	0.4397
0.3104	0.3262	0.3422	0.3581	0.3741	0.3900	0.4058	0.4214	0.4370	0.4524
0.3278	0.3429	0.3582	0.3735	0.3888	0.4042	0.4194	0.4346	0.4497	0.4647
0.3447	0.3591	0.3736	0.3883	0.4031	0.4178	0.4326	0.4473	0.4619	0.4765
0.3611	0.3747	0.3886	0.4026	0.4168	0.4310	0.4453	0.4595	0.4737	0.4878
0.3769	0.3898	0.4030	0.4165	0.4301	0.4438	0.4575	0.4713	0.4851	0.4987
0.3923	0.4044	0.4170	0.4298	0.4429	0.4561	0.1693	0.4826	0.4959	0.5092
0.4613	0.4703	0.4799	0.4900	0.5005	0.5112	0.5222	0.5334	0.5447	0.5560
0.5188	0.5553	0.5326	0.5404	0.5488	0.5575	0.5666	0.5760	0.5856	0.5953
0.6067	0.6101	0.6142	0.6190	0.6243	0.6301	0.6363	0.6430	0.6499	0.6571

Of course, this is much higher than the net present value of $-\$30.62$ calculated using traditional techniques. Apparently, there is significant economic value associated with the real option that is created by investing in Phase One and then delaying the decision about whether to invest in Phase Two of this project for 3 years. Traditional logic suggests that a firm should not invest in this project. Real options logic suggests that it should.[18]

Valuing Real Options Subjectively

In many circumstances, it is possible to use the techniques discussed here to value the real options associated with a strategic investment in quantitative terms. However, over and above the specific quantitative valuation of a real option, it is possible to use the attributes of real options to describe the conditions under which real options will be more or less valuable. This is done in Table 8.8. Firms can use this subjective information about real option value to help make strategic choices that have more rather than less option value.

First, the lower the cost of exercising a real option (X), the greater is the value of that real option. This is because it is more likely for real options with low exercise prices, other things being equal, to be exercised—that is, to be "in the money." Because a real option is exercised only when the value created by that option exceeds the cost of exercising the option, a low exercise price suggests a higher probability of being exercised. Conversely, the higher the exercise price of a real option, the lower is that option's value. If a firm has to choose between two strategies, one of which has a low cost of implementation some time in the future and the other a high cost of implementation some time in the future, this attribute of real options suggests—other things being equal—that the first strategy is preferred over the second.

Second, the higher the cash flows generated by exercising a real option (S), the greater is the value of that real option. It is these cash flows that must offset the cost of exercising a real option if a real option is to pay off for a firm. If these cash flows are much larger than the exercise price of a real option, then the value of that real option can be very large. Other things being equal, a strategy that generates large cash flows sometime in the future is preferred over a strategy that generates small cash flows sometime in the future.

Third, the longer the time to maturity (T), the more valuable a real option is. Real options are all about the flexibility afforded a firm under conditions of uncertainty. The further into the future a firm can delay its decision, the more flexibility it retains. Of course, in most circumstances, a firm does not have to wait until the maturity date to exercise a real option.[19] Thus, a long maturity date provides a firm with greater flexibility with no real additional costs. If, during this long time to maturity, it becomes appropriate for a firm to exercise its real option, it can almost always do so. If it is only appropriate to exercise a real option on its maturity date, firms can wait to do so. Long

TABLE 8.8 Characterizing the Value of a Real Option Subjectively	
Attribute of a Real Option	*Effect on Value of Real Option*
Exercise price (X)	The lower the exercise price, the greater is the value of a real option.
Cash flows generated	The higher the cash flows generated by exercising an option, the greater is the value of a real option.
Time to maturity (T)	The longer the time to maturity, the greater is the value of a real option.
Risk-free interest rate (r_f)	The higher the risk-free interest rate, the greater is the value of a real option.
Uncertainty about future cash flows (σ^2)	The greater the uncertainty about future cash flows, the greater is the value of a real option.

maturity dates provide a firm with increased flexibility and consequently are associated with more valuable real options.

Fourth, the higher the risk-free interest rate (r_f), the more valuable the option is. However, because the risk-free rate is usually outside the direct control of managers making strategic choices, its effect on those choices is not as important to strategic decision makers. If the risk-free rate of interest is expected to change (go either up or down), this can have an effect on the value of a real option compared to making an investment without any flexibility components.

Finally, the greater the uncertainty (σ^2), the more valuable a real option is. Intuitively, the relationship between uncertainty and the value of a real option turns on the importance of flexibility in these conditions. When it is not clear what specific strategic actions a firm should take, flexibility is the best strategic choice. Flexibility implies the ability of a firm to keep its options open. Therefore the ability to retain options is likely to be more valuable as uncertainty about which strategy to pursue increases.

Analytically, the effect of uncertainty on the value of a real option is extremely important. Firms gain economic value from real options when the cash flows generated from exercising those options are greater than the cost of exercising them (that is, when $S > X$). However, the cost of creating this option is fixed and equal to the investment required to create the option to defer, grow, expand, and so forth. The upside potential of a real option depends on the cash flows that exercising that option may create. The downside risk of a real option, on the other hand, is fixed. In this setting, highly uncertain cash flows are preferred over less uncertain cash flows. This is because highly uncertain cash flows have the chance of generating very high returns for a firm, whereas the downside risk associated with gaining access to those cash flows is fixed. Put differently, under high uncertainty, the chance of gain is greater and the chance of loss no larger. Therefore, the greater the uncertainty, the more valuable is the real option.

These subjective characteristics of real options can be used by firms to decide when real options analysis is likely to be important (that is, when uncertainty is high). They can also be used to choose among several different real options investments (that is, low exercise prices are preferred over high exercise prices; high cash flows are preferred over low cash flows; long time to maturity is preferred over short time to maturity; and high risk-free interest rates are preferred over low risk-free interest rates). All this can be done whether or not the actual value of a real option is calculated.

Return again to the example of the pharmaceutical firm deciding whether to invest in Product A, given the effect that producing A may have on its ability to create Products B and C. The criteria presented in Table 8.8 can be used to help make the decision about whether to invest in Product A, in order to have the option of investing in Products B and C in the future, even if it is not possible to value this option in a formal manner. Questions that managers should ask when subjectively valuing the real option value of investing in Product A include: How much additional investment will be required to develop Products B and C? What kinds of cash flows are Products B and C likely to generate? How long can the firm delay its decision to invest in Products B and C? What is the current risk-free rate of return and how is it likely to evolve? How uncertain are the cash flows associated with Products B and C? If the additional investment required to develop Products B and C is small, if the potential cash flows associated with these products is large, if the firm can delay its final decision about whether to invest in Products B and C for a very long time, if the current and future risk-free rates are high, and if the uncertainty associated with the cash flows from Products B and C is large, then the option value associated with investing in Product A is likely to be very large. In this setting, even if Product A does not generate positive net present value as a stand-alone investment, it may still be wise for a firm to invest in Product A in order to gain access to the opportunities associated with Products B and C.

Real Options Thinking

Both objective and subjective approaches to valuing real options can help managers understand the value of flexibility in their strategic decision making. Others have argued that the most important aspect of real options is not valuing these options per se, but the effect of real options thinking on managerial behavior.[20]

In particular, McGrath and MacMillan argue that, under conditions of uncertainty, managers should invest in a diversified range of projects. These projects can be arrayed as in Figure 8.1.

In this figure, **technical uncertainty** refers to the extent to which managers understand the process by which a new product or service will be developed before that process is undertaken. Low technical uncertainty exists when managers know what kinds of skills and other resources they will need to develop a new product or service, the cost of acquiring these skills and resources, how to manage them effectively, and so forth. High technical uncertainty exists when managers do not know these things about a new product or service. **Market uncertainty,** in Figure 8.1, refers to the extent to which managers understand how a new product or service will be received in the market. Low market uncertainty exists when managers know the price at which a product or service is likely to sell, the likely size of the market that a new product or service will address, the likely competitive responses to a new product or service, and so forth. High market uncertainty exists when managers do not know these things about a new product or service.

FIGURE 8.1　Categorizing Your Register of Opportunities

Source: McGrath, R. G., and I. MacMillan (2000). *The Entrepreneurial Mindset.* Boston: Harvard Business School Press.

Under conditions of low market uncertainty and low technical uncertainty, investments in new products and services have limited real option value. As suggested in the figure, such new products or services are typically more like simple enhancements of a firm's current products or services. Although such investments may clearly be valuable in traditional present value terms, they have limited value in creating options for a firm.

Under conditions of moderate market uncertainty and moderate technical uncertainty, the value of the real options associated with introducing new products or services increases. In such settings, new product or service offerings may look like the introduction of new technology platforms. Such platforms may be related to a firm's previous products or services, and thus the level of uncertainty in these investments is higher than for single enhancement launches. Moreover, such platform investments may give the firm the opportunity to introduce additional new products or services, but a firm is not required to do so.

Finally, when both market uncertainty and technical uncertainty are high, new investments made by firms typically have substantial real option value. McGrath and MacMillan identify three of these options: positioning options (when technical uncertainty is high and market uncertainty is low), scouting options (when market uncertainty is high and technical uncertainty is low), and stepping-stone options (when both types of uncertainty are high). The definition of these options is summarized in Table 8.9.

Positioning Options

Positioning options give a firm the opportunity to wait and see what technological standard or standards will emerge in an industry. Such options are created when a firm makes limited investments, through, say, strategic alliances or small acquisitions in several competing technologies. This occurred, for example, in the U.S. cellular telephone industry in the 1990s, in which several different technical standards were competing and it was not clear which, if any, of these standards would prevail. Several large telephone companies established positions in several of these different standards so that, once the technical uncertainty was resolved, they would have at least some experience in the winning standard that they could build on rapidly.

Creating a positioning option may ensure a firm's survival in the face of technical uncertainty, but such a firm might find itself at least at a temporary competitive

TABLE 8.9 Real Options Under Technical Uncertainty and Market Uncertainty	
Positioning options	Technical uncertainty is high: Take multiple small positions in alternative technologies and wait until technological uncertainty resolves, then invest.
Scouting options	Market uncertainty is high: Put several new offerings in consumer hands to gauge their reactions; once consumer preferences are clear, invest.
Stepping-stone options	Technical uncertainty and market uncertainty are high: Avoid fixing on a particular design or set of features early; fail fast, fail cheap; learn fast, and try again.

Source: McGrath, R. G., and I. MacMillan (2000). *The Entrepreneurial Mindset.* Boston: Harvard Business School Press.

disadvantage to a firm that made one technological bet that turned out to be the right bet. This firm will have more experience in the winning technology, and may be able to use that experience to gain cost or product differentiation advantages in this market. In this sense, the potential trade-offs between the real options listed in Table 8.2 and other business-level strategies can also exist for the real options listed in Table 8.9.

Scouting Options

According to McGrath and MacMillan, scouting options can be thought of as entrepreneurial experiments. They enable a firm to explore new markets with new capabilities, to gauge the size of these markets and the potential value of their new capabilities. However, as with all real options, investments in scouting options need to be kept small. The expectation that a scouting option will generate a positive net present value investment opportunity directly is small. Thus, to keep the costs of building this option low, investments need to be kept small.

However, though it is unlikely that any one scouting option will generate positive economic profit for a firm directly, among all the scouting options in which a firm invests, the probability that at least some of them may generate real profit opportunities directly is higher. Moreover, even if a scouting option does not generate profit opportunities directly, it may generate such opportunities indirectly by suggesting other scouting options that may ultimately generate profit opportunities.

Stepping-Stone Options

This last possibility—that a scouting option might suggest another scouting option that could lead to creating superior performance for a firm—suggests the final type of option listed in Table 8.9: a stepping-stone option. Stepping-stone options are the classic sequential investments originally discussed in the context of the Black-Scholes evaluation model. In this sense, most of the options listed in Table 8.2 can be thought of as special cases of stepping-stone options.

Firms seeking to create and realize the value associated with stepping-stone options must exercise great discipline in identifying decision-making milestones. Examples of such milestones might include, for example, dates by which a decision to invest or not invest in a new plant will be made, conditions under which a decision about whether or not investments in a new product will be made, and so forth. Without such strong milestones, and the discipline to enforce them, the stepping stones embedded in real options logic can lead down an infinitely long path. Sometimes, firms are so intent on keeping their options open, that they fail to exercise their options. Such firms never actually *do* anything, although they may have the ability to do something, sometime.

Alternatively, without these milestones and the discipline to enforce them, firms may exercise their options too soon, before the uncertainty that led them to invest in flexibility in the first place is resolved. Such premature execution of options also destroys value.

Indeed, research in the exercise of *financial* options suggests that brokerage customers sometimes exercise their options before their full value is realized Another study showed that corporate officers who hold stock options also tend to exercise these options earlier than they should if there had been a recent run-up in their firm's stock price.[21]

If financial options are not already exercised in an optimal manner, it seems likely that real options are even more likely to be exercised incorrectly. For example, research in the mining industry suggests that profitable firms are slower to close mines than less profitable firms are. If these mines are similar to each other, then they should have similar option value, and decisions about when to close a mine should not vary across firms. Put differently, a firm's current profitability should not affect the value of a firm's real options, but these mining firms behaved as if it did.[22]

Only when firms identify clear decision-making milestones with regard to either exercising or abandoning a real option, and then manifest the discipline required to use these milestones, will it be the case that the full value of real options thinking will be realized.

Building a Portfolio of Options

Firms that exclusively adopt a net present value approach to valuing new investments will rarely invest in new products or services beyond enhancement launches—relatively straightforward extensions of their current portfolio. Such investments will often create value for a firm's shareholders, but have limited ability to enable a firm to develop new technologies, resources, and capabilities. That is, such enhancement launches have limited agility to enable a firm to transform itself.

However, if a firm invests in a portfolio of options—some positioning options, some scouting options, and some stepping-stone options—some of these investments may pay off big for the firm. Not only may some of these investments generate direct profits for the firm's stockholders, they may also enable the firm to discover entirely new opportunities that could not otherwise have been anticipated.

Of course, such outcomes are uncertain. That is why the essential management task in building a portfolio of options is to invest broadly, but to keep the costs of those investments low. This is done by not committing to a particular technology, not making large and nontransferable investments in a particular set of product characteristics, and by employing strategic alliances and small acquisitions to keep a firm's options open as uncertainty resolves itself over time. Once the value of an investment becomes known, a firm thus positioned can act, by either divesting itself of an alliance or small acquisition (if the real option turns out not to be valuable) or by buying an alliance partner or increasing the investment in a small acquisition (if the real option turns out to be valuable).

8.4 FLEXIBILITY AND SUSTAINED COMPETITIVE ADVANTAGE

Under conditions of high uncertainty, flexibility is often valuable because it creates real options for firms. However, following the logic presented in Chapter 5, if several competing firms are all contemplating the same uncertain strategic decision and all value the flexibility and options embedded in this decision in the same way, then any actions they take as a result of this analysis will only be a source of competitive parity. These actions will be valuable, but they will not be rare or costly to imitate. When, if ever, can flexibility be a source of sustained competitive advantage for firms?

Rare and Costly-to-Imitate Flexibility

The concepts of flexibility and real options are closely related to the importance of history and path dependence described as potential sources of sustained competitive advantage in Chapter 5. Firms that are exploring options embedded in real assets that a firm possesses because it happened to be in the right place at the right time in history, or assets that grew up over time in an organization may be able to gain sustained competitive advantages because the options generated by these assets may be rare and costly to imitate. Consider, for example, the parallel between real options and flexibility, on the one hand, and history and path dependence, on the other, in the following example.[23] Imagine a biotechnology firm making a decision about its manufacturing strategy. Two manufacturing tasks must be accomplished in order for this firm ultimately to be able to bring the product it is developing to the market. The first task is to manufacture product prototypes that can be subjected to certification tests. Assuming the prototypes are certified, this product must then be manufactured for commercial sale. However, suppose that this manufacturing process is very complex, that the only way a firm can learn how to manufacture this product for commercial sale is to have developed its manufacturing skills during the process of manufacturing enough of this product for government tests. Finally, assume that the ultimate market value of this product is very uncertain. How can this firm make a decision about its manufacturing strategy?

As suggested in this chapter, the first step in this process (see Table 8.4) is to recognize that a real option exists in this situation: Under conditions of high uncertainty, the option to delay the decision about whether to build a plant for commercial production is valuable. The option, in this example, is represented in Figure 8.2.

However, notice that the branches on this simple decision tree are not all equally likely to occur. In fact, because of the importance of learning about manufacturing during the certification phase as preparation for commercial manufacturing, if this firm does not build the certification plant, it actually does not have an option to build the commercial plant. Put differently, the decision not to build the test plant is the same as the decision not to build the commercial plant. To retain its flexibility in this uncertain market, this firm must actually build the test plant.

The example in Figure 8.2 shows that, in some circumstances, the ability to create and exercise real options is very path-dependent. Only if a firm follows a specific path of decisions over time can it retain its flexibility. Once a firm has varied significantly

FIGURE 8.2   The Option to Defer Deciding Whether to Build a Commercial Plant

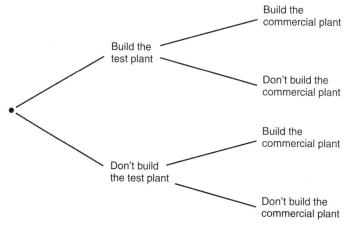

from this specific path, it can be very costly to turn back. A firm that decides not to build the test plant, but then later decides to build the commercial plant, will find itself at a significant competitive disadvantage compared to a firm that builds the test plant in the first place.

All this suggests that when the real options facing a firm are path-dependent, and when the ability to do real options analysis is not widely diffused among a set of competing firms, retaining flexibility can actually be a source of sustained competitive advantage for a firm. On the other hand, when real options are not path-dependent, or when the ability to do real options analysis is widely diffused among competing firms, this form of analysis is not likely to be a source of competitive advantage for a firm.

8.5 ORGANIZING TO IMPLEMENT FLEXIBILITY

It seems logical to assume that firms seeking to implement a strategy of flexibility under conditions of uncertainty should adopt flexible forms of organization. Although the U-form structure and associated control and compensation policies can provide some flexibility for firms, firms engaging in real options approaches to strategic analysis often need additional flexibility to realize the full potential of this strategy. Thus, while the traditional tools for implementing business-level strategies are used by firms implementing flexibility strategies, these tools are normally augmented with more flexible organizing mechanisms.

As will be described in more detail in Chapter 10, vertically integrating into an exchange is generally less flexible, that is, more costly to change, than using market contracts or strategic alliances to manage an exchange. In particular, when the latter mechanisms are used to manage an uncertain exchange that turns out not to be valuable, these exchanges are simply cancelled, usually at low cost. However, if the type of exchange is brought within the boundaries of the firm, the costs of backing out of it can be much greater. Thus, other things being equal, exchanges characterized by high uncertainty, where flexibility is important, are more likely to be managed through various forms of strategic alliances than be vertically integrated. These issues will be discussed in more detail in Chapters 10 and 13.

From the point of view of management control, flexible controls are preferred over less flexible controls. Highly bureaucratic systems of rules, unchangeable accounting budgets, and rigidly defined committees and task forces all seem inconsistent with this need for flexibility. Rather, some of the control mechanisms originally described in Chapter 7's discussion of organizing to implement product differentiation seem likely to be more appropriate under conditions of high uncertainty. These might include highly developed sets of guiding principles that define the acceptable range of decision making within a firm. Within the range defined by these principles, employees are free to make decisions. Outside this range, decision making is extremely limited.

Finally, compensation in firms that seek to implement flexibility strategies under conditions of uncertainty must also be flexible. Both nonmonetary forms of compensation and incentive compensation seem likely to be the most important in these uncertain settings. In particular, stock and stock options provide the same flexibility in compensating employees as the firm seeks in making its strategic choices. In this sense, incentive compensation aligns the interests of employees and the firm. For this reason, it is not surprising that firms operating in very uncertain settings—entrepreneurial firms—often use incentive compensation as an important component of employee compensation.

8.6 SUMMARY

Thus far, most of the discussion of strategic decision-making tools in this book has ignored the effect of uncertainty on strategic choice. Risk can be introduced into traditional strategic choice methods, including present value analysis. However, this approach can be misleading under conditions of uncertainty.

Instead of attempting to modify traditional tools, it may be more appropriate to develop new tools. In finance, this was done using financial option theory. Using analogies to financial option theory, real option theory has been developed. Real option theory can be the basis of strategic decision making under conditions of high uncertainty.

An option is the right, but not obligation, to buy or sell a specified asset at a pre-specified price on a prespecified date. When that asset is financial in character (that is, a stock or bond), the option is called a financial option. When that asset is real (that is, a manufacturing plant, a product), the option is called a real option. Firms looking to implement flexibility as a strategy should create real options in their strategic choices.

Flexibility can take numerous forms in an uncertain strategic investment, including the option to defer, the option to grow, the option to contract, the option to shut down and restart, the option to abandon, and the option to expand. There often exist trade-offs between retaining these options and other business strategies. For example, a manufacturing plant designed to implement a low-cost leadership strategy may be very different than a plant designed to maximize flexibility. Thus flexibility should only be a strategic objective for a firm when it is likely to be valuable, that is, under conditions of high uncertainty.

Real options can be valued by drawing an analogy between the attributes of real options and the attributes of financial options and then using the logic of financial options to value real options. Even when real options are not explicitly valued, it is possible to use information about the determinants of the value of real options to assist in strategic decision making. For example, real options are likely to be more valuable under conditions of high uncertainty. If a firm is making strategic choices in these settings, the real options and flexibility components of these choices should be highlighted.

Beyond valuing real options, some authors have suggested that options thinking can help a firm create a portfolio of projects, some of which extend current products or services in a relatively low-risk way, and others of which may create significant growth opportunities. Treating the discovery of these growth opportunities as the process of investing in real options can allow a firm to explore opportunities it otherwise would not explore.

Flexibility and real options can be a source of sustained competitive advantage to the extent that they are rare and costly to imitate. Rarity and imitability depend on the path-dependent nature of some of the assets that create real options. When the ability to exercise a real option is path-dependent, it can be a source of sustained competitive advantage for a firm.

Organizing to implement flexibility requires flexible forms of organization. Thus, firms pursuing this strategy typically augment traditional U-form structures with various strategic alliances, emphasize flexible management controls, and compensate employees with non-monetary and incentive forms of compensation.

REVIEW QUESTIONS

1. In the semiconductor industry, Moore's law suggests that the power and computational speed of microprocessors will double about every 19 months. Assuming that Moore's law is correct, is R&D in the microprocessor industry uncertain or risky? Justify your answer.

2. Identify a recent acquisition in the business literature. Are there likely to have been any real options associated with this acquisition? If yes, what are they? If not, why not? What effect, if any, does your analysis have for the price at which this acquisition was completed?

3. Suppose a firm is contemplating investing in a new distribution network to distribute over-the-counter drugs to pharmacies around the world. Also, suppose that the investments and cash flows associated with this distribution network are as follows. Finally, suppose that this distribution network, with some additional investment, could be used to distribute prescription drugs as well. The investments and cash flows associated with these strategies are as described later. Assume that the discount rate for these investments is 13 percent. First, what real options, if any, are embedded in the investment in the over-the-counter drug distribution network? Second, given the following data, what is the exercise price, the price of the underlying asset, and the time to maturity of these real options? Assume that the risk-free rate this firm is facing is 5.5 percent and that the level of uncertainty of the cash flows associated with investing in the prescription drug network is .25. What is the value of creating a new distribution network to distribute over-the-counter drugs without considering the value of any real options embedded in that investment? What is the real option value of this investment? In your view, should this firm invest in this distribution network? Why or why not?

Over-the-Counter Drug Distribution Network Investment									
Year	0	1	2	3	4	5	6	7	8
Cash flow	0	7.0	8.5	11.2	11.3	12.0	12.3	12.4	13.0
Terminal value									87.8
Investment	(72.0)								
Prescription Drug Distribution Network Investment									
Year	0	1	2	3	4	5	6	7	8
Cash flow					0	32.4	48.2	65.7	68.4
Terminal value									428.3
Investment					(275)				

4. How are the investment attributes that make it possible to characterize subjectively the value of a real option related to the attractiveness of an industry? For example, when the threat of entry into an industry is high, are real options likely to be more or less valuable? When the level of rivalry in an industry is high, are real options more or less likely to be valuable?

5. Over the last couple of years, several large U.S. technology-based firms have begun to create venture capital funds. Usually these venture capital funds are not as profitable as independent venture capital funds. In your view, does this mean that the technology-based firms should abandon their venture capital efforts? Why or why not?

ENDNOTES

1. The first author to distinguish between risk and uncertainty was Frank Knight. See Knight, F. H. (1921). *Risk, Uncertainty and Profit,* London: London School of Economics.

2. Even strategies that have "guaranteed" cash flows associated with them may still be subject to uncertainty or risk. For example, a firm may receive a "guarantee" that another firm will buy a certain number of its products at an agreed price. However, this contract is subject to the purchasing firm remaining in business. Thus, the uncertainty and risk in this "guaranteed" cash flow is a function of the probability of the purchasing firm going out of business.

3. Capital markets are strong-form efficient when the price of a firm's financial assets fully reflects all information about the value of those assets. Capital markets are semistrong form-efficient when these prices reflect all publicly available information about their value. In this context, only semi-strong capital market efficiency need exist. See Fama, E. F. (1970). "Efficient capital markets: A review of theory and empirical work," *Journal of Finance,* 25(2), pp. 383–417. Most research suggests that capital markets in developed economies are semi-strong efficient. See the evidence presented in Copeland, T. E., and J. F. Weston (1983). *Financial Theory and Corporate Policy,* Reading, MA: Addison-Wesley.

4. See Sick, G. A. *(*1986). "A certainty equivalent approach to capital budgeting," *Financial Management,* 15, pp. 23–32.

5. See Black, F., and M. Scholes (1973). "The pricing of options and corporate liabilities," *Journal of Political Economy,* 81, pp. 637–658.

6. This is an example of an American call option. Options that can be exercised on or before their expiration date are called American options. Options that can only be exercised on their expiration date are called European options. Options to buy an asset are called call options. Options to sell an asset are called put options.

7. As before, this is an example of an American call option. For general strategic discussions of real options theory, see Bowman, E., and D. Hurry (1993). "Strategy through the options lens," *Academy of Management Review,* 18(4), pp. 760–782; Sanchez, R. (1997). "Strategic flexibility, firm organization, and managerial work in dynamic markets: A strategic options perspective," in *Advances in Strategic Management, Volume 8,* New York: JAI Press, pp. 251–291; and Hurry, D., A. T. Miller, and E. H. Bowman (1992). "Calls on high technology: Japanese exploration of venture capital investments in the United States," *Strategic Management Journal,* 13(2), pp. 85–102. In the finance literature, some important discussions of real options include Dixit, A. K., and R. S. Pindyck (1998). *Investment Under Uncertainty,* Princeton, NJ: Princeton University Press; and Trigeorgis, L., ed. (1995). *Real Options in Capital Investment,* Westport, CT: Praeger.

8. See Mueller, B. (1996). "The buzzword for carmakers is flexibility," *World Business,* 2, p. 12; and Gray, D. (1998). "When might a distressed firm share work?" *British Journal of Industrial Relations,* 36, pp. 43–72, on the costliness of laying off full-time employees in Germany and France.

9. Research is beginning to show that an important determinant of the percentage of a firm's employees that have temporary status is the uncertainty a firm faces in its market place. See Barney, J. B., and D. Miller (forthcoming, 2006). "Employer Perspectives: Strategic Thinking or Reactive Responses?" in Gleason, S. E., ed., *The Shadow Workforce: Perspectives on Contingent Work in the United States, Japan and Europe,* Kalamazoo, MI: W. E. Upjohn Institute for Employment Research.

10. See Kamrad, B., and R. Ernst (1995). "Multiproduct manufacturing with stochastic input prices and output yield uncertainty," in Trigeorgis, L., ed., *Real Options in Capital Investment,* Westport, CT: Praeger, pp. 281–302.

11. One possible resolution of this conflict is to recognize that a firm may be able to develop a reputation for being able to rapidly reposition its products in a market. Thus, in this setting, the basis of product differentiation is flexibility in how a product or service is differentiated.

12. Black, R., and M. Scholes (1973). "The pricing of options and corporate liabilities," *Journal of Political Economy*, 81, pp. 637–658. These authors, along with Robert Merton, won the Nobel Prize in economics for this work. The model presented here is for valuing European call options, although it can be generalized to value American call and put options as well.

13. This example is taken from Copeland, T. E., and J. F. Westen (1983). *Financial Theory and Corporate Policy,* Reading, MA: Addison-Wesley, pp. 255–256.

14. Techniques originally developed by Luehrman, T. (1998). "Investment opportunities as real options: Getting started on the numbers," *Harvard Business Review*, 26, July/August, pp. 51–67.

15. For example, suppose the present value of the cost of exercising a real option (X) was $275 million, the present value of the cash flow generated by exercising that real option (S) was $300 million, the time before this option had to be exercised (T) was 4 years, but that the uncertainty of the cash flows associated with this option was unknown. Also, suppose that this real option is part of a two phase investment, and that the present value of Phase One of this investment, by itself, is −$52 million, and the present value of both phases of this investment, without considering the real options embedded in Phase Two, is −$20 million. Using equations 8.8 and 8.10, the option value metrics for this real option are

$$S/PV(X) = 300/275 = 1.09$$
$$\sigma\sqrt{T} = \sigma\sqrt{4} = 2\sigma$$

Suppose that σ^2 can vary from .02 (very low uncertainty) to .20 (moderate uncertainty) to .5 (very high uncertainty). Substituting these values into the option value metric equations generates

(1.09; .283)

(1.09; .894)

(1.09; 1.414)

The corresponding percentages in the Black-Scholes option pricing table are approximately

.1556

.3726

.535

Note that the value for (1.09; 1.414) was obtained from a larger Black-Scholes option value table than appears in this chapter. The value of this real option, under these different levels of uncertainty, is

$46.68 million

$111.78 million

$160.5 million

Thus, the present value of Phase One and the real option value of Phase Two of this investment are

$$(-52 + 46.68) = -5.32$$
for the low-uncertainty case
$$(-52 + 111.78) = +58.78$$
for the moderate-uncertainty case
$$(-52 + 160.5) = +108.5$$
for the high-uncertainty case.

Only when the level of uncertainty of the cash flows in this investment is moderate or high is the value created by the Phase One investment and the real option of making the Phase Two investment positive. Thus, if the managers considering this investment are very risk-averse, they should not make the Phase One investment in order to create the option of making the Phase Two investment, because the option for making the Phase Two investment is valuable only under conditions of uncertainty that are inconsistent with the risk preferences of these managers.

16. Option value metrics of financial options are described in Brealy, R., and S. Myers (1988). *Principles of Corporate Finance*, 3rd ed., New York: McGraw-Hill.

17. This approach can also be used to value financial options.

18. An alternative approach to valuing real options is presented by Copeland and Tufona (2004). "A real-world way to manage real options," *Harvard Business Review,* 82(3), pp. 90–99. This approach—called the binomial method—does not build directly on Black-Scholes logic, and thus avoids some

of the strong assumption built into the method developed by Luerhrman (1998). For example, the binomial method does not assume that the value of the real asset on which an option (*s*) is being written is known at the time initial investment is being made. However, this binomial valuation approach makes its own strong assumptions. That said, using both the Black-Scholes and binomial approaches may provide valuable information about the value of real options embedded in an investment.

19. That is, most real options are American options, not European options.

20. See, for example, McGrath, R. G., and I. MacMillan (2000). *The Entrepreneurial Mindset,* Boston: Harvard Business School Press.

21. Poteshman, A. M., and V. Serbin (2003). "Clearly irrational financial market behavior: Evidence from the early exercise of exchange traded stock options," *Journal of Finance,* 58(1), pp. 37–70; Heath, C.; S. Huddart; and M. Lang (1999). "Psychological factors and stock option exercise," *Quarterly Journal of Economics,* 114(2), pp. 601–627.

22. Moel, A., and P. Tufano (2000). "Bidding for the Antamina Mine: Valuation and incentives in a real options context," in Brennan, M. J., and L. Trigeorgis, eds., *Project Flexibility, Agency, and Competition: New Developments in the Theory and Application of Real Options,* New York: Oxford University Press.

23. This example is typical of biotechnology firms. See Pisano, G. (1991). "Nucleon," Harvard Business School Case no. 9-692-041; and Rossi, S. (1993). "Genzyme Corporation," Harvard Business School Case no. 9-793-120.

CHAPTER

Tacit Collusion: Cooperation to Reduce Competition

Each of the business-level strategies discussed so far in Part II of this book are competitive strategies. A firm implements a **competitive strategy** when it seeks to gain superior economic performance by contending with other firms. Competitive strategies, however, are not the only strategic options available. In this chapter and Chapter 13, two cooperative strategies, one at the business level and one at the corporate level, are discussed. The business-level cooperative strategy discussed in this chapter is tacit collusion; the corporate-level cooperative strategy discussed in Chapter 13 is strategic alliances. In general, **cooperative strategies** exist when firms work together to reach the common goal of obtaining superior economic performance.

Of course, there are numerous examples of cooperative strategies, including (illegal) explicit collusion, tacit collusion, joint ventures, licensing agreements, distribution agreements, and supply contracts. These different forms of cooperation can be organized into two broad categories: collusive strategies and strategic alliances. A **collusive strategy** exists when several firms in an industry cooperate to reduce industry competitiveness and raise prices above the fully competitive level. There are two types of collusion: explicit and tacit. **Explicit collusion** exists when firms negotiate production output and pricing agreements directly, in order to reduce competition. **Tacit collusion** exists when firms coordinate their production and pricing strategies indirectly, by observing the output and pricing decisions of other firms.

Tacit collusion exists when production output in an industry is below competitive levels and prices are above competitive levels, but firms have not actually negotiated agreements. A **strategic alliance** exists when several firms cooperate but industry competitiveness is not reduced. Examples include joint ventures, licensing agreements, and distribution agreements. Collusive strategies usually exist only among firms in a single industry and thus are examples of a business-level strategy. Strategic alliances, on the other hand, often exist between firms in different industries and thus are corporate strategies.

In this chapter, the causes and consequences of collusive strategies as a form of interfirm cooperation are examined. This chapter discusses the problem of cooperation more generally and begins by describing general solutions to this problem proposed in literature, discusses incentives to cooperate through collusion, incentives to cheat on cooperative agreements, the performance implications of different forms of cheating, and ends with an analysis of tacit collusion and sustained competitive advantage.

9.1 THE PROBLEM OF COOPERATION

The problem of cooperation can best be understood by analyzing a simple exchange game between two individuals.

A Simple Game

Imagine two individuals or organizations using the payoff matrix presented in Table 9.1 to choose between strategy A and strategy B. If both I and II choose strategy A, they each receive a payoff of $3,000. If I chooses strategy B and II chooses strategy A, I receives a payoff of $5,000 and II receives nothing. If II chooses B and I chooses A, II receives a payoff of $5,000 and I receives nothing. Finally, if both I and II choose strategy B, they both receive a payoff of $1,000. If I and II make a series of these strategic choices, what payoffs are associated with different patterns of choice, and what strategies are I and II likely to choose?

TABLE 9.1	Prisoner's Dilemma Game and Associated Payoff Matrix	
	Firm One	
	Strategy A	*Strategy B*
	I: $3,000	I: $5,000
Strategy A		
	II: $3,000	II: $0
	Firm Two	
	I: $0	I: $1,000
Strategy B		
	II: $5,000	II: $1,000

This, of course, is a simple "prisoner's dilemma" game.[1] At first, the answers to these questions seem clear enough. The maximum payoff that can be obtained in any one round of this game is $5,000. If the game is played five times, then the maximum payoff can be $25,000. This suggests that payoff-maximizing players should choose strategy B. However, if both firms choose strategy B over five rounds, each will obtain a *total* payoff of only $5,000.

Alternatively, each player might choose strategy A and receive a payoff of $3,000. If the game is played five times, both I and II will earn a total payoff of $15,000, less than the theoretically maximum (but very unlikely) payoff of $25,000, but greater than the $5,000 payoff if I and II choose strategy B on all five rounds.

Of course, various patterns of choice combine options A and B over several rounds. For example, if both players know that the game will be played for only five rounds, each may choose strategy A on the first four rounds (a $3,000 payoff per round) but then choose strategy B on the fifth round, hoping that the other player will stick with strategy A. This is an **end-game strategy.** If only one player chooses B in the fifth round, that player will earn a total payoff of $17,000 and the other player will earn a total payoff of only $12,000. However, if both players choose B in the fifth round, each will earn a total payoff of $13,000.

These patterns of choice represent decisions by players to compete, cooperate, or renege on a cooperative agreement. If both players in this simple game choose strategy B on all rounds, they are adopting a **competitive strategy.** Each time players choose strategy A, they are choosing to **cooperate** to maximize their payoff from the game. If players cooperate with each other on several rounds and then implement an end-game strategy, they are **cheating** on their (perhaps tacit) cooperative agreement. Ultimately, the payoff that one player obtains depends not just on that player's decisions but on decisions made by the other player as well.

Whether players in this kind of game choose to compete, cooperate, or cheat on a cooperative agreement depends on the broader context within which the game is played. For example, it has been shown that players are more likely to cooperate, and to continue cooperating, if they can communicate directly with one another, cheating does not lead to large payoffs, cheating leads to costly sanctions, or players are more interested in maximizing their payoffs than in beating the payoffs of other players.[2] When these conditions do *not* exist, competition and cheating on cooperative agreements is more likely.

The simple game presented in Table 9.1 reflects the dilemmas facing all firms contemplating cooperative strategies. There are often strong incentives to engage in cooperative behavior. Such behavior can generate substantial economic profits (a five-round payoff of $15,000), especially compared to the profits of purely competitive actions (a five-round payoff of $5,000). However, once cooperative agreements are in place, there are often strong incentives for firms that have agreed to cooperate to cheat on those agreements. In this game, a player who cheats in the fifth round can gain a total payoff of $17,000; if both players cheat in this round, each gains a total payoff of $13,000. In any case, the total payoffs to firms depend on decisions they make, as well as on decisions that other firms make. The simultaneous incentives of firms to cooperate *and* to cheat on cooperative agreements is known as the **problem of cooperation.**[3]

General Solutions to the Problem of Cooperation

Several authors have examined ways to resolve the problem of cooperation. Thomas Hobbes suggested the most traditional explanation of how cooperation develops in society.[4] Hobbes argued that, in the absence of some centralized authority, it is not possible to resolve the problem of cooperation and that cooperation will not emerge. According to Hobbes, cooperation develops only when a central authority (an individual or institution) forces other individuals or firms not to cheat on cooperative agreements. Put another way, the central authority implements sanctions (such as death, dismemberment, or banishment from the community) that make the cost of cheating very high.

Many authors have found Hobbes' analysis of cooperation unsatisfactory. For example, some have observed that most economic exchanges occur within a context of social relations that have norms of expected behavior associated with them.[5] When these social norms preclude cheating on cooperative relationships, their violation leads to the imposition of broad social sanctions. These sanctions, again, make cheating costly and help resolve the problem of cooperation. Notice that in this solution to the problem of cooperation, a central authority still exists and still acts to reduce cheating on cooperative agreements. However, this central authority is no longer an individual or institution but rather social norms of expected behavior.

Both Hobbes and some of his critics suggest that the problem of cooperation can be solved by central authorities imposing costly sanctions on cheating firms. However, firms may continue to cooperate even in the absence of these kinds of central authority, if both the returns to individual firms cooperating are high and the opportunity costs of individual firms cheating are high. This approach to the problem of cooperation is developed by Axelrod.[6]

Axelrod has observed that cooperation among firms is likely as long as firms anticipate numerous interactions and there are at least a few cooperative firms interacting with each other. Axelrod established these conclusions in a novel way. He invited professional and amateur game theorists to submit a decision rule strategy to play a series of games with a payoff matrix similar to the one in Table 9.1. A wide range of strategies designed to maximize a player's payoffs were proposed. Some were very complicated, involving sophisticated tools for estimating the probability that another player would cooperate on a given round. Of all these strategies, however, none generated a higher total payoff than a simple cooperative strategy called "tit for tat." In the tit-for-tat strategy, a player cooperates until another player "cheats," at which time the first player adopts a non-cooperative strategy as long as it is interacting with the cheating player.

According to Axelrod, tit-for-tat works well as long as at least a few other players are also implementing this strategy. In this way, tit-for-tat strategies gain very high payoffs when used in cooperation with other players using tit for tat, and they minimize losses when other players play non-cooperative strategies. Cooperation, according to Axelrod, is a good bet: If a firm cooperates with another cooperative firm, it does very well; and if it cooperates with a non-cooperative firm, it does not do badly. Axelrod concludes that the high payoffs, and low costs, associated with cooperation effectively resolve the problem of cooperation, all without reliance on any form of central authority—individual, institutional, or social.

Thus despite the emphasis in the strategic management literature on independent firm action and competitive strategy, cooperative strategies may, in some circumstances, be sources of competitive advantage for firms. Indeed, the analysis of returns to cooperative strategies generally parallels the analysis of returns to any strategic options facing a firm.

9.2 DEFINING COLLUSION

In December 1994, William Christie and Paul Schultz published an article in the *Journal of Finance* that brought into question certain trading practices at NASDAQ. NASDAQ is a multiple-dealer stock market designed to produce narrow bid–ask price spreads through the competition for stock order flow among individual dealers. Despite this supposed competition, Christie and Schultz found that 70 of the 100 most frequently traded NASDAQ stocks did not trade in "odd eighths" (for example, 18-3/8 or 23-3/8 or 45-7/8). Rather, these stocks traded only in "even eighths" (for example, 18-1/4 or 23-1/2 or 46). By not trading in odd eighths, Christie and Schultz suggested that NASDAQ dealers were appropriating extra profits for themselves. Moreover, this lack of "odd eighths" quotes could not be explained by any competitive process. They therefore concluded that NASDAQ dealers were engaging in tacit collusion at the expense of those buying and selling stocks on this market.

The conclusions of this paper had a sweeping effect in financial markets in general, and at NASDAQ in particular. Dozens of class-action lawsuits were filed against NASDAQ on behalf of those who lost money because of the lack of "odd eighths" quotes. The U.S. Department of Justice opened an investigation of collusion at NASDAQ, and the U.S. Securities and Exchange Commission began investigating other trading practices at NASDAQ, including the late reporting of trades and dealers backing away from quoted stock prices. In response, NASDAQ hired various economists, including a Nobel Prize winner, to demonstrate that Christie and Schultz's work was wrong. Finally, a group of economists called the "Shadow SEC" met and debated the veracity of the collusion charges leveled at NASDAQ. At the very least, the NASDAQ story suggests that collusion, as a cooperative business strategy, is an important topic that practicing strategic managers must understand.[7]

Collusion of any sort exists when firms in an industry agree to coordinate their strategic choices to reduce competition in an industry. In the extreme, collusion occurs when firms coordinate their output and pricing decisions. In some circumstances, such collusion can lead to economic profits. As suggested earlier in this chapter, explicit collusion exists when competition-reducing decisions are coordinated directly, through direct communication and negotiation. This kind of collusion is illegal in most developed economies. Tacit collusion exists when these decisions are not coordinated through direct communication and negotiation, but coordination develops nevertheless.

The case of "odd eighths" at NASDAQ is not the only example of firms possibly pursuing a collusion strategy. In 1990, Major League Baseball owners were found guilty of colluding in the market for baseball free agents, thereby trying to keep the price of hiring these free agents down. In 1991, MIT and Ivy League schools were accused of collusion by cooperating in the allocation of scholarships to needy applicants. In the early 1990s, U.S. airlines were found guilty of colluding on ticket prices. Archer Daniels Midland (ADM), a large agriculture products firm, was found guilty of colluding with its competitors in 1998. Recently, large appliance manufacturers, tire makers, and credit card companies have each been investigated by the Department of Justice for possibly collusive activities.[8]

9.3 THE ECONOMIC VALUE OF COLLUSION

To examine the value of collusive forms of cooperation, consider a simple two-firm industry (a duopoly) in which overall industry demand is expressed by the equation

$$P = 100 - Q \tag{9.1}$$

where P is the market-determined price and Q is industry output, equal to the sum of the two firm outputs: $Q = q_1 + q_2$. For ease of exposition, assume that production costs are zero and that the two firms have agreed to divide any profits resulting from collusion equally.

   If the two firms in this industry collude and act as a "cooperative monopolist," they will want to produce a quantity, Q, such that *industry* marginal revenue equals *industry* marginal cost. Because each firm's production costs are zero, the firms' marginal costs are zero, and industry marginal costs are zero. When a demand curve is linear, it is easy to calculate the corresponding marginal revenue curve, using the following relationship:[9]

$$\text{If } P = A - BQ, \text{ then } MR = A - 2BQ \tag{9.2}$$

In this example, $A = 100$ and $B = 1$. Thus the marginal revenue curve is $MR = 100 - 2Q$. Setting marginal costs equal to marginal revenue (to calculate the optimal level of production) leads to

$$\begin{aligned} MC &= MR \\ 0 &= 100 - 2Q \\ Q &= 50 \end{aligned} \tag{9.3}$$

Thus the profit-maximizing industry output in this example is 50 units. The profit-maximizing price on the demand curve can be calculated as

$$\begin{aligned} P &= 100 - Q \\ &= 100 - 50 \\ &= 50 \end{aligned} \tag{9.4}$$

along with total revenue,

$$\begin{aligned} R &= P \times Q \\ &= 50 \times 50 \\ &= 2{,}500 \end{aligned} \tag{9.5}$$

which, because production costs are zero, is also the industry total above-normal profit. Because these two firms agreed to divide this profit equally, each earns a profit of 1,250.

   The profit potential of collusion in this example can be seen by comparing these profit results to the situation in which each of these firms ignores the other in making price and output decisions. Instead of cooperating to set industry marginal cost equal to industry marginal revenue, purely competing firms act as price takers and set marginal costs equal to the market-determined price: $MC = P$.

By acting as a price taker, each firm sets marginal costs equal to price. However, marginal costs are still zero:

$$MC = P$$
$$0 = 100 - Q$$
$$Q = 100 \tag{9.6}$$

Thus the total quantity produced in this industry will be 100 units. If $Q = 100$, then the equilibrium price on the demand curve equals zero ($P = 100 - Q; P = 100 - 100$), total industry revenue equals zero ($R = P \times Q; R = 0 \times 100$), and each firm earns zero economic profit—not nearly as attractive as the collusive result. More realistically, if marginal costs are positive, then prices and marginal revenue will be greater than zero. However, at this quantity and price level, economic profits will still be zero.

Put another way, a firm that successfully implements a collusive strategy is exploiting an opportunity to neutralize the threat of rivalry. Left unchecked, rivalry can lead firms to gain zero economic profits, as is the case in this competitive duopoly. Collusion, on the other hand, enables a firm to neutralize the threat of rivalry and earn economic profits, as is the case in the cooperating duopoly. In this example, cooperating firms reduce output from the purely competitive level ($Q = 100$ in the competitive case, 50 in the cooperative case) and thereby earn economic profits (0 in the competitive case, 1,250 per firm in the cooperative case).

Incentives to Cheat on Collusive Agreements

Once firms collectively exploit the opportunity of neutralizing the threat of rivalry by colluding to restrict output and increase prices, individual firms have a strong incentive to cheat on this collusive agreement, especially if other firms stick to their agreements. This incentive to cheat on a collusive agreement is a major threat facing firms that attempt to implement this type of cooperative strategy.

Consider, for example, an industry with six firms, all selling undifferentiated products.[10] If five firms stick with an agreement to sell 1,000 widgets for $10 a piece but one firm breaks this agreement and sells 3,000 widgets for $9 a piece, each of the five colluding firms will have revenues of $10,000 (1,000 × $10), but the cheating firm will have revenues of $27,000 (3,000 × $9). Assuming economic costs are constant (at $3 per widget), the five colluding firms will all have economic profits of $7,000 [1,000 × ($10 − $3)], but the cheating firm will have an economic profit of $18,000 [3,000 × ($9 − $3)]. By increasing its output and lowering its price by $1 per widget, the cheating firm is able to increase its economic profit substantially.

Ways Firms Can Cheat on Collusive Agreements

Firms can cheat on their collusive agreements in a wide variety of ways. These different forms of cheating are based on different assumptions about colluding partners' reactions to cheating, and they have different effects on the performance of firms in an industry. Bertrand cheating and Cournot cheating—two of the most important

	Decision	Behavioral	Performance
TABLE 9.2 **Ways Firms Can Cheat on Collusive Agreements, Decision Variables, Behavioral Assumptions, and Equilibrium Performance Implications for Firms in a Duopoly Without Product Differentiation**			
Strategy	*Decision Variables*	*Behavioral Assumptions*	*Performance Implications*
Cooperation	Price/quantity	Both firms maintain agreements	Share monopoly profits
Price taking	Price/quantity	Both firms ignore all interdependence	Normal profits
Bertrand cheating	Price	One firm assumes other firm will maintain price from previous period; no learning across periods	Normal profits
Cournot cheating	Quantity	One firm assumes other firm will maintain quantity from previous period; no learning across periods	Profits fall between shared monopoly and normal profits

forms of cheating in collusive agreements—and their performance consequences are presented in Table 9.2. These forms of cheating are compared first with fully collusive strategies and then with fully competitive price-taking strategies.

Bertrand Cheating

Economist and mathematician Joseph Bertrand examined what happens to profits when colluding firms begin cheating by lowering prices below the cooperative price.[11] In his model, Bertrand makes the (unrealistic) assumption that each time cheating firms adjust their prices, they assume that other firms in the industry will continue cooperating. Bertrand's general conclusion is that, assuming little or no product differentiation among a small number of firms, if one firm decides to cheat on a collusive agreement by reducing its prices, others will as well and, in the long run, firms in this industry will earn no economic profits.

To see how this happens, consider the simple example presented in Table 9.3. In this industry, there are only two firms (a duopoly) and no product differentiation.

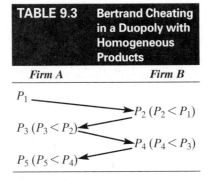

TABLE 9.3   **Bertrand Cheating in a Duopoly with Homogeneous Products**

Firm A	*Firm B*
P_1	
	$P_2\ (P_2 < P_1)$
$P_3\ (P_3 < P_2)$	
	$P_4\ (P_4 < P_3)$
$P_5\ (P_5 < P_4)$	

Imagine that Firm A and Firm B have decided to restrict output such that the prices they charge for their products are P_1. Firm B then decides to cheat on this agreement, increases its output, and sets its price equal to P_2. P_2 must be less than P_1, because any new price greater than or equal to P_1 will not increase Firm B's revenues. With the price equal to P_2, all customers switch to Firm B to buy its products. Firm A must respond and sets its new price at P_3 (where $P_3 < P_2$). Customers rapidly switch back to Firm A; Firm B responds, and so forth. This will continue until the prices charged by both firms generate revenues exactly equal to the firms' economic costs, at which point these firms will earn no economic profits.

Cournot Cheating

Bertrand's analysis suggests that the superior profits that can be obtained by colluding firms are very fragile—any price reductions by one firm will lead rapidly to zero economic profits for both firms. Antoine-Augustin Cournot took a slightly different approach to analyzing cheating in collusive arrangements.[12] Instead of focusing on reductions in price, Cournot examined the performance consequences if colluding firms cheat by adjusting the quantity of their output and let market forces determine prices.

The performance implications of competing on quantity are examined in Table 9.4 for firms in a duopoly with the same demand and other characteristics as in equation 9.1. The intuition behind this table is straightforward. Like Bertrand, Cournot adopts the simplification that Firm A and Firm B will assume that decisions made in a previous period will continue unchanged. Where Bertrand focused on prices, Cournot focused on quantity produced.

Given this assumption, when Firms A and B decide on their own quantity of output, assuming the other firm's quantity is fixed from an earlier decision, they become monopolists over the part of industry demand that is not filled by the other firm. Each of these firms then chooses a profit-maximizing quantity given this unmet demand. However, that quantity choice has an effect on the other firm, which adjusts the demand curve it faces to include demand not met by the first firm and chooses a new profit-maximizing quantity. This new quantity, of course, affects the first firm, which readjusts the demand curve it faces to include demand not met by the other firm, chooses a new profit-maximizing quantity, and so forth.

Other Forms of Cheating

The performance results associated with both Bertrand cheating and Cournot cheating depend on assumptions that firms make about how other firms will respond to their own cheating. Both Bertrand and Cournot assume that firms take other firms' prices/outputs in the previous period as fixed, and that firms never learn that other firms adjust their prices/outputs in response to their own decisions. These assumptions seem very unrealistic.

In response to these unrealistic assumptions, other models of cheating on collusive arrangements have been developed. Edgeworth, following Bertrand, examined price cheating.[13] However, Edgeworth introduced capacity constraints in his model (based on the observation that firms can change their prices faster than they can

TABLE 9.4   Performance Implications of Cournot Cheating in a Duopoly (Firm A and Firm B) with the Demand, Marginal Revenue, and Marginal Cost Characteristics Described in Equations 9.1 through 9.3

Firm A determines its optimal level of production by assuming Firm B's level of production from the previous period is fixed. In the next period, Firm B adjusts its quantity of production, assuming Firm A's quantity of production from the previous period is fixed, and so forth.[a]

Period	Firm Adjusting Its Quantity of Output, Assuming Other Firm's Output Is Fixed	Level at Which Other Firm's Output Is Assumed to Be Fixed	Optimal Output, Assuming Other Firm's Output Is Fixed	Firm A's Profits	Firm B's Profits
1	A	0	50	2,500	0
2	B	50	25	1,250	625
3	A	25	37.5	1,406	938
4	B	37.5	31.25	1,172	977
5	A	31.25	34.38	1,182	1,074
*	*	*	*	*	*
*	*	*	*	*	*
*	*	*	*	*	*
n	B	33.33	33.33	1,111	1,111

[a]Calculations in the table are done as follows. For example, in period 4, Firm B assumes that Firm A will produce the same quantity of output that it produced in Period 3, that is, that

$$q_1 = 37.5$$

Firm B then estimates the demand left in the industry by Firm A's decision to produce only 37.5 units,

$$P = 100 - Q$$
$$= 100 - (37.5 + q_2)$$

Firm B then determines its profit-maximizing quantity by setting marginal cost equal to marginal revenue.

$$MC = MR$$
$$0 = 62.5 - 2q_2$$
$$q_2 = 31.25$$

The market price is then calculated.

$$P = 100 - Q$$
$$= 100 - (q_1 + q_2)$$
$$= 100 - (37.5 + 31.25)$$
$$= 31.25$$

At this price, firm revenues for Firms A and B, respectively, can also be calculated.

$$R_A = P \times q_1$$
$$= 31.25 \times 37.5$$
$$= 1,172$$

$$R_B = P \times q_2$$
$$= 31.25 \times 31.25$$
$$= 977$$

Because marginal costs in the example are zero, revenue equals profit.

It can be shown that, in the long run, competition in quantity will lead to the situation in which one-third of total industry demand is provided by Firm A, one-third is provided by Firm B, and one-third is not produced, and therefore prices will be higher than a competitive level. Firms that cheat in quantity produced earn economic profits, but these profits are not as large as they would be if firms cooperated completely in making production decisions.

change their quantity of output). Because of these capacity constraints, the market share of the firm with a higher price does not go to zero, and firms are able to avoid the perfect competition outcome of pure Bertrand cheating—that is, both firms make positive profits, though not as large as the profits in Cournot cheating.

Stackelberg, following Cournot, focused on quantity decisions but adopted the assumption that one firm (the so-called Stackelberg leader) accurately anticipates how other firms will respond to its output decision, adopts a profit-maximizing quantity, and holds that quantity constant over time.[14] Other firms in this industry (Stackelberg followers) adjust their outputs accordingly. Firms in this kind of industry earn positive economic profits, but these profits are less than the profits earned by firms engaging in pure Cournot cheating.

Other authors have adopted different assumptions about the behavior of rivals. Some authors have examined the profits associated with Bertrand and Cournot cheating when firms sell differentiated products; when there are time lags in discovering that a firm has cheated; when firms interact simultaneously in several markets; when other firms are unable to observe price or quantity cheating; when prices cannot be adjusted quickly; when firms have a reputation for not retaliating against cheaters; and so forth.[15] Generally, long-run profits for firms that cheat on purely collusive agreements in these ways fall somewhere between the perfect competition, zero-economic-profit solution and the perfect cooperation, shared-monopoly-profit solution.

That the performance implications of cheating for colluding firms are so sensitive to assumptions that firms make about the motives and intentions of other firms is a significant limitation of this class of models. Many of these models represent very sophisticated applications of game theory.[16] Although game theory can be used to test the performance implications of alternative sets of these behavioral assumptions, it cannot be used to specify which of these assumptions are most appropriate in different market and industry contexts. Indeed, there is no good reason to assume that all of a firm's rivals will have the same response to cheating on cooperative agreements, let alone good reason to know what these responses will be in different economic contexts. To develop a complete model of collusion strategies, a model that specifies which game-theoretic assumptions apply will need to be developed.

Explicit and Tacit Collusion

Because the performance implications of cheating on collusion depend so critically on the particular assumptions that firms make about how their rivals will respond to cheating, an important question becomes: "How can a firm learn what its rivals' intentions are?" The easiest way to answer this question is for firms to communicate directly with each other about their current price and output decisions and their future price and output decisions. This kind of direct communication will allow firms to judge the likely responses of others and enable them to negotiate price and output strategies that jointly maximize profits. In a sense, direct communication solves the problems associated with game-theoretic analyses of collusion by enabling firms to develop reasonably accurate ideas about how other firms will behave. Once a firm has this information, it can choose the game-theoretic model that best fits, and it can perfectly anticipate the performance results of alternative actions.

Of course, this form of direct communication and negotiation—explicit collusion—is illegal in most developed economies. Managers in firms that collude explicitly may go to jail, and their firms may be subject to significant fines.[17]

Instead of engaging in direct communication and explicit collusion, colluding firms seeking to choose joint profit-maximizing cooperative strategies must use tacit collusion. Instead of communicating directly, tacitly colluding firms send and interpret signals of intent to cooperate (or intent not to cooperate) sent by potential collusion partners.[18]

Sometimes, signals of intent to collude are very ambiguous. For example, when firms in an industry do not reduce their prices in response to a decrease in demand, they may be sending a signal that they want to collude, or they may be attempting to exploit their product differentiation to maintain high margins. When firms do not reduce their prices in response to reduced supply costs, they may be sending a signal that they want to collude, or they may be individually maximizing their economic performance. In both cases, the organizational intent implied by a firm's behavior is ambiguous at best.

Other signals of intent to collude are less ambiguous. For example, when General Electric (GE) wanted to slow price competition in the steam turbine industry, it widely advertised its prices to customers and publicly committed not to sell products below these prices. Moreover, GE provided customers with price guarantees: If GE reduced prices on its turbines at some time in the future, its customers would receive a refund equal to these price reductions. These actions sent a clear message to GE's competitors that price reductions would be very costly to GE—a signal of an intent to collude on prices and one that helped reduce price competition in this industry. Both prices and margins in the steam turbine industry remained stable for approximately 10 years as GE and its major competitor, Westinghouse, learned how to survive together in this industry.[19]

However, even tacit collusion, with no direct communication between cooperating firms, can be illegal. Firms that consciously make price and output decisions in order to reduce competition may be engaging in what the courts call conscious parallelism and thus be subject to antitrust laws and penalties.[20] Indeed, the U.S. Department of Justice objected to the conscious parallelism engaged in by GE and Westinghouse in the steam turbine business and sued both firms for anti-competitive behavior. Firms contemplating tacit collusion as a form of cooperation should obtain competent legal counsel before proceeding, to see whether the signals of intent to cooperate that they plan to send are consistent with legal guidelines. This task is complicated by the fact that the probability of prosecution for tacit price/output collusion, at least in the United States, varies substantially, depending on the preferences and ideology of the administration in power in Washington, D.C.[21]

Strategic Choices That Reduce the Threat of Cheating

Whether cheating on collusive agreements focuses on prices (Bertrand cheating) or quantity (Cournot cheating), it is clear that firms that cheat on these agreements generally unleash competitive forces that have the effect of reducing their performance. In this context, an important question becomes: "What strategic actions can a firm take to signal to firms it is colluding with that it is not going to cheat on its collusive agreements?"

In general, strategic actions taken by a firm in this context send one of two signals to collusion partners: a **tough signal** (that if parties cheat on collusive agreements, the firm sending the signal will decrease prices more or increase output more than would have otherwise been the case) or a **soft signal** (that if parties cheat on collusive agreements, the firm sending the signal will decrease its prices less or increase its output less than would have otherwise been the case). Examples of strategic actions that send a tough signal to colluding partners include investing in a new production process that reduces a firm's marginal costs of production. By reducing its marginal costs, a firm could very easily lower its prices or increase its output should another colluding firm begin cheating. Examples of strategic actions that send a soft signal to a colluding partner include positioning a firm's product so that it does not compete directly with the products of a colluding firm. By positioning its product this way, a firm is suggesting that should its colluding partner cheat, it will simply shift more of its emphasis to the differentially positioned product. In this way, this firm would not have to decrease its prices or increase its output in the market in which it has been colluding with the other firm.[22]

Sometimes, the direct effects of these strategic actions may be to reduce a firm's economic performance. For example, the direct effect of investing in a tough new production process may be negative if the cost of creating this new process is greater than the cost savings that it generates. In the same way, the direct effect of investing in a soft new-product differentiation strategy may be negative if the cost of creating this new strategy is more than the revenues this product positioning generates.

However, in evaluating these strategic actions, both their direct and indirect strategic effects are important. In the context of implementing and maintaining collusion strategies, the critical indirect strategic effect of these actions is their effect on the likelihood that a colluding partner will decide to cheat on these tacit cooperative agreements. If the strategic actions a firm takes significantly reduce the likelihood of cheating on collusive agreements, then the strategic benefit of these actions in helping maintain the economic profits associated with collusion may more than offset their direct negative effects on the firm's performance.

The implications of tough and soft investments for maintaining collusive relationships when price is the primary basis of potential competition among colluding firms, and when quantity is the primary basis of potential competition among colluding firms, are summarized in Table 9.5.[23] When price is likely to be the major basis of competition in an industry, firms should *not* make investments that send a tough signal. Whatever the direct benefits of such investments, their strategic implications are quite negative. In particular, tough investments in this context send a signal that Bertrand cheating is about to unfold. This makes collusive arrangements very difficult to maintain. Instead of making investments that look "tough," firms in this setting should try to look non-aggressive. Some have called this the "puppy-dog ploy." A firm that follows this strategy would not invest in a new production process that reduces marginal costs, even if the direct effect of this investment was to enable the firm to implement a cost leadership strategy, in order to keep a tacit collusion agreement in place.

One firm that may have adopted this puppy-dog ploy is Ben & Jerry's Ice Cream, especially since the growth in demand for frozen yogurt. Since its inception, Ben & Jerry's had focused its marketing efforts on selling highly differentiated "premium" ice

TABLE 9.5	Strategic Implications of Soft and Tough Strategies when Collusive Agreements Are Threatened by Cheating on Prices and Quantities		
Strategic Logic	*Strategic Implication*	*Strategic Label*	*Example*
When cheating on collusive agreements is likely to focus on prices ...			
Investing in a tough strategy is likely to lead other firms to invest in a tough strategy.	Do not invest in tough strategies in order to avoid price competition.	*Puppy-dog ploy:* Maintaining a non-aggressive stance leads others to be non-aggressive.	Ben & Jerry's delays investing in frozen yogurt.
Investing in a soft strategy is likely to lead other firms not to invest in tough strategies.	Do invest in soft strategies so that competitors will not feel compelled to invest in tough strategies.	*Fat-cat effect:* Actively investing in ways that others will not find threatening leads others to be non-aggressive.	IKEA invests only in wooden, ready-to-assemble furniture.
When cheating on collusive agreements is likely to focus on quantities ...			
Investing in a tough-strategy is likely to lead other firms to invest in a soft strategy.	Do invest in tough strategies so that competitors know you will respond aggressively if they invest in tough strategies.	*Top-dog strategy:* Aggressive strategic investments threaten massive retaliation if another firm engages in aggressive behavior.	Korean memory chip firms invest in manufacturing capacity to discourage U.S. and Japanese firms from making similar investments.
Investing in a soft strategy is likely to lead other firms to invest in a tough strategy.	Do not invest in soft strategies because they signal your vulnerability to tough strategies pursued by others.	*Lean-and-hungry look:* Retaining the ability to make aggressive strategic investments has the effect of reducing the incentives of others to make these aggressive investments.	HP spins off its electronic instruments business in order to have the managerial resources necessary to exploit opportunities in the computer and printer industries.

cream. Most of Ben & Jerry's ice cream flavors include chunks of chocolate, nuts, fruit, or other additives. Beginning in the mid-1990s, demand for premium ice cream began to fall as consumers became more health-conscious. During this same period, demand for frozen yogurt—as a healthy alternative to ice cream—began to rise. Despite the increased popularity of frozen yogurt, Ben & Jerry's did not introduce a line of "premium" frozen yogurt at that time. Partially, the decision not to enter the frozen yogurt market reflected Ben & Jerry's traditional commitment to their ice cream product. However, from a competitive point of view, the decision not to enter the frozen yogurt market at that point was also a decision not to enter into direct competition with frozen yogurt firms. Had Ben & Jerry's entered into this competition, frozen yogurt firms might have felt compelled to enter into the premium ice cream market, and both the frozen yogurt and premium ice cream markets would have become more competitive. Because Ben & Jerry's delayed their entry into the frozen yogurt market, major frozen yogurt firms delayed their entry into the premium ice cream market. By delaying investment in an aggressive entry strategy, Ben & Jerry's may have been able to keep the level of competition in the premium ice cream industry lower than what would have been the case if it had adopted an aggressive entry strategy earlier.[24]

The decision *not* to invest in a tough signal is not the same as the decision to invest in a soft signal. After all, a firm that has decided not to invest in a tough signal could, in principle, decide to make no strategic investments to signal its intentions. In fact, when price is likely to be the basis of competition in an industry, firms should invest proactively in soft signals. These actions have the effect of reassuring collusion partners that price competition is not likely to be forthcoming in the market in which they are cooperating. This strategy has been called the "fat-cat effect," because firms that do this well send a signal that they will not compete aggressively in a market in which they have been colluding, but instead will act as a soft fat cat. Firms that follow this strategy try to differentiate their products in ways that do not threaten colluding partners.

Consider, for example, IKEA, the Swedish furniture firm. IKEA has developed a significant market presence in the wooden, ready-to-assemble segment of the furniture industry. Its extensive supply, manufacturing, and distribution capabilities in this segment of the furniture industry give it a significant competitive advantage. It is very likely that IKEA could extend this competitive advantage to the upholstered segments of the furniture by modifying the line of products its sells. However, IKEA's entry into the very competitive upholstered segment of the furniture industry could lead firms in the upholstery segment to aggressively enter the wooden, ready-to-assemble segment. And although IKEA's competitive advantage in this segment might remain, its level of profitability would probably fall. Thus, in order to keep competition in the wooden, ready-to-assemble segment of the furniture industry low, IKEA has an incentive not to invest in the upholstered segments of the industry. As was the case with Ben & Jerry's delayed entry into the frozen yogurt market, IKEA has an incentive to invest in a puppy-dog ploy with respect to the upholstered furniture market.

However, IKEA has gone beyond simply not investing in the upholstered furniture market. It has aggressively marketed itself in the wooden, ready-to-assemble market. Moreover, it has done so in ways that would be difficult to transfer to the upholstered furniture market. The reputation of being the lowest-cost, highest-quality, and most convenient supplier of wooden, ready-to-assemble furniture cannot be easily transferred to the upholstered furniture market. In this sense, marketing investments in positioning IKEA that are specific to the wooden, ready-to-assemble furniture market are not threatening to firms operating in the upholstered furniture market, and are examples of the fat-cat effect.[25]

On the other hand, when the primary basis of potential competition in an industry is quantity, then strategic investments that send tough signals can have very positive strategic consequences. In this setting, a firm must convince its collusion partners that if any of them begin to cheat, the consequences will be very negative for all. This has been called a "top-dog strategy." In this setting, firms may invest heavily in, say, manufacturing capacity, even if those investments do not generate positive economic profits directly. However, these investments send a clear signal to colluding firms that has the effect of reducing the likelihood that cheating will actually occur. Because these investments increase the likelihood that collusion will continue, they can have a positive effect on a firm's performance.

For example, in the worldwide memory chip manufacturing market, Korean firms such as Samsung and Hyundai spent billions of dollars on new chip manufacturing capacity in the early 1990s. Although these investments may have had a direct negative economic effect, they also had the effect of discouraging U.S. and Japanese firms from also investing in chip manufacturing capacity. By becoming "top dogs," the Korean firms were probably able to reduce total industry output below what it would have been had they not made these investments. This made it possible for these firms to potentially enjoy prices higher than what would have otherwise been the case.[26]

Finally, if the basis of competition in an industry is likely to focus on quantity, then making investments that send soft signals to colluding partners may actually increase their aggressiveness, reducing the likelihood that collusion will continue. In this setting, firms that make soft investments look like easy targets for colluding partners that decide to cheat. Rather than making these investments, firms in this setting should retain what has been called a "lean-and-hungry look."

Hewlett Packard's decision to spin off its electronic instruments business into a separate company may be, in many ways, an example of a firm that has adopted a lean-and-hungry-look strategy. By focusing all of its efforts on its computer and printer business, HP assures that it will have all the managerial resources it needs to respond to opportunities in this industry.[27] Firms contemplating entering into this industry, or firms currently in this industry and considering the pursuit of aggressive new technology and product offerings, may think twice before entering into a competitive struggle with the new HP. In this sense, HP's choice to focus its efforts, to become lean and hungry, has had the effect of reducing competition in the computer and printer industry below what would have been the case if it had not spun off its electronics instruments business.[28]

Industry Attributes and the Threat of Cheating

Beyond the strategic actions that a firm can take to signal its intentions about cheating on collusive arrangements in an industry, firms can also use a variety of attributes of an industry to estimate the probability of cheating on these agreements. In general, these industry attributes affect the probability that cheating, if it actually occurred in an industry, would be detected. Detected cheating is likely to lead to the competitive responses mentioned earlier in this chapter. Because these competitive outcomes are less attractive than collusive outcomes, if the probability of detecting cheating in a collusive industry is high, the likelihood that cheating in this industry will actually occur is low. On the other hand, if the probability of detecting cheating in a collusive industry is low, the likelihood that cheating in this industry will actually occur is high.

Several attributes of industries have been shown to affect the probability of cheating on collusive agreements.[29] The most important of these are listed in Table 9.6. Each of these industry attributes can be thought of as helping to define the level of opportunity and threat for pursuing a collusive strategy in an industry.

Small Number of Firms in an Industry

Tacit collusion is more likely to be successful if there are a small number of firms in an industry. As suggested earlier, tacit collusion depends on the sending and interpreting of signals of intent to cooperate. Because direct communication about prices and output is forbidden, coordination must be indirect and implicit. Intense monitoring of other firms' behavior helps make this coordination possible. However, as the number of firms in an industry increases, the number of firms whose subtle signals must be monitored and interpreted also increases. Indeed, as the number of firms in an industry increases arithmetically, the number of relationships among those firms that must be

TABLE 9.6	Industry Attributes That Facilitate the Development and Maintenance of Tacit Collusion

Small number of firms

Product homogeneity

Cost homogeneity

Price leaders

Industry social structure

High order frequency and small order size

Large inventories and order backlogs

Entry barriers

monitored and nurtured increases geometrically. As the number of relationships and subtle signals must be interpreted increases, judging the intent of firms sending these signals becomes more problematic (and it is never easy), and maintaining tacit collusion agreements becomes more difficult.

Having a large number of firms in an industry also reduces the effect of any one firm's cheating on the performance of other, still colluding, firms. If there are only two firms in an industry (a duopoly) and one reduces its prices (Bertrand cheating), then the increased sales of the cheating firm will significantly affect (reduce) the sales of the non-cheating firm. To maintain its share, the non-cheating firm will have to respond to the cheating firm, perhaps by reducing its prices, so that the zero-profit outcome is not far away. Because cheating hurts both firms very much, it is less likely that either firm will want to cheat on a tacit agreement.

However, if there are 50 firms in an industry and one cheats by reducing its prices, that one firm will not have a significant effect on the sales of other firms, and cheating may engender no response. If other firms are not likely to respond to isolated incidents of cheating, cheating is more likely. In the end, if the number of firms in an industry is very small, the interdependence among those firms is, on average, very clear to them, and tacit collusion is more likely. If the number of firms in an industry is large, the interdependence among those firms is less obvious, and tacit collusion is less likely.

Government regulators often use the number of firms competing in an industry as a signal that firms in an industry may decide to pursue collusive business strategies. For example, the charges leveled by a former GE executive that GE and DeBeers were colluding to raise prices in the industrial diamond market were more believable because GE and DeBeers together dominate over 80 percent of this $600 million market. The U.S. Department of Justice filed suit against GE for price-fixing in this market. These charges were dismissed in 1995, however, when a federal judge concluded that there was insufficient evidence to bring GE to trial.[30]

Other antitrust actions taken by the U.S. federal government have also been motivated by the small number of competing firms in an industry. These include antitrust suits against IBM (a firm that was dominating the mainframe computer market), AT&T (a firm that dominated the long-distance telephone market), Microsoft (a firm that dominated the personal computer operating systems market), and, most recently, Visa and MasterCard (two firms that dominate the credit card market).

Indeed, the relationship between the number of colluding firms and the ability to implement tacit collusion is so significant that most economists analyze collusion only under conditions of oligopoly. Research on government-sanctioned explicit price-fixing cartels in Western Europe, where (presumably) direct communication between colluding firms can occur, indicates that over 80 percent of these cartels occurred in industries with 10 or fewer firms. Thus even when explicit collusion is possible, a small number of firms seems to facilitate the implementation of this cooperative strategy. It is likely that small numbers are even more important for tacit collusion strategies. In general, having a small number of firms in an industry increases the probability that cheating firms will be discovered, and this likelihood reduces the payoffs associated with cheating.

Recent reviews of the empirical relationship between the number of firms competing in a geographic segment of an industry and prices found that as these geographic segments become more concentrated prices can rise significantly. In the retail gasoline industry, for example, when the three largest gasoline retailers in a geographic market sell 60 percent of the gasoline in that market, prices are approximately 5 percent higher than when the three largest gasoline retailers sell 50 percent of the gasoline in a market. This is consistent with the effect that a small number of competing firms can have on the ability to implement tacit collusion strategies.[31]

Product Homogeneity

Tacit collusion is also more likely when firms produce and sell similar products or services.[32] In general, changes in prices are easier to monitor than are changes in product characteristics or features. A firm may cheat on a tacit collusion strategy by charging the agreed price but providing more features, higher quality, or better service. These efforts at product differentiation are somewhat more difficult to monitor and thus create strong incentives for cheating.

However, if differentiating the products or services of firms in an industry is very costly, potential competition must focus on price reductions, a relatively easy-to-monitor effort at cheating. Once spotted, price reductions (Bertrand cheating) have significant negative consequences for all firms (zero economic profits). Thus, if firms in an industry produce homogeneous products or services, cheating on collusive agreements is more likely to be discovered, and this likelihood reduces the payoffs associated with cheating.

Product homogeneity may be a factor in the collusive activities of Archer Daniels Midland. The products that ADM sells are all agricultural commodities, or derived from agricultural commodities. There are limited opportunities to differentiate these kinds of products. Thus, any actions that colluding firms take to "cheat" on their collusive agreements would have to focus on reducing prices. Because price reductions are so easy to observe, it is unlikely that colluding firms will cheat on their tacit agreements, because to do so would almost certainly jeopardize any economic profits that could have been obtained through collusion. Thus, the fact that ADM sells only commodities may have made collusion a more viable strategy for this firm than if it had sold non-commodity products as well.[33]

Cost Homogeneity

Homogeneity of economic costs enhances the opportunities to implement tacit collusion. When firms have very different costs, their optimal level of output may be very different. This is because, in general, profit-maximizing firms should produce a quantity of products or services such that marginal costs equal marginal revenues. If marginal costs vary significantly among firms, the optimal level of production for these firms will also vary. These differences make it difficult for firms to find a level of output that jointly maximizes profits. In this situation, any tacit collusion agreement is very unstable, because each firm has even stronger incentives to cheat.

Cost heterogeneity is widely cited as one of the major reasons why the Organization of Petroleum Exporting Countries (OPEC), an explicitly colluding cartel, has generally been unable to maintain output and price discipline. Optimal levels of oil production vary sharply across members of OPEC, leading these countries to expand production beyond agreed-to collusive levels.[34]

When cooperating firms have similar economic costs, it may be relatively easy for them to discover an output level that is mutually satisfactory. This facilitates tacit collusion.

Price Leaders

Another industry characteristic that creates opportunities for tacit collusion is the existence of industry price leaders. A **price leader** is a firm that sets "acceptable" industry prices or "acceptable" profit margins in an industry. A price leader is often the firm with the largest market share, which helps create the order and discipline needed to make tacit collusion last over time. Also, a price leader can assist an industry adjusting to higher or lower prices, without jeopardizing an overall cooperative agreement, by defining industry standards for price or margin changes. In general, price leaders can be thought of as Stackelberg leaders.[35]

Through the 1950s and 1960s, General Motors acted as a price leader in the U.S. automobile market. Each Fall, with the introduction of new lines and models, GM publicized the percentage by which it planned to increase the price of its cars. Ford and Chrysler typically followed GM's lead, raising their prices by approximately the same percentage as had been announced by GM. Since the entry of Japanese and German firms as major players in the U.S. automobile industry (and thus the violation of the small-numbers requirement listed earlier), GM no longer plays this price leadership role.[36]

Industry Social Structure

Industry social structure can create opportunities for tacit collusion. **Industry social structure** refers to accepted norms of behavior and competition that often evolve in industries. These norms are usually implicit and constitute what might be called an **industry culture.** Spender calls this collection of expectations and norms an **industry recipe** and emphasizes its pervasive effect on firm behavior.[37] This industry recipe, in an important sense, defines the standard operating procedures, acceptable forms of competition, and norms of behavior for firms in an industry. Violation of these norms and expectations constitutes a major breach of "industrial etiquette."

Several factors may work together to help create an industry social structure. Some industries, when they first develop, are dominated by one or two firms with very large market shares. Because of this dominance, most managers in the industry receive their training and early experience in these dominant firms. In a sense, the culture within these dominant firms begins to define the culture in the industry as a whole, and expectations about acceptable forms of competition in the industry reflect expectations within the dominant firms. These industry expectations may continue long after dominant firms lose their share leadership. In the mainframe computer business, for example, IBM's dominance significantly affected the definition of acceptable competition. "White shirts and conservative ties" dominated the mainframe business well into the 1990s.

Managers in firms located in the same geographic area may come into contact at charity functions, private clubs, and in other social settings. These social interactions may lead to the development of mutual expectations concerning acceptable competitive behavior and help create a sense of trustworthiness among firms contemplating collusion.[38] Other social contacts among managers in an industry, including relationships developed at trade association meetings, can also help create an industry recipe.

However they evolve, these social expectations can facilitate tacit collusion by defining some forms of competition as unacceptable. If banned forms of competition would increase rivalry, an industry's culture can make tacit collusion easier to implement.

There is substantial evidence that industry social structure facilitated collusion among the owners of Major League Baseball franchises during the 1980s. Each Major League Baseball franchise in North America is independently owned. However, franchise owners must cooperate in leagues to establish playing schedules, a common set of rules, and other operating standards. While engaging in this legal cooperation, informal agreements not to bid aggressively on free agents were apparently struck. The effect of these agreements was to reduce payments to baseball players from 38 percent of team revenues to just 31 percent of team revenues by 1989.[39] In 1990, an arbitrator found that Major League Baseball owners had behaved collusively and violated their labor agreement with the players union. The owners were subsequently fined $102.5 million, and players' salaries have risen to over 40 percent of team revenues.

High Order Frequency and Small Order Size

Firms may have incentives to cheat on cooperative agreements when maintaining a collusive agreement has high opportunity costs. Imagine, for example, that a firm that has agreed to tacit collusion is seeking a very large contract to supply product to an important customer. Also, suppose that this contract will extend for several years. If this firm obtains this contract, it will have steady and profitable demand for its output for several years. If it does not obtain this contract, its profitability depends on uncertain industry demand and the willingness of other firms in the industry to maintain tacit collusion. Moreover, suppose the opportunity to gain this secure supply contract happens infrequently, once every 20 years.

Given unanticipated changes in demand, linked with the vagaries of maintaining tacit collusion, the present value of the secure supply contract is likely to be greater than the present value of tacit collusion.[40] In other words, the opportunity costs of maintaining a tacit collusion strategy in this context are likely to be substantial, and firms are likely to abandon this strategy in favor of competing for the longer-term contract. In this setting, a firm is likely to reduce prices below the collusive level in order to get the contract.

More generally, whenever firms in an industry gain sales opportunities through infrequent, large orders, the incentives to cheat on tacit collusion are usually stronger than the incentives to maintain tacit collusion. Conversely, when sales depend on numerous, small orders, firms have few incentives to cheat on tacit agreements to gain any one order, and thus tacit collusion is a more significant opportunity.

Numerous industries are characterized by infrequent, large orders. In military aircraft, the failure of a firm to obtain a major contract can have an adverse affect for 10 to 15 years.[41] In commercial aircraft, large orders for one company can have significant effect on another company. It is unlikely that tacit collusion agreements could survive the rivalry created by these infrequent, large orders, even though the number of firms in these industries is quite small.

Large Inventories and Order Backlogs

The ability of firms to produce for inventory and to create order backlogs helps facilitate tacit collusion.[42] Inventory and order backlogs create buffers between a firm and its environment. With these buffers in place, firms do not have to react to every change in market conditions with changes in output and price. Instead of reducing prices when demand drops, firms can produce for inventory and store the products they sell. Instead of increasing prices when demand increases, firms can create an order backlog. These buffers help firms maintain consistency in their output and prices over time, thereby facilitating tacit collusion.

In some industries, inventories may be technologically infeasible, and order backlogs may not satisfy customers. For example, in the fresh fruit business, production for inventory is likely to lead to large spoilage costs. To avoid such costs, firms facing unanticipated reductions in demand, or greater-than-anticipated supply, are likely to have to adjust their prices. These rapid changes in prices can have a very destabilizing effect on an industry's price/output structure and make tacit collusion very difficult.

Entry Barriers

Each of the industry attributes listed in Table 9.5 has an effect on the level of opportunity for tacit collusion in an industry. None, however, is more important for this strategy than the existence of barriers to entry. Without barriers to entry, the economic profits associated with tacit collusion create incentives for firms to enter into an industry. New entry into an industry reduces the collusion-enhancing attributes of each of the other industry characteristics listed in Table 9.5. New entry increases the number of firms in the industry. New entry is likely to create both product heterogeneity (as new firms introduce new products) and cost heterogeneity (new firms often have costs different from colluding incumbents'). New entrants are likely to ignore price leaders and often are not part of the industry social structure. New entrants are also likely to compete for all orders, small or large, to shrink order backlogs to satisfy customers, and to reduce inventories through stiff price competition. Overall, new entrants can be thought of as loose cannons in otherwise placid and calm industries. To reduce the threat of new entrants, tacitly colluding firms must be protected by barriers to entry. In Chapter 3, we discussed five common barriers to entry (see Table 3.1). Each barrier can reduce the threat of entry, and this can enable firms to implement and sustain tacit collusion strategies. However, if different firms pursue these different barriers to entry to varying degrees, these firm actions can actually make it difficult to create and sustain tacit collusion agreements.

For example, each firm in an industry can deter entry by reducing its costs as much as it can through exploiting economies of scale (barrier 1 in Table 3.1) and cost advantages independent of scale (barrier 3). However, unless firms in an industry reduce their costs at the same rate, and to the same level, such cost-reduction efforts are likely to lead to cost heterogeneity in an industry. If substantial cost heterogeneity exists, low-cost incumbent firms have a strong incentive to cheat on tacit collusion agreements to exploit their cost advantage. Therefore cost heterogeneity created by firms attempting to establish cost-based barriers to entry may lead to the breakdown of tacit collusion agreements.

The same conclusion applies to firms in an industry that attempt to deter entry through product differentiation (barrier 2). Unless all (or most) firms in an industry differentiate their products in the same way, and to the same extent, efforts to deter entry though product differentiation are likely to lead to product heterogeneity, which, in turn, is likely to make tacit collusion more difficult to create and maintain.

The costs associated with erecting the remaining two barriers to entry (barrier 4 and barrier 5) can also create cost heterogeneity and reduce the opportunity for tacit collusion. This is especially the case if these costs are borne by one or by a small number of incumbent firms. If the costs of creating these barriers are borne by one or by a small number of incumbent firms, these firms' costs can be greater, thereby creating cost heterogeneity in the industry. Cost heterogeneity, as suggested earlier, can reduce the likelihood of successful tacit collusion.

Consequently although the entry barriers listed in Table 3.1 are essential if firms in an industry seek to implement a tacit collusion strategy, differential investments in these barriers by different firms in an industry can lead to the failure of this cooperative effort. In general, entry barriers facilitate the implementation of a tacit collusion strategy only when they successfully deter entry and do not create significant levels of cost or product heterogeneity within an industry.

9.4 TACIT COLLUSION AND SUSTAINED COMPETITIVE ADVANTAGE

So far, the analysis of tacit collusion specifies the conditions under which this strategy can be used to exploit the opportunity of neutralizing the threat of rivalry. However, for tacit collusion to be a source of sustained competitive advantage, it must also be rare and costly to imitate, and a firm must organize itself successfully to implement this strategy.

The Rarity of Tacit Collusion

At first, it appears that tacit collusion strategies violate the rarity requirement of a sustained competitive advantage. After all, *rarity* in Chapters 6, 7, and 8 implied that a small number of firms in an industry have the resources needed to implement a vertical integration, low-cost, or product differentiation strategy. For tacit collusion to work, all or certainly the majority of firms in an industry must be involved. In what sense can a strategy implemented by all firms in an industry be considered rare?

The answer to this question depends on the first industry attribute listed in Table 9.5—the small-numbers requirement. From the perspective of firms currently in an industry, the tacit collusion strategy is not rare. However, the development of tacit collusion requires a small number of industry incumbents. So from the point of view of both incumbents *and* potential entrants, the tacit collusion strategy is rare. It is very unlikely that numerous firms, including incumbents and potential entrants, could successfully implement a tacit collusion strategy. Thus, from this broader perspective, tacit collusion must be rare in order to generate economic profits.

The Imitability of Tacit Collusion

As with the other business strategies discussed in this book, the imitability of tacit collusion depends both on the ability of firms to duplicate this strategy directly and on their ability to implement substitutes for it.

Direct Duplication

Tacit collusion seems to violate the costly-to-duplicate requirement of sustained competitive advantage. For tacit collusion to work in an industry, incumbent firms that have not joined in the collusion must *not* face a cost disadvantage if they choose to do so. If it is very costly for non-colluding incumbents to begin colluding, then collusion will break down, and the economic profits associated with this strategy will be lost. Therefore costly-to-duplicate strategies in this context appear to reduce the chance for sustained competitive advantage.

However, including potential entrants in the analysis resolves this apparent contradiction. Because all colluding incumbent firms are implementing the same strategy (tacit collusion), firm-level resources that are costly to duplicate are logically equivalent to industry-level barriers to entry. Industry barriers to entry are essential for the successful implementation of a tacit collusion strategy. Thus, if not only incumbent firms but also potential entrants into an industry are included in an analysis, the VRIO framework developed in Chapter 5 can be extended to cooperative tacit collusion strategies. In this context, the small-numbers industry attribute is equivalent to the rarity requirement, and the barrier-to-entry industry attribute is equivalent to the costly-to-duplicate requirement.

Substitutes for Tacit Collusion

There are few obvious close substitutes for tacit collusion. Certainly, vertical integration (Chapter 10), cost leadership, and product differentiation, rather than being substitutes for tacit collusion, are likely to prevent firms from cooperating with one another. Strategic alliances (discussed in Chapter 13) can sometimes be used to facilitate the development of collusive agreements. Put in this context, strategic alliances can help create the conditions necessary for collusion but are not substitutes for collusion. Moreover, most current research on alliances suggests that they are not usually associated with the development of collusive arrangements.[43]

Perhaps the closest substitute for tacit collusion is a particular form of diversification— horizontal diversification. A firm engaging in **horizontal diversification** acquires its rivals. If it does enough of this, it can begin acting as a monopolist in its industry. As we have seen, fully cooperating firms behave as if they were a "collective monopolist," but horizontal diversification that could lead to monopoly power is not allowed in most developed economies. Moreover, when monopolists do operate in these economies, they are usually subject to significant profit and activity regulations—regulations that limit their ability to earn monopoly profits. For these reasons, horizontal diversification is usually not a close substitute for tacit collusion.

9.5 ORGANIZING TO IMPLEMENT TACIT COLLUSION

As with all strategies, the return potential of tacit collusion depends on the ability of firms to organize themselves to implement this strategy. However, there are few organizational structures, management controls, or compensation policies that are unique to firms pursuing this strategy. Beyond these general categories, there are two organizational issues that are particularly important and unusual in implementing tacit collusion strategies: maintaining organizational efficiency and organizational self-discipline.

Organizational Efficiency

One of the most significant organizational issues facing tacitly colluding firms concerns the efficiency of their operations. Under competitive conditions, firms are forced to keep their head count and their overhead expenditures low and to cut out strategically unimportant spending. Thus competitive pressures tend to lead to lean and efficient organizations. Firms that do not meet these criteria either change or are forced out of business by more efficient firms.

Under tacit collusion, competitive pressures toward organizational efficiency are not as pronounced. Indeed, the profits associated with tacit collusion often depend on a firm *not* driving its cost to the lowest possible level, *not* differentiating products as much as possible, and so forth. Such competitive actions are likely to upset tacit collusion, especially if they create cost or product heterogeneity, rivalry, and price competition. In restraining these competitive tendencies, colluding firms may decrease their overall efficiency and effectiveness. This may not be a problem as long as tacit collusion continues, and as long as barriers to entry are in place. However, if collusion breaks down, or if entry occurs, inefficient organizations may be subject to intense competitive pressures.

Given the fragile character of tacit collusion, and the threat of potential entrants, colluding firms would be well advised to maintain an efficient organization—to act *as if* they were facing a competitive environment even though they are not. Of course, maintaining this efficiency is likely to be difficult, given the constraints that tacit collusion places on a firm. Moreover, such efficiency may be costly in the face of current collusion and may reduce (somewhat) a firm's current economic profit. However, if tacit collusion might break down sometime in the future, the ability to move quickly toward a more efficient organization may be worthwhile.

Research on tacitly colluding, explicitly colluding, and monopolistic firms suggests that most of these firms are unable to maintain high levels of organizational efficiency. They tend to become top-heavy with management, highly bureaucratic, risk-averse, over-invested in luxurious office buildings, and so forth. For these reasons, tacit collusion strategies appear to sow the seeds of their own destruction. As tacitly colluding firms become progressively more inefficient in their organization, they become more tempting prey for more efficient new entrants. At some point, the low cost of displacing inefficient incumbent firms may attract new entrants into an industry, despite substantial barriers to entry.

Organizational Self-Discipline

The other significant organizational challenge facing colluding firms concerns the maintenance of self-discipline. Once a firm has committed itself to a tacit collusion strategy, its willingness to stick to that strategy will almost certainly be tested. Thus, for example, once General Electric signaled that it would not engage in price competition in the steam turbine industry, Westinghouse (its major competitor) announced price reductions. In a sense, Westinghouse was testing GE's resolve to stick with its tacit collusion strategy. GE did reduce its prices but gave its customers substantial rebates on previously purchased products. This action indicated that GE would stick by its commitment to price stability. Shortly thereafter, Westinghouse increased its prices to match GE's original prices, and price stability continued in the industry for almost 15 years.[44]

Because tacitly colluding firms will almost certainly be tested in their resolve to maintain price and output stability, the ability to implement this strategy successfully depends on an unusual level of organizational self-discipline. Only when a tacitly colluding firm knows exactly what it is about, and is able to refrain from competitive actions in response to tests by its competitors, is this strategy likely to be successful. This self-discipline needs to be reinforced by appropriate management control systems and compensation policies.

9.6 SUMMARY

The problem of cooperation exists because firms, simultaneously, have strong incentives to cooperate and strong incentives to cheat on cooperative agreements. Traditional solutions to the problem of cooperation emphasize the role of some central authority, in the form of an individual or institution, in forcing cooperation (the Hobbesian solution). More recent solutions to this problem suggest that this central authority may be social norms. Alternatively, the benefits of cooperation, compared to the costs of cheating, may enable a firm to remain in cooperative agreements without any form of central authority.

The traditional way of examining cooperation in economic models focuses on explicit and tacit collusion. The primary benefit of collusion is that firms can establish prices and outputs that jointly maximize their profits. In some circumstances, such joint maximization is a much higher profit alternative than competing, acting as price takers, and earning superior profits. Put another way, explicit collusion and tacit collusion enable a firm to exploit the environmental opportunity of avoiding rivalry.

Although explicit and tacit collusion can present an important opportunity to firms, there are threats to this strategy as well. The threats depend on the incentives that cooperating firms have to cheat on collusive agreements. Colluding firms can cheat on their agreements in a variety of ways, including altering their prices (Bertrand cheating) and altering their output (Cournot cheating). Each of these alternative forms of cheating leads to long-run firm performance that falls somewhere between the zero economic profits of perfect competition and the shared monopoly profits of perfect cooperation. Which particular performance outcome occurs depends on the specific behaviors in which cooperating firms engage if others cheat.

If firms could communicate directly, they could judge the motives and intentions of other firms with reasonable accuracy. However, such explicit collusion is usually illegal. Instead, firms must rely on signals and other indicators of other firms' motives and intentions. Cooperation in this context is called tacit collusion.

A firm can send signals of its intention to cheat or not cheat on collusive agreements by investing in either tough or soft strategies. Alternatively, firms can use a variety of industry attributes to judge the likelihood that other firms will cheat on collusion agreements, thereby estimating the likelihood that tacit collusion is a viable strategic option.

Tacit collusion can also be examined for its ability to generate sustained competitive advantages. If both incumbent firms and potential entrants into an industry are considered, standard VRIO analysis can be applied to tacit collusion. The rarity criterion can be thought of as equivalent to the small-numbers requirement, and the costly-to-imitate criterion can be thought of as equivalent to the barriers-to-entry requirement.

Two critical organizational issues for firms implementing tacit collusion are the need for organizational efficiency and self-discipline in the face of other firms' testing of a firm's commitment to tacit collusion.

REVIEW QUESTIONS

1. Axelrod has shown that cooperation is likely as long as firms anticipate numerous interactions and as long as at least a few potentially interacting firms are willing to cooperate with each other. Others have argued that cooperation is likely to emerge in prisoner's dilemma games (a) as long as players can communicate directly, (b) if cheating does not lead to large payoffs, (c) if cheating leads to costly sanctions, and (d) if players are more interested in maximizing their payoffs than in beating the payoffs of other players. How are these two lists of the preconditions of cooperation related?

2. Both Granovetter and Axelrod argue that cooperation can emerge between firms, even in the absence of some central organizing institution. Does that mean that these authors believe that firms are somehow altruistic? Is there any room for altruism in these models of cooperation?

3. Firms that engage in Cournot cheating will achieve higher levels of performance than will firms that engage in Bertrand cheating. Why, then, would firms ever engage in Bertrand cheating?

4. Both cost homogeneity and product homogeneity enhance the ability of firms in an industry to implement tacit collusion strategies. Under what conditions, if any, would a firm be able to pursue a cost leadership strategy or a product differentiation strategy while simultaneously trying to implement a tacit collusion strategy? Are these strategies mutually exclusive?

5. At one level, the requirement that all firms in an industry be involved in a tacit collusion strategy in order for that strategy to be viable seems to contradict the rareness and imitability requirements for sustained competitive advantage, first discussed in Chapter 5. Is it possible to rationalize this apparent contradiction? If yes, how? If no, why not?

6. Some have argued that the implementation of a tacit collusion strategy will lead a firm to be relatively inefficient. Others have argued that the implementation of a tacit collusion strategy requires firms to be very efficient—at implementing this strategy. Which is it? Do firms implementing a tacit collusion strategy become less efficient or more efficient? Justify your answer.

ENDNOTES

1. The prisoner's dilemma game is named for the dilemma that faces two prisoners who have collaborated in perpetrating a crime. Before they are questioned by the police, these prisoners agree not to confess. However, they are questioned separately, so each prisoner has to decide whether to stick with their agreement or to defect, by confessing. Both prisoners are best off if neither confesses, but if one confesses while the other doesn't, the prisoner who does not confess will get a very harsh sentence. If both confess, both will get a harsh sentence. In this context, should a prisoner confess or not? This is this prisoner's dilemma.

2. See Fudenberg, D., and J. Tirole (1991). *Game Theory,* Cambridge, MA: MIT Press, for a detailed discussion of strategies in a prisoner's dilemma game.

3. This term was first introduced by Axelrod, R. M. (1984). *The Evolution of Cooperation,* New York: Basic Books.

4. Hobbes, T. (1952). *Leviathan,* Oxford, England: Oxford University Press.

5. See, for example, Granovetter, M. (1985). "Economic action and social structure: The problem of embeddedness," *American Journal of Sociology,* 3, pp. 481–510.

6. See Axelrod, R. M. (1984). *The Evolution of Cooperation,* New York: Basic Books.

7. See Christie, W. G., and P. Schultz (1994). "Why do NASDAQ market makers avoid odd-eighth quotes?" *Journal of Finance,* 49, pp. 1813–1840; Schroeder, M. (1995). "Who watches the watchdog at NASDAQ?" *Business Week,* May 15, pp. 102–109; Lux, H. (1995). "NASDAQ retains Nobel laureate for anti-trust case defense," *Investment Dealers Digest,* 61. March 13, pp. 3–4; and Lux, H. (1995). "An economists' supergroup will review NASDAQ charges," *Investment Dealers Digest,* 61, July 3, p. 5.

8. See Berstein, A. (1990). "The baseball owners get beaned," *Business Week,* October 15, p. 122; Carlton, D. W., G. Bamberger, and R. Epstein (1995). "Antitrust and higher education: Was there a conspiracy to restrict financial aid?" *Rand Journal of Economics,* 26, pp. 131–147; Burten, T., S. Kilman, and

R. Gibson (1995). "Investigators suspect a global conspiracy in Archer-Daniels case," *Wall Street Journal,* July 28, pp. A1+; Patterson, G. A., and R. Rose (1994). "U.S. Inquiry of big appliance makers involves cooperative ads with retailers," *Wall Street Journal,* December 5, p. A3; Narisetti, R. (1995). "Justice Department is investigating tire makers for possible price fixing," *Wall Street Journal,* August 24, p. A3; and Beckett, P. (2000). "Antitrust suit targeting MasterCard and Visa puts the pair at odds," *Wall Street Journal,* June 12, pp. B1+.

9. Hirshleifer, J. (1980). *Price Theory and Applications,* Upper Saddle, NJ: Prentice Hall, p. 339.

10. This analysis can be generalized to differentiated products. See Tirole, J. (1988). *The Theory of Industrial Organization,* Cambridge, MA: MIT Press.

11. Bertrand, J. (1883). "Theorie mathematique de la richesse sociale," *Journal des Savants,* pp. 499–508.

12. Cournot, A. (1938). *Recherches sur les principes mathematiques de la theorie des richesses;* English edition: Bacon, N. (1897). *Researches into the Mathematical Principles of the Theory of Wealth,* London: Macmillan. Both Bertrand and Cournot are excellent examples of dead economists.

13. Edgeworth, F. (1897). "La teoria pura del monopolio," *Giornale degli Economisti,* 40, pp. 13–31; in English: Edgeworth, F. (1925). "The pure theory of monopoly," in *Papers Relating to Political Economy,* 1, London: Macmillan.

14. von Stackelberg, H. (1934). *Marktform und Gleichgewicht,* Vienna, Austria: Julius Springer.

15. For Bertrand and Cournot cheating when firms sell differentiated products, see Hall, R. L., and C. J. Hitch (1939). "Price theory and business behavior," *Oxford Economic Papers,* 2, p. 1245; Sweezy, P. M. (1939). "Demand under conditions of oligopoly," *Journal of Political Economy,* 45, pp. 568–573; and Hotelling, H. (1929). "Stability in competition," *Economic Journal,* 39, pp. 41–57. When there are time lags in discovering

cheating, see Tirole, J. (1988). *The Theory of Industrial Organiztion,* Cambridge, MA: MIT Press. When firms interact simultaneously in several markets, see Bernheim, R. D., and M. D. Whinston (1990). "Multimarket contact and collusive behavior," *Rand Journal of Economics,* 12, pp. 605–617. When other firms can't observe price or quantity cheating, see Green, E. J., and R. H. Porter (1984). "Non-cooperative collusion under imperfect price information," *Econometrica,* 52, pp. 87–100. When prices cannot be adjusted quickly, see Maskin, E., and J. Tirole (1988). "A theory of dynamic oligopoly," *Econometrica,* 56, pp. 549–600, and Eaton, J., and M. Engers (1987). "International Price Competition," University of Virginia: mimeo. When firms have a reputation for not retaliating against cheaters, see Ortega-Reichert, A. (1967). "Models for competitive bidding under uncertainty," unpublished dissertation, Stanford University.

16. See Fudenberg, D., and J. Tirole (1991). *Game Theory,* Cambridge, MA: MIT Press.

17. See Slade, M. E. (1990). "Cheating on collusive agreements," *International Journal of Industrial Organization,* 8(4), pp. 519–543.

18. See Scherer, F. M. (1980). *Industrial Market Structure and Economic Performance,* Boston: Houghton Mifflin. Some of these signals of intent to collude are discussed later.

19. See Porter, M. E. (1979). "General Electric vs. Westinghouse in large turbine generators (A)," Harvard Business School Case no. 9-380-128.

20. See MacLeod, W. B. (1985). "A theory of conscious parallelism," *European Economic Review,* 27(1), pp. 25–44.

21. Sims, J., and R. H. Lande (1986). "The end of antitrust: Or a new beginning," *Antitrust Bulletin,* 31(2), pp. 301–322, shows the effect of the administration on antitrust enforcement.

22. See Besanko, D., D. Dranover, and M. Shanley (1996). *The Economics of Strategy,* New York: John Wiley & Sons.

23. This analysis was first developed by Fudenberg, D., and J. Tirole (1984). "The fat cat effect, the puppy dog ploy, and the lean and hungry look," *American Economic Review,* 74, pp. 361–366.

24. See Theroux, J., and J. M. Hurstak (1993). "Ben & Jerry's Homemade Ice Cream Inc.: Keeping the mission(s) alive," Harvard Business School Case no. 9-392-025.

25. See *Discount Merchandiser* (1999). "It's the IKEA way or no way," 39(1), January, pp. 51–53.

26. "Silicon duel: Korean move to grab memory chip market from the Japanese," *Wall Street Journal,* March 13, 1995, pp. A1+.

27. See Nee, E. (1999). "Lew Platt: Why I dismembered HP," *Fortune,* 139(6), March 29, pp. 167–170.

28. Of course, in the PC business, it turned out that the focused HP was not as efficient as some other PC manufacturers, including Dell (Brun, E. [1999]. "America's most admired corporations," *Fortune,* March 1, p. 68+). On the other hand, HP's "lean and hungry look" may have been more successful in the printer market.

29. Scherer, F. M. (1980). *Industrial Market Structure and Economic Performance,* Boston: Houghton Mifflin.

30. See Schiller, Z. (1992). "Diamonds and dirt," *Business Week,* August 10, pp. 20–23; Schiller, Z. (1994). "This diamond case had too many flaws," *Business Week,* December 19, p. 34; and Donoho, R. (1995). "GE off hook in price-fix case," *Sales and Marketing Management,* 147, p. 11.

31. Results that link the existence of price-fixing cartels and the number of colluding firms can be found in Edwards, C. D. (1964). *Cartelization in Western Europe,* Washington, DC: U.S. Department of State, Government Printing Office; Hay, G. A., and D. Kelly (1974). "An empirical survey of price fixing conspiracies," *Journal of Law and Economics,* 17, pp. 13–38. Research on the relationship between market concentration and prices is reviewed in Weiss, L., ed. (1989). *Concentration and Price,* Cambridge, MA: MIT Press; and Schmalansee, R. (1989). "Studies of structure and performance," in Schmalansee, R., and R. Willig, eds., *The Handbook of Industrial Organization,* Amsterdam: North-Holland.

32. Scherer, F. M. (1980). *Industrial Market Structure and Economic Performance,* Boston: Houghton Mifflin.

33. Burten, R., S. Kilman, and R. Gibson (1995). "Investigators suspect a global conspiracy in Archer-Daniels case," *Wall Street Journal,* July 28, pp. A1+.

34. El Mallakh, R. (1982). *OPEC: Twenty Years and Beyond,* Boulder, CO: Westview Press.

35. See Markham, J. W. (1951). "The nature and significance of price leadership," *American Economic Review,* 41, pp. 891–905; Scherer, F. M. (1980). *Industrial Market Structure and Economic Performance,* Boston: Houghton Mifflin; and von Stackelberg, H. (1934). *Marktform und Gleichgewicht,* Vienna, Austria: Julius Springer.

36. White, L. J. (1971). *The American Automobile Industry Since 1945,* Cambridge, MA: Harvard University Press.

37. Spender, J. C. (1989). *Industry Recipes: An Enquiry into the Nature and Sources of Managerial Judgement,* New York: Blackwell.

38. Granovetter, M. (1985). "Economic action and social structure: The problem of embeddedness," *American Journal of Sociology,* 3, pp. 481–510.

39. Berstein, A. (1990). "The baseball owners get beaned, *Business Week,* October 15, p. 122.

40. Tirole, J. (1988). *The Theory of Industrial Organization,* Cambridge, MA: MIT Press.

41. See Schine, E. (1991). "Northrop's biggest foe may have been its past," *Business Week,* May 6, pp. 30–31; and Cole, J. (1992). "Rising turbulence: Boeing's dominance of aircraft industry is beginning to erode, *Wall Street Journal,* July 10, p. A1.

42. Scherer, F. M. (1980). *Industrial Market Structure and Economic Performance,* Boston: Houghton Mifflin.

43. See Ordover, J. A., and R. D. Willig (1985). "Antitrust for high-technology industries: Assessing research joint ventures and mergers," *Journal of Law and Economics,* 28, pp. 311–343.

44. See Porter, M. E. (1979). "General Electric vs. Westinghouse in large turbine generators (A)," Harvard Business School Case no. 9-380-128.

C H A P T E R

10

Vertical Integration Strategies

In Part I, the analytical tools needed to evaluate a firm's environmental threats and opportunities and its organizational strengths and weaknesses were examined. Porter's five forces model was the major tool for analyzing threats, and generic industry structures was the major tool for analyzing opportunities. These tools built on the structure-conduct-performance paradigm in industrial organizational economics. The VRIO framework was the major tool for analyzing organizational strengths and weaknesses. This framework built on the resource-based view of the firm.

An understanding of the threats and opportunities facing a firm and a firm's strengths and weaknesses is an important precondition for making strategic choices. The strategic options facing firms are the subject of Parts II and III of the book. In Part II, the specific actions that firms can take within a particular market or industry, called **business strategies,** were examined. In Part III, our attention shifts from actions that firms can take within a single market or industry to gain competitive advantage to actions that firms can take to gain competitive advantage by leveraging their resources and capabilities across several markets or industries simultaneously. These types of strategies are called **corporate strategies.**

The first corporate strategy that we will examine is vertical integration. A firm's vertical integration choices define which business functions it will be in and which business functions it will not be in.

10.1 DEFINING VERTICAL INTEGRATION

The concept of a firm's value chain was first introduced in Chapter 5. As described in that chapter, a **value chain** is the set of discrete activities that must be accomplished to design, build, sell, and distribute a product or service. Each of the activities listed in a product's or service's value chain must be accomplished in order for that product or service to be sold to customers. Different firms, however, can make different decisions about which of those activities they would like to engage in on their own and which they would like other firms to engage in. The number of stages in a product's or service's value chain in which a particular firm engages defines that firm's level of **vertical integration.** The greater this number, the more vertically integrated a firm is; the smaller this number, the less vertically integrated a firm is.

The number of stages in the value chain in which a firm engages does not have to remain constant over time. Firms can become more vertically integrated by engaging in more stages of the value chain, and they can become less vertically integrated by engaging in fewer stages of the value chain. Whenever firms increase the number of value chain stages in which they engage, and those new stages bring them closer to direct interaction with a product's or service's ultimate customer, they are said to be engaging in **forward vertical integration.** When Coca-Cola began buying its previously franchised independent bottlers, it was engaging in forward vertical integration. Whenever firms increase the number of value chain stages in which they engage, and those new stages move them farther away from a product's or service's ultimate customer, they are said to be engaging in **backward vertical integration.** When Home Box Office, Inc., began producing its own movies for screening on the HBO cable channel, it was engaging in backward vertical integration.[1]

It is sometimes possible to observe directly which stages of the value chain a firm is engaging in and thus the level of that firm's vertical integration. This was the case with Dell Computer, as discussed in Chapter 5. Sometimes, however, it is more difficult to observe a firm's level of vertical integration directly. This is especially the case when a firm believes that its level of vertical integration is a potential source of competitive advantage and thus is not likely to reveal this information freely to competitors. In this situation, it is possible to get a sense of the degree of a firm's vertical integration—though not a complete list of the steps in the value chain integrated by the firm—from a close examination of the firm's **value added as a percentage of sales.** This measure of vertical integration can be computed directly from a firm's accounting performance numbers, which are widely available if a firm is publicly traded. Value added as a percentage of sales measures that portion of a firm's sales that are generated by activities conducted within the boundaries of the firm. A firm with a high ratio between value added and sales has brought many of the value-creating activities associated with its business inside its boundaries, consistent with a high level of vertical integration. A firm with a low ratio between value added and sales does not have, on average, as high a level of vertical integration.[2] Research has shown that value added as a percentage of sales is an appropriate approach to measuring the level of vertical integration of a firm in a wide range of situations.[3]

Value added as a percentage of sales is computed as

$$\text{vertical integration}_i = \frac{\text{value added}_i - (\text{net income}_i + \text{income taxes}_i)}{\text{sales}_i - (\text{net income}_i + \text{income taxes}_i)} \qquad \textbf{(10.1)}$$

where

$$\text{vertical integration}_i = \text{the level of vertical integration for firm}_i$$
$$\text{value added}_i = \text{the level of value added for firm}_i$$

$$\text{net income}_i = \text{the level of net income for firm}_i$$
$$\text{income taxes}_i = \text{firm}_i\text{'s income taxes}$$
$$\text{sales}_i = \text{firm}_i\text{'s sales}$$

The sum of net income and income taxes is subtracted in both the numerator and the denominator in equation 10.1 to control for inflation and changes in the tax code over time. Net income, income taxes, and sales can all be taken directly from a firm's profit-and-loss statement. Value added can be calculated as in equation 10.2:[4]

$$
\begin{aligned}
\text{Value added} = \ &\text{depreciation} + \text{amortization} + \text{fixed charges} \\
&+ \text{interest expense} + \text{labor and related expenses} \\
&+ \text{pension and retirement expenses} + \text{income taxes} \\
&+ \text{net income (after taxes)} + \text{rental expense} \qquad \textbf{(10.2)}
\end{aligned}
$$

Again, most of the accounting numbers for calculating value added can be found either in a firm's profit-and-loss statement or in its balance sheet.

10.2 THE ECONOMIC VALUE OF VERTICAL INTEGRATION

Vertical integration decisions can be understood as a particular example of governance choices that firms make in managing their economic exchanges. In all governance decisions, the question facing managers is, given a potentially valuable economic exchange, what is the most efficient way of managing or governing that exchange? Vertical integration is a valuable form of governance when its benefits outweigh its costs. A discussion on the benefits and costs of vertical integration as a governance strategy follows.

Vertical integration is an important way in which firms can govern their economic exchanges, but it is only one of a wide variety of governance choices available to managers. The broad range of possible governance mechanisms that managers can use to engage efficiently in potentially valuable exchanges is represented in Figure 10.1. At one extreme, parties to an exchange may interact across a faceless and nameless market and rely entirely on market-determined prices to manage an exchange. This approach is often called **market governance.** Parties to an exchange can also use a variety of approaches to managing exchanges that are not quite market governance but are also not quite vertical integration. This class of governance mechanisms includes joint ventures and other forms of strategic alliances and is often called **intermediate governance.** At the other extreme, an exchange may be managed in a vertically integrated way. When such an exchange involves different stages in a product's or service's value chain, this form of governance is called **vertical integration.** Bringing an exchange within the boundary of a firm has also been called **hierarchical governance.**[5] The term *hierarchical governance* suggests

FIGURE 10.1   The Range of Exchange Management Devices

that by bringing an exchange within the boundaries of a firm, an exchange that originally was managed directly between exchange partners is now managed by a third party—the "boss"—who has some power to control the behavior of these exchange partners.

This chapter reviews three explanations of when vertical integration, or hierarchical governance, can create value for a firm: transaction costs economics, capability theory, and real options theory. The latter two explanations build on ideas already discussed in the book—resource-based theory (in Chapter 5) for the capabilities perspective and flexibility theory (in Chapter 8) for real options theory.

Although these approaches vary in detail, they all begin with a common premise— that, barring compelling reasons to the contrary, *not* vertically integrating will be preferred over vertically integrating. This is because the costs of using market forms of governance to manage an exchange are generally much less than the costs of using either intermediate or hierarchical forms of governance. Thus, the central theme of research on vertical integration is, "Don't do it unless there are really good reasons to do so!"

Indeed, the founder of this entire tradition of research—Nobel Prize-winning economist Ronald Coase—first began the analysis of vertical integration by asking the question, "Given how efficient markets are in managing economic exchanges, why would firms *ever* exist?" A market such as the New York Stock Exchange can coordinate the trades of literally hundreds of millions of people each day—people who don't know each other, who can't even see each other—and does so very efficiently. Why would such efficient and elegant forms of exchange ever be replaced by the apparently inefficient and clumsy bureaucracies we see in so many modern corporations? Coase's answer to this question was that, sometimes, there are costs associated with using the market to manage an exchange. When these costs are high enough, markets fail, to be replaced by other forms of governance, including, perhaps, hierarchical governance and vertical integration.[6]

Thus, only when market governance fails to deliver acceptable outcomes will it be efficient for firms to adopt non-market forms of governance to make a particular exchange. In this sense, the three explanations of vertical integration presented in this chapter can all be understood as identifying different ways that the increased cost of using non-market forms of governance can be justified in comparison to the use of efficient market forms of governance.

The Threat of Opportunism and Vertical Integration: Transaction Costs Economics

One of the most important frameworks for making choices about whether or not to vertically integrate is called **transaction costs economics.**[7] Transaction costs economics is based on the assertion that, if a particular exchange is seen as being potentially valuable, then governance mechanisms—whether market, intermediate, or hierarchical—have two purposes: (1) to minimize the threat that exchange partners will be unfairly exploited in an exchange; and (2) to do this at the lowest cost possible. As was shown already in Chapter 9, in many economic exchanges, despite strong incentives to cooperate to realize gains from trade, there can also exist strong incentives to cheat. This threat of cheating can exist in any economic exchange, including those managed through market and hierarchical forms of governance. In transaction costs economics, this is called the threat of **opportunism.** Opportunism exists whenever parties to an exchange exploit the vulnerabilities of exchange partners.

Thus, the purpose of governance, at least according to transaction costs logic, is to create an institutional framework in which opportunistic behaviors can be discovered and appropriate remedies can be imposed on parties to an exchange who are behaving opportunistically. If the creation of exchange governance is done well, then parties to an exchange will find it in their rational self-interest not to behave opportunistically, for their opportunistic behaviors will be discovered and appropriately sanctioned. In this setting, parties to an exchange will find it too costly to engage in opportunistic behavior, and an exchange can go forward with little risk of opportunistic behavior.

In general, the more elaborate a governance device, the broader is the range of potential opportunistic behavior that it can discover, and the broader is the range of exchanges within which it can be used to manage opportunism. These observations suggest that intermediate forms of governance (see Figure 10.1) will be able to manage a broader range of potential opportunistic behaviors than will market forms of governance, and that hierarchical forms of governance will be able to manage a broader range of potential opportunistic behaviors than will intermediate forms of governance. If all exchange partners had to worry about was minimizing the threat of opportunism, they would choose more elaborate forms of governance over less elaborate forms of governance, and vertical integration would be the most common form of exchange governance.

However, minimizing the threat of opportunism is not the only thing that exchange partners need to consider. They must also concern themselves with the cost of managing opportunism. Governance is not costless. In general, the more elaborate the form of governance, the greater is the direct cost of governance.[8] That is, the direct costs of market forms of governance are less than the direct costs of intermediate forms of governance, and the direct costs of intermediate forms of governance are less than the direct costs of hierarchical forms of governance. Thus, if all exchange partners had to concern themselves with was minimizing the cost of governance in managing their economic exchanges, they would always choose market forms of governance.

Exchange partners, however, need to concern themselves with both minimizing the threat of opportunism *and* minimizing the cost of governance. Thus rational economic actors will choose just the level of governance needed to minimize the threat of opportunism in a particular exchange.

Determinants of the Threat of Opportunism

In the transaction costs framework, the appropriate form of governance for a particular economic exchange depends on the threat of opportunism in that exchange. Thus an important question is "What are the determinants of the threat of opportunism in a particular economic exchange?" A great deal of theoretical and empirical research has addressed this question.[9] This work has identified two primary determinants of the threat of opportunistic behavior in an economic exchange: the level of transaction-specific investment in an exchange and the level of uncertainty and complexity in an exchange. These two determinants of the threat of opportunism generate the two central propositions about vertical integration derived from transaction costs theory and are summarized in Table 10.1.

TABLE 10.1	Propositions About Vertical Integration Derived From Transaction Costs Economics

Proposition One:

Exchanges subject to high threats of opportunism due to high transaction-specific investments should be vertically integrated.

Proposition Two:

Exchanges subject to high threats of opportunism due to uncertainty and complexity should be vertically integrated.

Transaction-Specific Investment and Opportunism. An investment is said to be **transaction-specific** when its value in a particular exchange is much greater than its value in any alternative exchanges. Thus, if Firm A invests in a special technology that can be used only in an exchange with Firm B, then Firm A has made a transaction-specific investment. If Firm B has not made a similar investment, then Firm B can exploit the specific investment made by Firm A. The economic value of this exploitation can be as much as the difference between the value of this investment in its first best use and its value in its second best use. If the value of this investment in its highest-valued use (that is, in the exchange between Firm A and Firm B) is $10,000, and its value in its next-highest-valued use (that is, in an exchange between Firm A and any other firm) is only $500, then the firm that has not made this investment can appropriate economic value from the firm that has made this investment up to $9,500. As long as the value of the appropriation is less then $9,500, it is still better for Firm A, which made the specific investment, to continue in this exchange, rather than cancel the exchange and thereby gain only $500.

One of the implications of this threat of opportunistic behavior is that exchanges that require high levels of transaction-specific investment by parties to an exchange are more likely to be governed by more elaborate forms of exchange governance, including vertical integration, than are transactions that do not require this high level of specific investment. Hierarchical forms of governance have more elaborate mechanisms in place to discover and control opportunism, in the face of specific investment, than do nonhierarchical forms of governance. Thus, for example, market forms of governance must rely primarily on prices and simple contracts to discover and control the threat of opportunism, and intermediate forms of governance must rely on more elaborate forms of contract and cross-equity investments, but hierarchical forms of governance can employ not only price-like mechanisms (for example, the transfer prices discussed in detail in Chapter 12) and contracts but also managerial hierarchies to discover and control opportunism.

It has been argued that managerial hierarchies control the threat of opportunism through **managerial fiat.** If one or more parties to an exchange behave in ways that put the exchange at risk, managers in this hierarchy can ensure that the exchange will continue by engaging in close monitoring and by using their hierarchical authority to punish opportunistic parties. This is managerial fiat. In the extreme, in a hierarchical governance framework, individuals who engage in such behaviors can be fired and replaced by individuals who are less likely to engage in such activities.[10]

Consider, for example, the relationship between a firm that owns and operates an oil refinery and a firm that owns and operates oil pipelines, as depicted in Figure 10.2. Assume that this oil refinery is built on the edge of a deep-water bay and that it has been receiving supplies of crude oil from large tanker ships. Also, suppose that an oil field exists several miles distant from the refinery location, but the only way to transport crude oil from the oil field to the refinery is with trucks—a more costly means of transport than the tanker ships. Suppose too that an oil pipeline company approaches the refinery and indicates that it would be willing to build a pipeline from the oil field to the refinery if, in turn, the oil refinery would agree to buy a defined number of barrels of crude at an agreed-to price for some period of time—say five years—through the pipeline. If reasonable prices can be negotiated, the oil refinery is likely to find this offer attractive, for the cost of crude oil carried by the pipeline is likely to be lower than the cost of crude oil delivered by ship or by truck. Based on this analysis, the refinery and the oil pipeline firm are likely to explore this exchange opportunity.

However, look at this exchange from the point of view of the pipeline company. Suppose a contract is signed and things go along well for five years—most reasonable contingencies during this five-year period were anticipated, and appropriate contractual guarantees were in place. Now, however, it is time to renegotiate the supply contract. Who is at risk in this renegotiation? If the value of the refinery, with its pipeline

FIGURE 10.2   The Exchange Between an Oil Refinery and an Oil Pipeline Company

Oil refinery built on the edge of a deep-water bay

Oil tank truck

Oil tanker ship

Oil pipeline

Oil field

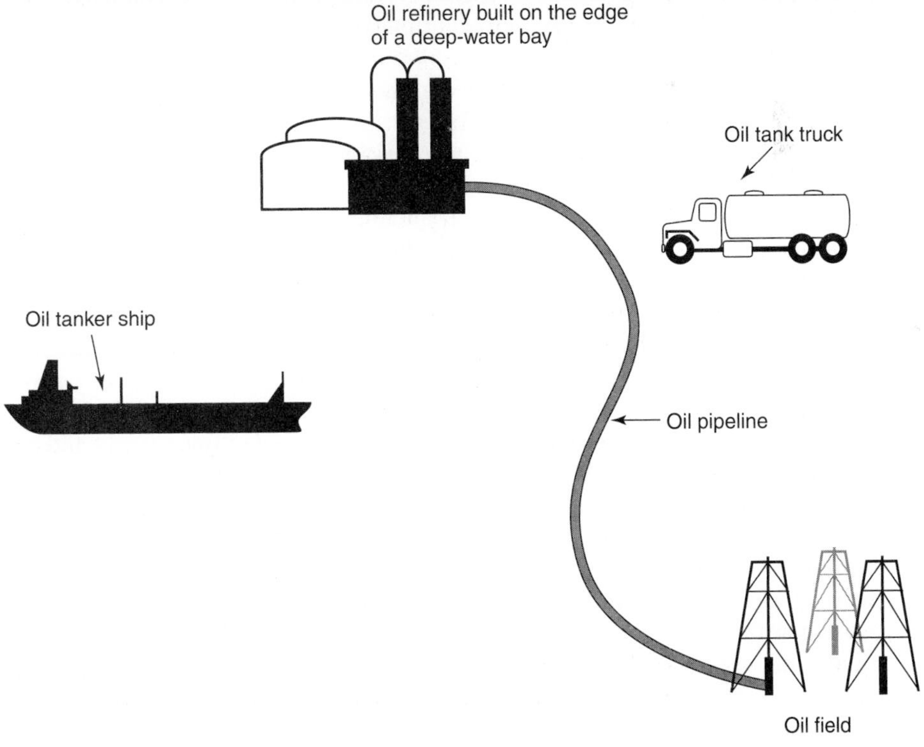

supply in place, is $1 million but drops to $900,000 if it has to start using oil supplied by tanker ships and trucks, the refiner has made some transaction-specific investments, but the specific investment made by the pipeline firm is substantially larger. The pipeline might be worth $750,000 as long as it is pumping oil to the refinery. However, if it is not pumping oil, it has very limited value—either as scrap or (perhaps) as the world's largest enclosed water slide. If the value of the pipeline is only $10,000 if it is not pumping oil to the refinery, the pipeline firm faces a significant risk of opportunism in the renegotiation process. This could take the form of, for example, the refiner demanding lower prices for crude oil pumped through the pipeline after a contract is renegotiated.

Of course, the pipeline firm is not likely to be managed by stupid people. These managers will have anticipated these potential problems in the renegotiation process and will have insisted on prices high enough on the crude oil pumped during the first contract period that the pipeline would be a profitable venture even if it had to be closed because of problems during renegotiation. Of course, this tactic would have had the effect of driving up the price of crude oil carried by the pipeline, perhaps to the point where piped crude was no longer less costly than oil delivered to the refinery by tanker ships or trucks.

Thus, on the one hand, this market contracting process is likely to put the pipeline firm at significant risk during renegotiation, after it has made its transaction-specific investments. On the other hand, efforts by the pipeline company to protect itself are likely to drive up the price of crude pumped through the pipeline, and the pipeline might not be built in the first place. This is a classic example of a market failure—where a market form of governance no longer protects parties to an exchange from threats of opportunism. If this exchange is to continue, some alternative to market governance must be created.

One option that the oil refinery and the pipeline firm can explore to manage this difficult situation is some sort of strategic alliance, perhaps even a joint venture in which each of these firms owns an equity position in an independent entity that, in turn, owns and operates the oil pipeline and the refinery. This governance alternative is described in more detail in Chapter 13. If an alliance cannot be used to solve the opportunism problems in this exchange, then these firms may have to opt for hierarchical governance and vertical integration, for example, by the refining company purchasing the oil pipeline company. If it is designed correctly, hierarchical governance could enable the pipeline to be built and could simultaneously minimize the threat of opportunism in this exchange.

Uncertainty, Complexity, and Opportunism.   The level of uncertainty and complexity in a transaction can also be an important determinant of the extent to which opportunism is a threat in an economic exchange. When parties to an exchange can anticipate, before the exchange actually occurs, how that exchange will unfold in all its detail, they will be able to anticipate all the different ways in which exchange partners can behave opportunistically. In this setting, it is usually possible to write a relatively complete contract that specifies all the ways in which the exchange will evolve and the rights and responsibilities of all parties in this relationship over time. In such certain and relatively simple exchanges, opportunism is not a significant threat, for there can be no unpleasant surprises.

However, when high levels of uncertainty and complexity characterize an exchange, it may be very difficult, if not impossible, for exchange partners to anticipate all possible ways in which an exchange might evolve. In particular, it may not be possible to anticipate how an exchange's evolution will affect the ability of different parties in the exchange to behave opportunistically. When possible sources of opportunistic behavior cannot be anticipated, the threat of opportunistic behavior may be greater than when all possible sources of opportunistic behavior in an exchange can be anticipated.

When the level of uncertainty and complexity in an exchange is high, the threat of opportunism may also be high, and more elaborate forms of costly governance—including vertical integration—may be appropriate. Vertical integration can be used to manage the problem of exchange uncertainty and complexity over time. Thus, although it may not be possible to anticipate all possible sources of opportunism when an exchange is begun, over time these sources of opportunistic threat can be revealed. Hierarchical governance creates a setting in which these sources of opportunism can be discovered and, once discovered, managed in a way that avoids the liabilities normally associated with opportunistic behavior.

Empirical Tests of the Transaction Costs Model of Vertical Integration

Transaction costs logic has been the object of a great deal of empirical research in economics, organization theory, and strategic management. Much of this empirical work supports the essential elements of transaction costs logic, including the notion that the threat of opportunism to a large extent determines the form of economic governance and that exchange partners will adopt the form of governance that, at the lowest possible cost, reduces the threat of opportunism.

For example several researchers have shown that when firms need to make transaction-specific capital investments (such as investments in plant and equipment) in order to engage in a particular economic exchange, these exchanges are more likely to be vertically integrated than exchanges that do not require these kinds of investments.[11] Others have examined the effect of transaction-specific human capital investments on vertical integration decisions and found that the more transaction-specific human capital investments are, the more likely are these exchanges to be managed through hierarchical forms of governance.[12] Still others have examined the effect of making site-specific investments, similar to the oil refinery/oil pipeline example described earlier, on vertical integration decisions, and have found that the greater the level of site specificity in an investment, the more likely an exchange is to be managed through hierarchical governance. Finally, other researchers have shown that when only a small number of qualified buyers and sellers exist for a particular exchange (a situation that often reflects the existence of transaction-specific investments), vertically integrated hierarchical forms of governance are more likely to be used than either intermediate or market forms of governance.[13]

Most of this research examines the effect of various forms of transaction-specific investment on vertical integration decisions. The perponderance of evidence suggests that, on average, the higher the required level of transaction-specific investment, the more likely it is that vertically integrated hierarchical forms of governance will be employed. The effect that uncertainty and complexity in an exchange have on vertical integration decisions has also been examined, although these results are not as consistent as research on transaction-specific investment. Sometimes, high levels of uncertainty and complexity lead exchange partners to choose vertical integration in order to minimize the threat of opportunism. On the other hand, some researchers have shown that under conditions of high uncertainty and complexity, exchange partners may want to retain flexibility in how they manage their exchanges. Vertically integrated hierarchical governance is usually less flexible than intermediate or market forms of governance.[14] Later in this chapter the trade-offs between using hierarchical governance to reduce the threat of opportunism in highly uncertain and complex exchanges and using non-hierarchical governance in this setting to retain strategic flexibility will be discussed.

Capabilities and Vertical Integration: The Resource-Based Perspective

Although transaction costs economics—with its emphasis on minimizing the threat of opportunism through governance while simultaneously minimizing the cost of governance—is an important approach to making vertical integration and governance choices, it is not the only approach to making these choices. Another approach builds on many of the ideas developed in Chapter 5 and suggests that capability differences among firms are also an important consideration for making governance decisions.[15] As suggested in Table 10.2, at least two propositions about vertical integration can be derived from the resource-based perspective. The first—that sometimes non-hierarchical governance should be chosen in spite of significant threats of opportunism— contradicts transaction costs logic. The second—that firms should vertically integrate into those business functions in which they enjoy a sustained competitive advantage— is consistent with transaction costs logic.

Non-hierarchical Governance Despite Significant Threats of Opportunism

As with the resource-based view discussed in Chapter 5, the capabilities approach to vertical integration begins with the assumption that different firms may have very different kinds of resources and capabilities. Previously, this was called the assumption of **resource heterogeneity.** As applied to vertical integration, what is particularly important about the assumption of resource heterogeneity is that different firms may have very different capabilities in the value chain of activities needed to bring a product or service to customers. Some firms may be particularly skilled in, say, research and

---

TABLE 10.2   Propositions About Vertical Integration Derived from Resource-Based Theory

Proposition Three:

When another firm has valuable, rare, and costly-to-imitate resources that are too costly to acquire, don't vertically integrate the exchange with this firm (despite threats of opportunism).

Proposition Four:

Vertically integrate in business functions in which a firm enjoys valuable, rare, and costly-to-imitate resources and capabilities.

development; other firms may be unusually skilled in manufacturing; others in distribution; others in sales and marketing; and still others in providing after-sales service.

One of the governance implications of this value chain heterogeneity in resources and capabilities is that, in addition to making governance choices that minimize the threat of opportunism, firms must also consider the potential value created by being able to work with other unusually skilled firms. Consider, for example, a firm deciding whether to vertically integrate into product distribution. If another firm exists that has valuable, rare, and costly-to-imitate distribution capabilities, the value that can be gained by working with this firm to distribute products must be weighed against any threat of opportunism that might exist by working with this firm.

This is exactly the situation that faces Wal-Mart's suppliers. Wal-Mart has developed very valuable, rare, and costly-to-imitate retail distribution capabilities, at least in North America. A firm that distributes its products through Wal-Mart is likely to see a much greater volume of sales than a firm that does not distribute its products through Wal-Mart. However, Wal-Mart requires most of its suppliers to make significant transaction-specific investments to distribute their products through Wal-Mart stores. For example, Wal-Mart requires most of its suppliers to invest in electronic data interchange (EDI) systems to facilitate order-processing. Because these EDI investments are usually very specific to Wal-Mart, they represent significant transaction-specific investments on the part of Wal-Mart's suppliers.[16]

Transaction costs logic suggests that specific investments are likely to lead to the threat of opportunism. Because transactions with Wal-Mart are likely to be plagued by opportunism problems, transaction costs logic seems to suggest that supply firms should either seek retail distribution outlets in addition to Wal-Mart, avoid making specific investments in their relationship with Wal-Mart, or, if these alternatives fail, seek to develop their own distribution functions.

Of course, most of these supply firms look for retail distribution outlets beyond Wal-Mart. However, given the size of Wal-Mart and its importance in the discount retail segment in North America, most of these firms must interact with Wal-Mart, and relations with other distribution networks do not provide much protection against any opportunistic actions that Wal-Mart may undertake. These supply firms would also like to avoid making specific EDI investments in Wal-Mart, but, in general, in order to gain access to Wal-Mart's retail distribution networks, such investments must be made. And while these supply firms might want to vertically integrate into retail distribution, it would be virtually impossible for any one of them to be able to develop the sophisticated and large distribution network that Wal-Mart has put in place in North America.

Put differently, the value of working with Wal-Mart for retail product distribution—as measured by an increased volume of sales—is simply greater than the value put at risk because of the specific investments that exist between these supply firms and Wal-Mart. Thus, contrary to transaction costs logic, the threat of opportunism is not the only determinant of a firm's governance choices. Rather, the costs associated with the threat of opportunism must be balanced against any value that is created by interacting with another uniquely skilled firm. When the value created by working with such a firm is greater than the cost of opportunism in this relationship, firms should not vertically integrate into these transactions, even though the threat of opportunism can be substantial.

In general, these capability considerations become important for firms making governance choices when the capabilities of a potential exchange partner are valuable, rare, costly to imitate, and costly to acquire.[17] Value and rarity are straightforward—if a potential exchange partner is one of the few firms that has value chain resources and capabilities that a particular firm needs to be successful, that firm becomes a potential exchange partner. These resources and capabilities may be costly to imitate for any of the reasons discussed in Chapter 5: They may reflect a firm's unique history, they may reflect numerous little decisions, or they may be socially complex. In this context, costly imitation means that vertical integration—at least through direct duplication or substitution—is too costly.

Of course, even if another firm has valuable, rare, and costly-to-imitate value chain resources and capabilities, it may still be possible to vertically integrate by acquiring a firm that possesses these capabilities. Acquisitions, as a corporate strategy, are discussed in detail in Chapter 14. However, in this context, it is important to recognize that sometimes the cost of acquiring valuable, rare, and costly-to-imitate resources and capabilities may be greater than the value of such an acquisition.

For example, it may be that in order to gain access to particular resources and capabilities, an entire firm—with numerous economically irrelevant resources and capabilities—will have to be acquired. The cost of disposing of all of these irrelevant resources and capabilities increases the cost of acquiring the relevant resources and capabilities, perhaps to the point that the acquisition is no longer valuable. In this setting, vertically integrating by acquiring another firm's valuable, rare, and costly-to-imitate resources and capabilities is not economically viable.

Moreover, sometimes a firm's resources and capabilities are valuable *because* they are not owned by another firm. For example, several U.S. advertising agencies were interested in acquiring the French advertising agency Publicis. Publicis had several large French accounts that appeared to be quite lucrative to the U.S. firms. However, one of the reasons why Publicis had these accounts was that it was French. If it had been acquired by a U.S. firm, it would no longer have been French and thus may have lost the very assets—its French accounts—that would have motivated an acquisition by a U.S. firm. In this setting, a vertical integration acquisition to gain access to valuable, rare, and costly-to-imitate resources and capabilities would not generate economic value.[18]

Finally, governments, for their own reasons, may prevent the acquisition of certain firms. In this setting, acquiring another firm in order to avoid any threat of opportunism associated with vertically interacting with this firm is not possible. This is a particularly common issue facing firms attempting to enter into new international markets. In such settings, interacting with a domestic firm may be important for successfully entering into a new country. However, such interactions, because of transaction-specific investment, uncertainty, or complexity, may be fraught with opportunism problems. Given government regulations, vertically integrating by acquiring this other firm is simply not an option. Firms seeking to enter into new markets by working with domestic partners must decide whether the value of interacting with these firms is greater than the potential costs associated with any opportunism that might emerge in this relationship. U.S. firms entering into the Japanese market have often faced this difficult choice.[19]

Of course, this capability reasoning does not suggest that threats of opportunism are irrelevant in making governance choices. However, it does suggest that minimizing the threat of opportunism must be balanced against the value that can be created by engaging in exchanges with firms that control valuable, rare, and costly-to-imitate resources that cannot be acquired in a cost-effective manner. In some settings, opportunism is simply a part of the cost of gaining access to another firm's special resources and capabilities.

Hierarchical Governance When Firms Possess Sources of Competitive Advantage

The first proposition in Table 10.2 examines vertical integration decisions when *another* firm possesses valuable, rare, and costly-to-imitate resources and capabilities. The second proposition focuses on vertical integration decisions when the firm in question possesses these kinds of resources and capabilities. This proposition suggests that firms should vertically integrate into business functions in which they currently enjoy competitive advantages.[20]

There are at least three reasons why a firm should vertically integrate into business functions in which it currently enjoys a competitive advantage. First, hierarchical governance can increase the possibility that a firm will be able to keep the sources of its competitive advantage proprietary, especially in comparison to nonhierarchical governance. To choose outside suppliers to provide a potential competitive advantage, a firm will generally have to contact several possible suppliers and share with them what needs to be done to create the advantage. This process of choosing outside suppliers increases the chance that the source of a firm's competitive advantage will become known to other competitors. This, in turn, reduces the chance that this source of competitive advantage will remain proprietary, and thus reduces the chance that it will become a source of sustained competitive advantage.[21]

Second, by vertically integrating into this function, a firm increases the chance that it will be able to appropriate the economic profits that a source of competitive advantage is likely to generate. When economic rents are generated from sources external to a firm, those sources—be they individuals or companies—have the ability to extract some of the profits their actions create. On the other hand, when a firm already controls its source of economic profits through its vertical integration actions, it can appropriate a larger portion of those profits for itself.[22]

Finally, in order for a business function to be a source of sustained competitive advantage, it must be valuable, rare, and costly to imitate. One of the reasons a business function may be valuable, rare, and costly to imitate is that resources and capabilities in that function have built up over long periods of time and are socially complex. Such resources and capabilities are highly firm-specific; that is, they exist in a particular firm at a particular time because of a firm's unique history. Investments in such firm-specific resources, thus, must necessarily also be highly firm-specific. According to transaction costs economics, managing the investment in highly firm-specific resources and capabilities through non-hierarchical means is subject to significant threats of opportunism and thus should be abandoned in favor of hierarchical governance. Therefore, when a firm has made specific investments in a particular function—investments that are a source of competitive advantage for that firm—both resource-base and transaction costs logic suggest that the firm should manage this function through vertical integration.

For example, suppose that a firm wants to increase its manufacturing capacity but would like to do so in a way that generates economic profits. To generate such profits, investments in new manufacturing capacity would have to be specific to this firm. That is, these investments would have to be more valuable to this particular firm than to competing firms. Outside manufacturing suppliers may be reluctant to invest in such specific manufacturing capacity, because in doing so they would know that they would be putting themselves at significant risk of opportunism. Thus, in order to gain access to this specific manufacturing capacity, a firm may have to invest internally. At the very least, this firm will have to make significant transaction-specific investments in its outside supplier if it expects the outside supplier to make significant transaction-specific investments in manufacturing capacity.[23]

Alternatively, if a firm wants to increase its manufacturing capacity but does not believe that manufacturing is likely to be a source of competitive advantage, it will be able to rely on outside suppliers to gain access to this capacity. This is because this additional manufacturing capacity would not have to be very specific to this firm—because the firm is not expecting to be able to gain economic profits from this manufacturing decision. Outside suppliers are willing to provide non-specific manufacturing capacity, because such investments will not put them at risk of opportunism.

Taken together, these arguments suggest that when a set of business functions is likely to be a source of sustained competitive advantage, firms have to manage the investment in those business functions through hierarchical forms of governance. On the other hand, when a set of business functions is not likely to be a source of sustained competitive advantage, it is possible to use non-hierarchical forms of governance to manage investments in those functions. As suggested earlier, this is perfectly consistent with transaction costs logic and, thus, Proposition Two in Table 10.2 is consistent with transaction costs logic.

Uncertainty and Vertical Integration: A Real Options Perspective

In the brief review of research on transaction costs economics presented earlier in this chapter, it was noted that although most of the work on the relationship between transaction-specific investment and governance choices is consistent with transaction costs theory, work on the relationship between uncertainty and governance is not always consistent with transaction costs expectations. In some situations, high levels of uncertainty in an economic exchange leads firms to choose more hierarchical forms of governance—in a way that is consistent with transaction costs logic. In other situations, however, high levels of uncertainty in an economic exchange lead firms to choose less hierarchical forms of governance—in a way that apparently contradicts traditional transaction costs logic.

These empirical anomalies have led scholars to search for alternative explanations of governance choice under conditions of high uncertainty. As was discussed in Chapter 8, an **option** is the right, but not the obligation, to buy or sell a specified asset at a pre-specified price on a pre-specified date. **Financial options** are options written on financial assets such as stock. Thus, a **stock option** gives a person the right, but not the obligation, to buy or sell a particular stock at a pre-specified price on a pre-specified date. A **real option** is an option written on a real asset, such as a factory, a distribution network, or a technology. For example, when a firm builds a new factory, not only does it have the opportunity to operate that new factory, it also has the right, but not the obligation, to expand that factory at some point in the future. The option to expand a factory is, in this sense, a real option.

Real options logic focuses on the ability of a firm to adjust its strategy in the future, depending on how that uncertain future evolves. Given the importance of this ability to adjust strategies over time, a real options analysis of governance suggests that when there is significant uncertainty about whether a particular investment will ultimately be valuable, choosing governance that maximizes strategic flexibility becomes an important consideration.[24]

In general, less hierarchical governance is more flexible than more hierarchical governance. This is because it is more costly to undo the investments necessary to create hierarchical governance than it is to undo the investments necessary to create non-hierarchical governance. To undo non-hierarchical governance, contracts can simply be cancelled. To undo hierarchical governance, business functions have to be outsourced, employees laid off, managers reassigned or laid off, and the unrealized value of an investment written off. All of this is more costly than undoing non-hierarchical governance. This logic leads to the proposition in Table 10.3.

Notice that the uncertainty that is emphasized by this real options logic is uncertainty about the future value of an investment. This is different than the uncertainty that is emphasized in transaction costs logic. That uncertainty is uncertainty about unanticipated sources of opportunism in an exchange. Although both kinds of uncertainty may exist in a particular exchange, they do not always coexist. This explains why previous empirical research on the relationship between uncertainty and governance has been inconsistent. When the uncertainty that exists in an exchange is uncertainty about possible sources of opportunism, transaction costs logic dominates and more hierarchical governance is preferred. When the uncertainty that exists in an exchange is uncertainty about the value of an investment, real options logic dominates and less hierarchical governance is preferred. When both types of uncertainty exist, the relative value of minimizing the threat of opportunism and retaining flexibility determines the optimal governance choice. Most previous empirical work on the relationship between uncertainty and governance has not examined these subtleties.[25]

However, empirical research on governance choices that has focused on conditions when the future value of a particular exchange is very uncertain *is* consistent with real options logic. For example, under these conditions, firms are more likely to choose intermediate forms of governance than hierarchical forms of governance, even though the threat of opportunism in an exchange is significant. The value of retaining the ability to change governance quickly at low cost is high in these uncertain conditions.[26]

Consider, for example, a pharmaceutical firm contemplating entry into the biotechnology drug industry by introducing a new drug developed through the application of biotechnology. The development of new drugs, in general, is a very uncertain business. Uncertainties exist about whether a new drug can be developed, whether it

---

TABLE 10.3   Propositions About Vertical Integration Derived from Real Options Theory

Proposition Five:

To retain flexibility, exchanges characterized by high levels of uncertainty should not be vertically integrated.

will work as hoped, whether it will have unanticipated negative side effects, whether it will receive government approval, and whether other firms are developing alternative competing drugs. These uncertainties are multiplied many times in the application of biotechnology to develop new drugs, because biotechnology is still new and underdeveloped.

In entering the biotechnology drug industry, an established pharmaceutical firm has at least two governance choices. First, it can decide to vertically integrate into this industry by building biotechnology capabilities and investing in biotechnology research to develop new drugs. Although this approach to managing this investment has some advantages, its main liability is that it commits a pharmaceutical firm to one, or a small number, of drug development research projects. In more mature research and development environments, a firm may be able to estimate the probability that a particular research project will yield a positive outcome. In the biotechnology industry, however, the probability that any one project will generate a successful new drug is unknown. Investing in a relatively small number of research projects by vertically integrating into biotechnology may commit a firm to a particular course of action that will turn out not to be valuable.

Second, a firm may decide not to vertically integrate into biotechnology, and instead develop relationships with several—perhaps even hundreds—of smaller biotechnology firms. Typically, these relationships will be some sort of strategic alliance, an intermediate governance device that will be discussed in more detail in Chapter 13. By establishing these relationships, the pharmaceutical firm avoids overcommitting to a particular course of action, and instead remains flexible to pursue only those R&D projects that turn out to be most promising. Once a particular small firm's research project shows unusual promise, a pharmaceutical firm may decide to vertically integrate into that project by acquiring its former small-firm partner. However, that vertical integration decision is made under conditions of much lower uncertainty compared to a pharmaceutical firm that decides to vertically integrate into biotechnology from the start.

Historically, most pharmaceutical firms pursuing opportunities in biotechnology have adopted this second approach to governance. Given the inability to know, *ex ante,* which particular projects to invest in, pharmaceutical firms develop relationships with hundreds of small biotechnology firms, each of which is pursuing several specific biotechnology research projects. This creates the flexibility for the large firm to invest in only those projects that are most likely to pay off. Only after the uncertainty in this industry is partially resolved do large firms make their final vertical integration decisions. In doing so, these large firms apply either the transaction costs or capabilities logic presented in this chapter.[27]

Integrating Transaction Costs, Capabilities, and Real Options Approaches to Vertical Integration Decisions

As suggested by this discussion, these three approaches to making vertical integration decisions—transaction costs, capabilities, and real options—are all well developed and tested. Unfortunately, at least in some circumstances, they are contradictory. To date, no "unified field theory" of vertical integration choices has been developed.

In this setting, those looking to make vertical integration choices must weigh the relative importance of these three models. One approach for doing this is presented in

Figure 10.3. For example, if the value of the threat of opportunism in a transaction is very high, then transaction costs logic should dominate, and more hierarchical forms of governance should be chosen. If the value of gaining access to another firm's valuable, rare, costly–to–imitate, and costly-to-acquire resources and capabilities is high, then capabilities logic should dominate, and less hierarchical forms of governance should be chosen—despite the threat of opportunism. Finally, if uncertainty about the future value of an investment is high, the value of flexibility in a transaction is very high. In this setting, real options logic should dominate and less hierarchical forms of governance should be chosen.

Consider, for example, the decision about whether to outsource the management of call centers.

Transaction-Specific Investments and the Management of Call Centers

When applying opportunism-based explanations of vertical integration, start by looking for actual or potential transaction-specific investments that would need to be made in order to complete an exchange. High levels of such investments suggest the need for vertical integration; low levels of such investment suggest that vertically integrating this exchange is not necessary.

In the context of call centers, when this approach to providing customer service was first developed in the 1980s, it required substantial levels of transaction-specific investment. First, a great deal of special-purpose equipment had to be purchased. And although this equipment could be used for any call center, it had little value except in a call center. Thus, this equipment was an example of a somewhat specific investment.

More important, in order to provide service in call centers, call center employees would have to be fully aware of all the problems that are likely to emerge with the use of a firm's products. This would require a firm to study its products very closely and then to

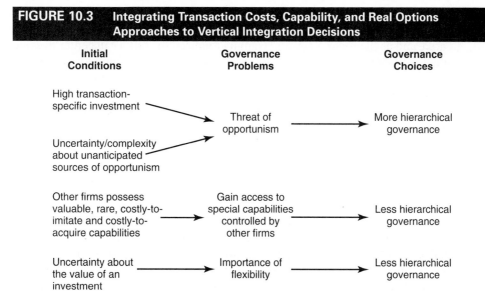

FIGURE 10.3   Integrating Transaction Costs, Capability, and Real Options Approaches to Vertical Integration Decisions

Initial Conditions	Governance Problems	Governance Choices
High transaction-specific investment	Threat of opportunism	More hierarchical governance
Uncertainty/complexity about unanticipated sources of opportunism		
Other firms possess valuable, rare, costly-to-imitate and costly-to-acquire capabilities	Gain access to special capabilities controlled by other firms	Less hierarchical governance
Uncertainty about the value of an investment	Importance of flexibility	Less hierarchical governance

train call center employees to be able to respond to any problems customers might have. This training was sometimes very complex and very time-consuming and represented substantial transaction-specific investments on the part of call center employees. Only employees who worked full time for a large corporation—where job security was usually high for productive workers—would be willing to make these kinds of specific investments. Thus, vertical integration into call center management made a great deal of sense.

However, as information technology improved, firms found that it was possible to train call center employees much more quickly. Now, all call center employees had to do was follow scripts that had been pre-written and pre-loaded on their computers. By asking a few pre-scripted questions, call center employees could diagnose most problems. And solutions to those problems were also included on an employee's computer. Only really unusual problems could not be handled by employees working off these computer scripts. Because the level of specific investment required to use these scripts was much lower, employees were willing to work for companies without the job security usually associated with large firms. Indeed, call centers became good part-time and temporary employment opportunities. Because the level of specific investment required to work in these call centers was much lower, not vertically integrating into call center management made a great deal of sense.

Capabilities Theory and the Management of Call Centers

In opportunism-based explanations of vertical integration, you start by looking for transaction-specific investments and then make vertical integration decisions based on these investments. In capability-based approaches, you start by looking for valuable, rare, and costly-to-imitate resources and capabilities, and then make vertical integration decisions appropriately.

In the early days of call center management, how well a firm operated its call centers could actually be a source of competitive advantage. During this period, the technology was new, and the training required to answer a customer's questions was extensive. Firms that developed special capabilities in managing these processes could gain competitive advantages and thus would vertically integrate into call center management.

Over time, however, as more and more call center management suppliers appeared, and as the technology and training required to staff a call center became more widely available, the ability of a call center to be a source of competitive advantage for a firm dropped. That is, the ability to manage a call center was still valuable, but it was no longer rare or costly to imitate. In this setting, it was not surprising that firms began getting out of the call center management business, outsourcing this business to low-cost specialist firms, and focusing on those business functions in which the firms might be able to gain a sustained competitive advantage.

The exception to this trend was call centers that support complex products. Such support may require complicated and even proprietary information. Such call centers are likely to be vertically integrated into a firm.

Flexibility and Management of Call Centers

Opportunism logic suggests starting with a search for transaction-specific investments; capabilities logic suggests starting with a search for valuable, rare, and costly-to-imitate resources and capabilities. Flexibility logic suggests starting by looking for sources of uncertainty in an exchange.

One of the biggest uncertainties in providing customer service through call centers is whether the people staffing the phones actually help the firm's customers. This is a particularly troubling concern for firms that are selling complex products that can have numerous different kinds of problems. A variety of technological solutions have been developed to try to address this uncertainty. However, if a firm vertically integrates into the call service center management business, it is committing to a particular technological solution. This solution may not work, or may not work as well, as some other solutions.

In the face of this uncertainty, maintaining relationships with several different call center management companies—each of which has adopted different technological solutions to the problem of how to use call center employees to assist customers who are using very complex products—gives a firm technological flexibility that it would not otherwise have. Once a superior solution is identified, then a firm no longer needs this flexibility and may choose to vertically integrate into call center management or not—depending on opportunism and capabilities considerations.

10.3 VERTICAL INTEGRATION AND SUSTAINED COMPETITIVE ADVANTAGE

Transaction costs economics, capabilities theory, and real options theory provide a powerful set of tools that firms can use to decide their level of vertical integration. Thus far, however, this analysis has adopted the assumption that the potential economic value of a particular exchange is independent of the form of governance used to manage that exchange. Put differently, these models all assume that the economic value of an exchange is given, and that the task facing managers is simply to choose the form of governance that extracts this value at the lowest cost possible. These analyses do not recognize the possibility that the way in which an exchange is governed can have a direct effect on the value that the exchange can create—that is, that governance itself can be a source of economic rents.

Consider the following examples. Suppose that two firms are evaluating the same transaction. Using transaction costs, capabilities, or real options, suppose these two firms come to similar conclusions about which forms of governance will be the best way to manage this exchange. In this setting, these two firms will adopt the same, or at least substitute, forms of governance. In this situation, governance per se cannot be a source of economic profits. However, if these two firms come to different conclusions about how to manage this exchange, they may come to different conclusions about the appropriate form of governance for this transaction. The identification of different governance mechanisms suggests that these firms will have different costs of governing this exchange and, perhaps, even come to different conclusions about the economic potential of this exchange. All these differences are potential sources of competitive advantage for these firms—advantages that derive from the differential ability of firms to apply the three types of vertical integration logic presented in this chapter.

Rare Vertical Integration Strategies

To derive competitive advantages from governance choices, it is necessary to introduce more heterogeneity into the application of these three models than has traditionally been introduced. Heterogeneity can be introduced by recognizing that economic actors may differ in their ability to analyze uncertain and complex economic transactions, their ability to conceive of and implement different governance mechanisms, and their propensity to behave opportunistically. If these differences in governance skills are valuable, rare, and costly to imitate, the vertical integration decisions they imply can be a source of sustained competitive advantage—if a firm is organized to exploit the full competitive potential of its special governance skills.

Differences in the Ability to Analyze Uncertain and Complex Transactions

It is widely recognized that individuals can vary in their ability to analyze different economic exchange opportunities. What is complex and uncertain to one person may be simple and obvious to another. Differences in analytical skills can exist in firms as well. One firm may conclude that a potential economic exchange is very complex and uncertain; another may conclude that the same economic exchange is actually quite simple and obvious.[28]

Differences in the ability to analyze uncertain and complex economic exchanges reflect numerous differences between individuals and between firms. Differences in native intelligence, training, and experience may lead individuals to come to very different conclusions about the complexity and uncertainty of an exchange. Analogies exist in the firm for each of these individual-level phenomena. For example, firms may differ in their ability to tap into the intelligence of their employees. As a result, some firms may behave as if they are more intelligent than others. Also, firms may vary with respect to the training of their employees and their experience in analyzing certain types of economic exchanges. For all these reasons, firms may come to very different conclusions about the level of uncertainty and complexity in a particular exchange.

Of course, these differences among individuals and firms are competitively relevant only to the extent that they have some implications for how firms make governance decisions. For example, suppose that two firms are contemplating the same economic transaction. Suppose that the "objective" properties of this transaction are constant across these two firms. However, if these firms differ in their ability to analyze these "objective" properties, they are likely to come to different conclusions about the level of uncertainty and complexity in these exchanges and thus to different conclusions about what the optimal level of governance for these exchanges is likely to be. Suppose that the actual (but difficult to observe) level of uncertainty in this exchange is quite low, and one firm comes to this conclusion but the second, less skilled firm concludes that the level of uncertainty in this exchange is actually quite high. The first (more accurate) firm will be able to choose a less elaborate and less costly form of governance and still be assured about reducing the threat of opportunism and maintaining required flexibility, compared to the second, less skilled firm.

The ability to use less costly governance to manage an exchange will give the more skilled firm at least a temporary competitive advantage because, relative to the only other firm in this simple example, these highly developed exchange analysis skills are rare. For these analysis skills to be a source of sustained competitive advantage, they must be immune from imitation, through either direct duplication or substitution. The imitability of these skills seems likely to depend on their source. For example, innate individual intelligence is probably a relatively fixed attribute and thus not subject to low-cost duplication, although individuals who are not endowed with high levels of intelligence might still be able to behave as if they were by surrounding themselves with highly skilled individuals, sophisticated databases, and related technologies. Organizational abilities to tap into the intelligence of employees seem likely to depend on the organizational culture and related attributes of a firm—attributes already shown to be not usually subject to low-cost duplication or easy substitution.[29] Individual and organizational training and experience can only accumulate over time and thus may not be subject to low-cost duplication or substitution. On the other hand, if there are decreasing returns to training and experience, then in the long run competing firms will develop strategically equivalent levels of training and experience.

Differences in the Ability to Conceive of and Implement Governance Mechanisms

Another potentially important difference among economic actors is the ability of individuals and firms to conceive of and implement different governance mechanisms. In a particular exchange, different economic actors may all come to exactly the same conclusion about the threat of opportunism, the importance of capabilities, or the level of uncertainty, but differ in their abilities to build governance mechanisms to respond to these exchange imperatives. If more skilled individuals and firms can develop less costly governance mechanisms to govern an exchange, compared to less skilled individuals and firms that have to develop more costly governance mechanisms, the more skilled individuals and firms can gain competitive advantages from their governance choices.

Differences in governance ability are not restricted to the ability that different economic actors might possess in building different governance mechanisms (for example, when one firm might be more skilled at using market contracts to manage exchanges while another might be more skilled at using strategic alliances). Economic actors might also vary with respect to their ability to use the same governance mechanism. Thus, for example, suppose that two competing firms decide to govern the same type of exchange by using a market contract. However, suppose that one of these firms is able to write and administer this form of governance at much lower cost compared to the other firm. Here, despite the fact that both firms have (apparently) come to the same conclusion about the nature of a particular transaction, and despite the fact that both have implemented the same governance mechanisms to manage this relationship, the fact that one firm is more skilled in implementing these governance mechanisms than the other suggests that a competitive advantage might exist.

For example, U.S. automakers have developed strategic alliances with Japanese automakers. If one asked only whether these U.S. firms have alliances with Japanese firms, one could conclude that these alliances are not rare and thus not a source of competitive advantage. However, when it is recognized that different U.S. automakers get different things from their alliances with Japanese automakers, it is clear that these alliances can be rare and thus a source of at least a temporary competitive advantage. These observations can be generalized by observing that, even when competing individuals and firms all choose the same governance devices for a transaction, differences in the ability to implement these devices can create important competitive advantages.

As was the case with different skills in analyzing uncertain economic exchanges, whether different skills in conceiving of and implementing governance devices will be a source of sustained competitive advantage depends on the sources of those skill differences. If those sources reflect an economic actor's unique history, if they reflect numerous "little" decisions in these actors, or if they are socially complex, they are likely to be immune from low-cost imitation and thus possible sources of sustained competitive advantage.

Differences in the Propensity to Behave Opportunistically

The first two ways in which governance choices can be sources of competitive advantage—differences in exchange analysis skills and differences in the ability to conceive of and implement governance mechanisms—focus primarily on the uncertainty and complexity of vertical integration decisions. Although the "objective" level of uncertainty and complexity in an exchange may be a constant property of that exchange, the perceived uncertainty and complexity of the exchange are likely to vary both with the exchange analysis skills of different actors and with the ability of these different actors to conceive of and implement governance devices. However, in addition to differences in the perceived level of uncertainty in an exchange, there may also be important differences in the propensity of different economic actors to behave opportunistically. If these differences exist and can be discovered at low cost, then, according at least to transaction costs logic, those exchanging with less opportunistically inclined exchange partners will be able to invest in less costly governance than will those exchanging with more opportunistically inclined exchange partners. This lower-cost governance can be a source of competitive advantage vis-à-vis firms that interact with opportunistically inclined exchange partners and thus require greater levels of costly governance to reduce the threat of opportunism.

Traditional transaction costs logic does not deny the possibility that different economic actors might vary in their propensity to behave opportunistically. However, this logic also suggests that it is very difficult to distinguish between individuals and firms that are *actually* less likely to engage in opportunistic behavior and those that only *claim* that they are less likely to engage in opportunistic behavior. To gain the lower governance-cost advantages associated with engaging in exchanges with less opportunistic exchange partners, it must be possible to distinguish reliably—and at low cost—between exchange partners who are actually less inclined to behave opportunistically and those who only claim to be less inclined to behave opportunistically.

If it were possible to observe the opportunistic tendencies of possible exchange partners directly, these problems would not exist. However, because the degree of willingness to behave opportunistically is not tattooed on exchange partners' foreheads, exchange partners must rely on market signals of a partner's intentions. **Market signals** are actions taken by an individual or firm that indicate the level of some attribute of that individual or firm that cannot be observed directly, such as willingness to behave opportunistically. For such an action to be a signal, two conditions must hold: (1) The action must be correlated with the underlying but unobservable attribute, and (2) investing in this signal must be less costly for those who possess this attribute than for those who do not possess it.[30]

A variety of behaviors can be used as market signals to indicate that a potential exchange partner is not likely to behave opportunistically. For example, such exchange partners are likely to be more willing to be open to outside auditors and more willing to commit themselves to transaction-specific investments in an exchange.[31] Such activities eliminate opportunistic behavior as an option for those individuals or firms that engage in them. Exchange partners who would not have engaged in opportunistic behavior anyway—that is, those with a low propensity to behave opportunistically—do not give up any options by engaging in these behaviors. On the other hand, exchange partners who might have behaved opportunistically forfeit this opportunity when they open themselves up to outside auditors and commit themselves to an exchange by making transaction-specific investments to that exchange. Thus the opportunity cost to exchange partners who might have behaved opportunistically is higher than the opportunity cost to exchange partners who would not have behaved opportunistically. In addition, the willingness to be open to outside auditors and to commit to an exchange by making transaction-specific investments can be thought of as signals of a low level of opportunism in a potential exchange partner. Engaging in exchanges with partners who are not likely to behave opportunistically will require less elaborate forms of governance—and thus less costly forms of governance—than engaging in exchanges with partners who may behave opportunistically.

Rare Uncertainty and Vertical Integration

Finally, a firm may be able to gain an advantage from vertically integrating when it resolves some uncertainty it faces sooner than its competition. Suppose, for example, that several firms in an industry all begin investing in a very uncertain technology. Flexibility logic suggests that, to the extent possible, these firms will prefer not to vertically integrate into the manufacturing of this technology until its designs and features stabilize and market demand for this technology is well established.

However, imagine that one of these firms is able to resolve these uncertainties before any other firm. This firm no longer needs to retain the flexibility that is so valuable under conditions of uncertainty. Instead, this firm might be able to, say, design special-purpose machines that can manufacture this technology very efficiently. Such machines are not flexible, but they can be very efficient.

Of course, for outside vendors to use these new machines, they would have to make substantial transaction-specific investments and they may be reluctant to make these investments. In this setting, this firm may find it necessary to vertically integrate to be able to use its machines to produce this technology. Thus, this firm, by resolving uncertainty faster than its competitors, is able to gain some of the advantages of vertical integration sooner than its competitors. While the competition is still focusing on flexibility in the face of uncertainty, this firm gets to focus on production efficiency in meeting customers' product demands. Obviously, this can be a source of competitive advantage.

Rare Vertical Disintegration

Each of the examples of vertical integration and competitive advantage described so far focus on a firm's ability to vertically integrate to create competitive advantage. However, firms can also gain competitive advantages through their decisions to vertically disintegrate, that is, through the decision to outsource an activity that used to be within the boundaries of the firm. Whenever a firm is among the first in its industry to conclude that the level of specific investment required to manage an economic exchange is no longer high, or that a particular exchange is no longer rare or costly to imitate, or that the level of uncertainty about the value of an exchange has increased, it may be among the first in its industry to vertically disintegrate this exchange. Such activities, to the extent they are valuable, will be rare, and thus a source of at least a temporary competitive advantage.

The Imitability of Vertical Integration

The extent to which these rare vertical integration decisions can be sources of sustained competitive advantage depends, as always, on the imitability of the rare resources that give a firm at least a temporary competitive advantage. Both direct duplication and substitution can be used to imitate another firm's valuable and rare vertical integration choices.

Direct Duplication of Vertical Integration

Direct duplication occurs when competitors develop or obtain the resources and capabilities that enable another firm to implement a valuable and rare vertical integration strategy. To the extent that these resources and capabilities are path-dependent, socially complex, or causally ambiguous, they may be immune from direct duplication and thus can be a source of sustained competitive advantage.

Consider, for example, outsourcing call centers to India. Recently, the number of firms engaging in this activity has increased. Indeed, the very popularity of this strategy suggests that it is highly imitable. This strategy is becoming so common that firms that move in the other direction by vertically integrating a call center and managing it in the United States make news.

However, the fact that many firms are outsourcing their call centers to India does not mean that they are all equally successful in doing so. These differences in performance may reflect some subtle and complex capabilities that some of these outsourcing firms possess that others do not. These are the kinds of resources and capabilities that may be sources of sustained competitive advantage.

Some of the resources that might enable a firm to implement a valuable and rare vertical integration strategy may not be susceptible to direct duplication. These might include a firm's ability to analyze the attributes of its economic exchanges and its ability to conceive and implement vertical integration strategies. Both of these capabilities may be socially complex and path-dependent—built up over years of experience.

Substitutes for Vertical Integration

The major substitute for vertical integration—strategic alliances—is the major topic of Chapter 13. So an analysis of how strategic alliances can substitute for vertical integration will be delayed until then.

10.4 ORGANIZING TO IMPLEMENT VERTICAL INTEGRATION

Organizing to implement vertical integration involves the same organizing tools as implementing any business or corporate strategy: organizational structure, management controls, and compensation policies.

Organizational Structure and Implementing Vertical Integration

The organizational structure that is used to implement a cost leadership and product differentiation strategy—the functional or U-form structure—is also used to implement a vertical integration strategy. Indeed, each of the exchanges included within the boundaries of a firm as a result of vertical integration decisions is incorporated into one of the functions in a functional organizational structure. Decisions about which manufacturing activities to vertically integrate determine the range and responsibilities of the manufacturing function within a functionally organized firm; decisions about which marketing activities to vertically integrate determine the range and responsibilities of the marketing function within a functionally organized firm; and so forth. Thus, in an important sense, vertical integration decisions made by the firm determine the structure of a functionally organized firm.

The CEO in this vertically integrated, functionally organized firm has the same two responsibilities that were first identified in Chapter 4: strategy formulation and strategy implementation. However, these two responsibilities take on added dimensions when implementing vertical integration decisions. In particular, while the CEO must take the lead in making decisions about whether each individual function should be vertically integrated into the firm, this person must also work to resolve conflicts that naturally arise between vertically integrated functions.

From a CEO's perspective, coordinating functional specialists to implement a vertical integration strategy almost always involves conflict resolution. Conflicts among functional managers in a U-form organization are both expected and normal. Indeed, if there is no conflict among certain functional managers in a U-form organization, then some of these managers probably are not doing their jobs. The task facing the CEO is not to pretend this conflict does not exist, or to ignore it, but to manage it in a way that facilitates strategy implementation.

Consider, for example, the relationship between manufacturing and sales managers. Typically, manufacturing managers prefer to manufacture a single product with long production runs. Sales managers, however, generally prefer to sell numerous customized products. Manufacturing managers generally do not like large inventories of finished products; sales managers generally prefer large inventories of finished products that facilitate rapid deliveries to customers. If these various interests of manufacturing and sales managers do not, at least sometimes, come into conflict in a vertically integrated U-form organization, then the manufacturing manager is not focusing enough on cost reduction and quality improvement in manufacturing or the sales manager is not focusing enough on meeting customer needs in a timely way, or both.

Numerous other conflicts arise among functional managers in a vertically integrated U-form organization. Accountants often focus on maximizing managerial accountability and close analysis of costs; R&D managers may fear that such accounting practices will interfere with innovation and creativity. Finance managers often focus on the relationship between a firm and its external capital markets; human resource managers are more concerned with the relationship between a firm and external labor markets.

In this context, the CEO's job is to help resolve conflicts in ways that facilitate the implementation of the firm's strategy. Functional managers do not have to "like" each other. However, if a firm's vertical integration strategy is correct, the reason that a function has been included within the boundaries of a firm is that this decision creates value for the firm. Allowing functional conflicts to get in the way of taking advantage of each of the functions within a firm's boundaries can destroy this potential value.

Management Controls and Implementing Vertical Integration

Although having the correct organizational structure is important for firms implementing vertical integration strategies, that structure must be supported by a variety of management control processes. Among the most important of these processes are the budgeting process and the management committee oversight process. These two processes can also help CEOs resolve the functional conflicts that are common within vertically integrated firms.

The Budgeting Process

Budgeting is one of the most important control mechanisms available to CEOs in vertically integrated U-form organizations. Indeed, in most U-form companies, enormous management effort goes into the creation of budgets and the evaluation of performance relative to budgets. Budgets are developed for costs, revenues, and a variety of other activities performed by a firm's functional managers. Often, managerial compensation and promotion opportunities depend on the ability of a manager to meet budget expectations.

Budgets are an important control tool, but they can also have unintended negative consequences. For example, the use of budgets can lead functional managers to overemphasize short-term behavior that is easy to measure and underemphasize longer-term behavior that is more difficult to measure. Thus, for example, the strategically correct thing for a functional manager to do might be to increase expenditures for maintenance and management training, thereby ensuring that the function will have both the technology and the skilled people needed to do the job in the future. An overemphasis on meeting current budget requirements, however, might lead this manager to delay maintenance and training expenditures. By meeting short-term budgetary demands, this manager may be sacrificing the long-term viability of this function and thereby compromising the long-term viability of the firm.

CEOs can do a variety of things to counter the "short-termism" effects of the budgeting process. For example, research suggests that evaluating a functional manager's performance relative to budgets can be an effective control device when (1) the process used in developing budgets is open and participative, (2) the process reflects the economic reality facing functional managers and the firm, and (3) quantitative evaluations of a functional manger's performance are augmented by qualitative evaluations of that performance. Adopting an open and participative process for setting budgets helps ensure that budget targets are realistic and that functional managers understand and accept them. Including qualitative criteria for evaluation reduces the chances that functional managers will engage in behaviors that are very harmful in the long run but enable them to make budget in the short run.[32]

The Management Committee Oversight Process

In addition to budgets, vertically integrated U-form organizations can use various internal management committees as management control devices. Two particularly common internal management committees are the **executive committee** and the **operations committee** (although these committees have many different names in different organizations).

The executive committee in a U-form organization typically consists of the CEO and two or three key senior functional managers. It normally meets weekly and reviews the performance of the firm on a short-term basis. Functions represented on this committee generally include accounting, legal, and other functions (such as manufacturing or sales) that are most central to the firm's short-term business success. The fundamental purpose of the executive committee is to track the short-term performance of the firm, to note and correct any budget variances for functional managers, and to respond to any crises that might emerge. Obviously, the executive committee can help avoid any functional conflicts in a vertically integrated firm before they arise.

In addition to the executive committee, another group of managers meet regularly to help control the operations of the firm. Often called the operations committee, this committee typically meets monthly and usually consists of the CEO and each of the heads of the functional areas included in the firm. The executive committee is a subset of the operations committee.

The primary objective of the operations committee is to track firm performance over time intervals slightly longer than the weekly interval of primary interest to the executive committee and to monitor longer-term strategic investments and activities. Such investments might include plant expansions, the introduction of new products, and the implementation of cost-reduction or quality improvement programs. The operations committee provides a forum in which senior functional managers can come together to share concerns and opportunities and to coordinate efforts to implement strategies. Obviously, the operations committee can help resolve functional conflicts in a vertically integrated firm when they arise.

In addition to these two standing committees, various other committees and task forces can be organized within the U-form organization to manage specific projects and tasks. These additional groups are typically chaired by a member of the executive or operations committee and report to one or both of these standing committees as warranted.

Compensation in Implementing Vertical Integration Strategies

Organizational structure and management control systems can have an important effect on the ability of a firm to implement its vertical integration strategy. However, a firm's compensation policies can be important as well.

We have already seen how compensation can play a role in implementing cost leadership and product differentiation, and how compensation can be tied to budgets to help implement vertical integration. However, the three explanations of vertical integration presented in this chapter have important compensation implications as well. We will first discuss the compensation challenges these three theories suggest and then discuss ways these challenges can be addressed.

Compensation Challenges

Opportunism-Based Vertical Integration and Compensation Policy.   When transaction costs theory is applied to the exchange between a firm and its employees, this theory suggests that employees who make firm-specific investments in their jobs will often be able to create more value for a firm than employees who do not make firm-specific investments. Firm specific investments are a type of transaction-specific investment. Whereas transaction-specific investments are investments that have more value in a particular exchange than in alternative exchanges, **firm-specific investments** are investments made by employees that have more value in a particular firm than in other firms.[33]

Examples of firm-specific investments include an employee's understanding of a particular firm's culture, his or her personal relationships with others in the firm, and an employee's knowledge about a firm's unique business processes. All this knowledge can be used by an employee to create a great deal of value in a firm. However, this knowledge has almost no value in other firms. The effort to create this knowledge is thus a firm-specific investment.

Despite the value that an employee's firm-specific investments can create, opportunism-based explanations of vertical integration suggest that employees are often reluctant to make these investments because, once they do, they become vulnerable in their exchange with this firm. For example, an employee who has made very significant firm-specific investments may not be able to quit and go to work for another company, even if this employee is passed over for promotion, does not receive a raise, or is even actively discriminated against. This is because by quitting this firm, this employee loses all the investment he or she made in this particular firm. Because this employee has few employment options other than his or her current firm, this firm can treat this employee badly and the employee can do little about it. This is why employees are often reluctant to make firm-specific investments.

However, the firm needs its employees to make such investments if it is to realize its full economic potential. Thus, one of the tasks of compensation policy is to create incentives for employees whose firm-specific investments could create great value to actually make those investments.

Capabilities and Compensation.   Capability explanations of vertical integration also acknowledge the importance of firm-specific investments in creating value for a firm. Indeed, many of the valuable, rare, and costly-to-imitate resources and capabilities that can exist in a firm are a manifestation of firm-specific investments made by a firm's employees. However, whereas opportunism explanations of vertical integration tend to focus on firm-specific investments made by individual employees, capabilities explanations tend to focus on firm-specific investments made by groups of employees.[34]

In Chapter 5 it was suggested that one of the reasons that a firm's valuable and rare resources may be costly to imitate is that these resources are socially complex in nature. Socially complex resources reflect the teamwork, cooperation, and culture that have evolved within a firm—capabilities that can increase the value of a firm significantly, but capabilities that other firms will often find costly to imitate, at least in the short to medium term. Moreover, these are capabilities that exist because several employees—not just a single employee—have made specific investments in a firm.

From the point of view of designing a compensation policy, capabilities analysis suggests that not only should a firm's compensation policy encourage employees whose firm-specific investments could create value to actually make those investments; this theory also recognizes that these investments will often be collective in nature—that, for example, until all the members of a critical management team make firm-specific commitments to that team, that team's ability to create and sustain competitive advantages will be significantly limited.

Flexibility and Compensation.   Flexibility explanations of vertical integration also have some important implications for compensation. In particular, because the creation of flexibility in a firm depends on employees being willing to engage in activities that have fixed and known downside risks and significant upside potential, it follows that compensation that has fixed and known downside risks and significant upside potential will encourage employees to choose and implement vertical integration strategies.

Compensation Alternatives

Table 10.4 lists several compensation alternatives and how they are related to each of the three explanations of vertical integration discussed in this chapter. Not surprisingly, opportunism-based explanations suggest that compensation that focuses on individual employees and how they can make firm-specific investments will be important for firms implementing their vertical integration strategies. Such individual compensation includes an employee's salary, cash bonuses based on individual performance, and **stock grants**—or payments to employees in the form of the firm's stock—based on individual performance.

Capabilities explanations of vertical integration suggest that compensation that focuses on groups of employees making firm-specific investments in valuable, rare, and costly-to-imitate resources and capabilities will be particularly important for firms implementing vertical integration strategies. Such collective compensation includes cash bonuses based on the firm's overall performance and stock grants based on the firm's overall performance.

Finally, flexibility logic suggests that compensation that has fixed and known downside risk and significant upside potential is important for firms implementing vertical integration strategies. **Stock options,** by which employees are given the right but not the obligation to purchase firm's stock at pre-determined prices, are a form of compensation that has these characteristics. Stock options can be granted based on an individual employee's performance or on the performance of the firm as a whole.

The task facing CEOs looking to implement a vertical integration strategy through compensation policy is to determine what kinds of employee behavior they need to have for this strategy to create sustained competitive advantages and then to use the appropriate compensation policy. Not surprisingly, most CEOs find that all three theories of vertical integration are important in their decision making and thus, not surprisingly, many firms adopt compensation policies that feature a mix of those policies listed in Table 10.4. Thus, most firms use both individual and corporate-wide compensation schemes along

TABLE 10.4	Types of Compensation and Approaches to Making Vertical Integration Decisions
Opportunism explanations	Salary
	Cash bonuses for individual performance
	Stock grants for individual performance
Capabilities explanations	Cash bonuses for corporate or group performance
	Stock grants for corporate or group performance
Flexibility explanations	Stock options for individual, corporate, or group performance

with salaries, cash bonuses, stock grants, and stock options for employees who have the greatest impact on a firm's overall performance.

10.5 SUMMARY

The number of stages in a product's or service's value chain in which a firm engages defines that firm's level of vertical integration. Sometimes a firm's level of vertical integration can be observed directly; sometimes it must be inferred from the firm's ratio of value added to sales.

Vertical integration is one of the governance options that firms can use to manage economic exchanges. Governance options can be grouped into three broad categories: market governance, intermediate governance, and hierarchical governance (vertical integration).

According to transaction costs logic, managers should choose the form of governance that, at the lowest cost possible, minimizes the threat of opportunistic behavior in an exchange. The threat of opportunism in an exchange depends, in turn, on the level of transaction-specific investment, uncertainty, and complexity in that exchange. In general the direct costs of governance increase as managers move from market forms of governance to hierarchical forms of governance.

According to a resource-based approach to making vertical integration decisions, firms should vertically integrate into business functions in which they currently enjoy a competitive advantage. Also, when another firm possesses valuable, rare, costly-to-imitate, and costly-to-acquire resources and capabilities, a firm may find it in its self-interest not to vertically integrate, even if there are significant threats of opportunism.

According to the real options approach to making vertical integration decisions, firms should not vertically integrate under conditions of high uncertainty. Not vertically integrating in these settings enhances a firm's flexibility.

These three approaches to making vertical integration decisions can be integrated by estimating which governance problems a firm is facing are likely to be most important in an exchange (the threat of opportunism, the need to gain or retain access to sources of competitive advantage, or the need to be flexible) and then making the appropriate governance choice.

For governance decisions to be a source of sustained competitive advantage, there must be differences in firm's ability to analyze uncertain and complex transactions, differences in a firm's ability to conceive of and implement governance devices, or differences in firm's propensity to behave opportunistically.

The most efficient organizational structure for implementing vertical integration strategies is the U-form structure. The CEO in U-form structure has two important responsibilities: strategy formulation and coordinating functions for strategy implementation. Resolving functional conflicts is likely to be particularly important in this context. A variety of management controls can also be important for implementing vertical integration. These include the budgeting process and management committees.

Compensation policy is also important in implementing vertical integration. The optimum form of compensation depends on how vertical integration is supposed to create economic value. Transaction costs, resource-based, and real options explanations of vertical integration each have different compensation implications.

REVIEW QUESTIONS

1. Some firms have engaged in backward vertical integration strategies in order to appropriate the economic profits that would have been earned by suppliers selling to them. How is this motivation for backward-vertical integration related to the transaction costs logic for vertical integration described in this chapter? (*Hint*: Compare the competitive conditions under which firms may earn economic profits to the competitive conditions under which firms will be motivated to minimize transaction costs through vertical integration.)

2. You are about to purchase a home. What kinds of opportunistic threats do you face in this purchase? What governance mechanisms can you put into place to minimize these threats?

3. Another popular explanation of vertical integration decisions made by firms is called "resource dependence theory." In this explanation, firms are assumed to pursue vertical integration strategies whenever the acquisition of a critical resource is uncertain and threatened. How is this theory of vertical integration related to the transaction costs theory, resource-based theory, and real options theory discussed in this chapter?

4. What are the competitive implications for firms if they assume that all potential exchange partners will behave opportunistically?

5. Under what conditions would you accept a lower-paying job instead of a higher-paying job? What implications does your answer have for your potential employer's compensation policy?

ENDNOTES

1. Porter, M. E., and R. Wayland (1991). "Coca-Cola vs. Pepsi-Cola and the soft drink industry," Harvard Business School Case no. 9-391-179.

2. See Adelman, M. A. (1955). "Concept and statistical measurement of vertical integration," in National Bureau for Economic Research, ed., *Business Concentration and Price Policy,* Princeton, NJ: Princeton University Press, pp. 281–322; Gort, M. (1962). *Diversification and Integration in American Industry,* Princeton, NJ: Princeton University Press; Laffer, A. (1969). "Vertical integration by corporations: 1929–1965," *Review of Economics and Statistics,* 51, pp. 91–93; Tucker, I., and R. P. Wilder (1977). "Trends in vertical integration in the U.S. manufacturing sector," *Journal of Industrial Economics,* 26, pp. 81–94; and Harrigan, K. (1986). "Matching vertical integration strategies to competitive conditions," *Strategic Management Journal,* 7, pp. 535–555.

3. Maddigan, R. (1979). "The Impact of Vertical Integration on Business Performance," unpublished doctoral dissertation, Indiana University at Bloomington.

4. Tucker, I., and R. P. Wilder (1977). "Trends in vertical integration in the U.S. manufacturing sector," *Journal of Industrial Economics,* 26, pp. 81–94.

5. See Williamson, O. E. (1975). *Markets and Hierarchies: Analysis and Antitrust Implications,* New York: Free Press.

6. See Coase, R. H. (1937). "The nature of the firm," *Economica,* 4, pp. 386–405.

7. Williamson, O. E. (1975). *Markets and Hierarchies: Analysis and Antitrust Implications,* New York: Free Press; Williamson, O. E. (1985). *The Economic Institutions of Capitalism,* New York: Free Press.

8. Williamson, O. E. (1975). *Markets and Hierarchies: Analysis and Antitrust Implications,* New York: Free Press.

9. See Barney, J. B., and W. G. Ouchi (1986). *Organizational Economics,* San Francisco: Jossey-Bass; and Barney, J. B., and W. Hesterly (1996). "Organizational economics: Understanding the relationship between organizations and economic analysis," in S. Clegg, C. Hardy, and W. Nord. eds., *Handbook of Organization Theory,* London: Sage, pp. 115–147.

10. Williamson, O. E. (1975). *Markets and Hierarchies: Analysis and Antitrust Implications,* New York: Free Press.

11. See MacDonald, J. M. (1985). "Market exchange or vertical integration: An empirical analysis," *Review of Economics and Statistics,* 67, pp. 327–331; MacMillan, I., D. C. Hambrick, and J. M. Pennings (1986). "Uncertainty reduction and the threat of supplier retaliation: Two views of the backward integration decision," *Organization Studies,* 7, pp. 263–278; and Caves, R. E., and R. M. Bradburd (1988). "The empirical determinants of vertical integration," *Journal of Economic Behavior and Organization,* 9, pp. 265–279.

12. See Armour, H. O., and D. J. Teece (1980). "Vertical integration and technological innovation," *Review of Economics and Statistics,* 60, pp. 470–474; Anderson, E., and D. Schmittlein (1984). "Integration of sales force: An empirical examination," *Rand Journal of Economics,* 15, pp. 385–395; Anderson, E. (1985). "The salesperson as outside agent or employee," *Marketing Science,* 4, pp. 234–254; John, G., and B. A. Weitz (1988). "Forward integration into distribution: An empirical test of the transaction cost analysis," *Journal of Law, Economics and Organization,* 4, pp. 337–355; and Masten, S., J. W. Meehan, and E. A. Snyder (1991). "The cost of organization," *Journal of Law, Economics and Organization,* 7, pp. 1–25.

13. See Levy, D. T. (1985). "The transactions cost approach to vertical integration: An empirical investigation," *Review of Economics and Statistics,* 67, pp. 438–445; MacDonald, J. M. (1985). "Market exchange or vertical integration: An empirical analysis," *Review of Economics and Statistics,* 67, pp. 327–331; and Caves, R. E., and R. M. Bradburd (1988). "The empirical determinants of vertical integration," *Journal of Economic Behavior and Organization,* 9, pp. 265–279.

14. See Joskow, P. L. (1988). "Asset specificity and the structure of vertical relationships," *Journal of Law, Economics and Organization,* 4, pp. 95–117; Mahoney, J. T. (1992). "The choice of organizational form: Vertical financial ownership versus other methods of vertical integration," *Strategic Management Journal,* 13, pp. 559–584; Walker, G., and D. Weber (1984). "A transaction cost approach to make-or-buy decisions," *Administrative Science Quarterly,* 29, pp. 373–391; Kogut, B. (1991). "Joint ventures and the option to expand and acquire," *Management Science,* 37, pp. 19–33; Balakrishnan, S., and M. Koza (1993). "Information asymmetry, adverse selection and joint-ventures," *Journal of Economic Behavior & Organization,* 20, pp. 99–117.

15. See Argyres, N. (1996). "Evidence on the role of firm capabilities in vertical integration decision," *Strategic Management Journal,* 17, pp. 129–150; and Barney, J. (1999). "How a firm's capabilities affect boundary decisions," *Sloan Management Review,* 40(3), pp. 137–145.

16. Collis, D. J. (1994). "Newell Company: Acquisition strategy," Harvard Business School Case no. 9-794-0610.

17. Barney, J. (1999). "How a firm's capabilities affect boundary decisions," *Sloan Management Review,* 40(3), pp. 137–145.

18. See Kanter, R. M. (1993). "FCB and Publicis (A): Forming the alliance." Harvard Business School Case no. 9-393-099.

19. Dyer, J., and W. Ouchi (1993). "Japanese style partnerships: Giving companies a competitive edge," *Sloan Management Review,* 31, 51–63.

20. See Argyres, N. (1996). "Evidence on the role of firm capabilities in vertical integration decision," *Strategic Management Journal,* 17, pp. 129–150.

21. Liebeskind, J. P. (1996). "Knowledge, strategy, and the theory of the firm," *Strategic Management Journal,* 17, pp. 93–108.

22. Coff, R. (1999). "When competitive advantage doesn't lead to performance. Resource-based theory and stakeholder bargaining power," *Organizational Science,* 10, pp. 119-133.

23. Riorden, M., and O. Williamson (1985). "Asset specificity and economic organization," *International Journal of Economic Organization,* 3, 365—378.

24. Kogut, B. (1991). "Joint ventures and the option to expand and acquire," *Management Science,* 37, pp. 19–33.

25. Mahoney, J. (1992). "The choice of organizational form: Vertical financial ownership versus other methods of vertical integration," *Strategic Management Journal,* 13, pp. 559–584.

26. Kogut, B. (1991). "Joint ventures and the option to expand and acquire," *Management Science,* 37, pp. 19–33.

27. Folta, T., and M. Leiblein, (1994). "Technology acquisition and the choice of governance by established firms: Insights from option theory in a multinomial logit model," in *Academy of Management Proceedings, 1994,* OMNIPRESS, Madison, WI: © Academy of Management, pp. 27–31.

28. Barney, J. B. (1994). "Bringing managers back in: A resource-based analysis of the role of managers in creating and sustaining competitive advantages for firms," in *Does Management Matter?* Lund, Sweden: Institute of Economic Research, Lund University, pp. 3–36; Busenitz, L., and J. Barney, (1997). "Differences between entrepreneurs and managers in large organizations: Biases and heuristics in strategic decision-making," *Journal of Business Venturing,* 12(1) pp. 9–30; and Tyler, B., and H. K. Steensma (1995). "Evaluating technological collaborative opportunities:

A cognitive modeling perspective," *Strategic Management Journal,* 16, pp. 43–70.

29. Barney, J. B. (1994). "Bringing managers back in: A resource-based analysis of the role of managers in creating and sustaining competitive advantages for firms," in *Does Management Matter?* Lund, Sweden: Institute of Economic Research, Lund University, pp. 3–310.

30. See Spence, A. M. (1973). *Market Signaling: Information Transfer in Hiring and Related Processes,* Cambridge, MA: Harvard University Press.

31. See Barney, J. B., and M. H. Hansen (1994). "Trustworthiness as a source of competitive advantage," *Strategic Management Journal,* 15 (Winter special issue), pp. 175–190.

32. See Gupta, A. K. (1987). "SBU strategies, corporate-SBU relations and SBU effectiveness in strategy implementation," *Academy of Management Journal,* 30(3), pp. 477–500.

33. Becker, G. S. (1993). *Human Capital: A Theoretical and Empirical Analysis, with Special Reference to Education,* Chicago: University of Chicago Press.

34. Barney, J. B. (1991). "Firm resources and sustained competitive advantage," *Journal of Management,* 17, pp. 99–120.

CHAPTER

11

Diversification Strategies

Chapter 10 began to explore the competitive implications of firms that operate in multiple business functions simultaneously. This chapter examines strategies under which firms broaden the range of activities even farther. However, rather than examining vertical integration and bringing additional stages of the value chain inside a firm, this chapter focuses on how bringing multiple different businesses within the boundaries of the firm can be used to create economic value. A firm that has brought multiple businesses within its boundaries has implemented a **corporate diversification strategy.** This chapter examines the economic value of corporate diversification strategies and the conditions under which they can be expected to generate competitive advantages for a firm. Chapter 12 focuses on organizing to implement a corporate diversification strategy.

11.1 TYPES OF CORPORATE DIVERSIFICATION

Firms vary in the extent to which they diversify the mix of businesses they pursue. Perhaps the simplest way of characterizing differences in the level of corporate diversification focuses on the relatedness of the businesses pursued within the boundaries of a firm. Firms can pursue a strategy of limited corporate diversification, of related corporate diversification, or of unrelated corporate diversification (see Figure 11.1).

Limited Corporate Diversification

A firm has implemented a strategy of **limited corporate diversification** when all or most of its business activities fall within a single industry (see Figure 11.1A). Two kinds of firms are included in this corporate diversification category: **single-business firms** (firms with more than 95 percent of their total sales in a single industry) and **dominant-business firms** (firms with between 70 percent and 95 percent of their total sales in a single industry). Differences between single-business and dominant-business firms are represented in Figure 11.1A. The firm that pursues a single-business corporate

FIGURE 11.1   Levels and Types of Diversification

A. Limited Diversification

• **Single business:** 95 percent or more of firm revenues comes from a single business.

• **Dominant business:** Between 70 and 95 percent of firm revenues comes from a single business.

B. Related Diversification

• **Related constrained:** Less than 70 percent of firm revenues comes from a single business, and different businesses share numerous links and common attributes.

• **Related linked:** Less than 70 percent of firm revenues comes from a single business, and different businesses share only a few links and common attributes or different links and common attributes.

C. Unrelated Diversification

• Less than 70 percent of firm revenues comes from a single business, and there are few, if any, links or common attributes among businesses.

diversification strategy, Business A, engages in only one business. The dominant-business firm, Business E, pursues two businesses, and a smaller Business F is tightly linked to Business E.[1]

In an important sense, firms that pursue a strategy of limited corporate diversification are not leveraging their resources and capabilities beyond a single market or industry. Therefore the analysis of limited corporate diversification is logically equivalent to the analysis of business-level strategies (discussed in Part II). Because these kinds of strategies have already been discussed, the remainder of this chapter focuses on corporate strategies that involve higher levels of diversification.

Related Corporate Diversification

As a firm begins to engage in businesses in more than one market or industry, it moves away from being a single-business or dominant-business firm and begins to adopt higher levels of corporate diversification. When less than 70 percent of a firm's revenues come from a single line of business and these multiple lines of business are linked, the firm has implemented a corporate strategy of **related diversification.**

The multiple businesses that a diversified firm pursues can be related in two ways (see Figure 11.1B). If all the businesses in which a firm operates share a significant number of inputs, production technologies, distribution channels, similar customers, and so forth, the corporate diversification strategy is called **related constrained.** The strategy is termed "constrained" because corporate managers pursue business opportunities in new markets or industries only if those markets or industries share numerous resource and capability requirements with the businesses the firm is currently pursuing. Commonalities across businesses in a strategy of related constrained diversification are represented by the linkages among Businesses K, L, M, and N in the related constrained section of Figure 11.1B.

If the different businesses that a single firm pursues are linked on only a couple of dimensions, or if different sets of businesses are linked along very different dimensions, the corporate diversification strategy is called **related linked.** For example, Business Q and Business R may share similar production technology, Business R and Business S may share similar customers, Business S and Business T may share similar suppliers, and Business Q and Business T may have no common attributes. This strategy is represented in the related linked section of Figure 11.1B by businesses with relatively few links between them and with different kinds of links between them (that is, straight lines and curved lines).

Unrelated Corporate Diversification

Firms that pursue a strategy of related corporate diversification have some type of linkages among most, if not all, the different businesses they pursue. However, it is possible for firms to pursue numerous different businesses and for there to be no linkages among these businesses (see Figure 11.1C). When less than 70 percent of a firm's revenues are generated by a single business, and when a firm's businesses share few, if any, common attributes, then that firm is pursuing a strategy of **unrelated corporate diversification.**

11.2 THE ECONOMIC VALUE OF CORPORATE DIVERSIFICATION

In order for corporate diversification to be economically valuable, two conditions must hold. First, there must be some economy of scope among the multiple businesses in which a firm is operating. Second, it must be more efficient to manage these economies of scope through hierarchical forms of governance than through alternative intermediate or market forms of governance.

Valuable Economies of Scope

Economies of scope are valuable when the value of the multiple businesses in which a firm operates is greater than the value of these businesses operating independently. This concept can be formalized as

$$NPV \sum_{i=1}^{n} B_i > NPV\,(B_1) + NPV\,(B_2) + \cdots + NPV(B_n) \qquad \textbf{(11.1)}$$

where

$$NVP(B_i) = \text{the present value of Business } i$$

Without the existen e of economies of scope, there can be no economic reason to operate in several businesses simultaneously.

In general, economies of scope exist because of the cost savings or revenue enhancements that a firm experiences because of the mix of business in which it operates. Certainly one of the ways that a firm operating in multiple businesses can reduce its costs is to realize economies of scale across its multiple businesses. This can occur, for example, if these multiple businesses all use a common input and if the cost of this common input falls as a function of its volume of production. Thus, economies of scale can be an example of an economy of scope. However, as will be shown later in this chapter, there are numerous examples of economies of scope that do not depend on economies of scale.

Hierarchical Governance and Economies of Scope

The existence of economies of scope—by itself—is only a necessary, not a sufficient, condition for corporate diversification to be economically valuable. Using the logic presented in Chapter 10, the existence of economies of scope, per se, does not mean that a firm must bring multiple businesses within its boundaries to realize these economies. Rather, in order for corporate diversification to be economically valuable, not only must economies of scope exist, it must be less costly to realize these economies within the boundaries of a single firm than through alternative forms of governance. These alternative forms of governance include both intermediate and hierarchical forms of governance.[2]

Thus, the logical apparatus originally developed in Chapter 10 for making vertical integration decisions is also important for making corporate diversification decisions. Whereas exchange value was an important prerequisite for making vertical integration decisions, the existence of economies of scope is an important prerequisite for making corporate diversification decisions. Given these prerequisites, the choice of how to organize an exchange—be it vertical integration or corporate diversification—depends on transaction costs, capabilities, and real options considerations.

If the level of transaction-specific investment in realizing an economy of scope across several businesses is likely to be high, then the threat of opportunism in realizing that economy through nonhierarchical means is also likely to be high, and transaction costs economics suggests that this exchange should be managed through hierarchical governance. In Chapter 10, hierarchical governance implied vertical integration. In this chapter, hierarchical governance implies corporate diversification.

If a firm already possesses valuable, rare, and costly-to-imitate resources and capabilities and seeks to use these capabilities to create economies of scope, then this effort should take place within the boundaries of that firm. Corporate diversification, in this context, enables a firm to keep the sources of its economy of scope–based competitive advantage more proprietary. Also, by managing these economies of scope within its own boundaries, a firm can appropriate more of the economic profits it generates. On the other hand, if another firm possess valuable, rare, and costly-to-imitate resources that can create an economy of scope, but the cost of acquiring or developing these resources is too high (because of their path-dependent, uncertain, or socially complex characteristics), corporate diversification and the use of hierarchical governance to realize these potential economies of scope may be too costly. In this context, an intermediate governance mechanism is the preferred form of governance for realizing these economies of scope. This may be the case even if there are significant threats of opportunism in this exchange. Such strategic alliances are discussed in more detail in Chapter 13.

Finally, if there is considerable uncertainty about the value of an economy of scope, then real options logic (as developed in both Chapter 8 and Chapter 10) suggests that a firm should opt for less hierarchical forms of governance to realize this economy, thereby maintaining its strategic flexibility.

Taken together, the application of the vertical integration logic developed in Chapter 10 to decisions about how to organize the realization of economies of scope suggests that corporate diversification is economically valuable only when alternative ways of realizing these economies are not effective. These other ways of realizing economies of scope are not likely to be effective when large transaction-specific investments are required to realize an economy of scope and when an economy of scope is likely to be a source of sustained competitive advantage for a diversifying firm.

Hierarchical Governance and Equity Holders' Interests in Corporate Diversification

The application of the governance logic originally developed in Chapter 10 to corporate diversification helps clarify the conditions under which a firm's outside equity holders find it in their self-interest to invest in a firm that is pursuing a corporate diversification strategy. In general, outside equity investors can gain many of the economies of scope associated with diversification on their own without the involvement of a firm's managers. They do this by investing in a diversified portfolio of stocks. Moreover, these equity investors can realize these economies of scope at almost zero cost. In this situation, it makes little economic sense for outside equity investors to "hire" managers in a firm to manage diversification for them, especially because organizing a diversified firm can be very costly (see Chapter 12). Rather, from the point of view of outside equity investors in a firm, it makes economic sense for a firm to engage in a corporate diversification strategy only when that strategy exploits economies of scope that these investors, on their own, would find too costly to realize by simply owning the stocks of different companies in a diversified portfolio.

When will a firm's equity investors find it too costly to realize an economy of scope on their own? Governance logic suggests that equity investors will find it too costly to realize an economy on scope of their own when the realization of that economy of scope by a particular firm is characterized by high levels of transaction-specific investment or when that economy of scope can be a source of sustained competitive advantage. When the realization of a particular economy of scope would be characterized by high transaction-specific investment, outside equity holders will want to hire managers to govern this exchange directly. In this setting, bringing multiple businesses within the boundaries of a firm creates economic value for outside equity holders because managers are in a much better position to deal with opportunism problems than outside equity holders would be able to. When an economy of scope has the potential for generating sustained competitive advantage, that economy of scope must be valuable, rare, and costly to imitate. As was suggested in Chapter 5, rare and costly-to-imitate resources and capabilities are often difficult for outsiders to understand and appreciate. In this context, outside equity investors will want to hire managers who can develop an intimate understanding of the valuable, rare, and costly-to-imitate economies of scope controlled in a firm. Thus, bringing multiple businesses within the boundaries of a firm in this setting also creates economic value for outside equity holders.

As an aside, the fact that outside equity holders will find it in their self-interest for a firm to pursue corporate diversification strategies only when these equity holders cannot pursue these strategies on their own creates some interesting organizational challenges. Because outside equity holders cannot pursue these opportunities on their own, they must rely on managers to pursue them. However, managerial interests and equity holders' interests in pursuing diversification strategies may not always coincide. This can lead to the agency problems discussed in more detail in Chapter 12.[3]

Several potential economies of scope that could lead to corporate diversification have been identified in the literature. Some of the most important of these motivations are listed in Table 11.1. These motivations can vary in how they meet the two value-creating criteria. Some of these motivations are based on real economies of scope, but outside investors can create them at low cost on their own. Some cannot be created by outside investors, but whether the inequality in equation 11.1 is met is less clear. And, some meet both criteria.

Diversification to Exploit Operational Economies of Scope

Sometimes, economies of scope may reflect operational links among the businesses in which a firm engages. **Operational economies of scope** typically take one of two forms: shared activities and shared core competencies.

Shared Activities

In Chapter 5 it was suggested that value-chain analysis can be used to describe the specific business activities of a firm. This same value-chain analysis can also be used to describe the business activities that may be shared across several different businesses within a diversified firm. These **shared activities** are potential sources of operational economies of scope for diversified firms.

Consider, for example, the hypothetical firm presented in Figure 11.2. This diversified firm engages in three businesses: A, B, and C. However, these three businesses share a variety of activities throughout their value chains. For example, all three draw on the same technology development operation. Product design and manufacturing

---

TABLE 11.1   Motivations for Implementing a Diversification Strategy

1. Operational economies of scope
   - Shared activities
   - Core competencies
2. Financial economies of scope
   - Internal capital allocation
   - Risk reduction
   - Tax advantages
3. Anticompetitive economies of scope
   - Multipoint competition
   - Exploiting market power
4. Employee and stakeholder incentives for diversification
   - Diversifying employees' human capital investments
   - Diversifying the risk of nonemployee stakeholders
   - Maximizing management compensation

FIGURE 11.2 A Hypothetical Firm Sharing Activities Among Three Businesses

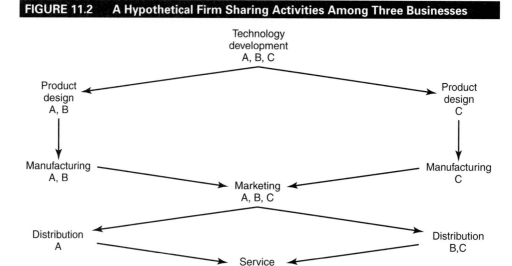

are shared in Businesses A and B and separate for Business C. All three businesses share a common marketing and service operation. Business A has its own distribution system.

These kinds of shared activities are quite common among both related-constrained and related-linked diversified firms. At Texas Instruments, for example, a variety of electronics businesses share some research and development activities and often share common manufacturing locations. Procter & Gamble's numerous different consumer products businesses often share common manufacturing locations and rely on a common distribution network (through retail grocery stores).[4]

A variety of lists of ways in which activities can link different businesses in a firm have been developed. Some of the most important of these activity linkages, and their position in a business's value chain, are summarized in Table 11.2. Shared activities can add value to a firm by reducing costs or by increasing the willingness of customers to pay.[5]

Shared Activities and Cost Reduction. Sources of cost advantage for firms were described in Chapter 6. Some of these sources of cost advantage may be obtained through activity sharing across businesses in a diversified firm. For example, if several businesses in a diversified firm manufacture similar products and services, and if there are important economies of scale in this manufacturing process, then a diversified firm may be able to capture the cost advantages associated with these economies of scale by sharing these manufacturing activities among its different businesses. Each business, then, can enjoy cost advantages that would otherwise be possible only if the business were large enough, as an independent entity, to exploit these economies of scale. Such savings are not restricted to manufacturing businesses.

Activity sharing can also enable a diversified firm to obtain cost reductions based on learning-curve economies. It may be that each business in a diversified firm, acting independently, does not have a sufficiently high level of cumulative volume of production to exploit learning and reduce costs. However, if these businesses are able to share

TABLE 11.2 Possible Shared Activities and Their Place in the Value Chain	
Value Chain Activity	*Shared Activities*
Input activities	Common purchasing chain
	Common inventory control system
	Common warehousing facilities
	Common inventory delivery system
	Common quality assurance
	Common input requirements system
	Common suppliers
Production activities	Common product components
	Common product components manufacturing
	Common assembly facilities
	Common quality control system
	Common maintenance operation
	Common inventory control system
Warehousing and distribution	Common product delivery system
	Common warehouse facilities
Sales and marketing	Common advertising efforts
	Common promotional activities
	Cross-selling of products
	Common pricing systems
	Common marketing departments
	Common distribution channels
	Common sales forces
	Common sales offices
	Common order processing services
Dealer support and service	Common service network
	Common guarantees and warranties
	Common accounts receivable management systems
	Common dealer training
	Common dealer support services

Source: Porter, M. E. (1985). *Competitive Advantage,* New York: Free Press; Rumelt, R. P. (1974). *Strategy, Structure, and Economic Performance.* Cambridge, MA: Harvard University Press; Ansoff, H. I. (1965). *Corporate Strategy.* New York: McGraw-Hill.

critical activities, the cumulative volume in these activities will rise more quickly, accelerating any learning opportunities that might exist and thereby reducing the costs of each business in the diversified firm.

Activity sharing may also enable a firm that has developed low-cost production technology in one of its businesses, or a common technology development laboratory, to reduce the direct production costs of each of the firm's businesses. Moreover, each business is spared the high costs associated with developing this production technology on its own.

Finally, it may be that one business in a diversified firm has obtained differential access to certain factors of production—raw materials, employees, managerial talent, and technology. If several of this firm's businesses draw on these same factors of production, then activity sharing can have the effect of reducing the supply costs of all these businesses. Again, these businesses will have lower costs than they would have had if they were not part of this diversified firm and thus did not have differential access to the factors of production through shared activities.

Failure to exploit shared activities across businesses can lead to out-of-control costs. For example, Kentucky Fried Chicken, when it was a division of PepsiCo, encouraged each of its regional business operations in North America to develop its own quality improvement plan. The result was enormous redundancy and at least three conflicting quality efforts—all leading to higher-than-necessary costs. In a similar way, Levi Strauss's unwillingness to centralize and coordinate order processing led to a situation in which six separate order-processing computer systems operated simultaneously. This costly redundancy was ultimately replaced by a single, integrated ordering system shared across the entire corporation.[6]

Shared Activities and Revenue Enhancement. Lower costs are often central to obtaining economies of scope through shared activities, but such sharing can also increase the revenues in diversified firms' businesses. This can happen in at least two ways.

First, shared product development and sales activities may enable two or more businesses in a diversified firm to offer a bundled set of products to customers. Sometimes, the value of these "product bundles" to customers is greater than the value of each product separately. This greater customer value can generate revenues for each business that are greater than what would have been the case if the businesses were not together and sharing activities in a diversified firm.

In the telecommunications industry, for example, separate firms sell telephones, access to telephone lines, equipment to route calls in an office, mobile telephones, and paging services. A customer who requires all these services could contact five different companies. Each of these five different firms would likely possess its own unique technological standards and software, making the development of an integrated telecommunications system for the customer difficult at best. Alternatively, a single diversified firm sharing sales activities across these businesses could significantly reduce the search costs of potential customers. This one-stop shopping is likely to be valuable to customers, who might be willing to pay a slightly higher price for this convenience than they would pay if they purchased these services from five separate firms. Moreover, if this diversified firm also shares some technology development activities across its businesses, it might be able to offer an integrated telecommunications network to potential customers. The extra value of this integrated network for customers is very likely to be reflected in prices that are higher than the prices that would have been possible if each of these businesses were independent or if activities among these businesses were not shared. Most of the remaining telephone operating companies in the United States are attempting to gain these economies of scope.[7]

Such product bundles are important in other types of firms as well. Many grocery stores now sell prepared foods alongside traditional grocery products, in the belief that busy customers want access to all kinds of food products in the same location.[8]

Second, shared activities can enhance business revenues by exploiting the strong, positive reputations of some of a firm's businesses in other of its businesses. For example, if one business has a strong positive reputation for high-quality manufacturing, other businesses sharing this manufacturing activity will gain some of the advantages of this reputation. And, if one business has a strong positive reputation for selling high-performance products, other businesses sharing sales and marketing activities with this business will gain some of the advantages of this reputation. In both cases, businesses that draw on another business's strong reputation through shared activities with that business will have larger revenues than if these businesses were operating on their own.

Shared Activities, Hierarchical Governance, and Outside Investors.   If shared activities in a diversified firm reduce the firm's costs or increase the willingness of customers to pay compared to a non-diversified firm, then the inequality in equation 11.1 holds—that is, shared activities are an operational economy of scope. However, for shared activities to be a valuable basis for corporate diversification, it must be more costly to manage this economy of scope through non-hierarchical means than hierarchical means, or, equivalently, it must be more costly for outside equity investors to realize this economy of scope than for the diversified firm to realize it.

In general, outside investors have limited ability to exploit shared activities among businesses. Such activity sharing typically requires a level of organizational control and integration that is characteristic of hierarchical governance. This usually cannot be duplicated in a diversified portfolio of stocks. Moreover, to the extent that this economy of scope may be a source of a sustained competitive advantage, its realization requires insights and information that are not typically available to outside equity investors.

The Limits of Activity Sharing

Despite the potential of activity sharing to be the basis of a valuable corporate diversification strategy, this approach has three important limits.[9] First, substantial organizational issues are often associated with a diversified firm's learning how to manage cross-business relationships. Managing these relationships effectively can be very difficult, and failure can lead to excess bureaucracy, inefficiency, and organizational gridlock. These organizational issues are discussed in detail in Chapter 12.

Second, sharing activities may limit the ability of a particular business to meet its specific customers' needs. For example, if two businesses share manufacturing activities, they may reduce their manufacturing costs by exploiting economies of scale. However, to exploit these economies of scale, these businesses may need to build products using somewhat standardized components that do not fully meet their individual customers' needs. Businesses that share distribution activities may have lower overall distribution costs but be unable to distribute their products to all their customers. Businesses that share sales activities may have lower overall sales costs but be unable to provide the specialized selling required in each business.

Third, activity sharing that exploits the reputation of one business in other firm businesses can go both ways. If one business in a diversified firm has a poor reputation, sharing activities with that business can reduce the quality of the reputation of other businesses in the firm.

Taken together, these limits on activity sharing can more than offset any possible gains. Indeed, over the last decade, more and more diversified firms have been abandoning efforts at activity sharing in favor of managing each business's activities independently. For example, ABB, Inc. (a Swiss engineering firm), and CIBA-Geigy (a Swiss chemicals firm) have adopted explicit corporate policies that restrict almost all activity sharing across businesses.[10] Other diversified firms, including Nestlé and General Electric, restrict activity sharing to just one or two activities (such as research and development or management training). However, to the extent that a diversified firm can exploit shared activities while avoiding these problems, shared activities can add value to a firm.

Core Competencies

Recently, a second operational linkage among the businesses of a diversified firm has been described. Unlike shared activities, this linkage is based on different businesses in a diversified firm sharing less tangible resources such as managerial and technical know-how, experience, and wisdom. This source of operational economy of scope has been called a firm's **core competence.**[11] Core competence has been defined by Prahalad and Hamel as "the collective learning in the organization, especially how to coordinate diverse production skills and integrate multiple streams of technologies." Core competencies are complex sets of resources and capabilities that link different businesses in a diversified firm through managerial and technical know-how, experience, and wisdom.

For example, some observers have argued that 3M has a core competence in substrates, adhesives, and coatings. Collectively, employees at 3M know more about applying adhesives and coatings on different kinds of substrates than do managers in any other organization. Over the years, 3M has applied these resources and capabilities in a wide variety of products, including Post-it notes, magnetic tape, photographic film, pressure-sensitive tape, and coated abrasives. At first glance, this widely diversified set of products seem to have little or nothing in common. Certainly these different businesses share few, if any, specific business activities. Yet they all draw on a single core set of resources and capabilities in substrates, adhesives, and coatings.

Honda also manufactures and sells a wide range of products—luxury automobiles, motorcycles, lawn mowers, and portable electric generators. These numerous products all draw on a single core competence in the manufacturing of engines and power trains. Some of these common resources and capabilities are exploited at Honda through shared activities among businesses. However, most of these businesses share few, if any, activities but are nevertheless linked by a core competence.

When a diversified firm exploits a core competence, the operations within each of its different businesses are significantly affected by the accumulated knowledge, experience, and wisdom gained from the firm's previous business activities. These different businesses may all exploit similar technologies, they may address similar kinds of customers, or they may adopt similar management principles. Although these businesses may differ in important ways, managers moving from one of these businesses to another will experience many common elements, despite the firm's diversification strategy.[12]

Core Competencies and Shared Activities. Core competencies may or may not exist in parallel with shared activities. For example, most observers would agree that Hanson Trust, PLC, had a well-defined core competence in the acquisition and management of

businesses in mature markets.[13] Indeed, the essential elements of this core competence can be described in a series of guiding principles (see Table 11.3). Over the
years, Hanson Trust has developed certain management principles and has applied
them to managing of each of the mature businesses it has acquired. Despite the clear
core competence that exists at Hanson Trust, the different businesses share virtually
no activities. Indeed, the lack of activity sharing among Hanson businesses is a manifestation of Hanson's core competence in acquiring and managing businesses in mature markets.

It would be easy to conclude that a firm such as Hanson Trust, which does not
share activities among its businesses, is pursuing a strategy of unrelated diversification.
However, the existence of a well-defined core competence at Hanson suggests that this
seemingly unrelated diversification is in fact a type of related diversification. Indeed,
because all of Hanson's businesses must meet all of the criteria in Table 11.3, from this
core competence perspective, Hanson is actually pursuing a strategy of related constrained diversification.

Core Competencies as an Economy of Scope   To understand how core competencies
can reduce a firm's costs or increase the willingness of customers to pay, it is necessary
to understand how core competencies emerge over time. Most firms begin operations
in a single business. Imagine that a firm has carefully evaluated all of its current business opportunities and has fully funded all of those with a positive net present value.

TABLE 11.3	Core Competencies at Hanson Trust—A Seemingly Unrelated Diversified Firm

When considering a potential acquisition:

1. Focus on mature, low-technology industries with low current performance where current management has made some progress toward improving performance.
2. Engage in intensive research, summarized on a single page, into a firm's performance and prospects, especially for firms contemplating a leveraged buyout.
3. Evaluate the size and likelihood of the downside risk of an acquisition—the implications for Hanson if everything goes wrong.
4. Evaluate the possibility of using the target's assets to secure debt for the acquisition effort.
5. Evaluate the ability of disposing of some of the target's current businesses to pay down the debt from the acquisition.
6. Evaluate how much excess overhead in a potential target can be eliminated after an acquisition.

After an acquisition has occurred:

1. Eliminate excess overhead, sell off unwanted businesses, and reduce debt.
2. Delegate to business managers all day-to-day operational decisions below capital expenditure limits set by Hanson.
3. Exercise tight financial controls through operating budgets and capital spending limits.
4. Create incentives, including bonuses, for business managers to meet their operating budget targets within their capital spending limits.
5. Do not appoint business managers to Hanson's board of directors.
6. De-emphasize any possible operating economies of scope among Hanson businesses.

Source: Adapted from Charles Hill, "Hanson PLC," in Charles Hill and Gareth Jones (1992). *Strategic Management,* 2nd ed. Boston: Houghton Mifflin, pp. 764–783.

Any of the economic profits that this firm has left over after fully funding all its current positive net present value opportunities can be thought of as **free cash flow.**[14] Firms can spend this free cash in a variety of ways: They can spend it on managerial perquisites; they can give it to shareholders; they can use it to invest in new businesses.

Suppose a firm chooses to use this cash to invest in a new business. In other words, suppose a firm chooses to implement a diversification strategy. If this firm is seeking to maximize the return from implementing this diversification strategy, which of all the possible businesses that it could invest in should it invest in? Obviously, a profit-maximizing firm will choose to begin operations in a business in which it has a competitive advantage. What kind of business is likely to generate this competitive advantage for this firm? The obvious answer is a business in which the same underlying resources and capabilities that gave this firm an advantage in its original business are still valuable, rare, and costly to imitate. Consequently, this first diversification move sees the firm investing in a business that is closely related to its original business, in that both businesses draw on a common set of underlying resources and capabilities in which the firm already has a competitive advantage.

Put another way, a firm that diversifies by exploiting its resource and capability advantages in its original business will have lower costs than a firm that begins a new business without these resource and capability advantages, or its customers will be willing to pay them more than firms that lack these advantages, or both. As long as this firm organizes itself to take advantage of these resources and capability advantages in its new business, it should earn an economic profit in its new business along with the profits it will still be earning in its original business.[15]

Of course, over time, this diversified firm is likely to develop new resources and capabilities through its operations in the new business. These new resources and capabilities enhance the entire set of skills that the firm may be able to bring to still another business. Using the profits it has obtained in its previous businesses, this firm is likely to enter another new business. Again, choosing from among all the new businesses it could enter, it is likely to begin operations in a business in which it can exploit its now-expanded resource and capability advantages to obtain a competitive advantage, and so forth.

After a firm has engaged in this diversification strategy several times, the resources and capabilities that enable it to operate successfully in several businesses are its core competencies. A firm develops these core competencies by transferring the technical and management knowledge, experience, and wisdom it developed in earlier businesses to its new diversified businesses. A firm that has just begun this diversification process has implemented a dominant-business strategy. If all of a firm's businesses share the same core competencies, then that firm has implemented a strategy of related constrained diversification. If different businesses exploit different groups of resources and capabilities, that firm has implemented a strategy of related linked diversification. In any case, these core competencies enable firms to have lower costs or increase their customers willingness to pay as they include more businesses in their diversified portfolio, compared to firms without these competencies.

Of course, not all firms develop core competencies in this logical and rational manner. As was the case with emergent strategies (discussed in Chapter 1), some core competencies emerge over time as firms attempt to rationalize their diversification moves. However, no matter how a firm develops core competencies, to the extent that it enables a diversified firm to have lower costs or larger revenues in its business operations, these competencies can be thought of as sources of economies of scope.

Core Competencies, Hierarchical Governance, and Outside Investors.   As with shared activities, outside investors have little ability to create or exploit core competence links between businesses on their own. Rather, they must "hire" firms to create and exploit these operational economies of scope for them. Therefore, if core competencies do create economies of scope, it is likely that they will have to be realized with firms that pursue a corporate diversification strategy.

If core competencies do not create economies of scope, however, they will not be economically valuable even though outside investors cannot exploit them on their own. For example, PepsiCo tried to leverage its marketing skills learned in the soft drink industry by entering the fast-food industry through its acquisition of Pizza Hut, Taco Bell, and Kentucky Fried Chicken. PepsiCo experienced only moderate success in these diversification moves. This level of success ultimately led PepsiCo to spin off its fast-food operations.[16] Kodak has had similar difficulties leveraging its imaging skills in the emerging digital-imaging industry, as has PolyGram in leveraging its entertainment expertise in the movie industry.[17] In all these cases, core competence–based economies of scope proved illusory.

The Limits of Core Competencies.   Just as there are limits to the value of shared activities as sources of economies of scope, so there are limits on core competencies as sources of these economies. The first of these limitations stems from important organizational issues to be discussed in Chapter 12. The way that a diversified firm is organized can either facilitate the exploitation of core competencies or prevent this exploitation from occurring.

A second limitation of core competencies is a result of the intangible nature of these economies of scope. Whereas shared activities are reflected in tangible operations in a diversified firm, core competencies may be reflected only in shared knowledge, experience, and wisdom across businesses. The intangible character of these relationships is emphasized when they are described as a **dominant logic** in a firm, or a common way of thinking about strategy across different businesses.[18] The intangibility of core competencies can lead diversified firms to make two kinds of errors in managing relatedness. First, intangible core competencies can be illusory inventions by creative managers to justify poor diversification moves. Managers can always find some intangible core competencies to link even the most completely unrelated businesses and thereby justify their diversification strategy. A firm that manufactures airplanes and running shoes can rationalize this diversification by claiming to have a core competence in managing transportation businesses. A firm operating in the professional football business and the movie business can rationalize this diversification by claiming to have a core competence in managing entertainment businesses. Such **invented competencies** are not real sources of economies of scope.

Finally, a diversified firm's businesses may be linked by a core competence, but this competence may affect these businesses in a trivial way. Thus, for example, all of a firm's businesses may be affected by government actions, but the effects of these actions on costs and revenues in different businesses may be quite small. A firm may have a core competence in managing relationships with the government, but this core competence will not reduce costs or enhance revenues for these particular businesses very much. Also, each of a diversified firm's businesses may use some advertising. However, if advertising does not have a major effect on revenues for these businesses, core competencies in advertising are not likely to reduce a firm's costs significantly or increase the willingness of its customers to pay. In this case, a core competence may be a source of economies of scope, but the value of those economies may be very small.

If a firm possesses core competencies and is able to avoid the limitations of this type of operational economy of scope, core competencies can be valuable for a firm pursuing corporate diversification.

Diversification to Exploit Financial Economies of Scope

A second class of motivations for diversification shifts attention away from operational linkages among a firm's businesses and toward financial advantages associated with diversification. Three financial implications of diversification have been studied: diversification and capital allocation, diversification and risk reduction, and tax advantages of diversification.

Diversification and Capital Allocation

Capital can be allocated to businesses in one of two ways. First, businesses operating as independent entities can compete for capital in the external capital market. They do this by providing a sufficiently high return to induce investors to purchase shares of their equity, by having a sufficiently high cash flow to repay principal and interest on debt, and in other ways. Alternatively, a business can be part of a diversified firm. That diversified firm competes in the external capital market and allocates capital among its various businesses. In a sense, diversification creates an **internal capital market** in which businesses in a diversified firm compete for corporate capital.[19]

Internal Capital Allocation as an Economy of Scope. For an internal capital market to create value for a diversified firm, it must offer some efficiency advantages over an external capital market. It has been suggested that a potential efficiency gain from internal capital markets depends on the greater amount and quality of information that a diversified firm possesses about the businesses it owns, compared with the information that external suppliers of capital possess. Owning a business gives a diversified firm access to detailed and accurate information about the actual performance of the business, its true future prospects, and thus the actual amount of capital that should be allocated to it. External sources of capital, in contrast, have relatively limited access to information and thus have limited ability to judge the actual performance and future prospects of a business.

Some have questioned whether a diversified firm, as a source of capital, actually has more and better information about a business it owns, compared to external sources of capital. After all, independent businesses seeking capital have a strong incentive to provide sufficient information to external suppliers of capital to obtain required funds. However, a firm that owns a business may have at least two informational advantages over external sources of capital.

First, although an independent business has an incentive to provide information to external sources of capital, it also has an incentive to downplay or even not report any negative information about its performance and prospects (recall the discussion on the limits of accounting measures of performance in Chapter 2). Such negative information would raise an independent firm's cost of capital. External sources of capital have limited ability to force a business to reveal all information about its performance and prospects and thus may provide capital at a lower cost than they would if they had full information. Ownership gives a firm the right to compel more complete disclosure, although even then full disclosure is not guaranteed. With this more complete information, a diversified firm can allocate just the right amount of capital, at the appropriate cost, to each business.

Second, an independent business may have an incentive not to reveal all the positive information about its performance and prospects. In Chapter 5, the ability of a firm to earn superior profits was shown to depend on the imitability of a firm's resources and capabilities. An independent business that informs external sources of capital about all of its sources of competitive advantage is also informing its potential competitors about these sources of advantage. This information sharing increases the probability that these sources of advantage will be imitated. Because of the competitive implications of sharing information, firms may choose not to share it, and external sources of capital may underestimate the true performance and prospects of a business.

A diversified firm, however, may gain access to this additional positive information about its businesses without revealing it to potential competitors. This information enables the diversified firm to make more informed decisions about how much capital to allocate to a business and about the cost of that capital, compared to the cost in the external capital market.[20]

Over time, there should be fewer errors in funding businesses through internal capital markets, compared to funding businesses through external capital markets. Fewer funding errors, over time, suggest a slight capital allocation advantage for a diversified firm compared to an external capital market. This advantage should be reflected in somewhat higher rates of return on invested capital for the diversified firm, compared to the rates of return on invested capital for external sources of capital.

However, the businesses within a diversified firm do not always gain cost-of-capital advantages by being part of a diversified firm's portfolio. Several authors have argued that because a diversified firm has lower overall risk (see the following discussion), it will have a lower cost of capital, which it can pass along to the businesses within its portfolio. Although the lower risks associated with a diversified firm may lower the firm's cost of capital, the appropriate cost of capital of businesses within the firm depends on the performance and prospects of each of those businesses. The firm's advantages in evaluating performance and prospects of it's businesses result in more appropriate capital allocation, not just in lower cost of capital for those businesses. Indeed, a business's cost of capital may be lower than what it could have obtained in the external capital market (because the firm is able to more fully evaluate the low-risk nature of that business), or it may be higher than what it could have obtained in the external capital market (because the firm is able to more fully evaluate the risky nature of that business).

Capital Allocation, Hierarchical Governance, and Outside Investors.   If diversified firms possess capital allocation advantages over external capital markets, then outside investors will typically be unable to duplicate this advantage. Consequently, to gain the benefits of these capital allocation economies of scope, outside investors will have to rely on the managers of a diversified firm.

An obvious exception to this generalization exists if an outside investor happens to possess the same type and quality of information about the prospects of a business as the managers of a diversified firm possess. Armed with such information, such investors could duplicate the advantages of internal capital markets on their own.

Limits on Internal Capital Markets. Although internal capital allocation has several potential advantages for a diversified firm, there are also several limits to this process. First, the level and type of diversification that a firm pursues can affect the efficiency of this allocation process. A firm that implements a strategy of unrelated diversification, in which managers have to evaluate the performance and prospects of numerous very different businesses, puts a greater strain on the capital allocation skills of its managers than does a firm that implements related diversification. Indeed, in the extreme, the capital allocation efficiency of a firm pursuing broad-based unrelated diversification will probably not be superior to the capital allocation efficiency of the external capital market.

Second, the increased efficiency of internal capital allocation depends on managers in a diversified firm having better information for capital allocation than the information available to external sources of capital. However, this higher-quality information is not guaranteed. The incentives that can lead managers to exaggerate their performance and prospects to external capital sources can also lead to this behavior within a diversified firm. Indeed, several examples of business managers falsifying performance records to gain access to more internal capital have been reported.[21] Research suggests that capital allocation requests by managers are routinely discounted in diversified firms in order to correct for these managers' inflated estimates of the performance and prospects of their businesses.[22]

Finally, not only do business managers have an incentive to inflate the performance and prospects of their business in a diversified firm, managers in charge of capital allocation in these firms may have an incentive to continue investing in a business despite its poor performance and prospects. The reputation and status of these managers often depend on the success of these business investments, because they often initially approved them. These managers often continue throwing good money at these businesses in the hope that they will someday improve, thereby justifying their original decision. Organizational psychologists call this process **escalation of commitment** and have presented numerous examples of managers becoming irrationally committed to a particular investment.[23]

Indeed, research on the value of internal capital markets in diversified firms suggests that, on average, the limitations of these markets often outweigh their advantages. For example, even controlling for firm size, excessive investment in poorly performing businesses in a diversified firm reduces the market value of the average diversified firm.[24] However, the fact that many firms do not gain the advantages associated with internal capital markets does not necessarily imply that no firms gain these advantages. If only a few firms are able to obtain the advantages of internal capital markets while successfully avoiding their limitations, this financial economy of scope may be a source of at least a temporary competitive advantage.

Diversification and Risk Reduction

Another possible financial economy of scope for a diversified firm has already been mentioned briefly—that is, the riskiness of the cash flows of diversified firms is lower than the riskiness of the cash flows of undiversified firms. Consider, for example, the risk of two businesses operating separately, compared to the risk of a diversified firm operating in those same two businesses simultaneously. If the risk of the cash flows in Business I (measured by the standard deviation of those cash flows over time) is sd_I, and the risk of cash flows in Business II (measured by the standard deviation of those cash flows over time) is sd_{II}, and if these two returns are distributed normally, then the risk of the cash flows of a diversified firm operating in both businesses simultaneously is given by

$$sd_{I, II} = \sqrt{w^2\, sd_I^{\,2} + (1 - w)^2\, sd_{II} + 2w(1 - w)COV_{I, II}} \qquad \textbf{(11.2)}$$

where

$sd_{I, II}$ = the riskiness of the combined business' cash flows
w = the percentage of the total investment in this diversified firm invested in Business I
$(1 - w)$ = the percentage of the total investment in this diversified firm invested in Business II
$COV_{I, II}$ = the correlation of the cash flows of Business I and Business II times the standard deviation of cash flows in Business I and Business II

or

$$COV_{I, II} = r_{I, II}\, sd_I\, sd_{II} \qquad \textbf{(11.3)}$$

where

$r_{I, II}$ = the correlation of the cash flows of Business I and Business II

If $sd_I = .8$, $sd_{II} = 1.3$, $w = .4$, and $r_{I, II} = -.8$, then equation 11.2 becomes

$$sd_{I, II} = \sqrt{(.4)^2(.8)^2 + (1 - .4)^2(1.2)^2 + 2(.4)(1 - .4)[(-.8)(.8)(1.3)]} = .558 \quad \textbf{(11.4)}$$

Notice that the risk of engaging in Business I and Business II simultaneously (.558) is less than the risk of engaging either in Business I by itself (.8) or in Business II by itself (1.3). This risk of engaging in both businesses simultaneously will be lower, compared to engaging in at least one of these businesses, as long as the cash flows from Business I and Business II are not perfectly and positively correlated—that is, as long as $r_{I,II} < 1.0$. For example, if $r_{I,II} = -.2$, then $sd_{I, II} = .782$ (the diversified firm is still less risky than either business operated separately); if $r_{I, II} = .7$, then $sd_{I,II} = 1.0296$ (the diversified firm is riskier than Business I by itself but less risky than Business II by itself). Of course, this analysis can be generalized to firms pursuing more than two businesses simultaneously. It can also be generalized to multiple businesses whose returns are not normally distributed.[25] The fundamental conclusion of this analysis remains unchanged: Firms can reduce their overall risk by engaging in multiple businesses with imperfectly correlated cash flows over time.

Diversifying to Reduce Risk and the Interest of Outside Equity Holders.   Although a firm can reduce its overall risk by engaging in a set of diversified businesses, such risk-reducing strategies are generally not *directly* valuable to a firm's outside equity investors. Outside equity investors generally have lower-cost ways to reduce their risk.[26]

Outside equity holders can reduce their risk by investing, either directly or through mutual funds, in a fully diversified portfolio of stocks and bonds. The cost of creating and maintaining this diversified portfolio (that is, commissions to brokers or management fees to mutual funds) is usually much less than the cost of conceiving and implementing a corporate diversification strategy (that is, salaries and bonuses for corporate managers, the cost of organizing to implement corporate diversification, and so on). Moreover, most equity holders can modify their portfolios at very low cost by buying or selling stocks. Modifying a diversified firm's portfolio of businesses, through mergers and acquisitions, internal development, or other means, is likely to be much more costly. For these reasons, outside equity holders will generally prefer to diversify their portfolios to reduce risk themselves, rather than have firm managers diversify to reduce risk for them.[27] Empirical research in several industries suggests that when firms pursue diversification strategies solely to reduce the risk of outside equity holders, these strategies, on average, reduce the economic performance of these firms.[28]

Diversification and Employees, Suppliers, and Customers.   Although diversifying in order to reduce risk generally does not directly benefit outside equity investors in a firm, it can benefit outside equity investors *indirectly* through its effect on the willingness of other stakeholders in a firm to make firm-specific investments. A firm's **stakeholders** include all those groups and individuals who have an interest in how a firm performs. In this sense, a firm's equity investors are one of its stakeholders. Other firm stakeholders include employees, suppliers, and customers.

Stakeholders make **firm-specific investments** when the value of the investments they make in a particular firm is much greater than the value of those same investments in other firms. Consider, for example, a firm's employees. An employee with long tenure in a particular firm has generally made substantial **firm-specific human capital investments.** These investments include understanding the particular firm's culture, policies, and procedures, knowing the "right" people to contact to complete a task, and so forth. Such investments have significant value in the firm in which they are made. Indeed, such firm-specific knowledge is generally necessary if an employee is to be able to help a firm conceive of and implement valuable strategies. However, the specific investments that an employee makes in a particular firm have almost no value in other firms. If a firm were to cease operations, employees would instantly lose almost all the value of any of the firm-specific investments they had made in that firm.

Suppliers and customers can also make these firm-specific investments. Suppliers make these investments when they customize their products or services to the specific requirements of a particular customer. They also make firm-specific investments when they forgo opportunities to sell to other firms in order to sell to a particular firm. Customers make firm-specific investments when they customize their operations to fully utilize the products or services of a particular firm. Also, by developing close relationships with a particular firm, customers may forgo the opportunity to develop relationships with other firms. These too are firm-specific investments made by customers. If a firm were to cease operations, suppliers and customers would instantly lose almost the entire value of the specific investments they have made in this firm.

Although the firm-specific investments made by employees, suppliers, and customers are risky—in the sense that almost their entire value is lost if the firm in which they are made ceases operations—they are extremely important if a firm is going to be able to generate economic profits. As was suggested in Chapter 5, valuable, rare, and costly-to-imitate resources and capabilities are more likely to be a source of sustained competitive advantage than resources and capabilities without these attributes. Firm-specific investments are more likely to have these attributes than non–firm-specific investments. Non–firm-specific investments are investments that can generate value in numerous different firms. Such investments, by definition, cannot be rare, and thus cannot be a source of even a temporary competitive advantage. Moreover, because most firm-specific investments made by employees, suppliers, and customers with a firm develop over time, and are based on socially complex relations that develop between these stakeholders and a firm, firm-specific investments are likely to be costly to imitate. If they are also valuable and rare, they are likely to be sources of sustained competitive advantage.[29]

Thus, valuable, rare, and costly-to-imitate firm-specific investments made by a firm's employees, suppliers, and customers can be the source of economic profits. And because a firm's outside equity holders are residual claimants on the cash flows generated by a firm, these economic profits benefit equity holders. Thus, a firm's outside equity holders generally want a firm's employees, suppliers, and customers to make specific investments in a firm because those investments are likely to be sources of economic wealth for the outside equity holders.

However, given the riskiness of firm-specific investments, employees, suppliers, and customers will generally be willing to make these investments only if some of the risk associated with making them can be reduced. Outside equity holders have little difficulty managing the risks associated with investing in a particular firm, because they can always create a portfolio of stocks that fully diversifies this risk at very low cost. This is why diversification that reduces the riskiness of a firm's cash flows does not generally benefit a firm's outside equity holders directly. However, a firm's employees, suppliers, and customers usually do not have these low-cost diversification opportunities. Employees, for example, are rarely able to make firm-specific human capital investments in a large enough number of different firms to fully diversify the risks associated with making these firm-specific human capital investments. And although suppliers and customers can diversify their firm-specific investments to a greater degree than employees—through selling to multiple customers and through buying from multiple suppliers—the cost of this diversification for suppliers and customers is usually greater than the costs that are borne by outside equity holders in diversifying their risk.[30]

Because it is often very costly for a firm's employees, suppliers, and customers to diversify the risks associated with making firm-specific investments on their own, these stakeholders often prefer that a firm's managers help manage this risk for them. Managers in a firm can do this by diversifying the portfolio of businesses in which the firm operates. If a firm is unwilling to diversify the portfolio of businesses within which it is operating, then that firm's employees, suppliers, and customers will generally be unwilling to make specific investments in that firm. Moreover, because these firm-specific investments can generate economic profits, and because economic profits can benefit a firm's outside equity holders directly, equity holders have an indirect incentive to encourage a firm to pursue a diversification strategy, even though that strategy does not benefit them directly.[31]

Put differently, a firm's diversification strategy can be thought of as compensation for the firm-specific investments that a firm's employees, suppliers, and customers make in the firm. Outside equity holders have an incentive to encourage this compensation in return for access to some of the economic profits that these firm-specific investments can generate. In general, the greater the impact of the firm-specific investment made by a firm's employees, suppliers, and customers on the ability of the firm to generate economic profits, the more likely it is that pursuing a corporate diversification strategy will be indirectly consistent with the interests of a firm's outside equity holders. In addition, the more limited the ability of a firm's employees, suppliers, and customers to diversify the risks associated with making firm-specific investments at low cost, the more that corporate diversification is consistent with the interests of outside equity investors.

Diversification and Debt Holders. So far, one key stakeholder for many firms has not been included in this discussion: debt holders. Many firms have significant debt on their balance sheet, either in the form of **bank debt, commercial paper,** or other forms of **corporate bonds.** Because the return on these investments depends on the ability of the firm to meet its debt service obligations, a firm's debt holders are primarily interested in the ability of that firm to generate sufficient cash flow to meet its debt obligations.

Generally, debt holders hold a portfolio of debt investments in a large number of different firms in different industries and countries. In this manner, debt holders can diversify away much of the firm-specific risk associated with investing in a particular firm. However, when the debt investment in a particular firm or a particular group of firms becomes very large, debt holders may not be able to efficiently diversify away all the firm-specific risk in their portfolio. In this setting, debt holders may look to managers in a firm to adopt a corporate diversification strategy to help reduce this riskiness of their debt investment.

In this context, corporate diversification, because it can reduce the variability of a firm's cash flows, also can reduce the likelihood that a firm will be unable to meet its debt repayment obligations. In this sense, corporate diversification can be consistent with debt holders' interests. And, because access to debt financing can also increase the value of a firm, diversification that benefits debt holders directly can benefit equity holders indirectly.

Types of Diversification and the Effects of Diversification on Equity Holders. Both unrelated and related diversification can have indirect benefits for a firm's outside equity holders. That is, both unrelated and related diversification can reduce the riskiness of firm-specific investments by a firm's employees, suppliers, and customers, thereby increasing the likelihood that these stakeholders will make such investments and generate economic profits that can increase equity holders' wealth. And both unrelated and related diversification can reduce the riskiness of debt investments in a firm, thereby increasing a firm's debt capacity and value and benefiting equity holders. However, between these two alternatives, outside equity holders will generally prefer that a firm pursue related corporate diversification rather than unrelated corporate diversification. Put differently, related diversification is likely to benefit a firm's outside equity holders—both directly and indirectly—much more than unrelated diversification.

The reason that equity holders generally prefer firms to pursue related diversification strategies is straightforward. Related diversification can benefit a firm's outside equity investors both directly, through exploiting shared activities, core competencies, or capital allocation efficiencies that outside equity investors cannot exploit on their own, and indirectly, through the willingness of employees, suppliers, and customers to make firm-specific investments and through the effect of diversification on a firm's debt capacity. Unrelated diversification can benefit a firm's outside equity investors only indirectly. Between these alternatives, related diversification, with its direct and indirect benefits, is clearly superior. Unrelated diversification is only consistent with outside equity investor interests when related diversification is not possible and when the indirect effects of diversification on a firm's equity holders are large.[32]

Tax Advantages of Diversification.   A final financial economy of scope from diversification stems from possible tax advantages of this corporate strategy. These possible tax advantages reflect one or a combination of two effects. First, a diversified firm can use losses in some of its businesses to offset profits in others, thereby reducing its overall tax liability. Of course, substantial losses in some of its businesses may overwhelm profits in other businesses, forcing businesses that would have remained solvent if they were independent to cease operation. However, as long as business losses are not too large, a diversified firm's tax liability can be reduced. Empirical research suggests that diversified firms do, sometimes, offset profits in some businesses with losses in others, although the tax savings of these activities are usually small.[33]

Second, as has already been suggested, diversification can increase a firm's debt capacity. This effect on debt capacity is greatest when the cash flows of a diversified firm's businesses are perfectly and negatively correlated. However, even when these cash flows are perfectly and positively correlated, there can still be a (modest) increase in debt capacity.

Debt capacity is particularly important in tax environments in which interest payments on debt are tax-deductible. In this context, diversified firms can increase their leverage up to their debt capacity and reduce their tax liability accordingly. Of course, if interest payments are not tax-deductible, or if the marginal corporate tax rate is relatively low, then the tax advantages of diversification can be quite small. Recent empirical work suggests that diversified firms do have greater debt capacity than undiversified firms. However, low marginal corporate tax rates, at least in the United States, make the accompanying tax savings on average relatively small.[34]

Diversification to Exploit Anti-competitive Economies of Scope

A third group of motivations for diversification is based on the relationship between diversification strategies and various anti-competitive activities by firms. Two specific examples of these activities are (1) multipoint competition to facilitate mutual forbearance and tacit collusion and (2) exploiting market power.

Multipoint Competition

Multipoint competition exists when two or more diversified firms compete in multiple markets simultaneously. For example, Michelin and Goodyear compete in both the U.S. automobile tire market and the European automobile tire market. Disney and AOL/Time Warner both compete in the movie production and book publishing businesses.

Multipoint competition can facilitate a particular type of tacit collusion called **mutual forbearance.** Consider the situation facing two diversified firms, A and B. These two firms operate in the same businesses, I, II, III, and IV (see Figure 11.3). In this

FIGURE 11.3   Multipoint Competition Between Hypothetical Firms A and B

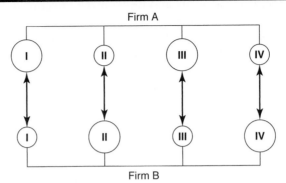

context, any decisions that Firm A might make to compete aggressively in Businesses I and III must take into account the possibility that Firm B will respond by competing aggressively in Businesses II and IV, and vice versa. The potential loss that each of these firms might experience in some of its businesses must be compared to the potential gain that each might obtain if it exploits competitive advantages in other of its businesses. If the present value of gains does not outweigh the present value of losses from retaliation, then both firms will avoid competitive activity. Refraining from competition is mutual forbearance.[35]

Mutual forbearance as a result of multipoint competition has occurred in several industries. For example, this form of tacit collusion has been described as existing between Michelin and Goodyear, Maxwell House and Folger's, Caterpillar and John Deere, and BIC and Gillette.[36] Another clear example of such cooperation can be found in the airline industry. For example, in November 1989, America West began service into the Houston Intercontinental Airport with very low introductory fairs. Continental Airlines, the dominant firm at Houston Intercontinental, rapidly responded to America West's low Houston fares by reducing the price of its flights from Phoenix, Arizona, to several cities in the United States. Phoenix is the home airport of America West. Within just a few weeks, America West withdrew its low introductory fares in the Houston market, and Continental withdrew its reduced prices in the Phoenix market. The threat of retaliation across markets apparently led America West and Continental to tacitly collude on prices.[37]

However, sometimes multipoint competition does not lead to mutual forbearance. Consider, for example, the conflict between The Walt Disney Company and AOL/Time Warner in the early 1990s. Disney operates in the theme park, movie and television production, and television broadcasting industries. AOL/Time Warner operates in the theme park and movie and television production industries and also operates a very large magazine business (*Time, People, Sports Illustrated,* and so forth). Disney spends millions of dollars in advertising its theme parks in AOL/Time Warner magazines. Despite this substantial revenue, AOL/Time Warner once began an aggressive advertising campaign aimed at wooing customers away from Disney theme parks to its own. Disney retaliated by canceling all of its advertising in AOL/Time Warner magazines. AOL/Time Warner responded to Disney's actions by canceling a corporate meeting to be held in Florida at Disney World. Disney responded to AOL/Time

Warner's meeting cancellation by refusing to broadcast AOL/Time Warner theme park advertisements on its Los Angeles television station.[38]

Some recent research investigates the conditions under which mutual forbearance strategies are pursued, as well as conditions under which multipoint competition does not lead to mutual forbearance.[39] In general, the value of the threat of retaliation must be substantial for multipoint competition to lead to mutual forbearance. However, not only must the payoffs to mutual forbearance be substantial, the firms pursuing this strategy must have strong strategic linkages among their diversified businesses. This strategic linkage requirement is recognized when mutual forbearance is modeled, assuming that firms choose optimal price/quantity levels across all the diversified businesses in which they invest, simultaneously. This suggests that firms pursuing mutual forbearance strategies based on multipoint competition are pursuing a form of related diversification.

To the extent that diversified firms use multipoint competition to implement mutual forbearance strategies, and to the extent that these strategies enable these firms to have lower costs or higher revenues than would be the case otherwise, this type of tacit collusion can be valuable for a diversified firm. Moreover, outside investors cannot generally create these synergies on their own. In this sense, mutual forbearance can be a source of valuable economies of scope.

Diversification and Market Power

Internal allocations of capital among a diversified firm's businesses may enable a firm to exploit in some of its businesses the market-power advantages it enjoys in other of its businesses. For example, suppose that a firm is earning monopoly profits in a particular business. This firm can use some of these monopoly profits to subsidize the operations of another of its businesses. This cross-subsidization can take several forms, including predatory pricing—that is, setting prices so that they are less than the subsidized business's costs. The effect of this cross-subsidy may be to drive competitors out of the subsidized business and then to obtain monopoly profits in that subsidized business. In a sense, diversification enables a firm to apply its monopoly power in several different businesses. Economists call this a **deep-pockets model of diversification.**[40]

Diversified firms with operations in regulated monopolies have been criticized for this kind of cross-subsidization. Indeed, when the original AT&T was broken up into smaller operating companies, one of the biggest concerns expressed by the court was that these regional companies would use their geography-based monopoly profits to subsidize the entry of these firms into other businesses. That is, the deep pockets created by their local monopolies would lead to diversification strategies.[41]

The distinction between cross-subsidies to exploit market power as an economy of scope and other economies of scope is subtle at best. For other economies of scope, especially operating economies and capital allocation economies, the objective of diversification is to reduce a firm's costs or increase the willingness of customers to pay. For market-power economies of scope, the objective is to enable a business to sustain losses caused by extremely low prices long enough to force competitors out of business. For all these economies of scope, competing independent firms may be at a competitive disadvantage. However, in the case of operating economies of scope and capital allocation economies of scope, that competitive disadvantage reflects a diversified firm's increased efficiency. In the anticompetitive case, that disadvantage reflects a diversified firm's market power.

Although these market power economies of scope may exist in principle, relatively little empirical work documents their existence. Indeed, research on regulated utilities diversifying into nonregulated businesses in the 1980s suggests not that these firms use monopoly profits in their regulated businesses to unfairly subsidize nonregulated businesses, but that the poor management skills developed in the regulated businesses tend to make diversification less profitable rather than more profitable.[42] Thus it is yet to be established that the inequality in equation 11.1 holds for diversification strategies designed to exploit market power.

Firm Size and Employee Incentives to Diversify

Employees may have incentives to diversify that are independent of any benefits from other sources of economies of scope. This is especially the case for employees in senior management positions and employees with long tenure in a particular firm. These employee incentives reflect the interest of employees to diversify because of the relationship between firm size and management compensation.

Research over the years has demonstrated conclusively that the primary determinant of the compensation of top managers in a firm is not the economic performance of the firm but the size of the firm, usually measured in terms of sales.[43] Thus, managers seeking to maximize their income should attempt to "grow" their firm. One of the easiest ways to grow a firm is through diversification, especially unrelated diversification through mergers and acquisitions. By making large acquisitions, a diversified firm can grow substantially in a short period of time, leading senior managers to earn higher incomes. All of this is independent of any economic profit that diversification may or may not generate. Senior managers need only worry about economic profit if the level of that profit is so low that unfriendly takeovers are a threat or so low that the board of directors may be forced to replace management.

Recently, the traditional relationship between firm size and management compensation has begun to break down. More and more, the compensation of senior managers is being tied to the economic performance of their firms. In particular, the use of stock options and other forms of deferred compensation makes it in management's best interest to be concerned with economic performance. These changes in compensation do not necessarily imply that firms will abandon all forms of diversification. They do suggest that firms will abandon those forms of diversification that do not generate real economies of scope.

Motives for Diversification and Types of Diversification

The different motives for diversification listed in Table 11.1 have implications for the type of diversification strategy a firm pursues. The relationships between motives for diversification and type of diversification are summarized in Table 11.4.

Operating economies of scope, including shared activities and core competencies, can be realized only under conditions of related diversification. Indeed, operational links among a related-diversified firm's businesses are the sources of these economies of scope. If all the businesses in a diversified firm share the same activities or build on the same core competencies, that firm is pursuing related constrained diversification. If different businesses share different activities or different core competencies, that firm is pursuing related linked diversification.

TABLE 11.4	Relationships Between Motivation for Diversification and Type of Diversification		
Motivation	*Related Diversification*	*Unrelated Diversification*	
Operating economies of scope			
Shared activities	X		
Core competencies	X		
Financial economies of scope			
Internal capital allocation	X		
Risk reduction	X	X	
Tax advantages	X	X	
Anticompetitive economies of scope			
Multipoint competition	X		
Exploiting market share	X	X	
Firm size and employee incentives for diversification	X	X	

Capital allocation, as a financial economy of scope, can usually be realized only when a firm implements a strategy of related diversification, either related constrained or related linked. For internal capital markets to have a capital allocation advantage over external capital markets, firm managers must have access to better information than the information available to external sources of capital. Moreover, internal managers must be able to evaluate and interpret this information in a more subtle and complex way, to understand a business's performance and prospects more completely than external sources of capital. These information-processing requirements are most likely to be met when a firm's multiple businesses are related along several important dimensions. In this case, evaluation experience developed in one business can be used in evaluating other businesses.

On the other hand, risk reduction, as a financial economy of scope, can be accomplished by both related and unrelated diversification. As long as a firm's businesses' cash flows are not perfectly and positively correlated, any form of diversification will reduce firm risk to some degree.

The same arguments apply to tax savings as a form of financial economy of scope. The chance that losses in some businesses will offset profits in other businesses exists as long as those businesses' cash flows are not perfectly and positively correlated over time. This can be the case for both related and unrelated diversification. Debt capacity and the ability to deduct interest payments can also be enhanced greatest in the related and unrelated case.

Multipoint competition leading to mutual forbearance is most likely to operate in conditions of related diversification. Recall that mutual forbearance requires firm managers to set price and output levels across all their diversified businesses simultaneously. This joint price/output determination process is a form of related diversification.

Exploiting market power as an anticompetitive economy of scope, on the other hand, can operate in either related or unrelated diversification strategies. Managers in a diversified firm seeking to exploit market-power advantages may adopt the joint price/output determination process described for multipoint competition. Alternatively, firms exploiting their market-power advantages may simply allocate monopoly profits from one business to support price competition in another business. This simple reallocation process assumes fewer linkages between firms than does joint price/output determination in mutual forbearance strategies.

Employees' efforts to grow a firm, in order to maximize compensation, can be accomplished through either related or unrelated diversification. Both strategies can lead to rapid growth in firm sales, although related diversification that exploits valuable economies of scope may, in the long run, generate profits more effectively than unrelated diversification.

The Limits of Unrelated Diversification

One of the interesting implications of Table 11.4 concerns the ability of unrelated diversification to add value to a firm. According to the table, a firm pursuing unrelated diversification can only realize four possible motives for diversifying: risk reduction, tax advantages, exploiting market power, and growing the firm to increase employee compensation. Of these motivations, diversifying to grow the firm solely to increase employee compensation is actually inconsistent with the interests of outside equity holders. Diversifying to gain tax advantages or to exploit market power may be consistent with equity holder interests, but most research has shown that the value created through these forms of diversification is usually quite small. Finally, diversifying to reduce risk may benefit equity holders, but only indirectly, through the effect that diversification has on the willingness of a firm's employees, suppliers, and customers to make firm-specific investments and through the effect that diversification can have on a firm's debt capacity.

A firm pursuing related diversification, on the other hand, can realize all of the motives for engaging in a corporate diversification strategy, including those motivations that can be realized through unrelated diversification. Indeed, some of the potentially most valuable motivations for pursuing a corporate diversification strategy—including exploiting operational economies of scope, core competencies, capital allocation efficiencies, and multipoint competition—can be realized only when a firm is pursuing a related diversification strategy. Because related diversification enables a firm to realize all the value-creating motives behind pursuing a corporate diversification strategy, related diversification will generally create more value for equity holders than unrelated diversification.

This observation is consistent with a very large body of literature that examines the relationship between diversification and firm performance. This literature generally shows that related diversified firms outperform unrelated diversified firms. Much of the corporate restructuring that occurred in the 1980s and 1990s can be understood as an effort by unrelated diversified firms to rationalize their portfolio of businesses to be consistent with the arguments presented in this chapter.[44]

The Limits of Diversification

The empirical literature overwhelmingly suggests that related diversification creates more economic value than unrelated diversification. However, much of this literature only compares related and unrelated diversification. It fails to compare the performance of diversified firms with the performance of firms that do not diversity at all, so-called focused firms.

Initially, while Rumelt showed that related diversifiers outperform unrelated diversifiers, he also showed that focused firms outperformed all types of diversified firms.[45] More recently, several scholars compared the economic performance of diversified firms with the average performance of a portfolio of focused firms that approximates the portfolio of businesses owned by diversified firms. This initial group of papers found that focused firms systematically outperform diversified firms.[46] One study found that diversified firms created approximately 24 percent less value than a portfolio of focused firms.[47]

A second group of papers suggested that returns from diversification are not independent of the decision to diversify. Thus, for example, a firm with limited growth options in its current industry may have relatively low levels of performance. This firm may thus be motivated to search for new growth options through diversification. Thus, while diversification and firm performance may be negatively correlated, that correlation may be due to the low level of performance that motivates a firm to seek to diversify in the first place. Several papers built on this insight and implemented sophisticated multistage statistical techniques to control for the effect of a firm's current level of performance on both its later level of performance and its decision to diversify.[48] None of these papers found a negative correlation between diversification and firm value; some even found a small diversification premium—suggesting that firms with limited options in their current business might actually create value through diversifying.

However, this conclusion has recently come under some additional scrutiny. In particular, none of this previous research controlled for all the options a firm has with its cash flow. Previous work examined the choice between diversifying and not diversifying. However, in addition to diversifying, firms can also return their excess cash flow to stockholders through dividends or stock buy-back plans. When this option is included in empirical models, the so-called diversification discount reappears, even after controlling for all the factors identified in previous papers.[49] Early work on including relatedness in this analysis does not change this basic finding: Given free cash flow, on average, the thing that maximizes the wealth of a firm's equity holders the most is to return this cash to them, in the form of a dividend or stock repurchase. The next most value-creating alternative is to diversify and return cash—although this alternative has only a very small effect on stockholder wealth. Finally, just diversifying actually reduces the wealth of a firm's shareholders.

11.3 DIVERSIFICATION AND SUSTAINED COMPETITIVE ADVANTAGE

Of course, all this work focuses on the average relationship between diversification and firm performance. Even if, on average, diversification destroys value, it may still be possible for some firms, some of the time, to create value through diversification. Indeed, for some firms, diversification might even be a source of sustained competitive advantage. In order for diversification to be a source of sustained competitive advantage, not only must it be valuable, it must also be rare and costly to imitate, and a firm must be organized to implement this strategy. The rarity and imitability of diversification are discussed in this section; organization questions are deferred until Chapter 12.

The Rarity of Diversification

At first glance, it seems clear that diversification per se is usually not a rare firm strategy. Most large firms have adopted some form of diversification, if only the limited diversification of a dominant-business firm. Even many small and medium-size firms have adopted various levels of diversification strategy. However, the rarity of diversification depends not on diversification per se but on how rare the particular economy of scope associated with that diversification is. If only a few competing firms have exploited a particular economy of scope, that economy of scope can be rare. If numerous firms have done so, it will be common and not a source of competitive advantage.

The Imitability of Diversification

Both forms of imitation—direct duplication and substitution—are relevant in evaluating the ability of diversification strategies to generate sustained competitive advantages even if the economies of scope that they create are rare.

Direct Duplication of Diversification

The extent to which a valuable and rare corporate diversification strategy is immune from direct duplication depends on how costly it is for competing firms to realize this same economy of scope. As suggested in Table 11.5, some economies of scope are, in general, more costly to duplicate than others.

Shared activities, risk reduction, tax advantages, and employee compensation bases for corporate diversification are usually relatively easy to duplicate. Because shared activities are based on tangible assets that a firm exploits across multiple businesses, these economies of scope are relatively easy for competing firms to describe and then duplicate. Thus, shared activities such as common R&D labs, common sales forces, and common manufacturing are usually relatively easy to duplicate. The only duplication issue for shared activities concerns developing the cooperative cross-business relationships that often facilitate the use of shared activities.

Because risk reduction, tax advantages, and employee compensation motives for diversification can be accomplished both through related and unrelated diversification, these motives for diversifying tend to be relatively easy to duplicate. As will be shown in detail in Chapter 12, unrelated diversification is more vulnerable to duplication than related diversification.

On the other hand, other economies of scope are much more difficult to duplicate. These difficult-to-duplicate economies of scope include core competencies, internal capital allocation efficiencies, multipoint competition, and exploiting market power. Because core competencies are often intangible, their direct duplication is often challenging. The realization of capital allocation economies of scope requires very substantial

TABLE 11.5 Costly Duplication of Economies of Scope	
Costly-to-Duplicate Economies of Scope	*Less Costly-to-Duplicate Economies of Scope*
Core competencies	Shared activities
Internal capital allocation	Risk reduction
Multipoint competition	Tax advantages
Exploiting market power	Employee compensation

information-processing capabilities. These capabilities are often very difficult to develop. Multipoint competition requires very close coordination among the different businesses in which a firm operates. This kind of coordination is socially complex, and thus may often be immune from direct duplication. Finally, exploiting market power may be costly to duplicate because it requires that a firm possess significant market power in one of its lines of business. A firm that does not have this market-power advantage has to obtain it. The cost of doing so, in most situations, will be prohibitive.

Substitutes for Diversification

There are two obvious substitutes for diversification. First, instead of obtaining advantages from exploiting economies of scope *across* businesses in a diversified firm, a firm may decide to simply grow and develop each of its businesses separately. In this sense, a firm that successfully implements a cost leadership strategy or a product differentiation strategy in a single business can obtain the same cost or customer willingness-to-pay advantages it could have obtained by exploiting economies of scope but without developing cross-business relations. Growing independent businesses within a diversified firm can be a substitute for exploiting economies of scope in a diversification strategy.

One firm that has chosen this course is Nestlé. Nestlé exploits few, if any, economies of scope among its different businesses. Rather, Nestlé has focused its efforts on growing each of its international operations to the point that they obtain advantages that could have been obtained in some form of related diversification. Thus, for example, Nestlé's operation in the United States is sufficiently large to exploit economies of scale in production, sales, and marketing, without relying on economies of scope between U.S. operations and operations in other countries.[50]

A second substitute for exploiting economies of scope in diversification can be found in strategic alliances. By using a strategic alliance, firms may be able to gain the economies of scope they could have obtained if they had carefully exploited economies of scope across businesses they own. Thus, for example, instead of a firm exploiting research and development economies of scope between two businesses it owns, it could form a strategic alliance with a different firm and form a joint research and development lab. Instead of a firm exploiting sales economies of scope by linking its businesses through a common sales force, it might develop a sales agreement with another firm and obtain cost or revenue advantages in that.

However, if a firm has done its diversification analysis correctly, then it is unlikely that strategic alliances will be a close substitute for a corporate diversification strategy. Recall that in order for corporate diversification to make sense, not only do economies of scope have to exist, it must be necessary to bring a transaction within the boundaries of the firm in order to realize these economies of scope. That is, if a firm has pursued a corporate diversification strategy and entered into businesses with economies of scope that can only be realized through hierarchical forms of governance, then it is unlikely that other firms will be able to realize these economies of scope through some non-hierarchical form of governance, including strategic alliances. Only if a firm has developed unusual governance skills (as described in Chapter 10) will it be able to use non-hierarchical forms of governance, to realize an economy of scope, as a substitute for a corporate diversification strategy that realizes that economy of scope.

11.4 SUMMARY

Firms implement corporate diversification strategies that range from limited diversification (single business, dominant business) to related diversification (related constrained, related linked) to unrelated diversification. In order to be valuable, corporate diversification strategies must exploit economies of scope that can be realized most efficiently through hierarchical governance. This implies that individual equity investors will find it too costly to create or exploit these economies of scope on their own.

There are several motivations for implementing diversification strategies, including exploiting operational economies of scope (shared activities, core competencies), exploiting financial economies of scope (internal capital allocation, risk reduction, obtaining tax advantages), exploiting anti-competitive economies of scope (multipoint competition, market power advantages), and employee incentives to diversify (diversifying employees' human capital investments, maximizing management compensation). These different motivations for diversification vary in their value. They also are associated with different types of diversification. Motivations that lead to related diversification are most likely to add value to a firm; motivations that lead to unrelated diversification are less likely to add value to a firm. Although research on the value of diversification compared to a focused firm strategy has generated contradictory results, the most recent work suggests that, on average, diversified firms create less value than focused firms.

The ability of a diversification strategy to create sustained competitive advantages depends not only on the value of that strategy but also on its rarity and imitability. The rarity of a diversification strategy depends on the number of competing firms that are exploiting the same economies of scope through diversification. Imitation can occur either through direct duplication or through substitutes. Costly-to-duplicate economies of scope include core competencies, internal capital allocation, multipoint competition, and exploiting market power. Other economies of scope are usually less costly to duplicate. Important substitutes for diversification are when relevant economies are obtained through the actions of independent businesses within a firm and when relevant economies are obtained through strategic alliances.

This discussion set aside important organizational issues in implementing diversification strategies. These issues are examined in detail in the next chapter.

REVIEW QUESTIONS

1. One simple way to think about relatedness is to look at the products or services a firm manufactures. The more similar these products or services are, the more related is the firm's diversification strategy. However, will firms that exploit core competencies in their diversification strategies always produce products or services that are similar to each other? Why or why not?

2. A firm implementing a diversification strategy has just acquired what it claims is a strategically related target firm but announces that it is not going to change this recently acquired firm in any way. Will this type of diversifying acquisition enable the firm to realize any valuable economies of scope that could not be duplicated by outside investors on their own? Why or why not?

3. One of the reasons why internal capital markets may be more efficient than external capital markets is that firms may not want to reveal full information about their sources of competitive advantage to external capital markets, in order to reduce the threat of competitive imitation. This suggests that external capital markets may systematically undervalue firms with competitive advantages that are subject to imitation. Do you agree with this analysis? If yes, how could you trade on this information in your own investment activities? If no, why not?

4. A particular firm is owned by members of a single family. Most of the wealth of this family is derived from the operations of this firm, and the family does not want to "go public" with the firm by selling its equity position to outside investors. Will this firm pursue a highly related diversification strategy or a somewhat less related diversification strategy? Why?

5. Under what conditions will a related diversification strategy not be a source of competitive advantage for a firm?

ENDNOTES

1. Richard Rumelt first developed this diversification categorization scheme; it has come to be the dominant diversification typology in the field. See Rumelt, R. (1974). *Strategy, Structure, and Economic Performance,* Cambridge, MA: Harvard University Press. See also Collis, D. J., and C. A. Montgomery (1997). *Corporate Strategy: Resources and the Scope of the Firm,* Chicago: Irwin.

2. See Williamson, O. E. (1975). *Markets and Hierarchies: Analysis and Antitrust Implication,* New York: Free Press; Williamson, O. E. (1985). *The Economic Institutions of Capitalism,* New York: Free Press; Teece, D. (1980). "Economy of scope and the scope of the enterprise," *Journal of Economic Behavior and Organization,* 1, pp. 223–245; and references in Chapter 6.

3. See Jensen, M. C., and W. H. Meckling (1976). "Theory of the firm: Managerial behavior, agency costs, and ownership structure," *Journal of Financial Economics,* 3, pp. 305–360, and references in Chapter 13.

4. See Burrows, P. (1995). "Now, TI means 'taking initiative,'" *Business Week,* May 15, pp. 120–121; and Rogers, A. (1992). "It's the execution that counts," *Fortune,* November 30, pp. 80–83, on TI; Wallas, J., and J. Erickson (1993). *Hard Drive: Bill Gates and the Making of the Microsoft Empire,* New York: Harper Business, on Microsoft; and Porter, M. E. (1981). "Disposable diaper industry in 1974," Harvard Business School Case no.

9-380-175, on Procter & Gamble. Whether Microsoft can continue to share activities across operating systems and applications software is one of the key issues at stake in the Microsoft antitrust suit. A more general discussion of the value of shared activities can be found in St. John, C. H., and J. S. Harrison (1999). "Manufacturing-based relatedness, Synergy, and coordination," *Strategic Management Journal,* 20, pp. 129–145.

5. Porter, M. E. (1985). *Competitive Advantage,* New York: Free Press; Rumelt, R. (1974). *Strategy, Structure, and Economic Performance,* Cambridge, MA: Harvard University Press; and Ansoff, H. I. (1965). *Corporate Strategy,* New York: McGraw-Hill.

6. See Fuchsberg, G. (1992). "Decentralized management can have its drawbacks," *Wall Street Journal,* December 9, p. B1.

7. See Crockett, R. (2000). "A Baby Bell's growth formula," *Business Week,* 3671, March 6, pp. 50–52; and Crockett, R. (1999). "The last monopolist," *Business Week,* 3624, April 12, p. 76.

8. de Lisser, E. (1993). "Catering to cooking-phobic customers, supermarkets stress carry-out, add cares," *Wall Street Journal,* April 5, B1.

9. See, for example, Davis, P., R. Robinson, J. Pearce, and S. Park (1992). "Business unit relatedness and performance: A look at the pulp and paper industry," *Strategic Management Journal,* 13, pp. 349–361.

10. Rapoport, C. (1992). "A tough Swede invades the U.S.," *Fortune,* June 29, pp. 776–779.

11. Prahalad, C. K., and G. Hamel (1990). "The core competence of the organization," *Harvard Business Review,* 90, p. 82.

12. See also Grant, R. M. (1988). "On 'dominant logic' relatedness and the link between diversity and performance," *Strategic Management Journal,* 9, pp. 639–642; Chatterjee, S., and B. Wernerfelt (1991). "The link between resources and type of diversification: Theory and evidence," *Strategic Management Journal,* 12, pp. 33–48; Markides, C., and P. J. Williamson (1994). "Related diversification, core competencies, and corporate performance," *Strategic Management Journal,* 15, pp. 149–165; Montgomery, C. A., and B. Wernerfelt (1991). "Sources of superior performance: Market share versus industry effects in the U.S. brewing industry," *Management Science,* 37, pp. 954–959; Liedtka, J. M. (1996). "Collaborating across lines of business for competitive advantage," *Academy of Management Executive,* 10(2), pp. 20–37; and Farjoun, M. (1998). "The independent and joint effects of the skill and physical bases of relatedness in diversification," *Strategic Management Journal,* 19, pp. 611–630.

13. Hill, C. W. L., and G. R. Jones (1992). *Strategic Management Theory: An Integrated Approach,* Boston: Houghton Mifflin.

14. Jensen, M. C. (1986). "Agency costs of free cash flow, corporate finance, and takeovers," *American Economic Review,* 76, pp. 323–329.

15. Nayyar, P. (1990). "Information asymmetries: A source of competitive advantage for diversified service firms," *Strategic Management Journal,* 11, pp. 513–519; and Robins, J., and M. Wiersema (1995). "A resource-based approach to the multibusiness firm: Empirical analysis of portfolio interrelationships and corporate financial performance," *Strategic Management Journal,* 16, pp. 277–299, for a discussion on the evolution of core competencies.

16. See Sellers, P. (1995). "Pepsico's shedding ugly pounds," *Fortune,* June 26, pp. 94–95, and Sellers, P. (1997). "Pepsi's eateries go it alone," *Fortune,* August 4, pp. 27–30.

17. See Nulty, P. (1995). "Digital imaging had better boom before Kodak film busts," *Fortune,* May 1, pp. 80–83, on Kodak, although very recently Kodak has begun experiencing some success in digital imaging [McClelland, D. (1997). "Midrange digital cameras," *Macworld,* 14(10), pp. 44–45]. See Trachtenberg, J., and K. Pope (1995). "Poly Gram's Levy puts music firm further into movie-making," *Wall Street Journal,* June 15, pp. A1+, on Poly Gram records.

18. Prahalad, C. K., and R. A. Bettis (1986). "The dominant logic: A new linkage between diversity and performance," *Strategic Management Journal,* 7(6), pp. 485–501.

19. See Williamson, O. E. (1975). *Markets and Hierarchies: Analysis and Antitrust Implications,* New York: Free Press.

20. See Liebeskind, J. P. (1996). "Knowledge, strategy, and the theory of the firm," *Strategic Management Journal,* 17 (Winter, Special Issue), pp. 93–107.

21. Perry, L. T., and J. B. Barney (1981). "Performance lies are hazardous to organizational health," *Organizational Dynamics,* 9(3), pp. 68–80.

22. Bethel, J. E. (1990). "The capital allocation process and managerial mobility: A theoretical and empirical investigation," unpublished doctoral dissertation, University of California at Los Angles.

23. Staw, B. M. (1981). "The escalation of commitment to a course of action," *Academy of Management Review,* 6, pp. 577–587.

24. See Comment, R., and G. Jarrell (1995). "Corporate focus and stock returns," *Journal of Financial Economics,* 37, pp. 67–87; Berger, P. G., and E. Ofek (1995). "Diversification's effect on firm value," *Journal of Financial Economics,* 37, pp. 39–65; Maksimovic, V., and G. Phillips (1999). "Do conglomerate firms allocate resources inefficiently?," working paper, University of Maryland; Matsusaka, J. G., and V. Nanda (1998). "Internal capital markets and corporate refocusing," working paper, University of Southern California; Palia, D. (1998). "Division-level overinvestment and agency conflicts in diversified firms," working paper, Columbia University; Rajan, R., H. Servaes, and L. Zingales (1997). "The cost of diversity: The diversification

discount and inefficient investment," working paper, University of Chicago; Scharfstein, D. S. (1997). "The dark side of internal capital markets II: Evidence from diversified conglomerates," NBER [National Bureau of Economic Research] working paper; Shin, H. H., and R. M. Stulz (1998). "Are internal capital markets efficient?" *Quarterly Journal of Economics,* May, pp. 551–552. However, Houston and James show that internal capital markets can create competitive advantages for firms: Houston, J., and C. James (1998). "Some evidence that banks use internal capital markets to lower capital costs," *Journal of Applied Corporate Finance,* 11(2), pp. 70–78.

25. See Copeland, T. E., and J. F. Weston (1983). *Financial Theory and Corporate Policy,* Reading, MA: Addison-Wesley.

26. See Chang, Y., and H. Thomas (1989). "The impact of diversification strategy on risk-return performance," *Strategic Management Journal,* 10, pp. 271–284; Williamson, O. E. (1975). *Markets and Hierarchies: Analysis and Antitrust Implications,* New York: Free Press; and Golbe, D. L. (1981). "The effects of imminent bankruptcy on stockholder risk preferences and behavior," *Bell Journal of Economics,* 12(1), pp. 321–328. A discussion of a firm's incentives to diversify when investors do not have low-cost diversification alternatives is presented later in this chapter.

27. These agency theory arguments are developed in Jensen, M. C. (1968). "The performance of mutual funds in the period 1945–64," *Journal of Finance,* May, pp. 389–416, and Jensen, M. C., and W. H. Meckling (1976); "Theory of the firm: Managerial behavior, agency costs, and ownership structure," *Journal of Financial Economics,* 3, pp. 305–360; and in Chapter 13.

28. Hill, C., and G. Hansen (1991). "A longitudinal study of the cause and consequence of changes in diversification in the U.S. pharmaceutical industry, 1977–1986," *Strategic Management Journal,* 12, pp. 187–199; Amit, R., and J. Livnat (1988). "Diversification and the risk-return trade-off," *Academy of Management Journal,* 31, pp. 154–166.

29. See Barney, J. B. (1991). "Firm resources and sustained competitive advantage," *Journal of Management,* 17, pp. 99–120.

30. See Stulz, R. M. (1996). "Rethinking risk management," *Journal of Applied Corporate Finance* (Fall), pp. 8–24; Miller, K. (1998). "Economic exposure and integrated risk management," *Strategic Management Journal,* 33, pp. 756–779; Amit, R., and B. Wernerfelt (1990). "Why do firms reduce business risk?" *Academy of Management Journal,* 33, pp. 520–533; Froot, K. A., D. S. Scharfstein, and J. C. Stein (1993). "Risk management: Coordinating corporate investment and financial policies," *Journal of Finance,* 8, 1629–1658; May, D. O. (1995). "Do managerial motives influence firm risk reduction strategies?" *Journal of Business,* 55(2), pp. 281–296; Smith, C. W., and R. M. Stulz (1985). "The determinants of firms' hedging policies," *Journal of Financial and Quantitative Analysis,* 20, pp. 391–405.

31. This argument is developed in Wang, H., and J. Barney (2006). "Employee incentives to make firm specific investments: Implications for resource-based theories of corporate diversification," *Academy of Management Review,* 31, pp. 466–476.

32. See also Wiseman, R. M., and A. H. Catanach, Jr. (1997). "A longitudinal disaggregation of operational risk under changing regulations: Evidence from the savings and loan industry," *Academy of Management Journal,* 40(4), pp. 799–830; Ruefli, T. W., J. M. Collins, and J. R. Lacugna (1999). "Risk measures in strategic management research: Auld Lang Syne?" *Strategic Management Journal,* 20, pp. 167–194; Gaynor, M., and P. Gertler (1995). "Moral hazard and risk spreading in partnerships," *Rand Journal of Economics,* 26(4), pp. 591–613; and Hill, C. W. L., and G. S. Hansen (1991). "A longitudinal study of the cause and consequences of changes in diversification in the U.S. pharmaceutical industry 1977–1986," *Strategic Management Journal,* 12, pp. 187–199, on risk reduction and value creation.

33. Scott, J. H. (1977). "On the theory of conglomerate mergers," *Journal of Finance,* pp. 1235–1250.

34. See Brennan, M. (1979). "The pricing of contingent claims in discrete time models," *Journal of Finance,* 34, pp. 53–68; Cox, J., S. Ross, and M. Rubinstein (1979). "Option pricing: A simplified approach," *Journal of Financial Economics,* 7, pp. 229–263; and Stapleton, R. C. (1982). "Mergers, debt capacity, and the valuation of corporate loans," in M. Keenan and L. J. White, eds., *Mergers and Acquisitions,* Lexington, MA: D. C. Heath, chap. 2; and Galai, D., and R. W. Masulis (1976). "The option pricing model and the risk factor of stock," *Journal of Financial Economics,* 3, pp. 53–82.

35. See Karnani, A., and B. Wernerfelt (1985). "Multi-point competition," *Strategic Management Journal,* 6, pp. 87–96; Bernheim, R. D., and M. D. Whinston (1990). "Multi-market contact and collusive behavior," *Rand Journal of Economics,* 12, pp. 605–617; Tirole, J. (1988). *The Theory of Industrial Organization,* Cambridge, MA: MIT Press; Gimeno, J., and C. Y. Woo (1999). "Multi-market contact, economies of scope, and firm performance," *Academy of Management Journal,* 43(3), pp. 239–259; Korn, H. J., and J. A. C. Baum (1999). "Chance, imitative, and strategic antecedents to multimarket contact," *Academy of Management Journal,* 42(2), pp. 171–193; Baum, J. A. C., and H. J. Korn (1999). "Dynamics of dyadic competitive interaction," *Strategic Management Journal,* 20, pp. 251–278; Gimeno, J. (1999). "Reciprocal threats in multimarket rivalry: Staking our 'spheres of influence' in the U.S. airline industry," *Strategic Management Journal,* 20, pp. 101–128; Gimeno, J., and C. Y. Woo (1996). "Hypercompetition in a multi-market environment: The role of strategic similarity and multimarket contact in competitive de-escalation," *Organization Science,* 7(3), pp. 322–341; Ma, H. (1998). "Mutual forbearance in international business," *Journal of International Management,* 4(2), pp. 129–147; McGrath, R. G., and M.-J. Chen (1998). "Multimarket maneuvering in uncertain spheres of influence: Resource diversion strategies," *Academy of Management Review,* 23(4), pp. 724–740; Chen, M.-J. (1996). "Competitor analysis and interfirm rivalry: Toward a theoretical integration," *Academy of Management Review,* 21(1), pp. 100–134; Chen, M.-J., and K. Stucker (1997). "Multinational management and multimarket rivalry: Toward a theoretical development of global competition," *Academy of Management Proceedings 1997,* pp. 2–6; and Young, G., K. G. Smith, and C. M. Grimm (1997). "Multimarket contact, resource heterogeneity, and rivalrous firm behavior," *Academy of Management Proceedings 1997,* pp. 55–59. This idea was originally developed by Edwards, C. D. (1955). "Conglomerate bigness as a source of power," in *Business Concentration and Price Policy,* NBER Conference Report, Princeton, NJ: Princeton University Press.

36. See Karnani, A., and B. Wernerfelt (1985). "Multi-point competition," *Strategic Management Journal,* 6, pp. 87–96.

37. This is documented by Gimeno, J. (1994). "Multipoint competition, market rivalry and firm performance: A test of the mutual forbearance hypothesis in the United States airline industry, 1984–1988," unpublished doctoral dissertation, Purdue University.

38. See Landro, L., P. M. Reilly, and R. Turner (1993). "Cartoon clash: Disney relationship with Time Warner is a strained one," *Wall Street Journal,* April 14, p. A1; and Reilly, P. M., and R. Turner (1993). "Disney pulls ads in tiff with Time," *Wall Street Journal,* April 2, p. B1.

39. The best work in this area has been done by Gimeno, J. (1994). "Multipoint competition, market rivalry and firm performance: A test of the mutual forbearance hypothesis in the United States airline industry, 1984–1988," unpublished doctoral dissertation, Purdue University. See also Smith, F., and R. Wilson (1995). "The predictive validity of the Karnani and Wernerfelt model of multipoint competition," *Strategic Management Journal,* 16, pp. 143–160.

40. See Tirole, J. (1988). *The Theory of Industrial Organization,* Cambridge, MA: MIT Press.

41. Carnevale, M. L. (1993). "Ring in the new: Telephone service seems on the brink of huge innovations," *Wall Street Journal,* February 10, p. A1.

42. See Russo, M. V. (1992). "Power plays: Regulation, diversification, and backward integration in the electric utility industry," *Strategic Management Journal,* 13, pp. 13–27. Recent work by Jandik and Makhija indicates that when a regulated utility diversifies out of a regulated industry, it often earns a more positive return than when an unregulated firm does this: Jandik, T., and A. K. Makhija (1999). "An empirical examination of the atypical diversification practices of electric utilities: Internal capital markets and regulation," Fisher College of Business, The Ohio State University, working paper (September). This work shows that regulators have the effect of making a regulated firm's internal capital market more efficient. Differences between Russo's (1992) findings and Jandik and Makhija's (1999) findings may have to do with when this work was done. Russo's (1992) research may have focused on a time period before regulatory agencies had learned how to improve a firm's internal capital market. However, even though Jandik and Makhija (1999) report positive returns from regulated firms diversifying, these positive returns do not reflect the market-power advantages of these firms.

43. Finkelstein, S., and D. C. Hambrick (1989). "Chief executive compensation: A study of the intersection of markets and political processes," *Strategic Management Journal,* 10, pp. 121–134.

44. See also William, J., B. L. Paez, and L. Sanders (1988). "Conglomerates revisited," *Strategic Management Journal,* 9, pp. 403–414; Geringer, J. M., S. Tallman, and D. M. Olsen (2000). "Product and international diversification among Japanese multinational firms," *Strategic Management Journal,* 21, pp. 51–80; Nail, L. A., W. L. Megginson, and C. Maquieira (1998). "How stock-swap mergers affect shareholder (and bondholder) wealth: More evidence of the value of corporate focus," *Journal of Applied Corporate Finance,* 11(2), pp. 95–106; Carroll, G. A., L. S. Bigelow, M.-D. L. Seidel, and L. B. Tsai (1996). "The fates of *de novo* and *de alio* producers in the American automobile industry 1885–1981," *Strategic Management Journal,* 17(7) (Special Summer Issue), pp. 117–137; Nguyen, T. H., A. Seror, and T. M. Devinney (1990). "Diversification strategy and performance in Canadian manufacturing firms," *Strategic Management Journal,* 11, pp. 411–418; and Amit, R., and J. Livnat (1988). "Diversification strategies, business cycles and economic performance," *Strategic Management Journal,* 9, pp. 99–110, for a discussion on corporate diversification in the economy over time. Major empirical studies on the relationship between diversification and firm performance include: Weston, J. F. and S. K. Mansinghka (1971). "Tests of the efficiency performance of conglomerate firms," *Journal of Finance,* 26, pp. 919–936; Rumelt, R. (1974). *Strategy, Structure, and Economic Performance,* Cambride, MA: Harvard University Press; Berry, C. H. (1975) *Corporate Growth and Diversification,* Princeton, NJ: Princeton University Press; Salter, M. S., and W. S. Weinhold (1979). - *Diversification Through Acquisition,* New York: Free Press; Jacquemin, A. P., and C. H. Berry (1979). "Entropy measure of diversification and corporate growth," *Journal of Industrial Economics,* 27(4), pp. 359–369; Amihud, Y., and B. Lev (1981). "Risk reduction as managerial motive for conglomerate mergers," *Bell Journal of Economics,* 12, pp. 605–617; Christensen, H. K., and C. A. Montgomery (1981). "Corporate economic performance: Diversification strategy versus market structure," *Strategic Management Journal,* 2, pp. 327–343; Bettis, R. A. (1981). "Performance differences in related and unrelated diversified firms," *Strategic Management Journal,* 2, pp. 379–393; Bettis, R. A., and W. K. Hall (1982). "Diversification strategy, accounting determined risk, and accounting determined return," *Academy of Management Journal,* 25, pp. 254–264; Rumelt, R. P. (1982). "Diversification strategy and profitability," *Strategic Management Journal,* 3, pp. 359–369; Backaitis, N. T., R. Balakrishnan, and K. R. Harrigan (1984). "The dimensions of diversification posture, market power, and performance: The continuing debate," Working paper, Columbia University; Michel, A., and I. Shaked (1984). "Multinational corporations vs. domestic

corporations: Financial performance and characteristics," *Journal of International Business,* 17 (Fall), pp. 89–100; Lecraw, D. J. (1984). "Diversification strategy and performance," *Journal of Industrial Economics,* 33(2), pp. 179–198; Montgomery, C. A., and H. Singh (1984). "Diversification strategy and systematic risk," *Strategic Management Journal,* 5(2), pp. 181–191; Bettis, R. A., and V. Mahajan (1985). "Risk/return performance of diversified firms," *Management Science,* 31, pp. 785–799; K. Palepu (1985). "Diversification strategy, profit performance and the entropy measure," *Strategic Management Journal,* 6(3), pp. 239–255; Varadarajan, P. R. (1986). "Product diversity and firm performance: An empirical investigation," *Journal of Management,* 50(3), pp. 43–57; Jose, M. L., L. M. Nichols, and J. L. Stevens (1986). "Contributions of diversification, promotion, and R&D to the value of multiproduct firms: A Tobin's *q* approach," *Financial Management* (Winter), pp. 33–42; Grant, R. M., and A. P. Jammine (1988). "Performance differences between the Wrigley/Rumelt strategic categories," *Strategic Management Journal,* 9, pp. 333–346; Galbraith, J. R., and R. K. Kazanjian (1986). "Organizing to implement strategies of diversity and globalization: The role of matrix designs," *Human Resource Management,* 25(1), pp. 37–54; Varadarajan, P. R., and V. Ramanujam (1987). "Diversification and performance: A reexamination using a new two-dimensional conceptualization of diversity in firms," *Academy of Management Journal,* 30(2), pp. 380–393; Dubofsky, P., and P. R. Varadarajan (1987). "Diversification and measures of performance: Additional empirical evidence," *Academy of Management Journal,* 30(3), pp. 597–608; Amit, R., and J. Livnat (1988). "Diversification strategies, business cycles and economic performance," *Strategic Management Journal,* 9, pp. 99–110; Amit, R., and J. Livnat (1988). "Diversification and the risk-return trade-off," *Academy of Management Journal,* 31, pp. 154–166; Simmods, P. (1990). "The combined diversification breadth and mode dimensions and the performance of large diversified firms," *Strategic Management Journal,* 11, pp. 399–410; Nguyen, T., and T. Devinney (1990). "Diversification strategy and performance in Canadian manufacturing firms," *Strategic Management Journal,* 11, pp. 411–418; Hill, C., and G. Hansen (1991). "A longitudinal study of the cause and consequence of changes in diversification in the U.S. pharmaceutical industry, 1977–1986," *Strategic Management Journal,* 12, pp. 187–199; Lang, H. P., and R. Stulz (1994). "Tobin's *q,* corporate diversification, and firm performance," *Journal of Political Economy,* 102, pp. 1248–1280; Markides, C., and P. J. Williamson (1994). "Related diversification, core competencies, and corporate performance," *Strategic Management Journal,* 15, pp. 149–165; Rotemberg, J. J., and G. Saloner (1994). "Benefits of narrow business strategies," *American Economic Review,* 84(5), pp. 1330–1349; Berger, P., and E. Ofek (1995). "Diversification effect on firm value," *Journal of Financial Economics,* 37, pp. 36–65; Comment, R., and G. Jarrell (1995). "Corporate focus and stock returns," *Journal of Financial Economics,* 37, pp. 67–87; Robins, J., and M. Wiersma (1995). "A resource-based approach to the multibusiness firm: Empirical analysis of portfolio interrelationships and corporate financial performance," *Strategic Management Journal,* 16, pp. 277–299; Denis, D. J., D. K. Denis, and A. Sarin (1997). "Managerial incentives and corporate diversification strategies," *Journal of Applied Corporate Finance,* 10(2), pp. 72–80; Palich, L. E., L. B. Cardinal, and C. C. Miller (2000). "Curvilinearity in the diversification-performance linkage: An examination of over three decades of research," *Strategic Management Journal,* 21(2), pp. 155–174.

45. Rumelt, R. P. (1974). *Strategy, Structure, and Economic Performance,* Cambridge, MA: Harvard University Press.

46. See Mackey, T., and J. B. Barney (2006). "Is there a diversification discount? Diversification, Payout policy, and the value of a firm," Working paper, The Ohio State University.

47. Lang, H. P., and R. Stulz (1994). "Tobin's *q,* corporate diversification, and firm performance," *Journal of Political Economy,* 102, pp. 1248–1280; Comment, R., and G. Jarrell

(1995). "Corporate focus and stock returns," *Journal of Financial Economics,* 37, pp. 67–87.

48. Miller, D. J. (2004). "Firms' technological resources and the performance effects of diversification: A longitudinal study," *Strategic Management Journal,* 25(11), pp. 1097–1119; Berger, P. G., and Ofek, E. (1995). "Diversification's effect on firm value," *Journal of Financial Economics,* 37, pp. 39–65; Villalonga, B. (2004). "Does diversification cause the 'diversification discount'?" *Financial Management,* 33, pp. 5–27.

49. See Mackey, T., and J. B. Barney (2006). "Is there a diversification discount? Diversification, Payout policy, and the value of a firm," Working paper, The Ohio State University.

50. The Nestlé story is summarized in Templeman, J. (1993). "Nestle: A giant in a hurry," *Business Week,* March 22, pp. 50–54.

Implementing Corporate Diversification

The arguments developed in Chapter 11 specify the conditions under which a corporate diversification strategy can add value to a firm (when it exploits real economies of scope that are realized most efficiently within the boundaries of a firm and thus cannot be duplicated easily by outside equity investors) and be a source of temporary and sustained competitive advantage (when these economies of scope are valuable, rare, and costly to imitate). Throughout that discussion, the importance of organizing efficiently to implement a diversification strategy was emphasized. A firm may choose a corporate diversification strategy for appropriate value-added and competitive reasons. However, if a firm does not organize itself to implement this strategy efficiently, this potential can be squandered and the firm will lose some of its economic profits, or it will earn only average or below-average profits with its corporate diversification strategy. Organizing issues are discussed in this chapter. We examine first the agency cost-reducing objectives of this organizing effort and then the organizational structure, management control systems, and compensation policies that can be used to implement a diversification strategy.

12.1 AGENCY COSTS

One of the criteria described in Chapter 11 for evaluating whether a particular economy of scope should be used as a basis of a diversification strategy is whether a firm's outside equity investors can duplicate that economy of scope at low cost. If independent equity investors, acting on their own behalf, can duplicate all the benefits of a particular economy of scope at very low cost, why would they want to "hire" managers in a firm to create this economy of scope for them? After all, hiring managers to create this economy of scope is a much more costly way of obtaining any benefits of this economy than equity investors' obtaining these benefits on their own would be.

When equity investors cannot realize an economy of scope on their own, it is in their best interest to delegate to managers the day-to-day management of their financial investment in a firm. As a result, managers can use these investors' financial capital to exploit economies of scope that investors cannot realize on their own. Any economic profits generated from these economies of scope can be transferred back to these investors in the form of dividends or capital gains on the value of their investment.

Several authors suggest that whenever one party to an exchange delegates decision-making authority to a second party, an **agency relationship** exists between these parties. The party delegating this decision-making authority is the **principal;** the party to whom this authority is delegated is the **agent.** In the context of corporate diversification, an agency relationship exists between a firm's outside equity holders (as principals) and its managers (as agents) to the extent that equity holders delegate the day-to-day management of their investment to those managers.[1]

Agency Relationships and Agency Costs

The agency relationship between equity holders and managers can be very effective as long as managers make investment decisions in ways that are consistent with equity holders' interests. Thus, if equity holders are interested in maximizing the rate of return on their investment in a firm, and if managers make their investment decisions with the objective of maximizing the rate of return on those investments, then equity holders will have few concerns about delegating the day-to-day management of their investments to managers.

Unfortunately, in numerous situations the interests of a firm's outside equity holders and its managers do not coincide. When parties in an agency relationship differ in their decision-making objectives, **agency problems** arise. Parties in an agency relationship can engage in a variety of actions to reduce these problems, but such actions are costly. Moreover, despite these actions, it may not be possible to resolve agency problems completely, and unresolved agency problems can also be costly. The cost of actions taken to reduce agency problems, and the cost of unresolved agency problems, are **agency costs.** Agency costs can substantially reduce the economic benefits that could have been created through an agency relationship.

Sources of Agency Costs

Equity holders are **residual claimants** to a firm's cash flow. These investors have a claim to a firm's cash flow after all other claims to that cash flow are satisfied. Other claimants include employees (through their wages and other forms of compensation), management (through their salaries and other forms of compensation), suppliers of raw materials (through cash payments), sources of debt capital (through principal and interest payments on bank debt, bonds, and other forms of debt), and government (through taxes). Given their status as residual claimants, equity holders have a strong interest in managers' making decisions that maximize the present value of the cash flow that a firm generates. By maximizing the present value of a firm's cash flow, managers maximize the amount of cash available to equity holders as residual claimants. As long as managers attempt to maximize the present value of their firm's cash flow, agency problems do not arise between managers and equity holders. However, managers can make numerous decisions that have the effect of reducing the present value of a firm's cash flow, thereby reducing the wealth of outside equity holders and creating agency problems between a firm's managers and equity holders. Sources of these agency costs include managerial perquisites and aversion to risk.

Managerial Perquisites

Managers can decide to take some of a firm's capital and invest it in perquisites that do not add economic value to the firm but do provide direct benefits to those managers. Examples of such investments include lavish offices, fleets of corporate jets, and corporate vacation homes. To the extent that such investments benefit managers directly and divert capital from positive-present-value investment opportunities, they create agency problems between a firm and its outside equity holders.

Of course, not all payments from a firm's cash flow to managers create agency problems. As a supplier of managerial talent to a firm, managers can claim some of a firm's cash flow. Moreover, sometimes lavish offices, corporate jets, corporate vacations homes, and similar perquisites can be positive-present-value investments for a firm. Lavish offices can send to customers a signal of a firm's profitability and thus its reliability.[2] Corporate jets can be used to transport critical decision makers to the right place at the right time. Corporate vacation homes can be made available to customers as part of a firm's marketing efforts. In order for these investments to be sources of agency costs, they must both benefit managers directly and have a negative present value.

Managerial Risk Aversion

Through negative-present-value investments in managerial perquisites, managers can reduce the residual cash flow available to equity holders. Managers may also be more risk-averse in their decision making than equity holders would prefer them to be. These different risk preferences can create agency problems.

As discussed in Chapter 11, equity holders can diversify their portfolio of investments at very low cost. Through their diversification efforts, they can eliminate all firm-specific risk in their portfolios. In this setting, equity holders are indifferent to the riskiness, per se, of investments made by individual firms. Rather, their interest is solely in the discounted present value of the cash flows created by these investments.

Managers, in contrast, have limited ability to diversify their human capital investments in their firm. Some portion of these investments are specific to a particular firm and have limited value in alternative uses. The value of a manager's human capital investment in a firm depends critically on the continued existence of the firm. Thus managers are *not* indifferent to the riskiness of investment opportunities in a firm. Very risky investments may jeopardize a firm's survival and thus eliminate the value of a manager's human capital investments. These incentives can lead managers to be more risk-averse in their decision making than equity holders would prefer them to be.

Consider, for example, two mutually exclusive investment opportunities being evaluated by a firm. The first investment has a very attractive cash flow pattern, although it is very risky (as reflected in a high discount rate of 35 percent applied to this investment). The present value of this first investment, despite its riskiness, is $500. The second investment has a less attractive cash flow pattern than the first, although this investment is considerably less risky than the first (as reflected in the relatively low discount rate of 15 percent applied to this investment). Despite the less attractive pattern of cash flow, the present value of the second investment is $400. Because these investments are mutually exclusive, managers must choose one of them.

Given the interest of equity holders to maximize the present value of a firm's cash flow, equity holders would prefer managers to choose the first investment, because its present value ($500) is greater than the present value of the second investment ($400). However, because managers cannot diversify their human capital investments as efficiently as equity holders can diversify their investment portfolios, managers are concerned about the relative riskiness of these alternative investments. Managers may choose the second investment, despite its lower present value, because it does not put their human capital investments at risk to the same extent as the first investment. To the extent that managers are more risk-averse in their decision making than outside equity holders would prefer, agency problems can arise between a firm and its equity holders.

Monitoring, Bonding, and Residual Agency Costs

Managers could safely ignore agency problems with equity holders if these conflicts did not adversely affect their ability to manage a firm's assets. However, it has been shown that as long as capital markets are semi-strong efficient, the cost of agency problems with equity holders will be reflected in the cost of equity capital for firms.[3] In the face of significant agency problems, firms will find their cost of capital rising, and their ability to take advantage of profitable opportunities will be limited.

The logic behind this assertion is straightforward. If capital markets are at least **semi-strong efficient,** then all public information about the value of investing in a firm's equity will be reflected in the cost of that firm's equity. Information about the divergence of managers' interests and equity holders' interests in the managing of a firm's assets is often public information. If managerial interests vary significantly from the interests of outside investors, those investors will require a higher rate of return on investing in that firm, compared to when managerial interests do not diverge from the interests of outside equity investors. This higher required rate of return is the higher cost of equity capital for a firm with significant agency problems.

This analysis suggests that managers seeking to reduce their firm's cost of capital have an incentive to reduce agency problems between themselves and their firm's outside equity holders. By doing so, managers can lower their firm's cost of capital and can explore a wider range of valuable economic opportunities. However, managers cannot reduce these agency problems by simply "assuring" outside investors that their interests will be considered during decision making. Outside equity holders will find it difficult to distinguish between managerial assertions that are sincere and those that are examples of "cheap talk." In reducing agency conflicts, talk is without value unless it is backed up by actions.[4]

Agency conflicts between managers and equity holders can be partially resolved in at least two ways: through the use of monitoring mechanisms or bonding mechanisms. **Monitoring mechanisms** are institutional devices through which a firm's equity holders can observe, measure, evaluate, and control managerial behavior. The purpose of monitoring mechanisms is not to enable outside investors to replace managers in their decision-making role, but rather to ensure that when managers engage in decision making, they do so in a way that is consistent with equity holders' interests. **Bonding mechanisms** are investments or policies that managers adopt to reassure outside equity holders that they will behave in ways consistent with equity holders' interests when making decisions.

Of course, monitoring and bonding are not costless, nor are they completely effective in eliminating all conflicts of interest between managers and outside equity holders. In semi-strong efficient capital markets, the costs of monitoring, the costs of bonding, and any **residual agency costs** will be reflected in a firm's cost of capital. Thus managers seeking to gain access to low-cost capital have a strong incentive to choose and implement effective and low-cost monitoring and bonding mechanisms.

In the context of agency problems between managers and outside equity holders, organizing to implement diversification strategies can be seen as the creation of monitoring and bonding devices to reassure outside equity holders that decisions being made throughout the firm are consistent with the interests of outside equity holders. Effective organizing efforts reduce perceived conflicts of interest between a firm's managers and outside investors, and do so at the lowest possible cost. A firm's organizational structure, management control systems, and compensation policies can all have important monitoring and bonding attributes.

12.2 ORGANIZATIONAL STRUCTURE

The most common organizational structure for implementing a corporate diversification strategy is the **M-form,** or **multi-divisional structure.** A typical M-form structure, as it would appear in a firm's annual report, is presented in Figure 12.1. This same structure is redrawn in Figure 12.2 to emphasize the roles and responsibilities of each of the major components of the M-form organization.[5]

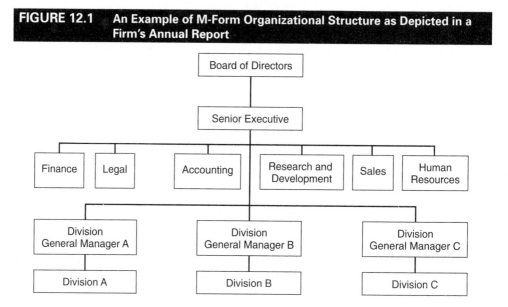

FIGURE 12.1 **An Example of M-Form Organizational Structure as Depicted in a Firm's Annual Report**

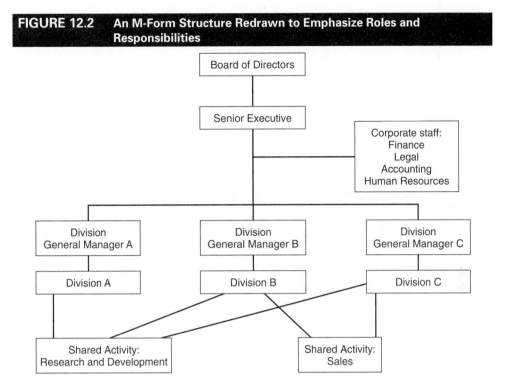

FIGURE 12.2   An M-Form Structure Redrawn to Emphasize Roles and Responsibilities

In the multidivisional structure, each business in which the firm engages is managed through a division. Different firms have different names for these **divisions**—strategic business units (SBUs), business groups, companies. Whatever their name, the divisions in an M-form organization are true **profit-and-loss centers:** Profits and losses are calculated at the level of the division in these firms.

Different firms use different criteria for defining the boundaries of profit-and-loss centers. For example, General Electric defines its divisions in terms of the types of products that each division manufactures and sells (for example, jet engines, medical imaging, and so forth). Nestlé defines its divisions with reference to the geographic scope of each of its businesses (North America, South America, and so forth). General Motors defines its divisions in terms of the brand names of its products (Cadillac, Chevrolet, Saturn, and so forth). However they are defined, divisions in an M-form organization should be large enough to represent identifiable business activities but small enough so that a division general manager can manage it effectively. Indeed, each division in an M-form organization typically adopts a U-form structure (see the discussion of the U-form structure in Chapters 6, 7, and 10), and the division general manager takes on the role of a U-form senior executive for his or her division.

As suggested in Section 12.1, the M-form organizational structure can be understood as a monitoring and bonding device. Each of the major components of this structure enables outside equity holders to observe the decision-making activities of managers (and thus facilitates monitoring), reassures outside equity holders that decision-making activities are consistent with their interests (and thus facilitates bonding), or both. The

monitoring and bonding activities of the major components of the M-form structure—
the board of directors, the senior executive, corporate staff, division general managers,
and shared activity managers—are summarized in Table 12.1 and discussed later.

Board of Directors

One of the major monitoring devices present in an M-form organization is the firm's
board of directors. In principle, all of a firm's senior managers report to the board. The
board's primary responsibility is to monitor decision making in the firm, to ensure that
it is consistent with the interests of outside equity holders.

TABLE 12.1 **Major Components of the M-Form Structure and Their Monitoring and Bonding Activities**

Component	Activity
Board of Directors	Evaluates the firm's decision making to ensure that it is consistent with the interests of equity holders (monitoring)
Institutional Investors	Evaluates the firm's decision making to ensure that it is consistent with the interests of major institutional equity investors (monitoring)
Senior Executive	Formulates corporate strategies consistent with equity holders' interests (bonding) and assures strategy implementation (monitoring)
	Strategy formulation:
	• Decides which businesses the firm should operate in
	• Decides how the firm should compete in those businesses
	• Specifies the economies of scope around which the diversified firm will operate
	Strategy implementation:
	• Encourages cooperation across divisions to exploit economies of scope
	• Evaluates performance of divisions
	• Allocates capital across divisions
Corporate Staff	Provides information to the senior executive about internal and external environments for strategy formulation and implementation (monitoring and bonding)
Division General Managers	Formulates divisional strategies consistent with corporate strategies (bonding) and assures strategy implementation (bonding)
	Strategy formulation:
	• Decides how the division will compete in its business, given the corporate strategy
	Strategy implementation:
	• Coordinates the decisions and actions of functional managers reporting to the division general manager to implement divisional strategy
	• Competes for corporate capital
	• Cooperates with other divisions to exploit corporate economies of scope
Shared Activity Managers	Supports the operations of multiple divisions (bonding)

A board of directors typically consists of 10 to 15 individuals drawn from a firm's top management group and from outside the firm. A firm's **senior executive** (often identified by the title of president or chief executive officer, CEO), its chief financial officer (CFO), and a few other senior managers are usually on the board—although managers on the board are typically outnumbered by non-managers. The firm's senior executive is often but not always the **chairman of the board** (a term used here to denote both female and male senior executives). The task of managerial board members including the board chair, is to provide other board members information and insights about critical decisions being made in the firm and the effect those decisions are likely to have on a firm's equity holders. The task of outsiders on the board is to evaluate the past, current, and future performance of the firm, and of its senior managers, to ensure that the actions taken within the firm are consistent with equity holders' interests.[6]

Boards of directors are typically organized into several sub-committees. An **audit committee** is responsible for ensuring the accuracy of accounting and financial statements. A **finance committee** maintains the relationship between the firm and external capital markets. A **nominating committee** nominates new board members. A **personnel and compensation committee** evaluates and compensates the performance of a firm's senior executive and other senior managers. Often, membership on these standing committees is reserved for external board members. Other standing committees reflect specific issues of a particular firm and are typically open to external and internal board members.[7]

Passive Versus Active Boards

For many years, the boards of major firms were relatively passive and would take dramatic action, such as firing the senior executive, only if a firm's performance was significantly below expectations for long periods of time. However, since the 1990s, boards have become more active proponents of equity holders' interests, taking more direct steps in influencing managerial actions and sometimes even firing a firm's CEO.[8] This recent surge in board activity reflects a new economic reality: If a board does not become more active in monitoring firm performance, then other monitoring mechanisms will. Consequently, the board of directors has become progressively more influential in representing the interests of a firm's equity holders.[9]

This new activity, however, can go too far. If boards begin actively managing a firm on a day-to-day basis, the efficiency advantages of the separation of ownership and control begin to break down. Recall that a firm that has chosen its corporate diversification strategy appropriately will be pursuing a strategy that outside investors cannot pursue on their own. This suggests that outside investors, or their representatives on a firm's board, will be limited in their ability to manage a firm's diversification strategy day to day. To the extent that a board attempts to manage a firm day to day, rather than simply monitoring the firm's actions and performance, it is unlikely that the full value of a corporate diversification strategy will be realized.

Some authors have suggested that most business decision making involves the four distinct activities listed in Figure 12.3.[10] Two of these activities, **initiation** and **implementation** of strategies, are thought to be the exclusive province of managers. The other two, **ratification** and **monitoring,** are the responsibility of boards of directors representing equity holders' interests. As long as board activity focuses on ratifying and

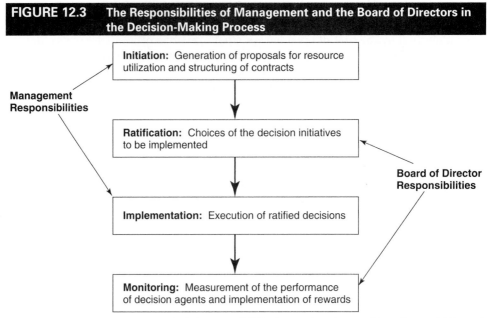

FIGURE 12.3 **The Responsibilities of Management and the Board of Directors in the Decision-Making Process**

Management Responsibilities

Initiation: Generation of proposals for resource utilization and structuring of contracts

Ratification: Choices of the decision initiatives to be implemented

Implementation: Execution of ratified decisions

Monitoring: Measurement of the performance of decision agents and implementation of rewards

Board of Director Responsibilities

Source: Adapted from Fama, E. F., and M. C. Jensen (1983). "Separation of ownership and control," *Journal of Law & Economics,* 2, pp. 301–325.

monitoring strategic decisions, such activity is likely to reduce potential agency conflicts in ways that preserve the efficiency benefits of the separation of ownership and control.

Insiders and Outsiders on the Board

Recent increases in board activity have refocused attention on the advantages and disadvantages of managers versus outsiders on the board. In one way, this seems to be a simple problem. Because the primary role of the board of directors is to monitor managerial decisions to ensure that they are consistent with the interests of equity holders, it follows that the board should consist mostly of outsiders because they face no conflict of interest in evaluating managerial performance. Obviously, managers, as inside members of the board, face significant conflicts of interest in evaluating their own performance.[11]

Research on outsider members of boards of directors tends to support this point of view. Outside directors, as compared to insiders, tend to focus more on monitoring a firm's economic performance rather than on monitoring other measures of firm performance. Obviously, a firm's economic performance is most relevant to its equity investors. Outside board members are also more likely than inside members to dismiss CEOs following poor performance. Also, outside board members have a stronger incentive than inside members to maintain their reputations as effective monitors. This incentive by itself can lead to more effective monitoring by outside board members. Moreover, the monitoring effectiveness of outside board members seems to be substantially enhanced when they personally own a substantial amount of a firm's equity.[12]

However, just because outside members face fewer conflicts of interest in evaluating managerial performance compared to management insiders on the board, it is not true that they face no conflicts of interest. Directors can receive substantial compensation for their service on a board—often as much at $100,000 per year—and the size of this cash compensation often has little relationship to the performance of the firm. In response to the conflicts of interest created by these fees, several groups have recommended, among other changes, that outside directors receive virtually all their board-related compensation in the form of stock and that other noncash benefits programs for board members be eliminated.[13]

Even if all conflicts of interest could be eliminated for outside board members, boards of directors should still include some inside/managerial members. Managers bring something to the board that cannot be easily duplicated by outsiders: detailed information about decision-making activities inside the firm. This is precisely the information that outsiders need in order to monitor the activities of a firm effectively, and it is information available to them only if they work closely with insiders (managers). Therefore, although most work suggests that a board of directors should be comprised primarily of outsiders, there is also an important role for insiders/managers as members of a firm's board.[14]

Institutional Owners

One of the reasons why boards of directors have become more active over the last several years is the growth of large institutional investors. Large institutional investors have very strong incentives to monitor the behavior of firms, to ensure that decisions are made in ways that enhance the value of their investment. Therefore large investors have begun to exercise more direct influence on a firm's board of directors, and thus on the decision-making processes in a firm.[15]

Institutional owners are usually pension funds, mutual funds, or other groups of individual investors that have joined together to manage their investments. In 1987, institutions owned 47 percent of the equity of the 1,000 largest firms in the United States. In 1999, institutions owned 60 percent of the equity of these firms. By the year 2002, institutional investors owned 62 percent of the equity traded in the United States.[16]

Are Institutional Investors Myopic?

Institutional investors can use their investment clout to insist that a firm's management behave in ways consistent with the interests of equity holders. Observers who assume that institutional investors are interested more in maximizing the short-term value of their portfolios than in the long-term performance of firms in those portfolios fear that such power will force firms to make only short-term investments. Recent research in the United States and Japan, however, suggests that institutional investors are not unduly myopic. Rather, as suggested earlier, equity investors apply standard discounted-present-value logic in valuing the performance of a firm. If the present value of a firm's activities is positive, these activities will be consistent with the interests of equity investors, even institutional investors, despite any short-term costs or losses associated with these activities.

For example, one group of researchers examined the effects of institutional ownership on research and development investments in R&D–intensive industries. R&D

investments tend to be longer-term in orientation. If institutional investors are myopic, they should influence firms to invest in relatively less R&D, in favor of investments that generate shorter-term profits. This research showed that high levels of institutional ownership did not adversely affect the level of R&D in a firm. These findings are consistent with the notion that institutional investors are not inappropriately concerned with the short term in their monitoring activities.[17]

More generally, other researchers have shown that high levels of institutional ownership lead firms to sell strategically unrelated businesses. This effect of institutional investors is enhanced if, in addition, outside directors on a firm's board have substantial equity investments in the firm. Given the discussion of the value of unrelated diversification in Chapter 11, it seems clear that these divestment actions are consistent with maximizing the present value of a firm.[18]

The Senior Executive

The senior executive (the president or CEO) in an M-form organization has the same two responsibilities as a senior executive in a U-form organization (see earlier discussions): strategy formulation and strategy implementation. The focus of these activities, however, is not the same. In a U-form organization, strategy formulation focuses on deciding how a firm should compete in its primary business. In an M-form organization, strategy formulation focuses on which businesses a firm should compete in and how the firm should compete in those businesses. In other words, in an M-form organization, the senior executive's primary strategy formulation task is to specify the economies of scope around which the diversified firm should operate. In a U-form organization, strategy implementation focuses on coordinating functions to implement strategy. In an M-form organization, strategy implementation focuses on encouraging appropriate cooperation among divisions in order to exploit valuable economies of scope. Senior executives in M-form organizations have several tools to assist in strategy implementation efforts, including processes for evaluating divisional performance and for allocating capital.

From the perspective of agency problems in a diversified firm, the senior executive's strategy formulation responsibilities can be understood as assuring outside investors that a firm is exploiting economies of scope that have the potential to reduce a firm's costs or increase its revenues in ways that cannot be duplicated by outside investors acting on their own (i.e., as a bonding mechanism). The senior executive's strategy implementation responsibilities can be understood as an effort to assure that this potential is realized through a firm's operations and activities (that is, as a monitoring mechanism).

Strategy Formulation

At the broadest level, deciding which businesses a diversified firm should operate in is equivalent to discovering and developing valuable economies of scope among a firm's current and potential businesses. If these economies of scope are also rare and costly to imitate, they can be a source of sustained competitive advantage for a diversified firm.

The senior executive is uniquely positioned to discover, develop, and nurture valuable economies of scope in a diversified firm. Every other manager in this kind of firm either has a divisional point of view (for example, division general managers and shared activity managers) or is a functional specialist (for example, corporate staff and functional managers within divisions). Only the senior executive has a truly corporate perspective. However, like the senior executive in a U-form organization, the senior executive in an M-form organization should involve numerous other divisional and functional managers in strategy formulation. This will ensure complete and accurate information as input to the process and a broad understanding of and commitment to the strategy once it has been formulated.

Strategy Implementation

As is the case for senior executives in a U-form structure, strategy implementation in an M-form almost always involves resolving conflicts among groups of managers. However, instead of simply resolving conflicts between functional managers (as is the case in a U-form structure), senior executives in M-form organizations must resolve conflicts within and between each of the major managerial components of the M-form structure: corporate staff, division general managers, and shared activity managers. Various corporate staff managers may disagree about the economic relevance of their staff functions; corporate staff may come into conflict with division general managers over various corporate programs and activities; division general managers may disagree with how capital is allocated across divisions; division general managers may come into conflict with shared activity managers about how shared activities should be managed; shared activity managers may disagree with corporate staff about their mutual roles and responsibilities, and so forth.

Obviously, the numerous and often conflicting relationships among groups of managers in an M-form organization can place significant strategy implementation burdens on the senior executive.[19] While resolving these numerous conflicts, however, the senior executive needs to keep in mind the reasons why the firm began pursuing a diversification strategy in the first place: to exploit real economies of scope that outside investors cannot realize on their own. Any strategy implementation decisions that jeopardize the realization of these real economies of scope are inconsistent with the underlying strategic objectives of a diversified firm. These issues are analyzed in detail in the discussion of management control systems in the M-form organization (Section 12.3).

The Office of the President: Chairman, CEO, and COO

The roles and responsibilities of the senior executive in an M-form organization are often more than what can be reasonably managed by a single individual. This is especially likely if a firm is broadly diversified across numerous complex products and markets. In this situation, it is not uncommon for the tasks of the senior executive to be divided among two or three people: the **chairman of the board,** the **chief executive officer,** and the **chief operating officer (COO).** The primary responsibilities of each of these roles in an M-form organization are listed in Table 12.2. Together, these roles are known as the **office of the president.** In general, as the tasks facing the office of the president become more demanding and complex, it is more likely that the roles and responsibilities of this office will be divided among two or three people.

TABLE 12.2   Responsibilities of Three Different Roles in the Office of the President

Chairman of the board	Supervision of the board of directors in its monitoring role
Chief executive officer	Strategy formulation
Chief operating officer	Strategy implementation

There is currently some debate about whether the roles of chairman of the board and CEO should be combined or separated, and if separated, what kinds of people should occupy these positions. Some have argued that the role of CEO and chairman of the board should definitely be separated and that the role of the chairman should be filled by an outside (non-managerial) member of the board of directors. These arguments are based on the assumption that only an outside member of the board of directors can ensure the independent monitoring required to resolve agency conflicts in the modern diversified corporation. Others have argued that effective monitoring often requires more information than what would be available to outsiders, and thus the roles of chairman of the board and CEO should be combined and filled by a firm's senior manager.[20]

Empirical research on this question suggests that whether these roles of CEO and chairman should be combined depends on the complexity of the information analysis and monitoring tasks facing the CEO and chairman. Some researchers have found that combining the two roles is positively correlated with firm performance when firms operate in slow-growth and simple competitive environments—environments that do not overtax the cognitive capability of a single individual.[21] This finding suggests that combining these roles does not necessarily increase agency conflicts between a firm and its equity holders. This research also found that separating the two roles is positively correlated with firm performance when firms operate in high-growth and very complex environments. In such environments, a single individual cannot fulfill all the responsibilities of both CEO and chairman, and thus the two roles need to be held by separate individuals. Other research on the effects of combining the positions of CEO and chairman indicates that such a combination can reduce agency costs in some settings and increase them in others.[22]

Corporate Staff

The primary responsibility of **corporate staff** is to provide information about the firm's external and internal environments to the firm's senior executive. This information is vital for both the strategy formulation and the strategy implementation responsibilities of the senior executive and makes effective monitoring and bonding possible. Corporate staff functions that provide information about a firm's external environment include finance, investor relations, legal affairs, regulatory affairs, and corporate advertising. The functions that provide information about a firm's internal environment include accounting and corporate human resources. These corporate staff functions report directly to a firm's senior executive and are a conduit of information to that executive.

Corporate and Divisional Staff

Many organizations re-create some corporate staff functions within each division of the organization. This is particularly true for internally oriented corporate staff functions such as accounting and human resources. At the division level, divisional staff managers usually have a direct, "solid-line" reporting relationship to their respective corporate staff functional managers and a less formal, "dotted-line" reporting relationship to their division general manager. The reporting relationship between the divisional staff manager and the corporate staff manager is the link that enables the corporate staff manager to collect the information that the senior executive requires for strategy formulation, strategy implementation, monitoring, and bonding. The senior executive can also use this corporate staff–division staff relationship to communicate corporate policies and procedures to the divisions, although these policies can also be communicated directly by the senior executive to division general managers.

Although divisional staff managers usually have a less formal relationship with their division general managers, in practice, division general managers can have an important influence on the activities of divisional staff. After all, divisional staff managers may formally report to corporate staff managers, but they spend most of their time interacting with their division general managers and with the other functional managers who report to these same managers. These divided loyalties can sometimes affect the timelines and accuracy of the information transmitted from divisional staff managers to corporate staff managers and thus affect the timeliness and accuracy of the information the senior executive uses for strategy formulation, strategy implementation, monitoring, and bonding.

Nowhere are these divided loyalties potentially more problematic than in accounting staff function. Obviously, it is vitally important for the senior executive in an M-form organization to receive timely and accurate information about divisional performance. If the timeliness and accuracy of that information are inappropriately affected by division general managers, the effectiveness of senior management can be adversely affected. In some situations, division general managers can have very strong incentives to affect the timeliness and accuracy of divisional performance information. This is especially true when a division general manager's compensation or if the capital allocated to a division depends on this information.

Efficient monitoring by the senior executive requires that corporate staff, true when especially the accounting corporate staff function, remain organizationally independent of division general managers (thus the importance of the solid-line relationship between divisional staff managers and corporate staff managers). Nevertheless, the ability of corporate staff to obtain accurate performance information from divisions also depends on close cooperative working relationships between corporate staff, divisional staff, and division general managers (thus the importance of the dotted-line relationship between divisional staff managers and division general managers). Maintaining the balance between, on the one hand, the distance and objectivity needed to evaluate a division's performance and, on the other hand, the cooperation and teamwork needed to gain access to the information required to evaluate a division's performance distinguishes excellent from mediocre corporate staff managers.

Over-involvement in Managing Division Operations

Over and above the failure to maintain a balance between objectivity and cooperation in evaluating divisional performance, the one sure way that corporate staff can fail in a multidivisional firm is to become too involved in the day-to-day operations of divisions. In an M-form structure, the management of such day-to-day operations is delegated to division general managers and to functional managers who report to division general managers. Corporate staff managers collect and transmit information; they do not manage divisional operations.

One way to ensure that corporate staff does not become too involved in managing the day-to-day operations of divisions is to keep corporate staff small. This is certainly true for some of the best-managed diversified firms in the world. For example, just 1.5 percent of Johnson & Johnson's 82,700 employees work at the firm's headquarters, and only some of those individuals are members of the corporate staff. Hanson Industries has in its U.S. headquarters 120 people who help manage a diversified firm with $8 billion in revenues. Clayton, Dubilier, and Rice, a management buyout firm, has only 11 headquarters staff members overseeing eight businesses with collective sales of over $6 billion.[23]

Numerous examples of corporate staff managers having an inappropriate influence on divisional operations can be cited. In many firms, corporate human resource departments specify wage and compensation schemes that, though appropriate in some divisions, make it impossible to attract labor or management for other divisions. It is not surprising that corporate human resource departments are often called the "antipersonnel" department in these types of firms. In other firms, staff accounting practices can lead division general managers to make decisions that are quite inconsistent with the long-term economic success of a division.

All of this is not to suggest that corporate staff managers never possess expertise that could benefit the operations of divisions. Obviously, they sometimes do, but when corporate staff begins to significantly influence day-to-day divisional activities, it ceases to be corporate staff and instead should be thought of as a shared activity. As will be described, the management challenge facing a shared activity is quite different from the management challenge facing a corporate staff function. For shared activity managers, the primary task is to engage in activities that satisfy the needs and requirements of division general managers. For corporate staff, the primary task is to engage in activities that satisfy the needs and requirements of the senior executive. Confusion between these two tasks often leads to difficulties for corporate staff managers.

Division General Manager

Division general managers in an M-form organization have primary responsibility for managing a firm's businesses day to day. Division general managers have full profit-and-loss responsibility and typically have multiple functional managers reporting to them. As general managers, they have both strategy formulation and strategy implementation responsibilities. On the strategy formulation side, division general managers choose strategies for their divisions, within the broader strategic context established by the senior executive of the firm. Many of the analytical tools described in this book can be used by division general managers to make these strategy formulation decisions.

The strategy implementation responsibilities of division general managers in an M-form organization parallel the strategy implementation responsibilities of senior executives in U-form organizations. In particular, division general managers must be able to coordinate the activities of often conflicting functional managers in order to implement a division's strategies.

In addition to their responsibilities as a U-form senior executive, division general managers in an M-form organization have two additional responsibilities: to compete for corporate capital and to cooperate with other divisions to exploit corporate economies of scope. Division general managers compete for corporate capital by obtaining high rates of return on capital invested in previous periods in their business by the corporations. In most firms, divisions that have demonstrated the ability to generate high rates of return on earlier capital investments gain access to more capital, or to lower-cost capital, compared to divisions that have not demonstrated a history of such performance.

Division general managers cooperate to exploit economies of scope by working with shared activity managers, corporate staff managers, and the senior executive in the firm to isolate, understand, and use the economies of scope around which the diversified firm was originally organized. Division general managers can even become involved in discovering new economies of scope that were not anticipated when the firm's diversification strategy was originally implemented but that nevertheless may be both valuable and costly for outside investors to create on their own.

A careful reader will recognize a fundamental conflict between the last two responsibilities of division general managers in an M-form organization. These managers are required to compete for corporate capital and to cooperate to exploit economies of scope at the same time. Competition is important, because it leads division general managers to focus on generating high levels of economic performance by their divisions. If each division is generating high levels of economic performance, then the diversified firm as a whole is also likely to do well. However, cooperation is important to exploit economies of scope that are the economic justification for implementing a diversification strategy in the first place. If divisions do not cooperate in exploiting these economies, there are few, if any, justifications for implementing a corporate diversification strategy, and the diversified firm should be split into multiple independent entities.

The need to compete and cooperate simultaneously puts significant managerial burden on division general managers. It is likely that this ability is both rare across most diversified firms and costly to imitate. This special managerial skill probably goes a long way in explaining both why most diversified firms do not earn economic profits from the diversification efforts and why a few such firms may.[24]

Shared Activity Managers

One of the potential diversification economies of scope identified in Chapter 11 is shared activities. Divisions in an M-form organization exploit this economy of scope when one or more of the stages in their value chains are managed in common. Typical examples of activities shared across two or more divisions in a multidivisional firm include common sales force, common distribution systems, common manufacturing facilities, and common research and development efforts (also see Table 11.2). The primary responsibility of the individuals who manage shared activities is to support the operations of the divisions that share the activity.

The way in which M-form structure is often depicted in company annual reports (as in Figure 12.1) tends to obscure the operational role of shared activities. In this version of the M-form organizational chart, no distinction is made between corporate staff functions and shared activity functions. Moreover, it appears that managers of shared activities report directly to a firm's senior executive, just as corporate staff do. These ambiguities are resolved by re-drawing the M-form organizational chart to emphasize the roles and responsibilities of different units within the M-form (as in Figure 12.2). In this more accurate representation of how an M-form actually functions, corporate staff groups are separated from shared activity managers, and each is shown reporting to its primary internal "customer"—the senior executive for corporate staff groups, and two or more division general managers for shared activity managers.

Shared Activities as Cost Centers

Shared activities are often managed as cost centers in an M-form structure. When that is the case, shared activity managers do not attempt to create profits when they provide services to the divisions they support. Rather, these services are priced to internal customers in such a way that the shared activity just covers its cost of operating.

Because cost center shared activities do not have to generate profits from their operations, the cost of the services they provide to divisions can be less than the cost of similar services provided either by a division itself or by outside suppliers. Well-managed cost center shared activities will provide lower-cost comparable services unless either of these situations exists: The services needed by a division require the managers of shared activities to acquire or develop costly resources and capabilities already possessed by that division or by an outside supplier; or the cost of providing services is highly sensitive to economies of scale, and shared activities do not enjoy the scale of outside suppliers.

If a shared activity is managed as a cost center, and the cost of services from this shared activity is *greater than* the cost of similar services provided by alternative sources, then either this shared activity is not being well managed, or it was not a real economy of scope in the first place. However, when the cost of services from a shared activity is *less than* the cost of comparable services provided by a division itself or by an outside supplier, then division general managers have a strong incentive to use the services of shared activities, thereby exploiting an economy of scope that may have been one of the original reasons why a firm implemented a corporate diversification strategy.

Although managing shared activities as cost centers can give division managers incentives to exploit an economy of scope in a diversified firm, this management approach can create problems as well. In particular, because cost center shared activities can often undercut the price of alternative sources of service available to divisions, the managers of shared activities have only limited incentives to compete for their internal customers (the divisions) with these other sources of service. This situation can lead the shared activity to supply the division with lower-quality services than the division could obtain on its own, either internally or from an outside supplier. It is not uncommon for division general managers to complain about poor service, shoddy quality, and indifferent responses from shared activities in a diversified firm.

These management difficulties are worsened when a firm's senior executive, in order to ensure that shared activity economies of scope are exploited in a diversified form, *requires* division general managers to use the services of shared activities, no matter what. In effect, the senior executive, in a desire to ensure that economies of scope are exploited, creates an internal monopoly for shared activities in the firm. In this monopoly setting, it is not uncommon for both the cost of services provided to divisions from a shared activity to rise and the quality of those services to fall.

Shared Activities as Profit Centers

In the face of these challenges, some diversified firms are beginning to manage shared activities as profit centers, rather than as cost centers. Moreover, rather than requiring divisions to use the services of shared activities, divisions retain the right to purchase services from internal shared activities or from outside suppliers or to provide services for themselves. In this setting, managers of shared activities are required to compete for their internal customers on the basis of the price and quality of the services they provide.[25]

Of course, the greatest risk associated with treating shared activities as profit centers and letting them compete for divisional customers is that divisions may choose to obtain no services or support from shared activities. Although this course of action may be in the self-interest of each division, it may not be in the best interest of the corporation if, in fact, shared activities are an important economy of scope around which the diversified firm is organized.

In the end, whether a shared activity is managed as a cost center or as a profit center, the task facing the managers of shared activities is the same: to provide such highly customized and high-quality services to divisional customers at a reasonable cost that those internal customers will not want to seek alternative suppliers outside the firm or provide those services themselves. In an M-form organization, the best way to ensure that shared activity economies of scope are realized is for shared activity managers to satisfy their internal customers.

12.3 MANAGEMENT CONTROL SYSTEMS

The M-form structure presented in Figures 12.1 and 12.2 is complex and multifaceted. No organizational structure by itself, however, is able to fully implement a corporate diversification strategy. The M-form structure must be supplemented with a variety of management control systems. At the broadest level, management controls fall into two categories: financial or output controls and strategic or process controls. **Financial** or **output controls** focus on the financial and other results of a manager's strategic and other decisions. Common examples of these controls include budgets and other measures of financial performance. **Strategic** or **process controls** focus on the quality of the strategic decision-making process in which a manager has engaged. A manager may make well-reasoned strategic decisions that turn out not to generate high levels of firm performance. A manager may also make poorly-reasoned strategic decisions that turn out to generate very high levels of firm performance. Strategic or process controls evaluate the quality of a manager's decisions, independent of the performance outcomes of these decisions.[26]

In general, firms that successfully implement a corporate diversification strategy apply both financial and strategic controls. Firms that apply only financial controls often create incentives for managers to do whatever is necessary—including, perhaps, falsifying the books—to meet their numbers. Strategic controls, because they focus on the quality of a manager's decision-making processes, can spot this kind of unethical behavior. On the other hand, firms with just strategic controls in place may have managers who never feel pressure to generate a high level of financial performance. In those firms, managers often "overprocess" decisions, delaying any final decisions to make sure that the decision-making process is good enough to pass inspection. These delays can ultimately cost a firm in terms of its actual financial performance.

Thus, well-managed diversified firms generally have both financial and strategic controls. How those controls are used to help implement a diversification strategy can be seen in three important managerial processes within these firms: evaluating divisional performance, allocating capital across divisions, and transferring intermediate products between divisions. Each of these processes can be thought of as monitoring and bonding mechanisms that firms can use to help reduce agency problems.

Evaluating Divisional Performance

Because divisions in an M-form structure are profit-and-loss centers, evaluating divisional performance should, in principle, be straightforward: Divisions that are very profitable should be evaluated more positively than divisions that are less profitable. In practice, this seemingly simple task is surprisingly complex. Two problems typically arise: (1) How should division profitability be measured, and (2) how should economy-of-scope linkages between divisions be factored into divisional performance measures?

Measuring Divisional Performance with Accounting Numbers

The most traditional approach to measuring and evaluating divisional profitability uses divisional versions of the accounting measures of performance first introduced in Section 2.3. In Chapter 2, such ratios as return on total assets , return on equity, gross profit margin, inventory turnover, and accounts receivable turnover were all calculated for the firm (see Table 2.3). These same ratios can also be calculated for divisions within a diversified firm.

Divisional performance can also be evaluated along numerous other accounting dimensions that the senior executive and the corporate staff think are important. For example, in addition to using traditional accounting ratios, General Electric (GE) has evaluated its divisions in terms of market share and sales growth. Apparently, senior management at GE believed that GE divisions were most likely to be successful in business where they were a market-share leader in a growing industry.[27]

Setting Accounting Performance Standards. Of course, accounting-based measures of performance do not, by themselves, indicate whether a division has performed well. To reach this conclusion, a division's accounting performance must be compared to some standard. Diversified firms typically use one of two standards to evaluate divisional accounting measures of performance.

Some firms simply require all their divisions to meet or exceed a common hurdle rate for the measures of performance that they designate as important. For example, in order to meet corporate expectations, all divisions in a firm might be expected to generate a return on investment (ROI) of at least 10 percent, or a return on sales (ROS) of at least 12 percent. GE has required that each of its divisions be either first or second in market share in a market growing at a specified rate if those divisions are to remain a part of the diversified portfolio of GE.[28]

The great advantage of the common-hurdle rate approach to evaluating divisional accounting performance is its simplicity. Every division general manager knows exactly what the performance standards are and exactly what the consequences are if those standards are not met. This simplicity, however, can be quite deceiving.

Suppose, for example, that a division is able to obtain an ROI of 125 percent. This huge ROI is almost certainly larger than whatever the common hurdle rate in this firm might be. However, simply because a division earned an ROI greater than the common hurdle rate, even if it earned an ROI of 125 percent, it does not follow that this division was managed well. It may be that, given changes in a division's industry structure or some other favorable economic circumstances, other firms in this industry earned an ROI of 250 percent. In this context, an ROI of 125 percent represents management failure, even though it is well above the common hurdle rate in that firm.

In the same way, if a division was able to earn an ROI of only 1.5 percent, well below the common hurdle rate in this firm, it does not necessarily follow that this division was managed poorly. If all the other firms in this industry earned an average ROI of −45 percent, then an ROI of 1.5 percent can be thought of as an enormous accomplishment.

These observations lead to the consideration of a second way of setting standards used to evaluate divisional accounting performance. In this second approach, the expected level of performance is adjusted across divisions to reflect the particular industry and economic conditions of different divisions. For example, some divisions may be expected to earn an ROI of 10 percent, others an ROI of 14 percent, and still others an ROI of 17 percent. Divisional performance expectations are established in a negotiation process that typically involves the division general manager, the senior executive of the firm, and various corporate staff functions.

The performance expectations of different divisions can reflect the unique circumstances of each division's business environment. Nevertheless, if the performance expectations of a business fall below some level for a sustained period of time, most diversified firms will take steps either to change the way business is conducted by that division or to divest themselves of that division.

Establishing Budgets.   Whether the first or second approach is used in establishing standards, they are usually reflected in a division's budget. A division's budget is usually negotiated among division general managers, the senior executive, and corporate staff. This budget reflects a division's expected revenues and costs over the next budgeting period and is a division's operating plan for that time period.

In most diversified firms, enormous time and energy are dedicated to budgeting. This process, when it works well, forces division managers to become explicit about their short- and long-term strategies and about the implications of those strategies for their division's revenues, costs, and profits. More often than not, division general managers are held accountable for the level of performance specified in their division's budget.

The budgeting process is not without pitfalls.[29] Managers throughout an M-form organization can "game" the budgeting process, to establish performance expectations that favor them. For example, division general managers might understate a division's expected performance in order to make it easier to meet or exceed budgeted expectations. Alternatively, divisions seeking additional capital may overstate a division's expected performance and thereby shift capital away from higher-return projects to their own lower-return projects.

Apparently, gaming the budgeting system is quite common in diversified firms. One study of the budget negotiation process among division general managers, a firm's senior executives, and corporate staff for a large sample of diversified firms in the United States found that senior executives and corporate staff routinely discount division sales projections, profitability projections, and capital requests. Some of this discounting reflects the belief that division general managers are systemically optimistic when they make budget requests. However, some of this discounting also reflects the belief that division general managers, anticipating discounting, inflate their budget requests.[30]

Limits of Accounting Measures of Divisional Performance

Aside from the budgeting process, which can create bizarre incentives inside a diversified firm, there are some additional limitations of accounting measures of divisional performance. Most reflect the limitations of accounting measures of firm performance described in Chapter 2.

Managerial Discretion. Just as managers often have some discretion in how they choose accounting methods in reporting a firm's performance, so too do division general managers often have some discretion in how they choose accounting methods in reporting a division's performance. Thus accounting measures of divisional performance reflect, to some degree at least, the interests and preferences of division general managers. For example, when a division general manager's compensation depends on a division's reported accounting performance, he or she can engage in a variety of activities to increase the reported performance of their division in a particular year.[31]

This managerial discretion is one reason why it is important for division-level accounting managers to have a solid-line relationship with the corporate accounting staff function but only a dotted-line relationship with the division general manager. This dual reporting relationship brings more objectivity to the process of accounting for a division's performance. However, even when this reporting relationship is in place, accounting abuses can go on. In some firms, division general managers simply lie about the level of performance in their division. Indeed, the size of this lying can be so large that, once it is discovered, the firm's overall accounting performance has to be restated. Throughout the early part of the twenty-first century, this kind of fraudulent accounting was not uncommon. Numerous diversified firms, including Tyco, WorldCom, HealthSouth, and, most famously, Enron, engaged in such behaviors. Accounting restatements during this time period were very common, and sometimes very substantial. Accounting fraud actually led several managers in these firms to serve time in prison.

Short-Term Bias. A second limitation of accounting measures of divisional performance is that they often have a short-term bias. The reason for this bias is that longer-term, multiple-year investments in a division are usually treated, for accounting purposes, as costs in the years in which they do not generate revenues that exceed costs. In this context, division general managers have limited incentives to invest in the longer-term health of their division—especially if division general managers can get promoted out of their division because of the (artificially) high accounting performance they report.

This short-term bias in accounting measures of divisional performance can manifest itself in a variety of ways. For example, divisions may delay or forgo maintenance on plant and equipment to prop up short-term accounting profitability. Divisions may systematically underinvest in developing new customers—customers that might not generate sales revenues for several years. Also, divisions may not invest in research and development, managerial training, and other capabilities in a division—capabilities that may be vital to the long-run success and viability of a division's business. An over-reliance on accounting-based measures of divisional performance can lead to a diversified firm to systematically underinvest in its long-run success and profitability.[32]

Agency Problems. In the end, the fundamental problem with using accounting measures of performance to evaluate divisions is that these measures can give division general managers incentives that are inconsistent with the interests of equity holders. As discussed previously, equity holders in a firm would like to see the firm managed in such a way that the present value of its future cash flow is maximized. As described in Chapter 2, there is surprisingly little relationship between accounting measures of performance, whether they are applied at the firm or the divisional level, and maximizing the present value of a firm's or division's cash flow. To the extent that divisions are evaluated by means of accounting measures of performance, a diversified firm is contributing to, not eliminating, agency problems between itself and its equity holders. As suggested earlier in this chapter, these agency problems will be reflected in a firm's cost of capital.

Measuring Divisional Economic Performance

Given the limitations of accounting measures of divisional performance, several firms have begun adopting alternative methods for evaluating this performance. These alternatives focus directly on the present value of the cash flow generated by a division and thus do not create the same agency problems as accounting-based approaches.

Perhaps the most popular of these economically oriented measures of division performance is economic value added (EVA).[33] EVA is calculated by subtracting the cost of capital employed in a division from that division's earnings:

$$EVA = \text{adjusted accounting earnings} - (\text{weighted average cost of capital} \times \text{total capital employed by a division}) \qquad (12.1)$$

Several of the terms in the EVA formula require some discussion. For example, the calculation of economic value added begins with a division's "adjusted" accounting earnings. These are a division's traditional accounting earnings adjusted so that they approximate what would be a division's economic earnings.

Given the discussion of accounting and economic performance in Chapter 2, it is clear that numerous adjustments will have to be applied to accounting earnings to make them more closely approximate economic earnings. For example, traditional accounting practices require R&D spending to be deducted each year from a division's earnings. As described earlier, this can lead division general managers to underinvest in longer-term R&D efforts. In the EVA measure of divisional performance, R&D spending is added back into a division's performance, treated as an asset, and then depreciated over some period of time.

One consulting firm (Stern Stewart) that specializes in implementing EVA-based divisional evaluation systems in multidivisional firms makes up to 40 "adjustments" to a division's standard accounting earnings so that they more closely approximate economic earnings. Many of these adjustments are proprietary to this consulting firm.

The terms in parentheses in equation 12.1 reflect the cost of investing in a division. Rather than using some accounting-based measure of the value of this investment, EVA applies financial theory and multiplies the amount of money invested in a division by a firm's weighted average cost of capital. In other words, the cost of its equity is multiplied by the percentage of its capital that takes the form of equity plus the cost of its debt multiplied by the percentage of its capital that takes the form of debt. This number can be thought of as the opportunity cost of investing in a particular division, as opposed to investing in any other division of the firm.

By adjusting a division's earnings and accounting for the cost of investing in a division, economic value added is a much more accurate estimate of a division's economic performance than are traditional accounting measures of performance. In an important sense, EVA is equivalent to calculating return on invested capital or economic profit—measures of firm performance discussed in Chapter 2—of divisions within a firm.

The number of diversified firms evaluating their divisions with EVA-based measures of divisional performance is impressive and growing. These firms include AT&T, Coca-Cola, Quaker Oats, CSX, Briggs and Stratton, and Allied Signal. At Allied Signal, divisions that do not earn their cost of capital are awarded the infamous "leaky bucket" award. If this performance is not improved, division general managers are replaced. The use of EVA has been touted as the key to creating economic wealth in a diversified corporation. Even the U.S. Postal Service has explored the application of EVA to its operations.[34]

The Ambiguity of Divisional Performance

Whether a firm uses accounting measures to evaluate the performance of a division or uses economic measures of performance such as EVA, divisional performance in a well-managed diversified firm can never be evaluated unambiguously. Consider a simple example.

Suppose that in a particular multidivisional firm there are only two divisions (Division A and Division B) and one shared activity (research and development). Also, suppose that the two divisions are managed as profit-and-loss centers and that the R&D shared activity is managed as a cost center. To support this R&D effort, each division pays $10 million per year and has been doing so for 10 years. Finally, suppose that after 10 years of effort (and investment), the R&D group develops a valuable new technology that perfectly addresses Division A's business needs.

Obviously, no matter how divisional performance is measured, it is likely that Division A's performance will rise relative to Division B's performance. In this situation, what percentage of Division A's improved performance should be allocated to Division A, what percentage should be allocated to the R&D group, and what percentage should be allocated to Division B? The managers in each part of this diversified firm can make compelling arguments in their favor. Division general manager A can reasonably argue that without Division A's efforts to exploit the new technology, the full value of the technology would never have been realized. The R&D manager can reasonably argue that without the R&D effort, there would not have been a technology to exploit in the first place. Finally, division general manager B can reasonably argue that without the dedicated long-term investment by Division B in R&D, there would have been no new technology and no performance increase for Division A.

That all three of these arguments can be made suggests that, to the extent that a firm exploits real economies of scope in implementing a diversification strategy, it will not be possible to evaluate the performance of individual divisions in that firm unambiguously. The fact that there are economies of scope in a diversified firm means that all of the businesses in which a firm operates are more valuable bundled together than they would be if kept separate from one another. Efforts to evaluate the performance of these businesses as if they were separate from one another are futile.

One solution to this problem is to force businesses in a diversified firm to operate independently of each other. If each business operates independently, then it will be possible to evaluate its performance unambiguously. Of course, to the extent that this independence is enforced, the diversified firm is unlikely to be able to realize the very economies of scope that were the justification for the diversification strategy in the first place.

Divisional performance ambiguity is bad enough when shared activities are the primary economy of scope that a diversified firm is trying to exploit. This ambiguity increases dramatically when the economy of scope is based on intangible core competencies. In this situation, it is shared learning and experience that justify a firm's diversification efforts. The intangible nature of these economies of scope multiplies the difficulty of the task of divisional evaluation.

Even firms that apply rigorous EVA measures of divisional performance are unable to fully resolve these difficulties of performance ambiguity. For example, the Coca-Cola division of the Coca-Cola Company has made enormous investments in the Coke brand name over the years, and the Diet Coke division has exploited some of that brand-name capital in its own marketing efforts. Of course, it is not clear that all of Diet Coke's success can be attributed to the Coke brand name. After all, Diet Coke has developed its own creative advertising, has developed its own loyal group of customers, and so forth. How much of Diet Coke's success—as measured through that division's economic value added—should be allocated to the Coke brand name (an investment made long before Diet Coke was even conceived), and how much should be allocated to the Diet Coke division's efforts? EVA measures of divisional performance do not resolve ambiguities created when economies of scope exist across divisions.[35]

In the end, the quantitative evaluation of divisional performance—with either accounting or economic measures—must be supplemented by the experience and judgment of senior executives in a diversified firm. Only by evaluating a division's performance numbers in the context of a broader and more subjective strategic evaluation, can a true picture of its performance be developed.

Allocating Corporate Capital

Another potentially valuable economy of scope outlined in Chapter 11 (besides shared activities and core competencies) is internal capital allocation. In that discussion (see Chapter 11), it was suggested that for internal capital allocation to be a justification for diversification, the information made available to senior executives allocating capital in a diversified firm must be superior, in both amount and quality, to the information available to external sources of capital in the external capital market. Both the quality and the quantity of the information available in an internal capital market depend on the organization of the diversified firm.

As suggested in Chapter 11, one of the primary limitations of internal capital markets is that division general managers have a strong incentive to overstate their division's prospects and understate its problems, in order to gain access to more capital at lower costs. Having an independent corporate accounting function in a diversified firm can help address this problem. However, given the ambiguities inherent in evaluating divisional performance in a well-managed diversified firm, independent corporate accountants do not resolve all these informational problems.

Zero-Based Capital Budgeting

One process for allocating capital in this corporate context is for the senior executives to create a list of all capital allocation requests from divisions in a firm, rank them from "most important" to "least important," and then fund all the projects a firm can afford given the amount of capital it has available. This is **zero-based budgeting.** In principle, with zero-based budgeting, no project will receive funding for the future simply because it received funding in the past. Rather, each project has to stand on its own merits each year by being included among the important projects the firm can afford to fund.

Zero-based budgeting has some attractive features, but it has some important limitations as well. First, evaluating and ranking all projects in a diversified firm from "most important" to "least important" is a very difficult task. It not only puts unrealistic analysis and decision-making demands on the senior managers, it also can be fraught with political intrigue and "backroom" capital-allocation deals.

Second, even if such a ranking could be developed, the assumption that the amount of capital available for allocation is fixed can lead either to investing in projects that do *not* have a positive present value or not investing in projects that do have a positive present value. Zero-based budgeting leads to investing in projects that do *not* have a positive present value when the sum of all capital requests with a positive present value is less than the total (fixed) amount of capital available. In this situation, negative-present-value projects are funded simply because a firm has sufficient capital to make the investment. Also, this type of budgeting leads to a failure to invest in projects that have a positive present value when the sum of all positive-net-present-value projects in a firm is greater than the total (fixed) amount of capital available. In this situation, positive-present-value projects are not funded, simply because a firm assumes it has insufficient capital to make the investment. In both cases, the internal market for capital allocation will be less efficient than an external capital market in which the amount of capital available for allocation to positive-present-value projects is not fixed.

Cross-Divisional Capital Allocation

To avoid the problems of zero-based budgeting, some firms manage capital allocation as a cross-divisional process. Rather than requiring a senior executive to rank all of a firm's capital projects from "most important" to "least important," some firms bring their division general managers (with their staffs) together with the senior executive (with the corporate staff) and the shared activity managers, to decide collectively how capital should be allocated. In this setting, division general managers take turns summarizing their division's performance, prospects, and capital requests. After each presentation, the senior executive, corporate staff, shared activity managers, and other division general managers have an opportunity to ask difficult, pointed questions in an attempt to fully understand a division's capital needs. In this context, it is difficult for backroom capital allocation deals to remain intact. Moreover, the strengths and weaknesses of each division's performance and prospects can be revealed.

With this more accurate information in place, managers in a diversified firm can apply present-value criteria and choose to invest in just those activities that have positive present value and not to invest in projects with negative present value. If this process is managed well, the amount of capital to be allocated across divisions is not fixed. Rather, the amount of capital to be allocated depends entirely on the sum of the positive-present-value investments available in a firm.

This type of cross-divisional meeting requires a fair amount of cooperation, trust, and teamwork among the different parts of a diversified organization.[36] This is a high standard for managing the capital allocation process. The difficulty of managing this process effectively may be one of the reasons why internal capital allocation often fails to qualify as a valuable economy of scope in diversified firms.[37]

Transferring Intermediate Products

The existence of economies of scope across multiple divisions in a diversified firm often means that products or services produced in one division are used as inputs for products or services produced by a second division. Intermediate products or services can be transferred between any of the units in an M-form organization. This transfer is, perhaps, most important and problematic when it occurs between profit center divisions. The transfer of intermediate products or services among divisions is usually managed through a **transfer-pricing system:** One division "sells" its product or service to a second division for a transfer price.

Setting Optimal Transfer Prices

From an economic point of view, the rule for establishing the optimal transfer price in a diversified firm is quite simple: The transfer price should be the value of the opportunities forgone when one division's product or service is transferred to another division. Consider the following example: Division A's marginal cost of production is $5 per unit, but Division A can sell all of its output to outside customers for $6 per unit. If Division A can sell all of its output to outside customers for $6 per unit, the value of the opportunity forgone of transferring a unit of production from Division A to Division B is $6. This is the amount of money that Division A forgoes by transferring its production to Division B instead of selling it to the market.

However, if Division A is selling all the units it can to external customers for $6 per unit but still has some excess manufacturing capacity, the value of the opportunity forgone in transferring the product from Division A to Division B is only $5 per unit which is Division A's marginal cost of production. Because the external market cannot absorb any more of Division A's product at $6 per unit, the value of the opportunity forgone when Division A transfers units of production to Division B is not $6 per unit (Division A can't get that price), but only $5 per unit.[38]

When transfer prices are set equal to opportunity costs, selling divisions will produce output up to the point that the marginal cost of the last unit produced equals the transfer price. Moreover, buying divisions will buy units from other divisions in the firm as long as the net revenues from doing so just cover the transfer price. If there are no interdependencies between divisions, these transfer prices will lead profit-maximizing divisions to optimize the diversified firm's profits.

Difficulties in Setting Optimal Transfer Prices

Setting transfer prices equal to opportunity costs sounds simple enough, but it is very difficult to do in real diversified firms. Establishing optimal transfer prices requires information about the value of the opportunities forgone by the "selling" division. This, in turn, requires information about this division's marginal costs, its manufacturing capacity, external demand for its products, and so forth. Much of this information is difficult to calculate. Moreover, it is rarely stable. As market conditions change, demand for a division's products can change, marginal costs can change, and the value of opportunities forgone can change. Also, to the extent that a selling division customizes the products or services for sale to other divisions—that is, to the extent that interdependencies exist between divisions within a firm—the value of the opportunities forgone by this selling division become even more difficult to calculate.

Even if this information could be obtained and updated rapidly, division general managers in selling divisions have strong incentives to manipulate the information in ways that increase the perceived value of the opportunities forgone by their division. These division general managers can thus increase the transfer price for the products or services they sell to internal customers and thereby appropriate for themselves profits that should have been allocated to buying divisions.

Setting Transfer Prices in Practice

Because it is rarely possible for firms to establish an optimal transfer-pricing scheme, most diversified firms must adopt some form of transfer pricing that attempts to approximate optimal prices. Several of these transfer-pricing schemes are described in Table 12.3. However, no matter what particular schemes a firm uses, the transfer prices it generates will, at times, create inefficiencies and conflicts in a diversified firm. Some of these inefficiencies and conflicts are described in Table 12.4.[39]

The inefficiencies and conflicts created by transfer pricing schemes that only approximate optimal transfer prices means that few diversified firms are ever fully satisfied with how they set transfer prices. Indeed, one study found that as the level of resource sharing in a diversified firm increases (thereby increasing the importance of transfer-pricing mechanisms), the level of job satisfaction for division general managers decreases.[40]

It is not unusual for a diversified firm to change its transfer-pricing mechanisms every few years in an attempt to find the "right" transfer-pricing mechanism. Economic theory tells us what the "right" transfer-pricing mechanism is: Transfer prices should equal opportunity cost. However, this "correct" transfer-price mechanism cannot be

TABLE 12.3 Alternative Transfer Pricing Schemes	
Exchange Autonomy	• Buying and selling division general managers are free to negotiate transfer price without corporate involvement.
	• Transfer price is set equal to the selling division's price to external customers.
Mandated Full Cost	• Transfer price is set equal to the selling division's actual cost of production.
	• Transfer price is set equal to the selling division's standard cost (that is, the cost of production if the selling division were operating at maximum efficiency).
Mandated Market Based	• Transfer price is set equal to the market price in the selling division's market.
Dual Pricing	• Transfer price for the buying division is set equal to the selling division's actual or standard costs.
	• Transfer price for the selling division is set equal to the price to external customers or to the market price in the selling division's market.

Source: Adapted from Eccles, R. (1985). *The Transfer Pricing Problem: A Theory for Practice,* Lexington, MA: Lexington Books.

TABLE 12.4	**Weaknesses of Alternative Transfer-Pricing Schemes**

1. Buying and selling divisions negotiate transfer price
- What about the negotiating and haggling costs?
- The corporation risks not exploiting economies of scope if the right transfer price cannot be negotiated.

2. Transfer price is set equal to the selling division's price to external customers
- Which customers? Different selling division customers may get different prices.
- Shouldn't the volume created by the buying division for a selling division be reflected in a lower transfer price?
- The selling division doesn't have marketing expenses when selling to another division. Shouldn't that be reflected in a lower transfer price?

3. Transfer price is set equal to the selling division's actual costs
- What are those actual costs, and who gets to determine them?
- *All* the selling division's costs, or only the costs relevant to the products being purchased by the buying division?

4. Transfer price is set equal to the selling division's standard costs
- Standard costs are the costs the selling division would incur if it were running at maximum efficiency. This hypothetical capacity subsidizes the buying division.

5. Transfer price is set equal to the market price
- If the product in question is highly differentiated, there is no simple "market price."
- Shouldn't the volume created by the buying division for a selling division be reflected in a lower transfer price?
- The selling division doesn't have marketing expenses when selling to a buying division. Shouldn't that be reflected in a lower transfer price?

6. Transfer price is set equal to actual costs for the selling division and to market price for the buying division
- This combination of schemes simply combines the problems of setting transfer price.

implemented in most firms. Firms that continually change their transfer-pricing mechanisms generally find that all these systems have some weaknesses. In choosing which system to use, a firm should be less concerned about finding the right transfer-pricing mechanism and more concerned about choosing a transfer-pricing policy that creates the fewest management problems, or at least the kinds of problems that the firm can manage effectively. Indeed, some scholars have suggested that the search for optimal transfer pricing should be abandoned in favor of treating transfer pricing as a conflict-resolution process. Viewed in this way, transfer pricing highlights differences between divisions and thus makes it possible to begin to resolve those differences in a mutually beneficial way.[41]

12.4 COMPENSATION POLICIES

A firm's compensation policies constitute a final set of monitoring and bonding mechanisms for implementing a diversification strategy. Many of the compensation issues raised in the discussion of U-form organizational structures apply equally as well to compensation in M-form organizations.

Traditionally, the compensation of senior managers in a diversified firm has been only loosely connected to the firm's economic performance. One important study examined the relationship between executive compensation and firm performance, and found that differences in CEO cash compensation (salary plus cash bonus) are not very responsive to differences in firm performance.[42] In particular, this study showed that a CEO of a firm, whose equity holders collectively lost $400 million in a year, earned average cash compensation worth $800,000, while a CEO of a firm, whose equity holders collectively gained $400 million in a year, earned average cash compensation worth $1,040,000. Thus an $800 million difference in the performance of another firm only had, on average, a $204,000 impact on the size of a CEO's salary and cash bonus. Put differently, for every million dollars of improved firm performance, CEOs, on average, get paid an additional $255. After taxes, increasing a firm's performance by a million dollars is roughly equal in value to a good dinner at a four-star restaurant—without wine!

However, this same study was able to show that if a substantial percentage of a CEO's compensation came in the form of stock and stock options in the firm, changes in compensation would be closely linked with changes in the firm's performance. In particular, the $800 million difference in firm performance just described would be associated with a $1.2 million difference in the value of CEO compensation, if CEO compensation included stock and stock options in addition to cash compensation. In this setting, an additional million dollars of firm performance increases a CEO's salary by $667.

These and similar findings reported elsewhere have led more and more diversified firms to include stock and stock options as part of the compensation package for the CEO. As important, many firms now extend this noncash compensation to other senior managers in a diversified firm, including division general managers. For example, the top 1,300 managers at General Dynamics receive stock and stock options as part of their compensation package. Moreover, the cash bonuses of these managers also depend on General Dynamics' stock market performance. At Johnson & Johnson, all division general managers receive a five-component compensation package. The level of only one of those components, salary, does not depend on the economic profitability of the business over which a division general manager presides. The level of the other four components—a cash bonus, stock grants, stock options, and a deferred income package—varies with the economic performance of the particular division. Moreover, the value of some of these variable components of compensation also depends on Johnson & Johnson's long-term economic performance.[43]

As reported previously, by 1991, 86 percent of the compensation of the 19 highest-paid CEOs in the United States came in the form of stock grants and other stock options. Only 47 of the 200 highest-paid CEOs in 1991 did not receive at least some of their compensation in the form of stock.[44] Less complete information exists about the compensation package of division general managers and other senior managers in diversified firms, but it is very likely that much of the compensation of these managers also comes in the form of stock and stock options. The trend to compensate CEOs and other senior managers through stock and stock options accelerated through the 1990s. By 1996, the total market value of stock reserved for stock option compensation programs in U.S. companies totaled over $600 billion. Fifteen of the 200 largest firms in the United States in 1996 had at least 24 percent of their shares set aside for options and other stock awards.[45]

To the extent that compensation in diversified firms gives managers incentives to make decisions consistent with stockholders' interests, these policies can be thought of as bonding mechanisms that reduce agency problems. However, given the dollar value of some CEO compensation packages, one must wonder if these forms of compensation, rather than reducing agency costs, are, in fact, a manifestation of agency problems. A recent extensive review of determinants of CEO compensation suggests that the type and amount of CEO compensation continues to be only loosely related to firm performance. Rather, executive compensation is often determined by, among other things, the interpersonal relationships between a CEO and his or her board of directors and a CEO's ability to manage the board's impressions of his or her performance. Although agency theory suggests that the determination of CEO salaries should be an economic process, research on the actual determinants of CEO compensation suggests that assessment of CEO performance is a social process affected by group decision-making forces in the board.[46]

12.5 SUMMARY

To be valuable, diversification strategies must exploit economies of scope that are not available to outside investors. One implication of this requirement is that outside investors must delegate the day-to-day management of their investments in a firm to the firm's managers. This practice creates an agency relationship between a firm's outside investors (as principals) and its managers (as agents). As long as managers make decisions in ways that are consistent with investors' interests, no agency problems arise. However, it is not uncommon for conflicts of interest between these two parties to emerge and thus for agency problems to exist.

Both managers and outside investors can engage in a variety of activities to minimize agency problems. In general, these activities can be described as either monitoring activities or bonding activities. Organizing to implement a corporate diversification strategy can be understood as an effort to create low-cost and effective monitoring and bonding mechanisms.

A diversified firm's organizational structure is a particularly important monitoring and bonding device. The best organizational structure for implementing a diversification strategy is the multidivisional, or M-form, structure. The M-form structure has several critical components that have both monitoring and bonding implications. These components include the board of directors, institutional investors, the senior executive, corporate staff, division general managers, and shared activity managers.

This organizational structure is supported by a variety of management control processes. Three critical management control processes for firms implementing diversification strategies are (1) evaluating the performance of divisions, (2) allocating capital across divisions, and (3) transferring intermediate products between divisions. The existence of economies of scope in firms implementing corporate diversification strategies significantly complicates the management of these processes in ways that facilitate monitoring and bonding.

Finally, a firm's compensation policies can also act as monitoring and bonding mechanisms for implementing a diversification strategy. Historically, management compensation has been only loosely connected to a firm's economic performance, but the last few years have seen the increased popularity of using stock and stock options to help compensate managers. Such compensation schemes act as bonding mechanisms and help reduce agency conflicts between managers and outside investors.

REVIEW QUESTIONS

1. Agency theory has been criticized for assuming that managers, left on their own, will behave in ways that reduce the wealth of outside equity holders when, in fact, most managers are highly responsible stewards of the assets they control. This alternative view of managers has been called *stewardship theory*. Do you agree with this criticism of agency theory? Why or why not?

2. Suppose that the concept of the stewardship theory is correct and that most managers, most of the time, behave responsibly and make decisions that maximize the present value of the assets they control. What implications, if any, does this supposition have on organizing to implement diversification strategies?

3. The M-form structure enables firms to pursue complex corporate diversification strategies by delegating different management responsibilities to different individuals and groups within a firm. Will there come a time when a firm becomes too large and too complex to be managed even through an M-form structure? In other words, is there a natural limit to the efficient size of a firm?

4. Most observers agree that centrally planned economies fail because it is impossible for bureaucrats in large government hierarchies to coordinate different sectors of an economy as efficiently as market mechanisms do. Many diversified firms, however, are as large as some economies and use private-sector hierarchies to coordinate diverse business activities in a firm. Are these large private-sector hierarchies somehow different from the government hierarchies of centrally planned economies? If yes, in what way? If no, why do these large private-sector hierarchies continue to exist?

5. Suppose that the optimal transfer price between one business and all other business activities in a firm is the market price. What does this condition say about whether this firm should own this business?

ENDNOTES

1. The arguments summarized in this section were originally developed by Jensen, M. C., and W. H. Meckling (1976). "Theory of the firm: Managerial behavior, agency costs, and ownership structure," *Journal of Financial Economics,* 3, pp. 305–360.

2. An argument made by Klein, B., and K. Leffler (1981). "The role of market forces in assuring contractual performance," *Journal of Political Economy,* 89, pp. 615–641.

3. See Fama, E. F. (1970). "Efficient capital markets: A review of theory and empirical work," *Journal of Finance,* 25, pp. 383–417.

4. See Williamson, O. E. (1975). *Markets and Hierarchies: Analysis and Antitrust Implications,* New York: Free Press; and Barney, J. B., and W. G. Ouchi (1986). *Organizational Economics,* San Francisco, CA: Jossey-Bass. This is yet another example of the "lemons" problem discussed by Akerlof, G. A. (1970). "The markets for 'lemons': Qualitative uncertainty and the market mechanism," *Quarterly Journal of Economics,* 84 (August), pp. 488–500.

5. The structure and function of the multi-divisional firm was first described by Chandler, A. (1962). *Strategy and Structure: Chapters in the History of the Industrial Enterprise,* Cambridge, MA: MIT Press. The economic logic underlying the multi-divisional firm was first described by Williamson, O. E. (1975). *Markets and Hierarchies: Analysis and Antitrust Implications,* New York: Free Press. Empirical examinations of the effect of the M-form structure on firm performance include Armour, H. O., and D. J. Teece (1980). "Vertical integration and technological innovation," *Review of Economics and Statistics,* 60, pp. 470–474. There continues to be some debate about the efficiency of the M-form structure. See Freeland, R. F. (1966). "The myth of the M-form? Governance, consent, and organizational change," *American Journal of Sociology,* 102(2), pp. 483–626; and Shanley, M. (1996). "Straw men and M-form myths: Comment on Freeland," *American Journal of Sociology,* 102(2), pp. 527–536.

6. See Finkelstein, S., and R. D'Aveni (1994). "CEO duality as a double-edged sword: How boards of directors balance entrenchment avoidance and unity of command," *Academy of Management Journal,* 37, pp. 1079–1108.

7. Kesner, I. F. (1988). "Director's characteristics and committee membership: An investigation of type, occupation tenure and gender," *Academy of Management Journal,* 31, p. 66–84; Zahra, S. A., and J. A. Pearce II (1989). "Boards of directors and corporate financial performance: A review and integrative model," *Journal of Management,* 15, pp. 291–334.

8. This evolution has been documented by Magnet, M. (1983). "What activist investors want," *Fortune,* March 8, pp. 59–63; and Kesner, I. F., and R. B. Johnson (1990). "An investigation of the relationship between board composition and stockholder suits," *Strategic Management Journal,* 11, pp. 327–336.

9. See, for example, Kosnik, R. D. (1990). "Effects of board demography and directors' incentives on corporate greenmail decisions," *Academy of Management Journal,* 33, pp. 129–150; and Lublin, J. S., and C. Duff (1995). "How do you fire a CEO? Very, very slowly," *Wall Street Journal,* January 20, p. B1.

10. Fama, E. G., and M. C. Jensen (1983). "Separation of ownership and control," *Journal of Law and Economics,* 26, pp. 301–325.

11. These conflicts are discussed in Lorsch, J. W. (1989). *Pawns or Potentates: The Reality of America's Corporate Boards,* Boston: Harvard Business School Press; and Weidenbaum, M. L. (1986). "Updating the corporate board," *Journal of Business Strategy,* 7, pp. 77–83.

12. See, for example, Boyd, B. (1990). "Corporate linkages and organizational environment: A test of the resource dependence model," *Strategic Management Journal,* 11, pp. 419–430; Johnson, R. A., R. E. Hoskisson, and M. A. Hitt (1993). "Board of director involvement in restructuring: The effects of board versus managerial controls and characteristics," *Strategic Management Journal,* 14, pp. 33–50; Fama, E. G., and

M. C. Jensen (1983). "Separation of ownership and control," *Journal of Law and Economics,* 26, pp. 301–325; Coughlan, A. T., and R. M. Schmidt (1985). "Executive compensation, managerial turnover, and firm performance," *Journal of Accounting and Economics,* 7, pp. 43–66; Warner, J. B., R. Watts, and K. Wruck (1988). "Stock prices and top management changes," *Journal of Financial Economics,* 20, pp. 461–493; Weisbach, M. S. (1988). "Outside directors and CEO turnover," *Journal of Financial Economics,* 20, pp. 431–460; Baysinger, B. D., and H. N. Butler (1985). "The role of corporate law in the theory of the firm," *Journal of Law and Economics,* 28(1), pp. 179–191; and Shleifer, A., and R. W. Vishny (1986). "Large shareholders and corporate control," *Journal of Political Economy,* 94, pp. 461–488.

13. See Lublin, J. S. (1995). "Give the board fewer perks, a panel urges," *Wall Street Journal,* June 19, p. B1.

14. Zajac, E., and J. Westphal (1994). "The costs and benefits of managerial incentives and monitoring in large U.S. corporations: When is more not better?" *Strategic Management Journal,* 15, pp. 121–142; Baysinger, B., and R. E. Hoskisson (1990). "The composition of boards of directors and strategic control: Effects on corporate strategy," *Academy of Management Review,* 15, pp. 72–87; Hoskisson, R. E., and T. A. Turk (1990). "Corporate restructuring: Governance and control limits of the internal capital market," *Academy of Management Review,* 15, pp. 459–477; Cochran, P. L., R. A. Wood, and T. B. Jones (1985). "The composition of board of directors and incidence of golden parachutes," *Academy of Management Journal,* 28, pp. 664–671; Vance, S. C. (1964). *Board of Directors: Structure and Performance,* Eugene, OR: University of Oregon Press.

15. See Rediker, K., and A. Seth (1995). "Boards of directors and substitution effects of alternative governance mechanisms," *Strategic Management Journal,* 16, pp. 85–99; Magnet, M. (1993). "What activist investors want," *Fortune,* March 8, pp. 59–63; Allen, F. (1993). "Strategic management and financial

markets," *Strategic Management Journal,* 14, pp. 11–22; Lipin, S. (1995). "A list of laggards appears to back investor activism," *Wall Street Journal,* October 3, pp. C1+.

16. Anonymous (2000). "Reversal of fortune: Institutional ownership is declining," *Investor Relations Business,* May 1, pp. 8–9.

17. See Hansen, G. S., and C. W. L. Hill (1991). "Are institutional investors myopic? A time-series study of four technology-driven industries," *Strategic Management Journal,* 12, pp. 1–16.

18. See Bergh, D. (1995). "Size and relatedness of units sold: An agency theory and resource-based perspective," *Strategic Management Journal,* 16, pp. 221–239; and Bethel, J., and J. Liebeskind (1993). "The effects of ownership structure on corporate restructuring," *Strategic Management Journal,* 14, pp. 15–31.

19. These burdens are well described by Westley, F., and H. Mintzberg (1989). "Visionary leadership and strategic management," *Strategic Management Journal,* 10, pp. 17–32.

20. Those that argue that the role of CEO and chairman should be separate and the chairman should be an outsider, include Neff, T. J. (1990). "Outside directors and the CEO: Changing the rules," *The Corporate Board,* 11, pp. 7–10; Lorsch, J. W. (1989). *Pawns or Potentates: The Reality of America's Corporate Boards,* Boston: Harvard Business School Press; Dobrzynski, J. (1991). "How America can get the 'patient' capital it needs," *Business Week,* October 21, p. 112; Rechner, P., and D. Dalton (1991). "CEO duality and organizational performance: A longitudinal analysis," *Strategic Management Journal,* 12, pp. 155–160; and Harris, D., and C. E. Helfat (1991). "CEO dualilty, succession, capabilities, and agency theory: Commentary and research agenda," *Strategic Management Journal,* 19(9), pp. 901–904. Those who argue the opposite include Donaldson, L. (1990). "The ethereal hand: Organizational economics and management theory," *Academy of Management Review,* 15, pp. 369–381; Fama, E. G., and M. C. Jensen (1983). "Separation of ownership and control," *Journal of Law and Economics,*

26, pp. 314–315. A good review of these issues can be found in Finkelstein, S., and R. D'Aveni (1994). "CEO duality as a double-edged sword: How boards of directors balance entrenchment avoidance and unity of command," *Academy of Management Journal,* 37, pp. 1079–1108.

21. See Boyd, B. K. (1995). "CEO duality and firm performance: A contingency model," *Strategic Management Journal,* 16, pp. 301–312; and Rechner, P., and D. Dalton (1991). "CEO duality and organizational performance: A longitudinal analysis," *Strategic Management Journal,* 12, pp. 155–160.

22. See Finkelstein, S., and R. D'Aveni (1994). "CEO duality as a double-edged sword: How boards of directors balance entrenchment avoidance and unity of command," *Academy of Management Journal,* 37, pp. 1079–1108.

23. See Dumaine, B. (1992). "Is big still good?" *Fortune,* April 20, pp. 50–60.

24. See Golden, B. (1992). "SBU strategy and performance: The moderating effects of the corporate-SBU relationship," *Strategic Management Journal,* 13, pp. 145–158; Berger, P., and E. Ofek (1995). "Diversification's effect on firm value," *Journal of Financial Economics,* 37, pp. 36–65; Lang, H. P., and R. Stulz (1994). "Tobin's q, corporate diversification, and firm performance," *Journal of Political Economy,* 102, pp. 1248–1280.

25. See Halal, W. (1994). "From hierarchy to enterprise: Internal markets are the new foundation of management," *Academy of Management Executive,* 8(4), pp. 69–83.

26. Hoskisson, R. E., and M. A. Hitt (1988). "Strategic control systems and relative R&D investment in multi-product firms," *Strategic Management Journal,* 9(6), pp. 605–621; and Simons, R. (1994). "How new top managers use control systems as levers of strategic renewal," *Strategic Management Journal,* 15, pp. 169–189.

27. Tichy, N., and S. Sherman (1993). *Control Your Destiny or Someone Else Will: How Jack Welch Is Making General Electric the World's Most Competitive Corporation,* New York: Doubleday.

28. See Loeb, M. (1995). "Jack Welch lets fly on budgets, bonuses, and buddy boards," *Fortune,* May 29, pp. 145–147.

29. Some of these are described in Duffy, M. (1989). "ZBB, MBO, PPB, and their effectiveness within the planning/marketing process," *Strategic Management Journal,* 12, pp. 155–160.

30. Bethel, J. E. (1990). "The capital allocation process and managerial mobility: A theoretical and empirical investigation," unpublished doctoral dissertation, University of California, Los Angeles.

31. See Watts, R. L., and J. L. Zimmerman (1986). *Positive Accounting Theory,* Upper Saddle River, NJ: Prentice Hall; Healy, P. M. (1985). "The effect of bonus schemes on accounting decisions," *Journal of Accounting and Economics,* 7, pp. 85–107; and Bowen, R. M., E. W. Noreen, and J. M. Lacey (1981). "Determinants of the corporate decision to capitalize interest," *Journal of Accounting and Economics,* August, pp. 151–179.

32. See Hoskisson, R., and M. Hitt (1988). "Strategic control systems and relative R&D investment in large multi-product firms," *Strategic Management Journal,* 9, pp. 605–621.

33. See Stern, J., B. Stewart, and D. Chew (1995). "The EVA financial management system," *Journal of Applied Corporate Finance,* 8, pp. 32–46; and Tully, S. (1993). "The real key to creating wealth," *Fortune,* 128, September 20, pp. 38–50.

34. Applications of EVA are described in Tully, S. (1993). "The real key to creating wealth," *Fortune,* 128, September 20, pp. 38–50; Tully, S. (1995). "So, Mr. Bossidy, we know you can cut. Now show us how to grow," *Fortune,* 3, August 21, pp. 70–80; Tully, S. (1995). "Can EVA deliver profits to the post office?" *Fortune,* July 10, p. 22.

35. A special issue of the *Journal of Applied Corporate Finance* in 1994 addressed many of these issues.

36. See Priem, R. (1990). "Top management team group factors, consensus, and firm performance," *Strategic Management Journal,* 11, pp. 469–478; and Wooldridge, B., and S. Floyd (1990). "The strategy process, middle management involvement, and organizational performance," *Strategic Management Journal,* 11, pp. 231–241.

37. A point made by Westley, F. (1900). "Middle managers and strategy: Microdynamics of inclusion," *Strategic Management Journal,* 11, pp. 337–351; Lamont, O. (1997). "Cash flow and investment: Evidence from internal capital markets," *The Journal of Finance,* 52(1), pp. 83–109; Shin, H. H., and R. M. Stulz (1998). "Are internal capital markets efficient?" *The Quarterly Journal of Economics,* May, pp. 531–552; and Stein, J. C. (1997). "Internal capital markets and the competition for corporate resources," *The Journal of Finance,* 52(1), pp. 111–133.

38. See Brickley, J., C. Smith, and J. Zimmerman (1996). *Organizational Architecture and Managerial Economics Approach,* Homewood, IL: Irwin; and Eccles, R. (1985). *The Transfer Pricing Problem: A Theory for Practice,* Lexington, MA: Lexington Books.

39. See Cyert, R., and J. G. March (1963). *A Behavioral Theory of the Firm,* Upper Saddle River, NJ: Prentice Hall; Swieringa, R. J., and J. H. Waterhouse (1982). "Organizational views of transfer pricing," *Accounting, Organizations & Society,* 7(2), pp. 149–165; and Eccles, R. (1985). *The Transfer Pricing Problem: A Theory for Practice,* Lexington, MA: Lexington Books.

40. Gupta, A. K., and V. Govindarajan (1986). "Resource sharing among SBUs: Strategic antecedents and administrative implications," *Academy of Management Journal,* 29, pp. 695–714.

41. A point made by Swieringa, R. J., and J. H. Waterhouse (1982). "Organizational views of transfer pricing," *Accounting, Organizations & Society,* 7(2), pp. 149–165.

42. Jensen, M. C., and K. J. Murphy (1990). "Performance pay and top management incentives," *Journal of Political Economy,* 98, pp. 225–264.

43. See Dial, J., and K. J. Murphy (1995). "Incentives, downsizing, and value creation at General Dynamics," *Journal of Financial Economics,* 37, pp. 261–314, on General Dynamics' compensation scheme; and

Aguilar, F. J., and A. Bhambri (1983). "Johnson & Johnson (A)," *Harvard Business School Case no. 384-053*, on Johnson & Johnson's compensation scheme.

44. Tully, S. (1992). "What CEOs really make," *Fortune,* June 15, pp. 94–99. By the late 1990s, stock-based CEO compensation was very common.

45. See Fox, J. (1997). "The next best thing to free money," *Fortune,* July 7, pp. 52+; and Colvin, G. (1999). "How to be a great E-CEO," *Fortune,* May 24, pp. 104+.

46. This very interesting perspective is presented in Gomez-Mejia, L., and R. Wiseman (1997). "Reframing executive compensation: An assessment and outlook," *Journal of Management,* 23(3), pp. 291–374. See also Finkelstein, S., and D. C. Hambrick (1996). *Strategic Leadership: Top Executives and Their Effects on Organizations,* Minneapolis/St. Paul: West Publishing; and Rosen, S. (1982). "Authority, control, and distribution of earnings," *Bell Journal of Economics,* 13, pp. 311–323.

C H A P T E R

$$\boxed{13}$$

Strategic Alliance Strategies

As described in Chapter 9, interfirm cooperation that takes the form of tacit collusion is a difficult strategy to develop and maintain. Firms often have strong economic incentives to collude tacitly, but there are also strong incentives to cheat on these cooperative agreements once they are established. Moreover, because explicit collusion is typically illegal, the ability of firms to collude depends on some rather special industry characteristics, such as small numbers of competing firms, homogeneous costs, homogeneous products, and entry barriers, together with some highly developed organizational skills in reading and interpreting signals that may indicate a willingness to collude. In the end, it becomes clear that although tacit collusion is not impossible, it is also probably not widely implemented.

However, other forms of cooperation are more common. Among these are a wide class of cooperative strategies called *strategic alliances,* the subject of this chapter.

13.1 TYPES OF STRATEGIC ALLIANCES

A **strategic alliance** exists whenever two or more independent organizations cooperate in the development, manufacture, or sale of products or services. Strategic alliances can be grouped into three broad categories: non-equity alliances, equity alliances, and joint ventures (see Figure 13.1). In a **non-equity alliance,** cooperating firms agree to work together to develop, manufacture, or sell products or services, but they do not take equity positions in each other or form an independent organizational unit to manage their cooperative efforts. Rather, these cooperative relations are managed through the use of various forms of contracts. **Licensing agreements** (by which one firm allows others to sell products), **supply agreements** (by which one firm agrees to supply others), and **distribution agreements** (by which

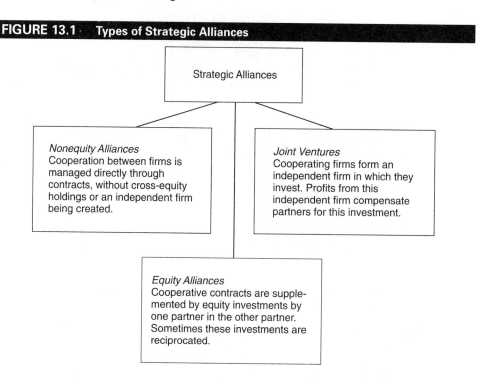

FIGURE 13.1 **Types of Strategic Alliances**

one firm agrees to distribute the products of others) are examples of non-equity strategic alliances.

In an **equity alliance,** cooperating firms supplement contracts with equity holdings in alliance partners. For example, when General Motors began importing small cars manufactured by Isuzu, not only did these partners have supply contracts in place, GM purchased 34.2 percent of Isuzu's stock.[1] In a **joint venture,** cooperating firms create a legally independent firm in which they invest and from which they share any profits that are created.

13.2 THE ECONOMIC VALUE OF STRATEGIC ALLIANCES

The use of non-equity alliances, equity alliances, and joint ventures is becoming a very common strategy. Indeed, one widely used database lists over 20,000 alliances of various kinds from around the world.[2]

Strategic Alliances and Economic Performance

In general, firms have an incentive to cooperate in strategic alliances when the value of their resources and assets combined is greater than the value of their resources and assets separately. This notion of resource complementarity is the same as the definition of an **economy of scope** that was seen in Chapter 11's discussion of corporate diversification and exists as long as the inequality in equation 13.1 holds:

$$NPV(A + B) > NPV(A) + NPV(B) \qquad \textbf{(13.1)}$$

where

$NPV(A + B)$ = the net present value of Firm A's and Firm B's assets combined
$NPV(A)$ = the net present value of Firm A's assets alone
$NPV(B)$ = the net present value of Firm B's assets alone

Alliance Opportunities

Several sources of interfirm economies of scope in strategic alliances have been discussed in literature. Some of the most important are listed in Table 13.1 and discussed below. These interfirm economies represent opportunities that can be exploited through strategic alliances.[3]

Exploiting Economies of Scale

One of the most often cited reasons for the development of strategic alliances is the exploitation of economies of scale by firms that, if acting independently, would not be large enough to obtain these cost advantages. In this context, the complementary resources and assets that alliance partners possess are their development, manufacturing, or distribution activities. The cost of these activities, when combined in a strategic alliance, can be less than the cost of the activities done separately.

An example of a strategic alliance to exploit economies of scale can be found in the aluminum industry.[4] The efficient scale of a bauxite mine is substantially larger than the efficient scale of an aluminum smelter. A single firm operating a bauxite mine efficiently is likely to generate many times more bauxite than it can process in its efficient aluminum smelters. To run its smelters efficiently, this single firm would have to mine bauxite in a less efficient, smaller-scale way or sell its excess bauxite on the open market. However, because of transaction-specific methods that are required to refine bauxite obtained from different mines, selling excess bauxite on the open market is difficult. Thus, to obtain all the economies of scale associated with bauxite mining while keeping their smelters efficiently small, many aluminum firms have joined in joint-venture mining operations. Indeed, joint ventures currently account for over half of the world's bauxite mining capacity.

Learning from Competitors

Firms can also use strategic alliances to learn important skills and abilities from their competitors.[5] These otherwise competing firms may have an incentive to cooperate

TABLE 13.1	Sources of Interfirm Economies of Scope That Can Motivate Strategic Alliances

1. Exploiting economies of scale
2. Learning from competitors
3. Managing risk and sharing costs
4. Facilitating tacit collusion
5. Low-cost entry into new markets
6. Low-cost entry into new industries and new industry segments
7. Low-cost exit from industries and industry segments
8. Managing uncertainty

even though cooperation may help a firm compete in all of its business activities, not just in the strategic alliance.

The joint venture between General Motors and Toyota has been widely cited for its potential to help GM learn from Toyota about manufacturing high-quality small cars at a profit.[6] To take advantage of this learning potential, GM rotates managers from its other manufacturing facilities to the joint venture and then back to GM plants. Of course, Toyota would not have been willing to become associated with GM in this strategic alliance (and risk sharing its knowledge about manufacturing small cars) unless it also gained from this relationship. From Toyota's point of view, this joint venture enables Toyota to gain a stronger foothold in the U.S. market by providing access to GM's impressive U.S. distribution network and by reducing the political liabilities associated with importing numerous cars into the U.S. market. Learning from this alliance can also facilitate Toyota's continued entry into the U.S. market. Moreover, Toyota may believe that GM's ability to learn about manufacturing small cars is limited, for much of this ability is tacit, socially complex, and difficult to imitate.[7]

Although learning from competitors through strategic alliances can be an important opportunity, at least three risks are associated with this type of alliance. First, as just suggested, this form of alliance can allow a competing firm to develop the skills and abilities it needs to compete more effectively in all segments of its business. This development, in the long run, can hurt the alliance partner who is serving as the instructor. Some have argued that strategic alliances between U.S. and Japanese firms have given the Japanese firms access to critical technologies that they have then used to generate important competitive advantages.[8] According to this line of thought, by cooperating with Japanese firms, U.S. firms transferred their skills and abilities to these Japanese firms, which then used these abilities to compete against their former partners. Of course, U.S. firms have gained some access to closed Japanese markets through their strategic alliances with local Japanese partners. The question facing all firms contemplating alliances with firms competing in their industry is: "Is the value of learning greater than the competitive threat that may be created through this form of cooperation?"

A second risk of this form of strategic alliance is that competing firms seeking to learn from each other may appear to be violating antitrust laws. Indeed, as will be discussed later, the traditional way of analyzing the benefits of strategic alliances with competitors has been to assume that such alliances are created to facilitate tacit collusion.[9] Government regulators may conclude that strategic alliances designed to facilitate learning from competitors are actually forms of tacit or even explicit collusion, and they may subject these alliances to intense legal scrutiny. This was the case in GM's alliance with Toyota.[10]

Finally, if the primary motivation for engaging in an alliance is to learn from competitors, a dynamic called a **learning race** can develop in an alliance. Learning races can have the effect of reducing the ability of an alliance to improve the performance of at least one partner to an alliance.[11]

Suppose that two competing firms want to learn from each other, but it is likely that it will be more difficult for Firm I to learn what it wants to learn from Firm II than it will be for Firm II to learn what it wants to learn from Firm I. In the GM/Toyota joint venture, for example, GM wants to learn how to manufacture small cars efficiently, while Toyota wants to learn how to operate in the U.S. marketplace. By virtue of creating the alliance with GM, Toyota is assured of gaining valuable experience in the U.S. market. On the other hand, in order for GM to learn about manufacturing small cars efficiently, it must carefully study the Toyota manufacturing process over a long period of time. It then must discover how to transfer parts of that process to the rest of GM. It is likely that it will be more difficult for GM to learn what it wants to learn from Toyota than it will be for Toyota to learn what it wants to learn from GM.

Similar asymmetries exist in alliances between large pharmaceutical firms and small biotechnology companies. Large firms typically want to learn about the new technology or technologies that small biotech firms bring to an alliance. Small firms, on the other hand, need to learn about the marketing, sales, manufacturing, and distribution skills that large firms bring to an alliance. Clearly, in most settings, it is much more difficult for small firms to learn all they can from large firms than it is for large firms to learn about the technology that a small firm brings to an alliance.

When these learning asymmetries are significant, they can lead to the premature dismantling of an alliance, at least from the point of view of one of the parties to that alliance. In particular, once one firm has learned all it needed to learn from an alliance, it has a strong incentive to underinvest in the continuing alliance. Thus, the alliance becomes a race to learn quickly. The first firm that learns what it wanted to learn from the alliance can then effectively dismantle the alliance. The firm that learns more slowly never learns all that it wanted to from the alliance. Engaging in a learning race and dismantling an alliance before your alliance partner learns all it wanted to learn can have the effect of sustaining the fast-learning firm's competitive advantage over the slow-learning firm. Later in this chapter, this type of behavior is described as *moral hazard*.

Of course, a firm that anticipates that it will be a slow learner in an alliance can engage in activities to reduce this threat of opportunism that might exist in a learning alliance. For example, it can try to slow the learning of its alliance partner. It can insist on a variety of contractual protections that force the fast-learning firm to continue investing in the alliance. It can try to develop resources and capabilities that will take some time for its alliance partners to learn about. However, these actions all have the effect of increasing the cost of using a strategic alliance as a way to learn from competitors. If these costs are sufficiently high, a firm might decide not to use an alliance to facilitate learning, but rather simply acquire its former competitor. The challenges associated with acquiring competitors are discussed in detail in Chapter 14.

Managing Risk and Sharing Costs

Strategic alliances can also help a firm manage the risks and share the costs associated with new business investments. Sometimes, the investment required to exploit an opportunity can be very large. Acting alone, a firm making this investment may be "betting the company," substantially increasing the probability of bankruptcy. Even when failure will not lead to bankruptcy of a firm, the downside risks of some costly investments can be substantial.

In this context, forming strategic alliances spreads the risk of failure by sharing the costs among several firms. Reports from the semiconductor-manufacturing industry suggest that the sheer size of the investment required to build a full service, vertically integrated semiconductor fabrication plant is so large that few, if any, single firm plants will be built in the future. Instead, several firms are likely to form joint ventures to fund and manage these facilities. Similarly, the high risk of offshore oil drilling has led most firms in this industry to join in drilling consortia to explore possible sites.[12]

Risk management and cost sharing seem to be at the heart of new alliances created in the automobile industry. The "Big Three" auto companies continue to compete in product markets but have alliances to invest in risky but high-potential research efforts. Such research and development alliances include a cooperative effort to develop composite materials, cleaner-burning engine technologies, and at least four other joint efforts.[13]

Alliances to manage risk and share costs can also be important in industries in which industry-wide technology and communication standards are important. In Chapter 4, these were called network industries. As these industries emerge, several competing standards may exist. These multiple standards can be allowed to compete until the standard that will predominate the industry emerges. Alternatively, firms in an industry can cooperate to create a standard that meets the needs of the cooperating firms. By cooperating, firms manage the risks and reduce the costs associated with "going it alone." This cooperative approach to standard setting was used in the emerging high-definition television industry to create a technology standard acceptable to many of the key players.[14]

Facilitating Tacit Collusion

Another incentive for cooperating in strategic alliances is that such activities may facilitate the development of tacit collusion. Recall that tacit collusion is made more difficult by legal restrictions on communication between firms. However, separate firms, even if they are in the same industry, can form strategic alliances. Although communication between these firms cannot legally include sharing information about prices and costs of products or services that are produced outside the alliance, such interaction does help create the social setting within which tacit collusion can develop.[15]

As suggested earlier, most early research on strategic alliances focused on the implications of these actions for tacit collusion. Several authors concluded that joint ventures, as a form of alliance, do increase the probability of tacit collusion. For example, one study found that joint ventures created two industrial groups, besides U.S. Steel, in the U.S. iron and steel industry in the early 1900s. In this sense, joint ventures in the steel industry were a substitute for U.S. Steel's vertical integration and have had the effect of creating an oligopoly in what (without joint ventures) would have been a more competitive market.[16] Other studies found that over 50 percent of joint venture partners belong to the same industry.[17] After examining 885 joint venture bids for oil and gas leases, one study found only 16 instances in which joint venture partners competed with one another on another tract in the same sale.[18] These results suggest that joint ventures might encourage subsequent tacit collusion among firms in the same industry.[19]

Another study found that joint ventures were most likely in industries of moderate concentration. This study suggested that in highly concentrated industries, joint ventures were not needed to create conditions conducive to collusion (that is, the small-numbers condition discussed in Chapter 9 already holds), and in nonconcentrated industries these conditions could not be created by joint ventures. Only when joint-venturing activity could effectively create conditions conducive for collusion—under conditions of moderate concentration—were joint ventures seen as likely.[20]

More recent work, however, disputes these findings. Joint ventures between firms in the same industry may be valuable for a variety of reasons that have little or nothing to do with collusion.[21] Moreover, by using a lower level of aggregation, several authors have disputed the finding that joint ventures are most likely in moderately concentrated industries. The original study defined industries by using two-digit Standard Industrial Classification (SIC) codes; by using three-digit SIC-code industry definitions, subsequent work found that 73 percent of the joint ventures had parent firms coming from different industries. Although joint ventures between firms in the same industry (defined at this lower level of aggregation) may have collusive implications, subsequent work has shown that these kinds of joint ventures are relatively rare.[22]

Low-Cost Entry into New Markets

Another motivation for strategic alliances cited in literature is the effect of these relationships on the cost of entry into new markets, especially entry into foreign markets. In this context, one partner typically brings products or services (as resources) to the alliance, and the other partner brings local knowledge, local distribution networks, and local political influence (as resources) to the relationship. Low-cost entry into new markets is the primary motivation behind the numerous international alliances in the telecommunications industry.[23]

Even in the absence of government regulations on entry, the development of local distribution networks can be a costly and difficult process. Such activities generally require a great deal of knowledge about local conditions. Local alliance partners may already possess this knowledge. By cooperating with local partners, firms can substantially reduce the cost of entry into these markets. Alliances can be even more important when government regulations favor local firms over firms from other countries. In this context, alliances with local partners may be the only economically viable means of entry into a market.[24]

Some empirical results support these observations. For example, one study found that when entry into a foreign market was based on a product differentiation strategy (a strategy that presumably requires a great deal of local knowledge), joint ventures with local partners (presumably to obtain local knowledge) were more likely, compared to entry into foreign markets based on low-cost or other strategies. Also, when the culture of a firm's country of origin is very different from the culture of the country it is seeking to enter, it has been shown that entering firms are more likely to use joint ventures, thereby obtaining the cultural expertise of the local partner.[25]

A strategic alliance with a local partner is almost the only way to enter into some new markets. For example, virtually all entry by U.S. firms into the Chinese and Japanese domestic markets has been with Chinese and Japanese alliance partners. The possible creation of trade barriers to protect European and other markets has made strategic alliances between North American firms and local partners in these protected markets much more important and frequent. Government restrictions on entry into India have required foreign firms, in many circumstances, to obtain local strategic alliance partners, as do the increased use of local-content laws in several European countries and the United States. Overall, the increased globalization of the world's industry, linked with heterogeneous cultures and political systems and barriers to free trade, makes international strategic alliances more valuable and common.[26]

Low-Cost Entry into New Industries and New Industry Segments

Strategic alliances can also facilitate a firm's entry into a new industry or into new segments in an industry. Entry into an industry can require skills, abilities, and products that a potential entrant does not possess. Strategic alliances can help a firm enter a new industry, by avoiding the high costs of creating these skills, abilities, and products.

For example, recently DuPont wanted to enter into the electronics industry. However, building the skills and abilities needed to develop competitive products in this industry can be very difficult and costly. Rather than absorbing these costs, DuPont developed a strategic alliance (DuPont/Phillips Optical) with an established electronics firm, Phillips, to distribute some of Phillips's products in the United States. In this way DuPont was able to enter into a new industry (electronics) without having to absorb all the costs of creating the needed resources and abilities from the ground up.

Of course, for this joint venture to succeed, Phillips must have had an incentive to cooperate with DuPont. Whereas DuPont was looking to reduce its cost of entry into a new industry, Phillips was looking to reduce its cost of continued entry into a new market: the United States. Phillips used its alliance with DuPont to sell in the United States the compact discs it already was selling in Europe.[27]

Notice that alliance partners do not have to obtain the same advantages from cooperation in order for the complementary resources and assets condition described in equation 13.1 to hold. All that is required is that the present value of the combined resources and assets be greater than the present value of each of these resources and assets separately. The sources of this increased value to alliance partners may or may not be the same.

Alliances to facilitate entry into new industries can be valuable even when the skills needed in these industries are not as complex and difficult to learn as skills in the electronics or movie industries. For example, rather than developing their own frozen novelty foods, Welch Foods, Inc., and Leaf, Inc. (maker of Heath candy bars) asked Eskimo Pie to formulate products for this industry. Eskimo Pie developed Welch's frozen grape-juice bar and the Heath toffee ice-cream bar. These firms then split the profits derived from these products.[28] As long as the cost of using an alliance to enter a new industry is less than the cost of learning new skills and capabilities, an alliance can be a valuable strategic opportunity.

Entry facilitated by alliances need not be restricted to entry into new industries. Often, firms cooperate in order to facilitate entry into a new segment within an industry. For example, Coca-Cola and Nestlé recently formed a joint venture to begin manufacturing and distributing coffee in aluminum cans in the Korean market. This represents a new industry segment for both firms.[29]

Low-Cost Exit from Industries or Industry Segments

Some firms use strategic alliances as a mechanism to withdraw from industries or industry segments in a low-cost way. Firms are motivated to withdraw from an industry or industry segment when their level of performance in that business is less than what was expected, and when there are few prospects of improvement. Often, when a firm desires to exit an industry or industry segment, it will need to dispose of the assets it has developed to compete in that industry or industry segment. These assets often include tangible resources and capabilities such as factories, distribution centers, and product technologies, and intangible resources and capabilities such as brand name, relationships with suppliers and customers, a loyal and committed workforce, and so forth.

Firms often have difficulty in obtaining the full economic value of these tangible and intangible assets as they exit an industry or industry segment. This reflects an important information asymmetry that exists between the firms that currently own these assets and firms that may want to purchase these assets—an asymmetry that leads to what some authors have called *the lemons problem*.[30]

Consider the used-car market. At the time a person purchases a used car, it is often difficult to tell whether this car is a "lemon," that is, a low-quality car. Full information about the quality of the used car one purchases only becomes available later, after the car is purchased. Of course, anyone selling a used car has a strong incentive to describe the car as not being a lemon. This way, the seller can get the highest price possible for the car. This is true both for those who are selling a high-quality used car and those who are selling what, in fact, is a lemon. Because potential buyers cannot easily tell the difference between sellers who are selling good used cars and sellers who are selling lemons that are merely described as good cars, they tend to discount all these descriptions. This means that high-quality used cars are valued at about the same level as low-quality used cars, and thus that high-quality used cars do not yield their full value when they are sold. In equilibrium, rational owners of high-quality used cars will not sell them, because they cannot obtain their full value in the used-car market. Thus, the only used cars that are sold will be lemons.

When a firm is trying to exit an industry or industry segment, and therefore is trying to sell the assets it developed in this industry or industry segment, it faces a similar lemons problem—especially if it is difficult for a potential buyer to value these assets independently. In general, it will be more difficult for a potential buyer to value intangible assets independently, as compared to tangible assets. Consequently, when the value of the assets a firm is looking to dispose of as part of its exit strategy depends primarily on intangible resources and capabilities, it will be very difficult for a firm to realize the full economic value of those assets upon exit. Potential buyers have a strong incentive to discount the quality of these assets, as described by the selling firm, because the selling firm has a strong incentive to exaggerate the quality of these intangible assets. This is the case even though, as suggested in Chapter 5, intangible assets are more likely to be a source of sustained competitive advantage than tangible assets.

In the market for used cars, those who are selling high-quality used cars can use a variety of mechanisms to signal the quality of their used cars to buyers. For example, they can sell guarantees associated with their used cars. Guarantees signal the quality of a used car because they are less costly to offer when selling high-quality used cars than when selling low-quality used cars. In this sense, guarantees reduce the information symmetry between those selling used cars and those buying them.

Firms looking to exit an industry or industry segment can use strategic alliances to reduce this information asymmetry about the value of their industry specific or segment specific tangible and intangible assets. By forming an alliance with another firm that may want to enter into the industry or industry segment that a particular firm wants to exit, the focal firm provides its alliance partner an opportunity to observe directly the quality of the tangible and intangible assets it controls in that industry or industry segment. Because it no longer has to rely on unreliable assertions about the quality of the resources and capabilities a firm possesses, the firm that seeks to acquire these assets will not discount them below their actual value. This enables the selling firm to obtain more of the full value of its tangible and intangible assets upon exiting an industry or industry segment. In this sense, a firm that is willing to form an alliance prior to exiting an industry or industry segment is giving a potential buyer of the assets a "guarantee" about the quality of the assets.

One firm that has used strategic alliances to facilitate its exit from an industry or industry segment is Corning. In the late 1980s, Corning entered into the medical diagnostics industry. After several years, however, Corning concluded that its resources and capabilities could be more productively used in other businesses. For this reason, it began to extract itself from the medical diagnostics business. However, to make sure it received the full value of the assets it had created in the medical diagnostics business upon exiting this business, it formed a strategic alliance with the Swiss specialty chemical company, Ciba-Geigy. Ciba-Geigy paid $75 million to purchase half of Corning's medical diagnostics business. A couple of years later, Corning finished exiting from the medical diagnostics business by selling its remaining assets in this industry to Ciba-Geigy. However, whereas Ciba-Geigy had paid $75 million for the first half of Corning's assets in the medical diagnostics business, it paid $150 million for the second half of these assets. Corning's alliance with Ciba-Geigy made it possible for Ciba-Geigy to fully value Corning's capabilities in medical diagnostics. Any information asymmetry that might have existed was reduced, and Corning was able to get more of the full value of its assets upon exiting this industry.[31]

Using the language developed in Chapter 8, Corning's alliance with Ciba-Geigy created a real option for Ciba-Geigy. Once Ciba-Geigy understood the full value of this real option, it struck the option by purchasing the rest of Corning's medical diagnostics assets. This way of characterizing the relationship between Corning and Ciba-Geigy leads to the last motivation for pursuing a strategic alliance.

Managing Uncertainty

Finally, firms may use strategic alliances to manage uncertainty. Under conditions of high uncertainty, firms may not be able to tell, at a particular point in time, which of the several different strategies should they pursue. As explained in Chapter 8, firms in this setting have an incentive to retain the flexibility to move quickly into a particular market or industry once the full value of that strategy is revealed. In this sense, strategic alliances enable a firm to maintain a point of entry into a market or industry, without incurring the costs associated with full-scale entry.

Based on this logic, strategic alliances have been analyzed as real options.[32] In this sense, a joint venture is an option that a firm buys, under conditions of uncertainty, to retain the ability to move quickly into a market or industry if valuable opportunities present themselves. One way in which firms can move quickly into a market is simply to buy out their partner(s) in the joint venture. Moreover, by investing in a joint venture, a firm may gain access to the information it needs to evaluate full-scale entry into a market.[33]

In this approach to analyzing strategic alliances, firms that invest in alliances as options will acquire their alliance partners only after the market signals an unexpected increase in value of the venture—that is, only after uncertainty is reduced and the true positive value of entering into a market is known. Empirical findings are consistent with these expectations.

The real option nature of many strategic alliances can be seen in the payoffs that are associated with purchasing an alliance partner. Suppose a firm forms an equity alliance with another firm, and this first firm buys a percentage of the equity of the second. Let the percentage of this other firm's equity that has been purchased equal α, the value of the cash flows created by this partially owned business equal V_t, and the price that would have to be paid to complete the acquisition of this other firm equal P. If this firm decided to purchase the rest of its alliance partner, the economic return from that purchase would be

$$(1 - \alpha)V_t - P \tag{13.2}$$

Alternatively, if this firm decides to not acquire the rest of its partner, it earns zero additional profit (although it may have positive cash flows from the percentage of its partner it does own). What the alliance between these firms does is create the option to either buy or not buy the rest of an alliance partner, depending on how V_t and P evolve. Moreover, by having a stake in an alliance partner, a firm is probably in a better position to know the value of these two variables, compared to the case when a firm does not have an alliance with a partner.

Strategic Alliances and Generic Industry Structures

Some of the incentives to cooperate in strategic alliances listed in Table 13.1 exist only when cooperating firms have similar strategic goals and objectives. For example, firms seeking economies of scale through strategic alliances must find partners that are also searching for economies of scale and have production or distribution processes that can be conveniently linked within a strategic alliance to obtain cost reductions. Also, firms seeking to develop tacit collusion through strategic alliances must find partners with whom collusion is likely to develop, and with whom collusion is likely to have the effect of reducing industry output and increasing industry prices. A strategic alliance in which all parties are seeking the same advantages from the alliance is called a **symmetric alliance.**

Some of the other incentives to cooperate in strategic alliances can be realized only when cooperating firms have different strategic goals and abilities. For example, an alliance that facilitates entry into new markets or into new industries and new industry segments presumes that at least one partner in the alliance is operating in a market or industry segment in which another firm in the alliance is not operating. Also, strategic alliances designed to facilitate learning presume that cooperating firms differ. If they did not differ along some strategically relevant dimension, one firm could not learn from another. These kinds of strategic alliances are called **asymmetric alliances.**

Other incentives to cooperate in strategic alliances can exist whether firms are similar to or different from one another. When alliances are used to manage uncertainty, that uncertainty can stem from factors within a firm's current market or industry or from factors associated with entering new markets or industries. The same can be said of alliances to manage risk. When uncertainty/risk exists within a single industry, partnering with other firms in that industry can help manage that uncertainty/risk. Such strategic alliances are likely to be symmetric. When managing uncertainty/risk requires partnerships across market or industry boundaries, asymmetric alliances are formed. Alliances in which firm interests can be similar to or different from one another are called **mixed alliances.**

The distinction among symmetric, asymmetric, and mixed strategic alliances helps clarify which kinds of strategic alliances are likely to be opportunities in some of the generic industry structures discussed in Chapter 4. These relationships are summarized in Table 13.2.[34]

Because symmetric alliances can exist only among similar firms, these kinds of alliances are most likely to generate advantages for firms in very mature industries (in which firms have similar products, technologies, customers, and so forth) or in fragmented industries with large groups of similar firms (in which firms within each group are similar to each other). These kinds of symmetric alliances are also most likely in network industries (in which firms cooperate to create a single *de facto* standard in an industry) and empty-core industries (in which firms cooperate to reduce the threat of cutthroat competition through tacit collusion or to influence government policy). In these industry settings, symmetric strategic alliances that are designed to exploit economies of scale or lead to the development or tacit collusion are most likely.

Asymmetric strategic alliances are most likely when cooperating firms are different from each other. Thus asymmetric alliances are most likely in emerging industries (before industry standards create firm homogeneity), in fragmented industries without strategic groups, in declining industries (in which firms pursue several different strategies), and in global industries (in which cultural and political heterogeneity exists). Asymmetric alliances are also the most likely form of alliance in hypercompetitive industries and in empty-core industries in which firms are pursuing product differentiation or demand management opportunities. In these industry settings, asymmetric alliances to gain entry into new markets or industries and alliances to facilitate learning are most likely to be important strategic opportunities.

Mixed strategic alliances can exist in any industry setting. Thus, alliances to manage risk and uncertainty can be opportunities in any generic industry structure.

TABLE 13.2 Types of Strategic Alliances and Generic Industry Structures

Type of Alliance	Generic Industry Structure
Symmetric alliance	Mature industries
Economies of scale	Fragmented industries (with strategic groups)
Tacit collusion	Network industries
	Empty-core industries
Asymmetric alliance	Emerging industries
Low-cost entry into new markets	Fragmented industries (with no strategic groups)
Low-cost entry into new industries and new industry segments	Declining industries
Learning from competitors	Global industries
Mixed alliance	All generic industry structures
Managing uncertainty	
Managing risks and sharing costs	

Alliance Threats: Incentives to Cheat on Strategic Alliance Agreements

Just as there are incentives to cooperate in strategic alliances, there are also incentives to cheat on these cooperative agreements. Cheating can occur in at least three different ways: adverse selection, moral hazard, and holdup (see Table 13.3).[35]

Adverse Selection

Potential cooperative partners can misrepresent the skills, abilities, and other resources that they will bring to an alliance. This form of cheating, called **adverse selection,** exists when an alliance partner promises to bring to an alliance certain resources that it either does not control or cannot acquire. For example, a local firm engages in adverse selection when it promises to make available to alliance partners a local distribution network that does not currently exist. Firms that engage in adverse selection are not competent alliance partners.

Adverse selection in a strategic alliance is likely only when it is difficult or costly to observe the resources or capabilities that a partner brings to an alliance. If potential partners can easily see that a firm is misrepresenting the resources and capabilities it possesses, they will not create a strategic alliance with that firm. Armed with such understanding, they will either seek a different alliance partner or develop the needed skills and resources internally, or perhaps forgo this particular business opportunity.

However, evaluating the veracity of the claims of potential alliance partners is often not easy. The ability to evaluate these claims depends on information that a firm may not possess. To fully evaluate claims about a potential partner's political contacts, for example, a firm needs its own political contacts; to fully evaluate claims about potential partners' market knowledge, a firm needs significant market knowledge. A firm that can completely, and at low cost, evaluate the resources and capabilities of potential alliance partners probably does not really need that strategic alliance. The fact that a firm is seeking an alliance partner is in some sense an indication that the firm has limited abilities to evaluate potential partners.

In general, the less tangible the resources and capabilities that are to be brought to a strategic alliance, the more costly it will be to estimate their value before an alliance is created, and the more likely is adverse selection to occur. Firms considering alliances with partners bringing intangible resources such as "knowledge of local conditions" or "contacts with key political figures" need to guard against this form of cheating.

There have been numerous examples of adverse selection in strategic alliances. BellSouth once formed an alliance with a software development company called Telesciences. The purpose of this alliance was to develop billing software to facilitate

TABLE 13.3	Ways to Cheat in Strategic Alliances
Adverse selection	Potential partners misrepresent the value of the skills and abilities they bring to the alliance.
Moral hazard	Partners provide to the alliance skills and abilities of lower quality than they promised.
Holdup	Partners exploit the transaction-specific investments made by others in the alliance.

BellSouth's international expansion in the cellular telephone business. BellSouth chose Telesciences as its alliance partner because Telesciences had acquired some software that accomplished some of the tasks that BellSouth ultimately wanted to have accomplished by the software it wanted to be developed. It was assumed that Telesciences would be able to build on its existing software and thus would be able to develop and deliver the entire software package in an efficient and effective manner. It turned out, however, that it was very difficult for Telesciences to re-engineer its old software and it did not possess all the programming skills it needed to deliver the software BellSouth needed in a timely manner. Software was ultimately delivered, but it was 18 months late and very difficult to use. From BellSouth's perspective, Telesciences engaged in adverse selection when it agreed to form the software-development alliance.[36]

Of course, Telesciences had a somewhat different interpretation. Telesciences asserted that the reason it was unable to deliver the software in a timely manner was that it did not receive the consistent support from BellSouth that it needed. Instead, BellSouth constantly changed the management team in charge of this alliance, continuously changed the specifications of the software to be developed, and in other ways made it difficult for Telesciences to be successful. From Telesciences' point of view, BellSouth engaged in the next form of cheating in strategic alliances discussed in this chapter—moral hazard.

Moral Hazard

Partners in an alliance may possess high quality resources and capabilities of significant value in an alliance but fail to make those resources and capabilities available to alliance partners. This form of cheating is called **moral hazard.** For example, a partner in an engineering strategic alliance may agree to send only its most talented and best-trained engineers to work in the alliance but then actually sends less talented, poorly trained engineers. These less-qualified engineers may not be able to contribute substantially to making the alliance successful, but they may be able to learn a great deal from the highly qualified engineers in other alliance partners. In this way, the less-qualified engineers effectively transfer wealth from other alliance partners to their own firm.[37]

Often both parties in a failed alliance accuse each other of moral hazard. For example, in the late 1980s, Boston Ventures, a New England investment firm, purchased Motown Records. Boston Ventures then entered into an alliance with MCA to distribute Motown's records. Unfortunately, sales of Motown's recordings through MCA's distribution networks never met expectations. Motown blamed MCA for failing to promote the recordings aggressively; MCA accused Motown of producing records that simply were not popular hits. After just a few years, this alliance crumbled and Motown signed a distribution agreement with Polygram Records.[38]

The existence of moral hazard in a strategic alliance does not necessarily mean that one or more parties to that alliance are malicious or dishonest. Rather, what often happens is that market conditions change after an alliance is formed, requiring one or more partners to an alliance to change their strategies.

For example, in the early days of the personal computer industry, Compaq Computer Corporation relied on a network of independent distributors to sell its computers. However, as competition in the personal industry increased, Internet, mail-order and electronics superstores became much more valuable distribution networks, and alliances between Compaq and its traditional distributors became strained. After a period of time, Compaq's traditional distributors were unable to obtain all the inventory they wanted in a timely manner. Indeed, to satisfy the needs of large accounts, some traditional distributors actually purchased Compaq computers from local computer superstores and then shipped them to their customers. Compaq's shift from independent dealers to alternative distributors looked like moral hazard at least from the point of view of the independent dealers. However, from Compaq's perspective, this change simply reflected economic realities in the personal computer industry.[39]

The learning race described earlier in this chapter can be seen as an example of moral hazard. One recent study estimated that almost 80 percent of entrepreneurial firms that enter into alliances with large firms experience moral hazard to a significant degree.[40]

Holdup

Even if alliance partners engage in neither adverse selection nor moral hazard, another form of cheating may evolve. Once a strategic alliance has been created, partner firms may make investments that have value only in the context of that alliance and in no other economic exchanges. These are the transaction-specific investments mentioned in Chapter 10. For example, managers from one alliance partner may have to develop close, trusting relationships with managers from other alliance partners. These close relationships are very valuable in the context of the alliance but have limited economic value in other economic exchanges. Also, one partner may have to customize its manufacturing equipment, distribution network, and key organizational policies to cooperate with other partners. These modifications have significant value in the context of the alliance but do not help the firm, and may even hurt it, in economic exchanges outside the alliance. As was the case in Chapter 10, whenever an investment's value in its first best use (in this case, within the alliance) is much greater than its value in its second best use (in this case, outside the alliance), that investment is said to be **transaction-specific.**[41]

When one firm makes more transaction-specific investments in a strategic alliance than other partner firms make, that firm may be subject to the form of cheating called **holdup.** Holdup occurs when a firm that has not made significant transaction-specific investments demands from an alliance returns that are higher than what the partners agreed to when they created the alliance.

For example, suppose two alliance partners agree to a fifty-fifty split of the costs and profits associated with an alliance. To make the alliance work, Firm A has to customize its production process. Firm B, however, does not have to modify itself to cooperate with Firm A. The value to Firm A of this customized production process, if it is used in the strategic alliance, is $5,000. Outside the alliance, however, this customized process is worth only $200 (as scrap).

Obviously, Firm A has made a transaction-specific investment in this alliance, and Firm B has not. Consequently Firm A may be subject to holdup by Firm B. In particular, Firm B may threaten to leave the alliance unless Firm A agrees to give Firm B part of the $5,000 value that Firm A obtains by using the modified production process in the alliance. Rather than lose all the value that could be generated by its investment, Firm A may be willing to give up some of its $5,000 to avoid gaining only $200. Indeed, if Firm B extracts up to the value of Firm A's production process in its next best use (here, only $200), Firm A will still be better off continuing in this relationship rather than dissolving it. Thus, even though Firm A and Firm B agree on a fifty-fifty split from this strategic alliance, the agreement may be modified if one party to the alliance makes significant transaction-specific investments. Research on international joint ventures suggests that the existence of transaction-specific investments in these relationships often leads to holdup problems.[42]

Although holdup is a form of cheating in strategic alliances, the threat of holdup can also be a motivation for creating an alliance. Bauxite-smelting companies often join in joint ventures with mining companies in order to exploit economies of scale in mining. However, these firms have another option: They could choose to operate large and efficient mines by themselves and then sell the excess bauxite (over and above their needs for their own smelters) on the open market. Unfortunately, however, bauxite is not a homogeneous commodity. Different kinds of bauxite require different smelting technologies. In order for one firm to sell its excess bauxite on the market, other smelting firms would have to make enormous investments, the sole purpose of which would be to refine that particular firm's bauxite. These investments would be transaction-specific and subject these other smelters to holdup problems.

In this context, a strategic alliance can be thought of as a way of reducing the threat of holdup by creating an explicit management framework for resolving holdup problems. In other words, although holdup problems might still exist in these strategic alliances, the alliance framework may still be a better way to manage these problems than attempts to manage them in arm's-length market relationships.

In all three forms of cheating in a strategic alliance, the cheating firm effectively extracts wealth from its partners and transfers this wealth to itself. How these forms of cheating can be controlled is discussed later in this chapter.

13.3 STRATEGIC ALLIANCES AND SUSTAINED COMPETITIVE ADVANTAGE

The ability of strategic alliances, like all the other strategies discussed in this book, to be sources of sustained competitive advantage can be analyzed by using the VRIO framework developed in Chapter 5. An alliance is economically valuable when the inequality in equation 13.1 is greater than the costs imposed in an alliance if one or more partners cheat. In addition, for a strategic alliance to be a source of sustained competitive advantage, it must be rare and costly to imitate, and the firm must be organized to fully exploit the alliance. These issues are considered later.

The Rarity of Strategic Alliances

The rarity of strategic alliances depends not only on the number of competing firms that have already implemented an alliance, but also on the rarity of the benefits that firms obtain from their alliances. Consider, for example, the automobile industry in the United States. Over the last several years, strategic alliances have become very common in this industry, especially with Japanese auto firms. Ford has developed an alliance with Mazda, Daimler-Chrysler has developed an alliance with Mitsubishi, and General Motors has developed an alliance with Toyota. Given the frequency with which alliances have developed in this industry, it is tempting to conclude that strategic alliances are not rare and thus not a source of competitive advantage.

Closer examination, however, suggests that these alliances may have been created for different reasons. For example, until recently, GM and Toyota have cooperated only in building a single line of cars, the Chevrolet Nova. GM has been less interested in learning design skills from Toyota and has been more interested in learning about manufacturing high-quality small cars profitably. Ford and Mazda, in contrast, have worked closely together in designing new cars and have contemplated joint manufacturing operations. Mitsubishi has acted primarily as a supplier to Daimler-Chrysler, and (until recently) there has been relatively little joint development or manufacturing. Thus, although all three U.S. firms have strategic alliances, the alliances serve different purposes and therefore each may be rare.[43]

One of the reasons why the benefits that accrue from a particular strategic alliance may be rare is that relatively few firms may have the complementary resources and abilities needed to form an alliance. This is particularly likely when an alliance is formed to enter into a new market and especially a new foreign market. In many less developed economies, only one local firm or a very few local firms may exist with the local knowledge, contacts, and distribution network needed to facilitate entry into that market. Moreover, sometimes the government acts to limit the number of these local firms. In such cases, even if several firms seek entry into this market, only a very small number will be able to form a strategic alliance with a local entity, and therefore the benefits that accrue to the allied firms will likely be rare.

The Imitability of Strategic Alliances

As discussed in Chapter 5, the resources and capabilities that enable firms to conceive of and implement valuable strategies may be imitated in two ways: direct duplication and substitution. Both duplication and substitution are important considerations in analyzing the imitability of strategic alliances.

Direct Duplication of Strategic Alliances

Recent research suggests that successful strategic alliances are often based on socially complex relations among alliance partners.[44] In this sense, successful strategic alliances often go well beyond simple legal contracts. They are characterized by socially complex phenomena such as a trusting relationship between alliance partners, friendship, and even (perhaps) a willingness to suspend narrow self-interest for the longer-term good of the relationship.

Some research has shown that the development of trusting relationships between alliance partners is both difficult to do and essential to the success of strategic alliances. In one study, approximately one-third of 49 alliances failed to meet the expectations of partner firms. The most common cause of failure was the partners' inability to trust one another. Interpersonal communication, tolerance for cultural differences, patience, and willingness to sacrifice short-term profits for longer-term success were all important determinants of the level of trust among alliance partners.[45]

Of course, not all firms in an industry are likely to have the organizational and relation-building skills required for successful alliances. If these skills and abilities are rare among a set of competing firms and are costly to develop, then firms that are able to exploit these abilities by entering into alliances may gain competitive advantages.

Examples of firms that have developed these specialized skills include Corning, a firm with several hundreds of strategic alliances.[46]

Substitutes for Strategic Alliances

Even if the purpose and objectives of a strategic alliance are valuable and rare, and even if the relationships based on which an alliance is created are socially complex and costly to imitate, that alliance will still not generate a sustained competitive advantage if low-cost substitutes are available. There are least two possible substitutes for strategic alliances: internal development and acquisitions.[47]

Internal Development.   In some situations, the cost of realizing a particular economy of scope through internal development efforts may approximately equal the cost of realizing this same economy through a strategic alliance. When this is the case, internal development will be a substitute for a strategic alliance. In other situations, the cost of realizing this economy through internal development may be greater than the cost of realizing it through an alliance, in which case internal development is not a substitute for a strategic alliance. The relative costs of using internal development and using strategic alliances to realize a particular economy depend on the cost of gaining access to the resources and capabilities needed to create this economy and on the costs of managing the links between these resources to realize this economy.[48]

In some circumstances, alliances will be a less costly way of gaining access to resources and capabilities than internal development. This will be the case when the marginal cost of using another firm's resources and capabilities through an alliance is almost zero. For example, if one firm already has a distribution network in place, and if that network could be used to distribute another firm's products or services, then the marginal cost of using that network to distribute the additional product or service is almost zero. In this context, even if a firm could develop its own distribution network at relatively low cost, the extremely low cost of using the established network makes a strategic alliance preferred over internal development, and internal development is not a substitute for a strategic alliance. It is not surprising to see relatively recent entrants into the U.S. automobile market, for example, use alliances with established GM, Ford, and Daimler-Chrysler dealers to distribute their products. Nor is it surprising that as U.S. telecommunications firms have expanded operations overseas, they have formed alliances with firms that already possess distribution networks in these markets. In these cases, the cost of gaining access to distribution capabilities is much lower through an alliance than it would be if these firms developed their own distribution networks.[49]

More generally, when the internal realization of an economy of scope requires the development of resources or capabilities that are path-dependent, uncertain, or socially complex, it is often less costly to gain access to these resources through an alliance with a firm that already possesses them rather than attempting to develop these resources from scratch. In this situation, internal development efforts are not a substitute for strategic alliances. However, when the realization of an economy of scope does not require the development of such resources, internal development and strategic alliances can be strategic substitutes.

Of course, the relative costs of gaining access to resources and capabilities through internal development and strategic alliances are not the only relevant issue in evaluating these as strategic substitutes. The relative costs of managing the links needed to realize a particular economy of scope in these different ways are also important. For example, it might be much less costly for a particular firm to use an alliance to gain access to another firm's distribution network, rather than developing such a network from scratch. However, if the cost of managing this alliance is very high, internal development might be preferred over the strategic alliance despite the low cost of gaining access to another firm's resources or capabilities through an alliance.[50]

There is a significant amount of research on the ability of firms to develop cooperative and synergistic relationships within their boundaries, and there is an ever-increasing amount of research on the importance of cooperative relationships in strategic alliances. Moreover, there is little consensus about the cost of cooperating within a firm to realize an economy of scope, compared to the cost of managing links between firms in a strategic alliance to realize a synergy.

On the one hand, some economists have assumed that cooperation is probably less costly to develop within a firm than between firms. The fact that managers in a firm operate within a single hierarchy suggests, for these economists at least, that formal authority can be used to ensure low-cost cooperation. This suggests that even when gaining access to the resources and capabilities needed to create an economy of scope is more costly through internal development than it is through a strategic alliance, the additional costs may be more than offset by the lower cost of managing the links between these resources to realize these synergies internally.[51]

On the other hand, others have criticized the assumption that cooperation within a firm is less costly to create than is cooperation between firms. They suggest that bringing a transaction within the boundaries of a firm does not "magically" reduce the cost of developing cooperation. This argument suggests that developing cooperative relations between firms and developing cooperative relations between units within a firm are about equally costly, and thus that the choice between internal development and strategic alliances should depend only on the relative cost of gaining access to the relevant resources and capabilities through these mechanisms. If internal development and strategic alliances do not differ in the cost of gaining access to the resources needed to create synergies, then they will be strategic substitutes.[52]

Whether the costs of managing the links between the resources in order to create economies of scope vary between internal development and strategic alliances probably depends on the **cooperative capabilities** of firms. Some firms may be very skilled at developing high levels of intra-organizational cooperation and thus pursue this as a low-cost approach to exploiting potential economies of scope. The well-known cooperative cultures at Hewlett-Packard and several Japanese firms may make internal cooperation to exploit synergies a preferred approach for these firms (see Chapter 12). Other firms may have become very skilled at developing inter-organizational cooperation and thus pursue strategic alliances as a low-cost approach to exploiting potential economies. The success of Corning and Dow Chemical in developing and nurturing strategic alliances with numerous partners suggests that these firms may prefer this approach to exploiting potential synergies.

If these different types of relationship-building skills enable several firms to exploit the same potential economies at equally low cost, then internal development and strategic alliances are likely to be close strategic substitutes. However, if different firms have very different costs in exploiting the same kinds of economies of scope, then these two approaches are not likely to be strategic substitutes.

Acquisitions. The acquisition of other firms can also be a substitute for alliances. In this case, rather than developing a strategic alliance or attempting to develop and exploit the relevant resources internally, a firm seeking the economies listed in Table 13.1 may simply acquire another firm that already possesses the relevant resources and capabilities and attempt to exploit the potential synergies in that way. Such acquisitions have the effect of diversifying the portfolio of businesses in which a firm is operating. However, diversifying acquisitions have four characteristics that often limit the extent to which they can act as substitutes for strategic alliances. These are summarized in Table 13.4.[53]

First, there may be legal constraints on acquisitions. These are especially likely if firms are seeking advantages by combining with other firms in their own industry. For example, using acquisitions as a substitute for strategic alliances in the aluminum industry would lead to a very concentrated industry and subject some of these firms to serious antitrust liabilities. Thus, firms have acquisitions foreclosed to them and must look elsewhere to gain the advantages from cooperation.

Second, strategic alliances enable a firm to retain its flexibility either to enter or not to enter into a new business. Acquisitions limit this flexibility, because they represent a strong commitment to engage in a certain business activity. Consequently, consistent with the discussion in Chapter 8 of flexibility under conditions of high uncertainty, firms may choose strategic alliances over acquisitions as a way to obtain synergies from complementary resources while maintaining the flexibility that alliances create.

Third, firms may choose strategic alliances over acquisitions because of the unwanted organizational baggage that often comes with an acquisition. Sometimes, economies of scope between firms depend on the combining of particular functions, divisions, or other assets in the firms. A strategic alliance can focus on exploiting economies just between the related parts of the firms. Acquisitions, in contrast, generally include the entire organization, both the parts of a firm in which economies of scope exist and the parts in which they do not exist.

From the point of view of the acquiring firm, parts of a firm in which economies of scope do not exist are essentially unwanted baggage. These parts of the firm may be sold off subsequent to an acquisition. However, this sell-off can be costly and time-consuming. If enough baggage exists, firms may determine that an acquisition is not a viable option, even though important economies of scope exist between the firm and the potential acquisition target. To gain these economies, an alternative approach such as a strategic alliance—will be required.

Finally, sometimes a firm's resources and capabilities are valuable because that firm is independent. In this setting, the act of acquiring a firm may actually reduce the

TABLE 13.4	Reasons Why Strategic Alliances May Be More Attractive than Acquisitions to Realize Valuable Economies of Scope

1. There may be legal constraints on acquisitions.
2. Under conditions of high uncertainty, acquisitions may limit firm flexibility.
3. An acquired firm may carry unwanted organizational "baggage."
4. The value of a firm's resources and capabilities may depend on its independence.

value of the firm. When this is the case, the realization of an economy of scope between two firms is best realized through an alliance, not an acquisition.

For example, the international growth of numerous marketing-oriented companies in the 1980s led to strong pressures on advertising agencies to develop global marketing capabilities. During the 1990s, many domestic advertising firms acquired non-domestic agencies to form a few large international advertising agencies. However, one firm that was reluctant to be acquired in order to be part of an international advertising network was the French advertising company Publicis. Over and above the personal interests of Publicis' owners to retain control of the company, Publicis wanted to remain an independent French agency in order to retain its stable of French and French-speaking clients, including Renault and Nestlé. These firms had indicated that they preferred working with a French advertising agency, and that they would look for alternative suppliers if Publicis were to be acquired by a foreign firm. Because much of the value that Publicis created in a potential acquisition depended on obtaining access to its stable of clients, the act of acquiring Publicis would have had the effect of destroying the very thing that made the acquisition attractive. For this reason, rather than allowing itself to be acquired by a foreign advertising agency, Publicis developed a complex equity strategic alliance and joint venture with a U.S. advertising firm, Foote, Coyne, and Belding. Although, ultimately, this alliance was not successful in providing an international network for either of these two partner firms, an acquisition of Publicis by Foote, Coyne, and Belding would almost certainly have destroyed some of the economic value that Publicis enjoyed as a stand-alone company.

13.4 ORGANIZING FOR STRATEGIC ALLIANCES

One of the most important determinants of the success of strategic alliances is their organization. The primary purpose of organizing a strategic alliance is to enable partners in the alliance to gain all the benefits associated with cooperation while minimizing the probability that cooperating firms will cheat on their cooperative agreements. The organizing skills required in managing alliances are, in many ways, unique. It often takes some time for firms to learn these skills and thus to realize the full potential of their alliances. This is why Apple Computer, as it anticipated a large and complex alliance with IBM and Motorola to develop a new personal computer architecture, began first developing less elaborate and complex alliances. By cooperating, for example, with Sony in the development of the PowerBook, Apple began to learn the organizational skills it would need to make its more complex alliance with IBM and Motorola successful.[54]

A variety of tools and mechanisms can be used to minimize the probability of cheating in interfirm exchanges: non-equity alliances, equity alliances, firm reputations, joint ventures, and trust.

Non-Equity Alliances: Explicit Contracts and Legal Sanctions

One way to avoid cheating in strategic alliances is for parties to an alliance to anticipate the ways in which cheating may occur (including adverse selection, moral hazard, and holdup) and to write explicit contracts that define legal liability if cheating does occur.

Writing these contracts, together with close monitoring of contractual compliance and the threat of legal sanctions, can reduce the probability of cheating. In Section 13.1 such strategic alliances were called *non-equity alliances*.

However, contracts sometimes fail to anticipate all forms of cheating that might occur in a relationship and firms may cheat on cooperative agreements in subtle ways that are difficult to evaluate in terms of contractual requirements. Thus, for example, a contract may require parties in a strategic alliance to make available to the alliance certain proprietary technologies or processes. However, it may be very difficult to communicate the subtleties of these technologies or processes to alliance partners. Does this failure in communication represent a clear violation of contractual requirements, or does it represent a good-faith effort by alliance partners? Moreover, how can one partner tell whether it is obtaining all the necessary information about a technology or process when it is unaware of all the information that exists in another firm? Hence, although contracts are an important component of most strategic alliances, they do not resolve all the problems associated with cheating.

Although most contracts associated with strategic alliances are highly customized, these different contracts do have some common features. These common features of alliance contracts are described in detail in Table 13.5. In general, firms contemplating a strategic alliance that will be at least partially governed by a contract will have to include clauses that address the issues presented in Table 13.5.

TABLE 13.5   Common Clauses Involved in Contracts Governing Strategic Alliances

Establishment Issues

Shareholdings

If an equity alliance or joint venture is to be formed, what percentage of equity is to be purchased by each firm involved in the alliance

Voting rights

The number of votes assigned to each partner in an alliance. May or may not be equal to shareholding percentages

Dividend percentage

How the profits from an alliance will be allocated among cooperating firms. May or may not be equal to shareholding percentages

Minority protection

Description of the kinds of decisions than can be vetoed by firms with a minority interest in an alliance

Board of directors

Initial board of directors, plus mechanisms for dismissing and appointing board members

Articles of association

Procedures for passing resolutions, share issuance, share disposal, etc.

Place of incorporation

If a joint venture, geographic location of incorporation

Advisors

Lawyers, accountants, and other consultants to the alliance

Identification of parties

Legal entities directly involved in an alliance

TABLE 13.5   continued

Operating Issues

Performance clauses

Duties and obligations of alliance partners, including warranties and minimum performance levels expected

Non-compete clauses

Partners are restricted from entering the primary business of the alliance

Non-solicitation clauses

Partners are restricted from recruiting employees from each other

Confidentiality clauses

Proprietary information from partners or from the alliance cannot be shared outside the alliance

Licensing of intellectual property rights

Who owns the intellectual property created by an alliance and how this property may be licensed to other firms

Liability

Liability of the alliance and liability of cooperating partners

Changes to the contract

Process by which the contract can be amended

Dispute resolution

Process by which disputes among partners will be resolved

Termination Issues

Pre-emption rights

If one partner wishes to sell its shares, it must first offer them to the other partner

Variations on preemption rights

Partners are forbidden from ever discussing the sale of their shares to an outsider without first informing their partner of their intention to do so

Call options

When one partner can force the other partner to sell its shares to it. Includes discussion on how these shares will be valued and the circumstances under which a call option can be exercised

Put options

A partner has the right to force another partner to buy its alliance shares

Drag-along rights

One partner can arrange a sale to an outside firm and force the other partner to sell shares as well

Tag-along rights

A partner can prevent the sale of the second partner's shares to an outside firm unless that outside firm also buys the first partner's shares

Initial public offering (IPO)

Circumstances under which an IPO will be pursued

Termination

Conditions under which the contract can be terminated, and consequences of termination for partners

Source: Adapted from Campbell, E. and J. Reuer (2001). "Note on the legal negotiation of strategic alliance agreements," Business Horizons 44(1), pp. 19–26.

Equity Alliances: Contracts and Equity Investments

If contracts do help resolve the threat of cheating to some extent, the control power of contracts can be enhanced by having partners in an alliance make equity investments in each other. When Firm A buys a substantial equity position in its alliance partner, Firm B, the market value of Firm A now depends, to some extent, on the economic performance of that partner. The incentive of Firm A to cheat Firm B falls, for to do so would reduce the economic performance of Firm B and thus the value of Firm A's investment in its partner. In Section 13.1 these kinds of strategic alliances were called *equity alliances*.

Many firms use cross-equity investments to help manage their strategic alliances. These arrangements are particularly common in Japan, where a firm's largest equity holders often include several of its key suppliers, including its main banks. These equity investments, because they reduce the threat of cheating in alliances with suppliers, can reduce these firms' supply costs. In turn, not only do firms have equity positions in their suppliers, but suppliers often have substantial equity positions in the firms to which they sell.[55]

Firm Reputations

A third constraint on incentives to cheat in strategic alliances is the effect that a reputation for cheating has on a firm's future opportunities. Although it is often difficult to anticipate all the different ways in which an alliance partner might cheat, it is often easier to describe after the fact how an alliance partner has cheated. Information about an alliance partner that has cheated is likely to become widely known. A firm with a reputation as a cheater will likely not be able to develop strategic alliances with other partners in the future, despite any special resources or capabilities that it might be able to bring to an alliance. In this way, cheating in a current alliance may foreclose opportunities for developing valuable alliances. Therefore, firms may decide not to cheat in their current alliances.[56]

There is substantial evidence that the effect of reputation on future business opportunities is important. Firms go to great lengths to make sure that they do not develop a negative reputation. Nevertheless, this reputational control of cheating in strategic alliances does have several limitations.[57]

First, subtle cheating in a strategic alliance may not become public; and even if it does become public, the responsibility for the failure of the strategic alliance may not be totally unambiguous. In one equity joint venture, created with the goal of perfecting the design of a new turbine for power generation, financial troubles made one partner considerably more anxious than the other partner to complete product development. The financially healthy and thus patient partner believed that if the alliance required an additional infusion of capital, the financially troubled partner would have to abandon the alliance and would have to sell its part of the alliance at a relatively low price. The patient partner thus encouraged alliance engineers to work slowly and carefully in the guise of developing the technology to reach its full potential. The financially troubled and thus impatient partner encouraged alliance engineers to work quickly, perhaps sacrificing some quality to develop the technology sooner. Eventually, the impatient partner ran out of money, sold its share of the alliance to the patient partner at a reduced price, and accused the patient partner of not acting in good faith to facilitate the rapid development of the new technology. The patient partner accused the other firm of pushing the technology too quickly, thereby sacrificing quality and, perhaps, worker safety. In some sense, both firms were cheating on their agreement to develop the new technology cooperatively. However, this cheating was subtle and difficult to spot and had relatively little effect on the reputation of either firm or on the ability of either firm to establish alliances in the future. It is likely that most observers would simply conclude that the patient partner obtained a windfall because of the impatient partner's bad luck.[58]

Second, although one partner to an alliance may be unambiguously cheating on the relationship, one or both firms may not be sufficiently connected into a network with other firms to make this information public. When information about cheating remains private, public reputations are not tarnished and future opportunities are not forgone. This is especially likely to happen if one or both alliance partners operate in less developed economies, where information about partner behavior may not be rapidly diffused to other firms or to other countries.

Finally, the effect of a tarnished reputation, as long as cheating in an alliance is unambiguous and publicly known, may foreclose future opportunities for a cheating firm, but it does little to address the current losses experienced by the firm that was cheated. Moreover, any of the forms of cheating discussed earlier—adverse selection, moral hazard, or holdup—can result in substantial losses for a firm currently in an alliance. Indeed, the wealth created by cheating in a current alliance may be large enough to make a firm willing to forgo future alliances. This would be the case if the present value of cheating in the current alliance is greater than the present value of engaging in future alliances. In this case, a tarnished reputation may be of minor consequence to a cheating firm.[59]

Joint Ventures

A fourth way to reduce the threat of cheating is for partners in a strategic alliance to invest in a *joint venture*. Creating a separate legal entity in which alliance partners invest and from whose profits they earn returns on their investments, reduces some of the risks of cheating in strategic alliances. When a joint venture is created, the ability of partners to earn returns on their investments depends on the economic success of the joint venture. Partners in joint ventures have limited interests in behaving in ways that hurt the performance of the joint venture because such behaviors end up hurting themselves. Moreover, unlike reputational consequences of cheating, cheating in a joint venture does not just foreclose future alliance opportunities; it can hurt the cheating firm in the current period as well.

Given the advantages of joint ventures in controlling cheating, it is not surprising that when the probability of cheating in a cooperative relationship is greatest, a joint venture is usually the preferred form of cooperation. There are some clear economies of scale in bauxite mining, for example. However, transaction-specific investments would lead to significant holdup problems in selling excess bauxite in the open market, and legal constraints prevent the acquisition of other smelter companies to create an intra-organizational demand for excess bauxite. Holdup problems would continue to exist in any mining strategic alliances that might be created. Non-equity alliances, equity alliances, and reputational effects are not likely to restrain cheating in this situation, because the returns to holdup, once transaction-specific investments are in place, can be very large. Thus most of the strategic alliances created to mine bauxite take the form of joint ventures. Only this form of strategic alliance is likely to create incentives strong enough to reduce the probability of cheating significantly.[60]

Despite these strengths, joint ventures are not able to reduce all cheating in an alliance except at some cost. Sometimes the present value of cheating in a joint venture is sufficiently large that a firm cheats even though doing so hurts the joint venture and forecloses future opportunities. For example, through a joint venture, a particular firm may gain access to a technology that would be valuable if used in another of its lines of business. This firm may be tempted to transfer this technology to this other line of business even if it has agreed not to do so and even if doing so would limit the performance of its joint venture. Because the above-normal returns earned in this other line of business may have a greater present value than the returns that could have been earned in the joint venture and the returns that could have been earned in the future with other strategic alliances, cheating may occur in a joint venture.

Trust

Alliance partners sometimes rely only on legalistic and narrowly economic approaches to manage their alliance. Recent work, however, suggests that although successful alliance partners do not ignore legal and economic disincentives to cheating, they strongly support these narrower linkages with a rich set of interpersonal relations and trust. These "relational contracts" help reduce the threat of cheating. More importantly, trust may enable partners to explore exchange opportunities that they could not explore if only legal and economic organizing mechanisms were in place.[61]

At first glance, this argument may seem far-fetched. However, both theory and research offer support for this approach to managing strategic alliances. In theory, a firm investing in a large number of strategic alliances over time can be thought of as playing a large number of prisoner's dilemma games of the sort described in Chapter 10. As discussed there, Axelrod has shown that a cooperative tit-for-tat strategy has the highest total payoffs in this situation. As applied to strategic alliances, tit for tat would take the following form: Firms entering into alliances continue in them as long as their partners behave in a trustworthy manner; if a partner behaves in an untrustworthy manner, the alliance is severed. As long as at least a few potential alliance partners are also using tit-for-tat strategies, the benefits gained from long-lasting and valuable alliances more than compensate for the short-lived costs endured by a firm that is cheated by an alliance partner.[62]

Empirical, research suggests that successful alliance partners typically do not specify all the terms and conditions in their relationship in a legal contract and do not specify all possible forms of cheating and their consequences. Moreover, when joint ventures are formed, partners do not always insist on simple fifty–fifty splits of equity ownership and profit sharing. Rather, successful alliances involve trust, a willingness to be flexible, a willingness to learn, and a willingness to let the alliance develop in ways that the partners could not have anticipated.[63]

Commitment, coordination, and trust are all important determinants of alliance success. Put another way, a strategic alliance is a relationship that evolves over time. Allowing the lawyers and economists to too rigorously define, a priori, the boundaries of that relationship may limit it and stunt its development.[64]

This "trust" approach also has implications for the extent to which strategic alliances may be sources of sustained competitive advantage for firms. The ability to move into strategic alliances in this trusting way may be very valuable over the long run. There is strong reason to believe that this ability is not uniformly distributed across all firms that might have an interest in forming strategic alliances, and that this ability may be history-dependent and socially complex and thus costly to imitate. Firms with these skills may be able to gain sustained competitive advantages from their alliance relationships. The observation that just a few firms are well known for their successful strategic alliances is consistent with the observation that these alliance management skills may be valuable, rare, and costly to imitate.

13.5 SUMMARY

Tacit collusion, as a form of interfirm cooperation, is difficult to create and maintain. Strategic alliances, in contrast, are much more common and growing in frequency. Strategic alliances exist whenever two or more organizations cooperate in the development, manufacture, or sale of products or services. Strategic alliances can be grouped into three large categories: non-equity alliances, equity alliances, and joint ventures.

There are many reasons to join in strategic alliances: exploiting economies of scale, learning from competitors, managing risk and sharing costs, facilitating tacit collusion, low-cost entry into new markets, low-cost entry into new industries or industry segments, and managing uncertainty. In all these cases, a strategic alliance is an attempt to exploit a potential synergy between independent firms.

Just as there are incentives to cooperate in strategic alliances, there are also incentives to cheat. Cheating generally takes one or a combination of three forms: adverse selection, moral hazard, or holdup.

The value of strategic alliances can be analyzed by using the model of generic industry structures discussed in Chapter 4. Symmetric alliances are most common in mature industries, in fragmented industries with large strategic groups of firms, in network industries, and in empty-core industries in which firms are pursuing collusion or government regulation opportunities. Asymmetric alliances are most common in emerging industries, in fragmented industries without strategic groups, in global industries, in hypercompetitive industries, and in empty-core industries in which firms are pursuing product differentiation or demand management opportunities. Mixed alliances can exist in any industry structure.

Strategic alliances can be a source of sustained competitive advantage. The rarity of alliances depends not only on the number of competing firms that have developed an alliance but also on the benefits that firms gain through their alliances.

Imitation through direct duplication of an alliance may be costly because of the socially complex relations that underlie an alliance. However, imitation through substitution is more likely. Two substitutes for alliances may be internal development, by which firms develop and exploit the relevant sets of resources and capabilities on their own, and diversifying acquisitions. Internal development is a substitute for a strategic alliance only when it is no more costly to develop the required resources inside a firm, compared to cooperating to use another firm's resources, and when it is no more costly to develop cooperative relations inside the firm, compared to the cost of developing cooperative relations with other firms. Diversifying acquisitions may be a substitute for strategic alliances when there are no legal constraints in acquisitions, strategic flexibility is not an important consideration, the acquired firm has relatively little unwanted organizational baggage, and when the value of an acquired firm's resources and capabilities do not depend on its remaining independent.

The key issue facing firms in organizing their alliances is to facilitate cooperation while avoiding the threat of cheating. Non-equity alliances, equity alliances, firm reputations, joint ventures, and trust can all reduce the threat of cheating in different contexts.

REVIEW QUESTIONS

1. One reason why firms might want to pursue a strategic alliance strategy is to exploit economies of scale. Exploiting economies of scale should reduce a firm's costs. Does this mean that a firm pursuing an alliance strategy to exploit economies of scale is actually pursuing a cost leadership strategy? Why or why not?

2. Consider the joint venture between General Motors and Toyota. GM has been interested in learning how to manufacture profitably high-quality small cars from its alliance with Toyota. Toyota has been interested in gaining access to GM's U.S. distribution network and in reducing the political liability associated with local-content laws. Which of these firms do you think is more likely to accomplish its objectives, and why?

3. Some have argued that strategic alliances are one way in which firms can help facilitate the development of a tacit collusion strategy. In your view, what are the critical differences between tacit collusion strategies and strategic

alliance strategies? How can one tell whether two firms are engaging in alliances to facilitate collusion or are engaging in an alliance for other purposes?

4. Some have argued that alliances can be used to help firms evaluate the economic potential of entering into a new industry or market. Under what conditions will a firm seeking to evaluate these opportunities need to invest in an alliance to accomplish this evaluation? Why couldn't such a firm simply hire some smart managers, consultants, and industry experts to evaluate the economic potential of entering into a new industry? What, if anything, about an alliance makes this a better way to evaluate entry opportunities than alternatives?

5. If adverse selection, moral hazard, and holdup are such significant problems for firms pursuing alliance strategies, why do firms even bother with alliances? Why don't they instead adopt an internal development strategy to replace strategic alliances?

ENDNOTES

1. Badaracco, J. L., and N. Hasegawa (1988). "General Motors' Asian alliances," Harvard Business School Case no. 9-388-094.

2. The database mentioned is Thomson Financial. See Ernst, D., and J. Bleeke (1993). *Collaborating to Compete: Using Strategic Alliances and Acquisitions in the Global Marketplace,* New York: John Wiley & Sons; Alvarez, S., and J. B. Barney (2001). "How entrepreneurial firms can benefit from alliances with large partners," *Academy of Management Executive,* 15(1), pp. 139–148; and Burgers, W. P., C. W. L. Hill, and W. C. Kim (1993). "A theory of global strategic alliances: The case of the global auto industry," *Strategic Management Journal,* 14,

pp. 419–432, for further information on the growth of the number of alliances.

3. See Harrigan, K. R. (1988). "Joint ventures and competitive strategy," *Strategic Management Journal,* 9, pp. 141–158; Hagedoorn, J. (1993). "Understanding the rationale of strategic technology partnering: Interorganizational modes of cooperation and sectoral differences," *Strategic Management Journal,* 14, pp. 371–385; Ernst, D., and J. Bleeke (1993). *Collaborating to Compete: Using Strategic Alliances and Acquisitions in the Global Marketplace,* New York: John Wiley & Sons; Kogut, B. (1988). "Joint ventures: Theoretical and empirical perspectives," *Strategic Management Journal,* 9,

pp. 319–332; Hennart, J. F. (1988). "A transaction cost theory of equity joint ventures," *Strategic Management Journal*, 9, pp. 361–374; Dyer, J. H., and H. Singh (1998). "The relational view: Cooperative strategy and sources of interorganizational competitive advantage," *Academy of Management Review*, 23(4), pp. 660–679; Spekman, R. E., T. M. Forbes III, L. A. Isabella, and T. C. MacAvoy (1998). "Alliance management: A view from the past and a look to the future," *Journal of Management Studies*, 35(6), pp. 747–772; Newburry, W., and Y. Zeira (1999). "Autonomy and effectiveness of equity international joint ventures (EIJV's): An analysis based on EIJV's [sic] in Hungary and Britain," *Journal of Management Studies*, 36(2), pp. 263–285; Day, G. S. (1995). "Advantageous alliances," *Journal of the Academy of Marketing Science*, 23(4), pp. 297–300; Varadarajan, P. R., and M. H. Cunningham (1995). "Strategic alliances: A synthesis of conceptual foundations," *Journal of the Academy of Marketing Science*, 23(4), pp. 282–296, for a discussion on motives for forming strategic alliances.

4. Stuckey, J. (1983). *Vertical Integration and Joint Ventures in the Aluminum Industry*, Cambridge, MA: Harvard University Press; and Hennart, J. F. (1988). "A transaction cost theory of equity joint ventures," *Strategic Management Journal*, 9, pp. 361–374.

5. See Shan, W., G. Walker, and B. Kogut (1994). "Interfirm cooperation and startup innovation in the biotechnology industry," *Strategic Management Journal*, 15, pp. 387–394; Hamel, G. (1991). "Competition for competence and inter-partner learning within international strategic alliances," *Strategic Management Journal*, 12, pp. 83–103; Si, S. X., and G. D. Bruton (1999). "Knowledge transfer in international joint ventures in transitional economies: The China experience," *Academy of Management Executive*, 13(1), pp. 83–90; Simonin, B. L. (1999). "Ambiguity and the process of knowledge transfer in strategic alliances," *Strategic Management Journal*, 20, pp. 595–623; Leroy, F., and B. Ramanantsoa (1997). "The

cognitive and behavioural dimensions of organizational learning in a merger: An empirical study," *Journal of Management Studies*, 34, pp. 871–894; Hagedoorn, J. (1993). "Understanding the rationale of strategic technology partnering: Interorganizational modes of cooperation and sectoral differences," *Strategic Management Journal*, 14, pp. 371–385; Kraatz, M. S. (1998). "Learning by association? Interorganizational networks and adaptation to environmental change," *Academy of Management Journal*, 41(6), pp. 621–643; and Inkpen, A. (1998). Learning and knowledge acquisition through international strategic alliances," *Academy of Management Executive*, 12(4), pp. 69–80.

6. Badaracco, J. L., and N. Hasegawa (1988). "General Motors' Asian alliances," Harvard Business School Case no. 9-388-094.

7. These are issues discussed in Chapter 5. In Chapter 12, the costly-to-imitate nature of these kinds of resources and capabilities is seen as a primary motivation of firm diversification strategies. See Teece, D. (1977). "Technology transfer by multinational firms," *Economic Journal*, 87, pp. 242–261.

8. Reich, R. (1986). "Joint ventures with Japan give away our future," *Harvard Business Review*, 64, March/April, pp. 78–86.

9. See Pfeffer, J., and P. Nowak (1976). "Patterns of joint venture activity: Implications for antitrust research," *Antitrust Bulletin*, 21, pp. 315–339.

10. Badaracco, J. L., and N. Hasegawa (1988). "General Motors' Asian alliances," Harvard Business School Case no. 9-388-094.

11. See Hamel, G. (1991). "Competition for competence and inter-partner learning within international strategic alliances," *Strategic Management Journal*, 12, pp. 83–103, and Alvarez, S. A., and J. B. Barney (2001). "How entrepreneurial firms can benefit from alliances with large partners," *Academy of Management Executive*, 15(1), pp. 139–148.

12. Personal communication (1998); and Hennart, J. F. (1988). "A transaction cost theory of equity joint ventures," *Strategic Management Journal*, 9, pp. 361–374.

13. See Stertz, B. A. (1991). "In a U-turn from past policy, Big Three at Detroit speed into era of cooperation," *Wall Street Journal,* June 28, p. B1+; and Suris, O. (1993). "Big Three win joint patent, marking a first," *Wall Street Journal,* April 13, p. B1+, for a discussion on the automotive alliances; and Jensen, E. (1993). "ABC and BBC pool their radio-TV news coverage," *Wall Street Journal,* March 26, p. B1+, for a discussion of the news-gathering alliance.

14. See Carnevale, M. L. (1993). "HDTV bidders agree to merge their systems," *Wall Street Journal,* May 24, p. B1+. This standard also puts other firms at a competitive disadvantage.

15. See Burgers, W. P., C. W. L. Hill, and W. C. Kim (1993). "A theory of global strategic alliances: The case of the global auto industry," *Strategic Management Journal,* 14, pp. 419–432.

16. Fusfeld, D. (1958). "Joint subsidiaries in the iron and steel industry," *American Economic Review,* 48, pp. 578–587.

17. See Pate, J. (1969). "Joint venture activity, 1969–1968," *Economic Review,* Federal Reserve Bank of Cleveland, pp. 16–23; and Boyle, S. E. (1968). "Estimate of the number and size distribution of domestic joint subsidiaries," *Antitrust Law and Economics Review,* 1, pp. 81–92.

18. Mead, W. J. (1967). "Competitive significance of joint ventures," *Antitrust Bulletin,* 12, pp. 300–315.

19. A point made by Kent, D. H. (1991). "Joint ventures vs. non-joint ventures: An empirical investigation," *Strategic Management Journal,* 12, pp. 387–393; and Bloch, F. (1995). "Endogenous structures of association in oligopolies," *Rand Journal of Economics,* 26, pp. 537–556.

20. Pfeffer, J., and P. Nowak (1976). "Patterns of joint venture activity: Implications for antitrust research," *Antitrust Bulletin,* 21, pp. 315–339.

21. See Kent, D. H. (1991). "Joint ventures vs. non-joint ventures: An empirical investigation," *Strategic Management Journal,* 12, pp. 387–393; Kogut, B. (1988). "Joint ventures: Theoretical and empirical perspectives," *Strategic Management Journal,* 9,

pp. 319–332; and Hennart, J. F. (1988). "A transaction cost theory of equity joint ventures," *Strategic Management Journal,* 9, pp. 361–374.

22. Duncan, L. (1982). "Impacts of new entry and horizontal joint ventures on industrial rates of return," *Review of Economics and Statistics,* 64, pp. 120–125.

23. Keller, J. J. (1993). "Sprint hangs back as its rivals forge global alliances," *Wall Street Journal,* June 4, p. B4.

24. See Tomlinson, J. W. L. (1970). *The Joint Venture Process in International Business,* Cambridge, MA: MIT Press; Friedman, W., and G. Kalmanoff (1961). *Joint International Business Ventures,* New York: Columbia University Press; Johansson, J. K. (1995). "International alliances: Why now?" *Journal of the Academy of Marketing Science,* 23(4), pp. 301–304; Xin, K. R., and J. J. Pearce (1996). "*Guanxi:* Connections as substitutes for formal institutional support," *Academy of Management Journal,* 39(6), pp. 1641–1658, on the importance of alliances for entering new markets, especially international markets.

25. Stopford, M., and L. Wells (1972). *Managing the Multinational Enterprise,* New York: Basic Books; and Kogut, B., and H. Singh (1986). "Entering the United States by acquisition or joint venture: Country patterns, and cultural characteristics," working paper, Department of Management, Wharton School of Business of the University of Pennsylvania.

26. See Pope, K., and D. Hamilton (1993). "U.S. computer firms, extending PC wars, charge into Japan," *Wall Street Journal,* March 31, p. A1+, on Japan; Jacob, R. (1992). "India is opening for business," *Fortune,* November 16, pp. 128–130, on India; and Hennart, J. F. (1988). "A transaction cost theory of equity joint ventures," *Strategic Management Journal,* 9, pp. 361–374, on the effects of globalization on the use of alliances.

27. See Freeman, A., and R. Hudson (1980). "DuPont and Phillips plan joint venture to make, market laser disc products," *Wall Street Journal,* December 22, p. 10.

28. See Teitelbaum, R. J. (1992). "Eskimo Pie," *Fortune,* June 15, p. 123.

29. Darlin, D. (1991). "Coke and Nestle Launch First Coffee Drink," *Wall Street Journal,* October 1, p. B1+.

30. This term was originally developed by Akerlof, G. A. (1970). "The markets for 'lemons': Qualitative uncertainty and the market mechanism," *Quarterly Journal of Economics,* 84, pp. 488–500, with reference to buying a used car.

31. Nanda, A., and C. A. Bartlett (1990). "Corning Incorporated: A network of alliances," Harvard Business School Case no. 9-391-102.

32. See Knight, F. H. (1965). *Risk, Uncertainty, and Profit,* New York: John Wiley & Sons, on uncertainty; Kogut, B. (1991). "Joint ventures and the option to expand and acquire," *Management Science,* 37, pp. 19–33; Burgers, W. P., C. W. L. Hill, and W. C. Kim (1993). "A theory of global strategic alliances: The case of the global auto industry," *Strategic Management Journal,* 14, pp. 419–432; Noldeke, G., and K. M. Schmidt (1998). "Sequential investments and options to own," *Rand Journal of Economics,* 29(4), pp. 633–653; and Folta, T. B. (1998). "Governance and uncertainty: The tradeoff between administrative control and commitment," *Strategic Management Journal,* 19, pp. 1007–1028.

33. See Kogut, B. (1991). "Joint ventures and the option to expand and acquire," *Management Science,* 37, pp. 19–33; and Balakrishnan, S., and M. Koza (1993). "Information asymmetry, adverse selection and joint-ventures," *Journal of Economic Behavior & Organization,* 20, pp. 99–117.

34. Hennart, J. F. (1988). "A transaction cost theory of equity joint ventures," *Strategic Management Journal,* 9, pp. 361–374; and Nielsen, R. P. (1988). "Cooperative strategy," *Strategic Management Journal,* 9, pp. 475–492.

35. These terms are defined in Barney, J. B., and W. G. Ouchi (1986). *Organizational Economics.* San Francisco, CA: Jossey-Bass; and Holmstrom, B. (1979). "Moral hazard and observability," *Bell Journal of Economics,* 10(1), pp. 74–91. Problems of cheating in economic exchanges, in general, and in

alliances in particular, are discussed by Gulati, R., and H. Singh (1998). "The architecture of cooperation: Managing coordination costs and appropriation concerns in strategic alliances," *Administrative Science Quarterly,* 43, pp. 781–814; Williamson, O. E. (1991). "Comparative economic organization: The analysis of discrete structural alternatives," *Administrative Science Quarterly,* 36, pp. 269–296; Osborn, R. N., and C. C. Baughn (1990). "Forms of interorganizational governance for multinational alliances," *Academy of Management Journal,* 33(3), pp. 503–519; Hagedoorn, J., and R. Narula (1996). "Choosing organizational modes of strategic technology partnering: International and sectoral differences," *Journal of International Business Studies,* second quarter, pp. 265–284; Hagedoorn, J. (1996). "Trends and patterns in strategic technology partnering since the early seventies," *Review of Industrial Organization,* 11, pp. 601–616; Kent, D. H. (1991). "Joint ventures vs. non-joint ventures: An empirical investigation," *Strategic Management Journal,* 12, pp. 387–393; and Shane, S. A. (1998). "Making new franchise systems work," *Strategic Management Journal,* 19, pp. 697–707.

36. Keil, M., and S. Simonson (1993). "Bell-South Enterprises: The Cellular Billing Project," Harvard Business School Case no. 9-193-150.

37. Such alliance difficulties are described by Ouchi, W. G. (1984). *The M-Form Society: How American Teamwork Can Capture the Competitive Edge,* Reading, MA: Addison-Wesley; and Bresser, R. K. (1988). "Cooperative strategy," *Strategic Management Journal,* 9, pp. 475–492.

38. Turner, R. (1991). "How MCA's relations with Motown Records went so sour so fast," *Wall Street Journal,* September 25, p. A1+.

39. Pope, K. (1993). "Dealers accuse Compaq of jilting them," *Wall Street Journal,* February 26, p. 8, B1+.

40. Alvarez, S. A., and J. B. Barney (2001). "How entrepreneurial firms can benefit from alliances with large partners," *Academy of Management Executive,* 15(1), pp. 139–148.

41. Williamson, O. E. (1975). *Markets and Hierarchies: Analysis and Antitrust Implications,* New York: Free Press; Klein, B., R. Crawford, and A. Alchian (1978). "Vertical integration, appropriable rents, and the competitive contracting process," *Journal of Law and Economics,* 21, pp. 297–326.

42. See, for example, Yan, A., and B. Gray (1994). "Bargaining power, management control, and performance in United States–China joint ventures: A comparative case study," *Academy of Management Journal,* 37, pp. 1478–1517.

43. See Badaracco, J. L., and N. Hasegawa (1988). "General Motors' Asian alliances," Harvard Business School Case no. 90-388-094, on GM and Toyota; Patterson, G. A. (1991). "Mazda hopes to crack Japan's top tier," *Wall Street Journal,* September 20, p. B1+; and Williams, M., and M. Kanabayashi (1993). "Mazda and Ford drop proposal to build cars together in Europe," *Wall Street Journal,* March 4, p. A14, on Ford and Mazda; and Ennis, P. (1991). "Mitsubishi group wary of deeper ties to Chrysler," *Tokyo Business Today,* 59, July, p. 10, on Daimler-Chrysler and Mitsubishi.

44. See, for example, Ernst, D., and J. Bleeke (1993). *Collaborating to Compete: Using Strategic Alliances and Acquisition in the Global Marketplace,* New York: John Wiley & Sons,; and Barney, J. B., and M. H. Hansen (1994). "Trustworthiness as a source of competitive advantage," *Strategic Management Journal,* 15, Winter (special issue), pp. 175–190.

45. Ernst, D., and J. Bleeke (1993). *Collaborating to Compete: Using Strategic Alliances and Acquisitions in the Global Marketplace,* New York: John Wiley & Sons.

46. Bartlett, C., and S. Ghoshal (1993). "Beyond the M-form: Toward a managerial theory of the firm," *Strategic Management Journal,* 14, pp. 23–46.

47. See Nagarajan, A., and W. Mitchell (1998). "Evolutionary diffusion: Internal and external methods used to acquire encompassing, complementary, and incremental technological changes in the lithotripsy industry," *Strategic Management Journal,* 19, pp. 1063–1077; Hagedoorn, J., and B. Sadowski (1999). "The transition from strategic technology alliances to mergers and acquisitions: An exploratory study," *Journal of Management Studies,* 36(1), pp. 87–107; and Newburry, W., and Y. Zeira (1997). "Generic differences between equity international joint ventures (EIJVs), International acquisitions (IAs), and International Greenfield investments (IGIs): Implications for parent companies," *Journal of World Business,* 32(2), pp. 87–102, on alliance substitutes.

48. Barney, J. B. (1999). "How a firm's capabilities affect boundary decisions," *Sloan Management Review,* 40(3), pp. 137–145.

49. See Patterson, G. A. (1991). "Mazda hopes to crack Japan's top tier," *Wall Street Journal,* September 20, p. B1+, on alliances in the automobile industry; and Keller, J. J. (1993). "Sprint hangs back as its rivals forge global alliances," *Wall Street Journal,* June 4, p. B4, on alliances in the telecommunications industry.

50. See Shortell, S., and E. J. Zajac (1988). "Internal corporate joint ventures: Development processes and performance outcomes," *Strategic Management Journal,* 9, pp. 527–542.

51. Williamson, O. E. (1975). *Markets and Hierarchies: Analysis and Antitrust Implications,* New York: Free Press; and Teece, D. (1977). "Technology transfer by multinational firms," *Economic Journal,* 87, pp. 242–261.

52. See Grossman, S., and O. Hart (1986). "The costs and benefits of ownership: A theory of vertical and lateral integration," *Journal of Political Economy,* 94, pp. 691–719.

53. See Hennart, J. F. (1988). "A transaction cost theory of equity joint ventures," *Strategic Management Journal,* 9, pp. 361–374; Kogut, B. (1988). "Joint ventures: Theoretical and empirical perspectives," *Strategic Management Journal,* 9, pp. 319–332; and Barney, J. B. (1999). "How a firm's capabilities affect boundary decisions," *Sloan Management Review,* 40(3), pp. 137–145, for a discussion on these limitations.

54. See Schlender, B. R. (1991). "Apple's Japanese ally," *Fortune,* November 4, pp. 151–152; and Corcoran, C. (1993). "At last, users can

inspect IBM's PowerPC systems," *Infoworld,* 15, November 15, pp. 1, 6.

55. See Ouchi, W. G. (1984). *The M-Form Society: How American Teamwork Can Capture the Competitive Edge,* Reading, MA: Addison-Wesley; and Barney, J. B. (1990). "Profit sharing bonuses and the cost of debt: Business finance and compensation policy in Japanese electronics firms," *Asia Pacific Journal of Management,* 7, pp. 49–64.

56. This is an argument developed by Barney, J. B., and M. H. Hansen (1994). "Trustworthiness as a source of competitive advantage," *Strategic Management Journal,* 15, Winter (special issue), pp. 175–190; Weigelt, K., and C. Camerer (1988). "Reputation and corporate strategy: A review of recent theory and applications," *Strategic Management Journal,* 9, pp. 443–454; and Granovetter, M. (1985). "Economic action and social structure: The problem of embeddedness," *American Journal of Sociology,* 3, pp. 481–510.

57. See, for example, Eichenseher, J., and D. Shields (1985). "Reputation and corporate strategy: A review of recent theory and applications," *Strategic Management Journal,* 9, pp. 443–454; Beatty, R., and R. Ritter (1986). "Investment banking, reputation, and the underpricing of initial public offerings," *Journal of Financial Economics,* 15, pp. 213–232; Kalleberg, A. L., and T. Reve (1992). "Contracts and commitment: Economic and sociological perspectives on employment relations," *Human Relations,* 45(9), pp. 1103–1132; Larson, A. (1992). "Network dyads in entrepreneurial settings: A study of the governance of exchange relationships," *Administrative Science Quarterly,* March, pp. 76–104; Stuart, T. E., H. Hoang, and R. C. Hybels (1999). "Interorganizational endorsements and the performance of entrepreneurial ventures," *Administrative Science Quarterly,* 44, pp. 315–349; Stuart, T. E. (1998). "Network positions and propensities to collaborate: An investigation of strategic alliance formation in a high-technology industry," *Administrative Science Quarterly,* 43(3), pp. 668–698; and

Gulati, R. (1998). "Alliances and networks," *Strategic Management Journal,* 19, pp. 293–317.

58. Personal communication, November 1989.

59. This same theoretic approach to firm reputation is discussed by Tirole, J. (1988). *The Theory of Industrial Organization,* Cambridge, MA: MIT Press.

60. Scherer, F. M. (1980). *Industrial Market Structure and Economic Performance,* Boston: Houghton Mifflin.

61. See, again, Ernst, D., and J. Bleeke (1993). *Collaborating to Compete: Using Strategic Alliances and Acquisitions in the Global Marketplace,* New York: John Wiley & Sons; and Barney, J. B., and M. H. Hansen (1994). "Trustworthiness as a source of competitive advantage," *Strategic Management Journal,* 15, Winter (special issue), pp. 175–190. In fact, there is a great deal of literature on the role of trust in strategic alliances. Some of the most interesting of this work can be found in Holm, D. B., K. Eriksson, and J. Johanson (1999). "Creating value through mutual commitment to business network relationships," *Strategic Management Journal,* 20, pp. 467–486; Lorenzoni, G., and A. Lipparini (1999). "The leveraging of interfirm relationships as a distinctive organizational capability: A longitudinal study," *Strategic Management Journal,* 20(4), pp. 317–338; Blois, K. J. (1999). "Trust in business to business relationships: An evaluation of its status," *Journal of Management Studies,* 36(2), pp. 197–215; Chiles, T. H., and J. F. McMackin (1996). "Integrating variable risk preferences, trust, and transaction cost economics," *Academy of Management Review,* 21(1), pp. 73–99; Larzelere, R. E., and T. L. Huston (1980). "The dyadic trust scale: Toward understanding interpersonal trust in close relationships," *Journal of Marriage and the Family,* August, pp. 595–604; Butler, J. K., Jr. (1983). "Reciprocity of trust between professionals and their secretaries," *Psychological Reports,* 53, pp. 411–416; Zaheer, A., and N. Venkatraman (1995). "Relational governance as an interorganizational strategy: An empirical test of the role of trust in economic

exchange," *Strategic Management Journal,* 16, pp. 373–392; Butler, J. K., Jr., and R. S. Cantrell (1984). "A behavioral decision theory approach to modeling dyadic trust in superiors and subordinates," *Psychological Reports,* 55, pp. 19–28; Carney, M. (1998). "The competitiveness of networked production: The role of trust and asset specificity," *Journal of Management Studies,* 35(4), pp. 457–479.

62. See Axelrod, R. M. (1984). *The Evolution of Cooperation,* New York: Basic Books; and Ring, P. S., and A. Van de Ven (1992). "Structuring cooperative relationships between organizations," *Strategic Management Journal,* 13, pp. 483–498.

63. Ernst, D., and J. Bleeke (1993). *Collaborating to Compete: Using Strategic Alliances and Acquisitions in the Global Marketplace,* New York: John Wiley & Sons.

64. See Mohr, J., and R. Spekman (1994). "Characteristics of partnership success: Partnership attributes, communication behavior, and conflict resolution techniques," *Strategic Management Journal,* 15, pp. 135–152; and Zaheer, A., and N. Venkatraman (1995). "Relational governance as an interorganizational strategy: An empirical test of the role of trust in economic exchange," *Strategic Management Journal,* 16, pp. 373–392.

CHAPTER

14

Merger and Acquisition Strategies

14.1 The Value of Merger and Acquisition Strategies
14.2 Mergers and Acquisitions and Sustained Competitive Advantage
14.3 Organizing to Implement a Merger or Acquisition
14.4 Summary

Thus far, we have focused on the economic consequences of corporate strategies once they have been implemented. We have shown that, in some circumstances, diversification can be a source of competitive advantage. We have given less attention to the performance implications of the process through which firms become diversified. This is the primary topic of Chapter 14.

That merger and acquisition strategies are an important strategic option for firms pursuing diversification strategies can hardly be disputed. The number of firms that have used merger and acquisition strategies to become diversified over the last few years is staggering. Indeed, from 1995 to 2004, the total value of acquisitions in the United States fell below $500 billion in only one year, 2002. In each year 1998, 1999, and 2000, the total value of U.S. acquisitions topped $1.5 trillion. In 2004, the total value of U.S. acquisitions was "only" $800 billion. However, this "urge to merge" was not limited just to the United States. In 2005, there were 538 acquisitions in Latin America, with a total value of $44.5 billion. In India, the first half of 2005 saw 277 acquisitions, valued at $6 billion. And in 2004, 587 acquisitions were completed in Europe, with a value equal to 80.2 billion euros.[1]

That mergers and acquisitions are a very common, and economically important, corporate strategy is clear. What is less clear is whether these strategies create superior profits for the firms that pursue them. The purpose of this chapter is to highlight the conditions under which merger and acquisition strategies will, and will not, be a source of economic profits for firms pursuing them.

14.1 THE VALUE OF MERGER AND ACQUISITION STRATEGIES

Like the value of all the other strategies discussed in this book, the value of merger and acquisition strategies depends on the market context within which these strategies are implemented. To the extent that a merger or acquisition enables a firm to exploit competitive opportunities or neutralize threats, that merger or acquisition will enable the firm to reduce its costs or increase its revenues, and that strategy will be economically valuable. In this section, two merger and acquisition contexts are discussed: mergers and acquisitions between strategically unrelated firms and mergers and acquisitions between strategically related firms.

Mergers and Acquisitions: The Unrelated Case

Imagine the following scenario: One firm (B: the target) is the object of an acquisition effort, and 10 firms (the bidders) are interested in making this acquisition. The current market value of the target firm is $10,000, the current market value of the bidding firms is $15,000, and the capital market within which the bidding firms operate is semi-strong efficient.[2] There is no strategic relatedness between these bidding firms and the target. This means that the value of any one of these bidding firms when combined with the target firm exactly equals the sum of the value of these firms as separate entities—that is,

$$NPV(A + B) = NPV(A) + NPV(B) \tag{14.1}$$

where

$$
\begin{aligned}
NPV(A) &= \text{net present value of Firm A as a stand-alone entity} \\
NPV(B) &= \text{net present value of Firm B as a stand-alone entity} \\
NPV(A + B) &= \text{net present value of Firms A and B as a combined entity}
\end{aligned}
$$

At what price will this target be acquired, and what are the economic performance implications for bidding and target firms at this price?

In this, and all acquisition situations, bidding firms will be willing to pay a price for a target up to the value that the target firm adds to the bidder once it is acquired. This price, P, is

$$P = NPV(A + B) - NPV(A) \tag{14.2}$$

Notice that P does not depend on the value of the target firm acting as an independent business but, rather, depends on the value that the target firm creates when it is combined with the bidding firm. Any price for a target less than P will be a source of economic profit for a bidding firm; any price greater than P will be a source of economic losses for the bidding firm that acquires the target.

In this specific scenario, the present value of each bidding firm is $15,000, and the present value of the bidding firms combined with the target firm is $25,000 ($15,000 from the bidding firm plus $10,000 from the target firm, assuming that the bidding and target firms are not strategically related). The maximum price that a bidding firm will be willing to pay for this target is $10,000 ($25,000 − $15,000). Any price greater than $10,000 will lead to economic losses for a bidder; a price less than $10,000 will generate economic profits.

It is not hard to see that the price of this acquisition will rise quickly to $10,000 and that, at this price, the bidding firm that acquires the target will only break even, economically. The price of this acquisition will rise quickly to $10,000 because any bid less than $10,000 will generate economic profits for a successful bidder. These potential profits, in turn, will generate entry into the bidding war for a target. Moreover, because the capital market for bidding firms is semi-strong efficient, these firms will be able to gain access to any capital they might need to make investments that have a positive net present value. Because entry into the acquisition contest is assured, the price of the acquisition will rise quickly to its value, and economic profits will not exist.

Moreover, at this $10,000 price, the target firm's equity holders will also not gain superior economic profits. Indeed, for them, all that has occurred is that the market value of the target firm has been capitalized in the form of a cash payment from the bidder to the target. The target was worth $10,000, and that is exactly what these equity holders will receive.

Mergers and Acquisitions: The Related Case

The conclusion that the acquisition of strategically unrelated targets will not generate superior economic profits for both the bidding and the target firms is not surprising. It is very consistent with the discussion of the economic consequences of unrelated diversification in Chapter 11. In that chapter, it was argued that there is limited economic justification for a corporate diversification strategy that does not build on some type of economy of scope across the businesses within which a firm operates, and thus that unrelated diversification is not an economically viable corporate strategy.

Types of Strategic Relatedness

The literature describes a wide variety of ways that bidding and target firms can be strategically related. Three particularly important lists of these potential linkages are discussed here.[3]

The FTC Categories.   Because mergers and acquisitions can have the effect of increasing (or decreasing) the level of concentration in an industry, the Federal Trade Commission (FTC) is charged with the responsibility of evaluating the competitive implications of proposed mergers or acquisitions. In principle, the FTC will disallow any acquisition involving firms with headquarters in the United States that could have the potential for generating monopoly (or oligopoly) profits in an industry. To help in this regulatory effort, the FTC has developed a typology of mergers and acquisitions (see Table 14.1). Each category in this typology can be thought of as a different way in which a bidding firm and a target firm can be related in a merger or acquisition.

According to the FTC, a firm engages in a **vertical merger** when it vertically integrates through its acquisition efforts. Vertical mergers could include a firm purchasing critical suppliers of raw materials (**backward vertical integration**) or acquiring customers and distribution networks (**forward vertical integration**).

TABLE 14.1 **FTC Categories of Mergers and Acquisitions**	
Vertical merger	A firm acquires former suppliers or customers
Horizontal merger	A firm acquires a former competitor
Product extension merger	A firm gains access to complementary products through an acquisition
Market extension merger	A firm gains access to complementary markets through an acquisition
Conglomerate merger	There is no strategic relatedness between a bidding and a target firm

A firm engages in a **horizontal merger** when it acquires a former competitor. Obviously, the FTC is particularly concerned with the competitive implications of horizontal mergers, because these strategies can have the most direct and obvious anticompetitive implications in an industry (see Chapter 9's discussion of tacit collusion in oligopolies). For example, the FTC raised antitrust concerns in the merger between Bank One and JP Morgan Chase, because these firms, together, dominated some geographic markets. Similar concerns were raised in the proposed merger between British Petroleum and Arco, and the merger between Mobil and Exxon.

The third type of merger identified by the FTC is a **product extension merger.** In a product extension merger, firms acquire complementary products through their merger and acquisition activities.

The fourth type of merger identified by the FTC is a **market extension merger.** Here, the primary objective is to gain access to new geographic markets.

The final type of merger or acquisition identified by the FTC is a **conglomerate merger.** For the FTC, conglomerate mergers are a residual category. If there are no vertical, horizontal, product extension, or market extension links between firms, the FTC defines the merger or acquisition activity between firms as a conglomerate merger.

Given the earlier conclusion that mergers or acquisitions between strategically *unrelated* firms will not generate economic profits for either bidders or targets, it should not be surprising that there are currently relatively few examples of conglomerate mergers or acquisitions. However, at various times in history, conglomerate mergers and acquisitions have been relatively common. In the 1960s, for example, many acquisitions took the form of conglomerate mergers. Research has shown that the fraction of single-business firms in the *Fortune* 500 dropped from 22.8 percent in 1959 to 14.8 percent in 1969, while the fraction of firms in the *Fortune* 500 pursuing unrelated diversification strategies rose from 7.3 percent to 18.7 percent during the same time period. These findings are consistent with an increase in the number of conglomerate mergers and acquisitions during the 1960s.[4]

Despite the popularity of conglomerate mergers in the 1960s, most strategically unrelated mergers or acquisitions are divested shortly after they are completed. One study estimated that over one-third of the conglomerate mergers of the 1960s were divested by the early 1980s. Another study showed that over 50 percent of these acquisitions were subsequently divested. These results are all consistent with our earlier conclusion that strategically unrelated mergers or acquisitions are not a source of economic profits.[5]

Because firms can be strategically related in multiple ways, it is often the case that a particular merger or acquisition can be simultaneously categorized into two or more of the FTC merger and acquisition categories. For example, Crown Cork & Seal's (CC&S) acquisition of CarnaudMetalbox is a market extension merger (it provided CC&S assess to a new geographic market—Europe), but it also is a product extension merger (it provided CC&S access to some unique CarnaudMetalbox packaging technology).

Other Types of Strategic Relatedness.   Although the FTC categories of mergers and acquisitions provide some information about possible motives underlying these corporate strategies, they do not capture the full complexity of the links that might exist between bidding and target firms. Several authors have attempted to develop more complete lists of possible sources of relatedness between bidding and target firms. One

TABLE 14.2	Lubatkin's (1983) List of Potential Sources of Strategic Relatedness Between Bidding and Target Firms
Technical economies	Scale economies that occur when the physical processes inside a firm are altered so that the same amounts of input produce higher quantity of outputs. Sources of technical economies include marketing, production, experience, scheduling, banking, and compensation.
Pecuniary economies	Economies achieved by the ability of firms to dictate prices by exerting market power.
Diversification economies	Economies achieved by improving a firm's performance relative to its risk attributes or lowering its risk attributes relative to its performance. Sources of diversification economies include portfolio management and risk reduction.

Source: Adapted from Lubatkin, M. (1983). "Mergers and the performance of the acquiring firm," *Academy of Management Review,* 8(2), pp. 218–225.

of these lists is summarized in Table 14.2. This list includes **technical economies** (in marketing, production, and similar forms of relatedness), **pecuniary economies** (market power), and **diversification economies** (in portfolio management and risk reduction) as possible bases of strategic relatedness between bidding and target firms.

A second important list of possible sources of strategic relatedness between bidding and target firms was developed by scholars after a comprehensive review of empirical research on the economic returns to mergers and acquisitions. This list is summarized in Table 14.3 and includes the following factors as possible sources of economic gains in mergers and acquisitions: potential reductions in production or distribution costs (from economies of scale, vertical integration, reduction in agency costs,

TABLE 14.3	Jensen and Ruback's (1983) List of Reasons Why Bidding Firms Might Want to Engage in Merger and Acquisition Strategies

To reduce production or distribution costs
1. Through economies of scale
2. Through vertical integration
3. Through the adoption of more efficient production or organizational technology
4. Through the increased utilization of the bidder's management team
5. Through a reduction of agency costs by bringing organization-specific assets under common ownership

Financial motivations
1. To gain access to underutilized tax shields
2. To avoid bankruptcy costs
3. To increase leverage opportunities
4. To gain other tax advantages

To gain market power in product markets
To eliminate inefficient target management

Source: Adapted from Jensen, M. C., and R. S. Ruback (1983). "The market for corporate control: The scientific evidence," *Journal of Financial Economics,* 11, pp. 5–50.

and so forth), the realization of financial opportunities (such as gaining access to un-derutilized tax shields, avoiding bankruptcy costs), the creation of market power, and the ability to eliminate inefficient management in the target firm.

To be economically valuable, links between bidding and target firms must meet the same criteria as diversification strategies (see Chapter 11). First, these links must build on real economies of scope between bidding and target firms. If these economies of scope exist between these firms, then the equality in equation 14.1 becomes an inequality:

$$NPV(A + B) > NPV(A) + NPV(B) \tag{14.3}$$

If this inequality holds, these two firms are more valuable cooperating through some sort of corporate strategy than they are as separate entities. This additional value can reflect either cost savings or revenue enhancements that are created by economies of scope. Second, not only must these economies of scope exist, they must be less costly for the merged firm to realize than for outside equity holders to realize on their own. As with corporate diversification strategies, by investing in a diversified portfolio of stocks, outside equity investors can gain many of the economies associated with a merger or acquisition on their own. Moreover, investors can realize some of these economies of scope at almost zero cost. In this situation, it makes little sense for in-vestors to "hire" managers in firms to realize these economies of scope for them through a merger or acquisition. Rather, firms should pursue merger and acquisition strategies only to obtain economies of scope that outside investors find too costly to create on their own.

Economic Profits in Related Acquisitions
If the bidding and target firms are strategically related, then the economic value of these two firms combined is greater than the economic value of these two firms as sep-arate entities. To see how the inequality in equation 14.3 affects returns to merger and acquisition strategies, consider the following scenario: As before, there is one target firm and 10 bidding firms. The market value of the target firm as a stand-alone entity is $10,000, and the market value of the bidding firms as stand-alone entities is $15,000. However, unlike the earlier scenario in this chapter, the bidding and target firms are strategically related. Any of the types of relatedness identified in Tables 14.1, 14.2, or 14.3 could be the source of these economies of scope. They imply that when any of the bidding firms and the target are combined, the market value of this combined entity will be $32,000—note that $32,000 is greater than the sum of $15,000 plus $10,000, and thus the inequality in equation 14.3 holds. Assuming that the capital market within which the bidding firms are operating is semi-strong efficient, at what price will this target firm be acquired, and what are the economic profit implications for bidding and target firms at this price?

As before, bidding firms will be willing to pay a price for a target up to the value that a target firm adds once it is acquired. Thus, the formula for determining the maxi-mum price, P, that bidding firms are willing to pay for a target—equation 14.2—remains unchanged. Applying that formula to this strategically related scenario implies that bidding firms will be willing to pay up to $17,000 ($P = $32,000 − $15,000) to acquire this target.

As was the case for the strategically unrelated acquisition, it is not hard to see that the price for actually acquiring the target firm in this scenario will rise rapidly to

$17,000. The price will rise quickly to $17,000 because any bid less than $17,000 has the potential for generating profits for a bidding firm. Suppose that one bidding firm offers $13,000 for the target. For this $13,000, the bidding firm gains access to a target that will generate $17,000 of value once it is acquired. Thus, to this bidding firm, the target is worth $17,000, and a bid of $13,000 will generate $4,000 economic profit. Of course, these potential profits will motivate entry into the competitive bidding process. Entry will be possible because each of the 10 bidding firms can realize the same economy of scope with this target, and because capital markets are semi-strong efficient.

At this $17,000 price, the successful bidding firm does not earn superior economic profits. After all, this firm has acquired an asset that will generate $17,000 of value and has paid $17,000 to do so. However, the owners of the target firm will earn an economic profit worth $7,000. As a stand-alone firm, the target is worth $10,000; when combined with a bidding firm, it is worth $17,000. The difference between the value of the target as a stand-alone entity and its value in combination with a bidding firm is the value of the economic profit that can be appropriated by the owners of the target firm.

Thus the existence of strategic relatedness between bidding and target firms, as defined in equation 14.3, is not a sufficient condition for the equity holders of bidding firms to earn profits from their acquisition strategies. If the economic potential of acquiring a particular target firm is widely known, if several potential bidding firms can all obtain this value by acquiring a target, and if semi-strong capital market efficiency holds, the equity holders of bidding firms will, at best, only "break even" by implementing an acquisition strategy. In this setting, a "strategically related" merger or acquisition will create economic value, but this value will be distributed in the form of economic profits to the equity holders of acquired target firms.

Note that the fact that a particular target is not the object of multiple bids does not necessarily imply that a bidding firm will be able to earn superior economic performance from its acquisition of a target. A bidding firm, in anticipation of other potential bidders, may make an initial bid equal to the full value of the target. With such a bid, this bidding firm will be able to acquire the target but will not earn superior profits from doing so. In this case, the threat of anticipated competition for a target leads to no economic profits for a bidding firm.

Also, different bidding firms may have different types of strategic relatedness with target firms, and these performance implications of mergers and acquisitions will still be unchanged. All that is required is that the different bidding firms value targets at the same level. When this is the case, bidding firms will break even and targets will earn economic profits. However, in real merger and acquisition situations, it seems likely that when different bidding firms value the acquisition of targets at the same level, the type of relatedness that exists between one bidder and targets is likely to be quite similar to the type of relatedness that exists between other bidders and targets. This homogeneity in relatedness leads to a homogeneity in the valuation of targets, which in turn leads to zero economic profits for bidders upon acquisition.

Empirical Research on the Performance Implications of Mergers and Acquisitions

This discussion of returns to bidding and target firms in strategically related and strategically unrelated mergers and acquisitions leads to a variety of important empirical questions. Several of these questions, including whether most acquisitions occur between strategically related or strategically unrelated firms, and the return implications of these different acquisition contexts for returns to bidding and target firms, have been addressed in the empirical literature.

For example, one study reviewed over 40 empirical merger and acquisition studies in finance literature. This study examined acquisitions that were negotiated between a bidding firm's management and a target firm's management, and offers to buy a target firm's shares made directly to the target firm's equity holders. This study concluded that the completion of the first type of acquisition, on average, increased the market value of target firms by 20 percent, and left the market value of bidding firms unchanged. In contrast, acquisition offers made directly to a target firm's equity holders, on average, increased the market value of a target firm by 30 percent and had a small positive effect (4 percent) on the value of the successful bidding firm. Judging from the empirical evidence in finance, Jensen and Ruback, the authors of this report, concluded that "corporate takeovers generate positive gains, . . . target firm equity holders benefit, and . . . bidding firm equity holders do not lose."[6]

However, this study was less confident about the sources of value creation in mergers and acquisitions. Although the study cited numerous potential economies of scope between bidding and target firms in mergers and acquisitions (see Table 14.3), most of the research that was reviewed examined only how much value mergers and acquisitions create and who appropriates that value, not the sources of that value. The only two studies reviewed that examine potential sources of value creation focused only on the ability of horizontal acquisitions to generate economic profits through the creation of market power (see Chapter 9's discussion of industry concentration and tacit collusion). However, both these studies concluded that horizontal mergers do not create market power or economic profits and thus are not a source of value creation in mergers and acquisitions.[7] This extensive review of the finance merger and acquisition literature concluded that "knowledge of the source of takeover gains still eludes us."

Strategy researchers have attempted to examine in more detail the sources of value creation in mergers and acquisitions and the question of whether these sources of value creation affect whether bidders or targets appropriate this value. For example, two well-known studies examined the effect of the type and degree of strategic relatedness (defined using the FTC typology summarized in Table 14.1) between bidding and target firms on the economic consequences of mergers and acquisitions.[8] These studies found that the more strategically related bidding and target firms are, the more economic value mergers and acquisitions create. However, like the finance studies, this work found that this economic value was appropriated by the owners of the target firm, regardless of the type or degree of relatedness between bidding and target firms. On average, bidding firms—even when they attempt to acquire strategically related targets—earn normal economic profits from their merger and acquisition strategies.

Thus, despite some variance in the empirical research, on the whole, this work is remarkably consistent. On average, most mergers and acquisitions do create economic value. Consequently it appears that most firms pursuing merger and acquisition strategies attempt to acquire strategically related targets, where the inequality in equation 14.3 holds. In most cases, however, the economic value of these acquisition strategies is appropriated by the owners of the target firms, and the owners of bidding firms usually just break even. Thus it appears that most mergers and acquisitions take place in highly competitive markets for corporate control, in which multiple potential bidders compete to acquire strategically related targets.

Why Are There So Many Mergers and Acquisitions?

Given the overwhelming empirical evidence that most of the economic value created in mergers and acquisitions is appropriated by the owners of the target firm most of the time, an important question becomes: Why do managers of bidding firms continue to engage in merger and acquisition strategies? Some possible explanations are summarized in Table 14.4 and discussed later.

Ensuring Survival

Even if mergers and acquisitions, on average, do not generate superior economic profits for bidding firms, it may still be necessary for bidding firms to engage in these activities to ensure their survival. In particular, if all of a bidding firm's competitors have been able to improve their efficiency and effectiveness through a particular type of acquisition, then failing to make such an acquisition may put a firm at a competitive disadvantage. Here, the purpose of a merger or acquisition is not to gain competitive advantages, but rather to gain competitive parity.

Of course, engaging in a merger or acquisition is not the only way in which a firm can realize these efficiencies. A firm may decide to obtain these efficiencies on its own without the involvement of another firm, or a firm may decide that it can obtain these efficiencies by developing a strategic alliance with another firm. In this sense, internal development and strategic alliances can be seen as potential substitutes for merger and acquisition strategies.

Many recent mergers among banks in the United States seem to have had competitive parity as an objective. Most bank managers recognize that changing bank regulations, increased competition from non-bank financial institutions, and soft demand are likely to lead to a consolidation of the U.S. banking industry. To survive in this consolidated industry, many U.S. banks will have to merge. As the number of banks engaging in mergers and acquisitions goes up, the ability to earn profits from those strategies goes down. These lower returns from acquisitions have already reduced the economic value of some of the most aggressive acquiring banks. Despite these lower returns, acquisitions are likely to continue for the foreseeable future, as banks seek survival opportunities in a consolidated industry. Phelps Dodge Mining Company's bid to acquire both Cyprus Amax Minerals and Asarto, once these firms agreed to merge, can be seen as an effort by Phelps Dodge not to be left behind in a rapidly consolidating metals mining market. Pfizer's efforts to snatch Warner-Lambert Co. from an acquisition by American Home Products had similar defensive overtones.[9]

TABLE 14.4	Possible Motivations to Engage in Mergers and Acquisitions
1. Ensuring survival	
2. Free cash flow	
3. Agency problems	
4. Managerial hubris	
5. The potential for above-normal profits	

Free Cash Flow

Another reason why firms may continue to invest in merger and acquisition strategies is that these strategies, on average, can be expected to generate at least competitive parity for bidding firms. This level of profit may be a more attractive investment for some firms than alternative strategic investments. This is particularly the case for firms that generate free cash flow.[10]

Free cash flow is simply the amount of cash a firm has to invest after all positive net present value investments in a firm's ongoing businesses have been funded. Free cash flow is created when a firm's ongoing business operations are very profitable but offer few opportunities for additional investment. One firm that seems to have generated a great deal of free cash flow over the last several years is Philip Morris. Philip Morris's retail tobacco operations are extremely profitable. However, regulatory constraints, health concerns, and slowing growth in demand limit investment opportunities in the tobacco industry, at least in the United States. Thus, the amount of cash generated by Philip Morris's ongoing tobacco business has probably been larger than the sum of its positive net present value investments in that business. This difference is free cash flow for Philip Morris.[11]

A firm that generates a great deal of free cash flow must decide what to do with this money. One obvious alternative is to give it to stockholders in the form of dividends or a stock buyback (see Chapter 11). However, in some situations (for example, when stockholders face high marginal tax rates), stockholders may prefer a firm to retain this cash flow and invest it for them. When this is the case, how should a firm invest its free cash flow? In this context, merger and acquisition strategies are a viable option, because bidding firms, on average, can expect at least not to destroy value by implementing them.

Agency Problems

Another reason why firms might continue to engage in mergers and acquisitions, despite not earning superior economic profits from doing so, is that mergers and acquisitions benefit managers directly, independent of any value they may or may not create for a bidding firm's stockholders. As suggested in Chapter 11, these conflicts of interest are a manifestation of agency problems between a firm's managers and its stockholders.

Merger and acquisition strategies can benefit managers, even if they do not benefit a bidding firm's equity holders directly, in at least two ways. First, managers can use mergers and acquisitions to help diversify their human capital investments in their firm. As discussed in Chapter 11, managers have difficulty diversifying their firm-specific human capital investments when the firm operates in a narrow range of businesses. By acquiring firms with cash flows that are not perfectly correlated with the cash flows of the firm's current businesses, managers can reduce the probability of bankruptcy for their firm and thus partially diversify their human capital investments in their firm. However, as was also discussed in Chapter 11, to the extent that this diversification leads managers to make firm-specific human capital investments, and to the extent that these investments can be a source of economic profits, this kind of diversification can benefit equity holders indirectly.

Second, managers can use mergers and acquisitions to quickly increase firm size, measured in either sales or assets. If management compensation is closely linked to firm size, managers who increase firm size can increase their compensation. Of all the ways to increase the size of a firm quickly, growth through mergers and acquisitions is perhaps the easiest. Even if there are no economies of scope between a bidding and a target firm, an acquisition ensures that the bidding firm will grow by the size of the target (measured in either sales or assets). If there are economies between a bidding and a target firm, the size of the bidding firm can grow at an even faster rate, as can the value of management's compensation, even though, on average, acquisitions do not generate wealth for the owners of the bidding firm.

Managerial Hubris

Another reason why managers may choose to continue to invest in mergers and acquisitions, despite the fact that, on average, they do not gain superior profits from doing so, is the existence of what might be called *managerial hubris*.[12] This is the unrealistic belief, held by managers in bidding firms, that they can manage the assets of a target firm more efficiently than the target firm's current management can. This notion can lead bidding firms to engage in acquisition strategies even though there may not be positive economic profits from doing so.

The existence of managerial hubris suggests that the economic value of bidding firms will fall once they announce a merger or acquisition strategy. Although managers in bidding firms might truly believe that they can manage a target firm's assets more efficiently than the target firm's managers can, investors in the capital markets are much less likely to be caught up in this hubris. In this context, a commitment to a merger or acquisition strategy is a strong signal that a bidding firm's management has deluded itself about its abilities to manage a target firm's assets. Such delusions will certainly adversely affect the economic value of the bidding firm.

Of course, empirical work on mergers and acquisitions discussed earlier in this chapter has concluded that, although bidding firms do not obtain superior profits from their merger and acquisition strategies, they also do not, on average, reduce their economic value by implementing these strategies. This is inconsistent with the "hubris hypothesis." However, simply because, on average, bidding firms do not lose economic value does not mean that some bidding firms do not lose economic value. Thus, although it is unlikely that all merger and acquisition strategies are motivated by managerial hubris, it is likely that at least some of these strategies are. In fact, several studies have found that bidding firms significantly reduced their economic value by implementing merger and acquisition strategies, studies that are consistent with the existence of managerial hubris in at least some bidding firms pursuing merger and acquisition strategies.[13]

The Potential for Superior Profits

A final reason why managers might continue to pursue merger and acquisition strategies is the potential these strategies offer for generating superior profits for at least some bidding firms. The empirical research on returns to bidding firms in mergers and acquisitions is very strong. On average, bidding firms break even from their merger and acquisition strategies. However, that bidding firms, *on average,* break even on these strategies does not mean that all bidding firms will always earn such low profits. In some situations bidding firms may be able to earn superior performance from merger and acquisition activities. These situations are discussed in the following section.

14.2 MERGERS AND ACQUISITIONS AND SUSTAINED COMPETITIVE ADVANTAGE

We have already seen that the economies of scope that motivate mergers and acquisitions between strategically related bidding and target firms can be valuable. However, the ability of these economies to generate superior profits and competitive advantages for bidding firms depends not just on their economic value but also on the competitiveness of the market for corporate control through which these valuable economies are realized. Only when the market for corporate control is imperfectly competitive might it be possible for bidding firms to earn superior profits from implementing a merger or acquisition strategy. To see how the competitiveness of the market for corporate control can affect returns to merger and acquisition strategies, three scenarios involving bidding and target firms and their implications for bidding firm and target firm managers are considered.[14]

Valuable, Rare, and Private Economies of Scope Between Bidding and Target Firms

An imperfectly competitive market for corporate control can exist when a target is worth more to one bidder than it is to any other bidders and when no other firms, including both bidders and targets, are aware of this additional value. In this setting, the price of a target will rise to reflect public expectations about the value of the target. Once the target is acquired, however, the performance of the special bidder that acquires the target will be greater than generally expected, and this level of performance will generate economic profits for the equity holders of the bidding firm.

Consider a simple case. The present value of the bidder Firm A combined with target firms is $12,000, whereas the present value of all other bidders combined with targets is $10,000. No other firms (bidders or targets) are aware of Firm A's unique relationship with these targets, but they are aware of the value of all other bidders combined with targets (that is, $10,000). The present value of all bidding firms, as stand-alone entities, is $6,000. In this setting, Firm A will be willing to pay up to $6,000 to acquire a target ($P = \$12,000 - \$6,000$), and all other bidders will be willing to pay up to only $4,000 to acquire a target ($P = \$10,000 - \$6,000$).

Because publicly available information suggests that acquiring a target is worth $4,000, the price of targets will rise rapidly to this level, ensuring that if bidding firms, apart from Firm A, acquire a target, they will not obtain superior economic profits. If there is only one target in this market for corporate control, then Firm A will be able to bid slightly more than $4,000 (perhaps $4,001) for this target. No other firms will bid higher than Firm A because, from their point of view, the acquisition is simply not worth more than $4,000. At this $4,001 price, Firm A will earn an economic profit of $1,999—Firm A had to spend only $4,001 for a firm that brings $6,000 in value. Alternatively, if there are multiple targets, then several bidding firms, including Firm A, will pay $4,000 for their targets. At this price, more of these bidding firms will earn zero economic profits, Firm A will earn a greater economic profit equal to $2,000.

In order for Firm A to obtain this economic profit, the value of Firm A's economy of scope with target firms must be greater than the value of any other bidding firms with that target. This special value will generally reflect unusual resources and capabilities possessed by Firm A—resources and capabilities that are more valuable in combination with target firms than are the resources and capabilities that other bidding firms possess. Put differently, to be a source of economic profits and competitive advantage, Firm A's link with targets must be based on firm resources and capabilities that are rare among those firms competing in this market for corporate control.

However, not only does Firm A have to possess valuable and rare links with bidding firms to gain economic profits and competitive advantages from its acquisition strategies, information about these special economies of scope must not be known to other firms. If other bidding firms know about the additional value associated with acquiring a target, they are likely to try to duplicate this value for themselves. Typically, they would accomplish this by imitating the type of relatedness that exists between Firm A and its targets, by acquiring the resources and capabilities that enabled Firm A to have valuable economies of scope with its targets. Once other bidders acquire the resources and capabilities necessary to obtain this more valuable economy of scope, they would be able to enter into bidding, thereby increasing the likelihood that the equity holders of successful bidding firms would not earn superior economic profits.

The acquisition or development of these resources and capabilities would not even have to be completed before bidding for target firms begins. This is because bidding firms could anticipate that they would be able to acquire or develop these resources and capabilities at some point in the future, and thus the present value of acquiring these targets for these bidders would be the same as for Firm A. In this setting, the price of an acquisition will rise to equal its full value for Firm A and for those bidders who anticipate the ability to acquire the resources and capabilities controlled by Firm A. Firm A can be shielded from this competition only if other bidding firms are unaware of the higher-valued strategic relatedness available to Firm A and the sources of this higher-valued strategic relatedness.

Target firms must also be unaware of Firm A's special resources and capabilities if Firm A is to obtain superior profits from an acquisition. If target firms were aware of this extra value available to Firm A, along with the sources of this value, they could inform other bidding firms. These bidding firms could then adjust their bids to reflect this higher value, and competitive bidding would reduce superior profits to bidders. Target firms are likely to inform other bidding firms in this way because increasing the number of bidders with more valuable economies of scope increases the likelihood that target firms will extract all the economic value created in a merger or acquisition.[15] Though there may be many different managerial motives behind target firms' seeking out "white knights" as alternative merger partners after an acquisition attempt has been made, the effect of such actions is to increase the number of fully informed bidders for a target. This, in turn, reduces the economic profit that bidding firms obtain.

Thus far, it has been assumed that only one firm has a more valuable source of strategic relatedness with targets (in this example, worth $12,000 compared to all other bidding firms' strategic relatedness, worth only $10,000). However, the argument also applies to the more complex case in which several bidding firms have more valuable economies of scope with targets than are the economies of scope whose value is publicly known. As long as the number of targets is greater than, or equal to, the number of firms with these more valuable sources of strategic relatedness, each of the bidding firms can complete an acquisition, and each can earn varying amounts of economic profits. The actual amount of economic profit depends on the value of each of these bidding firms' economies of scope with specific targets.

TABLE 14.5	Present Value of Strategic Relatedness Between Four Firms and Targets			
	Firm A	*Firm B*	*Firm C*	*Firm D*
Present value of strategic relatedness with targets	$12,000	$11,000	$10,000	$9,000
Present value of firm as a stand-alone entity	3,000	5,000	3,000	2,000

The effects of valuable, rare, and private economies of scope on economic profits for the equity holders of bidding firms holds even when different bidding firms have different values as stand-alone entities and in combination with different targets—that is, when each bidding firm acting in a market for corporate control is unique. Consider the example in Table 14.5. The present value of the four firms in this table (A, B, C, and D) as stand-alone entities ranges from $2,000 to $5,000, and the present value of these firms when combined with targets ranges from $9,000 to $12,000. From equation 14.2 it is clear that Firm A must pay less than $9,000 for a target in order to gain economic profits, Firm B less than $6,000, Firm C less than $7,000, and Firm D less than $7,000.

If publicly available information suggests that firms with the right resources and capabilities can obtain an incremental growth in their economic value worth $7,000 by acquiring a target, then several things are likely to occur. First, Firm B is likely to acquire or develop the resources and capabilities that enable Firms C and D to obtain a $7,000 present value increase from acquiring a target. Next, the price of a target is likely to rise to $7,000. If several target firms are available, all the firms in Table 14.5 will be able to acquire a target, but only Firm A will make an economic profit from doing so (worth $2,000). If only one target is available, only Firm A will complete the acquisition or merger, and its profit, though still positive, will be slightly smaller ($2,000 less some small amount). If there are not enough targets for all bidding firms, then which firms (B, C, or D) will complete an acquisition is indeterminate, although whichever of these firms does so will not obtain an economic profit. Also, Firm A will complete an acquisition and still earn a superior return for its equity holders equal to $2,000 (minus some small amount).

Adding a firm (Firm E) that is identical to Firm A in Table 14.5 highlights the requirement that the number of firms with a more valuable economy of scope with targets must be less than, or equal to, the number of targets in order for these bidding firms to earn economic profits. If there are two or more targets, then both Firm A and Firm E can execute an acquisition for economic profits. However, if there is only one target, then Firms A and E are likely to engage in competitive bidding, perhaps driving the price of this target up to the point that acquiring it will no longer be a source of economic profits (that is, setting P equal to $9,000). In this process, Firms A and E will be ensuring that the equity holders of this acquired firm earn substantial economic profits.

Valuable, Rare, and Costly-to-Imitate Economies of Scope Between Bidding and Target Firms

The existence of firms that have valuable, rare, and private economies of scope with targets is not the only factor that can result in an imperfectly competitive market for corporate control. If other bidders cannot imitate one bidder's valuable and rare economies with targets, then competition in this market for corporate control will be imperfect, and the equity holders of this special bidding firm will earn economic profits. In this case, the existence of valuable and rare economies does not need to be private, because other bidding firms cannot imitate these economies, and therefore bids that substantially reduce the profits for the equity holders of the special bidding firm will not be forthcoming.

Typically, bidding firms will be unable to imitate one bidder's valuable and rare economies of scope with targets when the strategic relatedness between the special bidder and the targets stems from some rare and costly-to-imitate resources or capabilities controlled by the special bidding firm. Any of the costly-to-imitate resources and capabilities discussed in Chapter 5 could create costly-to-imitate economies of scope between a firm and a target. If, in addition, these economies are valuable and rare, they can be a source of economic profit to the equity holders of the special bidding firm. This can happen even if all firms in this market for corporate control are aware of the more valuable economies of scope (and their services) available to this firm and its sources. Although information about this special economy is publicly available, equity holders of special bidding firms will earn an economic profit when acquisition occurs. The equity holders of target firms will not obtain all of this profit, because competitive bidding dynamics cannot unfold when the sources of a more valuable economy of scope are costly to imitate.

As before, the number of firms with this special economy of scope must be less than the number of targets, in order for the equity holders of these firms to obtain above-normal profits. If there are more of these special bidders than there are targets, then these firms are likely to engage in competitive bidding for targets, once again shifting above-normal profits from bidding firm to target firm equity holders.

If the number of bidding firms with these special attributes is less than the number of target firms, then the level of economic profit they obtain will be approximately the same as for bidding firms with valuable, rare, and private economies of scope with targets. However, if the number of special bidders and number of targets are the same, the market for corporate control takes on many of the attributes of a bilateral monopoly. In this setting, the level of superior profits that the equity holders of bidding firms obtain depends on their negotiation skills and is somewhat indeterminate. When all bidders and targets know the value of a target for a particular bidder that has valuable, rare, and costly-to-imitate economies of scope with targets, the negotiated price is likely to fall somewhere between the value of targets for firms that have the high-value economy of scope and the value of targets for other bidding firms.

Of course, it may be possible for a valuable, rare, and costly-to-imitate economy of scope between a bidding and a target firm also to be private. Indeed, it is often the case that those attributes of a firm that are costly to imitate are also difficult to describe and thus can be held as proprietary information. In that case, the analysis of economic profits associated with valuable, rare, and private economies of scope presented earlier applies.

Unexpected Valuable Economies of Scope Between Bidding and Target Firms

The discussion of profits to bidding firms implementing merger and acquisition strategies had adopted, for convenience, the strong assumption that the present value of the strategic relatedness between bidders and targets is known with certainty by individual bidders. This is, in principle, possible but certainly not likely. Most modern acquisitions and mergers are massively complex, involving numerous unknown and complicated relationships between firms. In these settings, unexpected events after an acquisition has been completed may make an acquisition or merger more valuable than bidders and targets anticipated it would be. The price that bidding firms will pay to acquire a target will equal the expected value of the target only when the target is combined with the bidder. The difference between the unexpected value of an acquisition actually obtained by a bidder and the price the bidder paid for the acquisition is an economic profit for the equity holders of the bidding firm.

Of course, by definition, bidding firms cannot expect to obtain unexpected value from an acquisition. Unexpected value, in this context, is a surprise, a manifestation of a bidding firm's good luck, not its skill in acquiring targets. For example, when the British advertising firm WPP acquired J. Walter Thompson for $550 million, it discovered some property owned by J. Walter Thomson in Tokyo. No one knew of this property when the firm was acquired. It turned out to be worth over $100 million after taxes, a financial windfall that helped offset the high cost of this acquisition. When asked, Martin Sorrel, president of WPP and the architect of this acquisition, admitted that this $100 million windfall was simply good luck.[16]

Implications for Bidding Firm Managers

The existence of valuable, rare, and private economies of scope between bidding and target firms, and of valuable, rare, and costly-to-imitate economies of scope between bidding and target firms, suggests that although, on average, most bidding firms do not generate economic profits from their acquisition strategies, in some special circumstances it may be possible for bidding firms to create such profits. Thus the task facing managers in firms contemplating merger and acquisition strategies is to choose these strategies in a manner that they have the greatest likelihood of generating superior returns for their equity holders. Several important managerial prescriptions can be derived from this discussion. These "rules" for bidding firm managers are summarized in Table 14.6.

Search for Rare Economies of Scope

One of the main reasons why bidding firms do not obtain superior performance from acquiring strategically related target firms is that several other bidding firms value the target firm in the same way. When multiple bidders value a target in the same way, competitive bidding is likely. Competitive bidding, in turn, drives out the potential for superior performance. To avoid this problem, bidding firms should seek to acquire targets with which they enjoy valuable and rare linkages.

TABLE 14.6   Rules for Bidding Firm Managers
1. Search for valuable and rare economies of scope
2. Keep information away from other bidders
3. Keep information away from targets
4. Avoid winning bidding wars
5. Close the deal quickly
6. Operate in "thinly traded" acquisition markets

Operationally, the search for rare economies of scope suggests that managers in bidding firms need to consider not only the value of a target firm when combined with their own company, but also the value of the target firm when combined with other potential bidders. This is important because it is the difference between the value of a particular bidding firm's relationship with a target and the value of other bidding firms' relationships with that target that defines the size of the potential economic profits from an acquisition.

In practice, the search for valuable and rare economies of scope is likely to become a search for valuable and rare resources already controlled by a firm that are synergistically related to a target. For example, if a bidding firm has a unique reputation in its product market, and if the target firm's products could benefit by association with that reputation, then the target firm may be more valuable to this particular bidder than to other bidders (firms that do not possess this special reputation). Also, if a particular bidder possesses the largest market share in its industry, the best distribution system, or restricted access to certain key raw materials, and if the target firm would benefit from being associated with these valuable and rare resources, then the acquisition of this target may be a source of economic profits.

The search for valuable and rare economies of scope as a basis for mergers and acquisitions tends to rule out certain interfirm linkages as sources of economic profits. For example, most acquisitions can lead to a reduction in overhead costs, because much of the corporate overhead associated with the target firm can be eliminated subsequent to acquisition. However, the ability to eliminate these overhead costs is not unique to any one bidder, and thus the value created by these reduced costs will usually be captured by the equity holders of the target firm.

Keep Information Away from Other Bidders

One of the keys to earning superior profits in an acquisition strategy is to avoid multiple bidders for a single target. One way to accomplish this is to keep information about the bidding process, and about the sources of economies of scope between a bidder and target that underlie this bidding process, as private as possible. To become involved in bidding for a target, other firms must be aware of the value of the economies of scope between themselves and that target. If only one bidding firm knows this information, and if this bidding firm can close the deal before the full value of the target is known, then this bidding firm may earn above-normal economic profits from completing this acquisition.

Of course, in many circumstances, keeping all this information private is difficult. Often, it is illegal. For example, when seeking to acquire a publicly traded firm, potential bidders must meet disclosure requirements that effectively reduce the amount of private information a bidder can retain. In these circumstances, unless a bidding firm has some valuable, rare, and costly-to-imitate economy of scope with a target firm, the possibility of economic profits coming from an acquisition is very low. It is not surprising that the research conducted on mergers and acquisitions of firms traded on public stock exchanges governed by U.S. Securities and Exchange Commission (SEC) disclosure rules suggests that, most of the time, bidding firms do not earn economic profits from implementing their acquisition strategies.

However, not all potential targets are publicly traded. Privately held firms may be acquired in an information environment that can create opportunities for superior performance for bidding firms. Moreover, even when acquiring a publicly traded firm, a bidder does not have to release all the information it has about the potential value of that target in combination with itself. Indeed, if some of this value reflects a bidding firm's taken-for-granted "invisible" assets, it may not be possible to communicate this information. In this case, as well, there may be opportunities for superior profits to bidding firms.

Keep Information Away from Targets

Not only should bidding firms keep information about the value of their economy of scope with a target away from other bidders, they also should keep this information away from target firms. Suppose that the value of a target firm to a bidding firm is $8,000 but the bidding firm, in an attempt to earn economic profits, has bid only $5,000 for the target. If the target knows that it is actually worth $8,000, it is very likely to hold out for a higher bid. In fact, the target may contact other potential bidding firms and tell them of the opportunity created by the $5,000 bid. As the number of bidders goes up, the possibility of superior economic performance for bidders goes down. Therefore, to keep the possibility of these profits alive, bidding firms must not fully reveal the value of their economies of scope with a target firm.

Again, in some circumstances, it is very difficult, or even illegal, to attempt to limit the flow of information to target firms. In these settings, superior economic performance for bidding firms is very unlikely.

Limiting the amount of information that flows to the target firm may have some other consequences as well. For example, it has been shown that a complete sharing of information, insights, and perspectives before an acquisition is completed increases the probability that economies of scope will actually be realized once an acquisition is completed.[17] By limiting the flow of information between itself and a target, a bidding firm may actually be increasing the cost of integrating the target into its ongoing business, thereby jeopardizing at least some of the superior economic performance that limiting information flow is designed to create. Bidding firms need to balance carefully the economic consequences of limiting the information they share with the target firm in order to generate superior economic performance against the costs that limiting information flow may create.

Avoid Winning Bidding Wars

It should be reasonably clear that if a number of firms bid for the same target, the probability that the firm that successfully acquires the target will earn superior profits is very low. Indeed, to ensure that competitive bidding occurs, target firms can actively encourage other bidding firms to enter the bidding process. The implications of these arguments are clear: Bidding firms should generally avoid winning a bidding war. To "win" a bidding war, a bidding firm often will have to pay a price at least equal to the full value of the target. Many times, given the emotions of an intense bidding contest, the winning bid may actually be higher than the true value of the target. Completing this type of acquisition will certainly reduce the economic performance of the bidding firm.

The only time it might make sense to "win" a bidding war is when the winning firm possesses a rare and private or a rare and costly-to-imitate economy of scope with a target that is more valuable than the strategic relatedness that exists between any other bidders and that target. In this setting, the winning firm may be able to earn an economic profit if it is able to fully realize the value of its relationship with the target.

Close the Deal Quickly

Another rule of thumb to obtain superior performance when implementing a merger and acquisition strategy is to close the deal quickly. All the economic processes that make it difficult for bidding firms to earn economic profits from acquiring a strategically related target take time to unfold. It takes time for other bidders to become aware of the economic value associated with acquiring a target; it takes time for the target to recruit other bidders; information leakage becomes more of a problem over time; and so forth. A bidding firm that begins and ends the bidding process quickly may forestall some of these processes and thereby retain some superior performance for itself from an acquisition.

The admonition to close the deal quickly should not be taken to mean that bidding firms need to make their acquisition decisions quickly. Indeed, the search for valuable and rare economies of scope should be undertaken with great care. There should be little rush in isolating and evaluating acquisition candidates. However, once a target firm has been located and valued, bidding firms have a strong incentive to reduce the period of time between the first bid and the completion of the deal. The longer this period of negotiation is, the less likely is the bidding firm to earn economic profits from the acquisition.

Complete Acquisitions in "Thinly Traded" Markets

Finally, an acquisition strategy can be a source of economic profits to bidding firms if these firms implement this corporate strategy in what could be described as "thinly traded markets." In general, a **thinly traded market** is a market in which there are only a small number of buyers and sellers; in which information about opportunities in this market are not widely known; and in which interests besides purely maximizing the value of a firm can be important. In the context of mergers and acquisitions, thinly traded markets are markets in which only a few (often only one) firms are implementing acquisition strategies. These unique firms may be the only firms that understand the full value of the acquisition opportunities in this market. Even target firm managers may not fully understand the value of the economic opportunities in these markets, and even if they do, they may have other interests besides maximizing the value of their firm if it becomes the object of a takeover.

In general, thinly traded merger and acquisition markets are highly fragmented. Competition in these markets occurs at the local level, as one local small firm competes with other local small firms for a common group of geographically defined customers. Most of these small firms are privately held. Many are sole proprietorships. Examples of these thinly traded markets have included, at various points in history, the printing industry, the fast-food industry, the used-car industry, the dry cleaning industry, and the barber shop/hair salon industry. As was suggested in Chapter 4, the major opportunity in all highly fragmented industries is consolidation. In the context of mergers and acquisitions, consolidation can occur by one firm (or a small number of firms) buying numerous independent firms to realize economies of scope in these industries. Often, these economies of scope reflect economies of scale in these industries— economies of scale that were not realized in a highly fragmented setting. As long as the number of firms implementing this consolidation strategy is small, then the market for corporate control in these markets will probably be less than perfectly competitive, and opportunities for superior profits from implementing an acquisition strategy may be possible.

More generally, if a merger or acquisition contest is played out through full-page ads in *The Wall Street Journal,* the ability of bidding firms to earn above-normal returns from their acquisitions is limited. Such highly public acquisitions are likely to lead to very competitive markets for corporate control. Competitive markets for corporate control, in turn, assure that the equity holders of the target firm will appropriate any value that might be created by an acquisition. However, if these contests occur in obscure, out-of-the-way industries, it is more likely that bidding firms will be able to earn superior profits from their acquisitions.

Service Corporation International: An Example

Empirical research on mergers and acquisitions suggests that it is not easy for bidding firms to earn economic profits from these strategies. However, it may be possible for some bidding firms, some of the time, to do so. One firm that has been successful in earning such profits from its merger and acquisition strategies is Service Corporation International (SCI). SCI is in the funeral home and cemetery business. It grew from a collection of five funeral homes in 1967 to being the largest owner of cemeteries and funeral homes in the United States today. It has done this through an aggressive and what was until recently a highly profitable acquisitions program in this historically fragmented industry (see the discussion of consolidation strategies in fragmented industries in Chapter 4).

The valuable and rare economy of scope that SCI brought to the funeral home industry is the application of traditional business practices in a highly fragmented and not often professionally managed industry. SCI-owned funeral homes operate with gross margins approaching 30 percent, nearly three times the gross margins of independently owned funeral homes. Among other things, these higher margins reflect savings from centralized purchasing services, centralized embalming and professional services, and the sharing of underutilized resources (including hearses) among funeral homes within geographic regions. SCI's scale advantages made a particular funeral home more valuable to SCI than to one of SCI's smaller competitors, and more valuable than if a particular funeral home was left as a stand-alone business.

Moreover, the funeral homes that SCI targeted for acquisition were, typically, family owned and lacked heirs to continue the business. Many of the owner/operators of these funeral homes were not fully aware of the value of their operations to SCI (they were morticians more than business managers), nor were they just interested in maximizing the sale price of their funeral homes. Rather, they were often looking to maintain continuity of service in a community, secure employment for their loyal employees, and ensure a comfortable (if not lavish) retirement for themselves. Being acquired by SCI was likely to be the only alternative to closing the funeral home once an owner/operator retired. Extracting less than the full value of the home when selling to SCI often seemed preferable to other alternatives.

Because SCI's acquisition of funeral homes exploited real and valuable economies of scope, this strategy had the potential for generating superior economic performance. Because SCI was, for many years, the only firm implementing this strategy in the funeral home industry, because the funeral homes that SCI acquired were generally not publicly traded, and because the owner/operators of these funeral homes often had interests besides simply maximizing the price of their operation when they sold it, it seems likely that SCI's acquisition strategy generated superior economic performance for many years.

In the last several years, however, information about SCI's acquisition strategy has become widely known. This had led other funeral homes to begin bidding to acquire formerly independent funeral homes. Moreover, independent funeral home owners have become more aware of their full value to SCI. Although SCI's economy of scope with independent funeral homes is still valuable, it is no longer rare, and thus no longer a source of economic profits to SCI. Put differently, the imperfectly competitive market for corporate control that SCI was able to exploit for almost 10 years has become more competitive. Future acquisitions by SCI are not likely to be a source of sustained competitive advantage and economic profit. For these reasons, SCI is currently reevaluating its corporate strategy, attempting to discover a new way in which it might be able to generate superior profits.[18]

Implications for Target Firm Managers

Although bidding firm managers can do several things to attempt to maximize the probability of earning economic profits from their merger and acquisition strategies, target firm managers can attempt to counter these efforts to ensure that the owners of target firms appropriate whatever value is created by a merger or acquisition. These "rules" for target firm managers are summarized in Table 14.7.

Seek Information from Bidders

One way in which a bidder can attempt to obtain superior performance from implementing an acquisition strategy is to keep information about the source and value of the strategic relatedness that exists between the bidder and target private. If that relationship is actually worth $12,000 but targets believe it is worth only $8,000, then a target might be willing to settle for a bid of $8,000 and thereby forgo the extra $4,000 it could have extracted from the bidder. Once the target knows that its true value to the bidder is $12,000, it is in a much better position to obtain this full value when the acquisition is completed.

It is well known that bidding firms must fully inform themselves about the resources and capabilities of potential acquisition targets to ensure that they price those targets appropriately. However, what is not as well known is that target firms must also inform themselves about the resources and capabilities of current and potential bidders. In this way, target firms can become fully aware of the value that they hold for bidders, and they are more likely to be able to extract this full value in the acquisition process.

TABLE 14.7   **Rules for Target Firm Managers**
1. Seek information from bidders
2. Invite other bidders to join the bidding competition
3. Delay but do not stop the acquisition

Invite Other Bidders to Join the Bidding Competition

Once a target firm is fully aware of the nature and value of the economies of scope that exist between it and current bidding firms, it can exploit this information by seeking other firms that may have the same relationship with it and then informing these firms of a potential acquisition opportunity. By inviting other firms into the bidding process, the target firm increases the competitiveness of the market for corporate control, thereby increasing the probability that the value resulting from an acquisition will be fully captured by the target firm.

Delay but Do Not Stop the Acquisition

As suggested earlier, bidding firms have a strong incentive to expedite the acquisition process, to prevent other bidders from becoming involved in an acquisition. Of course, the target firm wants other bidding firms to enter the process. To increase the probability of receiving more than one bid, target firms have a strong incentive to delay an acquisition.

The objective, however, should be to delay an acquisition to create a more competitive market for corporate control, not to stop an acquisition. If a valuable economy of scope exists between a bidding and a target firm, the merger of these two firms will create economic value. If the market for corporate control within which this merger occurs is competitive, then the equity holders of the target firm will appropriate the full value of this economy of scope. Preventing an acquisition in this setting can be very costly to the equity holders of the target firm.

Target firm managers can engage in a wide variety of activities to delay the completion of an acquisition. Some of these actions have the effect of reducing the wealth of target firm equity holders; some have no effect on the wealth of target firm equity holders; and some increase the wealth of target firm equity holders. Some common responses of target firm management to takeover efforts, along with their economic implications for the equity holders of target firms, are summarized in Table 14.8.[19]

TABLE 14.8   The Wealth Effects of Target Firm Management Responses to Acquisition Efforts

1. Responses that reduce the wealth of target firm equity holders
   - Greenmail
   - Standstill agreements
   - Poison pills
2. Responses that do not affect the wealth of target firm equity holders
   - Shark repellents
   - The "Pac Man" defense
   - Crown jewel sale
   - Lawsuits
3. Responses that increase the wealth of target firm equity holders
   - Search for white knights
   - Creation of bidding auctions
   - Golden parachutes

Responses That Reduce the Wealth of Target Firm Equity Holders.   Greenmail, standstill agreements, and poison pills are anti-takeover actions that target firm managers can take to reduce the wealth of target firm equity holders. **Greenmail** is a maneuver in which a target firm's management purchases any of the target firm's stock owned by a bidder, and does so for a price that is higher than the current market value of that stock. Greenmail effectively ends a bidding firm's effort to acquire a particular target, and does so in a way that can greatly reduce the wealth of a target firm's equity holders. Not only do these equity holders not appropriate any economic value that could have been created if an acquisition had been completed, they also have to bear the cost of the premium price that management must pay to buy its stock back from the bidding firm.

Not surprisingly, target firms that resort to greenmail substantially reduce the economic wealth of their equity holders. One study found that the value of target firms paying greenmail drops, on average, 1.76 percent.[20] Another study reported a 2.85 percent drop in the value of such firms. These reductions in value increase if greenmail leads to the cancellation of a takeover effort. Indeed, this second study found that such episodes led to a 5.50 percent reduction in the value of target firms.[21] These reductions in the value of target firms as a response to their greenmail activities stands in marked contrast to the generally positive market response to efforts by a firm to repurchase its own shares in non-greenmail situations.[22]

Standstill agreements are often negotiated in conjunction with greenmail. A standstill agreement is a contract between a target and a bidding firm whereby the bidding firm agrees not to attempt to take over the target for some specified period of time. When a target firm negotiates a standstill agreement, it prevents the current acquisition effort from being completed, and it reduces the number of bidders that might become involved in future acquisition efforts. Thus the equity holders of this target firm forgo any value that could have been created if the current acquisition had occurred. In addition, they also lose some of the value that they could have appropriated in future acquisition episodes by the target's inviting multiple bidders into a market for corporate control.

Standstill agreements, either alone or in conjunction with greenmail, reduce the economic value of a target firm. One study found that standstill agreements that were unaccompanied by stock repurchase agreements reduced the value of a target firm by 4.05 percent. Such agreements, in combination with stock repurchases, reduced the value of a target firm by 4.52 percent.[23]

So-called **poison pills** include any of a variety of actions that target firm managers can take to make the acquisition of the target prohibitively expensive. In one common poison pill maneuver, a target firm issues rights to its current stockholders such that if the firm is acquired in an unfriendly takeover, it will distribute a special cash dividend to stockholders. This cash dividend effectively increases the cost of acquiring the target and can discourage otherwise interested bidding firms from attempting to acquire this target. Another poison pill tactic substitutes the distribution of additional shares of a target firm's stock, at very low prices, for the special cash dividend. Issuing this low-price stock to current stockholders effectively undermines the value of a bidding firm's equity investment in a target and thus increases the cost of the acquisition. Other poison pills involve granting current stockholders other rights, rights that effectively increase the cost of an unfriendly takeover.[24]

Although poison pills are creative devices that target firms can use to prevent an acquisition, they generally have not been very effective. If a bidding firm and a target firm are strategically related, the value that can be created in an acquisition can be substantial, and most of this value will be appropriated by the stockholders of the target firm. Thus target firm stockholders have a strong incentive to have the target firm be acquired, and they are amenable to direct offers made by a bidding firm to them, as individual investors. These offers to purchase a publicly traded firm's stock directly from stockholders are called **tender offers.** However, to the extent that poison pills actually do prevent mergers and acquisitions, they are usually bad for the equity holders of target firms.

Since the 1980s, most firms have become aware that greenmail, standstill agreements, and poison pills reduce the wealth of their equity holders. For this reason, these responses to takeover efforts are becoming less common. Every once in a while, however, a firm seeking to avoid a takeover does engage in these activities.

Responses That Do Not Affect the Wealth of Target Firm Equity Holders. Target firm management can engage in a wide variety of other actions to try to delay their acquisition by a bidding firm. Many of these actions, however, do not significantly delay or stop the completion of an acquisition, and therefore have little effect on the wealth of the target firm's equity holders.

One class of these responses was called "shark repellents" in the 1980s. **Shark repellents** include a variety of relatively minor corporate governance changes that, in principle, are supposed to make it somewhat more difficult to acquire a target firm. Common examples of shark repellents include supermajority voting rules (which specify that more than 50 percent of the target firm's board of directors must approve a takeover) and state incorporation laws (in some states, incorporation laws make it difficult to acquire a firm incorporated in that state). However, if the value created by an acquisition is sufficiently large, these shark repellents will neither slow an acquisition attempt significantly nor prevent it from being completed.

Another response that does not affect the wealth of target firm equity holders is known as the **"Pac Man" defense.** Targets that use this tactic fend off an acquisition by taking over the firm or firms bidding for them. Just as in the old video game, the hunted becomes the hunter; the target turns the tables on current and potential bidders. One firm that employed the Pac Man defense successfully was American Brands, a diversified tobacco products company.[25] American Brands fought off an acquisition by acquiring its suitor, E II Holdings, Inc. However, the Liggett Group then launched an unfriendly takeover bid for American Brands. At the time, it was speculated that the owners of the Liggett Group really wanted to sell Liggett and that their bid to acquire American Brands was designed to spur American Brands into implementing its Pac Man defense to acquire the Liggett Group.

It should not be too surprising that the Pac Man defense does not, on average, either hurt or help the stockholders of target firms. In this defense, targets become bidders, and we know from empirical literature that, on average, bidding firms earn only breakeven from their acquisition efforts. Thus one would expect that, on average, the Pac Man defense would not generate superior economic profits for the stockholders of target firms implementing it.

Another ineffective and inconsequential response is called a **crown jewel sale.** The idea behind a crown jewel sale is that, sometimes, a bidding firm is interested in just a few of the businesses currently being operated by the target firm. These businesses are the target firm's "crown jewels." To prevent an acquisition, the target firm can sell off these crown jewels, either directly to the bidding firm or by setting up a separate company to own and operate these businesses. Then the bidding firm will be likely to be less interested in acquiring the target.

Perhaps one of the most famous crown-jewel sale defenses was employed by Pillsbury in its attempt to stave off an unfriendly takeover by Grand Met. At the time, the general belief was that Grand Met was particularly interested in acquiring Pillsbury's Burger King business. By setting up Burger King as a separate business entity, management at Pillsbury apparently believed that the full value of its Burger King operating unit would be revealed to the stock market and Grand Met's ability to earn economic profits from the acquisition of Burger King would fall. Moreover, Pillsbury's management also apparently believed that Grand Met would no longer be interested in acquiring the rest of Pillsbury. Pillsbury was wrong on both counts, because Grand Met completed its acquisition of Pillsbury shortly after Pillsbury announced its crown-jewel sale defense.[26]

A final relatively ineffective defense that most target firm managers pursue is filing lawsuits against bidding firms. Indeed, at least in the United States, the filing of a lawsuit has been almost automatic as soon as an acquisition effort is announced. These suits, however, usually do not delay or stop an acquisition or merger.

As with target actions that reduce the wealth of equity holders, actions that do not have an impact on the wealth of target firm equity holders have become less common over the last several years. This reflects a general understanding that these actions are largely ineffective.

Responses That Increase the Wealth of Target Firm Equity Holders. As suggested in Table 14.7, some of the actions that the management of target firms can take to delay (but not stop) an acquisition actually benefit target firm equity holders. The first of these is the search for a **white knight**—another bidding firm that agrees to acquire a particular target in the place of the original bidding firm. Target firm management may prefer to be acquired by some bidding firms rather than by others. For example, some bidding firms may possess much more valuable economies of scope with a target firm than other bidding firms, or some bidding firms may be expected to take a longer-term view in managing a target firm's assets than other bidding firms. In both cases, target firm managers are likely to prefer some bidding firms over other bidding firms.

As suggested earlier, whatever the motivation of a target firm's management, inviting a white knight to bid on a target firm has the effect of increasing the number of firms bidding for a target by at least one. If there is currently only one bidder, inviting a white knight into the bidding competition doubles the number of firms actually bidding for a target. As the number of bidders increases, the competitiveness of the market for corporate control and the likelihood that the equity holders of the target firm will appropriate all the value created by an acquisition also increase. On average, the entrance of a white knight into a competitive bidding contest for a target firm increases the wealth of target firm equity holders by 17 percent.[27]

If adding one firm to the competitive bidding process increases the wealth of target firm equity holders some, then adding more firms to the process is likely to increase this wealth even more. Target firms can accomplish this outcome by creating an **auction** among bidding firms. On average, the creation of an auction among multiple bidders increases the wealth of target firm equity holders by 20 percent.[28]

A third action that the managers of a target firm can take to increase the wealth of their equity holders from an acquisition effort is the institution of **golden parachutes**. A golden parachute is a compensation arrangement between a firm and its senior management team that promises these individuals a substantial cash payment if their firm is acquired and they lose their jobs as a result. These cash payments can appear to be very large but are actually quite small in comparison to the total value that can be created if a merger or acquisition is completed. In this sense, golden parachutes are a small price to pay to give a potential target firm's top managers incentives not to stand in the way of completing a takeover of their firm. Put differently, golden parachutes reduce agency problems for the equity holders of a potential target firm by aligning the interests of top managers with the interests of that firm's stockholders. On average, when a firm announces golden-parachute compensation packages for its top management team, the value of this potential target firm's equity increases by 7 percent.[29]

Overall, there is substantial evidence that delaying an acquisition long enough to ensure that a competitive market for corporate control emerges can significantly benefit the equity holders of target firms. One study found that when target firms did not delay the completion of an acquisition, their equity holders experienced, on average, a 36 percent increase in the value of their stock once the acquisition was complete. If, on the other hand, target firms did delay the completion of the acquisition, this average increase in value jumped to 65 percent.[30]

Of course, target firm managers can delay too long. Delaying too long can create opportunity costs for their firm's equity holders, for these individuals do not actually realize the gain from an acquisition until it is completed. Also, long delays can jeopardize the completion of an acquisition, in which case the equity holders of the target firm do not realize any gains from the acquisition.

14.3 ORGANIZING TO IMPLEMENT A MERGER OR ACQUISITION

To realize the full value of any strategic relatedness that exists between a bidding and a target firm, the merged organizations must be appropriately organized. The realization of each of the types of strategic relatedness discussed earlier in this chapter requires at least some coordination and integration between the bidding and target firms after an acquisition has occurred. For example, to realize economies of scale from an acquisition, bidding and target firms must coordinate in the combined firm the functions that are sensitive to economies of scale. To realize the value of any technology that a bidding firm acquires from a target firm, the combined firm must use this technology in developing, manufacturing, or selling its products. To exploit underutilized leverage capacity in the target firm, the balance sheets of the bidding and target firms must be merged, and the resulting firm must then seek additional debt funding. To realize the opportunity of replacing the target firm's inefficient management with more efficient management from the bidding firm, these management changes must actually take place.

Post-acquisition coordination and integration is essential if bidding and target firms are to realize the full potential of the strategic relatedness that drove the acquisition in the first place. If a bidding firm decides not to coordinate or integrate any of its business activities with the activities of a target firm, then why was this target firm acquired? Just as corporate diversification requires the active management of linkages among different parts of a firm, mergers and acquisitions (as one way in which corporate diversification strategies can be executed) require the active management of linkages between a bidding and a target firm.

Given that most merger and acquisition strategies are used to create corporate diversification strategies, the organizational approaches previously described for implementing diversification strategies are relevant for implementing merger and acquisition strategies as well. Thus mergers and acquisitions designed to create diversification strategies should be managed through the M-form structure. The management control systems and compensation policies associated with implementing diversification strategies should also be applied in organizing to implement merger and acquisition strategies.

Although, in general, organizing to implement merger and acquisition strategies can be seen as a special case of organizing to implement corporate diversification strategies, implementing merger and acquisition strategies can create special problems. Most of these problems reflect the fact that operational, functional, strategic, and cultural differences between bidding and target firms involved in a merger or acquisition are likely to be much greater than these same differences between the different parts of a diversified business that was not created through acquisition. The reason for this difference is that the firms involved in a merger or acquisition have had a separate existence, separate histories, separate management philosophies, and separate strategies.

Differences between bidding and target firms can manifest themselves in a wide variety of ways. For example, bidding and target firms may own and operate different computer systems, different telephone systems, and other conflicting technologies. These firms might have very different human resource policies and practices. One firm might have a very generous retirement and health care program; the other, a less generous program. One firm's compensation system might focus on high salaries; the other firm's compensation system might focus on large cash bonuses and stock options. Also, these firms might have very different relationships with customers. At one firm, customers might be thought of as business partners; in another, the relationship with customers might be more arm's-length in character. Integrating bidding and target firms may require the resolution of numerous such differences.

Perhaps the most significant challenge in integrating bidding and target firms involves cultural differences.[31] In Chapter 5, it was suggested that it can often be difficult to change a firm's organizational culture. Simply because a firm has been acquired does not mean that the culture in that firm will rapidly change to become more like the culture of the bidding firm. Indeed, cultural conflicts can last for very long periods of time.

Operational, functional, strategic, and cultural differences between bidding and target firms can all be compounded by the merger and acquisition process, especially if that process was unfriendly. Unfriendly takeovers can generate anger and animosity in target firm management toward the management of the bidding firm. Research has shown that top-management turnover is much higher in firms that have been taken over compared to firms not subject to takeovers, reflecting one approach to resolving these management conflicts.[32]

The difficulties often associated with organizing to implement a merger and acquisition strategy can be thought of as an additional cost of the acquisition process. Bidding firms, in addition to estimating the value of the strategic relatedness between themselves and a target firm, also need to estimate the cost of organizing to implement an acquisition. The value that a target firm brings to a bidding firm through an acquisition should be discounted by the cost of organizing to implement this strategy. In some circumstances, the cost of organizing to realize the value of strategic relatedness between a bidding firm and a target may actually be greater than the value of that strategic relatedness, in which case the acquisition should not occur.

Although organizing to implement mergers and acquisitions can be a source of significant cost, it can also be a source of value and opportunity. Some scholars have suggested that value creation can continue to occur in a merger or acquisition long after the formal acquisition is complete.[33] As bidding and target firms continue to coordinate and integrate their operations, unanticipated opportunities for value creation can be discovered. These sources of value could not have been anticipated at the time a firm was originally acquired (and thus are, at least partially, a manifestation of a bidding firm's good luck), but bidding firms can influence the probability of discovering these unanticipated sources of value by learning to cooperate effectively with target firms while organizing to implement a merger or acquisition strategy.

14.4 SUMMARY

Firms can use mergers and acquisitions to create corporate diversification strategies. Mergers or acquisitions between strategically unrelated firms cannot be expected to generate superior economic profits for both bidders and targets. Thus firms contemplating merger and acquisition strategies must search for strategically related targets.

Several sources of strategic relatedness have been discussed in literature. On average, the acquisition of strategically related targets does create economic value, but most of that value is captured by the equity holders of target firms. The equity holders of bidding firms generally do not earn superior profits even when bidding firms acquire strategically related targets. Empirical research on mergers and acquisitions is consistent with these expectations. On average, acquisitions do create value, but that value is usually captured by target firms, and acquisitions generally do not hurt bidding firms.

Given that most mergers and acquisitions do not generate superior economic profits for bidding firms, an important question becomes: Why are there so many mergers and acquisitions? Explanations of the number of firms pursuing these strategies include (1) the desire to ensure firm survival, (2) the existence of free cash flow, (3) agency problems between bidding firm managers and equity holders, (4) managerial hubris, and (5) the possibility that some bidding firms might earn economic profits from implementing merger and acquisition strategies.

To gain competitive advantages and economic profits from mergers or acquisitions, these strategies must be either (1) valuable, rare, and private, or (2) valuable, rare, and costly to imitate. In addition, a bidding firm may exploit unanticipated sources of strategic relatedness with a target. These unanticipated sources of relatedness can also be a source of economic profits for a bidding firm. These observations have several implications for the managers of bidding and target firms.

Organizing to implement a merger or acquisition strategy can be seen as a special case of organizing to implement corporate diversification strategy. However, historical differences between bidding and target firms may make the integration of different parts of a firm created through acquisitions more difficult than if a diversified firm is not created through acquisitions. Cultural differences between bidding and target firms are particularly problematic. Bidding firms need to estimate the cost of organizing to implement a merger or acquisition strategy and discount the value of a target by that cost. However, organizing to implement a merger or acquisition can also be a way in which bidding and target firms discover unanticipated economies of scope.

REVIEW QUESTIONS

1. Consider the following scenario: A firm acquires a strategically related target after successfully fending off four other bidding firms. Under what conditions, if any, can the firm that acquired this target expect to earn an economic profit from doing so?

2. Consider this scenario: A firm acquires a strategically related target; there were no other bidding firms. Is this acquisition situation necessarily different from the situation described in Question 1? Under what conditions, if any, can the firm that acquired this target expect to earn an economic profit from doing so?

3. Some researchers have argued that the existence of free cash flow can lead managers in a firm to make inappropriate acquisition decisions. To avoid these problems, these authors have argued that firms should increase their debt-to-equity ratio and "soak up" free cash flow through interest and principal payments. Is free cash flow a significant problem for many firms? What are the strengths and weaknesses of increased leverage as a response to free cash flow problems in a firm?

4. The hubris hypothesis suggests that managers continue to engage in acquisitions even though, on average, they do not generate economic profits, because of the unrealistic belief on the part of these managers that they can manage a target firm's assets more efficiently than can that firm's current management. This type of systematic non-rationality usually does not last too long in competitive market conditions: Firms led by managers with these unrealistic beliefs change, are acquired, or go bankrupt in the long run. Are there any attributes of the market for corporate control that suggest that managerial hubris could exist in this market, despite its performance-reducing implications for bidding firms? If yes, what are these attributes? If no, can the hubris hypothesis be a legitimate explanation of continuing acquisition activity?

5. It has been shown that so-called poison pills rarely prevent a takeover from occurring. In fact, sometimes when a firm announces that it is instituting a poison pill, its stock price goes up. Why could that happen?

ENDNOTES

1. See money.cnn.com/2005/01/31/news/ economy/merger_mania; latinbusiness chronicle.com/reports/0206/mergers; thehindubusinessline.com/2005/08/14/ stories; deloitte.com/dft/press_release.

2. Fama, E. F. (1970). "Efficient capital markets: A review of theory and empirical work," *Journal of Finance,* 25, pp. 383–417.

3. See Trautwein, I. (1990). "Merger motives and merger prescriptions," *Strategic Management Journal,* 11, pp. 283–295; and Walter, G., and J. B. Barney (1990).

"Management objectives in mergers and acquisition," *Strategic Management Journal,* 11, pp. 79–86. The three lists of potential links between bidding and target firms were developed by the Federal Trade Commission; Lubatkin, M. (1983). "Mergers and the performance of the acquiring firm," *Academy of Management Review,* 8, pp. 218–225; and Jensen, M. C., and R. S. Ruback (1983). "The market for corporate control: The scientific evidence," *Journal of Financial Economics,* 11, pp. 5–50.

4. See Rumelt, R. (1974). *Strategy, Structure, and Economic Performance,* Cambridge, MA: Harvard University Press.

5. The first study was by Ravenscraft, D. J., and F. M. Scherer (1987). *Mergers, Sell-offs, and Economic Efficiency,* Washington, DC: Brookings Institution. The second study was by Porter, M. E. (1987). "From competitive advantage to corporate strategy," *Harvard Business Review,* 3, pp. 43–59.

6. This is Jensen, M. C., and R. S. Ruback (1983). "The market for corporate control: The scientific evidence, *Journal of Financial Economics,* 11, pp. 5–50.

7. This work on horizontal mergers and economic value creation was done by Eckbo, B. E. (1983). "Horizontal mergers, collusion, and stockholder wealth," *Journal of Financial Economics,* 11, pp. 241–273; and Stillman, R. (1983). "Examining antitrust policy toward horizontal mergers," *Journal of Financial Economics,* 11, pp. 225–240.

8. See Lubatkin, M. (1987). "Merger strategies and stockholder value," *Strategic Management Journal,* 8, pp. 39–53; and Singh, H., and C. A. Montgomery (1987). "Corporate acquisition strategies and economic performance," *Strategic Management Journal,* 8, pp. 377–386.

9. See Grant, L. (1995). "Here comes Hugh," *Fortune,* August 21, pp. 43–52; Serwer, A. E. (1995). "Why bank mergers are good for your savings account," *Fortune,* October 2, p. 32; and Deogun, N. (2000). "Europe catches merger fever as global volume sets record," *Wall Street Journal,* January 3, p. R8.

10. The concept of free cash flow has been emphasized by Jensen, M. C. (1986). "Agency costs of free cash flow, corporate finance, and takeovers," *American Economic Review,* 76, pp. 323–329; and Jensen, M. (1988). "Takeovers: Their causes and consequences," *Journal of Economic Perspectives,* 2, pp. 21–48.

11. See Miles, R. H., and K. S. Cameron (1982). *Coffin Nails and Corporate Strategies,* Upper Saddle River, NJ: Prentice Hall.

12. Roll, R. (1986). "The hubris hypothesis of corporate takeovers," *Journal of Business,* 59, pp. 205–216.

13. See Dodd, P. (1980). "Merger proposals, managerial discretion and stockholder wealth," *Journal of Financial Economics,* 8, pp. 105–138; Eger, C. E. (1983). "An empirical test of the redistribution effect in pure exchange merger," *Journal of Financial and Quantitative Analysis,* 18, pp. 547–572; Firth, M. (1980). "Takeovers, shareholder returns, and the theory of the firm," *Quarterly Journal of Economics,* 94, pp. 235–260; Varaiya, N. (1985). "A test of Roll's hubris hypothesis of corporate takeovers," working paper, Southern Methodist University, School of Business; Ruback, R. S., and W. H. Mikkelson (1984). "Corporate investments in common stock," working paper, Massachusetts Institute of Technology, Sloan School of Business; Ruback, R. S. (1982). "The Conoco takeover and stockholder returns," *Sloan Management Review,* 14, pp. 13–33.

14. This section of the chapter draws on Barney, J. B. (1988). "Returns to bidding firms in mergers and acquisitions: Reconsidering the relatedness hypothesis," *Strategic Management Journal,* 9, pp. 71–78.

15. See Turk, T. A. (1987). "The determinants of management responses to interfirm tender offers and their effect on shareholder wealth," unpublished doctoral dissertation, Graduate School of Management, University of California at Irvine. In fact, this is an example of an antitakeover action that can increase the value of a target firm. These antitakeover actions are discussed later in this chapter.

16. See Bower, J. (1996). "WPP—integrating icons," Harvard Business School Case no. 9-396-249.

17. See Jemison, D. B., and S. B. Sitkin (1986). "Corporate acquisitions: A process perspective," *Academy of Management Review,* 11, pp. 145–163.

18. Blackwell, R. D. (1998). "Service Corporation International," presented to The Cullman Symposium, October, Columbus, OH.

19. Most of the "colorful" terms listed in Table 14.8 were developed in the 1980s. Although these terms are not used as frequently today, the firm actions they describe are.

20. See Walkling, R., and M. Long (1984). "Agency theory, managerial welfare, and

takeover bid resistance," *Rand Journal of Economics,* 15(1), pp. 54–68; Kosnik, R. D. (1987). "Greenmail: A study of board performance in corporate governance," *Administrative Science Quarterly,* 32, pp. 163–185; and Walsh, J. (1989). "Doing a deal: Merger and acquisition negotiations and their impact upon target company top management turnover," *Strategic Management Journal,* 10, pp. 307–322.

21. Dann, L. Y., and H. DeAngelo (1983). "Standstill agreements, privately negotiated stock repurchases, and the market for corporate control, "*Journal of Financial Economics,* 11, pp. 275–300.

22. See Bradley, M., and L. Wakeman (1983). "The wealth effects of targeted share repurchases," *Journal of Financial Economics,* 11, pp. 301–328; Masulis, R. (1980). "Stock repurchases by tender offer: An analysis of the causes of common stock price changes," *Journal of Finance,* 35, pp. 305–319; and Dann, L. Y. (1981). "Common stock repurchases: An analysis of returns to bondholders and stockholders," *Journal of Financial Economics,* 9, pp. 113–138.

23. Dann, L. Y., and H. DeAngelo (1983). "Standstill agreements, privately negotiated stock repurchases, and the market for corporate control," *Journal of Financial Economics,* 11, pp. 275–300.

24. See Lamphier, G. (1980). "Inco 'poison pill' plan is producing broad opposition," *Wall Street Journal,* October 20, p. A5; Metz, T. (1988). "Promoter of the poison pill prescribes stronger remedy," *Wall Street Journal,* December 1, p. C1; and Turk, T. A. (1987). "The determinants of management responses to interfirm tender offers and their effect on shareholder wealth," unpublished doctoral dissertation, Graduate School of Management, University of California at Irvine, for description of poison pills.

25. Freedman, A. M., and B. Burrough (1988). "American brands rejects 'Pac-Man' ploy," *Wall Street Journal,* September 19, p. A3.

26. See Gibson, R., J. S. Lublin, and M. Allen (1988). "Proposal to stave off bid by Grand Met criticized; defense plan is upheld," *Wall Street Journal,* November 5, p. A3; and Helyar, J., and B. Burrough (1988). "Buy-out bluff: How underdog KKR won RJR Nabisco without highest bid," *Wall Street Journal,* December 2, p. A1.

27. See Turk, T. A. (1987). "The determinants of management responses to interfirm tender offers and their effect on shareholder wealth," unpublished doctoral dissertation, Graduate School of Management, University of California at Irvine.

28. See Turk, T. A. (1987). "The determinants of management responses to interfirm tender offers and their effect on shareholder wealth," unpublished doctoral dissertation, Graduate School of Management, University of California at Irvine.

29. See Singh, H., and F. Haricento (1989). "Top management tenure, corporate ownership and the magnitude of golden parachutes, "*Strategic Management Journal,* 10, pp. 143–156; and Turk, T. A. (1987). "The determinants of management responses to interfirm tender offers and their effect on shareholder wealth, "unpublished doctoral dissertation, Graduate School of Management, University of California at Irvine.

30. Turk, T. A. (1987). "The determinants of management responses to interfirm tender offers and their effect on shareholder wealth," unpublished doctoral dissertation, Graduate School of Management, University of California at Irvine.

31. Cartwright, S., and C. Cooper (1993). "The role of culture compatibility in successful organizational marriage," *Academy of Management Executive,* 7(2), pp. 57–70; Chatterjee, S., M. Lubatkin, D. Schweiger, and Y. Weber (1992). "Cultural differences and shareholder value in related mergers: Linking equity and human capital," *Strategic Management Journal,* 13, pp. 319–334.

32. See Walsh, J., and J. Ellwood (1991). "Mergers, acquisitions, and the pruning of managerial deadwood, "*Strategic Management Journal,* 12, pp. 201–217; and Walsh, J. (1988). "Top management turnover following mergers and acquisitions, " *Strategic Management Journal,* 9, pp. 173–183.

33. See Haspeslagh, P., and Jemison, D. (1991). *Managing Acquisitions: Creating Value Through Corporate Renewal,* New York: Free Press.

CHAPTER

15

International Strategies

15.1 The Value of International Strategies
15.2 International Strategies and Sustained Competitive Advantage
15.3 The Organization of International Strategies
15.4 Summary

Strategic alliances, corporate diversification, and mergers and acquisitions are different strategies that firms can use to leverage their resource and capability advantages in one business activity to gain advantages in other strategically related business activities. Thus far, most of our discussion of these opportunities has focused on how firms can leverage their resources and capabilities across different businesses in different industries.

However, firms can also leverage their resources and capabilities by engaging in business activities in multiple geographic markets. This possibility has already been discussed at various points in this book. One of the environmental opportunities described in Chapter 4 is the ability that some firms might have to engage in business operations in multiple geographic markets. One of the motivations for engaging in strategic alliances, discussed in Chapter 13, is to facilitate a firm's entry into a new geographic market. Finally, one of the Federal Trade Commission merger and acquisition categories discussed in Chapter 14 is market extension acquisitions in which bidding firms acquire targets to gain access to new geographic markets in which they can operate.

This chapter focuses on leveraging a firm's resources and capabilities across multiple geographic markets. In particular, we examine the performance and competitive implications of these strategies when they lead a firm to operate across country borders. Firms that operate in multiple countries are implementing **international strategies.** Because international strategies are actually a special case of the diversification strategies already discussed in this part of the book, much of the discussion in Chapters 10 through 14 applies to international strategies as well. In this chapter, the unique characteristics of international strategies will be emphasized.

At some level, international strategies have existed since before the beginning of recorded time. Certainly, trade across country borders has been an important determinant of the wealth of individuals, companies, and countries throughout history. The search for trading opportunities and trade routes was a primary motivation for the exploration of the Western Hemisphere. Therefore it would be inappropriate to argue that international strategies are an invention of the late twentieth century.

In the past, however, the implementation of international strategies was limited to relatively small numbers of risk-taking individuals and firms. Today these strategies are becoming remarkably common. In 2005, large firms with substantial international operations included ExxonMobile, General Electric, Microsoft, and Citigroup (all U.S.-headquartered firms); BP, HSBC, and Vodaphone (all firms headquartered in the United Kingdom); Toyota (Japan); Novartis Group and Nestlé (Switzerland); and Samsung Electronics (South Korea).

Moreover, this international trend is not limited to huge multinational companies. Smaller international firms also exist, including Arby's and Wendy's (U.S. fast-food restaurants), Domino's Pizza, DryClean USA, Page Boy Maternity, Otis Elevators, and Briggs and Stratton. Logitech, the world's leading manufacturer of personal computer mouses, had headquarters in California and Switzerland when it was first founded in 1982, and R&D and manufacturing operations in Taiwan and Ireland just a couple of years later. In an important sense, Logitech began operations pursuing an international strategy. Momenta Corporation (a firm in the pen-based computer industry), Oxford Instruments (which supplies high-field magnets to physics laboratories), SPEA (a firm in the graphics software business), and Technomed (a medical products firm) were all very small, and very new, companies when they began pursuing business opportunities in multiple country markets.[1]

The increased use of international strategies by both large and small firms suggests that the economic opportunities associated with operating in multiple geographic markets can be substantial. However, to generate economic profits for firms, these opportunities must exploit a firm's valuable, rare, and costly-to-imitate resources and capabilities. A firm must also be appropriately organized to realize the full competitive potential of these resources and capabilities. This chapter examines the conditions under which international strategies can create economic value, as well as the conditions under which they can be sources of sustained competitive advantages.

15.1 THE VALUE OF INTERNATIONAL STRATEGIES

International strategies are diversification strategies. So, to be economically valuable, they must meet the two value criteria originally introduced in Chapter 11's discussion of corporate diversification strategies: They must exploit real economics of scope, and it must be costly for outside investors to realize these economies of scope on their own. Many of the economies of scope discussed in the context of strategic alliances, corporate diversification, and merger and acquisition strategies can be created when firms operate across multiple businesses. These same economies can also be created when firms operate across multiple geographic markets.

More generally, like all the strategies discussed in this book, to be valuable, international strategies must enable a firm to exploit environmental opportunities or neutralize environmental threats. To the extent that international strategies enable a firm to respond to its environment, they also enable a firm to reduce its costs or increase the willingness of its customers to pay compared to what would have been the case if that firm did not pursue these strategies. Several potentially valuable economies of scope that are particularly relevant for firms pursuing international strategies are summarized in Table 15.1.

Gaining Access to New Customers for Current Products or Services

The most obvious economy of scope that may motivate firms to pursue an international strategy is the potential new customers for a firm's current products or services that such a strategy might bring. To the extent that customers outside a firm's domestic market are willing and able to buy a firm's current products or services, implementing an international strategy can increase a firm's revenues directly. Gaining access to these customers can also help a firm manage changes in domestic demand as its products or services evolve through different stages of their life cycle. Finally, gaining access to these new customers can increase a firm's volume of production. If production processes are subject to economies of scale, international strategies can also have the effect of decreasing a firm's costs.

Internationalization and Firm Revenues

If customers outside a firm's domestic market are willing and able to purchase its products or services, then selling into these markets will increase the firm's revenues. However, it is not always clear that the products and services that a firm sells in its domestic market will also sell in foreign markets.

Are Non-domestic Customers Willing to Buy?   Customer preferences may vary significantly between a firm's domestic and foreign markets. These different preferences may require firms seeking to internationalize their operations to change their current products or services substantially before nondomestic customers will be willing to purchase them.

Many U.S. home appliance manufacturers faced this challenge as they looked to expand their operations into Europe and Asia. In the United States, the physical size of most home appliances (washing machines, dryers, refrigerators, dishwashers, and so forth) has become standardized, and these standard sizes are built into new homes, condominiums, and apartments. Standard sizes have also emerged in Europe and Asia. However, these non-U.S. standard sizes are much smaller than the U.S. sizes, requiring U.S. manufacturers to substantially retool their manufacturing operations in order to build products that might be attractive to Asian and European customers.[2]

Different physical standards can require a firm pursuing international opportunities to change its current products or services to sell them to a nondomestic market. Physical standards, however, can easily be measured and described. Differences in

---

TABLE 15.1   Potential Sources of Economies of Scope for Firms Pursuing International Strategies

1. Gaining access to new customers for current products or services
2. Gaining access to low-cost factors of production
3. Developing new core competencies
4. Leveraging current core competencies in new ways
5. Managing corporate risk

---

tastes can be much more challenging for firms looking to sell their products or services outside the domestic market.

Disney discovered the challenges associated with differences in tastes across non-domestic markets in two of its international strategy efforts—Disneyland Tokyo and Euro-Disney. When Disneyland Tokyo opened in April 1983, several adjustments to the theme park formula that had been so successful in California and Florida were necessary. For example, the main entranceway into the Tokyo park did not adopt a turn-of-the-century "Main Street USA" theme; instead the Tokyo park features cultural and other exhibits from around the world. Nevertheless, Disneyland Tokyo featured Disney's traditional cartoon characters (Mickey Mouse, Goofy, Donald Duck) along with its movie-based fairy-tale characters (Pinocchio, Snow White, Cinderella) and many rides and attractions originally developed for its U.S. operations. Although Disneyland Tokyo has been a financial success almost since the day it opened, the Walt Disney Company at the outset limited its financial stake in this venture. Disney licensed the use of its characters and technologies to a group of Japanese investors in return for 10 percent of the park's gate receipts and 5 percent of its other receipts. These financial arrangements have severely limited Disney's profits from Disneyland Tokyo. Some of these financial restrictions have been eased recently as Disney has decided to increase its investments in Disneyland Tokyo.[3]

The Walt Disney Company was determined not to lose these profit opportunities when it began theme park operations in Europe. Buoyed by its success with one Disney-based theme park outside the United States, Disney approached its entry into the European theme park market with confidence. Again, efforts were made to modify the traditional Disney formula to be consistent with European tastes. However, this time the Walt Disney Company took a 49 percent ownership stake in its foreign venture (as large a stake as French law would allow). In return, Disney was to receive 10 percent of Euro-Disney's admission fees, 5 percent of Euro-Disney's food and merchandise revenues, management fees, incentive fees, and 49 percent of Euro-Disney's profits. Unfortunately, the kinds of modification to the traditional Disney formula that worked so well in Japan have not generated the demand for Euro-Disney that was anticipated when the theme park opened. The largely American themes in Euro-Disney were offensive to some European visitors. Hotel rooms near Euro-Disney were different from (and more expensive than) the kinds of hotel rooms that Europeans generally prefer. As a result, Disney has had to restructure the financial operations of Euro-Disney in an attempt to enhance its profit potential.[4]

The unwillingness of customers in nondomestic markets to purchase a firm's current products or services is not limited to attempts by U.S. firms to begin operations in non-U.S. markets. Yugo had difficulty selling its automobiles in the United States. Apparently, U.S. consumers were unwilling to accept poor-performing, poor-quality automobiles, despite their low price. Sony, despite its success in Japan, was unable to carve out significant market share in the U.S. video market with its Betamax technology. Most observers blame Sony's reluctance to license this technology to other manufacturers, together with the shorter recording time available on Betamax, for this product failure. Apparently, U.S. customers wanted a broad choice of manufacturers and longer recording capabilities than Betamax could provide. Marks and Spencer's efforts to enter the Canadian retail market with its traditional mix of clothing and food stores—a mix that has been extremely successful in the United Kingdom—also met with stiff consumer resistance.[5]

What becomes clear is that in order for access to new customers for a firm's current products or services to be an economy of scope for a firm implementing an international strategy, those products or services must address the needs, wants, and preferences of customers in foreign markets at least as well as, if not better than, alternatives. Firms pursuing international opportunities may have to implement many of the cost leadership and product differentiation business strategies discussed in Chapters 6 and 7, modified to address the specific market needs of a nondomestic market. Only then will customers in nondomestic markets be willing to buy a firm's current products or services.

Are Non-domestic Customers Able to Buy? Customers in foreign markets might be willing to buy a firm's current products or services but may be unable to buy them. This may happen for at least three reasons: inadequate distribution channels, trade barriers, and insufficient wealth to make purchases.

Inadequate distribution channels may make it difficult, if not impossible, for a firm to make its products or services available to customers outside its domestic market. In some nondomestic markets, adequate distribution networks exist but are tied up by firms already operating in these markets. Many European firms face this situation as they try to enter the U.S. market. In such a situation, firms pursuing international opportunities must either build their own distribution networks from scratch (a very costly endeavor) or work with a local partner to utilize the networks that are already in place. As was suggested in Chapter 13, the marginal cost of using already-established distribution networks in a new market is almost zero. Thus cooperating, through strategic alliances, with firms that already have access to distribution networks is often preferable to building networks from scratch.

However, the problem facing some firms pursuing international opportunities is not that distribution networks are tied up by firms already operating in a market. Rather, the problem is that distribution networks either do not exist or operate in ways that are very different from the operation of the distribution networks in a firm's domestic market. This problem can be serious when firms seek to expand their operations into developing economies. Inadequate transportation, warehousing, and retail facilities can make it difficult to distribute a firm's products or services into a new geographic market. These kinds of problems have hampered investment in Russia and China. For example, when Nestlé entered the Chinese dairy market, it had to build a network of gravel roads connecting the factory collection points and villages where dairy farmers produce milk. Obtaining the right to build this network of roads took 13 years of negotiations with Chinese government officials.[6]

Such distribution problems are not limited to developing economies. For example, Japanese retail distribution has historically been much more fragmented, and much less efficient, than the system that exists in either the United States or Western Europe. Rather than being dominated by large grocery stores, discount retail operations, and retail superstores, the Japanese retail distribution network has been dominated by numerous small, "mom-and-pop" operations. Many Western firms find this distribution network difficult to use, because its operating principles are so different from what they have seen in their domestic markets. However, Procter & Gamble and a few other firms have been able to crack this Japanese distribution system and exploit significant sales opportunities in Japan.[7]

Even if distribution networks exist in nondomestic markets, and even if international firms can operate through those networks if they have access to them, entry into these markets may still be restricted by various tariff and non-tariff trade barriers. Table 15.2 lists some of these trade barriers. Trade barriers, no matter what their specific form, have the effect of increasing the cost of selling a firm's current products or services in a new geographic market and thus make it difficult for a firm to realize this economy of scope from its international strategy.

Despite a worldwide movement toward free trade and reduction in trade barriers, trade barriers are still an important economic phenomenon for many firms seeking to implement an international strategy. Japanese automobile manufacturers have faced voluntary quotas and various other trade barriers as they have sought to expand their presence in the U.S. market; U.S. automobile firms have argued that Japan has used a series of tariff and non-tariff trade barriers to restrict their entry into the Japanese market. Kodak once asked the U.S. government to begin negotiations to facilitate Kodak's entry into the Japanese photography market, a market that Kodak argued is controlled by Fuji through a government-sanctioned monopoly. Historically, beginning operations in India was hampered by a variety of tariff and non-tariff trade barriers. Tariffs in India have averaged more than 80 percent; foreign firms have been restricted to a 40 percent ownership stake in their operations in India; and foreign imports have required government approvals and licenses that could take up to 3 years to obtain. Over the last several years, many of these trade barriers in India have been reduced but not eliminated. The same is true for the United States. The tariff on imported goods and services imposed by the U.S. government reached an all-time high of 60 percent in 1932. It averaged from 12 to 15 percent after World War II and now averages about 5 percent for most imports into the United States. Thus U.S. trade barriers have been reduced but not eliminated.[8]

Governments create trade barriers for a wide variety of reasons: to raise government revenue, to protect local employment, to encourage local production to replace imports, to

TABLE 15.2	Tariffs, Quotas, and Nontariff Trade Barriers	
Tariffs: Taxes Levied on Imported Goods or Services	*Quotas: Quantity Limits on the Number of Products or Services that can be Imported*	*Nontariff Barriers: Rules, Regulations, and Policies that Increase the Cost of Importing Products or Services*
Import duties	Voluntary quotas	Government policies
Supplemental duties	Involuntary quotas	Government procurement policies
Variable levies	Restricted import licenses	Government-sponsored export subsidies
Border levies	Minimum import limits	Domestic assistance programs
Countervailing duties	Embargoes	Customs policies
		Valuation systems
		Tariff classifications
		Documentation requirements
		Fees
		Quality standards
		Packaging standards
		Labeling standards

protect new industries from competition, to encourage foreign direct investment, and to promote export activity. However, for firms seeking to implement international strategies, trade barriers, no matter why they are erected, have the effect of increasing the cost of implementing these strategies. Indeed, trade barriers can be thought of as a special case of artificial barriers to entry, as discussed in Chapter 3. Such barriers to entry can turn what could have been economically viable strategies into unviable strategies.

Finally, customers may be willing but unable to purchase a firm's current products or services even if distribution networks are in place and trade barriers are not making internationalization efforts too costly. If these customers lack the wealth, or sufficient hard currency, to make these purchases, then the potential value of this economy of scope can go unrealized.

Insufficient consumer wealth limits the ability of firms to sell products into a variety of markets. For example, per capita gross national product in Bangladesh is $270, $240 in Chad, and $110 in the Congo. In these countries, it is unlikely that there will be significant demand for many products or services originally designed for affluent Western economies. This situation also exists in India. The middle class in India is large and growing (164 million people with the highest 20 percent of income in 1998), but the income of this middle class is considerably lower than the income of the middle class in other economies. These income levels are sufficient to create demand for some consumer products. For example, Gillette estimates that the market in India for its shaving products could include 240 million consumers, and Nestlé believes that the market in India for its noodles, ketchup, and instant coffee products could include over 100 million people. However, the potential market for higher-end products in India is somewhat smaller. For example, Bausch & Lomb believes that only about 30 million consumers in India can afford to purchase its high-end sunglasses and soft contact lenses. The level of consumer wealth is such an important determinant of the economic potential of beginning operations in a new country that McDonald's adjusts the number of restaurants it expects to build in a new market according to the per-capita income of people in that market.[9]

Even if there is sufficient wealth in a country to create market demand, lack of hard currency can hamper internationalization efforts. **Hard currencies** are currencies that are traded, and thus have value, on international money markets. When an international firm does business in a country with hard currency, the firm can take whatever after-tax profits it earns in that country and translate those profits into other hard currencies—including the currency of the country in which the firm has headquarters. Moreover, because the value of hard currencies can fluctuate in the world economy, firms can also manage their currency risk by engaging in various hedging strategies in world money markets. Some firms move beyond simply hedging their currency risk and attempt to generate profits from their currency-trading activities. For example, Nestlé's currency-trading operations often generate more than 5 percent of this company's worldwide profits.[10]

When firms begin operations in countries without hard currency, they are able to obtain few of these advantages. Indeed, without hard currency, cash payments to these firms are made with a currency that has essentially no value outside the country where the payments are made. Although these payments can be used for additional investments inside that country, an international firm has limited ability to extract profits from countries without hard currencies and even less ability to hedge currency fluctuation risks in this context. The lack of hard currency has discouraged firms from entering a wide variety of countries—India, Russia, China at various points in time despite the substantial demand for products and services in those countries.[11]

One solution to the lack of hard currency in a nondomestic market is called **countertrade.** When international firms engage in countertrade, they receive payment for the products or services they sell into a country, but not in the form of currency. They receive payment in the form of other products or services that they can sell on the world market. Countertrade has been a particularly important way by which firms have tried to gain access to the markets in the former Soviet Union. For example, Marc Rich and Company (a Swiss commodity-trading firm) once put together the following deal: Marc Rich purchased 70,000 tons of raw sugar from Brazil on the open market; shipped this sugar to Ukraine, where it was refined; then transported 30,000 tons of refined sugar (after using some to pay the refineries) to Siberia, where it was sold for 130,000 tons of oil products that, in turn, were shipped to Mongolia in exchange for 35,000 tons of copper concentrate, which was moved to Kazakhstan, where it was refined into copper and, finally, sold on the world market to obtain hard currency. This complicated countertrade deal is typical of the kinds of actions that international firms must take if they are to engage in business in countries without hard currency and if they desire to extract their profits from those countries. Indeed, countertrade in various forms is actually quite common. One estimate suggests that countertrade accounts for between 10 and 20 percent of world trade.[12]

Although countertrade can enable a firm to begin operations in countries without hard currency, it can create difficulties as well. In particular, in order to do business, a firm must be willing to accept payment in the form of some good or commodity that it can sell in order to obtain hard currency. This is not likely to be a problem for a firm that specializes in buying and selling commodities. However, a firm that does not have this expertise may find itself taking possession of natural gas, sesame seeds, or rattan in order to sell its products or services in a country. If this firm has limited expertise in these kinds of commodities, it may have to use brokers and other advisers to complete these transactions. This, of course, increases the cost of using countertrade as a way to facilitate international operations.

Internationalization and Product Life Cycles

Gaining access to new customers can not only increase a firm's revenues directly, it can also enable a firm to manage its products or services through their life cycle. A typical **product life cycle** is depicted in Figure 15.1. Different stages in this life cycle are defined by different growth rates in demand for a product. Thus, in the first emerging

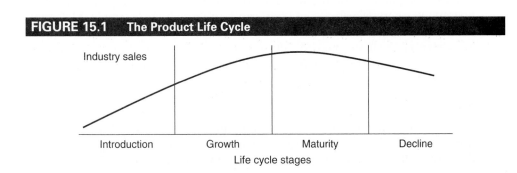

FIGURE 15.1   The Product Life Cycle

Industry sales

Introduction   Growth   Maturity   Decline

Life cycle stages

stage (called **introduction** in the figure), relatively few firms are producing a product, there are relatively few customers, and the rate of growth in demand for the product is relatively low. In the second stage (**growth**) of the product life cycle, demand increases rapidly, and many new firms enter to begin producing the product or service. In the third phase of the product life cycle (**maturity**), the number of firms producing a product or service remains stable, demand growth levels off, and firms direct their investment efforts toward refining the process by which a product or service is created and away from developing entirely new products. In the final phase of the product life cycle (**decline**), demand drops off when a technologically superior product or service is introduced. As described in Chapter 4, the product life cycle has a direct effect on the structure of opportunities in an industry.[13]

From an international strategy perspective, the critical observation about product life cycles is that a product or service can be at different stages of its life cycle in different countries. Thus a firm can use the resources and capabilities it developed during a particular product life cycle stage in its domestic market for that same stage of the life cycle in a nondomestic market. This can substantially enhance a firm's economic performance.

One firm that has been very successful in managing its product life cycles through its international efforts is Crown Cork & Seal. This firm had a traditional strength in the manufacturing of three-piece metal containers, when the introduction of two-piece metal cans into the U.S. market rapidly made three-piece cans obsolete. However, rather than abandoning its three-piece manufacturing technology, Crown Cork & Seal moved many of its three-piece manufacturing operations overseas, into developing countries where demand for three-piece cans was just emerging. In this way, Crown Cork & Seal was able to extend the effective life of its three-piece manufacturing operations and substantially enhance its economic performance.[14]

Internationalization and Cost Reduction

Gaining access to new customers for a firm's current products or services can increase a firm's volume of sales. If aspects of a firm's production process are sensitive to economies of scale, this increased volume of sales can reduce the firm's costs and enable the firm to gain cost advantages in both its nondomestic and its domestic markets (see Chapter 6).

Many scholars, over many years, have pointed out the potential of international operations to generate economies of scale.[15] Most of these authors recognize that the realization of economies of scale from international operations requires a high degree of integration across firm borders. Integration must focus on those aspects of a firm's operations where economies of scale can be realized. For example, McDonald's attempts to generate training-based economies of scale through the operation of a single management training center for all of its international operations. Firms in the float glass, color television, and chemical industries have all attempted to exploit manufacturing economies of scope through their international operations.[16]

Many firms in the worldwide automobile industry have attempted to realize manufacturing economies of scale through their international operations. According to one estimate, the minimum efficient scale of a single compact-car manufacturing plant is 400,000 units per year.[17] Such a plant would produce approximately 20 percent of all the automobiles sold in Britain, Italy, or France. Obviously, to exploit this 400,000-cars-per-year manufacturing efficiency, European automobile firms have had to sell cars in more than just a single country market. Thus the implementation of an international strategy has enabled these firms to realize an important manufacturing economy of scale.[18]

Although there are numerous potential sources of economies of scale from international operations, some recent empirical research suggests the most likely sources of these economies include exploiting international economies of scale in research and development and in marketing. This same research found that, as technological change has made it possible to operate smaller plants efficiently, manufacturing economies of scale have become less important sources of economic value in these same industries. Overall, this research suggested that exploiting economies of scale, no matter what their source, is becoming a more important source of economic value in most international industries.[19]

Gaining Access to Low-Cost Factors of Production

Just as gaining access to new customers can be an important economy of scope for firms pursuing international opportunities, so is gaining access to low-cost factors of production such as raw materials, labor, and technology.

Raw Materials

Gaining access to low-cost raw materials is, perhaps, the most traditional reason why firms began international operations. For example, in 1600, the British East India Company was formed with an initial investment of $70,000 to manage trade between England and the Far East, including India. In 1601, the third British East India Company fleet sailed for the Indies to buy cloves, pepper, silk, coffee, saltpeter, and other products. This fleet generated a return on investment of 234 percent. These profits led to the formation of the Dutch East India Company in 1602 and the French East India Company in 1664. Similar firms were organized to manage trade in the New World. The Hudson Bay Company was chartered in 1670 to manage the fur trade, and the rival North West Company was organized in 1784 for the same purpose. All these organizations were created to gain access to low-cost raw materials that were available only in nondomestic markets.[20]

Gaining access to low-cost raw materials is still an important reason why some firms engage in international enterprise. In some industries, including the oil and gas industries, virtually the only reason why firms have begun international operations is to gain access to low-cost raw materials.

Labor

In addition to gaining access to low-cost raw materials, firms also begin international operations in order to gain access to low-cost labor. After World War II, Japan had some of the lowest labor costs, and highest labor productivity, in the world. Over time, however, the improving Japanese economy and the increased value of the yen have had the effect of increasing labor costs in Japan, and South Korea, Taiwan, Singapore, and Malaysia all emerged as geographic areas with inexpensive and highly productive labor. In the last few years, China, Mexico, and Vietnam have taken this role in the world economy.[21]

Numerous firms have attempted to gain the advantages of low labor costs by moving their manufacturing operations. For example, Mineba, a Japanese ball-bearing and semiconductor manufacturer, has attempted to exploit low labor costs by manufacturing ball bearings in Japan in the 1950s and early 1960s, in Singapore in the 1970s, and since 1980 in Thailand. Hewlett-Packard operates manufacturing and assembly operations in Malaysia and Mexico; Japan's Mitsubishi Motors recently opened an automobile assembly plant in Vietnam; General Motors operates assembly plants in Mexico; and Motorola has begun operations in China. All these investments were motivated, at least partly, by the availability of low-cost labor in these countries.[22]

Although gaining access to low-cost labor can be an important determinant of a firm's international efforts, this access by itself is usually not sufficient to motivate entry into particular countries. After all, relative labor costs can change over time. For example, South Korea used to be the country in which most sports shoes were manufactured. In 1990, Korean shoe manufacturers employed 130,000 workers in 302 factories. By 1993, however, only 80,000 Koreans were employed in the shoe industry, and only 244 factories (most employing fewer than 100 people) remained. A significant portion of the shoe manufacturing industry had moved from Korea to China because of the labor cost advantages of China (approximately $40 per employee per month) compared to Korea (approximately $800 per employee per month).[23]

Moreover, low labor costs are not beneficial if a country's workforce is not able to produce high-quality products efficiently. In the sport shoe industry, until recently, China did not have access to some of the manufacturing technology and supporting industries available in Korea (for example, synthetic fabrics) to produce high-end sports shoes and high-technology hiking boots efficiently. As a result, Korea had been able to maintain a presence in the shoe manufacturing industry. However, when a country's labor force is highly educated and highly motivated, and when supporting technology and industries are in place, relatively low-cost labor can lead firms to begin operations in that country.

One interesting example of firms gaining access to low-cost labor through their international strategies is *maquiladoras*—manufacturing plants that are owned by non-Mexican companies and operated in Mexico near the U.S. border. The primary driver behind *maquiladora* investments is lower labor costs than for similar plants located in the United States. In addition, firms exporting from *maquiladoras* to the United States have to pay duties only on the value added that was created in Mexico; *maquiladoras* do not have to pay Mexican taxes on the goods processed in Mexico; and the cost of land on which plants are built in Mexico is substantially lower than what would be the case in the United States. However, a study by the Banco de Mexico suggests that without the 20 percent cost-of-labor advantage, most *maquildoras* would not be profitable operations.[24]

Given the cost advantages of operating *maquildoras*, it is not surprising that investment in this particular international strategy has increased substantially over time. In 1965 there were only 12 *maquildora* plants. By 1990, approximately 1,700 of them were in operation. By the turn of the twenty-first century, over 3,100 maquildoras employing over 1 million people were in operation, most resulting from investments made by U.S. firms. For example, TRW has a *maquildora* plant that assembles seat belts, and Mattel has a *maquildora* plant that assembles toys. Only oil generates more foreign currency for Mexico than *maquildoras*.[25]

Technology

Another factor of production to which firms can gain low-cost access through international operations is technology. Historically, Japanese firms have tried to gain access to technology by partnering with non-Japanese firms. Although the non-Japanese firms have often been looking to gain access to new customers for their current products or services by operating in Japan, the Japanese firms have used this entry into the Japanese market to gain access to foreign technology.[26]

Recently, however, some Japanese firms have begun to use entry into various U.S. markets as a way to gain access to additional technology. For example, in 1986, the Sumitomo Corporation announced investments in two venture capital firms operating in the United States (Grace Venture Partnership and Hambro Venture Fund) in order "to obtain new technologies and new business opportunities." By 1992, approximately 50 Japanese firms were engaged in venture capital investments in new technology in the United States. One study has shown that the primary goal of these investments in the United States has been to gain access to new technologies that Japanese firms could use in other products or services. This objective stands in marked contrast to U.S. venture capital firms, whose primary goal in making new venture investments is to maximize their current performance.[27]

Of course, the use of international strategies to gain low-cost access to technology is not limited to Japanese firms. Another study cites one Japanese manager's comments about his European strategic alliance partner: "The only motivation for [our European partner] is to get mass manufacturing technology. They see [the alliance] as a short circuit. As soon as they have this they'll lose interest in [in the alliance]."[28]

Developing New Core Competencies

One of the most compelling reasons for firms to begin operations outside their domestic markets is to refine their current core competencies and to develop new core competencies. By beginning operations outside their domestic markets, firms can gain a greater understanding of the strengths and weaknesses of their core competencies. By exposing these competencies to new competitive contexts, traditional competencies can be modified, and new competencies can be developed.

Of course, for international operations to affect a firm's core competencies, the firm must learn from their experiences in nondomestic markets. Moreover, once these new core competencies are developed, they must be exploited in a firm's other operations in order to realize their full economic potential.

Learning from International Operations

Learning from international operations is anything but automatic. Many firms that begin operations in a nondomestic market encounter challenges and difficulties and then immediately withdraw from their international efforts. Other firms continue to try to operate internationally but are unable to learn how to modify and change their core competencies.

One study examined several strategic alliances in an effort to understand why some firms in these alliances were able to learn from their international operations, modify their core competencies, and develop new core competencies, while others were not. This study identified the intent to learn, the transparency of business partners, and receptivity to learning as determinants of a firm's ability to learn from its international operations (see Table 15.3).

The Intent to Learn. A firm that has a strong intent to learn from its international operations is more likely to learn than a firm without this intent. Moreover, this intent must be communicated to all those who work in a firm's international activities. Compare, for example, a quote from a manager whose firm failed to learn from its international operations with a quote from a manager whose firm was able to learn from these operations.[29]

> Our engineers were just as good as [our partner's]. In fact, theirs were narrower technically, but they had a much better understanding of what the company was trying to accomplish. They knew they were there to learn; our people didn't.

> We wanted to make learning an automatic discipline. We asked the staff every day, "What did you learn from [our partner] today?" Learning was carefully monitored and recorded.

Obviously, the second firm was in a much better position than the first to learn from its international operations and to modify its current core competencies and develop new core competencies. Learning from international operations takes place by design, not by default.

Transparency and Learning. It has also been shown that firms are more likely to learn from their international operations when they interact with what have been called **transparent business partners.** Some international business partners are more open and accessible than others. This variance in accessibility can reflect different organizational philosophies, practices, and procedures, as well as differences in the culture of a firm's home country. For example, knowledge in Japanese and most other Asian cultures tends to be context-specific and deeply embedded in the broader social system. This makes it difficult for many Western managers to understand and appreciate the subtlety of Japanese business practices and Japanese culture. This, in turn, limits the ability of Western managers to learn from their operations in the Japanese market or from their Japanese partners.[30]

In contrast, knowledge in most Western cultures tends to be less context-specific, less deeply embedded in the broader social system. Such knowledge can be written down, can be taught in classes, and can be transmitted, all at a relatively low cost. Japanese managers working in Western economies are more likely to be able to appreciate and understand Western business practices and thus more able to learn from their operations in the West and from their Western partners.

TABLE 15.3 Determinants of the Ability of a Firm to Learn from Its International Operations

1. The intent to learn
2. The transparency of business partners
3. Receptivity to learning

Source: Adapted from Hamel, G. (1991). "Competition for competence and inter-partner learning within international strategic alliances," *Strategic Management Journal*, 12, pp. 83–103.

Receptivity to Learning.   Firms also vary in their receptiveness to learning. A firm's receptiveness to learning is affected by its culture, its operating procedures, and its history. Research on organizational learning suggests that, before firms can learn from their international operations, they must be prepared to unlearn. **Unlearning** requires a firm to modify or abandon traditional ways of engaging in business. Unlearning can be difficult, especially if a firm has a long history of success using old patterns of behavior and if those old patterns of behavior are reflected in a firm's organizational structure, its management control systems, and its compensation policies.[31]

Even if unlearning is possible, a firm may not have the resources it needs to learn. If a firm is using all of its available managerial time and talent, capital, and technology just to compete on a day-to-day basis, the additional task of learning from international operations can get neglected. Although managers in this situation often acknowledge the importance of learning from their international operations in order to modify their current core competencies or build new ones, they simply may not have the time or energy to do so.[32]

The ability to learn from operations can also be hampered if managers perceive that there is too much to be learned. It is often difficult for a firm to understand how it can evolve from its current state to a position where it operates with new and more valuable core competencies. This difficulty is exacerbated when the distance between where a firm is and where it needs to be is large. One Western manager who perceived this large learning gap after visiting a state-of-the-art manufacturing facility operated by a Japanese partner was quoted as saying:[33]

> It's no good for us to simply observe where they are today. What we have to find out is how they got from where we are to where they are. We need to experiment and learn with intermediate technologies before duplicating what they've done.

Leveraging New Core Competencies in Additional Markets

Once a firm has been able to learn from its international operations and modify its traditional core competencies or develop new core competencies, it must then leverage those competencies across its operations, both domestic and international, in order to realize their full value. Firms that have a history of leveraging their core competencies across multiple businesses, by implementing the organizational structures, control systems, and compensation policies discussed in Chapter 13, will often be able to exploit the opportunities associated with international operations.

Leveraging Current Core Competencies in New Ways

International operations can also create opportunities for firms to leverage their traditional core competencies in new ways. This capability is related to, though different from, using international operations to gain access to new customers for a firm's current products or services. When firms gain access to new customers for their current products, they often leverage their domestic core competencies across country boundaries. When they leverage core competencies in *new* ways, they not only extend operations across country boundaries, they also leverage their competencies across products and services in ways that might not be economically viable in their domestic market.

Consider, for example, Honda. As suggested in Chapter 11, there is widespread agreement that Honda has developed core competencies in the design and manufacture of power trains. Honda has used this core competence to facilitate entry into a variety of product markets—including motorcycles, automobiles, and snow blowers—both in its domestic Japanese market and in nondomestic markets such as the United States. However, Honda has begun to explore some competence-leverage opportunities in the United States that are not available in the Japanese market. For example, Honda has begun to design and manufacture lawn mowers of various sizes for the home in the U.S. market—lawn mowers clearly build on Honda's traditional power train competence. However, given the crowded living conditions in Japan, consumer demand for lawn mowers in that country has never been very great. Lawns in the United States, however, can be very large, and consumer demand for high-quality lawn mowers in that market is substantial. The opportunity for Honda to begin to leverage its power train competencies in the sale of lawn mowers to U.S. homeowners exits only because Honda operates outside its Japanese home market.

Managing Corporate Risk

The value of risk reduction for firms pursuing a corporate diversification strategy was evaluated in Chapter 11. There it was suggested that although diversified operations across businesses with imperfectly correlated cash flows can reduce a firm's risk, outside equity holders can manage this risk more efficiently on their own by investing in a diversified portfolio of stocks. Consequently, equity holders have little direct interest in hiring managers to operate a diversified portfolio of businesses, the sole purpose of which is risk diversification. This kind of diversification can benefit equity holders indirectly to the extent that it facilitates employees and other firm stake holders in making specific investments in a firm and to the extent that these specific investments generate economic profits for a firm.

Similar conclusions apply to firms pursuing international strategies but with one qualification. Certainly, firms that pursue business opportunities with imperfectly correlated cash flows across multiple markets in order to reduce their risk, when equity holders could reduce that risk more efficiently on their own, are not pursuing a strategy that equity holders will find directly valuable. In some circumstances, however, it may be difficult for equity holders in one market to diversify their portfolio of investments across multiple markets. To the extent that such barriers to diversification exist for individual equity holders but not for firms pursuing international strategies, risk reduction can benefit equity holders directly. In general, whenever barriers to international capital flows exist, individual investors may not be able to diversify their portfolios across country boundaries optimally. In this context, individual investors can indirectly diversify their portfolio of investments by purchasing shares in diversified multinationals.[34]

There is empirical evidence that suggests that barriers to international capital flows, in fact, exist for at least some countries. These barriers have the effect of increasing the cost to individual investors of investing in a nondomestic capital market. Such barriers include different tax structures across countries, different accounting standards, different securities regulations, and different political and economic systems. These barriers to capital flow lead investors to hold more domestic stocks in their portfolio than they would hold if they were able, at low cost, to hold a worldwide market portfolio of stocks.[35]

There is also empirical evidence suggesting that pursuing an international corporate diversification strategy when barriers to capital flows exist, can benefit equity holders directly. The stock prices of firms that pursue these strategies in this situation are higher, controlling for other factors, than the stock prices of firms that do not provide this service to their investors.[36]

However, firms pursuing international strategies should approach this risk reduction motivation with caution. Barriers to capital flows across countries are not stable. Over time, it seems reasonable to expect that these barriers will be reduced as the level of economic integration in the world economy increases. Various monetary markets already exist, and individual investors can gain access to these markets at low cost (either directly or indirectly through mutual funds). When barriers to capital flow disappear, risk reduction per se will no longer be a direct benefit to equity holders. This suggests that international strategies designed primarily to reduce the level of a firm's risk are not likely, in the long run, to add significant economic value to a firm directly. However, as was the case with risk-reducing corporate diversification motives described in Chapter 11, if a firm is pursuing an international strategy in order to exploit another valuable economy of scope, the pursuit of that strategy will also have the effect of reducing the firm's level of risk.

The Local Responsiveness/International Integration Trade-off

As firms pursue the economies of scope listed in Table 15.1, they constantly face a trade-off between the advantages of being responsive to market conditions in their nondomestic markets and the advantages of integrating their operations across the multiple markets in which they operate. This trade-off was originally discussed in Chapter 4.

On the one hand, **local responsiveness** can help firms be successful in addressing the local needs of nondomestic customers, thereby increasing demand for a firm's current products or services. Moreover, local responsiveness enables a firm to expose its traditional core competencies to new competitive situations, thereby increasing the chances that those core competencies will be improved or will be augmented by new core competencies. Finally, detailed local knowledge is essential if firms are going to leverage their traditional competencies in new ways in their nondomestic markets. Honda was able to begin exploiting its power train competencies in the U.S. lawn mower market only because of its detailed knowledge of, and responsiveness to, that market.

On the other hand, the full exploitation of the economies of scale that can be created by selling a firm's current products or services in a nondomestic market often can occur only if there is tight integration across all the markets in which a firm operates. Gaining access to low-cost factors of production may not only help a firm succeed in a particular nondomestic market, it may also help it succeed in all its markets, as long as those factors of production are used by many parts of the international firm. Developing new core competencies and using traditional core competencies in new ways can certainly be beneficial in a particular domestic market. However, the full value of these economies of scope is realized only when they are transferred from a particular domestic market into the operations of a firm in all its other markets.

Traditionally, it has been thought that firms have to choose between local responsiveness and international integration. For example, firms such as CIBA-Geigy (a Swiss chemical company), Nestlé (a Swiss food company), and Phillips (a Dutch consumer electronics firm) have chosen to emphasize local responsiveness. Nestlé, for example, owns nearly 8,000 brand names worldwide. However, of those 8,000 brands, only 750 are registered in more than one country, and only 80 are registered in more than 10 countries. Nestlé adjusts its product attributes to the needs of local consumers, adopts brand names that resonate with those consumers, and builds its brands for long-run profitability by country. In the United States, for example, Nestlé's condensed milk carries the brand name Carnation (obtained through the acquisition of the Carnation Company); in Asia, this same product carries the brand name Bear Brand. Nestlé delegates brand management authority to country managers, who can (and do) adjust traditional marketing and manufacturing strategies in accordance with local tastes and preferences. For example, Nestlé's Thailand management group dropped traditional coffee marketing efforts that focused on taste, aroma, and stimulation and instead began selling coffee as a drink that promotes relaxation and romance. This marketing strategy resonated with Thais experiencing urban stress, and it prompted Nestlé coffee sales in Thailand to increase dramatically.[37]

Of course, all this local responsiveness comes at a cost. Firms that emphasize local responsiveness are often unable to realize the full value of the economies of scope and scale that they could realize if their operations across country borders were more integrated. Numerous firms have focused on appropriating this economic value and have pursued a more integrated international strategy. Examples of such firms include IBM, General Electric, Toyota Motor Corporation, and most major pharmaceutical firms, to name just a few.

Internationally integrated firms locate business functions and activities in countries that have a comparative advantage in these functions or activities. For example, the production of components for most consumer electronics is research-intensive, capital-intensive, and subject to significant economies of scale. To manage component manufacturing successfully, most internationally integrated consumer electronics firms have located their component operations in technologically advanced countries such as the United States and Japan. Because the assembly of these components into consumer products is labor-intensive, most internationally integrated consumer electronics firms have located their assembly operations in countries with relatively low labor costs, such as Mexico and China.

Of course, one of the costs of locating different business functions and activities in different geographic locations is that these different functions and activities must be coordinated and integrated. Operations in one country might manufacture certain components very efficiently. However, if the wrong components are shipped to the assembly location, or if the right components are shipped at the wrong time, any advantages that could have been obtained from exploiting the comparative advantages of different countries can be lost. Shipping costs can also reduce the return to international integration.

To ensure that the different operations in an internationally integrated firm are appropriately coordinated, these firms typically manufacture more standardized products, using more standardized components, than do locally responsive firms. Standardization enables these firms to realize substantial economies of scale and scope, but it can limit their ability to respond to the specific needs of individual markets. When international product standards exist, as in the personal computer industry and the semiconductor chip industry, such standardization is not problematic. Also, when local responsiveness requires only a few modifications of a standardized product (for example, changing the shape of the electric plug or changing the color of a product), international integration can be very effective. However, when local responsiveness requires a great deal of local knowledge and product modifications, international integration can create problems for a firm pursuing an international strategy.

The Transnational Strategy

Recently, it has been suggested that the traditional trade-off between international integration and local responsiveness can be resolved by a **transnational strategy** that exploits all the advantages of both strategies.[38] Firms implementing a transnational strategy treat their international operations as an integrated network of distributed and interdependent resources and capabilities. In this context, a firm's operations in each country are not simply independent activities attempting to respond to local market needs; they are also repositories of ideas, technologies, and management approaches that the firm might be able to use and apply in its other international operations. Put differently, operations in different countries can be thought of as "experiments" in the creation of new core competencies. Some of these experiments will work and generate important new core competencies; others will fail to have such benefits for a firm.

When a particular country operation develops a competence in manufacturing a particular product, providing a particular service, or engaging in a particular activity that can be used by other country operations, the country operation with this competence can achieve international economies of scale by becoming the firm's primary supplier of this product, service, or activity. In this way, local responsiveness is retained as country managers constantly search for new competencies that will enable them to maximize profits in their particular markets, and international integration and economies are realized as country operations that have developed unique competencies become suppliers for all other country operations.

Managing a firm that is attempting to be both locally responsive and internationally integrated is not an easy task. Some of these organizational challenges are discussed later in this chapter.

Financial and Political Risks in Pursuing International Strategies

There is little doubt that the realization of the economies of scope listed in Table 15.1 can be a source of economic value for firms pursuing international strategies. However, the nature of international strategies can create significant risks that these economies of scope will never be realized. Beyond the implementation problems (to be discussed later in this chapter), both financial circumstances and political events can significantly reduce the value of international strategies.

Financial Risks: Currency Fluctuation and Inflation

As firms begin to pursue international strategies, they may begin to expose themselves to financial risks that are less obvious within a single domestic market. In particular, currency fluctuations can significantly affect the value of a firm's international investments. Such fluctuations can turn what had been a losing investment into a profitable investment (the good news). They can also turn what had been a profitable investment into a losing investment (the bad news). In addition to currency fluctuations, different rates of inflation across countries can require very different managerial approaches, business strategies, and accounting practices. Certainly, when a firm first begins international operations, these financial risks can seem daunting.

Fortunately, it is now possible for firms to hedge most of these risks, through the use of a variety of financial instruments and strategies. The development of money markets, together with growing experience in operating in high-inflation economies, has substantially reduced the threat of these financial risks for firms pursuing international strategies. Of course, the benefits of these financial tools and experience in high-inflation environments do not accrue to firms automatically. Firms seeking to implement international strategies must develop the resources and capabilities they will need to manage these financial risks. Moreover, these hedging strategies can do nothing to reduce the business risks that firms assume when they enter into nondomestic markets. For example, consumers in a nondomestic market may simply not want to purchase a firm's products or services, in which case this economy of scope cannot be realized. Also, these financial strategies cannot manage political risks that can exist for firms pursuing an international strategy.

Political Risks

The political environment is an important consideration in all strategic decisions. Changes in the political rules of the game can have the effect of increasing some environmental threats, reducing others, and thereby changing the value of a firm's resources and capabilities. However, the political environment can be even more problematic as firms pursue international strategies.

Types of Political Risks. Politics can affect the value of a firm's international strategies at the macro and micro levels. At the macro level, broad changes in the political situation in a country can change the value of an investment. For example, after World War II, nationalist governments came to power in many countries in the Middle East. These governments expropriated, for little or no compensation many of the assets of oil and gas companies located in their countries. Expropriation of foreign company assets also occurred when the Shah of Iran was overthrown, when a communist government was elected in Chile, and when new governments came to power in Angola, Ethiopia, Peru, and Zambia.[39]

Government upheaval and the attendant risks to international firms are facts of life in some countries. Consider, for example, oil-rich Nigeria. Since its independence in 1960, Nigeria has experienced several successful *coups d'états,* one civil war, two civil governments, and six military regimes.[40] The prudent course of action for firms engaging in business activities in Nigeria is to expect the current government to change and to plan accordingly.

Of course, government changes are not always bad for international firms. The fall of the Soviet Union and the emergence of capitalism into Eastern Europe have created enormous opportunities for firms pursuing international strategies. For example, Volkswagen has invested $6 billion in a Czech automobile firm; Opel (General Motors' European division) has invested $680 million in a car manufacturing facility in the former East Germany; and General Electric has invested $150 million in a light bulb manufacturing operation in Hungary—each one an investment that has taken place since the fall of the Soviet Union.[41]

At the micro level, politics in a country can affect the fortunes of particular firms in particular industries. For example, the success of Japanese automobile companies in the U.S. market has subjected these firms to a variety of political challenges, including local-content legislation and voluntary import quotas. These political risks exist even though there have been no major macro changes in the political system in the United States.[42]

Quantifying Political Risks. Political scientists have attempted to quantify the political risk that firms seeking to implement international strategies are likely to face in different countries. Although different studies vary in the level of detail, the country attributes listed in Table 15.4 summarize most of the important determinants of political risk for firms pursuing international strategies.[43] Firms can apply the criteria listed in the table for evaluating the political and economic conditions in a country and by adding up the scores associated with these conditions. For example, a country that has a very unstable political system (14 points), a great deal of control of the economic system

TABLE 15.4 Quantifying Political Risks from International Operations		
Increments to Country Risk if Risk Factor Is:	*Low*	*High*
The political environment		
1. Stability of the political system	3	14
2. Imminent internal conflicts	0	14
3. External threats to stability	0	12
4. Degree of control of the economic system	5	9
5. Reliability of country as a trade partner	4	12
6. Constitutional guarantees	2	12
7. Effectiveness of public administration	3	12
8. Labor relations and social peace	3	15
Domestic economic conditions		
1. Size of the population	4	8
2. Per-capita income	2	10
3. Economic growth over the last 5 years	2	7
4. Potential growth over the next 3 years	3	10
5. Inflation over the last 2 years	2	10
6. Availability of domestic capital markets to outsiders	3	7
7. Availability of high-quality local labor force	2	8
8. Possibility of employing foreign nationals	2	8
9. Availability of energy resources	2	14
10. Environmental pollution legal requirements	4	8
11. Transportation and communication infrastructure	2	14
External economic relations		
1. Import restrictions	2	10
2. Export restrictions	2	10
3. Restrictions on foreign investments	3	9
4. Freedom to set up or engage in partnerships	3	9
5. Legal protection for brands and products	3	9
6. Restrictions on monetary transfers	2	8
7. Revaluation of currency in the last 5 years	2	7
8. Balance-of-payments situation	2	9
9. Drain on hard currency through energy imports	3	14
10. Financial standing	3	8
11. Restrictions of the exchange of local and foreign currencies	2	8

Source: Adapted from Dichtl, E., and H. G. Koeglmayr (1986). "Country risk ratings," *Management Review*, 26(4), pp. 2–10. Reprinted with permission.

(9 points), and significant import restrictions (10 points) represents more political risk than a country that does not have these attributes, holding all other attributes constant.

Managing Political Risk. Unlike financial risks, there are relatively few tools for managing the political risks associated with pursuing an international strategy. Obviously, one option is to pursue international opportunities only in countries where political risk is very small. However, significant business opportunities often exist in politically risky countries precisely because they are politically risky. Alternatively, firms can limit their investment in politically risky environments. However, these limited investments may not enable a firm to take full advantage of whatever economies of scope might exist by engaging in business in that country.

One approach to managing political risk is to see each of the determinants of political risk, listed in Table 15.4, as a negotiation point as a firm enters into a new country market. In many circumstances, those in a non-domestic market have just as much an interest in seeing a firm begin doing business in their market as does the firm contemplating entry. International firms can sometimes use this bargaining power to negotiate entry conditions that reduce, or even neutralize, some of the sources of political risk in a country. Of course, no matter how skilled a firm is in negotiating these entry conditions, a change of government or changes in laws can quickly nullify any agreements.

A final approach to managing political risk is to turn this risk from a threat into an opportunity. One firm that has been successful in this way is Schlumberger, an international oil services company. Schlumberger has headquarters in New York, Paris, and the Caribbean and it is a truly international company. Schlumberger management has adopted a policy of strict neutrality in interactions with governments in the developing world. Because of this policy, Schlumberger has been able to avoid political entanglements and continues to do business where many firms find the political risks too great. Put differently, Schlumberger has developed valuable, rare, and costly-to-imitate resources and capabilities in managing political risks and is using these resources to generate high levels of economic performance.[44]

The Value of International Strategies: The Empirical Evidence

Overall, research on the economic consequences of implementing international strategies is mixed. Some research has found that the performance of firms pursuing international strategies is superior to the performance of firms operating only in domestic markets.[45] However, most of this work has not examined the particular economies of scope that a firm is attempting to realize through its internationalization efforts. Moreover, several of these studies have attempted to evaluate the effect of international strategies on firm performance by using accounting measures of performance. Other research has found that the risk-adjusted performance of firms pursuing an international strategy is not different from the risk-adjusted performance of firms pursuing purely domestic strategies.[46]

These ambivalent findings are not surprising, since the economic value of international strategies depends on whether a firm pursues valuable economies of scope when implementing this strategy. Most of this empirical work fails to examine the economies of scope on which a firm's international strategy might be based. Moreover, even if a firm is able to realize real economies of scope from its international strategies, to be a source of sustained competitive advantage, this economy of scope must also be rare and costly to imitate, and the firm must be organized to fully realize it.

15.2 INTERNATIONAL STRATEGIES AND SUSTAINED COMPETITIVE ADVANTAGE

As suggested earlier in this chapter, much of the discussion of rarity and imitability in strategic alliance, diversification, and merger and acquisition strategies also applies to international strategies. However, some aspects of rarity and imitability are unique to international strategies. Such aspects are discussed below.

The Rarity of International Strategies

In many ways, it seems likely that international strategies are becoming less rare among most competing firms. There are, of course, several reasons for the increased popularity of international strategies. Not the least of these are the substantial economies of scope that internationalizing firms can realize. In addition, several changes in the organization of the international economy have facilitated the growth in popularity of international strategies. For example, the recently negotiated World Trade Organization agreement in conjunction with the development of the European Community (EC), the Andean Common Market (ANCOM), the Association of Southeast Asian Nations (ASEAN), the North American Free Trade Agreement (NAFTA), and other free-trade zones, has substantially reduced both tariff and nontariff barriers to trade. These changes have helped facilitate trade among countries included in an agreement; they have also spurred firms that wish to take advantage of these opportunities to expand their operations into these countries.

Improvements in the technological infrastructure of business are also important contributors to the growth in the number of firms pursuing international strategies. Transportation (especially air travel) and communication (via computers, fax, telephones, pagers, cellular telephones, and so forth) have evolved to the point where it is now much easier for firms to monitor and integrate their international operations than it was just a few years ago. This infrastructure helps reduce the cost of implementing an international strategy and thus increases the probability that firms will pursue these opportunities.

Finally, the emergence of various communication, technical, and accounting standards is facilitating international strategies. For example, there is currently a de facto world standard in personal computers. Also, most of the software that runs off these computers is flexible and interchangeable. Someone can write a report on a PC in India and print that report out on a PC in France with no real difficulties. There is also a de facto world standard business language—English. Although fully understanding a non–English-speaking culture requires managers to learn the native tongue, it is nevertheless possible to manage international business operations by using English.

Even though it seems that more and more firms are pursuing international strategies, it does not follow that these strategies will never be rare among a set of competing firms. Despite the increased popularity of these strategies, rare international strategies can exist in at least two ways. Given the enormous range of business opportunities that exist around the globe, it may very well be that huge numbers of firms can implement international strategies and still not compete head to head when implementing these strategies. Recall that the rarity requirement is that the resources and capabilities that a firm brings to implementing a strategy must be rare among competing firms. If, for a particular international opportunity, there happen to be few direct competitors, this rarity criterion can be met.

Even if several firms are competing to exploit the same international opportunity, the rarity criterion can still be met if the resources and capabilities that a particular firm brings to this international competition are rare. Examples of these rare resources and capabilities might include unusual marketing skills, highly differentiated products, special technology, superior management talent, and economies of scale.[47] To the extent that a firm pursues one of the economies of scope listed in Table 15.1 using resources and capabilities that are rare among competing firms, that firm can gain at least a temporary competitive advantage from its international strategy.

The Imitability of International Strategies

Like all the strategies discussed in this book, both the direct duplication of and substitutes for international strategies are important in evaluating the imitability of these actions.

Direct Duplication of International Strategies

In evaluating the possibility of the direct duplication of international strategies, two questions must be asked: (1) Will firms try to duplicate valuable and rare international strategies? (2) Will firms be able to duplicate these valuable and rare strategies?

There seems little doubt that, in the absence of artificial barriers, the profits generated by one firm's valuable and rare international strategies will motivate other firms to try to imitate the resources and capabilities required to implement these strategies. This rush to internationalization has occurred in numerous industries, including the telecommunications industry and the processed-food industry.

However, simply because competing firms often try to duplicate a successful firm's international strategy does not mean that they are always able to do so. To the extent that a successful firm exploits resources or capabilities that are path-dependent, uncertain, or socially complex in its internationalization efforts, direct duplication may be too costly, and thus international strategies can be a source of sustained competitive advantage. Indeed, there is some reason to believe that at least some of the resources and capabilities that enable a firm to pursue an international strategy are likely to be costly to imitate.

For example, the ability to develop detailed local knowledge of nondomestic markets may require firms to have management teams with a great deal of foreign experience. Some firms may have this kind of experience in their top management teams; other firms may not. A recent survey of 433 chief executive officers from around the world reported that 14 percent of U.S. CEOs had no foreign experience and that the foreign experience of 56 percent of U.S. CEOs was limited to vacation travel. An even more recent survey has shown that only 22 percent of the CEOs of multinational companies have extensive international experience.[48] Of course, it can take a great deal of time for a firm that does not have much foreign experience in its management team to develop that experience. Firms that lack this kind of experience will have to bring managers in from outside the organization, invest in developing this experience internally, or both. Of course, these activities are costly. The cost of creating this experience base in a firm's management team can be thought of as the cost of direct duplication.

Substitutes for International Strategies

Even if direct duplication of a firm's international strategies is costly, there may still be substitutes that limit the ability of that strategy to generate sustained competitive advantages. In particular, because international strategies are just a special case of corporate strategies in general, any of the other corporate strategies discussed in this book—including some types of strategic alliances, diversification, and mergers and acquisitions—can be at least partial substitutes for international strategies.

For example, a firm may be able to gain at least some of the economies of scope listed in Table 15.1 by implementing a corporate diversification strategy within a single country market, especially if that market is large and geographically diverse. One such market, of course, is the United States. A firm that originally conducted business in the northeastern United States can gain many of the benefits of internationalization by beginning business operations in the southern United States, on the West Coast, or in the Pacific Northwest. In this sense, geographic diversification within the United States is at least a partial substitute for internationalization and is one reason why many U.S. firms have lagged behind European and Asian firms in their international efforts.

However, some economies of scope listed in Table 15.1 can be gained only through international operations. For example, because there are usually few limits on capital flows within most countries, risk management is directly valuable to a firm's equity holders only for firms pursuing business opportunities across countries where barriers to capital flow exist. Moreover, the potential value of some of the economies listed in Table 15.1 is substantially greater in an international context, compared to the value of those economies in a purely domestic context. For example, the ability to develop new core competencies is, on average, much greater for firms pursuing international opportunities than for firms pursuing a substitute strategy.

15.3 THE ORGANIZATION OF INTERNATIONAL STRATEGIES

To realize the full economic potential of a valuable, rare, and costly-to-imitate international strategy, firms must be appropriately organized.

Becoming Internationalized: Organizational Options

A firm implements an international strategy when it diversifies its business operations across country boundaries. In doing so, firms can organize their international business operations in a wide variety of ways. Some of the most common, ranging from simple export operations to managing a wholly owned foreign subsidiary, are listed in Table 15.5. These options can be thought of as different levels of integration into international activities available to a firm. As firms become more integrated into international

TABLE 15.5	**Organizing Options for Firms Pursuing International Strategies**	
Market Governance	*Intermediate Market Governance*	*Hierarchical Governance*
Exporting	Licensing	Mergers
	Non-equity alliances	Acquisitions
	Equity alliances	Wholly owned subsidiaries
	Joint ventures	

operations, their level of direct investment in nondomestic markets increases. This investment is called **foreign direct investment.**

Market Governance, Exporting, and International Strategies. Firms can maintain traditional arm's-length market relationships between themselves and their nondomestic customers and still implement international strategies. They do this by simply exporting their products or services to nondomestic markets and limiting any foreign direct investment into nondomestic markets. Of course, exporting firms generally have to work with some partner or partners to receive, market, and distribute their products in a nondomestic setting. However, it is possible for exporting firms to use complete contracts to manage their relationship with these foreign partners and thereby maintain arm's-length relationships with them (see Chapter 10 for a thorough discussion)—all the time limiting foreign direct investment.

The advantages of adopting exporting as a way to manage an international strategy includes its relatively low cost and the limited risk exposure faced by firms that pursue international opportunities in this manner. Firms that are just beginning to consider international strategies can use market-based exporting to test international waters to find out if there is demand for their current products or services, to develop some experience operating in nondomestic markets, or to begin to develop relationships that might be valuable in subsequent international strategy efforts. If firms discover that there is not much demand for their products or services in a nondomestic market, or if they discover that they do not have the resources and capabilities to compete effectively in those markets, they can simply cease their exporting operations. The direct cost of ceasing export operations can be quite low, especially if a firm's volume of exports is small and the firm has not invested in plant and equipment designed to facilitate exporting. Certainly, if a firm has limited its foreign direct investment, it does not risk losing this investment if it ceases export operations.

However, the opportunity costs associated with restricting a firm's international operations to exporting can be significant. Of the economies of scope listed in Table 15.1, only gaining access to new customers for a firm's current products or services can be realized through exporting. Other economies of scope that hold some potential for firms exploring international business opportunities are out of the reach of firms that restrict their international operations to exporting. For some firms, realizing economies from gaining access to new customers is sufficient, and exporting is a viable long-run strategy. However, to the extent that other economies of scope might exist for a firm, limiting international operations to exporting can limit the firm's economic profit.

Intermediate Market Governance, Strategic Alliances, and International Strategies. If a firm decides to move beyond market governance and exporting in pursuing international strategies, a wide range of intermediate market governance devices—called **strategic alliances** in Chapters 10 and 13—are available. These alliances range from simple licensing arrangements, by which a domestic firm grants a firm in a nondomestic market the right to use its products and brand names to sell products in that nondomestic market, to full-blown joint ventures, by which a domestic firm and a nondomestic firm create an independent organizational entity to manage international efforts. As suggested in Chapter 13, the recent growth in the number of firms pursuing strategic alliance strategies is a direct result of the growth in popularity of international strategies. Strategic alliances are one of the most common ways that firms manage their international efforts.

Most of Chapter 13's discussion of the value, rarity, imitability, and organization of strategic alliances applies to the analysis of strategic alliances to implement an international strategy. However, many of the opportunities and challenges of managing strategic alliances as cooperative strategies, discussed in Chapter 13, are exacerbated in the context of international strategic alliances.

For example, it was suggested that opportunistic behavior (in the form of adverse selection, moral hazard, or holdup) can threaten the stability of strategic alliances domestically. Opportunistic behavior is a problem because partners in a strategic alliance find it costly to observe and evaluate the performance of one another. Obviously, the costs and difficulty of evaluating the performance of an alliance partner in an international alliance are greater than those in a purely domestic alliance. Geographic distance, differences in traditional business practices, language barriers, and cultural differences can make it very difficult for firms to evaluate the performance and intentions of international alliance partners.

These challenges can manifest at multiple levels in an international strategic alliance. For example, one study has shown that managers in U.S. organizations, on average, have a negotiation style that is very different from that of managers in Chinese organizations. Chinese managers tend to interrupt each other and ask many more questions during negotiations than do U.S. managers. As U.S. and Chinese firms begin to negotiate collaborative agreements, it will be difficult for U.S. managers to judge whether the Chinese negotiation style reflects Chinese managers' fundamental distrust of U.S. managers or is simply a manifestation of traditional Chinese business practices and culture.[49]

Similar management style differences have been noted between Western and Japanese managers. One Western manager was quoted as saying:[50]

> Whenever I made a presentation [to our partner], I was one person against 10 or 12. They'd put me in front of a flip chart, and then stop me while they went into a conversation in Japanese for 10 minutes. If I asked them a question they would break into Japanese to first decide what I wanted to know, and then would discuss options in terms of what they might tell me, and finally would come back with an answer.

During those 10-minute breaks in the conversation, it would be very difficult for this manager to know whether the Japanese managers were trying to develop a complete and accurate answer to his question or scheming to provide an incomplete and misleading answer. In this ambiguous setting, to prevent potential opportunism, Western managers might demand greater levels of governance than were actually necessary. In fact, one study has shown that differences in the perceived trustworthiness of international partners affects the kind of governance mechanisms that are put into place when firms begin international operations. If partners are not perceived as being trustworthy, then elaborate governance devices, including joint ventures, are created—even if the partners are in fact trustworthy.[51]

Cultural and style conflicts leading to perceived opportunism problems are not restricted to alliances between Asian and Western organizations. U.S. firms operating with Mexican partners often discover numerous subtle and complex cultural differences.

For example, a U.S. firm operating a steel conveyor plant in Puebla, Mexico, implemented a three-stage employee grievance policy. An employee who had a grievance first went to his or her immediate supervisor and then continued up the chain of command until the grievance was resolved one way or another. U.S. managers were satisfied with this system and pleased that no grievances had been registered—until the day the entire plant walked out on strike. It turns out that there had been numerous grievances, but Mexican workers had felt uncomfortable confronting their supervisors directly with these problems. Such confrontations are considered antisocial in Mexican culture.[52]

Although significant challenges are associated with managing strategic alliances across country boundaries, there are significant opportunities as well. Strategic alliances can enable a firm pursuing an international strategy to realize any of the economies of scope listed in Table 15.1. Moreover, if a firm is able to develop valuable, rare, and costly-to-imitate resources and capabilities in managing strategic alliances, the use of alliances in an international context can be a source of sustained competitive advantage.

Hierarchical Governance, Integration, and International Strategies. Firms may decide to integrate in their international operations by acquiring a firm in a nondomestic market or by forming a new wholly owned subsidiary to manage their operations in a nondomestic market. Obviously, both of these international investments involve substantial direct foreign investment by a firm over long periods of time. These investments are subject to both political and economic risks and should be undertaken only if the economies of scope that can be realized through international operations are significant and other ways of realizing these economies of scope are not effective or not efficient.

Although hierarchical governance and integration in international operations can be expensive and risky, it can have some important advantages for internationalizing firms. First, like strategic alliances, this approach to internationalization can enable a firm to realize any of the economies of scope listed in Table 15.1. Moreover, integration enables managers to use a wider range of organizational controls to limit the threat of opportunism than are normally available in market forms or intermediate market forms of international governance. Finally, unlike strategic alliances, in which any profits from international operations must be shared with international partners, integrating into international operations enables firms to capture all the economic profits from their international operations.

Managing the Internationally Diversified Firm

In many ways, the management of international operations can be thought of as a special case of managing a diversified firm. Thus many of the issues discussed in Chapter 12 apply here. However, managing an internationally diversified firm does create some unique challenges and opportunities.

Organizational Structure. Firms pursuing an international strategy have four basic organizational structural alternatives, listed in Table 15.6 and discussed later. Although each of these structures has some special features, they are all special cases of the multidivisional structure first introduced in Chapter 12.[53]

TABLE 15.6	Structural Options for Firms Pursuing International Strategies
Decentralized federation	Strategic and operational decisions are delegated to divisions/country companies
Coordinated federation	Operational decisions are delegated to divisions/country companies; strategic decisions are retained at corporate headquarters
Centralized hub	Strategic and operational decisions are retained at corporate headquarters
Transnational structure	Strategic and operational decisions are delegated to those operational entities that maximize responsiveness to local conditions and international integration

Source: Adapted from Bartlett, C. A., and S. Ghoshal (1989). *Managing Across Borders: The Transnational Solution*, Boston: Harvard Business School Press.

Some firms organize their international operations as a **decentralized federation.** In this organizational structure, each country in which a firm operates is organized as a full profit-and-loss division headed by a division general manager, who is typically the president of the company in a particular country. In a decentralized federation, there are very few shared activities or other economies of scope among different divisions/country companies, and corporate headquarters plays a limited strategic role. Corporate staff functions are generally limited to the collection of accounting and other performance information from divisions/country companies and to reporting this aggregate information to appropriate government officials and to the financial markets. Most employees within the divisions/country companies in a decentralized federation may not even be aware that they are part of a larger internationally diversified firm. Both strategic and operational decision making are delegated to division general managers/country company presidents in a decentralized federation organizational structure. There are relatively few examples of pure decentralized federations in today's world economy, but firms such as Nestlé, CIBA-Geigy, and Electrolux have many of the attributes of this type of structure.[54]

A second structural option for international firms is the **coordinated federation.** In a coordinated federation, each country operation is organized as a full profit-and-loss center, and division general managers can be presidents of country companies. However, in a coordinated federation, strategic and operational decisions are not fully delegated to division general managers. Operational decisions are delegated to division general managers/country presidents, but broader strategic decisions are made at corporate headquarters. Moreover, coordinated federations attempt to exploit various shared activities and other economies of scope among their divisions/country companies. It is not uncommon for coordinated federations to have corporately sponsored central research and development laboratories, manufacturing and technology development initiatives, and management training and development operations. There are numerous examples of coordinated federations in today's world economy, including General Electric, General Motors, IBM, and Coca-Cola.

A third structural option for international firms is the **centralized hub**. In centralized hubs, operations in different countries may be organized into profit-and-loss centers, and division general managers may be country company presidents. However, most of the strategic and operational decision making in these firms takes place at the corporate center. The role of divisions/country companies in centralized hubs is simply to implement the strategies, tactics, and policies that have been chosen at headquarters. Of course, divisions/country companies are also a source of information for headquarters staff when these decisions are being made. However, in centralized hubs, strategic and operational decision rights are retained at the corporate center. Many Japanese and Korean firms are managed as centralized hubs, including Toyota, Mitsubishi, and NEC (in Japan), and Goldstar, Daewoo, and Hyundai (in Korea).[55]

A fourth structural option for international firms is the **transnational structure.** This structure is most appropriate for implementing the transnational strategy described in Section 15.1. In many ways, the transnational structure is similar to the coordinated federation. In both, strategic decision-making responsibility is largely retained at the corporate center, and operational decision making is largely delegated to division general managers/country presidents. However, there are also important differences.

In a coordinated federation structure, shared activities and other cross-divisional/cross-country economies of scope are managed by the corporate center. Thus, for many of these firms, if research and development is seen as a potentially valuable economy of scope, a central research and development laboratory is created and managed by the corporate center. In the transnational structure, these centers of corporate economies of scope may be managed by the corporate center. However, they are more likely to be managed by specific divisions/country companies within the corporation. Thus, for example, if one division/country company develops valuable, rare, and costly-to-imitate research and development capabilities in its ongoing business activities in a particular country, that division/country company could become the center of research and development activity for the entire corporation. If one division/country company develops valuable, rare, and costly-to-imitate manufacturing technology development skills in its ongoing business activities in a particular country, that division/country company could become the center for manufacturing technology development for the entire corporation.

The role of corporate headquarters in a transnational structure is constantly to scan business operations across different countries for resources and capabilities that might be a source of competitive advantage for other divisions/country companies in the firm. Once these special skills are located, corporate staff must then determine the best way to exploit these economies of scope—whether they should be developed within a single division/country company (to gain economies of scale) and then transferred to other divisions/country companies, or developed through an alliance between two or more divisions/country companies (to gain economies of scale) and then transferred to other divisions/country companies, or redeveloped for the entire firm at corporate headquarters. These options are not available to decentralized federations (which always let individual divisions/country companies develop their own competencies), coordinated federations, or centralized hubs (which always develop corporate-wide economies of scope at the corporate level). Firms that have been successful in adopting this transnational structure include Ford (Ford Europe has become a leader in automobile design for all of the Ford Motor Company) and Ericsson (Ericsson's

Australian subsidiary developed this Swedish company's first electronic telecommunication switch, and corporate headquarters was able to help transfer this technology to other Ericsson subsidiaries).[56]

Organizational Structure, Local Responsiveness, and International Integration.   It should be clear that the choice among these four approaches to managing international strategies depends on the trade-offs that firms are willing to make between local responsiveness and international integration (see Figure 15.2). Firms that seek to maximize their local responsiveness tend to choose a decentralized federation structure. Firms that seek to maximize international integration in their operations typically opt for centralized hub structures. Firms that seek to balance the need for local responsiveness and international integration typically choose coordinated federations. Firms that attempt to optimize both local responsiveness and international integration often choose a transnational organizational structure.

Management Control Systems and Compensation Policies.   Like the multidivisional structure discussed in Chapter 13, none of the organizational structures described in Table 15.5 can stand alone without the support of a variety of management control systems and management compensation policies. All the management control processes discussed in Chapter 13, including evaluating the performance of divisions, allocating capital, and managing the exchange of intermediate products among divisions, are also important for firms organizing to implement an international strategy. Moreover, the same management compensation challenges and opportunities discussed in that chapter apply in the organization of international strategies as well.

However, as is often the case when organizing processes originally developed to manage diversification within a domestic market are extended to the management of

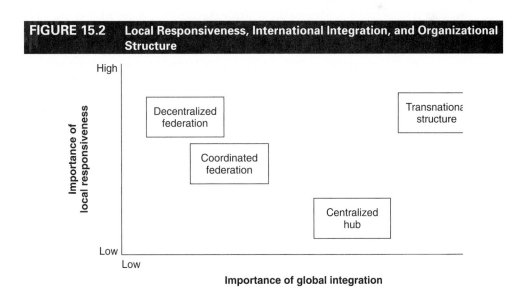

FIGURE 15.2   Local Responsiveness, International Integration, and Organizational Structure

Source: Adapted from Grant, R. (1991). *Comtemporary Strategy Analysis*, Cambridge, MA: Basil Blackwell. Reprinted with permission.

international diversification, many of the management challenges highlighted in Chapter 12 are exacerbated in an international context. This puts an even greater burden on senior managers in an internationally diversified firm to choose control systems and compensation policies that create incentives for division general managers/country presidents to cooperate appropriately to realize the economies of scope that originally motivated the implementation of an international strategy.

15.4 SUMMARY

International strategies can be seen as a special case of diversification strategies. Firms implement international strategies when they pursue business opportunities that cross country borders. Like all diversification strategies, international strategies must exploit real economies of scope that outside investors find too costly to exploit on their own in order to be valuable. Five potentially valuable economies of scope in international strategies are (1) to gain access to new customers for a firm's current products or services, (2) to gain access to low-cost factors of production, (3) to develop new core competencies, (4) to leverage current core competencies in new ways, and (5) to manage corporate risk.

As firms pursue these economies of scope, they must evaluate the extent to which they can be responsive to local market needs and obtain the advantages of international integration. Firms that attempt to accomplish both these objectives are said to be implementing a transnational strategy. Both economic and political risks can affect the value of a firm's international strategies.

To be a source of sustained competitive advantage, a firm's international strategies must be valuable, rare, and costly to imitate, and the firm must be organized to realize the full potential of its international strategies. Even though more and more firms are pursuing international strategies, these strategies can still be rare, for at least two reasons: (1) Given the broad range of international opportunities, firms may not compete head to head with other firms pursuing the same international strategies that they are pursuing; and (2) firms may bring valuable and rare resources and capabilities to the international strategies they pursue. Both direct duplication and substitution can affect the imitability of a firm's international strategy. Direct duplication is not likely when firms bring valuable, rare, and costly-to-imitate resources and capabilities to bear in their international strategies. There are several substitutes for international strategies, including some strategic alliances, vertical integration, diversification, and mergers and acquisitions, especially if these strategies are pursued in a large and diverse single-country market. However, some potential economies of scope from international strategies can be exploited only by operating across country borders.

Firms have several organizational options as they pursue international strategies, including market forms of governance (for example, exports), intermediate forms of governance (for example, strategies alliances), and hierarchical forms of governance (for example, wholly owned subsidiaries). Four alternative structures, all special cases of the multidivisional structure introduced in Chapter 13, can be used to manage these international operations: a decentralized federation structure, a coordinated federation structure, a centralized hub structure, and a transnational structure. These structures need to be consistent with a firm's emphasis on being responsive to local markets, on exploiting international integration opportunities, or both.

REVIEW QUESTIONS

1. Are international strategies always just a special case of diversification strategies that a firm might pursue? What, if anything, is different about international strategies and diversification strategies?
2. In your view, is gaining access to low-cost labor a sufficient reason for a firm to pursue an international strategy? Why or why not? In your view, is gaining access to special tax breaks a sufficient reason for a firm to pursue an international strategy? Why or why not?
3. The transnational strategy is often seen as one way in which firms can avoid the limitations inherent in the local responsiveness/international integration trade-off. However, given the obvious advantages of being both locally responsive and internationally integrated, why do only a relatively few firms seem to be implementing a transnational

strategy? What implications does your analysis have for the ability of a transnational strategy to be a source of sustained competitive advantage for a firm?
4. On average, is the threat of adverse selection and moral hazard in strategic alliances greater for firms pursuing an international strategy or for those pursuing a domestic strategy? Why?
5. How are the organizational options for implementing an international strategy, listed in Table 15.6, related to the M-form structure described in Chapter 13? Are these international organizational options just special cases of the M-form structure with slightly different emphases, or are these international organizational options fundamentally different from the M-form structure?

ENDNOTES

1. See Moffett, M. (1993). "U.S. firms yell Ole to future in Mexico," *Wall Street Journal*, March 8, p. B1; and Oviatt, B. M., and P. P. McDougall (1995). "Global start-ups: Entrepreneurs on a worldwide stage," *Academy of Management Executive*, 9, pp. 30–44. Logitech, Oxford, SPEA, and Technomed are all still operating successfully. Momenta no longer exists.
2. See Yoshino, M., S. Hall, and T. Malnight (1991). "Whirlpool Corp.," Harvard Business School Case no. 9-391-089.
3. See Jones, G., and C. W. Jones (1991). "Michael Eisner's Disney Company," in *Strategic Management*, Boston: Houghton-Mifflin, pp. 784–805; and Tanikawa, M. (1997). "Fun in the sun," *Far Eastern Economic Review*, 160(22), May 29, pp. 56–57.
4. See Greenhouse, S. (1991). "Playing Disney in the Parisian fields," *New York Times*, February 17, Section 3, pp. 1, 6; Toy, S., and P. Dwyer (1994). "Is Disney headed to the Euro-trash heap?" *Business Week*, January 24, p. 52; and Solomon, J. (1994). "Mickey's trip to trouble," *Newsweek*, February 14, pp. 34–39.

5. See Perry, N. J. (1991). "Will Sony make it in Hollywood?" *Fortune*, September 9, pp. 158–166; and Montgomery, C. (1993). "Marks and Spencer Ltd. (A)," Harvard Business School Case no. 9-391-089.
6. See Rapoport, C. (1994). "Nestlé's brand building machine," *Fortune*, September 19, pp. 147–156.
7. See Yoshino, M. Y., and P. Stoneham (1992). "Procter & Gamble Japan (A)," Harvard Business School Case no. 9-793-035.
8. See Davis, B. (1995). "U.S. expects goals in pact with Japan to be met even without overt backing," *Wall Street Journal*, June 30, p. A3; Bounds, W., and B. Davis (1995). "U.S. to launch new case against Japan over Kodak," *Wall Street Journal*, June 30, p. A3; Jacob, R. (1992). "India is opening for business," *Fortune*, November 16, pp. 128–130; and Rugman, A., and R. Hodgetts (1995). *Business: A Strategic Management Approach*, New York: McGraw-Hill.
9. See Jacob, R. (1992). "India is opening for business," *Fortune*, November 16, pp. 128–130; Serwer, A. E. (1994). "McDonald's conquers the world," *Fortune*, October 17,

pp. 103–116; and World Bank (1999). *World Development Report*, Oxford: Oxford University Press.

10. See Rapoport, C. (1994). "Nestlé's brand building machine," *Fortune*, September 19, pp. 147–156.

11. See Jacob, R. (1992). "India is opening for business," *Fortune*, November 16, pp. 128–130, Ignatius, A. (1993). "Commodity giant: Marc Rich & Co. does big deals at big risk in former U.S.S.R.," *Wall Street Journal*, May 13, p. A1; and Kraar, L. (1995). "The risks are rising in China," *Fortune*, March 6, pp. 179–180.

12. See Ignatius, A. (1993). "Commodity giant: Marc Rich & Co. does big deals at big risk in former U.S.S.R.," *Wall Street Journal*, May 13, p. A1; and Marin, D. (1990). "Tying in trade: Evidence on countertrade," *World Economy*, 13(3), p. 445.

13. The life cycle is described in Utterback, J. M., and W. J. Abernathy (1975). "A dynamic model of process and product innovation," *Omega*, 3, pp. 639–656; Abernathy, W. J., and J. M. Utterback (1978). "Patterns of technological innovation," *Technology Review*, 80, pp. 40–47; and Grant, R. M. (1991a). *Contemporary Strategy Analysis*, Cambridge, MA: Basil Blackwell.

14. See Bradley, S. P., and Cavanaugh, S. (1994). "Crown Cork and Seal in 1989," Harvard Business School Case no. 9-793-035; and Hamermesh, R. G., and R. S. Rosenbloom (1989). "Crown Cork and Seal Co., Inc.," Harvard Business School Case no. 9-388-096. Of course, this strategy works only until nondomestic markets mature. This occurred for Crown Cork & Seal during the 1990s. Since then the firm has had to search elsewhere for growth opportunities.

15. See Fayerweather, J. (1969). *International Business Management: Conceptual Framework*, New York: McGraw-Hill; Fayerweather, J. (1982). *International Business Strategy and Administration*, Cambridge, MA: Ballinger; Fayerweather, J., and A. Kapoor (1975). *Strategy and Negotiation for the International Company*, Cambridge, MA: Ballinger; and Hout, T., M. E. Porter, and E. Rudden (1982). "How global companies win out," *Harvard Business Review*, September/October, pp. 98–108.

16. See Serwer, A. E. (1994). "McDonald's conquers the world," *Fortune*, October 17, pp. 103–116; Prahalad, C. K., and Y. Doz (1987). *The Multinational Mission*, New York: Free Press; and Bartlett, C. A., and S. Ghoshal (1989). *Managing Across Borders: The Transnational Solution*, Boston: Harvard Business School Press.

17. Porter, M. E. (1986). "Competition in international industries: A conceptual framework," in M. E. Porter, ed., *Competition in International Industries*, Boston: Harvard Business School Press, p. 43; Ghoshal, S. (1987). "Global strategy: An organizing framework," *Strategic Management Journal*, 8, p. 436.

18. See Kobrin, S. (1991). "An empirical analysis of the determinants of global integration," *Strategic Management Journal*, 12, pp. 17–31.

19. See Kobrin, S. (1991). "An empirical analysis of the determinants of global integration," *Strategic Management Journal*, 12, pp. 17–31.

20. See Trager, J. (1992). *The People's Chronology*, New York: Henry Holt.

21. Kraar, L. (1992). "Korea's tigers keep roaring," *Fortune*, May 4, pp. 108–110.

22. See Collis, D. J. (1991). "A resource-based analysis of international competition: The case of the bearing industry," *Strategic Management Journal*, 12 (Summer, Special Issue), pp. 49–68; and Engardio, P. (1993). "Motorola in China: A great leap forward," *Business Week*, May 17, pp. 58–59.

23. Gain, S. (1993). "Korea is overthrown as sneaker champ," *Wall Street Journal*, October 7, p. A14.

24. See Reibstein, L., and M. Levinson (1991). "A Mexican miracle?" *Newsweek*, May 20, p. 42; and de Forest, M. E. (1994). "Thinking of a plant in Mexico?" *Academy of Management Executive*, 8(1), pp. 33–40.

25. See DePalma, A. (1994). "Trade pact is spurring Mexican deals in the U.S.," *New York Times*, March 17, pp. C1, C3; and Celestino, M. (1999). "Manufacturing in Mexico," *World Trade*, 12, July, pp. 36–42.

26. See Zimmerman, M. (1985). *How to Do Business with the Japanese*, New York: Random House; and Osborn, R. N., and C. C. Baughn (1987). "New patterns in the formation of US/Japan cooperative ventures: The

role of technology," *Columbia Journal of World Business*, 22, pp. 57–65.

27. See Hurry, D., A. T. Miller, and E. H. Bowman (1992). "Calls on high-technology: Japanese exploration of venture capital investments in the United States," *Strategic Management Journal*, 13, pp. 85–101.

28. Quoted in Hamel, G. (1991) "Competition for competence and inter-partner learning within strategic alliances," *Strategic Management Journal*, 12, p. 86.

29. Quoted in Hamel, G. (1991) "Competition for competence and inter-partner learning within strategic alliances," *Strategic Management Journal*, 12, p. 86.

30. See Benedict, R. (1946). *The Chrysanthemum and the Sword*, New York: New American Library; Peterson, R. B., and H. F. Schwind (1977). "A comparative study of personnel problems in companies and joint ventures in Japan," *Journal of Business Studies*, 8(1), pp. 45–55; Peterson, R. B., and J. Y. Shimada (1978). "Sources of management problems in Japanese-American joint ventures," *Academy of Management Review*, 3, pp. 796–804; and Hamel, G. (1991). "Competition for competence and inter-partner learning within strategic alliances," *Strategic Management Journal*, 12, pp. 83–103.

31. See Burgelman, R. A. (1983). "A process model of internal corporate venturing in the diversified major firm," *Administrative Science Quarterly*, 28(2), pp. 223–244; Hedberg, B. L. T. (1981). "How organizations learn and unlearn," in P. C. Nystrom and W. H. Starbuck, eds., *Handbook of Organizational Design*, London: Oxford University Press; Nystrom, P. C., and W. H. Starbuck (1984). "To avoid organizational crisis, unlearn," *Organizational Dynamics*, 12(4), pp. 53–65; and Argyris, C., and D. A. Schon (1978). *Organizational Learning*, Reading, MA: Addison-Wesley.

32. A problem described in Burgelman, R. A. (1983). "A process model of internal corporate venturing in the diversified major firm," *Administrative Science Quarterly*, 28(2), pp. 223–244.

33. Quoted in Hamel, G. (1991) "Competition for competence and inter-partner learning

within strategic alliances," *Strategic Management Journal*, 12, p. 97.

34. See Agmon, T., and D. R. Lessard (1977). Investor recognition of corporate diversification," *Journal of Finance*, 32, pp. 1049–1056.

35. Adler, M., and B. Dumas (1983). "International portfolio choice and corporate finance: A synthesis," *Journal of Finance*, 38, pp. 925–984; Lessard, D. R. (1996). "World, country, and industry relationships in equity returns: Implications for risk reduction through international diversification," *Financial Analysts Journal*, 32, pp. 32–38; Senchack, A. J., and W. L. Beedles (1980). "Is indirect diversification desirable?" *Journal of Portfolio Management*, 6, pp. 49–57.

36. See Adler, M., and B. Dumas (1983). " International portfolio choice and corporate finance: A synthesis," *Journal of Finance*, 38, pp. 925–984; Errunza, V., and L. W. Senbet (1981). "The effects of international operations on the market value of the firm: Theory and evidence," *Journal of Finance*, 36, pp. 401–418; Errunza, V., and L. W. Senbet (1984). "International corporate diversification, market valuation and size-adjusted evidence," *Journal of Finance*, 39, pp. 727–745; Logue, D. E. (1982). "An experiment in diversification," *Journal of Portfolio Management*, 9, pp. 22–30; Rugman, A. (1979). *International Diversification and the Multinational Enterprise*, Lexington, MA: Lexington Books; and Severn, A. K. (1974). "Investor evaluation of foreign and domestic risk," *Journal of Finance*, 29, pp. 545–550.

37. Rapoport, C. (1994). "Nestlé's brand building machine," *Fortune*, September 19, pp. 147–156.

38. See Bartlett, C. A., and S. Ghoshal (1989). *Managing Across Borders: The Transnational Solution*, Boston: Harvard Business School Press.

39. See Rugman, A., and R. Hodgetts (1995). *International Business: A Strategic Management Approach*, New York: McGraw-Hill.

40. Glynn, M. A. (1993). "Strategic planning in Nigeria versus U.S.: A case of anticipating the (next) coup," *Academy of Management Executive* 7(3), pp. 82–83.

41. See Roth, T. (1990). "Bid size showed VW's eagerness to buy Skoda," *Wall Street*

Journal, December 11, p. A15; and Tully, S. (1990). "GE in Hungary: Let there be light," *Fortune*, October 22, pp. 137–142.

42. See Ring, P. S., S. A. Lenway, and M. Govekar (1990). "Management of the political imperative in international business," *Strategic Management Journal*, 11, pp. 141–151.

43. Dichtl, E., and H. G. Koeglmayr (1986). "Country risk ratings," *Management International Review*, 26(4), pp. 2–10.

44. See Auletta, K. (1983). "A certain poetry—Parts I and II," *The New Yorker*, June 6, pp. 46–109; and June 13, pp. 50–91.

45. See, for example, Leftwich, R. B. (1974). "U.S. Multinational companies: Profitability, financial leverage and effective income tax rates," *Survey of Current Business*, 54, May, pp. 27–36; Dunning, J. H. (1973). "The determinants of production," *Oxford Economic Papers*, 25, November, pp. 289–336; Errunza, V., and L. W. Senbet (1981). "The effects of international operations on the market value of the firm: Theory and evidence," *Journal of Finance*, 36, pp. 401–418; Grant, R. M. (1987). "Multinationality and performance among British manufacturing companies," *Journal of International Business Studies*, 18 (Fall), pp. 78–89; and Rugman, A. (1979). *International Diversification and the Multinational Enterprise*, Lexington, MA: Lexington Books.

46. See, for example, Brewer, H. L. (1981). "Investor benefits from corporate international diversification," *Journal of Financial and Quantitative Analysis*, 16, March, pp. 113–126; and Michel, A., and I. Shaked (1986). "Multinational corporations vs. domestic corporations: Financial performance and characteristics," *Journal of Business*, 17 (Fall), pp. 89–100.

47. See Caves, R. E. (1971). "International corporations: The industrial economics of foreign investment," *Economica*, 38, February, pp. 1–28; Dunning, J. H. (1973). "The determinants of production," *Oxford Economic Papers*, 25, November, pp. 289–336; Hymer, S. (1976). *The International Operations of National Firms: A Study of Direct Foreign Investment*, Cambridge, MA: MIT Press; Errunza, V., and L. W. Senbet (1981). "The

effects of international operations on the market value of the firm: Theory and evidence," *Journal of Finance*, 36, pp. 401–418.

48. Anders, G. (1989). "Going global: Vision vs. reality," *Wall Street Journal*, September 22, p. R21; and Carpenter, M. A., G. Sanders, and H. B. Gregerson (2001). "Bundling human capital with organizational context: The impact of international assignment experience on multinational firm performance and CEO pay," *Academy of Management Journal*, 44(3), pp. 493–511.

49. Adler, N., J. R. Brahm, and J. L. Graham (1992). "Strategy implementation: A comparison of face-to-face negotiations in the People's Republic of China and the United States," *Strategic Management Journal*, 13, pp. 449–466.

50. Hamel, G. (1991) "Competition for competence and inter-partner learning within international strategic alliances," *Strategic Management Journal*, 12, p. 95.

51. Shane, S. (1994). "The effect of national culture on the choice between licensing and direct foreign investment," *Strategic Management Journal*, 15, pp. 627–642.

52. See de Forest, M. E. (1994). "Thinking of a plant in Mexico?" *Academy of Management Executive*, 8(1), pp. 33–40.

53. See Bartlett, C. A. (1986). "Building and managing the transnational: The new organizational challenge," in M. E. Porter, ed., *Competition in International Industries*, Boston: Harvard Business School Press; pp. 367–401; and Bartlett, C. A., and S. Ghoshal (1989). *Managing Across Borders; The Transnational Solution*, Boston: Harvard Business School Press.

54. See Baden-Fuller, C. W. F., and J. M. Stopford (1991). "Globalization frustrated: The case of white goods," *Strategic Management Journal*, 12, pp. 493–507.

55. See Kraar, L. (1992). "Korea's tigers keep roaring," *Fortune*, May 4, pp. 108–110.

56. Bartlett, C. A., and S. Ghoshal (1989). *Managing Across Borders: The Transnational Solution*, Boston: Harvard Business School Press; and Grant, R. M. (1991a). *Contemporary Strategy Analysis,* Cambridge, MA: Basil Blackwell.

Bibliography

Abernathy, W. J., and J. M. Utterback (1978). "Patterns of technological innovation," *Technology Review,* 80, pp. 40–47.

Adelman, M. A. (1955). "Concept and statistical measurement of vertical integration," in National Bureau for Economic Research, eds., *Business Concentration and Price Policy,* Princeton, NJ: Princeton University Press; pp. 281–322.

Adler, M., and B. Dumas (1983). "International portfolio choice and corporate finance: A synthesis," *Journal of Finance,* 38, pp. 925–984.

Adler, N., J. R. Brahm, and J. L. Graham (1992). "Strategy implementation: A comparison of face-to-face negotiations in the People's Republic of China and the United States," *Strategic Management Journal,* 13, pp. 449–466.

Agmon, T., and D. R. Lessard (1977). Investor recognition of corporate diversification," *Journal of Finance,* 32, pp. 1049–1056.

Aguilar, F. J., and A. Bhambri (1983). "Johnson & Johnson (A)," Harvard Business School Case no. 9-384-053.

Aguilar, F. J., J. L. Bower, and B. Gomes-Casseres (1985). "Restructuring European petrochemicals: Imperial Chemical Industries, P.L.C.," Harvard Business School Case no. 9-385-203.

Akerlof, G. A. (1970). "The Markets for 'Lemons': Qualitative Uncertainty and the Market Mechanism," *Quarterly Journal of Economics,* 84, pp. 488–500.

Allen, F. (1993). "Strategic management and financial markets," *Strategic Management Journal,* 14, pp. 11–22;

Allen, M., and M. Siconolfi (1993). "Dell Computer drops planned share offering," *Wall Street Journal,* February 25, p. A3.

Alley, J. (1997). "The heart of Silicon Valley," *Fortune,* July 7, pp. 86+.

Alpert, M. (1992). "The care and feeding of engineers," *Fortune,* September 21, pp. 86–95.

Altman, E. I. (1968). "Financial ratios, discriminant analysis and the prediction of corporate bankruptcy," *Journal of Finance,* 23, pp. 589–609.

Altman, E. I., R. G. Haldemen, and P. Narayanan (1977). "Zeta analysis: A new model to identify bankruptcy risk of corporations," *Journal of Banking and Finance,* 1, pp. 29–54.

Alvarez, S. A., and J. B. Barney (2001). "How entrepreneurial firms can benefit from alliances with large partners," *Academy of Management Executive,* 15(1), pp. 139–148.

Amihud, Y., and B. Lev (1981). "Risk reduction as managerial motive for conglomerate mergers," *Bell Journal of Economics,* 12, pp. 605–617.

Amit, R., and J. Livnat (1988a). "Diversification strategies, business cycles and economic performance," *Strategic Management Journal,* 9, pp. 99–110.

Amit, R., and J. Livnat (1988b). "Diversification and the risk-return trade-off," *Academy of Management Journal,* 31, pp. 154–166.

Amit, R., and P. J. H. Schoemaker (1993). "Strategic assets and organizational rent," *Strategic Management Journal,* 14(1), pp. 33–45.

Amit, R., and B. Wernerfelt (1990). "Why do firms reduce business risk?" *Academy of Management Journal,* 33, pp. 520–533.

Anders, G. (1989). "Going global: Vision vs. reality," *Wall Street Journal,* September 22, p. R21.

Anderson, E. (1985). "The salesperson as outside agent or employee," *Marketing Science,* 4, pp. 234–254.

Anderson, E., and D. Schmittlein (1984). "Integration of sales force: An empirical examination," *Rand Journal of Economics,* 15, pp. 385–395.

Anonymous (1999). "Sweet success," *Harvard Business Review,* 77, May/June, p. 192.

Anonymous (1999). "The weakling kicks back," *The Economist,* 352(8126), p. 46.

Anonymous (2006). "The Fortune 500," *Fortune,* April 17, p. F1+.

Ansoff, H. I. (1965). *Corporate Strategy,* New York: McGraw-Hill.

Argyres, N. (1996). "Evidence on the role of Firm capabilities in vertical integration decision," *Strategic Management Journal,* 17, pp. 129–150.

Argyris, C., and D. A. Schon (1978). *Organizational Learning,* Reading, MA: Addison-Wesley.

Armour, H. O., and D. J. Teece (1980). "Vertical integration and technological innovation," *Review of Economics and Statistics,* 60, pp. 470–474.

Armstrong, L. (1991). "Services: The customer as 'honored guest,'" *Business Week,* October 25, p. 104.

Arnst, C. (1998). "AT&T: Will the bad news ever end?" *Business Week,* October 7, p. 122.

Arthur, W. B. (1989). "Competing technologies, increasing returns, and lock-in by historical events," *Economic Journal,* 99, pp. 116–131.

Auletta, K. (1983). "A certain poetry—Parts I and II," *The New Yorker,* June 6, pp. 46–109, and June 13, pp. 50–91.

Axelrod, R. M. (1984). *The Evolution of Cooperation,* New York: Basic Books.

Backaitis, N. T., R. Balakrishnan, and K. R. Harrigan (1984). "The dimensions of diversification posture, market power, and performance: The continuing debate," Working paper, Columbia University.

Badaracco, J. L., and N. Hasegawa (1988). "General Motors' Asian alliances," Harvard Business School Case no. 90-388-094.

Baden-Fuller, C. W. F., and J. M. Stopford (1991). "Globalization frustrated: The case of white goods," *Strategic Management Journal,* 12, pp. 493–507.

Bain, J. S. (1956). *Barriers to New Competition,* Cambridge, MA: Harvard University Press.

Bain, J. S. (1968). *Industrial Organization,* New York: John Wiley & Sons.

Baker, S. (1995). "A real steelman for USX," *Business Week,* May 15, p. 47.

Balakrishnan, S., and M. Koza (1993). "Information asymmetry, adverse selection and joint-ventures," *Journal of Economic Behavior & Organization,* 20, pp. 99–117.

Ball, R., and P. Brown (1968). "An empirical examination of accounting income numbers," *Journal of Accounting Research,* Autumn, pp. 159–178.

Banz, R. W. (1981). "The relationship between return and market value of common stocks," *Journal of Financial Economics,* March, pp. 3–18.

Barnett, W. P., H. R. Greve, and D. Y. Park (1994). "An evolutionary model of organizational performance," *Strategic Management Journal,* 15 (Winter, Special Issue), pp. 11–28.

Barney, J. (1999). "How a firm's capabilities affect boundary decisions," *Sloan Management Review,* 40(3), pp. 137–145.

Barney, J., and P. Wright (1998). "On becoming a strategic partner," *Human Resource Management,* 37, pp. 31–46.

Barney, J. B. (1986). "Organizational culture: Can it be a source of sustained competitive advantage?" *Academy of Management Review,* 11, pp. 656–665.

Barney, J. B. (1986). "Strategic factor markets: Expectations, luck and business strategy," *Management Science,* 32, pp. 1512–1514.

Barney, J. B. (1986c). "Types of competition and the theory of strategy: Toward an integrative framework," *Academy of Management Review,* 1, pp. 791–800.

Barney, J. B. (1988). "Returns to bidding firms in mergers and acquisitions: Reconsidering the relatedness hypothesis," *Strategic Management Journal,* 9, pp. 71–78.

Barney, J. B. (1990). "Profit sharing bonuses and the cost of debt: Business finance and compensation policy in Japanese electronics firms," *Asia Pacific Journal of Management,* 7, pp. 49–64.

Barney, J. B. (1991). "Firm resources and sustained competitive advantage," *Journal of Management,* 17, pp. 99–120.

Barney, J. B. (1994). "Bringing managers back in: A resource-based analysis of the role of managers in creating and sustaining competitive advantages for firms," in *Does Management Matter?* Lund, Sweden: Institute of Economic Research, Lund University, pp. 3–36.

Barney, J. B., and M. H. Hansen (1994). "Trustworthiness as a source of competitive advantage," *Strategic Management Journal,* 15 (Winter, Special Issue), pp. 175–190.

Barney, J. B., and W. Hesterly (1996). "Organizational economics: Understanding the relationship between organizations and economic analysis," in Clegg, S., C. Hardy, and W. Nord, eds., *Handbook of Organization Theory,* Thousand Oaks, CA: Sage, pp. 115–147.

Barney, J. B., and R. E. Hoskisson (1990). "Strategic groups: Untested assertions and research proposals," *Managerial and Decision Economics,* 11, pp. 187–198.

Barney, J. B., and D. Miller (2006). "Employer Perspectives: Strategic Thinking or Reactive Responses?" in S. Gleason (ed.), *The Shadow Workforce: Perspectives on Contingent Work in the United States, Japan and Europe,* Kalamazoo, MI: W. E. Upjohn Institute for Employment Research.

Barney, J. B., and W. G. Ouchi (1986). *Organizational Economics,* San Francisco: Jossey-Bass.

Barney, J. B., and B. Tyler (1990). "The attributes of top management teams and sustained competitive advantage," in M. Lawless and L. Gomez-Mejia, eds., *Managing the High Technology Firm,* Greenwich, CT: JAI Press, pp. 33–48.

Bartlett, C., and S. Ghoshal (1993). Beyond the M-form: Toward a managerial theory of the firm," *Strategic Management Journal,* 14, pp. 23–46.

Bartlett, C. A. (1986). "Building and managing the transnational: The new organizational challenge," in M. E. Porter, ed., *Competition in International Industries,* Boston: Harvard Business School Press; pp. 367–401.

Bartlett, C. A., and S. Ghoshal (1989). *Managing Across Borders: The Transnational Solution,* Boston: Harvard Business School Press.

Bartlett, C. A., and U. S. Rangan (1985). "Komatsu Ltd.," Harvard Business School Case no. 9-385-277.

Basu, S. (1977). "Investment performance of common stocks in relation to their price-earnings ratios: A test of the efficient markets hypothesis," *Journal of Finance,* June, pp. 663–682.

Baum, J. A. C., and H. J. Korn (1999). "Dynamics of dyadic competitive interaction," *Strategic Management Journal,* 20, pp. 251–278.

Baysinger, B., and R. E. Hoskisson (1990). "The composition of boards of directors and strategic control: Effects on corporate strategy," *Academy of Management Review,* 15, pp. 72–87.

Baysinger, B. D., and H. N. Butler (1985). "The role of corporate law in the theory of the firm," *Journal of Law & Economics,* 28(1), pp. 179–191.

Beatty, R., and R. Ritter (1986). "Investment banking, reputation, and the underpricing of initial public offerings," *Journal of Financial Economics,* 15, pp. 213–232.

Becker, G. S. (1964). *Human Capital,* New York: Columbia University Press.

Becker, G. S. (1993). *Human Capital: A Theoretical and Empirical Analysis, with Special Reference to Education,* Chicago: University of Chicago Press.

Beckett, P. (2000). "Antitrust suit targeting MasterCard and Visa puts the pair at odds," *Wall Street Journal,* June 12, pp. B1+.

Benedict, R. (1946). *The Chrysanthemum and the Sword,* New York: New American Library.

Berger, P., and E. Ofek (1995). "Diversification effect on firm value," *Journal of Financial Economics,* 37, pp. 36–65.

Bergh, D. (1995). "Size and relatedness of units sold: An agency theory and resource-based perspective," *Strategic Management Journal,* 16, pp. 221–239.

Berman, P., and A. Alger (1994). "Reclaiming the patrimony," *Forbes.* March 14, p. 50.

Bernheim, R. D., and M. D. Whinston (1990). "Multimarket contact and collusive behavior," *Rand Journal of Economics,* 12, pp. 605–617.

Berry, C. H. (1975). *Corporate Growth and Diversification,* Princeton, NJ: Princeton University Press.

Berstein, A. (1990). "The baseball owners get beaned," *Business Week,* October 15, p. 122.

Bertrand, J. (1883). "Theorie mathematique de la richesse sociale," *Journal des Savants,* pp. 499–508.

Besanko, D., D. Dranove, and M. Shanley (1996). *The Economics of Strategy,* New York: John Wiley & Sons.

Besanko, D., D. Dranove, and M. Shanley (2001) "Exploiting a cost advantage and coping with a cost disadvantage," *Management Science,* 47(2), pp. 221–236.

Bethel, J., and J. Liebeskind (1993). "The effects of ownership structure on corporate restructuring," *Strategic Management Journal,* 14, pp. 15–31.

Bethel, J. E. (1990). "The capital allocation process and managerial mobility: A theoretical and empirical investigation," unpublished doctoral dissertation, University of California at Los Angeles.

Bettis, R. A. (1981). "Performance differences in related and unrelated diversified firms," *Strategic Management Journal,* 2, pp. 379–393.

Bettis, R. A. (1983). "Modern financial theory, corporate strategy and public policy: Three conundrums," *Academy of Management Review,* 8(3), pp. 406–415.

Bettis, R. A., and W. K. Hall (1982). "Diversification strategy, accounting determined risk, and accounting determined return," *Academy of Management Journal,* 25, pp. 254–264.

Bettis, R. A., and V. Mahajan (1985). "Risk/return performance of diversified firms," *Management Science,* 31, pp. 785–799.

Birnbaum, J. H., and M. Waldholz (1993). "Harsh medicine: Attack on drug prices opens Clinton's fight for healthcare plan," *Wall Street Journal,* February 16, p. A1.

Bittlingmayer, G. (1982). "Decreasing average cost and competition: A new look at the Addyston Pipe case," *Journal of Law and Economics,* 25, pp. 201–229.

Black, R., and M. Scholes (1973). "The pricing of options and corporate liabilities," *Journal of Political Economy,* 81, pp. 637–658.

Blackman, A. (1990). "Moscow's Big Mac attack," *Time,* February 5, p. 51.

Blackwell, R. D. (1998). "Service Corporation International," presented to The Cullman Symposium, October, Columbus, OH.

Bloch, F. (1995). "Endogenous structures of association in oligopolies," *Rand Journal of Economics,* 26, pp. 537–556.

Blois, K. J. (1999). "Trust in business to business relationships: An evaluation of its status," *Journal of Management Studies,* 36(2), pp. 197–215.

Blume, M. E. (1975). "Betas and their regression tendencies," *Journal of Finance,* 30, pp. 785–795.

Bond, R. S., and D. F. Lean (1977). *Sales, Promotion, and Product Differentiation in Two Prescription Drug Markets,* Washington, DC: U.S. Federal Trade Commission.

Boston Consulting Group (1970). *Perspectives on Experience,* Boston: BCG.

Bounds, W., and B. Davis (1995). "U.S. to launch new case against Japan over Kodak," *Wall Street Journal,* June 30, p. A3.

Bowen, R. M., E. W. Noreen, and J. M. Lacey (1981). "Determinants of the corporate decision to capitalize interest," *Journal of Accounting & Economics,* 3(2), pp. 151–179.

Bower, J. (1996). "WPP—Integrating icons," Harvard Business School Case no. 9-396-249.

Bowman, E., and D. Hurry (1993). "Strategy through the options lens," *Academy of Management Review,* 18(4), pp. 760–782.

Boyd, B. (1990). "Corporate linkages and organizational environment: A test of the resource dependence model," *Strategic Management Journal,* 11, pp. 419–430.

Boyd, B. K. (1995). "CEO duality and firm performance: A contingency model," *Strategic Management Journal,* 16, pp. 301–312.

Boyle, S. E. (1968). "Estimate of the number and size distribution of domestic joint subsidiaries," *Antitrust Law and Economics Review,* 1, pp. 81–92.

Bradley, M., and L. Wakeman (1983). "The wealth effects of targeted share repurchases," *Journal of Financial Economics,* 11, pp. 301–328.

Bradley, S. P., and S. Cavanaugh (1994). "Crown Cork and Seal in 1989," Harvard Business School Case no. 9-793-035.

Brandenburger, A., and B. Nalebuff (1998). *Co-opetition,* New York: Doubleday.

Brealey, R., and S. Myers (1988), *Principles of Corporate Finance,* 3rd ed., New York: McGraw-Hill.

Breen, B. (2003). "What's selling in America?" *Fast Company,* January, pp. 80+.

Brennan, M. (1979). "The pricing of contingent claims in discrete time models," *Journal of Finance,* 34, pp. 53–68.

Bresnahan, T. F. (1985). "Post-entry competition in the plain paper copier market," *American Economic Review,* 85, pp. 15–19.

Bresser, R. K. (1988). "Cooperative strategy," *Strategic Management Journal,* 9, pp. 475–492.

Brewer, H. L. (1981). "Investor benefits from corporate international diversification," *Journal of Financial and Quantitative Analysis,* 16, March, pp. 113–126.

Brickley, J., C. Smith, and J. Zimmerman (1996). *Organizational Architecture and Managerial Economics Approach,* Homewood, IL: Irwin.

Bright, A. A. (1949). *The Electric Lamp Industry,* New York: Macmillan.

Bromiley, P., M. Govekar, and A. Marcus (1988). "On using event-study methodology in strategic management research," *Technovation,* 8, pp. 25–42.

Brown, E., and L. Costa. (1999), "America's most admired companies," *Fortune,* March 1, pp. 68+.

Brown, S., and K. Eisenhardt (1998). *Competing on the Edge,* Cambridge, MA: Harvard Business School Press.

Brown, S. J., and J. B. Warner (1980). "Measuring security price performance," *Journal of Financial Economics,* 8, pp. 205–258.

Brown, S. J., and J. B. Warner (1985). "Using daily stock returns: The case of event studies," *Journal of Financial Economics,* 14(1), pp. 3–31.

Brush, T. H., and K. W. Artz (1999). "Toward a contingent resource-based theory," *Strategic Management Journal,* 20, pp. 223–250.

Brush, T. H., P. Bromiley, and M. Hendrickx (1999). "The relative influence of industry and corporation on business segment performance," *Strategic Management Journal,* 20, pp. 519–547.

Burgers, W. P., C. W. L. Hill, and W. C. Kim (1993). "A theory of global strategic alliances: The case of the global auto industry," *Strategic Management Journal,* 14, pp. 419–432.

Burgess, J. (1993). "Apple bets on Newton, new direction," *Washington Post,* July 30, p. A1.

Burgelman, R. A. (1983b). "A process model of internal corporate venturing in the diversified major firm," *Administrative Science Quarterly,* 28(2), pp. 223–244.

Burns, G. (1997). "What price the Snapple debacle?" *Business Week,* April 14, p. 42.

Burrows, P. (1995). "Now, TI means 'taking initiative,'" *Business Week,* May 15, pp. 120–121.

Burton, R., S. Kilman, and R. Gibson (1995). "Investigators suspect a global conspiracy in Archer-Daniels case," *Wall Street Journal,* July 28, pp. A1+.

Busenitz, L., and J. Barney, (1997). "Differences between entrepreneurs and managers in large organizations: Biases and heuristics in strategic decision-making," *Journal of Business Venturing,* 12(1) pp. 9–30.

Butler, J. K., Jr. (1983). "Reciprocity of trust between professionals and their secretaries," *Psychological Reports,* 53, pp. 411–416.

Butler, J. K., Jr., and R. S. Cantrell (1984). "A behavioral decision theory approach to modeling dyadic trust in superiors and subordinates," *Psychological Reports* 55, pp. 19–28.

Buzzell, R. D., B. T. Gale, and R. Sultan (1975). "Market share: A key to profitability," *Harvard Business Review,* 53(1), January/February, pp. 97–106.

Cameron, K. (1986). "Effectiveness as paradox: Consensus and conflict in conceptions of organizational effectiveness," *Management Science,* 32, pp. 539–553.

Caminiti, S. (1992). "The payoff from a good reputation," *Fortune,* February 10, pp. 74–77.

Carey, S. (1993), "USAir declares war over fares in California," *Wall Street Journal,* June 9, p. B1.

Carlton, D. W., G. Bamberger, and R. Epstein (1995). "Antitrust and higher education: Was there a conspiracy to restrict financial aid?" *Rand Journal of Economics,* 26, pp. 131–147.

Carnevale, M. L. (1993). "HDTV bidders agree to merge their systems," *Wall Street Journal,* May 24, pp. B1+.

Carnevale, M. L. (1993). "Ring in the new: Telephone service seems on the brink of huge innovations," *Wall Street Journal,* February 10, p. A1.

Carney, M. (1998). "The competitiveness of networked production: The role of trust and asset specificity," *Journal of Management Studies,* 35(4), pp. 457–479.

Carpenter, M., G. Sanders, and H. Gregerson (2001). "Building human capital with organizational context: The impact of international assignment experience on multinational firm performance and CEO pay," *Academy of Management Journal,* 44(3), pp. 493–511.

Carroll, G. A., L. S. Bigelow, M.-D. L. Seidel, and L. B. Tsai (1996). "The fates of *de novo* and *de alio* producers in the American automobile industry 1885–1981," *Strategic Management Journal,* 17(7) (Special Summer Issue), pp. 117–137.

Carroll, P. (1993). *Big Blues: The Unmaking of IBM,* New York: Crown.

Cartwright, S., and C. Cooper (1993). "The role of culture compatibility in successful organizational marriage," *Academy of Management Executive,* 7(2), pp. 57–70.

Carvell, T. (1998). "How Sony created a monster," *Fortune,* June 8, pp. 162+.

Casey, J. (1976). "High fructose corn syrup," *Research Management,* 19, pp. 27–32.

Caves, R. E. (1971). "International corporations: The industrial economics of foreign investment," *Economica,* 38, February, pp. 1–28.

Caves, R. E., and R. M. Bradburd (1988). "The empirical determinants of vertical integration," *Journal of Economic Behavior and Organization,* 9, pp. 265–279.

Caves, R. E., and M. E. Porter (1977). "From entry barriers to mobility barriers: Conjectural decisions and contrived deterrence to new competition," *Quarterly Journal of Economics,* 91, pp. 241–262.

Caves, R. E., and O. Williamson (1985). "What is product differentiation, really?" *Journal of Industrial Economics,* 34, pp. 113–132.

Celestino, M. (1999). "Manufacturing in Mexico," *World Trade,* 12, July, pp. 36–42.

Chamberlin, E. H. (1933). *The Theory of Monopolistic Competition,* Cambridge, MA: Harvard University Press.

Chandler, A. D. (1962). *Strategy and Structure: Chapters in the History of the Industrial Enterprise,* Cambridge, MA: MIT Press.

Chang, Y., and H. Thomas (1989). "The impact of diversification strategy on risk-return performance," *Strategic Management Journal,* 10, pp. 271–284.

Chappell, H. W., and D. C. Cheng (1984). "Firms' acquisition decisions and Tobin's *q* ratio," *Journal of Economics & Business,* 36(1), pp. 29–42.

Charan, R., and G. Colvin (1999). "Why CEOs fail," *Fortune,* June 21, pp. 69+.

Chartier, John (2002). "Burger battles," CNN/Money, http://money.cnn.com, December 11.

Chatterjee, S., M. Lubatkin, D. Schweiger, and Y. Weber (1992). "Cultural differences and shareholder value in related mergers: Linking equity and human capital," *Strategic Management Journal,* 13, pp. 319–334.

Chatterjee, S., and B. Wernerfelt (1991). "The link between resources and type at diversification: Theory and evidence," *Strategic Management Journal,* 12, pp. 33–48.

Chen, M. J. (1996). "Competitor analysis and interfirm rivalry: Toward a theoretical integration," *Academy of Management Review,* 21(1), pp. 100–134.

Chen, M. J., and K. Stucker (1997). "Multinational management and multimarket rivalry: Toward a theoretical development of global competition," *Academy of Management Proceedings 1997,* pp. 2–6.

Chiles, T. H., and J. F. McMackin (1996). "Integrating variable risk preferences, trust, and transaction cost economics," *Academy of Management Review,* 21(1), pp. 73–99.

Choi, F. D. S., and R. M. Levich (1990). *The Capital Market Effects of International Accounting Diversity,* Homewood, IL: Dow-Jones Irwin.

Christensen, C. R., K. R. Andrews, J. L. Bower, G. Hamermesh, and M. E. Porter (1980). *Business Policy: Text and Cases,* Homewood, IL: Irwin.

Christensen, C. R., N. A. Berg, and M. S. Salter (1980). *Policy Formulation and Administration: A Casebook of Senior Management Problems in Business,* 8th ed., Homewood, IL: Irwin, p. 163.

Christensen, H. K., and C. A. Montgomery (1981). "Corporate economic performance: Diversification strategy versus market structure," *Strategic Management Journal,* 2, pp. 327–343.

Christie, W. G., and P. Schultz (1994). "Why do NASDAQ market makers avoid odd-eighth quotes?" *Journal of Finance,* 49, pp. 1813–1840.

Chung, K. H., and S. W. Pruitt (1994). "A simple approximation of Tobin's q," *Financial Management,* 23(3), pp. 70–74.

Coase, R. H. (1937). "The nature of the firm," *Economica,* 4, pp. 386–405.

Cochran, P. L., R. A. Wood, and T. B. Jones (1985). "The composition of board of directors and incidence of golden parachutes," *Academy of Management Journal,* 28, pp. 664–671.

Coff, R. (1999). "When competitive advantage doesn't lead to performance: The resource-based theory and stakeholder bargaining power," *Organizational Science,* 10(2), pp. 119–132.

Cole, J. (1992). "Rising turbulence: Boeing's dominance of aircraft industry is beginning to erode," *Wall Street Journal,* July 10, p. A1.

Collins, J. (2003). "Bigger, better, faster," *Fast Company,* June, pp. 74+.

Collis, D. J. (1991). "A resource-based analysis of international competition: The case of the bearing industry," *Strategic Management Journal,* 12 (Summer, Special Issue), pp. 49–68.

Collis, D. J. (1994). "Newell Company: Acquisition Strategy," Harvard Business School Case no. 9-794-0610.

Collis, D. (1995). "The Walt Disney Company (A)," Harvard Business School Case no. 1-388-147.

Collis, D. J., and C. A. Montgomery (1997). *Corporate Strategy: Resources and the Scope of the Firm,* Chicago: Irwin.

Colvin, G. (1999). "How to be a great e-CEO," *Fortune,* May 24, pp. 104+.

Comment, R., and G. Jarrell (1995). "Corporate focus and stock returns," *Journal of Financial Economics,* 37, pp. 67–87.

Conner, K. (1995). "Obtaining strategic advantage from being imitated: When can encouraging 'clones' pay?" *Management Science,* 41, pp. 209–225.

Conner, K. R. (1991). "A historical comparison of resource based theory and five schools of thought within industrial organization economics: Do we have a new theory of the firm?" *Journal of Management,* 17(1), pp. 121–154.

Conner, K. R., and R. P. Rumelt (1991). "Software piracy: An analysis of protection strategies," *Management Science,* 37(2), pp. 125–139.

Cool, K. O., and I. Dierickx (1993). "Rivalry, strategic groups and firm profitability," *Strategic Management Journal,* 14, pp. 47–59.

Cool, K. O., and D. Schendel (1987). "Strategic group formation and performance: The case of the U. S. pharmaceutical industry, 1963–1982," *Management Science,* 33, pp. 1102–1124.

Copeland, T., T. Koller, and J. Murrin (1995). *Valuation: Measuring and Managing the Value of Companies,* 2nd ed., New York: John Wiley & Sons.

Copeland, T. E., and J. F. Westen (1983). *Financial Theory and Corporate Policy,* Reading, MA: Addison-Wesley.

Corcoran, C. (1993). "At last, users can inspect IBM's PowerPC systems," *Infoworld,* 15, November 15, pp. 1, 6.

Coughlan, A. T., and R. M. Schmidt (1985). "Executive compensation, managerial turnover, and firm performance," *Journal of Accounting and Economics,* 7, pp. 43–66.

Cournot, A. (1897). *Recherches sur les principes mathematiques de la theorie des richesses.* English edition: Bacon, N., transl. (1938).

Researches into the Mathematical Principles of the Theory of Wealth, New York: Macmillan.

Cox, J., S. Ross, and M. Rubinstein (1979). "Option pricing: A simplified approach," *Journal of Financial Economics,* 7, pp. 229–263.

Cox, M. (1993). "Electronic campus: Technology threatens to shatter the world of college textbooks," *Wall Street Journal,* June 1, p. A1.

Coyne, K. P., S. J. D. Hall, and P. G. Clifford (1997). "Is your core competence a mirage?" *McKinsey Quarterly,* Issue 1, pp. 40–54.

Crockett, R. (2000). "A Baby Bell's growth formula," *Business Week,* 3671, March 6, pp. 50–52; and Crockett, R. (1999). "The last monopolist," *Business Week,* 3624, April 12, p. 76.

Curran, J. (1997). "GE Capital: Jack Welch's secret weapon," *Fortune,* November 10, pp. 116+.

Cyert, R., and J. G. March (1963). *A Behavioral Theory of the Firm,* Upper Saddle River, NJ: Prentice Hall.

Dambolona, I. G., and S. J. Khoury (1980). "Ratio stability and corporate failure," *Journal of Finance,* 35(4), pp. 1017–1026.

Dann, L. Y. (1981). "Common stock repurchases: An analysis of returns to bondholders and stockholders," *Journal of Financial Economics,* 9, pp. 113–138.

Dann, L. Y., and H. DeAngelo (1983). "Standstill agreements, privately negotiated stock repurchases, and the market for corporate control," *Journal of Financial Economics,* 11, pp. 275–300.

Darlin, D. (1991). "Coke and Nestlé launch first coffee drink," *Wall Street Journal,* October 1, p. B1+.

D'Aveni, R. (1994). *Hypercompetition: Managing the Dynamics of Strategic Maneuvering,* New York: Free Press.

D'Aveni, R. (1995). "Coping with hypercompetition: Utilizing the new 7S's framework," *Academy of Management Executive,* 9(3), pp. 45–60.

Davids, M. (1997). "More attention to Kmart shoppers," *The Journal of Business Strategy,* 18, p. 36.

Davidson, J. H. (1976). "Why most new consumer brands fail," *Harvard Business Review,* 54, March/April, pp. 117–122.

Davis, B. (1995). "U.S. expects goals in pact with Japan to be met even without overt backing," *Wall Street Journal,* June 30, p. A3.

Davis, P., R. Robinson, J. Pearce, and S. Park (1992). "Business unit relatedness and performance: A look at the pulp and paper industry," *Strategic Management Journal,* 13, pp. 349–361.

Day, G. S. (1995). "Advantageous alliances," *Journal of Academy of Marketing Science,* 23(4), pp. 297–300.

de Forest, M. E. (1994). "Thinking of a plant in Mexico?" *Academy of Management Executive,* 8(1), pp. 33–40.

de Lisser, E. (1993). "Catering to cooking-phobic customers, supermarkets stress carry-out, add cares," *Wall Street Journal,* April 5, p. B1.

Demetrakakes, P. (1994). "Household-chemical makers concentrate on downsizing," *Packaging,* 39(1), p. 41.

Demsetz, H. (1973). "Industry structure, market rivalry, and public policy," *Journal of Law and Economics,* 16, pp. 1–9.

Denis, D. J., D. K. Denis, and A. Sarin (1997). "Managerial incentives and corporate diversification strategies," *Journal of Applied Corporate Finance,* 10(2), pp. 72–80.

Deogun, N. (2000). "Europe catches merger fever as global volume sets record," *Wall Street Journal,* January 3, p. R8.

DePalma, A. (1994). "Trade pact is spurring Mexican deals in the U.S.," *New York Times,* March 17, pp. C1, C3.

Deutsch, C. H. (1991). "How is it done? For a small fee . . . ," *New York Times,* October 27, p. 25.

DeWitt, W. (1997). "Crown Cork & Seal/Carnaud Metalbox," Harvard Business School Case no. 9-296-019.

Dial, J., and K. J. Murphy (1995). "Incentive, downsizing, and value creation at General Dynamics," *Journal of Financial Economics,* 37, pp. 261–314.

Dichtl, E., and H. G. Koeglmayr (1986). "Country risk ratings," *Management International Review,* 26(4), pp. 2–10.

Dierickx, I., and K. Cool (1989). "Asset stock accumulation and sustainability of competitive advantage," *Management Science, 35,* pp. 1504–1511.

Discount Merchandiser (1999). "It's the IKEA way or no way," 39(1), January, pp. 51–53.

Dixit, A. K. (1982). "Recent developments in oligopoly theory," *Papers and Proceedings of the American Economic Association,* 94th annual meeting, 72(2), pp. 12–17.

Dixit, A. K., and R. S. Pindyck (1998). *Investment Under Uncertainty,* Princeton, NJ: Princeton University Press.

Dobrzynski, J. (1991). "How America can get the 'patient' capital it needs," *Business Week,* October 21, p. 112.

Dodd, P. (1980). "Merger proposals, managerial discretion and stockholder wealth," *Journal of Financial Economics,* 8, pp. 105–138.

Doherty, J. (1997). "A sparkling strategy?" *Barron's,* 77, September 15, p. 12.

Donaldson, L. (1990). "The ethereal hand: Organizational economics and management theory," *Academy of Management Review,* 15, pp. 369–381.

Donoho, R. (1995). "GE off hook in price-fix case," *Sales and Marketing Management,* 147, p. 11.

Dubofsky, P., and P. R. Varadarajan (1987). "Diversification and measures of performance: Additional empirical evidence," *Academy of Management Journal,* 30(3), pp. 597–608.

Duffy, M. (1989). "ZBB, MBO, PPB, and their effectiveness within the planning/marketing process," *Strategic Management Journal,* 12, pp. 155–160.

Duke, J., and H. Hunt (1990). "An empirical examination of debt covenant restrictions and accounting-related debt proxies," *Journal of Accounting & Economics,* 12, pp. 45–63.

Dumaine, B. (1992). "Is big still good?" *Fortune,* April 20, pp. 50–60.

Duncan, L. (1982). "Impacts of new entry and horizontal joint ventures on industrial rates of return," *Review of Economics and Statistics,* 64, pp. 120–125.

Dunning, J. H. (1973). "The determinants of production," *Oxford Economic Papers,* 25, November, pp. 289–336.

Dyer, J., and W. Ouchi (1993). "Japanese style partnerships: Giving companies a competitive edge," *Sloan Management Review,* 31, pp. 51–63.

Dyer, J. H., and H. Singh (1998). "The relational view: Cooperative strategy and sources of interorganizational competitive advantage," *Academy of Management Review,* 23(4), pp. 660–679.

Eaton, J., and M. Engers (1987). "International price competition," Mimeo, University of Virginia.

Eccles, R. (1985). *The Transfer Pricing Problem: A Theory for Practice,* Lexington, MA: Lexington Books.

Edgeworth, F. (1897). "La Teoria Pura del Monopolio," *Giornale degli Economisti,* 40, pp. 13–31. English edition: "The pure theory of monopoly," in Edgeworth, F.,ed., *Papers Relating to Political Economy,* London: Macmillan, 1925.

Edwards, C. D. (1955). "Conglomerate bigness as a source of power," *Business Concentration and Price Policy, NBER Conference Report,* Princeton, NJ: Princeton University Press.

Edwards, C. D. (1964). *Cartelization in Western Europe,* Washington, DC: U.S. Department of State, Government Printing Office.

Eger, C. E. (1983). "An empirical test of the redistribution effect in pure exchange merger," *Journal of Financial and Quantitative Analysis,* 18, pp. 547–572.

Eichenseher, J., and D. Shields (1985). "Reputation and corporate strategy: A review of recent theory and applications," *Strategic Management Journal,* 9, pp. 443–454.

Eckbo, B. E. (1983). "Horizontal mergers, collusion, and stockholder wealth," *Journal of Financial Economics,* 11, pp. 241–273.

El Mallakh, R. (1982). *OPEC: Twenty Years and Beyond,* Boulder, CO: Westview Press.

Engardio, P. (1993). "Motorola in China: A great leap forward," *Business Week,* May 17, pp. 58–59.

Ennis, P. (1991). "Mitsubishi group wary of deeper ties to Chrysler," *Tokyo Business Today,* 59, July, p. 10.

Enright, M. J., and U. Bumbacher (1995). "Swiss watch industry," Harvard Business School Case no. 9792-046.

Ernst, D., and J. Bleeke (1993). *Collaborating to Compete: Using Strategic Alliances and Acquisition in the Global Marketplace,* New York: John Wiley & Sons.

Errunza, V., and L. W. Senbet (1981). "The effects of international operations on the market value of the firm: Theory and evidence," *Journal of Finance,* 36, pp. 401–418.

Errunza, V., and L. W. Senbet (1984). "International corporate diversification, market valuation and size-adjusted evidence," *Journal of Finance,* 39, pp. 727–745.

Fama, E. F. (1970). "Efficient capital markets: A review of theory and empirical work," *Journal of Finance,* 25, pp. 383–417.

Fama, E. F., L. Fisher, M. C. Jensen, and R. Roll (1969). "The adjustment of stock prices to new information," *International Economic Review,* 10(1), pp. 1–21.

Fama, E. G., and M. C. Jensen (1983). "Separation of ownership and control," *Journal of Law and Economics,* 26, pp. 314–315.

Farjoun, M. (1998). "The independent and joint effects of the skill and physical bases of relatedness in diversification," *Strategic Management Journal,* 19, pp. 611–630.

Farnham, A. (1997). "How safe are your secrets?" *Fortune,* September 8, pp. 114+.

Fatsis, S. (1995). "Major Leagues keep minors at a distance,' *Wall Street Journal,* November 8, pp. B1+.

Fayerweather, J. (1969). *International Business Management: Conceptual Framework,* New York: McGraw-Hill.

Fayerweather, J. (1982). *International Business Strategy and Administration,* Cambridge, MA: Ballinger.

Fayerweather, J., and A. Kapoor (1975). *Strategy and Negotiation for the International Company,* Cambridge, MA: Ballinger.

Finkelstein, S., and R. D'Aveni (1994). "CEO duality as a double-edged sword: How boards of directors balance entrenchment avoidance and unity of command," *Academy of Management Journal,* 37, pp. 1079–1108.

Finkelstein, S. and D. C. Hambrick (1989). "Chief executive compensation: A study of the intersection of markets and political processes," *Strategic Management Journal,* 10, pp. 121–134.

Finkelstein, S., and D. C. Hambrick (1996). *Strategic Leadership: Top Executives and Their Effects on Organizations,* Minneapolis/St. Paul: West.

Finn, E. A. (1987). "General Eclectic," *Forbes,* March 23, pp. 74–80.

Firth, M. (1980). "Takeovers, shareholder returns, and the theory of the firm," *Quarterly Journal of Economics,* 94, pp. 235–260.

Fisher, F. M. (1979). "Diagnosing monopoly," *Quarterly Review of Economics & Business,* 19, pp. 7–33.

Fisher, F. M., and J. J. McGowan (1983). "On the misuse of accounting rates of return to infer monopoly profits," *American Economic Review,* 73, pp. 82–97.

Folta, T., and M. Leiblein, (1994). "Technology acquisition and the choice of governance by established firms: Insights from option theory in a multinomial logit model," *Academy of Management Proceedings '94,* 27–31.

Folta, T. B. (1998). "Governance and uncertainty: The tradeoff between administrative control and commitment," *Strategic Management Journal,* 19, pp. 1007–1028.

Fortune (1995). "Can EVA deliver profits to the post office?" *Fortune,* July 10, p. 22.

Fortune (1995). "So, Mr. Bossidy, we know you can cut. Now show us how to grow," *Fortune,* 3, August 21, pp. 70–80.

Fox, J. (1997). "The next best thing to free money," *Fortune,* July 7, pp. 52+.

Freedman, A. M., and B. Burrough (1988). "American brands rejects 'Pac-Man' ploy," *Wall Street Journal,* September, p. A3.

Freeland, R. F. (1966). "The myth of the M-form? Governance, consent, and organizational change," *American Journal of Sociology,* 102(2), pp. 483–626.

Freeman, A., and R. Hudson (1980). "DuPont and Phillips plan joint venture to make, market laser disc products," *Wall Street Journal,* December 22, p. 10.

Friedland, J., and B. Ortega (1995). "U.S. copper producers are deeply worried as Chile surges ahead," *Wall Street Journal,* July 25, pp. A1+.

Friedman, W., and G. Kalmanoff (1961). *Joint International Business Ventures,* New York: Columbia University Press.

Froot, K. A., D. S. Scharfstein, and J. C. Stein (1993). "Risk management: Coordinating corporate investment and financial policies," *Journal of Finance,* 8, 1629–1658.

Fuchsberg, G. (1992). "Decentralized management can have its drawbacks," *Wall Street Journal,* December 9, p. B1.

Fudenberg, D., and J. Tirole (1984). "The fat cat effect, the puppy dog ploy, and the lean and hungry look," *American Economic Review,* 74, pp. 361–366.

Fudenberg, D., and J. Tirole (1991). *Game Theory,* Cambridge, MA: MIT Press.

Fuerst, B., F. Mata, and J. Barney (1996). "Information technology and sustained competitive advantage: Reason-based analysis," *MIS Quarterly,* 19, pp. 487–505.

Fusfeld, D. (1958). "Joint subsidiaries in the iron and steel industry," *American Economic Review,* 48, pp. 578–587.

Gain, S. (1993). "Korea is overthrown as sneaker champ," *Wall Street Journal,* October 7, p. A14.

Galai, D., and R. W. Masulis (1976). "The option pricing model and the risk factor of stock," *Journal of Financial Economics,* 3, pp. 53–82.

Galbraith, J. R., and R. K. Kazanjian (1986). "Organizing to implement strategies of diversity and globalization: The role of matrix designs," *Human Resource Management,* 25(1), pp. 37–54.

Garvin, D., and J. West (1995). "Time Life Inc. (A)," Harvard Business School Case no. 9-395-012.

Gaynor, M., and P. Gertler (1995). "Moral hazard and risk spreading in partnerships," *Rand Journal of Economics,* 26(4), pp. 591–613.

Geringer, J. M., S. Tallman, and D. M. Olsen (2000). "Product and international diversification among Japanese multinational firms," *Strategic Management Journal,* 21, pp. 51–80.

Ghemawat, P. (1984). "Capacity expansion in the titanium dioxide industry," *Journal of Industrial Economics,* 33(2), pp. 145–163.

Ghemawat, P. (1984). "Du Pont in titanium dioxide (A)," Harvard Business School Case no. 9-385-140.

Ghemawat, P. (1986). "Wal-Mart stores' discount operations," Harvard Business School Case no. 9-387-018.

Ghemawat, P. (1993). "Sears, Roebuck and Company: The Merchandise group," Harvard Business School Case no. 9-794-039.

Ghemawat, P., and A. McGahan (1995). "The U.S. airline industry in 1995," Harvard Business School Case no. 9-795-113.

Ghemawat, P., and H. J. Stander III (1992). "Nucor at a crossroads," Harvard Business School Case no. 9-793-039.

Ghoshal, S. (1987). "Global strategy: An organizing framework," *Strategic Management Journal,* 8, p. 436.

Gibson, R. (1991). "McDonald's insiders increase their sales of company's stock," *Wall Street Journal,* June 14, p. A1.

Gibson, R. (1995). "Food: At McDonald's, new recipes for buns, eggs," *Wall Street Journal,* June 13, p. B1.

Gibson, R. (1999). "'Star Wars' tie-in is more a menace than a hit at Tricon," *Wall Street Journal,* July 21, p. A5.

Gibson, R., J. S. Lublin, and M. Allen (1988). "Proposal to stave off bid by Grand Met criticized; Defense plan is upheld," *Wall Street Journal,* November 5, p. A3.

Gilbert, R. J., and D. M. Newbery (1982). "Preemptive patenting and the persistence of monopoly," *American Economic Review,* 72(3), pp. 514–526.

Gimeno, J. (1994). "Multipoint competition, market rivalry and firm performance: A test of the mutual forbearance hypothesis in the United States airline industry, 1984–1988," unpublished doctoral dissertation, Purdue University.

Gimeno, J. (1999). "Reciprocal threats in multimarket rivalry: Staking our 'spheres of influence' in the U.S. airline industry," *Strategic Management Journal,* 20, pp. 101–128.

Gimeno, J., and C. Y. Woo (1996). "Hypercompetition in a multimarket environment: The role of strategic similarity and multimarket contact in competitive de-escalation," *Organization Science,* 7(3), pp. 322–341.

Gimeno, J., and C. Y. Woo (1999). "Multimarket contact, economies of scope, and firm performance," *Academy of Management Journal,* 43(3), pp. 239–259.

Glueck, W. F. (1980). *Business Policy and Strategic Management,* McGraw-Hill: New York.

Glynn, M. A. (1993). "Strategic planning in Nigeria versus U.S.: A case of anticipating the (next) coup," *Academy of Management Executive* 7(3), pp. 82–83.

Golbe, D. L. (1981). "The effects of imminent bankruptcy on stockholder risk preferences and behavior," *Bell Journal of Economics,* 12(1), pp. 321–328.

Golden, B. (1992). "SBU strategy and performance: The moderating effects of the corporate-SBU relationship," *Strategic Management Journal,* 13, pp. 145–158.

Gomez-Mejia, L., and R. Wiseman (1997). "Reframing executive compensation: An assessment and outlook," *Journal of Management,* 23(3), pp. 291–374.

Gort, M. (1962). *Diversification and Integration in American Industry,* Princeton, NJ: Princeton University Press.

Granovetter, M. (1985). "Economic action and social structure: The problem of embeddedness," *American Journal of Sociology,* 3, pp. 481–510.

Grant, L. (1995). "Here comes Hugh," *Fortune,* August 21, pp. 43–52.

Grant, L. (1997). "Monsanto's bet: There's gold in going green," *Fortune,* April 14, p. 116.

Grant, R. M. (1987). "Multinationality and performance among British manufacturing companies," *Journal of International Business Studies,* 18 (Fall), pp. 78–89.

Grant, R. M. (1988). "On 'dominant logic' relatedness and the link between diversity and performance," *Strategic Management Journal,* 9, pp. 639–642.

Grant, R. M. (1991). *Contemporary Strategy Analysis,* Cambridge, MA: Basil Blackwell.

Grant, R. M. (1996). "Toward a knowledge-based theory of the firm," *Strategic Management Journal,* 17 (Winter, Special Issue), pp. 109–122.

Grant, R. M., and A. P. Jammine (1988). "Performance differences between the Wrigley/Rumelt strategic categories," *Strategic Management Journal,* 9, pp. 333–346.

Gray, D. (1998). "When might a distressed firm share work?" *British Journal of Industrial Relations,* 36, pp. 43–72.

Green, E. J., and R. H. Porter (1984). "Noncooperative collusion under imperfect price information," *Econometrica,* 52, pp. 87–100.

Greenhouse, S. (1991). "Playing Disney in the Parisian fields," *New York Times,* February 17, Section 3, pp. 1, 6.

Gross, N. (1995). "The technology paradox," *Business Week,* March 6, pp. 691–719.

Grossman, S., and O. Hart (1986). "The costs and benefits of ownership: A theory of vertical and lateral integration," *Journal of Political Economy,* 94, pp. 691–719.

Gulati, R. (1998). "Alliances and networks," *Strategic Management Journal,* 19, pp. 293–317.

Gulati, R. (1999). "Network location and learning," *Strategic Management Journal,* 20, pp. 397–420.

Gulati, R., and H. Singh (1998). "The architecture of cooperation: Managing coordination costs and appropriation concerns in strategic alliances," *Administrative Science Quarterly,* 43, pp. 781–814.

Gupta, A. K. (1987) "SBU strategies, corporate-SBU relations and SBU effectiveness in strategy implementation," *Academy of Management Journal,* 30(3), pp. 477–500.

Gupta, A. K., and V. Govindarajan (1986). "Resource sharing among SBUs: Strategic antecedents and administrative implications," *Academy of Management Journal,* 29, pp. 695–714.

Hackman, J. R., and G. R. Oldham (1980). *Work Redesign,* Reading, MA: Addison-Wesley.

Hagedoorn, J. (1993). "Understanding the rationale of strategic technology partnering: Interorganizational modes of cooperation and sectoral differences," *Strategic Management Journal,* 14, pp. 371–385.

Hagedoorn, J. (1996). "Trends and patterns in strategic technology partnering since the early seventies," *Review of Industrial Organization,* 11, pp. 601–616.

Hagedoorn, J., and R. Narula (1996). "Choosing organizational modes of strategic technology partnering: International and sectoral differences," *Journal of International Business Studies,* Second Quarter, pp. 265–284.

Hagedoorn, J., and B. Sadowski (1999). "The transition from strategic technology alliances to mergers and acquisitions: An exploratory study," *Journal of Management Studies,* 36(1), pp. 87–107.

Halal, W. (1994). "From hierarchy to enterprise: Internal markets are the new foundation of management," *Academy of Management Executive,* 8(4), pp. 69–83.

Hall, B. H. (1990). "The manufacturing sector master file: 1959–1987," National Bureau of Economic Research, Working Paper Series no. 3366.

Hall, G., and S. Howell (1985). "The experience curve from the economist's perspective," *Strategic Management Journal,* 6, pp. 197–212.

Hall, R. L., and C. J. Hitch (1939). "Price theory and business behavior," *Oxford Economic Papers,* 2, p. 1245.

Hambrick, D. (1987). "Top management teams: Key to strategic success." *California Management Review,* 30, pp. 88–108.

Hamel, G. (1991) "Competition for competence and inter-partner learning within strategic alliances," *Strategic Management Journal,* 12, p. 86–103.

Hamel, G., and J. Sampler (1998). "The e-corporation," *Fortune,* December 7, pp. 80+.

Hamermesh, R. G., and R. S. Rosenbloom (1989). "Crown Cork and Seal Co., Inc.," Harvard Business School Case no. 9-388-096.

Hansen, G. S., and C. W. L. Hill (1991). "Are institutional investors myopic? A time-series study of four technology-driven industries," *Strategic Management Journal,* 12, pp. 1–16.

Harrigan, K. (1986). "Matching vertical integration strategies to competitive conditions," *Strategic Management Journal,* 7, pp. 535–555.

Harrigan, K. R. (1980). *Strategies for Declining Businesses,* Lexington, MA: Lexington Books.

Harrigan, K. R. (1988). "Joint ventures and competitive strategy," *Strategic Management Journal,* 9, pp. 141–158.

Harris, L. C., and E. Ogbonna (1999). "Developing a market oriented culture: A critical evaluation," *Journal of Management Studies,* 36(2), pp. 177–196.

Haspeslagh, P., and Jemison, D. (1991). *Managing Acquisitions: Creating Value Through Corporate Renewal,* New York: Free Press.

Hatfield, D. D., J. P. Liebeskind, and T. C. Opler (1996). "The effects of corporate restructuring on aggregate industry specialization," *Strategic Management Journal,* 17, pp. 55–72.

Hatten, K. J., and M. L. Hatten (1988). *Effective Strategic Management: Analysis and Action,* Englewood Cliffs, NJ: Prentice Hall.

Hay, G. A., and D. Kelly (1974). "An empirical survey of price fixing conspiracies," *Journal of Law and Economics,* 17, pp. 13–38.

Hayes, R. H., and S. G. Wheelwright (1979). "The dynamics of process-product life cycles," *Harvard Business Review,* March/April, p. 127.

Healy, P. M. (1985). "The effect of bonus schemes on accounting decisions," *Journal of Accounting & Economics,* 7, pp. 85–107.

Hedberg, B. L. T. (1981). "How organizations learn and unlearn," in P. C. Nystrom and W. H. Starbuck, eds., *Handbook of Organizational Design,* London: Oxford University Press.

Helyar, J., and B. Burrough (1988). "Buy-out bluff: How underdog KKR won RJR Nabisco without highest bid," *Wall Street Journal,* December 2, p. A1.

Henderson, B. (1974). *The Experience Curve Reviewed III—How Does It Work?* Boston: Boston Consulting Group.

Henderson, R., and I. Cockburn (1994). "Measuring competence? Exploring firm effects in pharmaceutical research," *Strategic Management Journal,* 15, pp. 63–84.

Hennart, J. F. (1988). "A transaction cost theory of equity joint ventures," *Strategic Management Journal,* 9, pp. 361–374.

Heskett, J. L., and R. H. Hallowell (1993). "Southwest Airlines: 1993 (A)," Harvard Business School Case no. 9-695-023.

Hesterly, W. S. (1989). "Top management succession as a determinant of firm performance and de-escalation: An agency problem," unpublished doctoral dissertation, University of California, Los Angeles.

Hill, C., and G. Hansen (1991). "A longitudinal study of the cause and consequences of changes in diversification in the U.S. pharmaceutical industry, 1977–1986," *Strategic Management Journal,* 12, pp. 187–199.

Hill, C. W. L. (1988). "Differentiation versus low cost or differentiation and low cost: A contingency framework," *Academy of Management Review,* 13(3), pp. 401–412.

Hill, C. W. L., and G. R. Jones (1992). *Strategic Management Theory: An Integrated Approach,* Boston: Houghton Mifflin.

Hirshleifer, J. (1980). *Price Theory and Applications,* Upper Saddle, NJ: Prentice Hall, p. 339.

Hitt, M. A., and R. D. Ireland (1986). "Relationships among corporate-level distinct competencies, diversification strategy, corporate strategy and performance," *Journal of Management Studies,* 23, pp. 401–416.

Hitt, M. A., R. D. Ireland, and R. E. Hoskisson (1997). *Strategic Management: Competitiveness and Globalization,* Cincinnati, OH: Southwestern.

"Hitting the mail on the head," *The Economist,* April 30, 1994, pp. 69–70.

Hobbes, T. (1952). *Leviathan,* Oxford, England: Oxford University Press.

Holm, D. B., K. Eriksson, and J. Johanson (1999). "Creating value through mutual commitment to business network relationships," *Strategic Management Journal,* 20, pp. 467–486.

Holmstrom, B. (1979). "Moral hazard and observability," *Bell Journal of Economics,* 10(1), pp. 74–91.

Hoskisson, R., and M. Hitt (1988). "Strategic control systems and relative R&D investment in large multi-product firms," *Strategic Management Journal,* 9, pp. 605–621.

Hoskisson, R. E., M. A. Hitt, R. A. Johnson and D. D. Moesel (1993). "Construct validity of an objective (entropy) categorical measure of diversification strategy," *Strategic Management Journal,* 14, pp. 215–235.

Hoskisson, R. E., and T. A. Turk (1990). "Corporate restructuring: Governance and control limits of the internal capital market," *Academy of Management Review,* 15, pp. 459–477.

Hotelling, H. (1929). "Stability in competition," *Economic Journal,* 39, pp. 41–57.

Houston, J., and C. James (1998). "Some evidence that banks use internal capital markets to lower capital costs," *Journal of Applied Corporate Finance,* 11(2), pp. 70–78.

Hout, T., M. E. Porter, and E. Rudden (1982). "How global companies win out," *Harvard Business Review,* September/October, pp. 98–108.

Huey, J. (1997). "In search of Robert's secret formula," *Fortune,* December 29, p. 230.

Hunt, M. S. (1972). "Competition in the major home appliance industry 1960–1970," Unpublished doctoral dissertation, Harvard University.

Hurry, D., A. T. Miller, and E. H. Bowman (1992). "Calls on high technology: Japanese exploration of venture capital investments in the United States," *Strategic Management Journal,* 13(2), pp. 85–102.

Hymer, S. (1976). *The International Operations of National Firms: A Study of Direct Foreign Investment,* Cambridge, MA: MIT Press.

Hymon, M. (1999). "Pity the poor owners? That's rich," *Business Week,* November 22, pp. 91+.

Ignatius, A. (1993). "Commodity giant: Marc Rich & Co. does big deals at big risk in former U.S.S.R.," *Wall Street Journal,* May 13, p. A1.

Injiri, Y. (1980). "Recovery rate and cash flow accounting," *Financial Executive,* 48(3), pp. 54–60.

Inkpen, A. (1998). Learning and knowledge acquisition through international strategic alliances," *Academy of Management Executive,* 12(4), pp. 69–80.

Investor Relations Business (2000). "Reversal of fortune: Institutional ownership is declining," May 1, pp. 8–9.

Itami, H. (1987). *Mobilizing Invisible Assets,* Cambridge, MA: Harvard University Press.

Jacob, R. (1992). "India is opening for business," *Fortune,* November 16, pp. 128–130.

Jacob, R. (1992). "Service Corp. International: Acquisitions done the right way," *Fortune,* November 16, p. 96.

Jacobsen, R. (1988). "The persistence of abnormal returns," *Strategic Management Journal,* 9(5), pp. 415–430.

Jacquemin, A. P., and C. H. Berry (1979). "Entropy measure of diversification and corporate growth," *Journal of Industrial Economics,* 27(4), pp. 359–369.

Jandik, T., and A. K. Makhija (1999). "An empirical examination of the atypical diversification practices of electric utilities: Internal capital markets and regulation," Fisher College of Business, The Ohio State University, working paper (September).

Jemison, D. B., and S. B. Sitkin (1986). "Corporate acquisitions: A process perspective," *Academy of Management Review,* 11, pp. 145–163.

Jensen, E. (1993). "ABC and BBC pool their radio-TV news coverage," *Wall Street Journal,* March 26, p. B1+.

Jensen, E., and M. Robichaux (1993). "Fifth network sparks interest of TV industry," *Wall Street Journal,* June 28, p. B1.

Jensen, M. (1988). "Takeovers: Their causes and consequences," *Journal of Economic Perspectives,* 2, pp. 21–48.

Jensen, M. C. (1968). "The performance of mutual funds in the period 1945–64," *Journal of Finance,* May, pp. 389–416.

Jensen, M. C. (1986). "Agency costs of free cash flow, corporate finance, and takeovers," *American Economic Review,* 76, pp. 323–329.

Jensen, M. C., and W. H. Meckling (1976). "Theory of the firm: Managerial behavior, agency costs, and ownership structure," *Journal of Financial Economics,* 3, pp. 305–360.

Jensen, M. C., and K. J. Murphy (1990). "Performance pay and top management incentives," *Journal of Political Economy,* 98, pp. 225–264.

Jensen, M. C., and R. S. Ruback (1983). "The market for corporate control: The scientific evidence," *Journal of Financial Economics,* 11, pp. 5–50.

Johansson, J. K. (1995). "International alliances: Why now?" *Journal of the Academy of Marketing Science,* 23(4), pp. 301–304.

John, G., and B. A. Weitz (1988). "Forward integration into distribution: An empirical test of the transaction cost analysis," *Journal of Law, Economics and Organization,* 4, pp. 337–355.

Johnson, R. (1999). "Speed sells," *Fortune,* April 12, pp. 56–70.

Johnson, R. A., R. E. Hoskisson, and M. A. Hitt (1993). "Board of director involvement in restructuring: The effects of board versus managerial controls and characteristics," *Strategic Management Journal,* 14, pp. 33–50.

Jones, G., and C. W. Jones (1991). "Michael Eisner's Disney Company," in *Strategic Management,* Boston: Houghton-Mifflin, pp. 784–805.

Jose, M. L., L. M. Nichols, and J. L. Stevens (1986). "Contributions of diversification, promotion, and R&D to the value of multi-product firms: A Tobin's *q* approach," *Financial Management,* 15(4), pp. 33–42.

Joskow, P. L. (1988). "Asset specificity and the structure of vertical relationships," *Journal of Law, Economics and Organization,* 4, pp. 95–117.

Judge, P. (1996). "Is it rainforest crunch time?" *Business Week,* July 15, p. 70.

Kalay, A. (1982). "Stockholder-bondholder conflict and dividend constraints," *Journal of Financial Economics,* 10, pp. 211–233.

Kalleberg, A. L., and T. Reve (1992). "Contracts and commitment: Economic and sociological perspectives on employment relations," *Human Relations,* 45(9), pp. 1103–1132.

Kamrad, B., and R. Ernst (1995). "Multiproduct manufacturing with stochastic input prices and output yield uncertainty," in L. Trigeorgis, ed., *Real Options in Capital Investment,* Westport, CT: Prager, pp. 281–302.

Kanter, R. M. (1993). "FCB and Publicis (A): Forming the alliance," Harvard Business School Case no. 9-393-099.

Kaplan, R. S., and D. P. Norton (1996). *The Balanced Scorecard: Translating Strategy into Action,* Boston: Harvard Business School Press.

Karnani, A., and B. Wernerfelt (1985). "Multipoint competition," *Strategic Management Journal,* 6, pp. 87–96.

Kearns, D. T., and D. A. Nadler (1992). *Prophets in the Dark,* New York: Harper-Collins.

Keil, M., and S. Simonson (1993). "BellSouth Enterprises: The Cellular Billing Project," Harvard Business School Case no. 9-193-150.

Keller, J. J. (1993). "Sprint hangs back as its rivals forge global alliances," *Wall Street Journal,* June 4, p. B4.

Kent, D. H. (1991). "Joint ventures vs. non-joint ventures: An empirical investigation," *Strategic Management Journal,* 12, pp. 387–393.

Kesner, I. F. (1988). "Director's characteristics and committee membership: An investigation of type, occupation tenure and gender," *Academy of Management Journal,* 31, p. 66–84.

Kesner, I. F., and R. B. Johnson (1990). "An investigation of the relationship between board composition and stockholder suits," *Strategic Management Journal,* 11, pp. 327–336.

Kirkpatrick, D. (1997). "Now everyone in PCs wants to be like Mike," *Fortune,* 136(5), August 9, pp. 91–92.

Kirkpatrick, D. (1998). "The second coming of Apple," *Fortune,* November 8, pp. 886+.

Klebnikov, P. (1991). "The powerhouse," *Forbes,* September 2, pp. 46–52.

Klein, B., R. Crawford, and A. Alchian (1978). "Vertical integration, appropriable rents, and the competitive contracting process," *Journal of Law and Economics,* 21, pp. 297–326.

Klein, B., and K. Leffler (1981). "The role of market forces in assuring contractual performance," *Journal of Political Economy,* 89, pp. 615–641.

Klemperer, P. (1986). "Markets with consumer switching costs," doctoral thesis, Graduate School of Business, Stanford University.

Knight, F. H. (1921). *Risk, Uncertainty and Profit,* London: London School of Economics.

Kobrin, S. (1991). "An empirical analysis of the determinants of global integration," *Strategic Management Journal,* 12, pp. 17–31.

Kogut, B. (1988). "Joint ventures: Theoretical and empirical perspectives," *Strategic Management Journal,* 9, pp. 319–332.

Kogut, B. (1991). "Joint ventures and the option to expand and acquire," *Management Science,* 37, pp. 19–33.

Kogut, B., and H. Singh (1986). "Entering the United States by acquisition or joint venture: Country patterns, and cultural characteristics," Working Paper, Department of Management, Wharton School of Business, the University of Pennsylvania.

Kogut, B., and U. Zander (1992). "Knowledge of the firm, combinative capabilities, and the replication of technology,"*Organization Science,* 3, pp. 383–397.

Korn, H. J., and J. A. C. Baum (1999). "Chance, imitative, and strategic antecedents to multimarket contact," *Academy of Management Journal,* 42(2), pp. 171–193.

Kosnik, R. D. (1987). "Greenmail: A study of board performance in corporate governance," *Administrative Science Quarterly,* 32, pp. 163–185.

Kosnik, R. D. (1990). "Effects of board demography and directors' incentives on corporate greenmail decisions," *Academy of Management Journal,* 33, pp. 129–150.

Kotler, P. (1986). *Principles of Marketing,* Upper Saddle River, NJ: Prentice Hall.

Kraar, L. (1992). "Korea's tigers keep roaring," *Fortune,* May 4, pp. 108–110.

Kraar, L. (1995). "The risks are rising in China," *Fortune,* March 6, pp. 179–180.

Kraatz, M. S. (1998). "Learning by association? Interorganizational networks and adaptation to environmental change," *Academy of Management Journal,* 41(6), pp. 621–643.

Krafcik, J. K., and J. P. MacDuffie (1989). *Explaining High Performance Manufacturing: The International Automotive Assembly Plant Study,* Cambridge, MA: International Motor Vehicle Program, Massachusetts Institute of Technology.

Krogh, L., J. Praeger, D. Sorenson, and J. Tomlinson (1988). "How 3M evaluates its R&D programs," *Research Technology Management,* 31, pp. 10–14.

Kupfer, A. (1991) and Holder, D. (1989). "L. L. Bean, Inc.—1974," Harvard Business School Case no. 9-676-014.

Labich, K. (1992). "Airbus takes off," *Fortune,* June 1, pp. 102–108.

Laffer, A. (1969). "Vertical integration by corporations: 1929–1965;" *Review of Economics and Statistics,* 51, pp. 91–93.

Laing, J. R. (1999). "Blimey! Wal-Mart," *Barron's,* 79, p. 14.

Lamont, O. (1997). "Cash flow and investment: Evidence from internal capital markets," *The Journal of Finance,* 52(1), pp. 83–109.

Lamphier, G. (1980). "Inco 'poison pill' plan is producing broad opposition," *Wall Street Journal,* October 20, p. A5.

Landro, L., P. M. Reilly, and R. Turner (1993). "Cartoon clash: Disney relationship with Time Warner is a strained one," *Wall Street Journal,* April 14, p. A1.

Lang, H. P., and R. Stulz (1994). "Tobin's *q*, corporate diversification, and firm performance," *Journal of Political Economy,* 102, pp. 1248–1280.

Larson, A. (1992). "Network dyads in entrepreneurial settings: A study of the governance of exchange relationships," *Administrative Science Quarterly,* March, pp. 76–104.

Larzelere, R. E., and T. L. Huston (1980). "The dyadic trust scale: Toward understanding interpersonal trust in close relationships," *Journal of Marriage and the Family,* August, pp. 595–604.

latinbusinesschronicle.com/reports/0206/mergers.

Lau, L. J., and S. Tamura (1972). "Economies of scale, technical progress, and the non-homothetic Leontief production function," *Journal of Political Economy,* 80, pp. 1167–1187.

Lawrence, J., and P. Sloan (1992). "P&G plans big new Ivory push," *Advertising Age,* November 23, p. 12.

Leana, C. R., and H. J. Van Buren, III (1999). "Organizational social capital and employment practices," *Academy of Management Review,* 24(3), pp. 538–555.

Learned, E. P., C. R. Christensen, K. R. Andrews, and W. Guth (1969). *Business Policy,* Homewood, IL: Irwin.

Lecraw, D. J. (1984). "Diversification strategy and performance," *Journal of Industrial Economics,* 33(2), pp. 179–198.

Lee, L. (1999). "David S. Pottruck," *Businessweek Online,* September 7, www.businessweek.com/1999/99_39/63648018.htm.

Leftwich, R. B. (1974). "U.S. Multinational companies: Profitability, financial leverage and effective income tax rates," *Survey of Current Business,* 54, May, pp. 27–36.

Leroy, F., and B. Ramanantsoa (1997). "The cognitive and behavioural dimensions of organizational learning in a merger: An empirical study," *Journal of Management Studies,* 34, pp. 871–894.

Lessard, D. R. (1996). "World, country, and industry relationships in equity returns: Implications for risk reduction through international diversification," *Financial Analysts Journal,* 32, pp. 32–38.

Levinthal, D., and J. Myatt (1994). "Co-evolution of capabilities and industry: The evolution of mutual fund processing," *Strategic Management Journal,* 17, pp. 45–62.

Levy, D. T. (1985). "The transactions cost approach to vertical integration: An empirical investigation," *Review of Economics and Statistics,* 67, pp. 438–445.

Lieberman, M. (1984). "The learning curve and pricing in the chemical processing industries," *Rand Journal of Economics,* 15, pp. 213–228.

Lieberman, M., and C. Montgomery (1988). "First-mover advantages," *Strategic Management Journal,* 9, pp. 41–58.

Lieberman, M. B. (1982). "The learning curve, pricing and market structure in the chemical processing industries," unpublished doctoral dissertation, Harvard University.

Lieberman, M. B. (1987). "The learning curve, diffusion, and competitive strategy," *Strategic Management Journal,* 8, pp. 441–452.

Liebeskind, J. P. (1996). "Knowledge, strategy, and the theory of the firm," *Strategic Management Journal,* 17 (Winter, Special Issue), pp. 93–107.

Liedtka, J. M. (1996). "Collaborating across lines of business for competitive advantage," *Academy of Management Executive,* 10(2), pp. 20–37.

Light, L. (1999). "Now that's a Pepsi Challenge," *Business Week,* 3627, May 3, pp. 15+.

Lindenberg, E. B., and S. A. Ross (1981). "Tobin's q ratio and industrial organization," *Journal of Business,* 54(1), pp. 1–32.

Lipin, S. (1995). "A list of laggards appears to back investor activism," *Wall Street Journal,* October 3, pp. C1+.

Lippman, S., and R. Rumelt (1982). "Uncertain imitability: An analysis of interfirm differences in efficiency under competition," *Bell Journal of Economics,* 13, pp. 418–438.

Livingstone, J. L., and G. L. Salamon (1971). "Relationship between the accounting and the internal rate of return measures: A synthesis and analysis," in J. L. Livingstone and T. J. Burns, eds., *Income Theory and Rate of Return,* Columbus: Ohio State University Press.

Loeb, M. (1995). "Empowerment that pays off," *Fortune,* 131(5), pp. 145–146.

Loeb, M. (1995). "Jack Welch lets fly on budgets, bonuses, and buddy boards," *Fortune,* May 29, pp. 145–147.

Logue, D. E. (1982). "An experiment in diversification," *Journal of Portfolio Management,* 9, pp. 22–30.

Long, W. F., and D. J. Ravenscraft (1984). "The misuse of accounting rates of return: Comment," *American Economic Review,* 74, pp. 494–500.

Lorenzoni, G., and A. Lipparini (1999). "The leveraging of interfirm relationships as a distinctive organizational capability," *Strategic Management Journal,* 20, pp. 317–338.

Lorsch, J. W. (1989). *Pawns or Potentates: The Reality of America's Corporate Boards,* Boston: Harvard Business School Press.

Lubatkin, M. (1983). "Mergers and the performance of the acquiring firm," *Academy of Management Review,* 8, pp. 218–225.

Lubatkin, M. (1987). "Merger strategies and stockholder value," *Strategic Management Journal,* 8, pp. 39–53.

Lublin, J. S. (1995). "Give the board fewer perks, a panel urges," *Wall Street Journal,* June 19, p. B1.

Lublin, J. S., and C. Duff (1995). "How do you fire a CEO? Very, very slowly," *Wall Street Journal,* January 20, p. B1.

Luehrman, T. (1998). "Investment opportunities as real options: Getting started on the numbers," *Harvard Business Review,* 26, July/August, pp. 51–67.

Lux, H. (1995). "An economists' supergroup will review NASDAQ charges," *Investment Dealers Digest,* 61, July 3, p. 5.

Lux, H. (1995). "NASDAQ retains Nobel laureate for anti-trust case defense," *Investment Dealers Digest,* 61. March 13, pp. 3–4.

Ma, H. (1998). "Mutual forbearance in international business," *Journal of International Management,* 4(2), pp. 129–147.

MacDonald, J. M. (1985). "Market exchange or vertical integration: An empirical analysis," *Review of Economics and Statistics,* 67, pp. 327–33.

Mackey, T., and J. B. Barney (2006). "Is there a diversification discount? Diversification, payout policy, and the value of a firm," Working Paper, The Ohio State University.

MacLeod, W. B. (1985). "A theory of conscious parallelism," *European Economic Review,* 27(1), pp. 25–44.

MacMillan, I., D. C. Hambrick, and J. M. Pennings (1986). "Uncertainty reduction and the threat of supplier retaliation: Two views of the backward integration decision," *Organization Studies,* 7, pp. 263–278.

Maddigan, R. (1979). "The impact of vertical integration on business performance," unpublished doctoral dissertation, Indiana University at Bloomington.

Magnet, M. (1993). "What activist investors want," *Fortune,* March 8, pp. 59–63.

Mahoney, J. (1992). "The choice of organizational form: Vertical financial ownership versus other methods of vertical integration," *Strategic Management Journal,* 13, pp. 559–584.

Mahoney, J. T., and J. R. Pandian (1992). "The resource-based view within the conversation of strategic management," *Strategic Management Journal,* 13, pp. 363–380.

Maijoor, S., A. Van Witteloostuijn (1996). "An empirical test of the resource-based theory," *Strategic Management Journal,* 17, pp. 549–569.

Main, O. W. (1955). *The Canadian Nickel Industry,* Toronto: University of Toronto Press.

Majumdar, S. (1998). "On the utilization of resources," *Strategic Management Journal,* pp. 809–831.

Makadok, R. (1997). "Do inter-firm differences in capabilities affect strategic pricing dynamics?" *Academy of Management Proceedings '97,* pp. 30–34.

Maksimovic, V., and G. Phillips (1999). "Do conglomerate firms allocate resources inefficiently?" Working Paper, University of Maryland.

Mancke, R. B. (1974). "Causes of interfirm profitability differences: A new interpretation of the evidence," *Quarterly Journal of Economics,* 88(2), pp. 181–193.

Mancke, R. B. (1977). "Interfirm profitabilty differences: Reply," *Quarterly Journal of Economics,* 91(4), pp. 677–680.

Mandel, M. (2000). "Antitrust in the digital age," *Business Week,* 3681, May 15, pp. 46–48.

Mansfield, E. (1985). "How rapidly does new industrial technology leak out?" *Journal of Industrial Economics,* 34(2), pp. 217–223.

Mansfield, E., M. Schwartz, and S. Wagner (1981). "Imitation costs and patents: An empirical study," *Economic Journal,* 91, pp. 907–918.

Marcus, A., and D. Geffen (1998). "The dialectics of competency acquisition," *Strategic Management Journal,* 19, pp. 1145–1168.

Marin, D. (1990). "Tying in trade: Evidence on countertrade," *World Economy,* 13(3), p. 445.

Markham, J. W. (1951). "The nature and significance of price leadership," *American Economic Review,* 41, pp. 891–905.

Markides, C., and P. J. Williamson (1994). "Related diversification, core competencies, and corporate performance," *Strategic Management Journal,* 15, pp. 149–165.

Martin, J. (1996). "Are you as good as you think you are?" *Fortune,* September 30, pp. 142+.

Maskin, E., and J. Tirole (1988). "A theory of dynamic oligopoly," *Econometrica,* 56, pp. 549–600.

Mason, E. S. (1939). "Price and production policies of large scale enterprises," *American Economic Review,* 29, pp. 61–74.

Masten, S., J. W. Meehan, and E. A. Snyder (1991). "The cost of organization," *Journal of Law, Economics and Organization,* 7, pp. 1–25.

Masulis, R. (1980). "Stock repurchases by tender offer: An analysis of the causes of common stock price changes," *Journal of Finance,* 35, pp. 305–319.

Matsusaka, J. G., and V. Nanda (1998). "Internal capital markets and corporate refocusing," Working Paper, University of Southern California.

May, D. O. (1995). "Do managerial motives influence firm risk reduction strategies?" *Journal of Business,* 55(2), pp. 281–296.

McClelland, D. (1997). "Midrange digital cameras," *Macworld,* 14(10), pp. 44–45.

McCormick, J., and N. Stone (1990). "From national champion to global competitor: An interview with Thomson's Alain Gomez," *Harvard Business Review,* May/June, pp. 126–135.

McGahan, A. (1999). "The performance of U.S. Corporations: 1981–1994," *Journal of Industrial Economics,* 47, pp. 373–398.

McGahan, A., and J. Kou (1995). "The U.S. Airline Industry in 1995," Harvard Business School Case no. 9-795-113.

McGahan, A., and M. Porter (2002). "What do we know about variance in accounting profitability?" *Management Science,* 48, pp. 834–851.

McGahan, A., and M. Porter (2003). "The emergence and sustainability of abnormal profits," *Strategic Organization,* 1, pp. 79–108.

McGee, J., and H. Thomas (1986). "Strategic groups: Theory, research and taxonomy," *Strategic Management Journal,* 7, pp. 141–160.

McGrath, R. G., and M. J. Chen (1998). "Multimarket maneuvering in uncertain spheres of influence: Resource diversion strategies," *Academy of Management Review,* 23(4), pp. 724–740.

McGrath, R. G., and I. MacMillan (2000). *The Entrepreneurial Mindset,* Boston: Harvard Business School Press.

McHugh, J. (1999). "Emerging channels—sort of," *Fortune,* 163, p. 55.

McWilliams, A. (1990). "Rethinking horizontal market restrictions: In defense of cooperation in empty core markets," *Quarterly Review of Economics and Business,* 30, pp. 3–14.

McWilliams, A., and J. Barney (1994). "Managing cutthroat competition in empty core markets: An additional motive for inter-firm cooperation," unpublished manuscript, Arizona State University West.

McWilliams, A., and D. Siegel (1997). "Event studies in management research: Theoretical and empirical issues," *Academy of Management Journal,* 40(3), pp. 626–657.

McWilliams, G. (1998). "Mimicking Dell, Compaq to sell its PC directly," *Wall Street Journal,* November 11, pp. B1+.

Mead, W. J. (1967). "Competitive significance of joint ventures," *Antitrust Bulletin,* 12, New York: Federal Legal Publications, pp. 300–315.

Metz, T. (1988). "Promoter of the poison pill prescribes stronger remedy," *Wall Street Journal,* December 1, p. C1.

Meyer, M. W., and L. B. Zucker (1989). *Permanently Failing Organizations,* Newbury Park, CA: Sage.

Michel, A., and I. Shaked (1986). "Multinational corporations vs. domestic corporations: Financial performance and characteristics," *Journal of Business,* 17 (Fall), pp. 89–100.

Miles, R. H., and K. S. Cameron (1982). *Coffin Nails and Corporate Strategies,* Upper Saddle River, NJ: Prentice Hall.

Miller, A., and G. G. Dess (1996). *Strategic Management,* McGraw-Hill.

Miller, D., and J. Shamsie (1996). "The resource-based view of the firm in two environments," *Academy of Management Journal,* 39(3), pp. 519–543.

Miller, D. J. (2004). "Firms' technological resources and the performance effects of diversification: A longitudinal study," *Strategic Management Journal,* 25(11), pp. 1097–1119.

Miller, K. (1998). "Economic exposure and integrated risk management," *Strategic Management Journal,* 33, pp. 756–779.

Miller, M. W., and Berton, L. (1993). "Softer numbers: As IBM's woes grew, its accounting tactics got less conservative," *Wall Street Journal,* April 7, p. A1.

Mintzberg, H., and A. McHugh (1985). "Strategy formulation in an adhocracy," *Administrative Science Quarterly,* 30, pp. 160–197.

Moel, A., and P. Tufano (2000). "Bidding for the Antamina mine: Valuation and incentives in a real options context," in Brennan, M. J., and L. Trigeorgis, eds., *Project Flexibility, Agency, and Competition: New Developments in the Theory and Application of Real Options,* New York: Oxford University Press.

Moffett, M. (1993). "U.S. firms yell olé to future in Mexico," *Wall Street Journal,* August 9, p. B1.

Mohr, J., and R. Spekman (1994). "Characteristics of partnership success: Partnership attributes, communication behavior, and conflict resolution techniques," *Strategic Management Journal,* 15, pp. 135–152.

money.cnn.com/2005/01/31/ news/economy/ merger_mania.

Monteverde, K., and D. Teece (1982). "Supplier switching costs and vertical integration in the automobile industry," *Rand Journal of Economics,* 13(1), pp. 206–213.

Montgomery, C. (1993). "Marks and Spencer Ltd. (A)," Harvard Business School Case no. 9-391-Ò089.

Montgomery, C. A. (1989). "Sears, Roebuck and Co. in 1989," Harvard Business School Case no. 9-391-147.

Montgomery, C. A., and H. Singh (1984). "Diversification strategy and systematic risk," *Strategic Management Journal,* 5(2), pp. 181–191.

Montgomery, C. A., and B. Wernerfelt (1991). "Sources of superior performance: Market share versus industry effects in the U. S. brewing industry," *Management Science,* 37, pp. 954–959.

Montgomery, D. B. (1975). "New product distribution: an analysis of supermarket buyer decision," *Journal of Marketing Research,* 12, pp. 255–264.

Moore, F. T. (1959). "Economies of scale: Some statistical evidence," *Quarterly Journal of Economics,* 73, pp. 232–245.

Moritz, M., and B. Seaman (1984). *Going for Broke: Lee Iacocca's Battle to Save Chrysler,* Garden City, NY: Anchor/Doubleday.

Mueller, B. (1996). "The buzzword for carmakers is flexibility," *World Business,* 2, p. 12.

Mueller, D. C. (1977). "The persistence of profits above the norm," *Economica,* 44, pp. 369–380.

Nagarajan, A., and W. Mitchell (1998). "Evolutionary diffusion: Internal and external methods used to acquire encompassing, complementary, and incremental technological changes in the lithotripsy industry," *Strategic Management Journal,* 19, pp. 1063–1077.

Nail, L. A., W. L. Megginson, and C. Maquieira (1998). "How stock-swap mergers affect shareholder (and bondholder) wealth: More evidence of the value of corporate focus," *Journal of Applied Corporate Finance,* 11(2), pp. 95–106.

Nanda, A., and C. A. Bartlett (1990). "Corning Incorporated: A network of alliances," Harvard Business School Case no. 9-391-102.

Narisetti, R. (1995). "Justice Department is investigating tire makers for possible price fixing," *Wall Street Journal,* August 24, p. A3.

Nayyar, P. (1990). "Information asymmetries: A source of competitive advantage for diversified service firms," *Strategic Management Journal,* 11, pp. 513–519.

Nee, E. (1999). "Lew Platt: Why I dismembered HP," *Fortune,* 139, pp. 167–170.

Neff, T. J. (1990). "Outside directors and the CEO: Changing the rules," *The Corporate Board,* 11, pp. 7–10.

Nelson, E. (1998). "Wal-Mart accuses Amazon.com of stealing its secrets in lawsuit," *Wall Street Journal,* October 19, p. B10.

Nelson, R., and S. Winter (1982). *An Evolutionary Theory of Economic Change,* Cambridge, MA: Belknap.

Newburry, W., and Y. Zeira (1997). "Generic differences between equity international joint ventures (EIJVs), international acquisitions (IAs) and international greenfield investments (IGIs): Implications for parent companies," *Journal of World Business,* 32(2), pp. 87–102.

Newburry, W., and Y. Zeira (1999). "Autonomy and effectiveness of equity international joint ventures (EIJV's): An analysis based on EIJV's in Hungary and Britain," *Journal of Management Studies,* 36(2), pp. 263–285.

Nguyen, T., and T. Devinney (1990). "Diversification strategy and performance in Canadian manufacturing firms," *Strategic Management Journal,* 11, pp. 411–418.

Nguyen, T. H., A. Seror, and T. M. Devinney (1990). "Diversification strategy and performance in Canadian manufacturing firms," *Strategic Management Journal,* 11, pp. 411–418.

Nielsen, R. P. (1988). "Cooperative strategy," *Strategic Management Journal,* 9, pp. 475–492.

Noldeke, G., and K. M. Schmidt (1998). "Sequential investments and options to own," *Rand Journal of Economics,* 29(4), pp. 633–653.

Norton, E. and G. Stem (1995), "Steel and aluminum vie over every ounce in a car's construction," *Wall Street Journal,* May 9, pp. A1+.

Nulty, P. (1995). "Digital imaging had better boom before Kodak film busts," *Fortune,* May 1, pp. 80–83.

Nystrom, P. C., and W. H. Starbuck (1984). "To avoid organizational crisis, unlearn," *Organizational Dynamics,* 12(4), pp. 53–65.

Oates, B. (1992). "What happened to the run-and-shoot revolution?" *Football Digest,* 22(2), pp. 28.

O'Brien, B. (1993), "Losing altitude: After long soaring, Delta Air Lines runs into financial clouds," *Wall Street Journal,* June 25, p. A1.

"Only here for the biru," *The Economist,* May 14, 1994, pp. 69–70.

Ono, Y. (1996). "Who really makes that cute little beer? You'd be surprised," *Wall Street Journal,* April 15, pp. A1+.

Ordover, J. A., and R. D. Willig (1985). "Antitrust for high-technology industries: Assessing research joint ventures and mergers," *Journal of Law and Economics,* 28, pp. 311–343.

O'Reilly, B. (1990). "The inside story of AIDS drug," *Fortune,* November 5, pp. 112–129.

Ortega-Reichert, A. (1967). "Models for competitive bidding under uncertainty," unpublished dissertation, Stanford University.

Osborn, R. N., and C. C. Baughn (1987). "New patterns in the formation of US/Japan cooperative ventures: The role of technology," *Columbia Journal of World Business,* 22, pp. 57–65.

Osborn, R. N., and C. C. Baughn (1990). "Forms of interorganizational governance for multinational alliances," *Academy of Management Journal,* 33(3), pp. 503–519.

Osterland, A. (1999). "Fixing Rubbermaid is no snap," *Business Week,* 3647, September 20, p. 108.

Ouchi, W. G. (1981). *Theory Z: How American Business Can Meet the Japanese Challenge,* Reading, MA: Addison-Wesley.

Ouchi, W. G. (1984). *The M-Form Society: How American Teamwork Can Capture the Competitive Edge,* Reading, MA: Addison-Wesley.

Oviatt, B. M., and P. P. McDougall (1995). "Global start-ups: Entrepreneurs on a worldwide stage," *Academy of Management Executive,* 9, pp. 30–44.

Pacelle, M. (1996). "'Big boxes' by discounters are booming," *Wall Street Journal,* January 17, p. A2.

Palepu, K. (1985). "Diversification strategy, profit performance and the entropy measure," *Strategic Management Journal,* 6(3), pp. 239–255.

Palia, D. (1998). "Division-level overinvestment and agency conflicts in diversified firms," Working Paper, Columbia University.

Palich, L. E., L. B. Cardinal, and C. C. Miller (2000). "Curvilinearity in the diversification-performance linkage: An examination of over three decades of research," *Strategic Management Journal,* 21(2), pp. 155–174.

Paré, T. P. (1995). "Why the banks lined up against Gates," *Fortune,* May 29, p. 18.

Pascale, R. T. (1984). "Perspectives on strategy: The real story behind Honda's success," *California Management Review,* 26(3), pp. 47–72.

Pascale, R. T., and A. G. Athos (1981). *The Art of Japanese Management,* New York: Simon & Schuster.

Pate, J. (1969). "Joint venture activity, 1960–1968," *Economic Review,* Federal Reserve Bank of Cleveland, pp. 16–23.

Patterson, G. A. (1991). "Mazda hopes to crack Japan's top tier," *Wall Street Journal,* September 20, pp. B1+.

Patterson, G. A., and R. Rose (1994). "U.S. inquiry of big appliance makers involves cooperative ads with retailers," *Wall Street Journal,* December 5, p. A3.

Pearson, A. E., and C. L. Irwin (1988). "Coca-Cola vs. Pepsi-Cola (A)," Harvard Business School Case no. 9-387-108.

Penrose, E. T. (1959). *The Theory of the Growth of the Firm,* New York: John Wiley & Sons.

Perfect, S. B., and K. K. Wiles (1994). "Alternative constructions of Tobin's q: An empirical comparison," *Journal of Empirical Finance,* 1, pp. 313–341.

Perrow, C. (1984). *Normal Accidents: Living with High-Risk Technologies,* New York: Basic Books.

Perry, L. T., and J. B. Barney (1981). "Performance lies are hazardous to organizational health," *Organizational Dynamics,* 9(3), pp. 68–80.

Perry, N. J. (1991). "Will Sony make it in Hollywood?" *Fortune,* September 9, pp. 158–166.

Perry, N. J. (1993). "What's next for the defense industry," *Fortune,* February 22, pp. 94–100.

Peteraf, M. A. (1993). "The cornerstones of competitive advantage: A resource-based view," *Strategic Management Journal,* 14, pp. 179–191.

Peteraf, M. A., and J. B. Barney (2003). "Unraveling the resource-based tangle," *Managerial and Decision Economics,* 24(4), pp. 309–323.

Peters, L. J., and R. H. Waterman (1982). *In Search of Excellence,* New York: Harper & Row.

Peterson, R. B., and H. F. Schwind (1977). "A comparative study of personnel problems in companies and joint ventures in Japan," *Journal of Business Studies,* 8(1), pp. 45–55.

Peterson, R. B., and J. Y. Shimada (1978). "Sources of management problems in Japanese-American joint ventures," *Academy of Management Review,* 3, pp. 796–804.

Pfeffer, J. and P. Nowak (1976). "Patterns of joint venture activity: Implications for antitrust research," *Antitrust Bulletin,* 21, New York: Federal Legal Publications, pp. 315–339.

Pfeffer, J., and G. R. Salancik (1978). *The External Control of Organizations: A Resource Dependence Perspective,* New York: Harper & Row.

Pirrong, S. C. (1992). "An application of core theory to the analysis of ocean shipping markets," *Journal of Law and Economics,* 35, pp. 89–132.

Pisano, G. (1991). "Nucleon," Harvard Business School Case no. 9-692-041.

Pisano, G. P. (1994). "Knowledge, integration, and the locus of learning: An empirical analysis of process development," *Strategic Management Journal,* 15, pp. 85–100.

Polanyi, M. (1962). *Personal Knowledge: Towards a Post Critical Philosophy,* London: Routledge & Kegan Paul.

Pollock, E. (1999). "Why Mountain Dew is now the talk of the teen circuit," *Wall Street Journal,* October 14, pp. A1+.

Pollock, E. J. (1993). "Mediation firms alter the legal landscape," *Wall Street Journal,* March 22, p. B1.

Pope, K. (1993). "Dealers accuse Compaq of jilting them," *Wall Street Journal,* February 26, pp. 8, B1+.

Pope, K., and L. Cauley (1998). "In battle for TV ads, cable is now the enemy," *Wall Street Journal,* May 6, pp. B1+.

Pope, K., and D. Hamilton (1993). "U.S. computer firms, extending PC wars, charge into Japan," *Wall Street Journal,* March 31, pp. A1+.

Porras, J., and P. O. Berg (1978). "The impact of organizational development," *Academy of Management Review*, 3, pp. 249–266.

Porter, M. E. (1979). "General Electric vs. Westinghouse in large turbine generators (A)," Harvard Business School Case no. 9-380-128.

Porter, M. E. (1979). "How competitive forces shape strategy," *Harvard Business Review*, March/April, pp. 137–156.

Porter, M. E. (1980). *Competitive Strategy*, New York: Free Press.

Porter, M. E. (1981). "Disposable diaper industry in 1974," Harvard Business School Case no. 9-380-175.

Porter, M. E. (1981). "The contribution of industrial organization to strategic management," *Academy of Management Review*, 6, pp. 609–620.

Porter, M. E. (1985). *Competitive Advantage: Creating and Sustaining Superior Performance*, New York: The Free Press.

Porter, M. E. (1986). "Competition in international industries: A conceptual framework," in M. E. Porter, ed., *Competition in International Industries*, Boston: Harvard Business School Press, p. 43.

Porter, M. E. (1987). "From competitive advantage to corporate strategy," *Harvard Business Review*, 3, pp. 43–59.

Porter, M. E., and R. Wayland (1991). "Coca-Cola vs. Pepsi-Cola and the soft drink industry," Harvard Business School Case no. 9-391-179.

Poteshman, A. M., and V. Serbin (2003). "Clearly irrational financial market behavior: Evidence from the early exercise of exchange traded stock options," *Journal of Finance*, 58(1), pp. 37–70.

Powell, T. C., and A. Dent-Micallef (1997). "Information technology as competitive advantage," *Strategic Management Journal*, 18(5), pp. 375–405.

Prahalad, C. K., and R. A. Bettis (1986). "The dominant logic: A new linkage between diversity and performance," *Strategic Management Journal*, 7(6), pp. 485–501.

Prahalad, C. K., and Y. Doz (1987). *The Multinational Mission*, New York: Free Press.

Prahalad, C. K., and G. Hamel (1990). "The core competence of the organization," *Harvard Business Review*, May/June, pp. 79–93.

Press, E. G., and J. B. Weintrop (1990). "Accounting-based constraints in public and private debt agreements: Their association with leverage and impact on accounting choice," *Journal of Accounting & Economics*, 12, pp. 65–95.

Priem, R. (1990). "Top management team group factors, consensus, and firm performance," *Strategic Management Journal*, 11, pp. 469–478.

Prokesch, S. (1995). "Competing on customer service: An interview with British Airways' Sir Colin Marshall," *Harvard Business Review*, November/December, p. 101.

Quinn, J. (1995). "KitchenAid," *Incentive*, 169(5), pp. 46–47.

Quinn, J. B. (1980). *Strategies for Change: Logical Incrementalism*, Homewood, IL: Irwin.

Rajan, R., H. Servaes, and L. Zingales (1997). "The cost of diversity: The diversification discount and inefficient investment," Working Paper, University of Chicago.

Rankin, A. (1998). "Dave Matthews Band succeeds by marching to its own drummer," *Columbus Dispatch*, August 2, pp. F1+.

Rapoport, C. (1992). "A tough Swede invades the U.S.," *Fortune*, June 29, pp. 776–779.

Rapoport, C. (1994). "Nestlé's brand building machine," *Fortune*, September 19, pp. 147–156.

Ravenscraft, D. J., and F. M. Scherer (1987). *Mergers, Sell-offs, and Economic Efficiency*, Washington, DC: Brookings Institution.

Ray, G., J. Barney, and W. Muhanna (2004). "Capabilities, business processes, and competitive advantage. " *Strategic Management Journal*, 25, pp. 23–57.

Ray, G., W. Muhanna, and J. Barney (2005). "Information technology and the performance of the customer service process," *MIS Quarterly*, 29, pp. 625–651.

Rechner, P., and D. Dalton (1991). "CEO duality and organizational performance: A longitudinal analysis," *Strategic Management Journal*, 12, pp. 155–160.

Reda, S. (1995). "Motor oil: Hands-on approach," *Stores*, 77(5), pp. 48–49.

Rediker, K., and A. Seth (1995). "Boards of directors and substitution effects of alternative governance mechanisms," *Strategic Management Journal,* 16, pp. 85–99.

Reed, R., and R. J. DeFillippi (1990). "Causal ambiguity, barriers to imitation, and sustainable competitive advantage," *Academy of Management Review,* 15(1), pp. 88–102.

Reibstein, L., and M. Levinson (1991). "A Mexican miracle?" *Newsweek,* May 20, p. 42.

Reich, R. (1986). "Joint ventures with Japan give away our future," *Harvard Business Review,* 64, March/April, pp. 78–86.

Reilly, P. M. (1993). "At a crossroads: The instant-new age leaves Time Magazine searching for a mission," *Wall Street Journal,* May 12, p. A1.

Reilly, P. M., and R. Turner (1993). "Disney pulls ads in tiff with Time," *Wall Street Journal,* April 2, p. B1.

Reinganum, M. R. (1981). "Misspecification of capital asset pricing: Empirical anomalies based on earnings yields and market values," *Journal of Financial Economics,* March, pp. 19–46.

Ricardo, D. (1817). *Principles of Political Economy and Taxation,* London: J. Murray.

Ries, A., and J. Trout (1986). *Marketing Warfare,* New York: McGraw-Hill.

Rigdon, J. E. (1993). "Workplace: Using new kinds of corporate alchemy, some firms turn lesser lights into stars," *Wall Street Journal,* May 3, p. B1.

Ring, P. S., S. A. Lenway, and M. Govekar (1990). "Management of the political imperative in international business," *Strategic Management Journal,* 11, pp. 141–151.

Ring, P. S., and A. Van de Ven (1992). "Structuring cooperative relationships between organizations," *Strategic Management Journal,* 13, pp. 483–498.

Riorden, M., and O. Williamson (1985). "Asset specificity and economic organization," *International Journal of Economic Organization,* 3, pp. 365–378.

Roberts, P. (1999). "Product innovation, product-market competition and persistent profitability in the U.S. pharmaceutical industry," *Strategic Management Journal,* 20, pp. 655–670.

Robins, J., and M. Wiersema (1995). "A resource-based approach to the multibusiness firm: Empirical analysis of portfolio interrelationships and corporate financial performance," *Strategic Management Journal,* 16, pp. 277–299.

Robinson, E. (1998). "China spies target corporate America," *Fortune,* March 30, pp. 118+.

Robinson, J. (1934). "What is perfect competition?" *Quarterly Journal of Economics,* 49, pp. 104–120.

Robinson, W. T., and C. Fornell (1985). "Sources of market pioneer advantages in consumer goods industries," *Journal of Marketing Research,* 22(3), pp. 305–307.

Rogers, A. (1992). "It's the execution that counts," *Fortune,* November 30, pp. 80–83.

Rohwedder, C. (1993). "Europe's smaller food shops face finis," *Wall Street Journal,* May 12, p. B1.

Roll, R. (1977). "A critique of the asset pricing theory's tests; Part I: On past and potential testability of the theory," *Journal of Financial Economics,* March, pp. 129–176.

Roll, R. (1986). "The hubris hypothesis of corporate takeovers," *Journal of Business,* 59, pp. 205–216.

Rosen, S. (1982). "Authority, control, and distribution of earnings," *Bell Journal of Economics,* 13, pp. 311–323.

Rosenbloom, R. S., and C. Christensen (1990). "Continuous casting investments at USX Corporation," Harvard Business School Case no. 9-391-121.

Ross, S. A. (1976). "The arbitrage theory of capital asset pricing," *Journal of Economic Theory,* December, pp. 343–362.

Rossi, S. (1993). "Genzyme Corporation," Harvard Business School Case no. 9-793-120.

Rotemberg, J. J., and G. Saloner (1994). "Benefits of narrow business strategies," *American Economic Review,* 84(5), pp. 1330–1349.

Roth, T. (1990). "Bid size showed VW's eagerness to buy Skoda," *Wall Street Journal,* December 11, p. A15.

Roush, C. (1993). "At Timex, they're positively glowing," *Business Week,* July 12, p. 141.

Rowe, A. J., R. O. Mason, and K. E. Dickel (1982). *Strategic Management: A Methodological Approach,* Reading, MA: Addison-Wesley.

Ruback, R. S. (1982). "The Conoco takeover and stockholder returns," *Sloan Management Review,* 14, pp. 13–33.

Ruback, R. S., and W. H. Mikkelson (1984). "Corporate investments in common stock," Working Paper, Sloan School of Business, Massachusetts Institute of Technology.

Ruefli, T. W., J. M. Collins, and J. R. Lacugna (1999). "Risk measures in strategic management research: Auld Lang Syne?" *Strategic Management Journal,* 20, pp. 167–194.

Rugman, A. (1979). *International Diversification and the Multinational Enterprise,* Lexington, MA: Lexington Books.

Rugman, A., and R. Hodgetts (1995). *International Business: A Strategic Management Approach,* New York: McGraw-Hill.

Rukstad, M.G., and J. Horn (1989). "Caterpillar and the construction equipment industry in 1988," Harvard Business School Case no. 9-389-097.

Rumelt, R. (1974). *Strategy, Structure, and Economic Performance,* Cambridge, MA: .Harvard University Press.

Rumelt, R. P. (1982). "Diversification strategy and profitability," *Strategic Management Journal,* 3, pp. 359–369.

Rumelt, R. P. (1984). "Toward a strategic theory of the firm," in R. Lamb, ed., *Competitive Strategic Management,* Upper Saddle River, NJ: Prentice Hall, pp. 556–570.

Rumelt, R. P. (1991). "How much does industry matter?" *Strategic Management Journal,* 12, pp. 167–185.

Russo, M. V. (1992). "Power plays: Regulation, diversification, and backward integration in the electric utility industry," *Strategic Management Journal,* 13, pp. 13–27.

Salamon, G. L. (1985). "Accounting rates of return," *American Economic Review,* 75, pp. 495–504.

Salter, M. S., and W. S. Weinhold (1979). *Diversification Through Acquisition,* New York: Free Press.

Sanchez, R. (1997). "Strategic flexibility, firm organization, and managerial work in dynamic markets: A strategic options perspective," in *Advances in Strategic Management,* 8. New York: JAI Press, pp. 251–291.

Saporito, B. (1992). "Why the price wars never end," *Fortune,* March 23, pp. 68–78.

Scharfstein, D. S. (1997). "The dark side of internal capital markets II: Evidence from diversified conglomerates," Working Paper, National Bureau of Economic Research.

Schelling, T. C. (1960). *Strategies of Conflict,* Cambridge, MA: Harvard University Press.

Scherer, F. M. (1980). *Industrial Market Structure and Economic Performance,* Boston: Houghton Mifflin.

Schiller, Z. (1992). "Diamonds and dirt," *Business Week,* August 10, pp. 20–23.

Schiller, Z. (1994). "This diamond case had too many flaws," *Business Week,* December 19, p. 34.

Schine, E. (1991). "Northrop's biggest foe may have been its past," *Business Week,* May 6, pp. 30–31.

Schlender, B. (1997). "On the road with Chairman Bill," *Fortune,* May 20, pp. 72+.

Schlender, B. R. (1991). "Apple's Japanese ally," *Fortune,* November 4, pp. 151–152.

Schlender, B. R. (1992). "How Sony keeps the magic going," *Fortune,* February 24, pp. 75–84.

Schlesinger, J. M. (1993). "Tough gamble: A slot-machine maker trying to sell in Japan hits countless barriers," *Wall Street Journal,* May 11, p. A1.

Schmalensee, R. (1978). "Entry deterrence in the ready-to-eat breakfast cereal industry," *Bell Journal of Economics,* 9(2), pp. 305–327.

Schmalensee, R. (1985). "Do markets differ much?" *American Economic Review,* 75, pp. 341–351.

Schmalensee, R. (1989). "Studies of structure and performance," in R. Schmalensee and R. Willig, eds., *The Handbook of Industrial Organizations,* Amsterdam: North-Holland.

Schonfeld, E. (1998). "Can computers cure health care?" *Fortune,* March 30, pp. 111+.

Schroeder, M. (1995). "Who watches the watchdog at NASDAQ?" *Business Week,* May 15, pp. 102–109.

Schultz, E. (1989). "Climbing high with discount brokers," *Fortune,* Fall Special Issue, pp. 219–223.

Schumpeter, J. A. (1934). *The Theory of Economic Development*, Cambridge, MA: Harvard University Press.

Scott, J. H. (1977). "On the theory of conglomerate mergers," *Journal of Finance*, 32(4), pp. 1235–1250.

Sellers, P. (1995). "Pepsico's shedding ugly pounds," *Fortune*, June 26, pp. 94–95.

Sellers, P. (1995). "Sears: In with the new, out with the old," *Fortune*, October 16, pp. 98+.

Sellers, P. (1997). "Pepsi's eateries go it alone," *Fortune*, August 4, pp. 27–30.

Sellers, P. (1999). "Crunch time for Coke," *Fortune*, 140, July 19, pp. 72–78.

Selznick, P. (1957). *Leadership in Administration*, New York: Harper & Row.

Senback, A. J., and W. L. Beedles (1980). "Is indirect diversification desirable?" *Journal of Portfolio Management*, 6, pp. 49–57.

Serwer, A. E. (1994). "McDonald's conquers the world," *Fortune*, October 17, pp. 103–116.

Serwer, A. E. (1995). "Why bank mergers are good for your savings account," *Fortune*, October 2, p. 32.

Severn, A. K. (1974). "Investor evaluation of foreign and domestic risk," *Journal of Finance*, 29, pp. 545–550.

Shaffer, R. A. (1995). "Intel as conquistador," *Forbes*, February 27, p. 130.

Shan, W., G. Walker, and B. Kogut (1994). "Interfirm cooperation and startup innovation in the biotechnology industry," *Strategic Management Journal*, 15, pp. 387–394.

Shane, S. (1994). "The effect of national culture on the choice between licensing and direct foreign investment," *Strategic Management Journal*, 15, pp. 627–642.

Shane, S. A. (1998). "Making new franchise systems work," *Strategic Management Journal*, 19, pp. 697–707.

Shanley, M. (1996). "Straw men and M-form myths: Comment on Freeland," *American Journal of Sociology*, 102(2), pp. 527–536.

Sharpe, W. F. (1966). "Mutual fund performance," *Journal of Business*, January, pp. 119–138.

Shin, H. H., and R. M. Stulz (1998). "Are internal capital markets efficient?" *Quarterly Journal of Economics*, May, pp. 531–552.

Shleifer, A., and R. W. Vishny (1986). "Large shareholder and corporate control," *Journal of Political Economy*, 94, pp. 461–488.

Shortell, S., and E. J. Zajac (1988). "Internal corporate joint ventures: Development processes and performance outcomes," *Strategic Management Journal*, 9, pp. 527–542.

Si, S. X., and G. D. Bruton (1999). "Knowledge transfer in international joint ventures in transitional economies: The China experience," *Academy of Management Executive*, 13(1), pp. 83–90.

Sick, G. A. (1986). "A certainty equivalent approach to capital budgeting," *Financial Management*, 15, pp. 23–32.

"Silicon duel: Korean move to grab memory chip market from the Japanese," *Wall Street Journal*, March 13, 1995, pp. A1+.

Silverman, B. S., J. A. Nickerson, and J. Freeman (1997). "Profitability, transactional alignment, and organizational mortality in the U.S. trucking industry," *Strategic Management Journal*, 18 (Summer, Special Issue), pp. 31–52.

Simmonds, P. (1990). "The combined diversification breadth and mode dimensions and the performance of large diversified firms," *Strategic Management Journal*, 11, pp. 399–410.

Simonin, B. L. (1999). "Ambiguity and the process of knowledge transfer in strategic alliances," *Strategic Management Journal*, 20(7), pp. 595–623.

Simons, R. (1994). "How new top managers use control systems as levers of strategic renewal," *Strategic Management Journal*, 15, pp. 169–189.

Sims, J., and R. H. Lande (1986). "The end of antitrust: Or a new beginning," *Antitrust Bulletin*, 31(2), pp. 301–322.

Singh, H., and F. Haricento (1989). "Top management tenure, corporate ownership and the magnitude of golden parachutes," *Strategic Management Journal*, 10, pp. 143–156.

Singh, H., and C. A. Montgomery (1987). "Corporate acquisition strategies and economic performance," *Strategic Management Journal*, 8, pp. 377–386.

Sjostrom, W. (1989). "Collusion in ocean shipping: A test of monopoly and empty core models," *Journal of Political Economy*, 97, pp. 1160–1179.

Slade, M. E. (1990). "Cheating on collusive agreements," *International Journal of Industrial Organization,* 8(4), pp. 519–543.

Smirlock, M., T. Gillingan, and W. Marshall (1984). "Tobin's *q* and the structure-performance relationship," *American Economic Review,* 74(5), pp. 1051–1060.

Smith, C. W., and R. M. Stulz (1985). "The determinants of firms' hedging policies," *Journal of Financial and Quantitative Analysis,* 20, pp. 391–405.

Smith, D. K., and R. C. Alexander (1988). *Fumbling the Future,* New York: William Morrow.

Smith, F., and R. Wilson (1995). "The predictive validity of the Karnani and Wernerfelt model of multipoint competition," *Strategic Management Journal,* 16, pp. 143–160.

Smith, L. (1993). "Can defense pain be turned to gain?" *Fortune,* February 8, pp. 84–96.

Smith, T. K., and E. Norten (1993). "Throwing curves: One baseball statistic remains a mystery," *Wall Street Journal,* April 2, p. A1.

Solomon, E. (1970). "Alternative rate of return concepts and their implications for utility regulation," *Bell Journal of Economics,* 1, pp. 65–81.

Solomon, J. (1994). "Mickey's trip to trouble," *Newsweek,* February 14, pp. 34–39.

Spekman, R. E., T. M. Forbes III, L. A. Isabella, and T. C. MacAvoy (1998). "Alliance management: A view from the past and a look to the future," *Journal of Management Studies,* 35(6), pp. 747–772.

Spence, A. M. (1973). *Market Signaling: Information Transfer in Hiring and Related Processes,* Cambridge, MA: Harvard University Press.

Spence, A. M. (1981). "The learning curve and competition," *Bell Journal of Economics,* 12, pp. 49–70.

Spender, J. C. (1989). *Industry Recipes: An Enquiry into the Nature and Sources of Managerial Judgement,* New York: Blackwell.

Spender, J. C. (1996). "Making knowledge the basis of a dynamic theory of the firm," *Strategic Management Journal,* 17 (Winter, Special Issue), pp. 109–122.

Stalk, G., P. Evans, and L. Shulman (1992). "Competing on capabilities: The new rules of corporate strategy," *Harvard Business Review,* March/April, pp. 57–69.

Stapleton, R. C. (1982). "Mergers, debt capacity, and the valuation of corporate loans," in M. Keenan and L. J. White, eds., *Mergers and Acquisitions,* Lexington, MA: D. C. Heath, chap. 2.

Starr, C. (1993). "Orphan Drug Act: Celebration a decade and 87 drugs later," *Drug Topics,* April 5, pp. 26–31.

Statman, M. (1981). "Betas compared: Merrill Lynch vs. Value Line," *Journal of Portfolio Management,* 7(2), pp. 41–44.

Stauffer, T. R. (1971). "The measurement of corporate rates of return: A generalized formulation," *Bell Journal of Economics,* 2, pp. 434–469.

Staw, B. M. (1981). "The escalation of commitment to a course of action," *Academy of Management Review,* 6, pp. 577–587.

Stecklow, S. (1999). "Gallo woos French, but don't expect Bordeaux by the jug," *Wall Street Journal,* March 26, pp. A1+.

Stein, J. C. (1997). "Internal capital markets and the competition for corporate resources," *Journal of Finance,* 52(1), pp. 111–133.

Steiner, G. A., and J. B. Miner (1977). *Management Policy and Strategy: Text, Readings and Cases,* New York: Macmillan.

Stern, J., B. Stewart, and D. Chew (1995). "The EVA financial management system," *Journal of Applied Corporate Finance,* 8, pp. 32–46.

Stertz, B. A. (1991). "In a U-turn from past policy, Big Three at Detroit speed into era of cooperation," *Wall Street Journal,* June 28, pp. B1+.

Steven, L. (1992). "Front line systems," *Computerworld,* March 2, pp. 61–63.

Stewart, T. (1995). "Getting real about brain power," *Fortune,* November 27, pp. 201+.

Stewart, T. (1995). "Mapping corporate knowledge," *Fortune,* October 30, pp. 209+.

Stillman, R. (1983). "Examining antitrust policy toward horizontal mergers," *Journal of Financial Economics,* 11, pp. 225–240.

St. John, C. H., and J. S. Harrison (1999). "Manufacturing-based relatedness, Synergy, and coordination," *Strategic Management Journal,* 20, pp. 129–145.

Stopford, M., and L. Wells (1972). *Managing the Multinational Enterprise,* New York: Basic Books.

Stuart, T. E. (1998). "Network positions and propensities to collaborate: An investigation of strategic alliance formation in a high-technology industry," *Administrative Science Quarterly,* 43(3), pp. 668–698.

Stuart, T. E., H. Hoang, and R. C. Hybels (1999). "Interorganizational endorsements and the performance of entrepreneurial ventures," *Administrative Science Quarterly,* 44, pp. 315–349.

Stuckey, J. (1983). *Vertical Integration and Joint Ventures in the Aluminum Industry,* Cambridge, MA: Harvard University Press.

Stulz, R. M. (1996). "Rethinking risk management," *Journal of Applied Corporate Finance,* Fall, pp. 8–24.

Suris, O. (1993). "Big Three win joint patent, marking a first," *Wall Street Journal,* April 13, pp. B1+.

Suris, O. (1993). "IndyCar 'Honda rule' blocks fast track," *Wall Street Journal,* May 28, p. B1.

Sweezy, P. M. (1939). "Demand under conditions of oligopoly," *Journal of Political Economy,* 45, pp. 568–573.

Swieringa, R. J., and J. H. Waterhouse (1982). "Organizational views of transfer pricing," *Accounting, Organizations & Society,* 7(2), pp. 149–165.

Symonds, W. (1998). "Paddling harder at L.L. Bean." *Business Week,* 3607, p. 72.

Takeuchi, H., and P. P. Merliss (1981). "L. L. Bean, Inc.: Corporate Strategy," Harvard Business School Case no. 9-581-159.

Tanikawa, M. (1997). "Fun in the sun," *Far Eastern Economic Review,* 160(22), pp. 56–57.

Taylor, A., III (1994). "Iacocca's minivan," *Fortune,* 129(11), pp. 56–66.

Taylor, D., and J. S. Archer, (1994). *Up Against the Wal-Marts,* New York: Amacon.

Teece, D. (1977). "Technology transfer by multinational firms," *Economic Journal,* 87, pp. 242–261.

Teece, D. (1980). "Economy of scope and the scope of the enterprise," *Journal of Economic Behavior and Organization,* 1, pp. 223–245.

Telser, L. (1978). *Economic Theory and the Core,* Chicago: University of Chicago Press.

Telser, L. (1987). *A Theory of Efficient Cooperation and Competition,* Cambridge, MA: MIT Press.

Templeman, J. (1993). "Nestlé: A giant in a hurry," *Business Week,* March 22, pp. 50–54.

Tetzeli, R. (1993). "Johnson controls: Mining money in mature markets," *Fortune,* 127(6), pp. 77–80.

thehindubusinessline.com/2005/08/14/stories.

Theroux, J., and J. M. Hurstak (1993). "Ben & Jerry's Homemade Ice Cream Inc.: Keeping the mission(s) alive," Harvard Business School Case no. 9-392-025.

Thompson, A. A., Jr., and A. J. Strickland, III (1987). *Strategic Management: Concepts and Cases,* 4th ed., Plano, TX: Business Publications.

Thurm, S. (1998). "Copy this typeface? Court ruling counsels caution," *Wall Street Journal,* July 15, pp. B1+.

Tichy, N., and S. Sherman (1993). *Control Your Destiny or Someone Else Will: How Jack Welch Is Making General Electric the World's Most Competitive Corporation,* New York: Doubleday.

Tichy, N. M., and M. A. Devanna (1986). *The Transformational Leader,* New York: John Wiley & Sons.

"Time Warner, Inc.: HBO unit expands push into original programming," *Wall Street Journal* January 16, 1992, p. 136.

Tirole, J. (1988). *The Theory of Industrial Organization,* Cambridge, MA: MIT Press.

Titman, S. (1984). "The effect of capital structure on a firm's liquidation decisions," *Journal of Financial Economics,* 13(1), pp. 137–151.

Tobin, J. (1969). "A general equilibrium approach to monetary theory," *Journal of Money, Credit and Banking,* 1, pp. 15–29.

Tobin, J. (1978). "Monetary policies and the economy: The transmission mechanism," *Southern Economic Journal,* 37, pp. 421–431.

Tobin, J., and W. Brainard (1968). "Pitfalls in financial model building," *American Economic Review,* 58, pp. 99–122.

Tomer, J. F. (1987). *Organizational Capital: The Path to Higher Productivity and Well-Being,* New York: Praeger.

Tomlinson, J. W. L. (1970). *The Joint Venture Process in International Business,* Cambridge, MA: MIT Press.

Toy, S., and P. Dwyer (1994). "Is Disney headed to the Euro-trash heap?" *Business Week,* January 24, p. 52.

Trachtenberg, J., and K. Pope (1995). "Poly Gram's Levy puts music firm further into movie-making," *Wall Street Journal,* June 15, pp. A1+.

Trager, J. (1992). *The People's Chronology,* New York: Henry Holt.

Trautwein, I. (1990). "Merger motives and merger prescriptions," *Strategic Management Journal,* 11, pp. 283–295.

Treynor, J. L. (1965). "How to rate mutual fund performance." *Harvard Business Review,* January/February, pp. 63–75.

Trigeorgis, L., ed. (1995). *Real Options in Capital Investment,* Westport, CT: Praeger.

Tucker, I., and R. P. Wilder (1977). "Trends in vertical integration in the U.S. manufacturing sector," *Journal of Industrial Economics,* 26, pp. 81–94.

Tuller, L. W. (1991). *Going Global: New Opportunities for Growing Companies to Compete in World Markets,* Homewood, IL: Irwin.

Tully, S. (1990). "GE in Hungary: Let there be light," *Fortune,* October 22, pp. 137–142.

Tully, S. (1992). "What CEOs really make," *Fortune,* June 15, pp. 94–99.

Tully, S. (1993). "The real key to creating wealth," *Fortune,* September 20, pp. 38–50.

Turk, T. A. (1987). "The determinants of management responses to interfirm tender offers and their effect on shareholder wealth," unpublished doctoral dissertation, Graduate School of Management, University of California at Irvine.

Turner, R. (1991). "How MCA's relations with Motown Records went so sour so fast," *Wall Street Journal,* September 25, pp. A1+.

Tyler, B., and H. K. Steensma (1995). "Evaluating technological collaborative opportunities: A cognitive modeling perspective," *Strategic Management Journal,* 16, pp. 43–70.

Utterback, J. M., and W. J. Abernathy (1975). "A dynamic model of process and product innovation," *Omega,* 3, pp. 639–656.

Van de Ven, A., D. Polley, R. Garud, and S. Venkatraman (1999). *The Innovation Journey,* New York: Oxford University Press.

Vance, S. C. (1964). *Board of Directors: Structure and Performance,* Eugene, OR: University of Oregon Press.

Varadarajan, P. R. (1986). "Product diversity and firm performance: An empirical investigation," *Journal of Management,* 50(3), pp. 43–57.

Varadarajan, P. R., and M. H. Cunningham (1995). "Strategic alliances: A synthesis of conceptual foundations," *Journal of the Academy of Marketing Science,* 23(4), pp. 282–296.

Varadarajan, P. R., and V. Ramanujam (1987). "Diversification and performance: A reexamination using a new two-dimensional conceptualization of diversity in firms," *Academy of Management Journal,* 30(2), pp. 380–393.

Varaiya, N. (1985). "A test of Roll's hubris hypothesis of corporate takeovers," Working Paper, Southern Methodist University, School of Business.

Villalonga, B. (2004). "Does diversification cause the 'diversification discount'?" *Financial Management,* 33, pp. 5–27.

Von Clausewitz, K. (1976). *On War,* volume I. London: Kegan Paul.

Von Neumann, J., and O. Morgenstern (1944). *The Theory of Games and Economic Behavior,* New York: John Wiley.

von Stackelberg, H. (1934). *Marktform und Gleichgewicht,* Vienna, Austria: Julius Springer.

Wahlgreen, E. (2005). "Salads days for burger joints," *Business Week Online,* June 3, 2005.

Walker, G., and D. Weber (1984). "A transaction cost approach to make-or-buy decisions," *Administrative Science Quarterly,* 29, pp. 373–391.

Walkling, R., and M. Long (1984). "Agency theory, managerial welfare, and takeover bid resistance," *Rand Journal of Economics,* 15(1), pp. 54–68.

Wallas, J., and J. Erickson (1993). *Hard Drive: Bill Gates and the Making of the Microsoft Empire,* New York: Harper Business.

Walsh, J. (1988). "Top management turnover following mergers and acquisitions," *Strategic Management Journal*, 9, pp. 173–183.

Walsh, J. (1989). "Doing a deal: Merger and acquisition negotiations and their impact upon target company top management turnover," *Strategic Management Journal*, 10, pp. 307–322.

Walsh, J., and J. Ellwood (1991). "Mergers, acquisitions, and the pruning of managerial deadwood," *Strategic Management Journal*, 12, pp. 201–217.

Walter, G., and J. B. Barney (1990). "Management objectives in mergers and acquisition," *Strategic Management Journal*, 11, pp. 79–86.

Wang, H., and J. Barney (2006). "Employee incentives to make firm specific investments: Implications for resource-based theories of corporate diversification," *Academy of Management Review*, 31, pp. 466–476.

Waring, G. F. (1996). "Industry differences in the persistence of firm-specific returns," *American Economic Review*, 86, pp. 1253–1265.

Warner, J. B., R. Watts, and K. Wruck (1988). "Stock prices and top management changes," *Journal of Financial Economics*, 20, pp. 461–493.

Watts, R. L., and J. L. Zimmerman (1978). "Towards a positive theory of determination of accounting standards," *Accounting Review*, 53, pp. 112–133.

Watts, R. L., and J. L. Zimmerman (1986). *Positive Accounting Theory*, Upper Saddle River, NJ: Prentice Hall.

Watts, R. L., and J. L. Zimmerman (1990). "Positive accounting theory: A ten-year perspective," *Accounting Review*, 65, pp. 131–156.

Weidenbaum, M. L. (1986). "Updating the corporate board," *Journal of Business Strategy*, 7, pp. 77–83.

Weigelt, K., and C. Camerer (1988). "Reputation and corporate strategy: A review of recent theory and applications," *Strategic Management Journal*, 9, pp. 443–454.

Weimer, D. (1998). "The softest side of Sears," *Business Week*, 3610, December 8, p. 6.

Weiner, S. (1987). "The road most traveled," *Forbes*, October 19, pp. 60–64.

Weisbach, M. S. (1988). "Outside directors and CEO turnover," *Journal of Financial Economics*, 20, pp. 431–460.

Weiss, L., ed. (1989). *Concentration and Price*, Cambridge, MA: MIT Press.

Welbourne, T., and A. Andrews (1998). "Predicting the performances of initial public offerings," *Academy of Management Journal*, 39, pp. 891–919.

Welsh, J. (1998). "Office-paper firm pursue elusive goal: Brand loyalty," *Wall Street Journal*, September 21, p. B6.

Wernerfelt, B. (1984). "A resource-based view of the firm," *Strategic Management Journal*, 5, pp. 171–180.

Wernerfelt, B. (1986). "A special case of dynamic pricing policy," *Management Science*, 32, pp. 1562–1566.

Wernerfelt, B., and A. Karnani (1987). "Competitive strategy under uncertainty," *Strategic Management Journal*, 8, pp. 187–194.

Westley, F. (1900). "Middle managers and strategy: Microdynamics of inclusion," *Strategic Management Journal*, 11, pp. 337–351.

Westley, F., and H. Mintzberg (1989). "Visionary leadership and strategic management," *Strategic Management Journal*, 10, pp. 17–32.

Weston, J. F. and S. K. Mansinghka (1971). "Tests of the efficiency performance of conglomerate firms," *Journal of Finance*, 26, pp. 919–936.

White, L. J. (1971). *The American Automobile Industry Since 1945*, Cambridge, MA: Harvard University Press.

William, J., B. L. Paez, and L. Sanders (1988). "Conglomerates revisited," *Strategic Management Journal*, 9, pp. 403–414.

Williams, M., and M. Kanabayashi (1993). "Mazda and Ford drop proposal to build cars together in Europe," *Wall Street Journal*, March 4, p. A14.

Williamson, O. E. (1975). *Markets and Hierarchies: Analysis and Antitrust Implications*, New York: Free Press.

Williamson, O. E. (1985). *The Economic Institutions of Capitalism*, New York: Free Press.

Williamson, O. E. (1991). "Comparative economic organization: The analysis of discrete structural alternatives," *Administrative Science Quarterly*, 36, pp. 269–296.

Williamson, O. E. (1991). "Strategizing, economizing, and economic organization," *Strategic Management Journal*, 12 (Winter), pp. 75–94.

Wilson, J. H. (1981). "A note on scale economies in the savings and loan industry," *Business Economics,* January, pp. 45–49.

Wiseman, R. M., and A. H. Catanach, Jr. (1997). "A longitudinal disaggregation of operational risk under changing regulations: Evidence from the savings and loan industry," *Academy of Management Journal,* 40(4), pp. 799–830.

Womack, J. P., D. I. Jones, and D. Roos (1990). *The Machine That Changed the World,* New York: Rawson.

Woods, W. (1991). "Misery in the air," *Fortune,* December 16, pp. 88–89.

Wooldridge, B., and S. Floyd (1990). "The strategy process, middle management involvement, and organizational performance," *Strategic Management Journal,* 11, pp. 231–241.

World Bank (1999). *World Development Report,* Oxford, England: Oxford University Press.

Xin, K. R., and J. J. Pearce (1996). "*Guanxi*: Connections as substitutes for formal institutional support," *Academy of Management Journal,* 39(6), pp. 1641–1658.

Yan, A., and B. Gray (1994). "Bargaining power, management control, and performance in United States-China joint ventures: A comparative case study," *Academy of Management Journal,* 37, pp. 1478–1517.

Yeoh, P.-L., and K. Roth (1999). "An empirical analysis of sustained advantage in the U.S. pharmaceutical industry," *Strategic Management Journal,* 20, pp. 637–653.

Yoder, S. K. (1991). "A 1990 reorganization at Hewlett Packard is already paying off," *Wall Street Journal,* July 22, pp. 1+.

Yoffie, D. (1994). "Swissair's Alliances (A)," Harvard Business School Case no. 9-794-152.

Yoshino, M., S. Hall, and T. Malnight (1991). "Whirlpool Corp.," Harvard Business School Case no. 9-391-089.

Yoshino, M. Y., and P. Stoneham (1992). "Procter & Gamble Japan (A)," Harvard Business School Case no. 9-793-035.

Young, G., K. G. Smith, and C. M. Grimm (1997). "Multimarket contact, resource heterogeneity, and rivalrous firm behavior," *Academy of Management Proceedings 1997,* pp. 55–59.

Yukl, G. (1989). "Managerial leadership: A review of theory and research," *Journal of Management,* 15(2), pp. 251–289.

Zaheer, A., and N. Venkatraman (1995). "Relational governance as an interorganizational strategy: An empirical test of the role of trust in economic exchange," *Strategic Management Journal,* 16, pp. 373–392.

Zahra, S. A., and J. A. Pearce II (1989). "Boards of directors and corporate financial performance: A review and integrative model," *Journal of Management,* 15, pp. 291–334.

Zajac, E. J., and J. D. Westphal (1994). "The costs and benefits of managerial incentives and monitoring in large U.S. corporations: When is more not better?" *Strategic Management Journal,* 15, pp. 121–142.

Zimmerman, J. L. (1983). "Taxes and firm size," *Journal of Accounting & Economics,* 5(2), pp. 119–149.

Zimmerman, M. (1985). *How to Do Business with the Japanese,* New York: Random House.

Zmijewski, M. E., and R. L. Hagerman (1981). "An income strategy approach to the positive theory of accounting standard setting/choice," *Journal of Accounting & Economics,* 3(2), pp. 129–149.

Index

In this index, page numbers in *italics* designate figures; page numbers followed by the letter "t" designate tables. *See also* cross-references designate related topics or more detailed subtopic breakdowns.

A

ABB, Inc., 348
Accounting measures, 20–25.
    See also Measures
  adjusted, 24–44
  agency problems, 396–397
  divisional performance, 396–397
  intangible resources and
      capabilities limitation, 25
  limitation effects, 25
  limitations, 22
  managerial discretion, 22–23, 396
  ratio analysis, 21t
  ratio types, 20
  short-term bias, 23, 396
  user challenges, 23
Accounting performance standards,
    394–395
Acquisitions. *See also* Mergers
    and acquisitions
  completing in "thinly traded"
    markets, 463–464
  delaying, 466–470
  economic profits related to,
    450–451
  legal constraints, 430
  postacquisition coordination, 470
  SCI, 464–465
  strategic alliances and, 430–431
Adjusted accounting measures,
    24–44. *See also* Accounting
    measures
  cost of capital, 25
  economic profit (EP), 25
  intangible resources and
    capabilities and, 40–41
  market value added (MVA),
    25
  return on invested capital
    (ROIC), 25
  weaknesses, 39–41

Adverse selection
  defined, 423
  in strategic alliances, 423–424
Agency costs, 376–380
  agency relationships and, 377
  defined, 377
  managerial perquisites, 378
  managerial risk aversion, 378–379
  residual, 380
  sources, 377–379
Agency problems, 377
  divisional performance accounting
    measures, 396–397
  mergers and acquisitions
    and, 454–455
Agency relationships, 377
Agents, 377
Alliances. *See* Strategic alliances
Allied Signal, 398
Alternative market measures,
    41–44. *See also* Measures
  event study method, 41–44
  Jensen's alpha, 43–44
  limitations, 44
  Sharpe's measure, 43
  Treynor index, 43
Altman's estimated equation, 20
American Brands, 468
Andean Common Market
    (ANCOM), 497
Anticompetitive economies of
    scope, 359–362. *See also*
    Economies of scope
  diversification to exploit, 359–362
  market power, 361–362
  multipoint competition, 359–361
Antitrust actions, 292
Apple Computer, 47t, 227, 431
Arbitrage pricing theory (APT), 31
Archer Daniels Midland (ADM),
    181, 293
Architectural competence, 205

Asset mass efficiencies, 145
Association of Southeast Asian
    Nations (ASEAN), 497
Asymmetric alliances. *See also*
    Strategic alliances
  defined, 421
  occurrence, 422
AT&T, 228–229, 292
Audit committee, 383

B

Backlogs, 296
Backward vertical integration, 76, 306
Balance sheets, 26t
Balanced scorecard, 233–235
  business strategy implementation,
    234–235
  defined, 234
  for product differentiation, *235*
Bank debt, 358
Barriers to entry. *See also* Entry;
    Entry threat
  contrived deterrence as, 64–68
  cost advantages independent of
    scale as, 62–64
  cost of capital as, 69
  customer-switching costs as, 70
  defined, 59
  distribution channel access as, 70
  economies of scale as, 59–61
  favorable access to raw materials
    as, 63–64
  favorable geographic locations as,
    63, 64
  government policy as, 68–69
  know-how as, 63
  learning-curve cost advantages
    as, 63, 64
  natural, 64
  product differentiation, 61–62
  proprietary technology as, 62–63